# A Life With Dogs

# A Life With Dogs

Roger Welsch

MBI

First published in 2004 by MBI, an imprint of MBI Publishing Company, Galtier Plaza, Suite 200, 380 Jackson Street, St. Paul, MN 55101-3885 USA



ISBN 0-7603-2045-4

On the front cover: Illustration by Linda Hotovy Welsch.

Edited by Darwin Holmstrom
Designed by Rochelle Schultz

Printed in the United States of America

For Dick and Deb . . .

**"FIRST DOG"**

16 x 20

oil

by Linda Hotovy Welsch

*Linda Welsch has lived and worked with Roger since their marriage in 1981. Inspiration for her paintings can be found in the things she knows and loves at home. Her illustrations for this book were based on the Welsch household pets over the last 23 years.*

# CONTENTS

*Recollect that the Almighty,*
*who gave the dog to be companion*
*of our pleasures and our toils,*
*hath invested him with a nature noble*
*and incapable of deceit.*

**SIR WALTER SCOTT, *THE TALISMAN (1825)***

# ACKNOWLEDGMENTS

I want to thank the good folks at the Central Nebraska Humane Society for their kind help in locating other agencies that help good humans and good dogs come together for a continuing relationship. And I want to thank my own human life partners, Linda and Antonia, for their invaluable help in preparing this manuscript.

# INTRODUCTION

*Had a dog and his name was Blue*
*Had a dog and his name was Blue*
*Had a dog and his name was Blue*
*Bet you ten dollars he's a good one too.*
*Come on, Blue, you're a good dog, you.*

*Grabbed my gun and tooted my horn*
*Grabbed my gun and tooted my horn*
*Grabbed my gun and tooted my horn*
*Gonna get me a 'possum in the new-grown corn.*
*Come on, Blue, you're a good boy, you.*

*Blue treed a 'possum in a 'simmon tree*
*Blue treed a 'possum in a 'simmon tree*
*Blue treed a 'possum in a 'simmon tree*
*'Possum looked at Blue, Blue looked at me*
*Good ol' Blue, you're a good one, you.*

*Baked that 'possum all nice and brown*
*Baked that 'possum all nice and brown*
*Baked that 'possum all nice and brown*
*Sweet pertaters layin' all around*
*Come on, Blue, you can have some too.*

*When ol' Blue died he died so hard*
*When ol' Blue died he died so hard*
*When ol' Blue died he died so hard*
*He jarred the ground in my backyard.*
*Go on, Blue, I'm a-comin' too.*

*I dug his grave with a silver spade*
*I dug his grave with a silver spade*
*I dug his grave with a silver spade*
*And I let him down on a golden chain.*
*Goodbye, ol' Blue, you're a good one, you.*

*When I get to Heaven first thing I'll do*
*When I get to Heaven first thing I'll do*
*When I get to Heaven first thing I'll do*
*I'll grab my horn and I'll blow for Blue.*
*Come on, Blue, finally got here too.*

*Then when I hear that Blue dog bark*
*Then when I hear that Blue dog bark*
*Then when I hear that Blue dog bark*
*I'll know he's treed a 'possum in Noah's Ark.*
*Ah, Blue, you're a good one, you.*

*Had a dog and his name was Blue*
*Had a dog and his name was Blue*
*Had a dog and his name was Blue*
*Bet you ten dollars he's a good one too.*
*Come on, Blue . . .*

I've been singing that song for 40 years now and I never can get through it without shedding tears. God, I do love a good dog (as if there were any other kind). And that old, traditional song pretty well sums it up in my mind. Men who can get through a funeral service for their father bravely, with little more than a shaky lip, fall to pieces and cry like babies when they're burying a good dog. There are a lot of people who die and leave the world a better place simply by going away, but in my long life I haven't met many dogs of whom that same thing could be said.

Nope, dogs are special. I have often joked—even wrote it now and then in various publications myself—that it's hard to believe the fact that the word "dog" spelled backward is "god" is a mere coincidence. (Nor that the phrase "kitty cat" spelled backward is "ticky tacky," sort of.)

My youngest daughter recently visited a church whose theology interested her. She wanted to know what sort of questions she should ask to determine the depth and truth of what she was about to hear. I told her, "Ask if they think dogs go to heaven." Any church that thinks dogs don't go to heaven isn't worth the glass in its windows as far as I'm concerned. In fact, when it comes right down to it, I guess I'd be more inclined to accept a theology that has dogs going to heaven but has far more restrictive admission policies for human beings.

I am writing this book about dogs not out of any expertise. Maybe it's not even based on my unique canine experiences. No, I am writing only out of my passion for these wonderful creatures that grace us with their devotion and service. Just yesterday I came out of the house beset with a world of what seemed like very important problems. I just wanted to sit down on the back-porch swing and work some things out in my mind. But Abigail, our crossbreed black Lab/Saint Bernard, wouldn't let me be. She jumped up into my face again and again. Finally she jumped up and pushed off my front, almost knocking me down. I was about ready to pop her on the head with the notebook I was carrying when she caught my eye and with an instant message told me that all she really wanted was to get me back on track, remind me what is important ("*Throw the Frisbee! Throw the Frisbee!*"), and help me smile again.

I felt momentarily dreadful, thinking that I could have thumped her for nothing more than her exuberance for life. That's my most basic human nature, I guess. Her basic nature, on the other hand, was to seize the moment and celebrate each other's presence here on earth yet another day. And that's why I (and you!) should treasure the invaluable perspective brought into our lives by dogs.

No, I'm not a dog expert. My dogs have not been exceptional. I guess they've just been an assortment of dogs, some mutts, some with papers. My hope is not that my words will teach you anything new about dogs or dog ownership, but that you resonate with my experiences and feelings and maybe give your own best friend an extra pat on the head or scratch behind the ear today.

I haven't had a lot of dogs in my life, but there haven't been many times in my 60-some years that I have been without a canine companion. Life just isn't right without a dog around, in my experience. I've lived alone without another human being and found it really quite comfortable—at times even preferable. But man, it's hard to get by without a dog to talk to after a hard day's work. Or more precisely, it's hard to set off on a day's work with the lower species of mammal—man—without a dog to offer up a sense of perspective.

The following pages are without scientific basis or value. These are things I know and feel about dogs. Your experience might be different. Doesn't matter. I want to tell you about my dogs and dogs I've known, and then you can tell me about yours. Never met a man who wasn't ready to compare good dogs. I know less about training and raising dogs than just about anyone you know. My dogs are and have been unexceptional.

Which is to say, then, I am writing in these pages about almost all of you and almost all of your dogs. My intention is to strike a sympathetic vibration with you and your dogs so you can be reassured that there are a lot of us out here just like you, that you don't need to feel the least bit guilty about loving an ordinary dog that everyone else thinks is an idiot, that even the very most macho of men cry when their dogs die.

CHAPTER ONE

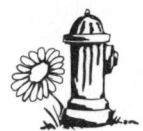

# WHAT'S IN A NAME

*No blithe Irish lad was so happy as I;*
*No harp like my own could so cheerily play,*
*And wherever I went was my poor dog Tray.*

**–THOMAS CAMPBELL, *THE HARPER***

Man's respect for dogs is nothing new. The origins of our animal terms are often buried in ancient history. For example, the Romans called cows *bos*, and to this very day we call for our cows with that word. An ancient Germanic word *su* became our word "swine" and provides the shout we still use to call our hogs to slops—"sooEE!" What is the ultimate, climactic, most clichéd name for a dog in any cartoon or joke? "Fido." Of course. Fido. Again, it almost brings tears to my eyes when I remember that this most common of all dog names seems to bring it all together for us: Fido is Latin for "I am faithful." Isn't that perfect? Isn't that the motto of every dog that's ever lived? Aren't those precisely the words you read in your dog's eyes every time you look into them? "I am faithful." Ah, if only mankind could approach that kind of ideal!

People can be pretty unimaginative when naming their dogs, but my impression is that they put a good deal more thought, love, and creativity into naming their dogs than they do their children. Look at the lists of the most popular names for children these days. It's pretty obvious that modern parents are at least realistic about the prospects of their children amounting to anything important. I mean, jeez, you know for a fact that someone named Chelsey, Rusty, Heather, or Jamool is not destined to be President of the US of A!

I am always interested in what other people name their dogs: Pearl, Hillary, Fala, Him and Her, Harley, Priscilla, Freckles, Doowa, Odie, Buddy, Ricky Lee Anderson, Jr., Pearl, Chico, Patch, Jim, Yoni, Zeke, Emma, Elvis. I've always liked names like "Bill," "Joe," "Fred," and "Bob." I think giving a dog a plain ol' people name may be a trifle disrespectful to the dog, but it also says something about how the dog is seen as a peer, a human friend, even if maybe a little too good to be a human.

I think it is a terrific idea and tribute to name a dog "Fido"— "I am faithful"—or "Rex " or "King." One of these days I imagine I'll name a good black dog Fido, or maybe Blue.

"Spot" may seem a pedestrian name for a dog, but I have always wanted to name a black Lab retriever Spot. Wouldn't that lend the word a new import? I mean, you know, a 150-pound black Lab would be one really *big* spot. My next choice as a name for a black Lab is Snowball. My wife, Linda, does not have a flair for naming dogs; she named our golden retriever "Goldie." Uh-huh. Good. Golden retriever named Goldie. I reserve the right to name our real dogs, which is to say, our black Labs. At this point we have only two.

I believe that two is a subminimum number of black Labs anyone should have. Everyone should have one black Lab as the main dog, and then a codog for immediate assistance in welcoming the FedEx man, sniffing strange dog butts, cleaning out a food bowl, that kind of thing. You need a backup black dog in reserve behind those two so that if something should happen to your main dog and the codog moves up the hierarchy, you have your immediate replacement for the number two slot.

I would say those three dogs constitute your basic canine critical mass. Another two or three would provide a safety cushion that would certainly ease *my* mind and let me sleep more easily at night, but in our household the word has been let down that any more than two black dogs and there'll be one less helpmate woman. So, we have a rock-bottom base at this point of two black Labs. I have made few absolute proclamations in my life but one of them that I take very seriously is that life is too short to spend one single day without a black dog—so a second-string black dog is absolutely critical.

Our oldest black Lab is Thud. You'll hear a lot more about Thud as this book moves along. Thud is a bear of a dog (and at one time "Bear" was a name under consideration for him). "Thud," as we often note, is a name this big boy earned with his head. I don't believe it's a matter of clumsiness that causes him to bonk into things with such apparently contemptuous frequency. No, I prefer to believe that Thud simply doesn't care. Running into things with his head is for him a kind of signature behavior trait; moreover, I get the clear impression that Thud knows it amuses me when he runs into things with his head, so he just goes ahead and does it. He does whatever he thinks will please me. Thud is that way about things.

Our current codog is Abigail von der Pooper. The name "Abigail" came from my favorite brand of single-malt Scotch, Abelour, which is particularly and peculiarly feminine Scotch, much like Abigail herself. The name carries with it a certain sense of haughty royalty, even elegance, and she is that. The "von der Pooper" part is a result of her earliest demonstrated innate talent: Abbie is a half-black Lab retriever, although, as my son, Chris, has pointed out, she is more of a "retainer" than a retriever. While she is willing to run after and seize whatever you throw to her, she is less enthusiastic about bringing it back or releasing it. And she is half Saint Bernard. But when we got her we had no idea that the half of her that is Saint Bernard would be the part that eats and poops.

Before Thud, we had Goldie and Lucky. As I noted before, Goldie was a golden retriever and without doubt the sweetest dog that ever lived . . . and perhaps one of the most devious. She was way too smart for her own good. Goldie had some delightful peculiarities about her. One of my favorites was that when I walked the dogs down to the river, she would walk calmly into the water to the depth of her neck (while the Labs ran insanely back and forth on the sandbars and plunged madly in and out of the water) and then . . . lie down. That left only her head, held as high as it would go, nose pointing straight up, out of the water. And she would just lie there, enjoying the water running over and around her. It was her joy: simple, quiet, calm.

There's an old joke about the dog that was so lazy he would wait for the neighbor's dogs to bark and then he would just nod. Goldie was like that, except instead of being lazy, she was smart. She'd go running up the outside stairs when anyone drove into our yard and bark twice, maybe three times. That would be enough to get everyone else barking, whereupon Goldie would retreat to a safer place under a cedar tree from where she could watch the action. She relaxed while the other dogs went nuts, us yelling at them to shut up, delivery people scrambling back into their vehicles seeking refuge, that kind of thing.

Contemporaneously with Goldie was Lucky. Lucky was a black Labrador retriever, and, man, was he ever a retriever! He *lived* to retrieve. Sticks, Frisbees, balls, ropes, whatever; it didn't make a whit of difference to Lucky what you threw, just as long as you were throwing. The most bewildering thing Lucky ever encountered in his life was someone who just sat there and wasn't throwing. He couldn't imagine a human being not throwing. A human being alive and not throwing made no sense whatsoever to him.

We got Lucky on a New Year's Day one year. I can't remember why we did that, but we did. I imagine it's because we knew somewhere in the back of our minds that if something evil happened to this new fuzzy black puppy, there'd be no veterinarian anywhere to help us. And of course that's what happened. There is a rule written down somewhere, maybe in the Bible, that when a dog gets hurt or sick it will always be late on a Friday or on a Saturday when your veterinarian is not in the office.

We never did figure out what happened to Lucky. One minute this new little fuzz-ball of a puppy was running around the yard with our other dog, Goldie, and the next minute he was spitting blood and having seizures. We guessed that maybe he fell off the patio retaining wall, or maybe Goldie accidentally stepped on him in the furor of welcoming him (Goldie would never have hurt a soul on purpose, even this annoying forcible insertion into her life). Whatever it was, he was mighty sick within hours of coming to us.

We finally found our vet and got the puppy to him, where the problem was diagnosed as way too serious for a small country clinic. Something was broken internally—bones, lungs—so we needed to get the new puppy to the nearest large city and find a vet with an X-ray unit. Many hours later, deep into the night, Linda and I were still sitting there, worried sick about this new little soul that was just clinging to life after only just arriving. We were crushed.

The recovery, both Lucky's and ours, was long and painful, and there were plenty of other problems along the way, too: falls, getting lost, nips from an overtaxed Goldie, cat slashes across a curious black nose. So when it came time to give the new Welsch a name, the choice seemed obvious. "Lucky" it was.

Before Goldie there was Blackjack, a huge bear of a Lab on whose flat head you could set two or three cans of beer, which he would have accepted with total equanimity. Blackjack was the first real black Labrador I ever owned. You won't be surprised to hear that Linda came up with this name. He (and Thud and Goldie) came "with papers." (So did Abbie and the rest of our dogs but the papers they came with were newspapers.)

Before Blackjack there was Slump, also black and sold to us as a Lab, but clearly *not* a Lab, a pinhead like hers only possible from Irish setter blood. The name "Slump" came from a wonderful dog I saw in a James Garner film, and I tried to fit the dog into the name in this case rather than the much more reasonable and successful reverse. Slump was a nervous, crazy dog, not your typical black Labrador. I loved her nonetheless, probably in part because she was my first black dog. My buddy Mick was once doing some work on our house, looked at Slump, and then looked over the fence into the yard of an African-American neighbor of ours. He had a poodle. Mick wisely noted an important feature of the relationship between human beings and their dogs: "Why is that?" Mick asked rhetorically. "The white guy has a black dog . . . and the black guy has a white dog."

Slump was important to Linda and me because he was our first dog together. And my first dog after losing my previous dog in a fractious divorce. Jonathon Livingston Beagle, a.k.a. Fleagle, was as fine a dog as you can get by way of a nonblack dog. And a dog that was absolutely beyond reason. Fleagle simply refused to listen. He had his own ideas and he followed them without second thought. He did what he felt needed to be done. He might as well have been deaf. He wasn't at all belligerent about his defiance; he simply did not want you or anyone else to get the idea that he cared about what you wanted or were thinking. Nor did he have any regard for the works of man and God: fences, walls, doors, bogs, swamps, rivers, and distance meant nothing at all to Fleagle.

When I left my first wife, along with my home and all my belongings, not to mention my children and my dog, I lived in an apartment for a couple years and then a house about three miles away. As I recall, Fleagle traveled to my new digs a couple times in a car, but being a beagle he didn't get to see much of the trip since his eye level was well below the car window. But being a beagle, his eyes were pretty much an afterthought anyway; Fleagle lived by and followed his nose.

That's the only solution, at least, that I can imagine to the mystery that one morning I heard a scratching at my front door, opened it . . . and there was Fleagle. He was three miles from home, having traveled utterly unknown streets and neighborhoods, crossing several very busy, wide avenues. He didn't seem to think his trip was at all remarkable, but I was amazed. I fed him, watered him, greeted him heartily. I was a lonely, hurt man at the time, and Fleagle's grand dedication (the phrase "I am faithful" comes to mind) brought tears to my eyes. All I can figure is that he *smelled* his way through busy city streets from my old home to the new. Perhaps the hygiene of a new bachelor aided him in his quest.

How did Fleagle do it? Why didn't he get lost? How did he find my house? I penned him into my fenced backyard, figuring I'd drive him back home when I got home from work, but as I noted already Fleagle considered fences minor and momentary distractions. So by the time I returned from work, Fleagle was no longer in the yard. I called my former home and the children told me that they had in fact not even noticed that Fleagle had been gone, since he was now already back home, none the worse for wear, sound asleep on the front room couch.

Several more times during Fleagle's life in the city he got the whim to come visit me and he did. In yet another thoughtless and unwise decision, my erstwhile wife eventually exiled him to live with a farm family. A city-bred and -raised beagle on a farm. Yeah, that makes sense.

The first and only previous dog of that earlier marriage was, significantly, a nervous wreck of a dog we named Pooter in honor of her remarkable gastric reactions when eating leftover corn fritters. And because of the natural consequences that we very quickly realized and appreciated, we probably ate corn fritters more in our marriage and Pooter's tenure than any other single meal.

All dogs fart, I suppose, but some bring it off much better than others. Pooter wasn't much of anything else, but she was a sublime and industrial-grade farter. It wasn't simply that she farted more than most dogs (although she did) or that her products were audible (few dogs' are, despite braggarts' claims to the contrary) and otherwise notable (in an olfactory manner of speaking). No, the best part about Pooter's emissions was not so much the items themselves as her reaction to them. She could absolutely drive me into paroxysms of laughter because whenever she farted, she would haughtily jump up or to one side and look back at the offending place in the air where the bubble of stink now resided. . . *as if she had had nothing to do with it!* Other dogs I've known seem not to notice their social gaffes, although this may be a ruse to avoid the responsibility of the ecological damage they have wrought, but not Pooter. She was always the most offended by her own work and she made this disgust very clear.

She did ignore my glee, however.

In all my experiences with dogs, only Fleagle and Pooter were not with me until death did us part. My soul simply cannot stand discarding a dog. I find that a betrayal beyond any other. I mean that and, God knows, I've had plenty of the other kinds. I lost Fleagle in a divorce and then to a cold heart, so I guess I won't take responsibility for that treason, but Pooter . . . we gave Pooter away and I was a part of that conspiracy.

Pooter was with us for five years. We loved her even though she was a nasty, nervous, barky, bitey dog. It was just us—my wife, me, and Pooter—so her bitchy behavior (I am speaking here of Pooter's) was not a problem. But then along came our son, Chris. And then in rapid order, two daughters came. One daughter was adopted, so there were three infants introduced into our household within a little over two years. We feared this might be a problem for Pooter, and it was. It got to the point where we were worried about the welfare and safety of the children. We couldn't be angry with Pooter—she was there first, after all. And the children were obnoxious, startlingly loud, and stinky a lot of the time.

But it was obvious that something was going to have to be done, which is to say Pooter was going to have to go. Since she was nothing but a mutt, and a mutt with an evil disposition at that, and not at all a puppy, we knew it was not going to be easy to find her a new home. But since we couldn't bring ourselves to "put her to sleep," as the euphemism tends to go with pets, we started with what even we recognized as a vain effort to deal with her humanely—we put an ad in the paper.

Pooter wasn't like a used car whose faults could be concealed with sawdust in the transmission, a new paint job, and a dose of radiator sealant. Anyone who bothered to respond to our advertisement would eventually have to come to our house and meet this snarly little yapper. Her disposition simply could not be concealed.

Well, a little old lady telephoned in response to our posting, and I couldn't even try to promote Pooter as anything but what she was. I explained that she barked, yipped, nipped, and snarled every time anyone came to the door and there would be no way to stop her. We had tried and failed. To our astonishment, our caller absolutely giggled with glee; that was exactly what she wanted, she gushed, a little dog that would let her know when someone came to the door and give any visitor pause about coming in.

She drove immediately to our home and to our astonishment instantly fell in love with this most unlovable of dogs. And what's even more astonishing—miraculous, even—Pooter fell instantly in love with her. Pooter didn't go with her unwillingly. No, you could almost hear Pooter begging, "Gray-haired old lady, take me with you! Take me away from these loonies and their wretched children! I will yap and nip and bark at your pleasure! Let us spend the rest of our lives being nasty old snarlers together! Take me! Take me! Take me!"

They drove off and my wife and I sat there in our living room, surrounded by our squalling children, and we were amazed. And maybe just a little envious. Pooter had gotten off easy.

Now we're going to go back further in time to the brink of my tear-threshold, back to the first real love of my life, my first dog, the unfortunately named Toodles. I didn't name her Toodles. She came to me with that name. Sometimes that happens. I suppose one can call a dog anything one wants. People change their names after all and manage to deal with that. But I would feel, even to this day, terribly presumptuous doing that unless the dog changed the name his- or herself. Sometimes people name a pet and that name simply changes to fit the animal, just as Jonathan Livingston Beagle eventually (rather quickly, actually) became Fleagle. Our daughter Antonia was just four years old when she named our new farm kitty Love-Heart Love-Angel Love-Kitty; that ponderous moniker very quickly evolved to "Hairball." Toodles' name didn't do that. That's the name she came to us with and that's the name she kept. She seemed quite comfortable in fact with the name, so that was it.

I was home from school, maybe six years old, and I had the whooping cough. In those days when you got something like the measles, whooping cough, anything major, you were quarantined. No kidding, you had to stay at home and they put a big yellow sign on your front door warning people not to come in. Not only was I home sick from school, none of my friends could come visit me for weeks. It was a terrible isolation for a kid like me who normally ran the streets with his friends every day.

My family—Mom, Dad, some uncles and aunts—worked as domestics for the rich folks in town, sometimes as a first job, or in the case of my parents, as a second. Dad was a power engineer at the university powerhouse but, he also did lawn care for rich businessmen in town. Mom occasionally worked as a cleaning lady or cook for special occasions like parties at the same homes. My Aunt Edith was a live-in maid for a family of wealthy Jewish clothing store owners in Lincoln, Nebraska. Somewhere along the line Aunt Edith told these people . . . oh, what the heck. I'm going to tell you their names because they were such wonderful and generous people, and they are now gone, and I think they deserve credit for what they did next. Somewhere along the line Aunt Edith mentioned to Harry and Helen Simon that I was sick and lonely and would be for several weeks to come.

Now, the Simons were bright, well-educated people, and I can't help but think they must have known what they were doing when they offered to let my Aunt Edith bring their own beloved, new little puppy, a toy Boston terrier—their "Toodles"—to me to keep me company for a week or two. You don't lend a kid a dog for a week or two. Or an hour or two. You know what is going to happen. You're going to lose your dog. And the Simons did. I remember taking Toodles to my grandmother's house to return her to Aunt Edith when I was well so she could take Toodles back "home" to the Simons.

I thought I was going to die. I can still these 60 years later remember the anguish. My family is 100 percent German and not notably softhearted. We are disciplined people. Our kids don't get their way by crying. We do what needs to be done. And this borrowed dog needed to be returned. That was my father's absolute rule: Never borrow anything; but if you do, always return it in better condition in which than you received it. And here was his son, attempting not to return a loan at all! But I'm sure my obvious and utterly spontaneous pain—these were not the tears of a spoiled child!—must have been hard even for him to bear.

We returned home with Toodles and somehow, sometime, my folks must have talked with the Simons about what had happened. And the Simons let me keep their dog. Many years later I happened to encounter the Simons in a Lincoln restaurant and had a chance to thank them again for their incredible kindness. As if any thanks could ever be adequate to the gesture.

Toodles was my best friend all through my youth, from that point until my senior year in high school. When I walked home from elementary school, I always knew that when I rounded the corner at the bottom of the long hill at 12th and Lake Streets, I would instantly see a small black-and-white bundle of muscle launch itself from our front porch two blocks away and carry itself on scurrying legs all the way down to me, welcoming me back home.

I guess that's one of the reasons I love that old folk song "Old Blue." When Toodles died, she jarred the ground in my backyard for damn sure. I lost the best friend I'd had all my life. She was the only one who understood me through my adolescence. She was the very embodiment of love through my developmental years. It took me a long time to get over losing her; I never lost sight of her sense of dignity and devotion.

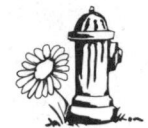

CHAPTER TWO

# THE WAY THEY ARE

*Some of my best leading men have been dogs and horses.*

—ELIZABETH TAYLOR

The earliest lessons we learn about animal behavior are almost always and most surely from our pets. Every kid figures out pretty quickly that animals do some things because they are the things those animals do. Cats stalk, parakeets preen, fish, well, fish swim. Two things amaze me about dog behavior. Make that at least two things: First, the miracle that they actually are born with behaviors locked in place in their brains and, second, that those behaviors differ from breed to breed and dog to dog.

Lucky was a retriever and he, by God, retrieved to a fair-thee-well. Goldie too was a retriever, obviously a water retriever, and she took to water knowing it was an element that spoke to her most primal instincts. Fleagle's nose was not just what he breathed through; it was what he *lived* through. His nose was never more than an inch from the ground in front of him. You could look at him in action and simply *know* that he was reading a thousand things about which we humans had not the slightest inkling.

Now, that doesn't mean he was necessarily more in tune with things than we were. In fact, sometimes Fleagle's nose got in the way of his reading of the world around him. I remember on one occasion driving into the yard of my river cabin and letting Fleagle out of the car. This was to him the sublime moment of freedom. The sensory input must have been incredible. He spent most of his life tied up or in a yard, sniffing pretty much the same odors day after day, but when we drove the two hours out to our river property, suddenly it was a new world, a new *universe*! Turkeys, coyotes, 'possums, coons, mice, beavers, foxes, squirrels, rabbits—imagine what that catalog of whiffs must have been! He exploded from the car, switched his nose onto autopilot, and ran until his stubby little legs gave out on him and turned to jelly.

On this one occasion, however, he launched himself from the car, put his nose to the ground, and went olfactory ballistic. I turned just as he approached the edge of a low slough area near the cabin and watched as a white-tailed deer exploded from the brush not five feet away from him and ran full tilt away in a roar of breaking brush and branches. Now, all sense—literally, all *senses*—tell us that Fleagle should have spun on his low-slung torso and been amazed at this huge wild creature so near him. But no, Fleagle didn't see the deer with his eyes. Nor did he hear the deer with his ears. He smelled the deer, and with his nose still to the ground he tracked the deer 10 or 20 feet, not even noticing that the creature itself was still within sight. And then he ran across the scent trail of something else and went on track for it.

I have often wondered what the world must be like for dogs and their noses. I have read now and again about how much more sensitive a dog's nose is than a human being's, and it's pretty astonishing. Almost scary. I mean, jeez, the world must be an absolute riot of screaming odors to dogs. Aside from hunting and running down escaped prisoners in movies escapes from southern prisons (who can ever forget the bloodhound floating by in the flood of *O Brother, Where Art Thou?*), dogs' noses are finding application and appreciation even in a modern world where electronics rule all. Law enforcement and security agencies use drug- and bomb-sniffing dogs in even the most genteel situations, such as airports, for example. Dogs are being used to detect dangerous molds hiding behind the walls of houses. There are even experiments that use dogs to detect cancer, for Pete's sake!

My love for herding dogs transcends my already goofy affection for dogs in general. I have no idea why. Maybe it's the passion, the obsession they seem to have with what they are doing. I have never been fond of cool, dispassionate people; no dogs are cool and dispassionate. Working dogs that are working have no time whatsoever for nonsense—human beings being a perfect example of the nonsense for which they have no time. Insofar as the human being(s) with them are not doing *their* jobs, they are of no consequence.

When I was an essayist for CBS News *Sunday Morning*, I did one of my television stories on a working dog that herded cows. Now, sheep are one thing; they are medium-sized, meek, and pretty tractable. Cows, on the other hand, are big and can be belligerent. Think "bull fight." But this little dog took no nonsense from cows or people. Her owner said she was easily worth three good men on horseback, and I didn't doubt that assertion.

At one point in moving a herd of maybe 150 head of cattle 10 miles from one pasture to another, this dog accidentally hit the bottom strand of a barbed-wire fence and got a nasty cut in her paw. Her owner spotted the injury, dismounted, called over the supply pickup truck, and got out an emergency medical kit. He called the dog over with some difficulty—she really didn't want to take the time from her job of herding cows to take care of her wound. Her owner daubed disinfectant on the gash and, to our astonishment and horror, sewed the wound shut. The dog showed no pain; she was so completely disgusted with having to sit out even a minute of the action for which she had been born that she only pulled and fought to get out of his arms so she could get back to work. Her dedication to her calling was, no kidding, an inspiration. In fact, she eventually died at work, not seeing a cow behind her that kicked her and killed her. I suspect she died cursing the damned cow for cutting her workday short.

That dog's intensity was intimidating. And like most herders, she did most of her work with her eyes. She stared down cows, no matter how big or how many, and made them do pretty much what she wanted them to do. I was once told that you can spot good herding dogs even when they're puppies simply by looking them in the eye. If they look straight back and stare you down, you may have a good working dog on your hands. If not, well, perhaps the dog will make some kid a good pet. It's all in their eyes.

The best example of the inbred herding instinct I've ever seen was in Yorkshire, England, where working dogs are more common than working men. I was staying with my old friend Jay Anderson at a country house near Leeds. I awoke one morning to hear something of a fuss coming from the neighbor's farmstead, not 200 yards away. A dog was barking, sheep were bleating, obviously in some distress. I looked out the window and saw a curious sight in the field. Some large, darkish sheep, and some much smaller, lighter-colored sheep milled around. I didn't remember that contrast in ovine colors and textures from the day before. Then I saw a collie working dog, moving some of the larger, darker sheep toward the farm buildings.

Oh . . . I get it! The farmer is shearing! The big, dark sheep are as yet unshorn, and those smaller, lighter ones have had all their wool cut off. Jay and I quickly dressed and with his family hotfooted it over to the neighbor's place. We found there a wonderfully pleasant old gent who not only tolerated us as an audience but actually seemed to enjoy showing us the shearing process and telling us about his life on the farm. (He said he'd spent all his life in farming. When we chuckled about that line "all his life," he added that, okay, the first three years all he'd actually done was milk and spread manure!)

His collie working dog knew his job. He didn't need to be told to bring the unshorn sheep into the pens and take the others back out to the pastures. He was not only doing his job, he was doing it with an exuberance that bordered on mania. In fact, the one thing that dog needed to be told was when to stop doing his job. When he ran out of unshorn sheep, he started bringing back the shorn sheep for a second pass under the shears. The farmer patiently scolded the dog and told him no, that there would be no repeats.

You could read the dog's expression as clear as if it were a printed headline: *I'm just getting started! You can't stop me now! I was born to herd, and I'm going to herd!* But the dog trotted off and didn't bring back any more shorn sheep, so for the moment things were quiet and the farmer could continue his demonstrations for us of proper shearing, hoof trimming, and wound treatment on his sheep.

Suddenly there was a loud uproar from behind the farmer's barn; it was a howling of anguished children—Jay's children. We all (except perhaps the farmer) had visions of the collie gutting the children and devouring their still warm and quivering flesh. The dog had *seemed* gentle enough, but once a bad dog tastes blood. . . .

We ran as fast as we could to rescue the children, and the Anderson kids needed rescuing in the worst possible way. The dog was herding them from one end of a sheep pen to another. They were wailing and howling, and he was pushing them first to one corner and then to the next. I was half surprised he hadn't brought them through the dip pit to the farmer to be sheared.

We all laughed, except the children and the dog, and the farmer again scolded and instructed his dog to calm down, that the workday was over, that he had done his job well, and now it was done. We returned to the pens where the shearing continued, and Jay's kids slowly sobbed their way out of their traumatic experience as sheep. All was quiet for a while and then the barking started again. We all looked at each other, wondering what trouble the dog's instincts had gotten him into now. Again we hurried to the back of the barn and out into the pastures beyond it.

I won't blame you if you don't believe what I am going to tell you now. If you've never known a working dog or seen them working, you might well presume I am pulling your leg on this one. But I'm not. There was that collie, so help me, herding clouds of grasshoppers from one side of the field to the other. He would head them off and move them to the barn, and then back out to the field, utterly gleeful with his skill. "Let him run himself weary," the old farmer said, laughing. There was no sense in trying to keep that dog from herding because that dog's life *was* herding, even if he was herding nothing but grasshoppers. If he had had to, that gloriously dedicated dog would have herded the wind in the grass.

Without question, the high point in my life (next to my wedding day with Lovely Linda, I hasten to add) was when I realized a lifelong dream and had the chance to fly straight north out of Baltimore for hour after hour after hour to Thule, Greenland. Then another couple hours even farther north to what is touted as the northernmost human habitation on Earth, Qaanaaq. (Actually, it's not; I hopped a ride an hour even farther north of Qaanaaq to Sioropoluk, a small seal-hunters' village, and probably the truly northernmost human habitation on Earth, but . . . ) Inuit culture—Eskimo life, if you like—centers on dogs just as surely as American culture revolves around automobiles. Everything in Qaanaaq, in fact, everything in most places north of the Arctic Circle, depends on dogs.

This dependence has its advantages and its problems. The dogs of Qaanaaq are all of the same breed: Eskimo sled dogs. There is in fact a law (at least that's what I was told) that no dogs of any other breed may be brought north of the Arctic Circle in Greenland so that the truly grand and glorious character of that breed won't be watered down by dachshunds, Pomeranians, or Chihuahuas. When the need is felt to enrich the canine gene pool in a small community like Sioropoluk (maybe 100 inhabitants) or Qaanaaq (maybe 350), sled dogs are staked overnight well out of town where they might be visited by their not too distant kinfolk, Arctic wolves.

Sled dogs are beautiful beasts, and clearly dogs. But they are also about as close to being wild beasts as any other dog on Earth except those that are truly wild, like coyotes, dingoes, and wolves. There are strictly enforced laws in Inuit villages that all dogs but very small pups must be kept on chains. Not on ropes, not in fences, but on chains. Sled dogs are pack dogs more than any of their southern cousins; they work, travel, and hunt as a unit. I'll be blunt here: if sled dogs were running loose, in a pack, and some little Inuit kid happened to fall down on his way to school some morning, well, there is every chance in this world that the dogs would see the child as vulnerable prey and tear it apart with the ferocity expected of wolves. As is the case with most human habitations, the lives of children outweigh those of even good dogs. Visitors are cautioned never to approach chained dogs no matter how friendly they might seem. Loose dogs are shot on sight in Qaanaaq. There are no warnings, no second chances. And no hard feelings. It's not that loose dogs are bad dogs; they're just doing what they do, resulting in Inuits doing what Inuits have to do.

Inuit sled dogs in Qaanaaq are staked everywhere around the village because everyone has a full sled's complement of dogs, anywhere from 5 to 20. The sea ice immediately off Qaanaaq—the ocean is frozen solid enough for airplanes to land on all but a few weeks a year—is well populated with packs of sled dogs staked and chained. Locating the dog yards out on the sea ice carries with it the added advantage that for that short period every year when the ice does melt, the, uh, residue of all those dogs staked in one place all that time just kind of disappears with the outgoing tide.

I asked a Qaanaaq resident why people there don't simply use snowmobiles and avoid all the problems with dogs. I knew some of the answers, but I wanted to hear what an Inuit had to say, and I'm glad I did. I was told that, of course, it would be extremely difficult and therefore costly to haul motor vehicles so far north, not to mention spare parts, tools, maintenance equipment, and fuel. Moreover, the brutal cold is not the sort of environment that allows internal combustion engines to operate comfortably: at 60 below zero oil sets up like concrete, after all. But the most telling part of my Inuit friend's explanation was also the most subtle: "If you are out on the sea ice far from home, hunting seals or narwhal, and a storm comes up. And your snowmobile won't start. You cannot eat your snowmobile."

I'm still leading up to my main story about working dogs here, so be patient with me. My guide and friend, Ed Brimner, an Air Force officer stationed at Thule, and I were sitting at a Qaanaaq window one day eating breakfast and far out at the base of the little town, heading out onto the frozen sea, we saw several dog sleds heading out onto the cold and ice. Ed drifted idly into a brief summary of the kind of weapons and war tools his Air Force had at its command. I wondered where he was going with that line of conversation, but then he metaphorically banged my head on the table when he said, "But you know, Rog, there go the real men [pointing to the dog sleds now almost out of site], heading out to kill whales . . . with sticks."

This comment took on considerably more meaning later that same day when Ed got an invitation to take a dogsled ride out onto the sea ice himself, with a woman who was experienced at mushing and with a good team of dogs. I would have loved to have gone along, but I simply didn't have the clothes with me for such an adventure and a second sled was not offered. That's okay. Later that night—much later as it turned out—I got a full report of Ed's adventures.

Ed met his friend and her dogs about ten that evening. Now, you might wonder why anyone would set out on a sled behind a pack of dogs at the approach of night, but in April in Qaanaaq it really doesn't make much difference what time you do anything. When I called Linda from Thule, I could honestly assure her that I was not fooling around with the Inuit or Danish women—some stunningly beautiful, by the way—on the base and that, in fact, I was back to my room and in bed every day before the sun went down. She figured out fairly quickly that that far above the Arctic Circle in April, the sun doesn't go down.

Anyway, Ed and his friend set out on the sea ice, Ed tucked snugly into the sled, the woman standing behind on the sled's runners, "mushing." As I understand it, in Alaska, dogs are harnessed one behind the other in a line of traces, in part so they can go between trees and brush. In northern Greenland, however, there are no trees and brush. The dogs are independently harnessed so they can freely jump breaks in the sea ice; the teams are organized more like a large fan, each dog pulling on its own individual line attached to the sled.

At some point well away from civilization insofar as the tiny Inuit village of Qaanaaq constitutes civilization, maybe an hour or so into the mad dash, the woman brought her crazy dogs to a halt to sort out the twisted lines of the dog harness. This involved her getting out her whip and cowing them into a lying, sitting, or crouching position. You don't need to crack a whip to get sled dogs going—take it from me, they are ready to go! You use a whip to intimidate them and hold them in place while you do chores like straightening out their harness.

So that's what this woman was doing, while Ed huddled in the warmth of the blankets and skins on the sled. The system then is that the musher gives the word to the dogs to start running again, and then she takes a couple of running steps and jumps onto the back of the sled, and off they go again, flying across the ice and snow of an Arctic "night." Well, when Ed finally got back to our room in Qaanaaq at about four o'clock the next morning, he told me that's not quite the way it went this time. The woman straightened out the dogs all right, and then gave the word for them to take off. She took her running steps and jumped . . . but missed the sled and fell. Which means that Ed, lying there in the covers, was now moving full tilt across the Arctic ice alone, ever farther into the wild, frozen wilderness, at the total mercy of these crazy, half-feral dogs that lived for running and knew no pace but wide-open.

He had noted, fortunately, that when his friend had stopped the sled to untangle the lines, she had used a kind of "brake"—a short piece of heavy rope hawser with lighter lines running back to the rear of the sled. The heavy rope was thrown forward over the front of the sled and under the runners, creating enough drag to pull the ravening dogs to a stop.

Ed managed to work himself free enough to get hold of that "brake." He heaved it forward as best he could from his almost prostrate position and . . . it fell only halfway under *one* of the sled's runners. That was enough to make the sled unstable but not enough to stop it. Ed leaned hard over to the side with the brake rope under the runner to put as much pressure on it as possible. It was just beginning to slow down the sled when they hit a large crack in the sea ice and Ed was thrown completely out of the sled.

He rolled out onto the snow and ice and then sat up to see the dogs and the sled going even faster into the distance, away from him, away from the woman whose sled it was. She was now maybe a mile behind him somewhere over the horizon among the buckled ice and icebergs frozen in place since the year before. What was worse, they were also headed ever farther away from Qaanaaq and warmth and safety. The sea ice is not a friendly place under the best of conditions. There are wolves and polar bears, not to mention the cold, and when storms sweep off the ice cap, death is right there, only minutes away. Alone, without transportation, far from any potential rescue, is definitely *not* the best of conditions.

Ed walked back toward the woman whom he could see walking toward him. When they met, they took stock of their situation. The woman said that the dogs were headed up the fjord toward the glacier front, and when they reached there, they would do what runaway sled dogs do—tangled in their lines, confused, and leaderless, they would eventually tear each other to shreds. There was nothing to be gained by walking in the direction the dogs had gone. Their only hope was to follow their own tracks the long miles back to Qaanaaq. Which is what they started to do.

But an hour into their trek, they heard something behind them: barking dogs. Rescuers, perhaps? Someone coming back from a seal or narwhal hunt? Or . . . even better, their own dogs? The woman explained that another hope, not all that often realized in the emptiness of the Arctic, would be that hunters would spot the derelict dogs and stop them. If that happened, the standard practice was to sort out the dogs, straighten the harness again, and then turn them around and head them back down their own tracks. Given the option, the sled dogs will always follow another sled track. So, if you set them down a sled's twin tracks, it's like putting a train on rails; they will go right back from where they came.

And that was apparently what had happened. Somewhere out there on that endless ice, some hunters had seen the dogs charging across the ice pulling an empty sled and, of course, instantly realized what had happened. They had stopped the dogs, sorted them out, and sent them right back toward Ed and his friend, and now, here they were. They were happy as they could be to have had the incredible freedom to resonate to their spirit and heritage, oblivious to the trouble they had caused, happy to see a couple of old friends out here on the ice, and ready to pack up and start again down that trail back to home toward Qaanaaq and a dried fish supper.

Sled dogs do what they do. They know nothing else. And they do what they do with a joy that is so visible there is no way you could ever be angry that their enthusiasm for the run had almost killed you. What else could those dogs have done but run? They're Arctic sled dogs. That's what they do.

*L. Hotovy Welsch after "Night on the Volga"*

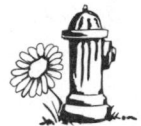

## CHAPTER THREE

# INNER CALLINGS

*The more I see of the representatives of the people,*
*the more I admire my dogs.*

**—COUNT D'ORSAY,**
***LETTER TO JOHN FORSTER***

My canine first love at the moment of this writing is Abbie. Her inborn peculiarities are partly—mostly—her Lab and Saint Bernard blood trying to reconcile with one another.

I have only recently discovered something that seems to be singularly hers—inborn, but not universal to her breed. Every dog I've ever had (I feel icky using the word "own" when it comes to a relationship with a dog) has been terrified by fireworks, thunder, and gunshots. We live in the country, near a river, on a highway, so the sound of shots is a fairly common thing, right down to the whizzing of errant bullets around our ears. Gun ownership and use in America is to no degree restricted to the sane, mature, responsible, or sensible, one should always keep in mind. Around here, starting about April 1, people who want to demonstrate their enthusiasm for America and the Constitution in the most irrational way possible start shooting off fireworks.

Of course not wanting to annoy any of their own neighbors in town, they come down to the river so they can annoy nature and those of us who came here to enjoy the peace and quiet of nature. Anyway, over a long life, I've grown used to otherwise courageous and strong-minded dogs cowering under a couch, drooling and shivering at every discharge of a weapon and/or every half-witted demonstration of pseudo-patriotism.

Well, the other day Linda came into the house and told me that Thud and Abbie had treed the rotten damned squirrel that has been tearing up our bird feeders, a habit that was getting to the point of being a bit too expensive for my otherwise animal-tolerant, easygoing ways. I grabbed a .410 shotgun and headed out the door, and sure enough, there was the squirrel, and there were Thud and Abbie. The squirrel was about to get what he deserved. It would have been one thing if he had simply gorged himself on corn and sunflower seeds, but no, he had ripped up Goldfinch thistle-seed feeders even though he had no interest in thistle seeds . . . but I sure hated what I was about to do to the dogs.

I understand how dogs feel about this. Gunshots are ferociously loud, especially shotgun blasts at close range. And while human beings know what's about to happen when they see a gun raised and can brace themselves for the explosion, dogs have no idea what is coming up. I can't imagine a situation like this *not* being traumatic to a dog inexperienced in the ways of guns, hunting, and shooting.

Yes, I know that dogs can be trained not only to accept shooting but actually to welcome it. If you fire a gun within earshot of my little town of Dannebrog, Nebraska, the next sound you hear is 400 dog feet scrambling into pickup truck beds because they think they are about to go hunting. My buddies here sometimes have to drive around with their dogs in their trucks because someone shot a gun somewhere within earshot. The dogs heard it, jumped into the truck all excited about going hunting, and now there's no way to get them back out. The dogs just have to sit in that truck long enough to figure out that no, this time *they* aren't going to be heading out into the corn fields or duck blinds!

I have often wondered how one does train a dog to handle the sound of shooting. My experience has always been that that first explosion, no matter how small—a .22-short cartridge fired away from the dog, a tiny little ladyfinger firecracker, doesn't matter—is enough to send any dog I've ever known into a fit of trembling, whining, drooling terror. One-hundred-fifty-pound brutes like Thud are not exempt.

So, there I stood, shotgun in hand, two dogs standing right there under the barrel, staring at that squirrel in the tree staring back at us. My only hope was that when I did fire the gun, I wouldn't so terrify them that they would tear through our heavy fence and wind up 12 miles away covered with burrs and mud before we could run them down. I raised the gun and shot the squirrel. Thud instantly ran down the stairs and toward the door to the dog porch, precisely as expected. But Abbie stood there, eyes glued to the squirrel. I hit the squirrel all right, but he was still clinging to a large branch over our heads.

"Shoot him again, Dad! Shoot him again!" Abbie urged. No kidding, she really did. She'd never heard or seen a gun fired, but she seemed to know instantly what was going on. I shot again and the squirrel fell. Abbie looked at me and said, "Thanks, God. Sorry I spoke with such disrespect. You are indeed the bringer of all good things."

At that point Thud came back to see what was going on. He suspected that Abbie was getting something he wasn't getting, and that is not acceptable to him under any circumstances. Seeing that she was not terrified, he decided he wouldn't be either. How did that happen? Why wasn't Abbie terrified? She should have been, but she wasn't. I suddenly had a new appreciation for her, reciprocating her new appreciation for me. Was she somehow born with an inherent tolerance for explosions? Even that would fall short of this newly discovered virtue of Abbie because she didn't just endure the astonishingly loud and sudden blast of that shotgun; she liked it!

To this day she scouts the yard with a passion. Now and then the gods smile and a squirrel ventures into the yard, misjudging the distance to the fence so that he suddenly finds that his only recourse is to scramble up a tree. And then Abbie not only sits at the base of that tree intent on converting that squirrel into a very special chew-toy. No! She actually comes and finds one of us and says so plainly that it might just as well be flashing in neon across her forehead, "*Get the damn gun and blow this arrogant little puke out of that tree! Come on, Dad, right now . . . Do your thing and get the gun get the gun get the gun!*" And it's all a gift. I'm not smart enough to train her to do that.

And I wonder what sorts of traits we human beings are born with. It makes no sense to me at all that all sorts of other creatures get shortcuts in life and we humans don't.

Current linguistic theories suggest that we are not born with the ability to use language but we are born with our circuits and dip switches set to learn how to use language. Is that all? Shouldn't we have some other things simply prewired in us at birth? Some of my Indian friends insist that we are indeed born with some spiritual, intellectual, cosmic sorts of connections but that white folks are educated out of them. I see no evidence to contradict that, with the single exception of the biological baby clock set to go off in all women at roughly 15 minutes after 30 years of age.

Perhaps the most eerie example I have witnessed of a dog's primal canine inheritance was with Slump. Linda and I and Slump were spending a weekend at our riverside cabin. Linda and I were asleep in the loft; Slump was sleeping on an old couch on the front porch. Suddenly I sat straight up in bed, awoken by the wonderful and spine-tingling sound of a coyote choir passing by within yards of the house in full howl, a sound that I love to my very heart and never hear without getting goose bumps. (And while we're speaking of hearing things and getting goose bumps, let's get it straight right now that the word "coyote" has two syllables, not three, and rhymes with "connote" rather than "Truman Capote." Only sportscasters and sleazy drinking establishments where no one has ever seen a coyote much less met one pronounce the word "kai-OAT-ee.")

Now, where was I? Oh yeah, Linda woke too because the coyotes were so close and so noisy it was not something easily missed. And Slump woke. We have found that while our dogs bark at other dogs, cats, birds, raccoons, opossums, and any other sort of creature that comes within sight or sound, they never go outside when coyotes come through, much less make a peep at them. I think it's a matter of that old saw about discretion being the better part of valor. And this time too there was not a peep from Slump outside on the porch . . . until the coyotes were well down our road, perhaps a quarter mile away and still screaming their mad laughter into the night.

Then Slump began to make sounds I had never heard him make before or after, or any other dog for that matter. They were coyote-like sounds, but muffled and strangled. I went down the loft ladder and called Slump in. He was obviously distraught and embarrassed. He was trying to stop himself from making these wild, primitive sounds that his civilized nature seemed to abhor. But he couldn't. The sounds kept coming out almost as if against his own will. Slump was clearly frightened, but not of the coyotes. He was deeply troubled, yes, even frightened, but frightened by what he found within his own soul that night when the coyotes passed so close. He tried to stop the sounds coming from within him but simply could not. His inner coyote was howling to escape.

His experience bothered me too. I wondered if maybe that's why I so thoroughly love the song of the coyote; it resonates somehow with a deeply buried primal part of my own soul. I do love the notion that wild dogs run through our farm regularly, just yards from our back door. I love that they survive, even prosper, although a major war is waged against them constantly; traps, guns, poison, even airplanes are used to kill coyotes around here. But they survive. I find that encouraging for us human beings too . . . at least for those of us lowest in the social hierarchy.

And just as I wonder if my own attraction to coyotes isn't because of their wonderful ability to survive and their defiant spirit, I also wonder if that isn't why some people are so intent on killing them. Unable to live a life with joy and freedom in it, some people try to snuff out whatever other expressions of joy and freedom they see around them. If you can't have a soul yourself, some people seem to think, then destroy those who do have souls. Once again when the canine universe comes up against human's, the dogs win, hands down, every time.

Apart from dog-wide traits and breed-specific talents, dogs have individual personalities. Toodles hated uniforms, any uniform—mail carrier, meter reader, police officer, Boy Scout. I have asked my mother if she can recall any sort of events that might have sparked this characteristic, but she says no, there was never any one event that could have explained it, but Toodles' antagonism toward anybody wearing a uniform was enormous and dangerous.

I understand why some dogs are afraid of some things. A dog that has been hurt or simply traumatized by a gunshot, automobile, bigger dog, or even a child is likely to carry that memory with him. But I don't at all understand why some dogs are just afraid for no particular reason, sometimes of something they have no reason to fear at all. Our Abbie is a wonderfully curious dog. She is the only dog I have ever seen look up into the sky to look at migrating cranes, geese, or even eagles. And she has no reason, absolutely *no* reason to be afraid of anything. She has never been hurt or threatened by anything or anyone. And yet she has a genuine fear of what she doesn't know. On various occasions I have come around a corner of the house carrying a big box, dragging a vacuum sweeper, or hauling a mattress and come upon Abbie relaxing in the shade or sun, as the season demands. She jumps straight up into the air and hits the ground running, with her tail between her legs. And it takes some reassurance to convince her that it's just her daddy lugging something. It's as if she doesn't recognize me in any unusual profile and she presumes the worst.

I think some dog behavior is simply to amuse us. I have no idea when Abbie jumped up beside me on the old car seat on our back porch and sat on her head, but now it's standard. She only sits on her head when she is sitting beside me, so far only on the back-porch car seat and the sofa in the front room. I think you know what I mean; you've seen other dogs do this. Instead of sitting sedately beside me on her fanny, which she can and sometimes does do, knowing that it amuses the heck out of me, she puts her head down on the seat and then pushes so that her rear end is over her head. Her head is now upside down and she can pretend to bite at me and Thud while I scratch her heinie. And no, this isn't her way of getting her heinie scratched. I do that anyway; I scratch her ears, her rear, her chest. She just knows it makes me laugh when she pulls this upside-down contortion. Thud, on the other hand, never does this, nor have any of our other dogs, ever. It's Abbie's trick and she does it for no other reason than that it makes me chuckle.

Behaviorists poo-poo this notion. They insist that animals do things for direct reward or pain avoidance. I am convinced otherwise. Abbie and Thud *both* know that they are going to be scolded for dragging laundry out of the utility room and into the front room, but they do it anyway because they *know* I think it's funny. Pavlov be damned, Abbie likes to make me laugh even though she doesn't understand either why I am laughing or why she likes it.

Lucky was downright prissy about his bathroom habits. If you said anything to him while he was pooping, you could almost see him blush. He'd cut off his activity and slink around to the other side of the house so he could continue with some dignity. Thud poops when and where the spirit moves him. We're sitting on the patio bench, maybe scratching Thud's ear. He walks 10 steps away, looks us right in the eye, and squats. Means nothing to him.

Our 60-acre tree farm runs along a Nebraska river, the Middle Loup. We have a zoo of wildlife here but my favorites, as I noted earlier, are the coyotes. We save our edible kitchen scraps for all the critters that live here, the real tenants, since they are long-term and we've only been here a couple dozen years. During the winter I can spot who's been visiting my refuse leavings: possums, skunks, coons, squirrels, turkeys, crows, and, sometimes, wonderfully, coyotes.

Even when there is not snow on the ground, I get signals that Coyote appreciates my offerings: he poops in our bottom road, right along the route where I drop off the food scraps. Now, I can imagine that some of those sitings could be coincidence: coyotes run down the low-grass of the road, so that's also where they poop. And some of it could be gastrological: he eats, he is moved to poop. But I am absolutely convinced that something more than that is going on with my coyotes. They also poop at our gate, where we are sure to see it but where they are never fed. When we moved into a building serve as Linda's art studio, the next morning in several spots in clear view around that new building was coyote poop. I never find coyote poop anywhere else. And believe me, I look. I find raccoon poop here and there now and then. (In case you wonder, there is no mistaking raccoon poop:

"They asked me if I knew/ Raccoon poop is blue;/ I of course then said/Bullshit you've been fed/ Raccoon poop is red . . ." as the fine old tune goes.) But I never find coyote poop *except on that road where I put the food.*

How do I know it's coyote poop? There's not much mistaking coyote poop. It's larger and firmer than raccoon, possum, or skunk poop. But more than that, it also reflects the omnivorous nature of coyote and generally canine cuisine. Sorting through coyote poop, one finds bug wings, little teeth and bones, large hairs, feathers, pits and seeds, an absolute buffet of whatever it is that crosses a coyote's path during his busy day. Or night, as the case may be.

What, after all, do dogs eat? Sticks, bones, lawn sprinklers, cat poop, house slippers, grass. (Q: What does it mean when a dog eats grass? A: It means the dog's going to puke.) Oh, your dog may be fussy about what kind of dog food it eats, or like Lucky, he may sort out any peas that happen to appear in his bowl and spit them contemptuously off to the side, but given any chance to eat anything *else* he *will* eat it. The more disgusting, the better.

As a former literary scholar and professor, the question naturally and instantly springs to my mind: what does this thing about coyote poop mean? Is it an insult, a gesture of defiance, an invitation to take my stinky household and inadequate household dogs and go back where I came from? Maybe, but I don't think so. I can't imagine that a coyote spends much time in his daily considerations being grateful, but I do know that coyotes are much, much too smart not to recognize that steak scraps, remnants of baloney sandwiches, fish skins, and overly ripe frankfurters are not, strictly speaking, the kind of natural fare that simply appears deep in Nebraska river woods, neatly placed time after time in the middle of a road.

I sleep with my windows open during winter and summer specifically so I can hear the coyote choirs as they pass through our place. So I know that they sometimes howl a mile or so to our west, sometimes to the east, across the river. Their choice of venues for any particular performance seems to be pretty much at random. But not *right* here. Not here where I put our scraps. Here, directly below our house, not a 100 yards away, they put on especially excellent and ornate rococo cadenzas. It simply cannot be a matter of chance that the coyotes stop so close to the house, in the very same place, summer and winter, whether I have left food for them or not . . . *and regardless of where I have thrown food for them on this 60 acres*!

That said, neither can I believe that it is pure circumstance that they select the very same place to poop. No, I believe ol' Br'er Coyote comes cruising by our house on his way somewhere, or on his way nowhere, he sees the lights at the house or smells those peculiar human smells, and he feels he needs to say something by way of greeting. He needs to acknowledge that we occasionally leave food for him down there on the road. "Let's see," he thinks to himself. "What could I leave here that the big guy who smells so bad would understand is my little token of gratitude. I don't have much. I'm only a coyote, after all. But let's see . . . I can sing. Sure, that's it. I'll sing him a couple bars of my latest composition, 'When the Moon Comes Up Over the Loup.'

"That still doesn't seem like much by way of an exchange. Surely I have something else. Nope. Nothing. It's too late for ticks, too early for pups. Let's see. What could

I leave here for him? Wait a minute! I feel an inspiration coming on! Yes, yes, yes! I know what I can leave him!"

And that's what Coyote leaves me.

Or maybe I'm spending too much time analyzing.

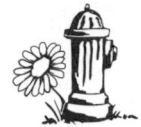

CHAPTER FOUR

# THE DEVIOUS COURSES OF DOGGIE THOUGHT

*Young blood must have its course, lad,*
*And every dog his day.*

—CHARLES KINGSLEY, ***WATER BABIES***

If you think dogs simply eat, you haven't been paying attention. We have to separate Thud and Abbie at meal times because Thud instantly eats everything. He inhales it. He throws himself into a meal. Lucky was like that too. Except that Lucky always sorted the peas out of any leftovers and carefully spit them out beside his bowl. Thud devours everything instantly without a moment to say grace. Abbie is more like Goldie—she eats slowly, almost delicately. Sometimes she has to be talked into eating. She doesn't hurry. She is careful not to get any food on her lips or whiskers. Abbie eats inside the dog porch; Thud eats outside on the patio, and almost always barks. He barks because he is very nervous about being alone outside. He's huge, and can even be ferocious, and is not a fearful sort of dog. But it just makes him uncomfortable to be outside alone. Abbie frequently goes off by herself and simply sits looking off into the distance, or plays with a toy all by herself, or sprawls and naps in the sun while Thud is indoors. Abbie likes company but she doesn't seem to need it to the extent that Thud does.

Thud likes to have his ears rubbed. Abbie doesn't like anything over her head, especially a hand. She likes to have her tummy rubbed. Lucky never looked you in the eye. Thud never fails to look you in the eye. Sometimes Abbie does, sometimes she doesn't. What is clear from all this is that dogs have very distinct personalities. Thud and Abbie are both dogs and do some things clearly canine- or breed-universal, but they also have their own minds and personalities. Nor are these two members of our family mere carbon copies of any previous dogs we've had, or of us. They have distinct personalities of their own, as do all dogs. I respect that about them. They are individuals no less certainly than we humans are.

One of the most distinctive characteristics of the dogs in my life has been the way they express their affection. There are those who insist that the notion that dogs have actual feelings like affection is an example of pathetic fallacy, an attribution of human emotions, feelings, and reactions to objects in nature. Like thinking a tree looks "sad" and calling it a "weeping" willow. Anyone who thinks dogs don't have very real emotions has never had much to do with dogs and is an idiot besides.

And no, it isn't just a matter of conditioning; that is, a dog doesn't like the people in his life simply because they feed him. If anything, I'd say that dogs have even stronger emotions than human beings, more tender feelings, and even express them more openly than most human beings—certainly more than most men.

Years ago we were having some work done on our house and the workmen accidentally left a part of our fence open. A visitor came through during the day and Blackjack went nuts; it turned out that this fellow's female dog was in heat and he carried with him the canine perfume of love. And Blackjack fell in love with this man's dog as only a dog can fall in love. (Note: I am not for a moment suggesting that Blackjack's lustings were emotional. I'm getting there. Stay with me a bit longer here.)

That night Blackjack's passion carried him out the gap in our fence and on his path to love. We think Goldie went with him, at least as far as the highway where Blackjack was hit and killed by a passing car. We think Goldie was with him because she wouldn't have missed a chance to go on an adventure like that, and the next day she had burrs and dirt in her fur and showed emotional trauma well beyond what would have been expected if she had simply noticed that Blackjack had exited our yard sometime during the night. They were inseparable. Goldie's sorrow is the love I am talking about here, not Blackjack's hormonal frenzy.

Anyway, I found Blackjack's huge dead body beside the highway. I picked him up, put him in my car, and took him down to our river cabin where my friend Mick was staying. I had to go to Lincoln and so, drenched in sorrow and tears, I had to ask Mick and Linda to bury my beloved friend

Blackjack for me. That night was a sad one in our house—Linda still hasn't recovered these 15 years later—but the worst was yet to come: that night, all night, we could hear from the dog porch downstairs the pitiful crying of Goldie, mourning her lost life partner. She never cried before or again like that. She had never before whined or cried like that. But that night she cried. She was heartbroken.

When Lucky died seven years later from a nasal tumor, it was simply too much for Goldie. She'd lost one big black friend in Blackjack, and now she had lost another. Lucky died the first of the month. Goldie died less than a month later. She had been in good health. Except that she was lonely. Don't tell me dogs don't have feelings like love. Don't tell me Goldie, who was so smart she knew everything we were going to do even before we did it, didn't know that Blackjack and Lucky had died.

The moral of all this is that animals in general, and dogs in particular, know a lot more about abstract things like death, love, fear, freedom, embarrassment, humiliation, revenge, even plotting and scheming than we humans have given them credit for.

This next story doesn't belong here, perhaps, since it is a cat story, but I guess even cats have feelings, albeit malevolent ones, and are perfectly capable of the most devious sort of plotting. My training, research, and work experience have all been in the area of folklore, traditional practices, and knowledge. Unfortunately, some people who don't know any better confuse the word "folklore" with "fiction," as in "the facts and folklore of PMS." The problem is, an astonishing amount of our traditional knowledge is based on experience over long periods of time and is therefore at least as accurate, sometimes even *more* truthful, than what passes for science, history, or truth.

All of which is to say, I cannot in good conscience dismiss out-of- hand notions like that of cats having nine lives. Okay, an idea like that may come from the incredible physical resilience of cats. Anyone who has had the experience of starting an automobile when a cat is sleeping soundly on the still-warm engine and witnessed how a cat that has been hit by the voltage from a spark plug wire, then hit the bottom side of the hood when startled, then fled through the spinning fan and/or fan belt of the running car, and then hit the pavement under the car with a velocity enhanced by the electrical shock, then rebounded off the hood's springy metal with extra force from the boost of a rotating fan blade, has almost assuredly been astonished to see that selfsame cat sitting on that very same car hood, licking its paws, leaving muddy tracks up and down the car windshield as if nothing even faintly unusual had happened to it earlier that same day.

My story about Homer the Cat is a different slant on the feline contempt for mortality. Homer was always an amazing member of our household. Linda first found him living with our chickens in the hen house. We are constantly plagued by dumped, lost, stray feral cats around here, and they are anything but candidates for domestication. They are mean, loud, ugly, belligerent, and aggressive. As a result, when such cats begin hanging around, they tend to be discreetly sent to kitty heaven.

Well, Homer was not like that. For one thing, he was just a kitty, too young to be a full-fledged, card-carrying savage beast. We certainly didn't need another cat but Linda felt sorry for him. She wouldn't let me trap him and send him to feral tomcat heaven. Instead she had me do something I had never done before or have done since. I took the cat and dumped him somewhere else. I know that abandoning an animal is unforgivable and I swear I won't do it again, but I did it this time. I took this kitten across the river to a small park area and left him there, hoping someone would come along and adopt him. I was drenched with guilt as I drove away, having done something I consider just about the lowest thing a human can do. But I didn't have a choice. And I needn't have worried. So help me, by the time I drove back across the bridge to our farm, there was Homer, sitting in the sun in front of the hen house, licking his paws.

No, it couldn't be. It must be a different cat. Yeah, that's it, a different cat. Linda checked. Nope, same cat. Somehow he had made it across a 100 yards of water and sand or across the bridge, or maybe he hung on the undercarriage of my pickup, I don't know, but there he was. And Linda said, "Rog, you have to get rid of this cat, but don't you dare hurt him."

Great. We boxed up the blasted cat and I went back across the river. And down the road six miles south, west another three, across creeks, past six mean dogs, over a slough. And once again I did the unthinkable and turned the cat loose on its own to starve and die or find a new home, anywhere but our place.

Three days later and after a ferocious weekend thunderstorm, of course there was Homer—that was now officially his name—sitting in front of the hen house in the sun, licking his paws. Well, that did it. There was no way we could reject someone that determined to live with us. Linda did insist that he be "customized," so she put him in the cat box once again and drove him over to our veterinarian's office in St. Paul, about 15 miles away. She says that Homer was very attentive the whole drive over, and she noticed he was scratching little kitty notes on the back wall of the pet caddy: "Siks meils north, tern east another ate meils, tirn north agin, . . ." just in case he once again was being tested. Homer lived with us—or as cats would have it, we lived with Homer—for many years after that, and I came to admire him mightily for his sheer gall, persistence, and disregard for others.

The point being, once Homer set his mind on something he pretty much insisted on having his way. He loved life and would go to astonishing ends to see that life was going his way. Homer was no dummy. In fact, if Homer had a fault, other than the usual inventory of failings that make all cats annoying as hell, it was that he was way, way too smart for his own good.

Linda doesn't like going away and leaving me here alone because she says something always goes wrong when she leaves me alone. Strictly speaking, that's not true: once 16 years ago she left me here alone for three days and nothing went wrong unless you count something like a bowl of beans exploding in the microwave as "going wrong" or, as Linda has just reminded me, forgetting I was babysitting and leaving the then three-year-old Antonia alone in town. I don't think that should really count because there have been plenty of times when I've blown up bowls of beans—also anchovies, potatoes, maple syrup, and coffee mugs—in the microwave or forgotten various family members when she *was* here. But along came an occasion when she decided to go to Lincoln to visit her family, and she left me here alone for three days. I resolved to do everything I could to regain her confidence in me; nothing, by God, *nothing* was going to go wrong this time.

I firmly believe that dogs can read human minds. Not only can cats read minds, they are better at it even than dogs. A cat can walk into a room full of people and instantly tell which of those people hates cats most—and that would be me—and jump up on that person's lap and rub against that person's face. All the while they know that the victim can't possibly fling her across the room and out the sixth-floor window as long as the hostess is standing right there cooing about what a precious darling Kitty-Koo is.

Anyway, on this occasion, completely unnoticed by either Linda or me, Homer was reading the situation like a Navy Seal scout. And laying his plans. Linda left. Everything went fine the rest of that day and through the evening. The next morning I fed the dogs and cats. Homer dug right in, never revealing the slightest hint of his plans for me. I went out to my office to work.

About noon I left the office to go to the house for lunch and was startled to find all three of our dogs at the time—Lucky, Thud, and Goldie—and our other cat, Hairball, standing in a little clump, looking at something on the ground. I went over to see what had attracted their curiosity. And there was Homer. Dead as a doornail.

I was flabbergasted, of course. I checked the corpse to see if I could figure out what had killed him. Nope . . . no wounds, nothing. There wasn't a mark on him. He wasn't old, he wasn't sick. He was just dead.

And I knew immediately that so was I. Never again was Linda going to leave me here alone. I put the corpse of that miserable yellow schemer in a box so I could show Linda I hadn't shot him or run over him or drowned him, that he had just died. Of course it really didn't make a difference. What mattered was that Homer had died while I was in charge, while I was here alone.

My theory is that Homer knew perfectly well what he was doing. He knew that he was mortal, that all creatures die. Perhaps he figured since he was a cat, he had other lives ahead of him. But whatever the case, even if this was the one single life Homer had to surrender, he also knew that this was the one chance he would have to die a death worthy of catdom immortality and legend. Simply by deciding to lie down and die right there in the yard, Homer knew that he would put me into a jam like no other situation he would ever be able to cook up, while at the same time appearing to be utterly blameless himself.

When Linda came home she did examine the body to be sure I hadn't murdered Homer, as if that would make any difference. When we buried him, I noticed that he had just a hint of a smile on his face.

Now, all that is to say that I believe animals think. They plot and scheme. They have feelings, they miss someone who's gone, they love us and each other. No, they don't have the words for it, but somehow they seem to figure out ways to express themselves. That is, I believe dogs and cats not only love us, they try to *tell* us they love us. Or in cases like Homer, hate us.

I first noticed this with good ol' Fleagle. It was my habit at that time to lie on the floor on my back in front of the television set during the evening. I'm not crazy about being licked by dogs so I disciplined Fleagle when he tried to demonstrate affection with that usual canine method. He gave that some considerable thought—you could tell he was thinking about it by the look on his face—and he decided that if I didn't want to be licked, then lick he wouldn't. And yet he also knew that he wanted to tell me something in his heart, something that he really needed to say somehow.

I have no recollection how it started, but at some point Fleagle came up to me lying there on the floor and stood with his front paws on my chest. He just stood there. Sometimes he'd look in my eyes, but that wasn't a crucial part of what he was trying to say. He just pressed down with his front paws. And that's where this really transcends a trick, like standing with his paws on my chest because someone somehow signaled it was cute, or because he got his ears scratched when he did that. He didn't *just* stand with his front paws on my chest: he pressed down as hard as he could with those paws. I have tried to analyze how he did that. I imagine he just shifted his long torso's weight forward, perhaps moving his legs back on his length to put added weight there. But it was more like a Zen thing.

Dick Cavett is a friend of mine and a student of martial disciplines and arts. He's no wimp. When we were in high school together, he was the state gymnastics champ. Anyway, Dick once demonstrated to me how the martial arts are as much mental as physical. He stood in front of me and told me to try to lift him off the ground. He's a fairly small guy and I'm fairly big; it wasn't really easy but I did manage to get him off the ground. He did some "focusing," shifted his inner weight mentally, and told me to try it again. I couldn't even come close to budging him. It was as if he were anchored to our floor with half-inch bolts.

That's what Fleagle did. While he may have made some actual physical adjustments in his stance to transfer weight to his front paws, that wasn't evident. But his much-increased weight was clearly there. He would just stand there, pressing down, and I don't think for a moment either one of us mistook what he was saying with that. He was telling me he loved and appreciated what we had by way of a friendship.

Thud sits on my foot. He will go out of his way, get up off a nice soft cushion, and come sit on my foot. He doesn't drag his butt (I knew that's what you were thinking!), and he doesn't seem to gain any particular advantage from that aside from sometimes getting his ear scratched in return. I think I know what Thud is saying.

When Lucky and Goldie were number one and number two of the Welsch pack, Thud was really truly third on the totem pole. He knew that. He was always the last at everything. But he devised a system for establishing a relationship with us beyond food, bed, and ear scratching. When we would let them into the house for the evening, which we try to do several times a week, he would make a beeline for the open door to the laundry room. We tried to get him to stop but he would not be deterred. He would reach into the laundry basket and pull out a sock and bring it to the front room. We tried to get him to stop that too but he insisted. He would bring the sock to us and give it to us. He didn't see it as a toy, or a chewie, or anything at all for his own personal enjoyment. He brought it to us as a gift.

Thing is, like ol' Coyote, Thud doesn't really have anything he can call his own, so what could he give us of *his*? Nothing really. But he could give us *something*, and that's what he did. Sometimes on a particularly pleasant evening, he would get off a nice comfortable bed, wander to the laundry room (we eventually stopped the formality of trying to get him to stop the habit), and bring out a sock for us. He would bring it to us, let us have it, and go back to lie down. He had something he wanted to say and he said it.

## CHAPTER FIVE

# WHAT THEY SEE, WHAT THEY HEAR, WHAT THEY KNOW

*Let dogs delight to bark and bite,*
*For God hath made them so . . .*

—ISAAC WATTS, "AGAINST QUARRELING AND FIGHTING," *DIVINE SONGS*

Now, here's what's curious. We have found that every one of our dogs is better than the last one. You have a dog or two so wonderful that you can't imagine there ever in your life—or in this world—being a better dog. But that dog dies. One of the true agonies of being a human being, I believe, is that we live longer lives than our dogs, so we see them die more than they send us off. But damned if the next dog isn't somehow better, and, here's the spooky part, somehow becoming in many ways an echo of what that previous super dog was. When we lost Goldie and Lucky within one month, we were devastated, in part because we knew there'd never be another dog quite like Goldie or Lucky, probably not one different than those two in better ways.

But along comes Abbie. And she is not only a better dog in many ways than Goldie and Lucky (which is not to take a single thing away from those two grand canine souls), but she somehow incorporates in an uncanny way the very same characteristics they had. What's even crazier is that she has also assumed some of the duties of Thud, lightening his load in his dotage. It was Thud's "job," or "trick," to bring us those socks. When Abbie came along, so full of youthful enthusiasm and nuttiness that she drove Thud to distraction (he adores her—that is also evident—but like any tired old guy with a young woman in his life, man, it can be wearing on the disposition!), Thud quit bringing us socks. He had other things on his mind, like ensuring that he had a space on the dog-porch bed before this wild woman Abigail von der Pooper took over the whole thing. And he just seemed to forget about bringing us socks. I can't help but wonder if it wasn't a matter of our much-increased affection and attention for him because (1) he was the survivor of the Lucky/Goldie Dynasty and (2) he was now beset with this new whirlwind of a puppy in his previously placid life.

Now, here's the spooky part: without ever having seen Thud bring us socks, Abbie started doing the exact selfsame thing. Exactly. It was as if she were doing a precise imitation of Thud's behavior . . . but without ever having seen him do it! And she astonishes us with that little gesture every evening we let the two of them into the house. They come in, greet us, Abbie brings us a sock, they both lie down on their pads for a little while, Thud gets bored, gets up, opens the door on his own (a trick he learned from Goldie), Abbie chews on a bonie for a while, goes to sleep, and then eventually gets up and leaves on her own too. Sometimes before she leaves, she brings us another sock.

While I'm on the subject, I'll never forget the evening when we—Linda, Goldie, Thud, Lucky, and I—were sitting in the front room when a couple of mealy moths from the pantry came fluttering into the front room and I took after them with a rolled-up newspaper. Well, Goldie hated violence of any kind—she was theologically speaking a Quaker—so she hated anything that had to do with a rolled-up newspaper. She watched this scene of my mad flailings for about a minute and then got up off her bed, went over to the back door, opened it, and left. Linda and I sat there in utter disbelief. No dog of ours had ever opened any door, much less left on its own. But Goldie just did it as if she'd done it all her life. And from that moment on, she always let herself out when she was bored with us. Or annoyed. Lucky never learned that trick. He'd sit there and watch Goldie leave and then ask us to let him out. Thud did learn it, and now he has taught it to Abbie.

What else do they know how to do? I don't know for sure. I have some suspicions, however, and it's almost scary. For example, I'm fairly sure that our dogs can read our minds. I imagine fancy behavioral scientists have theories about dogs picking up on the faintest sorts of clues in *our* behaviors that lead them to whatever it is *they* do in reaction. And in many cases, maybe even most cases, that's the way it works. We make the slightest little twitch every time we are thinking about heading to the refrigerator. Your dog has nothing better to do with his time than to try to read things in what you do that might lead to a piece of baloney, and pretty soon he notices that twitch. And so you twitch, he reacts, and you get to thinking he is reading your mind since he seems to know you are going to the fridge even before you make the first conscious move.

When my son, Chris, now a big galoot, was but a tad, he had a thing for horses. He didn't know a lot of things in this world, but he did know horsies, and he loved horsies, and so he could spot horsies much better than those of us who really don't care all that much about horsies. Certainly much better than those of us who have suffered the humiliations of being hated by horses all our long lives: bitten, kicked, stepped on, rubbed against trees, crushed by being leaned on, drooled on, pooped on, peed on, ignored or countermanded, bucked off. I'm not mentioning any names here, I hope you've noticed. Let's just say that I know there are people who've suffered these kinds of misbehavior at the evil whim of horses and take it from me, we don't really go out of our way to notice horsies.

Once when Chris was maybe two years old, we were visiting my parents and he started to make a fuss about horsies. "Horsies, horsies, horsies," he yelled wildly, pointing in the general direction of Mom's kitchen cupboards. "There are no horsies there, Chris," we explained as patiently as we could over his howling, dancing about, and pointing. "Horsies! Horsies! Horsies!" he insisted even louder. We tried to spot what he was pointing at . . . nothing. Finally, in an effort to bring some calm and quiet onto the scene, I picked him up and held him horizontally, scanning him around the room like a Geiger counter or metal detector, hoping I could get him to indicate more precisely what he was so excited about. Slowly but surely we worked our way into the corner of the kitchen, on a counter, under a cupboard, to the toaster. The closer we got, the more excited he got, beeping louder and faster, until his forefinger finally touched the toaster cover.

I still didn't spot any horsies. I pulled the toaster out onto the counter to get a closer look at it and finally, at long last, I could see that the abstract pattern on the toaster cover was actually small geometric, interlaced . . . horses. My mother, of course, interpreted this as a sure sign that her first grandchild had super genius vision. But the probable truth is that since his life centered on the few things he knew and loved, that's what he spotted in his environment. He didn't need to spot red traffic lights, children approaching a street, a suspicious-looking guy with his hands in his pockets approaching me while I withdrew money from an ATM, flashing red lights looking like little oil cans on my automobile control panel, wisps of smoke coming out from under a bathroom window, the veins in my erstwhile wife's temples swelling ever so slightly and throbbing just a little bit harder and faster. What Chris saw when he looked around his world was what he knew, and that included horsies.

On the American frontier, even my Indian friends admit, Indian scouts were not prized because they had some sort of mystic knowledge (but they might have, if my experience is anything close to accurate), or inbred information (which, again, they very well may have had), but because they simply saw the world in very different terms from the white man's vision. Where Fremont saw wilderness and desert, the Pawnee saw a lush paradise. Where Bill Cody saw an endless herd to be slaughtered for only the tongue or, for that matter, for fun, the Lakota saw an expression of God's generosity to be revered and respected. Where homesteaders saw a frontier where food was difficult to transport and maintain, the Omaha saw a garden where food was easily procured at every turn.

Chris saw the world in terms of horsies. The Pawnee saw the Plains in terms of easy living. And dogs see the world in terms of fascinating smells, things to be fetched and chewed, and the every movement of their pack leader, which is to say, *you*. (I urge the male reader to use some caution in applying the conventional, even scientific, term "alpha bitch" to the lady of the household when she has established her position within your own collection of pets. While you may be, strictly speaking, correct, you could find yourself, as I have, with some new problems in determining your own position within the pack after only once referring to the woman in your life as the alpha bitch. "Alpha leader" sounds *much* better and leads to far fewer complications. Trust me on this one.)

If you haven't been struck by it before, sooner or later you are going to be astonished at what your dog observes and therefore knows about you and your behavior. There's not a doubt in my mind that the very best anthropological study of human behavior will eventually be written by a dog. Dogs "read" when you are sad, happy, or sick. Anyone who has ever had a dog knows that the very best nursie a sick person can have is a dog. After Goldie died, Linda was completely bereft; Thud, despite his own pain at losing his foster mother Goldie, was adamant about being with Linda to ease her pain as she sobbed.

Dogs show enormous concern, do whatever they think will make you better, completely alter their own behavior to make you more comfortable. But dogs also know, for example, when you are going somewhere. Our dogs' behavior is clearly different when I go out the front door with a suitcase, or even when we get into the car to go to town for supper. Their ears drop as if laden with the added responsibilities of taking care of the house alone during our absence; they watch the car or truck leave the yard in such a way as they would never do if I were simply running to town to get the mail or pick up some bread. Somehow they *know* we are going *away*. They understand that the leadership of the pack has shifted to *them*, and that we expect something new and more of them in our absence.

There's more. We have an interior anteroom at our back door that serves as the dog porch, and it has a separate little door so they can go in and out at will. There is a large door for us to go in and out of our kitchen, into their porch, and then out into the yard. But we leave the house to go to the office, yard, shop, or cars through the *front* door, which is on the opposite side of the house. At some point years ago, Linda and I noticed that when we were about to go somewhere, the dogs would go busting out of the dog porch door and head for the front door to be a part of the departure.

It got to be a kind of amusement to say, "Well, I guess I'll be GOing, . . ." pick up the keys or a coffee cup, or have Linda zip her purse, and then laugh as the dogs exploded from that back door and ripped toward the front. But at some point we noticed that we didn't need to pick up the keys, or even say anything about going. If we carried on a normal conversation in which we discussed what we were going to do the next hour or so and then stood up, the dogs went roaring out their door.

Hmmm. So what would happen if we didn't say anything at all, but simply stood up and . . . out the door they went. Okay, how about if we were already standing and simply started toward the door would they . . . fa-woom! Out the door they go. What if we edged very quietly toward the door out of their sight and . . . out they went. If we leave their door closed so they can't hear or see a thing would they . . . gone. We finally gave up. There is nothing we can do or *not* do that successfully conceals our intentions from the dogs, it seems. They *know* when we are leaving the house. To this day, we have no idea what signals them. I'd like to think they can read our minds but then it would really be scary because I'm not sure souls as tender, wise, and honest should be subjected to human perfidy.

Human beings have been making pathetic stabs at reversing the process in the last few years, we should note. The "Bowlingual" is a Japanese-produced device that is attached to a dog's collar from which vantage point it offers up translations of its barks, whines, and snarls in either Japanese or English. Human and electronic limitations restrict the number of possible messages your dog can send you. For example, "Got some good stuff?" "I want to see the world," "I'm feeling a little odd," or "I've never been so embarrassed." Do we really need an electronic device to get this kind of message from our dog? Not in my experience.

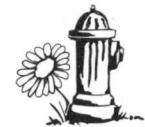

CHAPTER SIX

# TO SLEEP, PERHAPS TO DREAM

*A watchdog is a dog kept to guard your home, usually by sleeping where a burglar would awaken the household by falling over him.*

**—ANONYMOUS**

I don't spend a lot of time reading about animal behavior so I really don't know what I'm talking about here, but somewhere I recall having read or heard that dogs can't possibly be dreaming because dreaming depends on language, and obviously dogs don't have language. Of course that would be wrong. As the old saying goes, you don't have to be a chicken to know a bad egg, or a dog to know a dumb idea. Dogs dream. Five minutes with a sleeping dog will make that perfectly clear to anyone, even a psychologist. To my mind, the really sad thing is not being able to know what it is that our dogs are dreaming about. Some evenings we invite our current two canine companions in to share a couple hours with us, especially in the winter when their porch is cold. We have comfortable pads for them on our living room floor, and when they come in they chew on toys for a while and then settle down to nap. Along with some very impressive snoring and devastating SBD farting, they twitch, kick, curl their lips, yip, and, what's most fascinating, wag their tails. (Linda, being a woman—for which I am eternally grateful by the way—insists that I insert here a definition for SBD, although there isn't a male alive who doesn't know that is a common designation for a species of fart known notoriously as "silent but deadly.")

It doesn't matter much what Linda and I are watching on television, reading, or talking about, when one of the dogs goes into an overt dream mode, we stop and watch. Wondering what is going on in those heads is simply too fascinating to miss. Abbie has never had a thing to fear in her life. She has never been hurt or threatened, so what is she growling and baring her teeth at? What kinds of demons and ogres does she fight in her dreams? When she whimpers softly and wags her tail in her sleep as if greeting a beloved friend, is it one of us? Thud perhaps? A memory of her mother? A canine genie granting her three wishes?

There's an old folk belief that on Christmas Eve animals can talk, a kind of reward for their gracious reception of Joseph, Mary, and the newborn Jesus into the stable. My family jokes every Christmas, speculating what our animal family will say. We imagine that they will probably say pretty much what they always seem to say anyway. Lucky: "Throw the Frisbee! Throw the Frisbee!" Goldie: "Love me! Love me! Love me!" Thud: "What's for supper? Isn't it about time for supper?" Abbie: "I simply cannot believe how great this place is! God must surely love me. Why, here he comes now with yet another meal that is way too good for the likes of me!"

Some Christmas I'm going to stay up past my usual bedtime in hopes that the old folklore is right, and I'll have a chance to ask the dogs some questions and maybe get some answers. One of the first things I would ask is what they dream about. I would *love* to know what they are dreaming. What are they chasing? I imagine rabbits, squirrels, deer, the kinds of things they chase during the day. I can even imagine why they wag their tails since I pretty much know what it is that makes them happy: a thrown stick, goodies, a good ear scratch for Thud or belly scratch for Abbie. But what is it that makes them snarl and growl? What do they struggle against? They lead pretty safe and calm lives here. They are never threatened by anything. Our dogs face no real dangers through their entire lives in most cases. So, I can't help but wonder if dogs not only have dreams drawn from their own experiences but also have the capacity to imagine things they have not experienced. Isn't that a fascinating thought? Your dog's dreams suggest that given the time, a thesaurus, and a decent word processor he or she might be able to write a novel.

The mere activity of play-acting suggests to me that dogs have imaginations and understand very well the processes of inventing, pretending, thinking. Dogs create theatrical works. They "fight" with each other, clearly only pretending to fight. They have established an obvious understanding that they are not *actually* biting and clawing at each other, that when one falls down he is not *actually* injured, that the barking and growling is not *really* intended to warn or threaten.

And they do the same with us, their human friends. We all know how threatening dogs can be. Watch an episode of *Cops* television, if you doubt me. A miscreant who is fighting off 10 police officers with only a knife or his fists will fall to his face and surrender without further argument the second someone yells that if he doesn't comply at once, they are sending in the dog. There is something implacably unmerciful about a dog's attack and no one wants to deal with it.

So, why don't we cower in fear when we wrestle on the floor with our own pet dogs? They are growling, showing teeth, perhaps barking, snapping, advancing, retreating, trying to get at our soft and tender parts, but we only laugh until we pee our pants if we are little kids . . . or sometimes even adults, I suppose. We know that the dogs understand we are pretending. We trust their imagination. I think that says something wonderful about dogs.

Cats attack a string but I don't get the impression that they know they are amusing us. They are simply curious. They react to innate urges to attack. If your hand happens to be in the way, there is every likelihood the cat will bury needle-sharp claws or teeth in you and not have the foggiest notion why you object when they do. They don't understand it's a game. It's just another reality, which they think they understand but you apparently do not. Not dogs. They are intellectuals who understand the magic and usefulness of the hypothetical.

When I chase Abbie or Thud while they have a toy in their mouths, they may have a momentary relapse; their back hairs may stand up and their tails disappear between their back legs, but just a word of reassurance has them back running insane circles. They'll come just close enough to taunt me, perhaps even surrendering the toy so I can throw it. And we can start pretending all over again that I am Roger the Ogre and am about to tear their bodies apart to get at that rubber ball they have in their mouths.

DOGS

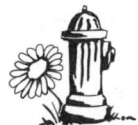

CHAPTER SEVEN

# THE OTHER DOG'S WHATEVER

*I loathe people who keep dogs.*
*They are cowards who haven't got the guts*
*to bite people themselves.*

—AUGUST STRINDBERG

There's no doubt that dogs have a strong sense of possession. Dogs know what is theirs, or at least their pack's, and they know that it is their job to protect it. They understand this in terms of territory, as well as in terms of possessions and fellow pack members. My buddy Dave lived across the street from us in my early days in Lincoln, Nebraska, and he had two huge Saint Bernards, Zeke and Emma. Like so many big dogs, Zeke and Emma were huge, lumbering, good-hearted oafs, even bigger in heart and love than they were in body. At that time Lincoln was more a town than a city and was just transitioning from being a place where dogs simply ran loose—as Toodles did through my entire youth and her entire life—and one where dogs had to be confined. Dave was something of a free soul anyway and didn't have a lot of regard for legal niceties. He was from Nebraska ranch country where freedom borders on anarchy, and his house sat in the middle of a large residential block, way back from the street and behind newer houses all around it. So, Zeke and Emma pretty much wandered at will through our neighborhood.

That wasn't much of a problem, actually. Mostly, they stayed close to home, a good 100 feet from any other residence or street, but sometimes they drifted out of their area, across a lightly traveled street, and over to our house, within view of their own home. When Dave was gone, I fed and watered the dogs, so they considered me a friend, and they had a special affection for my daughter Jenny, then about six years old. Jenny was one of those people like the "horse whisperer" everyone is now making so much of a fuss about; she had some sort of knack about her when it came to animals. They saw her instantly as one of them, more primal or basic or something than most of the human beings they encountered. So, as often as not, when Zeke and Emma went a-visiting, they came over to our house to visit and play with Jen.

It was a remarkable sight and I loved it. I worked at that time at a stand-up desk at a window, so I could watch pretty much everything that was going on around the neighborhood, including Zeke, Emma, and Jen's comings and goings. It was always a pleasing scene to me, this tiny, delicate child, playing dolls with these two huge dogs. And, no kidding, that's what they did. Zeke and Emma would sit or lie there patiently while Jen talked with them ("with them" not "to them"), put dolls in their arms or on their backs or bellies, used them as lounging pillows. . . .

Well, one day those three gay caballeros were on our front stoop playing dolls and I was working at my desk at the window, and up drove an animal control truck. My one and only thought was "Uh-oh. . . . "The uniformed enforcement officer got out of his truck, eyed the scene—Jen and the two Saint Bernards—and got a huge net on a pole out of his truck. Zeke and Emma stood up and watched him in gentle curiosity. He put on heavy gloves and advanced cautiously up our front sidewalk holding the net and pole out in front of him.

At that point I went out the front door to head off what was certainly about to become a disaster. I walked out to this genius and suggested that this might not be the way to handle things. "These dogs have been reported as running loose several times and they could be dangerous. I have to take them to the impoundment area," he told me officiously.

"Well, obviously they aren't dangerous," I said, laughing. "They're playing dolls with that little girl!"

"Could be dangerous to others," he snapped, "and they have to be taken in."

"In that case, what I would suggest is that you put away the net and pole and walk up to them, pat them on the head, and invite them to jump into the truck with you. If you really need to take them, I can bring out a couple of dog biscuits and they'll go with you quite willingly. Or I can take them back over to their home and put them inside. Or I can call their owner to come and talk with you."

"We have talked before with the dogs' owner and obviously he has not cooperated. Now we have to take the dogs in and our official policy is to exercise all caution and take the dogs by secure methods."

"If you hurt the girl, I'm going to have to warn you, that net better be big enough for me because I'm going to take care of whatever parts of you the dogs don't," I said with a growl. At this point Zeke and Emma must have sensed the threat because now they stood up and were making some serious noises themselves. I stepped back behind the dogs and told Jen to stand up and step back too because we were about to be entertained by the funny man in the white suit.

The animal control officer advanced. One man, one pole, two Saint Bernards—not a pretty equation. I had never seen Zeke or Emma so much as growl at each other. They had grown up to be the very picture of oafish gentility. But they apparently had kept deep within them an understanding of the importance of protecting their property—our house fell within their aegis—and their friends and family, of which Jen and I were close members. I imagine that what they saw was not this guy coming at *them*, but at our house and us. And they were not about to tolerate that.

First they took away the guy's stick and net. Then they took off some of his clothes. Then they took off most of his clothes. They helped him back to his truck; in fact, first he decided to check the top of his truck so he got way up on it and then crawled down the side and into a side window. When he drove out of sight, he didn't shout, "And to all a good-night." No, it was more like "You bragsnaggin' bladboodle stackrattle idjbod dogs, we're not done yet! You haven't heard the last of Duane Austerblotz!"

The moment he left, of course, Zeke and Emma cheerfully returned to Jen, figuring they hadn't finished in their roles as Mommy and Daddy in the doll story she had been working out with them before this whole fuss started with the guy in the white outfit. Or the guy who used to be in the white outfit, anyway. But I suggested that maybe we should all drift back over to Zeke and Emma's abode and call Dave as soon as possible. Which we did. It didn't take us long to figure out that the company of Z & M were in some pretty hot water now, having physically attacked one of Lincoln's finest (although I certainly was ready and willing to testify to the exact opposite in court, since it was clearly he who had disturbed *their* peace and attacked *them*). Dave had planned on going home to his family's remote ranch-country home that weekend anyway so he hastened his preparations, and by the time an army of animal control officers rolled up in front of my house with a whole new arsenal of weapons and renewed determination to bring the full force of the law down on those canine desperados, Zeke and Emma were long gone westward and Jen was reduced to playing dolls with whatever various pill bugs and crickets she could round up from under rocks around the porch.

I assumed the traditional deaf-mute, half-witted patterns my peasant people had always used to deal with authority figures in Germany before they went to Russia, and in Russia before they came here. And the animal control people left with their vicious prey still at large and their thirst for vengeance unslaked. And, I imagine, no new understanding of the enormous depth and breadth of a dog's sense of territory.

It's a matter of respect. They may be the most generous and hospitable dogs in the world, but they expect anyone venturing to step foot on their property, to address their colleagues, to eat at their bowl to also demonstrate appropriate gratitude and gentility in doing so. I've told you about our physical household arrangements here, that the dogs have their own sleeping porch that is within the walls of the house but not within the doors of the house proper. They have their own entrance and can come and go as they wish, but not into our living area. One of our sleeping areas is the porch immediately above the dogs' porch so for years we heard nighttime goings-on in that porch: bumps, thumps, growls, barks. We wondered what life was like in that canine world. One weekend Linda and Antonia went to Lincoln to see family so I thought this would be my chance to do some anthropological research. Or maybe caninopological research.

When bedtime came, I grabbed a blanket and pillow and instead of going up the stairs to our bedroom, I stepped out onto the dog porch. The dogs were surprised but not at all displeased to see me there. (Their porch and their bed are very clean, so it's not as if I was about to wallow in a flea-invested pile of hay, I want you to understand.) I made myself a bed on their bed. They were now astonished but in a curious way: I could read in their behavior that while they were surprised that I was joining them for the night, I was certainly welcome and in fact they wondered why I hadn't done it a long time ago.

There was some initial scrambling around—face licking, playing—but then things settled down very quickly and everyone went to sleep. I was surprised to find that it was not Lucky that made all the night noises, as we expected, but Thud and Goldie. Aside from snores and dream-induced yips, most of the noises came from their various comings and goings out the dog door: bathroom breaks, checks on noises in the backyard, that kind of thing. It was a little crowded on the bed, but everyone did what they could to accommodate their guest and it was really quite charming that everyone seemed to take special care not to step on me as they came and went. At one point I joined them outdoors to pee, and I think we all agreed that we had never so completely appreciated each other. In fact, I wound up feeling a little guilty that Linda and I had always been so stuffy with our own beds and lives since the dogs were never invited to share them quite as generously as they had accepted me that night.

Linda said no, we wouldn't be that generous either, and I understood. But what's more remarkable is that the dogs understood. That is, they didn't really expect us to reciprocate the hospitality. They said they were quite honored that I had seen fit to join them that night, and I would be welcome anytime in the future to do the same and even bring other members of the family.

On the other hand, that is not to say dogs don't have an intense sense of possessiveness even about objects. One of the most distinctive traits of dogdom is their insatiable lust to have whatever it is the other dog has. I have often invited friends to go ahead and get stinking, stomping rich using my idea to market a dog toy or dog food labeled "The Other Dog's Toy" or "The Other Dog's Food." There is nothing in this world any dog wants so much as the other dog's toy or food. Nothing.

While it might be obvious that if one dog has a wonderful, fresh bone and the other has none, well, of course the boneless dog is going to want that bone. But what might not be so clear in theory is that if each dog has a wonderful, fresh bone—*identically* wonderful, fresh bones—they will instantly and automatically prefer the other dog's bone.

(Precisely this same phenomenon is true with children, you have probably noted, but this is a book about dogs. My book about children will follow shortly.) Ultimately this becomes tail-chasing, of course, because whatever bone any one dog has, is *not* the bone he wants, even if it's the bone he previously had when he wanted nothing more in this world than the bone he now has.

To my devious mind this becomes all the more fascinating when dogs make a clear indication that they not only suffer from this syndrome, but they know they suffer from it. And they know that other dogs suffer from it. Thud is an older, quieter guy, and he is quite content lying in the sun, soaking up God's bounty. Abbie is much younger, much more active, and eager to have something going on. So, here's Thud quietly lounging in the sun, maybe even sleeping. Abbie will go to the toy box, shop around for something she knows is particularly attractive not simply to herself but, more importantly, to Thud, pull it out, and take it directly to where Thud is lying. She dangles it in front of him. She bangs it against his nose. She lies down with her mouth and oh-so desirable toy inches (if not fractions of an inch) from his nose, and she chews vigorously and with obvious relish. You can almost hear her saying, "Oh my God, this is soooo good! This is the best toy we've ever had and it's all mine. Nope, no other dog in this yard has a toy like this . . . and no other dog in this yard *will* have a toy like this. This is *my* toy. I think I'll just use it up and leave nothing behind for any other dog, in fact. I can't believe my good luck in having this toy. Did I already say that this is clearly the best toy we've ever had?"

Now, either Thud will continue to ignore this performance and go to sleep, whereupon Abbie too will most likely lose interest and go to sleep too, or Thud will take the bait and try to take the toy away from her, which is obviously exactly what she had in mind. Once he tries to take the toy from her, they have a lively tug of war or she goes off running a tritsy-trotsy run with the toy held high and visible, and Thud goes after her, now convinced that it *is* the best toy they have ever had and if he doesn't get some of it right now, she probably will completely destroy it and leave him with nothing but inferior toys, which is to say, whatever toys he happens to have.

Now, I consider it already a phenomenon worthy of study and admiration that Abbie understands there is this other-dog's-toy complex, but I find it even more interesting that she knows how to manipulate it in such a way that she can control Thud's behavior. But it gets even better, to this observer's mind: Thud is big, tired, old, and lumbering, so he only follows her around for a limited amount of time. Then she stops and they do the tug-of-war routine, or he somehow manages to get it away from her, whereupon it becomes *his* prize and now it is *her* turn to lust and *his* turn to flaunt, or—and this is the option I love—he grows tired of the chase and demonstrates his own understanding of canine psychology: he abandons the chase and ambles over to the dog toy box and begins to rummage around for his own best-toy-ever. Abbie stops. Her ears drop. Oh my God, what is Thud doing? He no longer wants the toy I have. He is apparently getting a toy of his own, and there is every chance in the world that now *his* toy is the most wonderful toy we have ever had!

Thud finds something that strikes his fancy and he pulls it out. It doesn't matter which toy it is. That's not the point.

The point is that whatever toy he picks is indeed now the very best toy they have ever had by far and now, of course, Abbie wants *that* toy.

See? Now the manipulation has come full circle. Abbie manipulated Thud because she understands the process of envy and coveting. Thud, realizing he is being manipulated, reverses the psychology and indulges in his own flaunting, and suddenly the entire conflict has been reversed! Don't tell *me* dogs don't think! During these transactions the dogs are not only thinking, they are *anticipating*. They know how the other dog is going to react, and they know they can generate exactly the response they want. That is, as creepy as it sounds, dogs *scheme*!

What's more, dogs know and love each other. The implications of that are not trivial: dogs understand that they are individuals, that there are others, and they understand fully when others are no longer there. Earlier I told you about the day Blackjack died and Goldie was devastated. It was both harder and easier when Lucky and Goldie died within four weeks of each other, leaving Thud alone with us.

All his life Thud had known Lucky and Goldie, and only Lucky and Goldie. Along with Linda and me (Antonia was pretty much gone out of the house and off to college by the time Thud was grown), those two were his family. They slept together every night. They did everything together but eat; as I said, Thud's voracity requires that he eat alone, or more precisely inhale whatever is in his bowl alone. When Lucky went, there was an enormous emptiness, but it seemed to be felt mostly by Goldie. Small wonder—Lucky had been her elder all her life. But when Goldie went, Thud became a different dog. He wasn't the impossibly energetic, constantly into mischief, ready to play, ready to bark dog he'd always been. Suddenly it was as if the weight of the world was on his shoulders. He wasn't just in mourning; he seemed burdened by a new sense of responsibility.

We weren't ready for another dog because we were pretty much devastated ourselves. Nobody could replace Lucky, nobody could replace Goldie, and sure as billy hell nobody could replace Lucky *and* Goldie! (Only later did we figure out that a new spirit like Abbie doesn't really replace her antecedents so much as she augments them, improves them, honors them.) Then Thud did something that made our broken spirits seem even more shattered: he adopted a sock monkey. He was so lonely, he was so bereft, he needed someone so badly that when Linda made a sock monkey for Thud from one of my orphan socks, that was exactly the ticket. For Linda and me it was less a comfort than a symbol of the Grand Canyon Lucky and Goldie's absence left in our lives, but it was nice to see Thud find his own new comfort even if tears came to our eyes every time he came moping into the house dragging his sock monkey.

And then, of course, along came Abbie. She certainly hasn't made any of us, including Thud I suspect, forget Lucky and Goldie, but she has presented herself as a living memorial to everything good about them . . . with a few new quirks of her own. (What kind of dog sleeps upside down on a regular basis, for Pete's sake?)

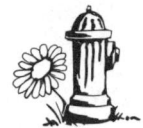

## CHAPTER EIGHT

# PASSING ON

> *...The dog, to gain some private ends,*
> *Went mad and bit the man.*
> *The man recovered of the bite,*
> *The dog it was that died.*
>
> **–OLIVER GOLDSMITH,**
> ***AN ELEGY ON THE DEATH OF A MAD DOG***

It's not going to be easy for me to get through this next chapter. I have it in my notes—"dogs sick and dying"—and I know I need to say something about how dogs approach their own mortality, but I sure am not looking forward to the next day or two of writing about it.

When Linda, Antonia, or I are sick or injured—and believe me, that happens a lot on a farm!—we usually just "suck it up" and try to get through the thing, knowing that sooner or later it will pass and we'll be up and around. We know that we can get pretty good medical attention, and that we have each other to take care of the others. We listen to our medical advisors and try to understand what is going on with our bodies. We hope that if we take our medicine and do as we're told we can even speed our recovery along.

Dogs don't know that. All they know is that something sure as hell isn't right. They don't know or care that it is going to improve over time because they don't know about time. All they know is right now. And it hurts.

Which makes it just as hard on us because we do know all that about the dog(s) just as surely as we know they don't know. I can imagine other peoples of this world quite reasonably being thoroughly disgusted with the obscene amounts of money we Americans spend on medical attention for our pets—even while our government doesn't seem to care much one way or the other about families impoverishing themselves within our wretched medical system to keep our own children and elderly alive and well. I'd even be embarrassed to tell you how much we have spent on one sick cat or dog at one time or another. But somehow when you have that wounded or sick animal in your arms and you know that they have no one but you to help them and they so trust and depend on you, well, money doesn't seem to be much of an object.

No, I don't like cats very much. And Homer was particularly annoying because he killed songbirds and bunnies. Nor did he waste a lot of time or love-energy on me. And when he lived in my shop he jumped at a bird and spilled two gallons of filthy waste oil all over my shop floor. Then he slipped and fell in it, wallowed and spun in it until he was thoroughly coated with the crap and then ran insanely around the shop until every single square inch of anything was also covered with it. And then like the cosmic idiot he was, he licked it all off and got so sick he threw up all the dead moles, voles, mice, and crickets he'd eaten for the last six years in a kind of waste-oil marinade all over the layer of oil he'd already applied generously to the shop floor. And then we had to catch him, wrap him in a blanket and make a mad run to the veterinarian's office on a Sunday (of course). And it cost us an amount something approaching a Republican budget deficit to get him cleaned up, flushed out, and back to normal health. But you know, however I felt about Homer and however he felt about me, it was worth whatever it took to take care of the obnoxious old howler. That's the way it is with pets. They're family after all.

We know when we are sick roughly what is going on, even if it's only that we are sick. What's more a blessing and curse for us humans is that we also know to one degree or another we are going to die. Some theologians and philosophers feel that knowing about our mortality is a unique human quality. That is the "knowledge" that Adam and Eve obtained from the tree in that garden so long ago, that we know we will die. As a hospice worker once wisely told me, from the moment of birth on, we are all "terminal." That is a terrible knowledge to have.

Maybe. More and more I'm convinced our fear of death, our inability or refusal to deal with it on a rational basis (and it is rational and inevitable, after all, that we *will* die) is more culture-specific than we might think. That is, I think Americans more than anyone else go to great pains to avoid the thought and certainty of death. Moreover, I am less and less convinced that we alone are able to grasp our own finiteness, yet understand it. A substantial proportion of our population, moreover, confesses a knowledge that they are going to die, but they then flit away from that reality like a butterfly in a tornado by insisting that, well, sure, yeah, they're going to die, *but they're going to heaven where they'll live forever*. And they are absolutely sure of that. Hmmm. Sure.

Well, you've read far enough along in this treatise by now to know what I'm leading up to, I suppose: I can't help but wonder, maybe even suspect, that dogs know about mortality. They don't show their understanding of death, they don't fret and fuss, fight its approach, resist admitting to it, deny it, avoid it, cower, cringe, cry because unlike those of us who do all those things, they are wiser and simply accept it.

I realize what a jump I am making here. It is one thing for Goldie to realize that Blackjack and then Lucky were gone; that is, it is one thing to recognize an absence. But is it really possible that dogs understand that they too will one day "be gone?" (Jeez, we human beings don't even like to use the word "die!") I don't know for certain—there's not much, bottom line, that I really know for certain about much of anything—but I sure have my suspicions about exactly how much dogs know about the concept of mortality.

Oh boy, I am now going to tell you some stories that already have my stomach tightening. One of the real curses of being a human being is that we live so much longer than our dogs. How much easier it would be to have a dog in our lives when we are born and still be there when we die 70 years or so later! But instead lives like mine are measured in the all-too brief lives of six or eight dogs I've had to bury. It doesn't help to talk about it, either, nor does time smooth the pain.

The first dog whose death I really had to face was Slump. Slump was anything but a great dog. He was, in fact, an idiot. He was supposed to be a black Lab when we got him as a puppy, but as his pointy little head and skittish personality emerged ever more, his Irish setter influences became ever more evident to us. And they drove us nuts. But you know as well as I do, problems like that really don't make much of a difference to a dog owner: you tend to forget the worst of your dog's traits and embrace the best. Owners of the most miserable, yappy, biting, snarling, pissing, stinky, foul-breathed, obnoxious dogs on Earth adore them and see nothing but man's best friend over there throwing up on the new carpet.

Which is to say, as miserable a beast as Slump was, he was the first dog Linda and I had together, and we loved him. And he loved us. But I can imagine what he must have looked like to others who didn't love him. Slump *was* an idiot. But the grace and dignity with which he died leads me to believe that beneath his buffoonery and lack of self-control, there was a wise and sensitive heart, with considerable pride.

Oh man, I hate to recall this more than you can imagine. Linda and I were in bed on our enclosed sleeping porch when Slump came into our room and woke us up. That sounds fairly mundane, but you can't imagine, although I hope you will try, the import of that simple sentence. Slump had never been upstairs in our house his entire life, and certainly not in a bedroom. But there he was. He didn't have to do anything special to wake us because his presence was so unexpected, so unlikely, we were instantly awake.

He had not been doing well. He seemed pretty listless, was not eating well, and was restless but not with any energy. But there was something about him that night that was compelling. I can't put my finger on anything at all in particular. I just knew something was really wrong. Maybe it was simply the incredible fact that he had come up the stairs where he had never been, down the hall he had never walked, and into that porch where we slept. Whatever it was, he made it clear that he wanted out, and right now. There is a door that leads out of our sleeping porch. I was uneasy about letting him out—the door led outside the fenced yard, so Slump was not only in our bedroom where he was never allowed, he also wanted to go out of our yard. It was not a squirrel-chasing kind of urgency he was showing on this occasion, however. No, Slump had something very serious on his mind and was asking our cooperation in no uncertain terms. I didn't even hesitate. Slump's urgency was so apparent and so forceful, I simply got up and let him out.

The next morning—just hours later—I went out to find him, pretty much knowing in advance what I was going to find. (Slump's communications to me that night were that clear.) I went directly to our river cabin, somehow sensing that's where he would be, and that's where he was. He was lying (oh God, am I going to get through this story?) on the porch of the cabin, covered with his own filth. He'd obviously been very sick. He raised his head and wagged his tail feebly when I came up to him. He was dying. He knew it and I knew it. And he told me with his eyes how embarrassed he was to be in this situation (I sit here crying like a baby as I write . . . damn . . . ), to have bothered me, to be in such a sad condition. I cleaned him up and through my tears and sobbing (okay, I am a man and I was 50 years old, but damn it, Slump was my *dog*!) I got him to a sofa cushion and got a good blanket to cover him. Linda came down after a bit and, realizing the situation and that Slump was really in enormous pain, she called our veterinarian to come end the suffering. Our vet is a good man—I can't imagine a bad person being a veterinarian any more than I can imagine a bad dog—so he came immediately after our call. He was diplomatic enough to ignore my own utter lack of dignity and self-control and gave Slump the shot that put him out of his misery. Slump seemed to know what was going on, and despite his long history of hysteria at the arrival or approach of any stranger, he again raised his head, wagged his tail, and embraced the comfort of death.

And I goddamn near died on the spot myself. And as I sit here writing this I am going through the whole misery again, still incapable of generating the dignity that seemed to come so easily even to the loony-tune Slump. The vet left me there in my misery with my now dead Slump. For the first time in my life I dug a hole for my dog and spent that day at his graveside in mourning. And damn it, I'm still not over the quiet dignity and grace of that dog's death.

I would have dug his grave with a silver spade and I would have let him down on a golden chain and for the first time in my life I understood the profound truth of that song's words. When ol' Slump died, he died so hard he jarred the ground in my backyard. And so would other dogs as I came to face the reality and pain of death, not my own, perhaps, but of those I love so much, my dogs.

Now there's a dilemma in my life: while I would like never again to have to see one of my dogs die, the incredible lesson that seems to come so naturally from that process is too important to us to miss when we have the chance. Blackjack died on the highway and I had to ask my buddy Mick to bury him, so while I had my share of agony from that departure (lifting his massive body into my car was the heaviest weight I have ever lifted in my life—something like 500 tons I would estimate), I didn't have to deal with the even-greater burden of lowering him into the ground.

Lucky had a long and lingering approach to his death. He had a bad cancer in his nose. The vet looked at it, found it inoperable, and we did what we could to give Lucky as long and comfortable a decline as we could. But the day came when he was sneezing blood, was again out of the house and in the backyard where he wouldn't cause anyone any trouble or make a mess, and we knew the time had come to deal with the situation. We called the vet again. I drove my pickup into the backyard so we could lift Lucky into it and get him away from Goldie and Thud before the vet came. We dreaded even these preliminaries. The only time Lucky had ever been in a vehicle was to take him to the vet's and it was never easy. How were we going to get him, reluctant and now sick on top of it, into the cab of that truck? We couldn't imagine but figured we'd deal with that once I was in the yard and got Lucky out to the truck door.

Lucky walked painfully out of the dog porch and to the truck. I opened the door, and with obvious resolution and enormous effort, he got up into the truck and then up on the seat. To this day I think he knew what was going on, he knew the immense pain we were in because of it, and he was determined to do whatever he could to make this whole process as easy on us as he could. There was no doubt in Linda's and my minds that Lucky's first thoughts at this incredibly painful moment were, as always, for us.

And then Linda, Lucky, and I sat in the pickup out at our gate on the highway. Lucky never traveled in the pickup, but he didn't resist at all or get overly excited. Once again, he gave every indication of knowing exactly what was going on, why he was in the truck, why we were at the gate, what was about to come. The vet arrived and once again demonstrated remarkable diplomacy in getting past this sobbing hulk of a man—now 65 years old but no better equipped to deal with the loss of a dog—and easing our pet into what lay over the horizon of the hills of mortality. Lucky, like Slump, had always gone nuts at the approach of a stranger to our yard, and he certainly would never have tolerated being actually touched by a stranger, but this time he wagged his tail a bit, raised his head, seemed to be saying for all the world, "It's okay. I know what we have to do here. It's been a good run. Lots of well-thrown Frisbees, some great swims in the river, and now I'd appreciate whatever you can do to help me deal with this nose problem of mine. See you, Dad. Mom. Tell Goldie and Thud I love them. . . . "Again, there was a remarkable dignity about this dog in death that made me wonder who indeed was the sentient, intellectual element in this mix of dog and humans.

Oh, I know how melodramatic this all seems. But God, you can't imagine how deeply it kills me to even tell you about this. Or if you've ever owned a dog yourself, maybe you can imagine. When the vet left and I'd pulled myself into some semblance of self-control (Linda, who seems much more fragile in the anticipation of and recovery from such trauma, deals much better than I do with the reality of the event itself), we carried Lucky to the frozen, snowy hill above our farm and put him into the grave I'd dug during a warm spell a month before . . . another occasion when I'd cried like a baby simply anticipating the loss of my beloved Lucky.

The very moment Lucky gave up his heroic ghost, a robin appeared on the wires over us and sang a cheering song. We like to think that had something to do with Lucky.

We hadn't even begun to come to grips with our sorrow at the loss of Lucky when Goldie died. But once again Goldie took her responsibilities to us more seriously than she did her own life and welfare. She was not feeling at all well since Lucky had died, but about a month after Lucky left us, she was really having trouble. She didn't eat, couldn't drink, simply wasn't doing well, so we decided to leave her inside for this bitter cold night so she would be warm and wouldn't be bothered by the then thoroughly annoying and puppylike Thud. Linda and I both knew as Goldie watched us go upstairs to bed that things were not right. Not at all.

The next morning we found that she had fouled the kitchen and dining room floor, which was utterly out of character for this oh-so polite and social creature. And she was mortified—consider that word for a moment—beyond belief. We cleaned up the mess and she retreated to her pad and collapsed in embarrassment. We comforted her because it was clear as hell that this lapse in etiquette was not a matter of defiance, not even a mistake. It was a tragedy in the making.

She was so sick through the day that we spent most of the day tending to her, comforting her, trying to find out what the problem was. She was alert and in no apparent pain, so we moved her indoor bed so she could better watch the activities of the household going on around her, hushed and cautious as a result of our enormous concern about our old friend Goldie. Linda got down on the floor early in the evening to sit with her. Goldie put her head in Linda's lap.

After several hours she died. Just like that. She gave up her spirit and died. I don't know if Linda and I have been that crushed in our lives—to have this wonderful friend die like that in our arms.

Along with what few other guilts I have in my life—I'm German and Protestant while Linda is Czech and Catholic, so her burdens of self-doubt make mine look silly in comparison—I really do wonder about my balance in matters like the deaths of Goldie, Lucky, and Slump. I haven't had a lot of death in my life—some uncles and aunts, mostly. I never knew any of my grandparents. I loved my uncles and aunts dearly, but in America death seems such a remote phenomenon that you can almost go on with your own life hardly noticing that someone is missing until a couple years later. I've had a couple buddies die, but mostly they were well prepared for their departure and therefore so was I. Most seemed to be pretty much on schedule rather than painfully early, so it's not the timing that is the problem.

My father died a little over a year ago, but again the long decline into his departure seemed to make his eventual step across the line almost a blessing, for all of us and for him. I miss my dad, but he had a good, long life. Besides, he was struck by lightning when he was just a kid and was unconscious for a full week, so we all, including him, always considered all the rest of his 75+ years to be a kind of gift. Maybe it's the many years of exposure I've had to Native American culture that have gentled my grief about the passing of friends and kin: the Omaha tribal understanding is that there are four hills of life: infancy, childhood, maturity, and old age. When you pass over that fourth hill, you simply go on down the path toward something else. None of us, not even all of us together, in the Omaha understanding, are equipped to understand what is beyond that fourth hill. So we simply accept it.

But damn, my friends, it is just not the same when we watch our canine friends die. Not for us. For them death seems to be even more an understandable stage, or step, or phase, or whatever it is. The bottom line for me is that while the pain of losing my canine companions and colleagues causes me pain beyond anything else I have ever felt in my life, I have on every occasion been struck by the incredible grace and dignity with which they approach and pass over the crest of that fourth hill. Maybe the embarrassment for me on such occasions is that I am brought face to face, without possible equivocation, with the obvious conclusion of which species is superior in this relationship, me in my bewilderment, fear, confusion, and self-delusion, or my dogs with their maturity and acceptance.

The only course for humankind is to do what we can to learn from dogs.

CHAPTER NINE

# CANINE EXISTENTIALISM

*If I have any beliefs about immortality,*
*it is that certain dogs I have known will go to heaven,*
*and very, very few persons.*

**—JAMES THURBER**

I read somewhere that blood pressure goes down when people are around animals, especially dogs, and that doesn't surprise me at all. Dogs offer us not just a new perspective but a sensible one. Sure, a dog in a hurry can be just as frantic, just as idiotic as any rush-hour, road-rage-drenched nine-to-fiver human being. But generally speaking, a dog has a much more finely refined set of priorities. And while a dog chasing a squirrel up a tree or trying to convince his owner to go for a ride can be fairly focused, that same dog can also be wonderfully instructive when it comes to the importance of soaking up the spring sun when one presents the opportunity.

The phrase "to work like a dog" makes some sense, I suppose, if you have ever seen a dog trying to join a rabbit in a burrow or a good hunter working a field. But it says something about our language (if not dogs) that human beings haven't come up with the much more important concept of "to rest like a dog." Our black Labs Abbie and Thud are worth studying in this regard. They know the importance of using the north side of a house in the summer, the south side in the winter. They can run, play, wrestle, pull on a rope, chase rabbits as long as you have the strength to keep track of them, but they then attack a good sleep with the same kind of enthusiasm. You just don't see a dog tossing and turning, worrying about unfinished jobs, social offenses suffered earlier, romantic disappointments, economic setbacks, or religious dilemmas. To a dog, work equals work but, just as importantly, play equals play, and rest equals rest.

It's perhaps easier to define dog philosophy in terms of what it isn't rather than what it is. That's because we Americans, maybe we European-British-Americans, are the ones with the peculiar grasp of how the world works. There is not, after all, a "reality." Everything we humans perceive around us is filtered through our eyes, and thus through our brains, and thus through our individual and collective experience, learning, beliefs, customs, and culture. That's really a hard concept to convey because everyone presumes that they see things exactly as they are. We can't imagine seeing things any other way than the way we see them. Well, actually, we can imagine it if we think about it, if we keep our minds open, if we don't presume that we know more than anyone else, or maybe even everything there is to know. And believe it or not, there are a lot of cultures that actually do allow for an admission that they don't know everything.

That, of course, is not the way of American or Western civilization. When we decide to go to war against someone and everyone else in the world says it's the wrong thing to do, there's no question about what is going on: we are right and everyone else is wrong. No one even stops to ask or considers that we might not be omniscient. The others are stupid, treasonous, naive, uneducated. We are wise, benevolent, smart, and most of all, right.

No dog thinks like that, and neither do most other people in the world. One of the reasons I love dogs is the same reason, or reasons, that I admire Native American cultures. American mainstream society, for example, is inductive and active. That is, we learn from asking, from being instructed, from doing; we are masters of our own fates. We can be anything we want to be, it is up to us, our futures are in our own hands, nothing is impossible with hard work and determination, anyone in this grand nation can be president, blah blah blah blah blah. . . .

A moment's rational thought tells us that is all so much bushwa. We are actually the product of many things outside our control. Very little we do is actually totally within our control. We can wish, work, believe, exert all we want and some things are simply not going to happen. Take it from me, *you* are not going to be president! Most people of the world know that. They do what they can, they control what little they can control, but most importantly, they accept what they cannot control. They accept and understand, which is a grasp of reality that serves a lot of human beings very well and in ways that the constant frustration of believing otherwise never will. Most cultures of the world understand that we as individuals, even as collective societies, ultimately as a species, are to a large degree little more than twigs in a raging river, simply going where the currents, eddies, wind, and water take us. To an American, to most Europeans, that is a very depressing notion.

Not to Native Americans. Not to me. Not to dogs.

Have you ever seen a dog truly unhappy with his lot? Sure, no dog wants to be hungry, cold, wet, unloved, or abused, but damn near every dog I've ever seen in my life pretty much accepts where he is as where he is. The poorest mutt on the poorest Indian reservation is really tickled when he gets a scrap of a baloney sandwich. He'd also be happy with a can of deluxe Alpo, but the baloney sandwich is pretty darn nice, he'll tell you. Would he like to sleep on a couch in a fancy mansion and not have fleas? Well, sure, okay, I suppose, but right now it's nice to have this pile of leaves in the sun and be able to scratch when and where it itches.

Dogs have a sense of acceptance that we should envy and acquire when we can, to my mind. And they don't simply give up and resign themselves to this miserable life they have, while envying other dogs for their good fortune. No, with the exception of other dogs' toys, dogs seem to figure that whatever they have, wherever they are, is probably just about the best thing to have and best place to be at the time, at least for them. And they deal with it.

Dogs are existentialists to the extent that they never ask what the meaning of all this is. It simply is. It's not so much that they think it has no meaning. They simply do not ask the question. They may presume there is meaning to all this, but whether there is or not does not strike them as being particularly important since their knowing about it won't make much difference one way or another. And if someone did try to explain the meaning of life to a dog, he wouldn't understand. As neither, I might note, would we. One of my favorite philosophers, John Kay, said it best: "If all of this should have a meaning, we would be the last to know."

Dog questions run along the lines of "Why is that guy sitting there and not throwing the stick? I brought him a stick, so why doesn't he throw it?" "I wonder what that butt smells like?" "I wonder what's for supper?" (No dog ever asks if there is going to *be* supper; there either is supper or there isn't.) "What does he want me to do? Because that's what I want to do."

I have given this idea some study and have compiled a list of questions, in fact, that dogs never ask. (You never know when this kind of information might come in handy for you so study it closely.)

**QUESTIONS DOGS NEVER ASK:**

How much does that cost?
Are you saved?
What time is it?
Is this deductible?
What did the Dow do today?
What would Jesus do?
Does this collar make my ass look big?
Which one is the salad fork?
What's on TV tonight?
Whose turn is it?
What was your name again?

What's in it for me?
What's 15% of $32.75?
Am I pulling my weight around here? (Any sort of self-doubt is never explored by the dog psyche.)
Is this relationship good for me/us?
How are you supposed to get a promotion in this place?
Does God love me?
Mutuals or utilities?
Did I leave the stove on?
Why don't other dogs like me?
What can I do with this hair to be more attractive?
Why does [fill in the blank] always have all the good luck?
Why?

There are things a dog wants—to go to the river, for example—and they may even ask, but mostly they ask if you are going to the river. If you are going to the river and they can't go with you, well, that is clearly a disappointment, maybe a mistake on your part, but a dog always gives you the benefit of the doubt. If you accidentally hit a dog on the head with a newspaper, he will be startled, confused, maybe even frightened, but he will understand when you explain that it was a mistake. In fact, if you hit a dog with a newspaper on purpose, he will also presume the same thing: You can't possibly have meant to hit *him* with that newspaper! What sense would it make for someone to hit *him*?

The words "That's my favorite!" have become a standard expression around our household to describe the wonderful enthusiasm dogs have for whatever they happen to be enjoying at any particular moment. A wonderful item was circulating on the Web not long ago that summed up dog thinking wonderfully. I wish I knew who had written it so I could ask permission to reproduce it here. The format of the piece was a doggy diary, hour by hour through a typical day. The gag was that whatever was recorded for any particular time—from "8:10 A.M. breakfast of dry food with three French fries from the human's Happy Meal of last night" to "The boss comes home from work and stops twice on the way to the house to scratch my ear"—is followed by the words over and over, "My favorite!" It's true and it's wonderful. Whatever a dog is doing at any particular moment in his day or life is quite clearly and quite grandly his "favorite!"

Now, this is the realization that many people may have but which they then mistakenly conclude means that dogs don't think. Well, that's wrong, and I hope I disabused you of that error many pages earlier. Dogs do think. They think a lot. Sometimes they think fairly profoundly—at least as profoundly as most human beings I know. But they don't waste a lot of time thinking about really dumb stuff like "What is the nature of God?" (a concept we are no better equipped to understand than our dogs, but that we are not smart enough to avoid, as do dogs) or "What is the meaning of the universe?" or "Why are cats so damned annoying?" They know there is a God, that there is a universe, and cats are annoying, and they know that is all any of us, canine or human, will ever know. "So why worry about it? What's for supper?" seems to be the traditional dogs' train of thought when such matters arise in conversation.

No human has ever heard a dog wish that some other dog had fleas. Moreover, no dog has ever wished that he didn't have fleas but some other dog—or all other dogs—did. In fact, most dogs I know don't even wish they didn't have fleas; they simply wish fleas weren't so annoying. Talk about Zen!

To get back to the notion of death, it is my clear impression that when it comes to that phenomenon, those in the mix who are most mystified by it—and therefore most frightened of it—are human beings. Dogs are touched by death, mourn a lost comrade or friend, but they accept its reality. I imagine one reason for this is that while we constantly read about dogs saving human beings, we don't often read about dogs being the cause of a death of someone in their life.

Yes, we unfortunately *do* read about dogs killing human beings out of their sense of duty or training, but it seems pretty clear to me that such horrible circumstances are the fault not of the dog but of the people involved. I don't mean the victims; I'm talking about the half-wits who keep dangerous dogs (actually, "dogs made dangerous") in inappropriate circumstances or even train dogs to do what is clearly not in their nature: kill human beings. And then of course we witness the ultimate irony. Someone keeps pit bulls in a suburban backyard, children approach and tease the dogs, the dogs break out and kill the children . . . and who is held responsible and destroyed? Yep, the dogs! I fail to see the dogs' responsibility in situations like this. The parents of the children, the children, the dog owners, sure, but the dogs? I don't get that one at all.

Okay, so dogs are more likely to rescue human beings than to be responsible, even accidentally, for a human's death. But human beings are far more likely to be responsible for the death of a dog than for rescuing one. Yes, humans do rescue dogs, and I am enormously grateful to those who perform such heroics: firefighters, police officers, animal control officers, just plain old citizens who go out of their way, even risk their own lives, to rescue an animal in a bad situation. But I'd still bet that if we kept track, more dogs are hit by cars, run over by farm machinery, poisoned, shot, or lost out of cars and trucks, and on and on, than are saved by courageous human action.

Nothing is more reprehensible than killing a good dog on purpose. I can understand killing another human being much more easily than I can imagine killing a good dog. (That is, not a sick dog or attacking dog.) On the other hand, nothing can be worse than accidentally killing a good dog. And this is where the agony of being human comes in. If it hurts to have to put a sick, dying, badly injured dog down—and believe you me, it hurts!—then I don't even want to think about what pain it must be to accidentally kill a good dog, especially your own.

I'm not going to dwell on this because I don't have the heart to do it, but one of the most painful stories in my life involves just such a set of circumstances. In this case, the dog was one of the finest I have ever known, and her owner is one of the finest friends I have ever had. So, I'm not writing here with any sense of blame, only with a mountain of pain so enormous I have never wanted to hear the entire story. I have never asked further about it; I never will. I don't even want to think about it. But I am going to for just a couple of seconds here by way of illustrating again how dogs deal better with death than we humans do.

Hillary Maun was an incredibly sweet dog, a black Lab, shepherd, maybe retriever in there somewhere. I'd ask her owner Mick about Hillary's family tree, but the last thing in this world I want to do is to remind him of this horror in his life. Hillary was a retriever of the most dogged (nice word, isn't it?) sort. When you drove into Mick's yard, there was Hillary, always with a stick or ball. All she asked in this world was for someone to throw something for her to fetch. But like most such dogs, while it was almost impossible to resist her inevitable invitations to play, once you threw that ball or stick for Hillary, you were doomed to throw it for as long as you and Hillary were in the same universe. Once you threw something for Hillary, there would be no sitting on the patio or porch and drinking beer or talking. She now knew that you (1) understood your responsibility in this relationship and (2) were capable of fulfilling that obligation.

Mick is a terrific guy. He loves dogs. He has gotten us some of our best dogs. And God, did Mick ever love Hillary. And there wasn't a single human being who didn't understand why. Hillary was just, well, just Hillary. Except maybe for that part about driving you nuts with sticks and balls, and that could wear on your nerves a little toward the end of an evening.

Mick did what he could to deal with this. Before guests came, he would throw until he thought he had worn Hillary out. Nope. Turned out you couldn't wear Hillary out when it came to fetching. He built slingshots that would throw tennis balls a 100 yards. That would give you maybe 10 seconds to talk, drink a beer, or eat a hot dog from the time the ball was launched until Hillary's return.

Then someone invented Super Balls. I don't know if they even still make Super Balls. They were made of some kind of extremely compact plastic substance that gives the ball incredible bounce. If you dropped it to the floor, it would fly back up almost exactly as high as the height from which it had been dropped. Mick had this great idea—all of us thought it was great—of batting a Super Ball out into a corn field bordering the farmhouse where he was living with Hillary. The ball would easily go a quarter mile, a little dark ball into a plowed and cluttered corn field. This was good for all of us—it gave Hillary plenty of long balls to chase, it gave her time while searching to rest up from the run, it gave the rest of us time to have some social life with each other even while keeping Hillary happy.

I wasn't there when it happened. Mick kind of told me about it, but he couldn't tell me much about it, and I sure as billy hell wasn't going to press him for details because I could see the pain the tragedy gave him even when he simply told me that Hillary had died. That was bad enough. Any man grieves for any dog. Any good man grieves for any good dog. Any good man dies a little when his own good dog dies. But this time . . . It was the most painful story I have ever sensed, since Mick couldn't bring himself to tell me much of it himself.

I suspect just knowing this much you will be in the same situation I was in when I heard Hillary was dead and saw the agony in Mick's eyes. He was batting the Super Ball for Hillary. He made the small, understandable mistake of trying to carry on a conversation with someone as he did this, and he paused a trifle too long before throwing the ball into the air to hit it. Hillary's impatience got the best of her and when Mick threw the ball into the air to hit it. . . .

I'm not going to go on with the story. That's all anyone needs to know about how a man feels when he is responsible for the death of a good dog, even if by the most totally unintentional accident.

## CHAPTER TEN

# A DOG DIET

*If you pick up a starving dog and make him prosperous, he will not bite you. This is the principal difference between a dog and a man.*

**—MARK TWAIN, PUDD'NHEAD WILSON, *PUDD'NHEAD WILSON'S CALENDAR***

It will almost certainly come to you as something of a startling turnabout when I confess that I have eaten dog. I have also eaten horse, whale, bear, and horseradish-coated dried peas, all of which were excellent fare. Believe me, I have thought this through with considerable care, quite a few times (I have two daughters who are vegetarians), and I find no contradiction between my omniverousness and my concern for animals. No matter what manner of creature we are on this world, we are only fooling ourselves if we think we can live without the sacrifice of our other fellow creatures. Every time we eat, something dies to feed us. That's the bottom, unchangeable line. If you live on nothing but milk and honey and replaceable leaves and flowers like day lilies, you can probably make a case that you are not exactly *killing* to live, but to me it's a moot point.

To my mind, the ultimate expression of love and respect is not denying the ways of life—eating—but to return full circle to the two words from where you start: love and respect. Did the Lakota hate the buffalo they lived on? Of course not. They didn't even just love the animals, they considered them brothers. Even more than that, they held their Father Bison to be a divine expression of The Great Mysterious. After all, Christians eat their God, so why shouldn't the Sioux? The secret was, and is, that decent people respect their food and the sources of that nourishment. It is understood to be part of a cycle. The Lakota (and Pawnee, Ponca, Omaha, and others) thanked the buffalo for providing so much: shelter, clothing, food, tools, weapons. At the same time, they accepted the gratitude of the bison. Just as the buffalo played a crucial role in the lives of the natives who lived on them, so too was it understood that even in the act of hunting and killing the buffalo, the Indians were fulfilling a necessary role by making the buffalo's life meaningful.

I therefore think that it is not at all the point that we not eat fellow creatures but that we acknowledge their sacrifice and gift, express our constant reliance on them, consider our gratitude, and understand that eventually we can return to the earth what we have taken. Americans work way too hard to avoid both ends of that occasion: we do what we can to avoid recognizing the sacrifices of our fellow creatures by disguising our food (calling cow meat "beef," for example, or pig meat "pork") and being disgusted at the very suggestion that what we eat was once a living being. And then, when it is our turn to return our borrowed resources to the earth, we spend huge amounts of money and energy to preserve ourselves in sealed coffins, vaults, mausoleums, even pyramids, to avoid the very injunctions of our gods that since we came from dust, we should return to dust.

All of which is to say, I'm not suggesting we should pamper dogs as if they were gods, saving them from earning their keep or being our provender. Far from it. Since we're all going to go sooner or later—mostly sooner—I am suggesting that we should go willingly and quickly into the inevitable bargain. No, I haven't willed my body to an Alpo factory. But I do make a point of acknowledging the contributions of my fellow earthlings to my living, including wheat, trees, yogurt bacteria, hops flowers, cows, squid, and, yes, on one occasion a dog. And I make a point of being grateful for their sacrifice to my well-being.

And since you asked, the dog was really quite good.

I understand that canine cuisine is still de rigueur in Asia. I don't know. I imagine that will disgust some readers, but then you might want to keep in mind that what you had for breakfast would make about a third of the world's population throw up on the spot—Canadian bacon, ham, scrambled eggs, maybe a bloody Mary, sausage. (God only knows what's in *that*!) Most of what various peoples of the world consider delicacies is revolting to others. Of course the reverse is true too. My own brush with dog meat was a Native American experience, back in the 1950s, and the family with whom I had this taste of what I found out later was dog was eating it not out of dire need but out of choice.

I have been told now, some 50 years later, that the family was just giving this white boy a bad time, telling me it was dog meat in my bowl, but I knew this family well and they weren't joking. Which is not to say that there isn't plenty of joking along this line even within Native circles. Just this morning I wrote to two Indian friends of mine that I am working on a book about dogs and wondered if they might not want to contribute some recipes.

One of my favorite stories in this life happened at a fairly serious occasion when we had the honor of hosting a half dozen Pawnee elders, political leaders, and spiritual men at our farm as they went on their search for a suitable resting place for their ancestors they were about to retrieve from archeologists' museum shelves. We had offered them a site here on our place—originally Pawnee country—and Linda had cooked a big meal in their honor. As is her custom, when we finished the meal, she said, "Where I come from, whoever does the cooking doesn't have to do the dishes." I automatically then added my usual response, "Where I come from, we just put the dishes on the floor and let the dogs clean up." One of the Pawnee elders instantly picked up on the humor of the moment and floored us all with "Where I come from, we didn't have any dishes. And we ate the dogs."

I have often wondered if Native peoples in Central or South America might still eat dog. It would stand to reason, right? A friend here once asked me, since I had been in the anthropology department at the University of Nebraska for many years although not strictly speaking an anthropologist, what kind of dogs Plains Indians had. That's an excellent question. There are few blurry photos of Indian encampments, villages, groups, and scenes with dogs in view, but of course they would have been taken very early in the history of photography and very late in the history of culturally untainted tribal peoples. It is clearly and often reported that Nebraska Indians kept dogs for food, carrying burdens, and serving as defensive warning systems for their villages. But not much is made of what kind of dogs they were: their size, color, dispositions.

I imagine they were close to their own roots, coyote, wolf, unrefined mutts? Well, I had that question still ricocheting around in my head when I happened to take a trip to the Yucatan peninsula and traveled deep into the interior to some Mayan pueblos. While I can't say they were peopled by Indians who had never before seen a white man—they had television and were watching a soccer game, as I recall—they were cooking over open fires, growing native crops, speaking their native language, and, remarkably, practicing the old religions.

I made a point of noting what kind of dogs they had, and the representation was pretty much unanimous: nondescript, grayish brown, medium-size (I'd guess 25 to 35 pounds, maybe a bit less) dogs that would be very hard to assign to any particular breed. A few had a spot here or there of black, white, or darker brown, but other than that I would be hard-pressed to conjure up much by way of a description of distinctive traits of those dogs—medium muzzle, short to medium hair, medium tail—pretty much your basic generic, plain label, average dog. And don't you suppose that's pretty much what would have been expected throughout the Western hemisphere? I suppose there might have been some regional variations—like longer hair in the North, shorter in the South—as a result not of selective breeding but of natural selection. Diet might have determined some size standards. Would Plains Indians living as they did on bison have made more meat scraps available to their dogs than peoples with less generous sources of animal protein? Those are only guesses; however; I do suspect that if you take a bus to Chichén Itzá from Cancun, as you pass through the villages of the Yucatan, you are going to see pretty much the same kind of dog early French and Spanish travelers saw on the Plains among the Pawnee and Omaha; that is, your fundamental, basic, all-purpose *dog*, suitable for petting, loading up with luggage, defending the camp, comforting the children, or functioning as an entrée.

That's part of the long history between dogs and human beings too, I guess, and we might just as well admit it. Over the long ages from the rise of man and the early associations of man and dog, I imagine that there is some kind of equation in the amount if not the number of dog-eats-man vis-à-vis man-eats-dog. As an old friend of mine once so eloquently if not delicately put it, "The Lord giveth and the Lord taketh away, and if that's not a square deal, I'll kiss your ass."

CHAPTER ELEVEN

# LAUGHING WITH THEM, NOT AT THEM

*In Dog We Trust.*

—BUMPER STICKER
SEEN IN GRAND ISLAND, NEBRASKA

I considered having a section of dog jokes in this book. Just by way of a test, I asked some cyber-friends at various websites for their favorite dog jokes, and a couple of interesting facts came quickly to light. First, everyone has a favorite dog joke. Second, one joke rose abruptly to the surface as America's favorite. A nice version of it was posted on the Yesterday's Tractors site by "Ludwig" on April 28, 2003:

> *My grandfather was sitting on the front porch and a city fellow pulled up in a big, fancy car. He leaned out of the window and asked Grandpop, "Does your dog bite?"*

*Grandpop replied, "Nope, my dog don't bite."*

*The city fellow got out of his car and the dog jumped up, bit him, and proceeded to chase him around the car three or four times. Finally, the fellow got into his car and yelled, "I thought you said your dog don't bite."*

*Grandpop replied, "That ain't my dog."*

During my long years of collecting, studying, and publishing the American folk tale, plenty of dog stories have passed over my desk, and most of them run pretty much along this same line. The theme is glaringly obvious: dogs are smart and people are dumb. I think this speaks well not only of dogs, who are indeed smart, but also of human beings, who all too rarely have a clear grasp of their own inherent inadequacies. Maybe the contrast is wider between dog and man than between one man and another, thus making the enormous gap all the more obvious.

A nice version of this common motif was posted on the Yesterday's Tractors site by "Brian/PA" on April 28, 2003:

*As a butcher is shooing a dog away from his shop, he sees $20 and a note in his mouth, reading, "10 pork chops, please." Amazed, he takes the money, puts a bag of chops in the dog's mouth, and quickly closes the shop. He follows the dog and watches him wait for a green light, look both ways, and trot across the road to a bus stop. The dog checks the timetable and sits on the bench. When a bus arrives, he walks around the front and looks at the number, then boards the bus. The butcher follows, dumbstruck.*

*As the bus travels out into the suburbs, the dog takes in the scenery. After a while he stands on his back paws to push the "stop" button, then the butcher follows him off. The dog runs up to a house and drops his bag on the stoop. He goes back down the path, takes a big run, and throws himself—Whap!—against the door. He does this again and again. No answer. So he jumps on a wall, walks around the garden, beats his head against a window, jumps off, and waits at the front door. A big guy opens it and starts yelling and pummeling the dog.*

*The butcher runs up and screams at the guy, "What the hell are you doing? This dog's a genius!"*

*The owner responds, "Genius? Listen, man, that dog's no genius! This is the second time this week he's forgotten his key!"*

I've gotten similar stories over the years of the miracle of a dog playing chess, but the owner argues he's not all that smart since he only wins three out of every four games. Then there's the dog that plays the piano at a karaoke bar but has to hum because he forgets the words. And there's the dog that, without fail, errantly points out exactly the kind of bird his owner is hunting for but during fishing has a problem with overshooting the limit or catching fish that don't meet the size requirements.

Decades ago* Russ Meints told me about the fellow who buys a new hunting dog that has the remarkable ability to run out of the blind and across the top of the water to retrieve downed ducks. When he shows off this fine dog to a friend, however, the friend snorts, "You were robbed! That dog is afraid of the water!"

Not all dogs have that fault, apparently. A winner in a 1925 Nebraska liars' contest was this nicely developed tale from Herman Neiman of Curtis:

> *This dog was half water spaniel and Irish setter. One day when I was fishing, my dog was sitting by my side looking into the water. All at once he dived into the creek and out of sight. I thought he was drowned. About 15 minutes later, I heard a dog barking a quarter of a mile down the stream, and saw to my surprise there were 10 catfish and 8 bass, which my dog had treed.*
>
> *This dog was good to hunt chickens with also. Whenever he found birds he just held them until I could come to shoot them. We had a 30-acre field of bluestem grass in which my brother and I were hunting. My dog set some chickens but the grass was so tall we could not find him. We gave it up and went home thinking the dog would soon follow. He didn't come, and so the next day we decided we would have to find the dog to keep him from starving to death, because we knew he would hold those chickens until he died. We couldn't find him and we finally decided to burn the field and drive him out that way. When the fire died down, there was my dog, holding a chicken about 30 feet from him, both burned to a crisp. I'd like to have a dog like that again.*

Time and time again folk humor suggests that our dogs are skilled to a fault. It was my old friend and colleague Bill Kloefkorn who told me he'd heard this tale duing his childhood near Attica, Kansas:

*There was once a guy who had a dog he was very proud of. He would hold a point on any bird for any length of time. He was in a bar with the dog and the dog suddenly jumped up and went into a point at another guy who had just walked into the bar. The dog's owner looked around but could not see anything that might have caused the dog's behavior. He asked the man, "Do you happen to have a bird in your pocket?"*

*"No," he answered.*

*"Have you been hunting recently? Could you have the scent of a bird on you somehow?"*

*"No."*

*"Well, I'm certainly sorry my dog is behaving like this," the dog's owner apologized. '"I hope it hasn't embarrassed you too much, Mr.? . . . Mr.? . . ."*

*"Partridge," the man answered.*

I guess such tales would be unbelievable if they weren't so common. Can we possibly believe that so many people have so many stories about so many dogs' skills and tenacity and that they are all incorrect? I think not! Dale Keag of Coal Valley, Illinois, submitted this story for judging in another, uh, liars' contest:

*Since I've retired farming, I spend a lot of time with my fox terrier, smartest dog that ever lived. When he sees I've got my rifle, he only hunts squirrels, and when he sees my shotgun, he only hunts rabbits. But the other day when I got out my fishing pole, my dog was nowhere to be found. Finally, I saw him behind the chicken house—he'd dug up a dozen worms, put them in a can, and was heading for the car!*

If there is a monkey wrench in the workings of such fine canines, it is inevitably the human element. My buddy Dan Selden once told me about an extra fine dog he had of much the same ilk as Farmer Keag's. If the prices were high on raccoons and Dan was thinking of doing some coon hunting, all he had to do was set out his pelt-stretching board for coons and his old dog Jim would go roaring into the woods along Oak Creek and tree a couple of coons for him. If he put out the fox-pelt stretcher, Jim would head out on the run and corner a couple foxes in a hollow log somewhere close to Dan's home in Nysted, Nebraska. Same with squirrels, mink, beaver—all Dan had to do was set out the appropriate hide stretching board and that dog would take care of the rest.

But one day Dan's bride, Kim, without thinking, set her ironing board outside the back door, and they never saw poor Jim again.

Kenny Lauritsen topped that one, or nearly so, however, when he told us about a dog he'd once had to herd his dairy cows. That dog would go out to the pasture twice a day and never fail to come back with every single cow of Kenny's fairly sizable herd. But one day Kenny was out hunting with that same dog when his wife, Linda, sold one of the cows to a buyer who came by the farm. Well, that night Kenny sent his dog out to bring home the cows, and the next morning that dog was still gone, still out there in the field looking for that one missing cow. Finally Kenny had to go back to the house and get the check from the buyer and show it to that dog to demonstrate for certain that she wasn't just losing her counting skills but that there was indeed one less cow in the herd!

The famous columnist Lowell Thomas once sponsored a mendacity contest and one of the winners was—surprise!—yet another story about a clever dog. This dog was so smart that when he was night-hunting, he'd catch a toad and feed him lightning bugs until he glowed like a lantern, which he then used to light his way home.

A very early frontier report from the April 29, 1881, Valley County, Nebraska, *Journal* verifies that particularly clever dogs are nothing new:

> *I had a dog once, back in Nebraska, that I kept to herd lumber. It was this way. Cottonwood boards warp like thunder in the sun. [And this author can verify the veracity of* **that** *statement! RW] A board would hump its back up about nine in the morning, and in half an hour, it would turn over. By eleven it would warp the other way with the heat and make another flop. Each time it turned, it moved a couple feet, always following the sun toward the west. The first summer I lived in Brownville, over 10,000 board feet of lumber skipped out to the hills the day before I had advertised a house raisin'. I went to the county seat to attend a lawsuit and when I got back, there wasn't a stick of timber left. It had strayed away into the uplands. An ordinary board would climb a two-mile hill during a hot week, and when it struck the timber it would keep wormin' in and out among the trees like a garter snake. Every farmer in the state*

*had to keep shepherd dogs to follow his lumber around the country, keep it together, and show where it was in the morning. We didn't need any flumes there for lumber. We sawed it east of the place we wanted to use it and let it warp itself to its destination, with men and dogs to head it off at the right time, and we never lost a stick.*

Sometimes what is apparently acknowledged by human beings to be a clear intellectual superiority of dog over man appears in very subtle forms. I have sworn a death oath to keep the source of this "blond joke" absolutely confidential, and small wonder! "There are of course intelligent blonds. They retrieve good too." And from the same anonymous death-wish source, a story commonly told around here but which I only as of this writing have realized is yet another admission of canine superiority, this time in the area of socially acceptable behavior:

*A country gal comes back to her parents' home for the first time with her new husband. The new husband sits down at the dinner table and the folks serve him up a fabulous, big, country meal. After dinner the Pa says, "Let's talk a spell so we can get to know ya." And the new husband talks. He listens. And pretty soon, as country eating can do, he feels a fart coming on. He sneaks off a quiet little squeak.*

*"Spot!" yells the father.*

*The new husband thinks, "Good. He thinks it was the dog." They talk some more, the gravy and beans start to working, and the young husband needs to fart again. He raises up a bit and lets another one squeak through.*

*"Spot!" yells Pa, looking under the table.*

*"Good, he still thinks it's the damn dog," thinks the new husband.*

*Finally he can't take it anymore. He really has to get rid of some buildup. He raises up and really fires one off. "Spot!" yells Pa. "Get out from under that table before this idiot craps on you!"*

One of my favorite Nebraska storytellers, Harry "The Fiddlin' Wheat Farmer" Hanson, once told me that his father was out in a field cutting hay when their favorite dog, running ahead of the mower, stopped to deal with a flea, and before Harry's father could hit the implement lift, that sickle bar had passed over the dog's back . . . and cut his tail off right at the base. Well, the dog was sitting there crying and whining so Harry's father said to his son, "Boy, run back to the house and bring me that bottle of Wizard Oil I keep by the sink." Which errand Harry promptly did. Well, Harry's dad—now, this is what Harry told me!—put some of that Wizard Oil on the dog's stump . . . and the dog grew another tail. Even more remarkably, he put some Wizard Oil on that amputated tail . . . and it grew another dog!

Sometimes it seems we simply are not deserving of our dogs. "Pogo" posted on my Successful Farming tall-tale site on April 28, 2003, the one ". . . about the guy who went to look at a bird dog offered for sale by an old southern gentleman. The prospective buyer asked, 'Does that dog have good bloodlines?' whereupon the seller sniffed, 'Suh, if this dog would talk, he wouldn't speak to either of us.'"

My favorite dog story is one an old-timer told me almost 40-years ago when I first became interested in traditional American folk humor. He was in his 90s then, in a nursing home, and for a couple of days he told me tall tale after tall tale, some of the best I'd heard before or that I've heard since. But he also told me about the hardships he'd seen in his lifetime: family members who died during the horrendous influenza plagues of 1918; fires that destroyed barns, towns, and crops; dust storms, grasshopper storms, blizzards, tornados, floods, hail; bank failures, crop failures. He told me one disaster after another until he had told me maybe 30 or 40 things worse than the things that had ever happened to me in my lifetime. So, I said to him that I didn't understand how he could tell me about a life so filled with tragedy and yet tell me at the same time some of the funniest stories I'd ever heard. The old gent thought over what I said a moment. Then he provided me with an explanation of the human condition and frontier humor that explained more to me than any 10 graduate seminars at any university possibly could have:

> *Roger, I'm not an educated man, so I can't tell you the psychology or the philosophy of the matter, but I can tell you another story. I was once hunting down in the Republican River bottoms with my good ol' dog. We came around a bend in the riverbank, and that dog ran right smack into a bobcat about three times his size. The bobcat took out after that dog and was gaining on him every jump. The dog looked over his shoulder, and he could see that that bobcat was just about to get him, so he ran up to one of those big old cottonwood trees that grows down in the bot-*

*toms, and he ran 50 feet right straight up the trunk. Now, that dog didn't climb the tree because he could. He climbed it because he had to.*

That old veteran was saying that pioneers, people in general, don't laugh because it's easy. They laugh because they have to. It's a survival technique. And I'm not sure whether it's the laughers who survive or the survivors who laugh, but there's a correlation there we can't ignore or deny. And yet another lesson from a good ol' dog.

If you would like to cheer your day with a couple of dog jokes, I highly recommend that you visit www.doghumor.com (as recommended to me by "Fair Cheryl" Rainford, Agriculture Online [www.agriculture.com], a part of Successful Farming's enormous cyber department). Lots of good laughs there, especially the ones about dog rules and the differences between dogs and cats.

A couple of years ago my son Chris e-mailed me a dozen dog haiku poems that were really terrific, and I sensed that a new art form would soon be sweeping the country. So, in preparation for this manuscript, I popped the term "dog haiku" into the Google search engine and came up with scores of sites touting the very best, the newest, and the largest collections of dog haiku. Oh boy! Is this going to be fun, or what? Well, it turns out that whoever invented that first assortment of canine haiku must have sopped up the well and left creative juices on low everywhere across the Web, because there's almost nothing new added to that original list. It's still one heck of a good laugh, but you'll only need to visit one of the many lists you'll find under "dog haiku," so don't be dismayed by the hundreds of sites that pop up in your search. The lists all start with the haiku beginning "I love my master . . ." so you can hardly go wrong with any list that shows that as its opening lines.

My favorite examples from this collection are:

*I am your best friend,*
*Now, always, and especially*
*When you are eating.*

And

*I sound the alarm!*
*Paperboy—come to kill us all—*
*Look! Look! Look! Look! Look!*

My own favorite form of dog humor is another classical form of art: the very famous nineteenth-century paintings by Cassius Marcellus Coolidge of dogs playing cards. The most famous version—and there are several—is titled "A Friend in Need" and features a cigar-smoking bulldog on the right of the frame passing an ace of clubs under the table to the dog on his left. Why am I telling you this? You all know the painting! It's at least as famous as the Mona Lisa or Grant Wood's *American Gothic*!

Coolidge was an interesting guy. He was born in upstate New York in 1844, was educated in the remarkably uncreative field of accounting, and began his life as a banker. He clearly was not a man to be confined by training and experience, however; from his teller's cage, during the rest of his life, he ventured into raising chickens, writing operas, running a drugstore, publishing a newspaper, inventing (he came up with a device to collect fares from streetcar riders), and collecting sap from maple trees. Have you ever posed for a photograph in one of those carnival devices where you stick your head through a hole and thus appear over the body of a muscular beach hero, a well-endowed babe, a cowboy, a firefighter, a police officer, or a clown? Well, Coolidge invented those too.

He also demonstrated his vitality by marrying a 29-year-old woman when he was 64 and fathering a child at the age of 66! He had always had some artistic skills, painting street signs and portraits, even studying under a New York portraitist, and in 1873 he came up with the bizarre but remarkably successful notion of painting images of dogs playing cards. At first his paintings were purchased by cigar companies, which distributed free prints of the paintings as premiums for their tobacco products, but Coolidge's real score came when a large New York printing firm started marketing his prints as calendars, posters, and prints. Cassius Coolidge's dogs may not be *fine* art, but I'm betting that money has been spent over the years buying his images of dogs playing cards (and pool and chess and whatever else he came up with) more than has been spent on Picasso's works. And what's more, I'd bet at least as much pleasure has been derived from them. Coolidge died January 13, 1934.

I am the very proud owner of an ancient example of the genre on a velvet tapestry, given to me by a pal who once ran a small-town-tavern where this objet d'art hung for many years as the *only* work of art on display. Then a buddy of mine, Mick Maun, gave me a set of four different Coolidge prints, which are now framed and prominently displayed in our home's hallway. In the intervening years, I have acquired tin placards of the paintings, playing cards, and at least two very nice shirts, one sporting the dogs playing cards, the an playing pool.

The closest our marriage came to collapse was a time when Linda came home from Grand Island, the closest town of any size to our tiny village (population 352), and told me with stunning sanguinity that she had driven past a filling station corner in that town and noticed a guy selling a bunch of paintings on velvet there . . . I was interested. I've always wanted an Elvis on velvet, or maybe the half-naked and buxom Aztec maiden about to be sacrificed by the cruel priest on an altar of stone, or even the sunset over a Yucatan beach. And, she said, there was a tapestry of . . . dogs playing cards. I was shocked and outraged. How could anyone simply drive by something like that without at least stopping to inquire about a price? Yet my *wife*? We roared full-speed back to Grand Island where, fortunately for her and our child, the ropes of the art exhibit were still bearing that tapestry of Coolidge's masterpiece. I asked about the price—$12—and bought the tapestry on the spot. It now hangs in our bedroom as an ostentatious flaunting of my willingness to spend obscene amounts of money to satisfy my elitist tastes in the arts.

Which is to say, Cassius Coolidge's inspiration is still alive, even flourishing. And I'm betting reproductions and originals still grace walls of discriminating art lovers all over America.

* The previous tall tales are from my own collection or from my books *Shingling the Fog and Other Plains Lies* (University of Nebraska Press, Lincoln), *Catfish at the Pump* (University of Nebraska Press, Lincoln), *The Liars Corner* (Plains Heritage, Dannebrog, Nebraska), *And Liars Too* (Lee Books, Lincoln, Nebraska).

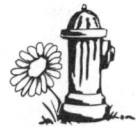

CHAPTER TWELVE

# WHO EXACTLY IS THE STABLE ONE IN THIS RELATIONSHIP?

*My favorite!*

**—FROM AN ANONYMOUS "DOG'S DAILY DIARY" SEEN ON THE WEB**

I started my history of dogs in my life by telling you about dear Toodles, a dog that came to me as a companion while I was very ill and lonely. That's part of the story of dogs and humans too. Dogs work with us as partners in hunting, mushing, law enforcement, herding, detection of all sorts, and guiding the blind, and everyone knows what a great nurse a dog can be. They just seem to know something is wrong with a human being, and they just seem to know that by their very presence they can do something about the problem. While their therapies may come in the form of some special gestures of love—a wagging tail or wet kiss—they also seem to understand that their very presence does something to soothe the human soul. To the credit of some human beings, we are learning to appreciate and systematically use that canine capacity.

I noticed early on that when everything seemed way too complicated—nothing was going right, people around me were anything but cooperative and friendly, the rain was falling only on me—all I needed to do was sit out on our back porch for a half hour with my good ol' dogs. Suddenly things popped into focus again like a slide warming up in a projector. My dogs love me. Nothing's complicated to them. They'd do whatever I had in mind. Rain? What rain? My mornings now start when, precisely at 7 A.M., I hear a bumblethump on the back stairs to our sleeping porch. It's Abbie, up and ready to enjoy life. Forget the *day*! This is *life* we're talking about here! There is a ritual: I let her in, she makes an insane leap for the bed—we have a very high, old-fashioned bed. (When it's wet outside, which in our area of the continent is depressingly rare, I step quickly outside so she doesn't get a shot at that bedspread!) She rolls over, her tongue lolls madly, she wiggles and squirms, she tries to lick me, she tries to nip me, she leaps off the bed and dashes back to the door insanely, then back on the bed. There are a couple of minutes of that, and then she's back out the door. She's said her piece: "Where the hell have you been, Dad? The sun's been up for hours (minutes, as the case may be)! We're alive and there are Frisbees to throw! Where's Mom? Let's go! Run run run! Throw throw throw! Scratch my tummy! Let's go go go!"

There simply is no way for me to go downstairs after that first greeting of the day from Abbie without a glow and a grin. No way. When it doesn't happen, when she is too busy with a squirrel or bit of rope or particularly tasty stick to come up for a morning greeting, I'll have to admit it, I miss her.

That's the therapy dogs are all about. It strikes me as being the most obvious, logical, inherently sensible program possible: take dogs into situations where human beings are sick, depressed, lonely, hurting. I can never understand why our local television stations treat these therapy dog events as some kind of news. Oh, boy, a dog can make a human feel better. Now, there's a scoop! Water slakes thirst, chocolate really tastes good, the sun comes up in the east, and dogs make humans feel better.

A number of excellent websites tell you more about the details of dog therapy (isn't the Web an absolutely amazing resource?), but in my opinion they really shortchange themselves. They talk about what great physical therapy petting a dog is, what a great distraction training a dog or even talking with a dog can be for those who are spending too much time focusing on the less positive sides of life, blah blah blah . . . I think the benefits are a good deal more intellectual than that: I think it does everyone good to have some intelligent conversation with a dog to take our minds off the prattle that is the usual fare of human conversation. Just a couple of days ago, there was a story on one of the network television news shows to the effect that children learn to read much more quickly if they read to dogs. Well, duh! Of course! How much more sense it makes for a kid to read a good story about the little engine that could or anything by Dr. Seuss to someone who is intellectually capable of grasping such concepts—for example, any dog who's ever lived—compared to some dumb adult who has nothing on his or her mind beyond the fact that while you're reading you're eating a crayon or peeing your pants!

Also, there truly is something spiritual about a dog's aura. Linda noticed earlier today she just feels more relaxed when she takes a moment to watch our dogs sleep. They don't even have to do anything but just lie there and sleep. And we don't have to do anything, not even touch them. We just look at 'em and drink in that sublime Zen acceptance they exude.

I am fortunate enough to have a good friend who is involved in the dog therapy program. Dr. Jan Anderson is a university librarian who also works with her own golden retriever, Buddy, as a therapy giver. I asked her about her experiences in the program, and I'm just going to pass her response along to you so you can read for yourself what a rewarding and effective notion this is:

*Hi, Roger,*

*I have an anecdote for you below, but for websites on therapy animals (not Seeing Eye dogs), try Delta Society and Intermountain Therapy Animals, ITA—the Delta affiliate that certified Buddy and me.*

*ITA started a great new program a few years ago called READ. Therapy dogs go to schools and libraries, and kids read books to them. In the ITA newsletter recently there was a great quote from a kid who'd done this. He said something like: "I really scared that big dog. (How did you do that?) I read him a story about a monster!" The READ program is designed to provide kids with noncritical listeners. When we get back [home], we have to get involved in this one!*

*Here golden retriever Buddy and I have been visiting a local nursing home two times a month since June or July. At first I wasn't sure I could handle all the old-ness, but I quickly got to know the residents and the staff as individuals and settled in. Buddy loved it from the start.*

*On our visiting days, Buddy and I have a morning routine that gets us both prepared and lets him know it's "his day." We start with brushing, ear cleaning, and doggie tooth brushing. Then the two of us take a walk around the block, and finally we put on our matching red "uniforms" with the ITA logo. Mine is a T-shirt, and Buddy's is a bandana, the final step that really gets him revved up. He stands up in the car all the way to the nursing home, and when we arrive, he pulls me up the steps and in the front door.*

*I have my favorites among the residents, and Buddy does too! He's very patient and loving with everyone. He sits or stands still for petting, sometimes offering a paw and occasionally giving doggie kisses (rare for him). But for his favorites, he literally tows me over to them or into their rooms and greets them with big-time wagging and smiling. Most of the time Buddy's favorites are the people who pet him most enthusiastically and who talk directly to him.*

*Among the residents is a woman named Rose who is in the later stages of Alzheimer's disease. Whenever we visit she is seated in her wheelchair at a table in the sitting room—the only person not facing the television. On the table in front of her she holds a baby doll or a Raggedy Ann and just looks at it without emotion. When you talk directly to her, Rose sometimes smiles and occasionally tries to speak, although she's unable to form words, and only sounds come out.*

*The activities director, Pat, accompanies Buddy and me on our visiting rounds. The first day we came, Pat introduced us to Rose and asked if she would like to pet "Buddy the dog." Rose looked up into Pat's face while she spoke but never knew we were right beside her wheelchair, even when Pat placed her [Rosie's] hand on Buddy's head. The next couple of visits Rose began to register that Buddy was there. She smiled when her hand was placed on his head and stiffly patted him. Still some days are good days, and some aren't for her.*

*On our fifth or sixth visit, Rose saw us across the room as we entered! As we approached, she actually reached out her hand to Buddy! And as she patted his head, she tried to speak. Pat bent close to her and said, "You like him, don't you?" Although I couldn't understand her, Rose said to Pat, "I don't like him, I love him."*

*Unbelievable. Made my whole . . . life. Interestingly, from the very start Rose has been one of Buddy's favorites, even when she is unresponsive.*

How's that for an endorsement for dog therapy? Gives me goose bumps. Brings tears to my eyes. And it makes me wonder how many other of our human afflictions, mental and physical, could be treated, maybe even cured, with the ministrations of our good canine friends. As I read Jan's letter again I get the feeling too that a not insignificant benefit of her work with Buddy accrues to her too. What do you think?

If you would like to support this kind of activity, know more about it, and subscribe to the companion animal magazine *PetLife*, check their website at www.petlifeweb.com.

Well, even if it's an exercise in the obvious, it's here, and it works, and I think it's great. If you would like to explore pet (or animal) therapy, maybe use a dog therapist (although let's face it—every dog is a therapist!), or get into training animal therapists or animal-assisted therapy, take a look at www.dog-play.com/therapy.html. Check out www.superdog.com for stories of therapy dogs and some of their most interesting cases. That should get you started.

Now, it's not all that hard to imagine how a warm, friendly, nonjudgmental dog can be a real salve for the sick soul, but there may be more to it than gooey sentimentality like mine. At Cambridge in England, scientists are conducting tests to determine if dogs can detect prostate cancer from urine samples. The early indications are that they can. In California, researchers have had remarkable success using dogs to detect lung cancer from victims' breath! Maybe doctors no longer make house calls and increasingly the American health-care system is sinking into what appears to be irredeemable political miasmas, but the cure may be on your back porch in the form of your family dog. For the price of an ear scratch and maybe a Milkbone, you have a psychiatrist, therapist, and general practitioner at your beck and call. "Hey, Abbie, I have this pain right here and. . ."

**CHAPTER THIRTEEN**

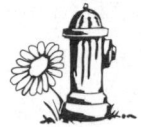

# TOGETHERNESS

*A boy can learn a lot from a dog:*
*obedience, loyalty, and the importance of turning around*
*three times before lying down.*

—ROBERT BENCHLEY

Those are the words of a very, very wise man. I grew up with a dog. My kids grew up with a dog. My wife grew up with a dog. I can't imagine growing up without a dog. At least not normally. Childhood and adolescence are pretty tough times to get through. No one understands you, your friends are jerks, and your enemies are aliens. It seems like nothing is ever going to change—your parents are always going to run your life and your big brother will be giving you wedgies for as far as you can see into the future. They say school will go on at least until after the 12th grade, and then maybe four years of college, and then possibly another two to six years of graduate school, and . . . and . . . and you're in the fourth grade! There's only one soul that can get you through tough spots like that, and of course it's your dog. People who have children but no dog should go to jail.

There is the problem of introducing a child into a home where a dog has been lord and master for some time already á la Pooter. Sometimes that simply does not work. I know that. But there's not a puppy in the world that won't adjust to a child, and a child who won't adjust to a puppy needs some major brain surgery. No doubt about it, adjusting to a new puppy is not easy. We had three dogs living here for some time, so not only did we live with dogs, they outnumbered us. Then Lucky and Goldie died and we got Abbie. We were surprised all over again at what an enormous adjustment that was.

For one thing, she's a puppy. A dog is a dog, but a puppy . . . Oh, man, a puppy is a puppy. Nothing is safe. Those razor teeth (why is it in the logic of evolution that little puppies that are going to be feeding off of tender mommy dog breasts have teeth like hypodermic needles?) are never at rest: shoes, furniture, fingers, food bowls, anything is fair game for chewing to a puppy. And they have no sense at all of your private person, your space, or your schedule. They do whatever occurs to them at whatever moment it happens to strike their fancy, requiring endless patience and discussion if you hope for any change.

Curiously, we have never had any real problem with housebreaking our dogs; they somehow figure out in a day or two that the best thing to do is pursue those particular biological demands elsewhere. Abbie peed twice in the house until we figured out that we had to make sure her auxiliary tanks were drained before we let her in and we had to watch for that very distinctive nose-to-the-ground, sense-of-urgency scramble signaling that she was about to unload again. I think she pooped once inside, and then not again even on the dog porch.

We are still, a year later, having to make adjustments and try to help her understand why we would just as soon she wouldn't do things like carry bras out of the laundry room and into the kitchen, dig holes the size of septic tanks in the backyard, chew the handles off of any tools left in the yard, and eat the kitty. But she is a bright dog, and she does want to please, and I really do have the impression that she is trying to do what she can to subvert her natural canine inclinations and cater to our far less fun and spontaneous human expectations. I explained to her just a few days ago what an inconvenience the new hole in the backyard is, and she actually listened. I could see that she understood that I wasn't happy and it had something to do with this hole she had so carefully crafted. And it may work: three days now and no new holes.

Thud had the toughest time adjusting to Abigail's new membership in our family. I think it's probably always tough for an adult dog, especially a male, to accept a new canine into the pack. That's only natural. But Thud is a big, good-hearted, gentle bear of a Lab, and we thought that since he was so desperate for companionship—he'd actually found solace in a sock monkey, for Pete's sake—he would love a sweet, little, cuddly, utterly harmless black puppy. (The time came all too quickly when we could set aside the notion of Abbie being "harmless," but at this point she was still quite young, newly separated from her mommy and sibs, and if anything a trifle shaky.)

I'm surprised that Abbie's first five minutes on our homestead didn't scar her psyche forever. (There's plenty of evidence it did not.) First she encountered Hairball the Cat (nee Love-Heart Love-Angel Love-Kitty). Hairball is a diminutive but no-nonsense, ancient but physically fit, outdoor, butt-kicker of a cat. She weighs, tops, three pounds. She's had to defend her turf for a decade against feral tom cats, stray dogs, *our* dogs, 'possums, coons, skunks, chickens, geese, ducks, deer, horses, cows, wild turkeys, belligerent squirrels, and countless other challengers. And she has won every battle she has taken on. (We have seen her stare down buck deer!) So, Hairball was curious when we came through the garage door with the tiny black bundle. We had a brief debate about what to do about the inevitable confrontation between Abbie and her new housemates and decided we might as well get it over with. So we put Abigail on the ground in front of Hairball first. Hairball approached cautiously. Abigail didn't so much as wiggle her tail or woof and Hairball laid four razor blades across her nose in one savage swipe of her paw. Abbie fell over backward and rolled frantically to escape this hissing, growling demon before her.

Before Linda or I could react even to the degree of seizing Abbie from this feline serial murderer, Thud came roaring up the stairs and went right straight at Abbie. Thud weighs 140 pounds. At that point Ab weighed maybe four pounds. The mere wind vector blast from Thud's first "woof" knocked her over backward and scared her to the point of piddling all over herself and the sidewalk.

Welcome to the Welsches, new puppy!

Two things had happened in regard to Thud's status in our family, we later theorized. First, from being the youngest, puppiest, most irresponsible, most carefree member of our pack, he had become not only the oldest dog, but our *only* dog. And he had been in that position for three months, long enough to get to like it. He was, in short, a little bit spoiled. And as small and insignificant as she was, he saw Abigail quite rightly as something of a threat to his new and exalted position.

Second, and quite seriously, the demands of his new situation *and its inherent responsibilities* had changed him from the puppy he'd been for years to an adult, heavily laden with all the obligations that come along with being *the* family dog. He could no longer hide behind Goldie and Lucky when it came to defending the house against threats like the UPS man, turtledoves at the feeder, stray cats, and fast-food wrappers blowing in the wind. And he couldn't be certain that this new intrusion wasn't some kind of threat. Or maybe he could be certain. . . .

It didn't take long for Abigail von der Pooper to hit her stride. Before long she was constantly chewing on whatever part of Thud happened to be close to her mouth; ragging him at every moment of his life, including those times when a man needs a certain amount of privacy, if you catch my drift; exploding in his face whenever he tried to collect his expected ear scratches or belly rubs from us; beating him to every Frisbee or bonie tossed into the yard for play; and challenging him for every snack and goodie; and on and on and on and on.

In short, Abbie was now fulfilling what had been Thud's role with Goldie and Lucky for many years! His slot as annoying young puppy had been taken over by Abbie. And slowly but wonderfully surely Thud eased into his new obligations as respected elder, calm and dignified senior pack male, backup UPS man greeter, the guy who sits on the bench with me and welcomes the *other* dog back from an insane run fetching a Frisbee. Which brings out the obvious but still surprising fact that a dog's personality is not simply a product of its genes or environment but also of its changing status within the family. Just as a dog adjusts to become an ad hoc nurse when someone in the family is ill, hurting, or depressed, a dog understands where it fits within the family unit and, apparently, has an explicit job description for that slot. If I throw a Frisbee for Thud when Abbie is not around and indicate to him that it is for him, now he simply looks me straight in the eye and clearly says, "Not my job anymore. Give a whistle for the kid. She'll get your Frisbee for you."

One of the surprising elements of pet ownership for me since the days of Fleagle and our cat Judy (a tom who hated me through his whole life for saddling him with the name) has been that cats and dogs get along just fine. There is often—okay, usually—a bit of adjustment fuss to get through: dog chases cat, cat slashes open dog's nose, cat and dog run wildly through house and demolish furniture and heirlooms, dog and cat damn near kill each other in fit of fury, and so on. But I have been surprised with every new dog/cat combination we've had by how quickly they adjust to each other. In fact, in every case, within a relatively short period of time, our dogs and cats have become so accustomed to each other that their relationship has passed the level of affection and become downright embarrassingly gooey. It's true: our cats lick our dogs and accept slobbery kisses in return. They not only sleep *together*, our cats have been known to sleep *on* our dogs on cold, winter nights.

Hairball never passes by one of our dogs without an affectionate rub, a bit of a purr. The dogs, admittedly, seem embarrassed when someone happens to be around to witness these displays of affection. I think they know what the expectation is, and it sure isn't this kind of lovey-dovey snuggling and necking they constantly indulge in.

Some pet combinations are, of course, more difficult than others. A bird and a cat may never wind up being friends until one eats the other, and the hierarchy of that process is pretty well set in stone. The secret is to get *big* birds. For example, Abbie loves chasing robins, wrens, and goldfinches away from our bird feeder. Or at least she did until the day seven adult wild turkeys drifted up to the yard from the bottom ground. A couple of them even flew over the fence and *into* the yard. Abbie spotted them and went ripping out of the dog porch to teach these invaders a lesson, but as her sense of perspective kicked in and the size of the birds became evident, her understanding of the situation changed.

You could see it on her face: "Think you can just come into our yard and strut around, do you? Well, you have another thing coming because . . . Uh, wow! You certainly are one big fellow, aren't you? Bigger than me, I guess. And hmmm, I see there are three of you—whoops—no, make that a whole mess of you. And each of you is bigger than me. And, I wonder whatever happened to that bone I buried on the other side of the house? I think I'll go check on that bone, but you guys better be gone by the time I get back. Unless you really want to stay. Thud! Hey, Thud! There are some birds out here that want to have a word with you. . . ."

Lucky was cured of chasing sparrows, however. We used to have chickens, you see. And a couple little black banty hens were Linda's favorites. And one day we came back from some errand or another to find Lucky sitting at the front gate, tail wagging like crazy, one of the little hens dead in his mouth. You could tell from his eyes he was just proud as hell of his accomplishment. He was at the gate to show us what a great job he had done in our absence, that he had finally rid us of this constant, noisy, and expensive annoyance we had endured for so long. Ta-da!

And then you could see in his eyes his utter astonishment and dismay at our reaction to his accomplishment. When we got done yelling at him and scolding him—he'd never heard the word "No" so often and so loud in his life—he had pretty much decided that birds, for whatever strange reasons we seemed to have about the issue, are best left alone.

Blackjack learned his big-bird lessons from some geese we acquired to weed our yard. If you are looking for household security but don't want to train a nice dog to be threatening or to bark, I have just the solution for you. Get yourself some geese. Nothing is nastier, more territorial, more physical than a couple of geese. And when a goose thumps you, you know you've been thumped.

If you need an audio warning system, then what you are looking for is guinea hens. Get yourself a half dozen guinea hens to sit in the trees over your farmyard parking area, and you will never again have to worry about someone sneaking up on you when you're not looking. Guinea hens are always looking, and their screams have been known to drive away determined bands of attacking ninja warriors.

## CHAPTER FOURTEEN

# WHENCE THEY COME

*There are three faithful friends—an old wife, an old dog, and ready money.*

**—BENJAMIN FRANKLIN, *POOR RICHARD'S ALMANAC [FOR 1738]***

I have experienced a fairly wide range of options in the process of acquiring dogs over my life. As I've told you, there's been charity, newspaper ads, the Humane Society, freebies at the feed and seed store, veterinarian's bulletin board, AKC registered breeders. And there's not a doubt in my mind where the best choices are to be made and what I would do the next time we needed a good dog: I'd take a freebie every time.

We really haven't found that a purebred dog is any more calm, bright, healthy, trainable, brave, reverent, true, thrifty, etc., than any mutt we picked out of a box in a filling station labeled *Good Dogs Free—Take One*. In fact, it's probably just coincidence, but our experience has been precisely the opposite. Or at least mixed. Goldie was a purebred golden retriever and she was everything good in a dog. Thud is purebred and he's a good boy and all, but bright? Well, he's a good boy. Slump was a mixed breed and he was an idiot. Abbie's a mutt and she's wonderful.

The telling factor for us is where the dog up for adoption stands in the world's larger scheme of things: a person who is breeding show dogs for sale is not going to make any more dogs he or she can't sell for $500. There is not a glut of registered dogs to speak of; on the other hand, there is a desperate and tragic surplus of just plain-dogs. The problem could be solved if there were no careless, cheap, ignorant, misguided, cruel dog owners, but what's the likelihood of the human race making *that* turnaround anytime soon?

So, the bottom line is, we have millions of dogs sitting in cages, boxes, pens, garages, feed and seed stores, taverns, and filling stations that really need good homes. And they need one fairly desperately because the alternative isn't pretty. The older they get, the less adoptable they are. The older they get, the more expensive they are to keep. The older they get, the closer they come to being killed as excess baggage. At the same time, there are so-called puppy mills where idiots are breeding dogs like crazy, not show dogs or purebreds or working dogs, just dogs with the intent of selling them, often through pet stores, farm stores, whatever. *Never* buy one of these dogs. In my mind there are two choices for obtaining a pet dog. First, you can go to a professional breeder if you really *have* to have a pedigreed dog (a waste of good money if you ask me, and a disservice to choice number two). Second, you can find a dog being given away to a good home, with the very best source of this being the

American Society for the Prevention of Cruelty to Animals (ASPCA) or your local Humane Society. I'll be telling you more about these wonderful organizations in the next chapter or so. Welsch dogs are lovable, friendly, bright, beautiful curs. Just like our kids.

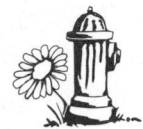

CHAPTER FIFTEEN

# BEING KNOWN BY THE COMPANY YOU KEEP

*Pomeranians speak only
to Poodles and Poodles speak only to God.*

—CHARLES KURALT

Probably the shakiest dimension of accepting a random dog into your household is size and breed. Advertised origins for free or cheap dogs are pretty much like that for free and cheap automobiles: distinctly unreliable. Slump was allegedly a black Lab mix. The operational word there is "mix." Like, uh, what would that black Lab be mixed with? Pomeranian? Pit bull? Rogue elephant? It's pretty hard to tell because as often as not, the owner doesn't have the slightest idea, not to mention that sitting there with eight more puppies to get rid of before next Friday, you can be damn sure he is going to put the very best spin on his pups' family tree as possible.

Everyone knows that the words "black Lab" and "golden retriever" carry a lot of weight. Everyone "knows" that black Labs and golden retrievers are everything you want in a dog, and so the gamble is which of this puppy's genes are going to hold true: the great-grandfather's one-fourth black Lab mix or the father's or the mother's Dalmatian-poodle's? As much as my left-wing, liberal, civil rights, we-shall-overcome history makes me hate to admit it, breeding does have something to say about what kind of result you get. I know stereotypes are not always true and are a terrible way to judge people and dogs, but well, uh, dang, let's face it. Dalmatians are really, really dumb. And pit bulls are really, really mean. And goldens shed. And black Labs don't. Yes, I know, you once had a Dalmatian that was invited to join the Mensa Society, and your brother-in-law had a Lab that hated water, and when your babysitter comes over, she brings her six pit bulls to play with the tots. The reason those are called exceptions is that they are, well, to put it bluntly, exceptions.

Abbie was billed as a Lab–Saint Bernard mix, and well she may be. We saw her mother and father, and they were sort of vaguely a Lab, kind of, and a relatively Saint Bernardish-looking large dog. I think any papers they might have had would never have held up in a probate court. Abbie looked terminally black Lab as a pup, but as she grew she mutated, though thankfully not into anything Saint Bernard-like, except that her eye sockets sag when she's tired, her salivary glands are hyperactive, and she has about three acres of spare skin under her chin. And when she was approaching her first birthday, she took on a funny brownish tinge. Sometimes when the sun hits him funny, Thud has a bit of brown to him, but Abbie's is far more pronounced. And it's mostly her body that is turning brown as of this writing (at which she is just a touch over a year old); her head and front shoulders are still as black as Thud's. Somehow I always thought that in a "mixed-breed" dog, there was truly a mixing process, but there Abbie is, her head as black as Thud's but her body with a distinctly brown overtone to it. And she is shedding whitish-brownish hair like Goldie used to do in the spring. So every day Abbie looks less and less like a black Lab. But every day she is also even smarter than a black Lab—more like a golden. And I don't sense much of anything about her that is Saint Bernard.

What does all that mean? Beats me. I guess it means you never can tell about people or dogs by their breeding. I just can't imagine that we could have been any more certain of her appearance or behavior if she had indeed come with a full set of papers, a church baptism, and a generous dowry. Or that our affection for her would have been either more or less. So, do we spend $500 for a beautiful dog we love that looks to all the world like a dog, or do we spend $5 for a beautiful dog we love that looks to all the world like a dog? I guess it depends on what kind of friends you want to impress: the kind who are dumb enough to be impressed by a $500 dog or the kind who aren't.

Now, size is to some degree a function of breed. Dogs are not like people in that regard. (Or in many other ways, now that I think of it, but for the moment we are considering size.) Okay, Mayans and Japanese are, generally speaking, smaller than Kansans and Poles, and just to make it clear, I'm talking people here. But the variation in the human format, I think we can all admit, doesn't approach the variety we see in dogdom. There are big dogs and there are little dogs. There may be bigger Chihuahuas and there may be smaller black Labs, but chances still are, your basic Lab is going to be bigger than your fundamental Chihuahua. I'm not going to get any argument on that, right?

Sticking a big dog that should be running insanely in a three-acre yard into a city apartment is downright cruel; leaving it chained to a stake in the ground day after day is criminal. Inflicting rural life on a cute little dog about the size of a rat is no better. Does it make sense to have a Siberian husky in Florida? A Mexican hairless in Michigan's Upper Peninsula? If it does, I don't get it. I think along the line somewhere someone needs to ask what makes sense for the *dog*.

To this end it makes some sense to try to find out something about the lineage of a puppy before taking it on as a member of the family. You know what your circumstances are and are likely to be, and it is not only good sense but common decency to consider an environment that is suitable for that situation—with at least as much care as it is to select a dog that you think fits your personality and personal wishes. So, even if Abbie's heritage is a bit clouded, from the clues we got—"black Lab," "Saint Bernard"—we knew that the little black bundle we were looking at in the sawdust-floored horse tank at the feed and seed store was likely to become a sizable dog. And we knew that we have the house, yard, finances, and inclination to deal with a sizable dog. When we visited her parents to pick her up a few weeks later, we had another chance to see that we were indeed looking at a puppy that was likely to be a big dog. Maybe she wouldn't be as huge, barrel-chested, and big-boned as Thud, but she would be a big dog nonetheless, and that is almost precisely what she has become.

I don't know quite what to say about color. Everything in my psyche, politics, and religion tells me color should make absolutely no difference one way or the other, but my prejudices when it comes to dogs are so blatant and consuming, I simply cannot deny or defy them: I adore *black* dogs. (This bias is clearly being tested at this very moment, however, as Abbie, bought as a backup black dog for Thud, turns ever so slowly but ever so definitely *brown*. I love ol' Ab, black or brown. I suspect that if she turned white or yellow or calico she'd still be my Abbie and I'd love her just the same.) Aside from prejudices like that, however, I suppose the only issue that comes to bear on what color dog should be your choice is what color clothes dominate your closet, so any shedding will be as unobtrusive as possible.

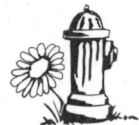

## CHAPTER SIXTEEN

# SCHOOL TIME, SCHOOL TIME

*In order to really enjoy a dog, one*
*doesn't merely try to train him to be semi-human.*
*The point of it is to open oneself to*
*the possibility of becoming partly a dog.*

**—EDWARD HOAGLAND, "DOGS AND THE TUG OF LIFE," *HARPER'S***

One distinct failure in my life with dogs and now of our lives with dogs (Linda's and mine) is undeniably our own fault. Despite a lot of well-intentioned fits and starts, we have never managed to train our dogs beyond "sit." For a while we had a trainer come to our home and help us—maybe "try to help us" would be a more accurate turn of phrase—leash-train the dogs. But it was clear to us very quickly that our dogs were too old for such training, or at least one or two of them were too old at the time, even if one was in the perfect range.

And there were too many of them. Trying to manage and train three dogs at the same time was madness. And our dogs were too big for us to muscle around the yard for very long at a time (and I'm a pretty big boy, understand).

We tried training tapes and books, but once again, while the dogs were always ready to go—they are always ready to go with anything we have in mind—our own schedules, inclinations, dispositions, whatever, quickly resulted in the training collars and leashes gathering dust in the coat closet by the front door.

We resolved to do better by Abigail von der Pooper. By God, *she* was going to go to a real dog-training school, and *we* were going to go with her, and she was going to be as wonderfully disciplined as the Lassie we had known and loved in our childhood. Yeah, right! We signed up for puppy training classes and marked down the dates on our calendar so there'd be no excuses. I built a ramp we could put up against the tailgate of Linda's pickup truck so we could easily load and unload Abbie, nice and wide, with carpet on it so she wouldn't slip.

And we went to the first class at Puppy College, Grand Island, Nebraska.

Well, it was fun. I have to say that. Our first trip was a hectic ride. Abbie was not at all happy about being in her doggy cage in the back of the truck all by herself and she, uh, embarrassed herself a trifle, but that was to be expected we decided (and she never did it again, in fact). There were maybe 15 puppies all told in the class, of every size, breed, and temperament, under almost no control whatsoever by 15 owners of every size, breed, and temperament. The four-month-old puppies were one thing, but the 70-pound one-year-olds didn't just act up—they ricocheted.

It was the closest thing to total chaos I have ever seen. The puppies loved it—lots of random piddling from the sheer delight of being there in the company of so many other puppies—but the owners, to a person, were in abject misery.

We were divided into two groups, one of which was to sit quietly (hahahahahahahahahahaha!) on the chairs arrayed around the outside of the room, an unused automobile show room, while the other half went through its paces (hahahahahahahahahaha!). The lady in charge seemed to know what she was doing even though it was only we humans who seemed to note and appreciate that, because the puppies couldn't have cared less who was saying or doing what. For an hour people marched back and forth around the circle, in one direction and then the next, stooping, pulling with the leash, guiding, coaxing, and eventually, inevitably, begging. There was a constant shuffle of owners running to the supplies table to get paper towels to clean up accidents, which it became ever clearer were not accidents at all.

At the end of our first hour of Puppy College some of our charges were showing a vague inclination if not strict ability to do what it was that was being asked of them, which was mostly "heel" and "sit" this early in the game. At the end of the session, we all sat down in various stages of exhaustion, frustration, fury, and embarrassment. (A basset hound named "Webster" was my favorite, utterly humiliating his flummoxed owner with his ability to apparently pee at will and demonstrate how totally smitten he was with our Abbie. He also drooled and pooped, but those emissions were not so clearly romantic in intent.) At the end of our session we were given handouts with hints about what we should do with our students until next week's seminar. We were all generally praised to buoy our flagging enthusiasm for dog training, and—here's the good part—a beautiful, shiny trophy went to the "Outstanding Student of the Week."

Well, okay, now we're talking. I was as discouraged about dog training as Linda was at this point, but the thought of being able to get a trophy to put on our mantle for a week acknowledging that Abigail von der Pooper was Outstanding Student of the Week at Puppy College, now *that* was something I could see working toward. I was determined to return to Puppy College, not only to have Abbie be all the dog she could be, but because I wanted that trophy, and I wanted it badly.

You might think that this is really a good sign: a firm dedication to the process, a firm desire for success, and it should have been. But two ugly elements started to creep into the situation. First, it became clear there were teacher's favorites, that the awarding of the trophy each week was not as objective a decision as we might have ideally hoped. For three weeks we watched a thoroughly undeserving winner walk off proudly with the trophy while our Abbie sobbed herself to sleep in her disappointment and disillusionment with the human race. (Well, okay, I'll admit it was *me* who was disappointed and disillusioned, and I didn't so much sob myself to sleep as I cursed the wretched perfidy and unfairness of it all.)

Finally, one week I worked with Abbie hours every day on our homework—I think it was "stay" and "come" that week—and by the time class time rolled around, we had this assignment nailed. We amazed the class: if Webster had been charmed by Abbie before, now he was utterly, slobbery in love. At the very sight of her, he lost control of every gland in his body. And when he managed to sneak in a sniff of her caboose, well. . .

We aced the hour and left the rest of Ab's classmates in her academic dust. This time we could not be denied. Her academic superiority was so overwhelming, the utter corruption that now infected the Outstanding Puppy College Student of the Week selection committee was swept away: that night Linda, Abbie, and I walked out of the classroom with the trophy.

The next day we took the expected portraits of our proud student and had T-shirts made saying "*My Abbie is outstanding student of the week*." The next week we went back to Puppy College wearing our T-shirts, returned the trophy, and never went back. For one thing, Linda and I were exhausted. For another, Abbie hadn't learned much. She was simply too young to grasp what we wanted of her, especially in the madhouse atmosphere of that lunatic scene. But finally (at least for us), because some people had totally lost control of their charges, it had gone beyond chaos to destruction and mayhem. People were being hurt; property was being destroyed.

Oh no, I'm not talking about the dogs. I'm talking about the children that some people insisted on bringing with them for the puppy school lessons. The irony was so thick you could have cut it with a chain saw. Here were people who were spending good money, taking time out of watching stealing hubcaps, driving quite some distance in their battered station wagons all the way from the trailer park, to train their *dogs* when it was all too obvious that they really needed to train their wretched, miserable, spoiled, destructive, derelict children before they wound up in reform school! We and our dogs were dutifully learning discipline and restraint, but right through the windows of the training room we could see the children of these selfsame people bouncing rocks off our cars, lighting fires in a dumpster, and firing random shots at pedestrians. Okay, it wasn't *that* bad but believe me, these kids were out of control. Linda had to restrain me on several occasions from seizing one of the little spawns of Satan, wrestling them to the ground, and putting a tight choke collar on them. I wanted to march them around the circle, slipping in the pee and drool, and making them sit, heel, and stay at the penalty of pain for misbehavior, a concept they had apparently never encountered before.

So, I guess you could say we pulled Abbie out of Puppy College because we didn't want her learning bad behavior patterns from the other dog owners' children. It was crazy. And the other inevitable, painful conclusion had to be that since Abbie is obviously plenty smart enough to learn whatever it is we would like her to learn, any failure in her socialization would be because the man in charge of her—me—is either too lazy or too dumb to teach her. While I am a little depressed by that admission, I do as I usually do and take what comfort I can from the fact that I am such a superior person I readily admit to all my inadequacies, especially when my own training is compared to your average dog's.

## CHAPTER SEVENTEEN

# ON THE ROAD AGAIN

*Dogs feel very strongly that they should always go with you in the car, in case the need should arise for them to bark violently at nothing right in your ear.*

—DAVE BARRY

One of our hopes in training Abbie was that she would be the very first of our dogs skilled in the art of motor vehicular travel. I'll admit it, I have a very bad case of pickup envy. I love coming up behind one of our locals driving along a gravel road in his pickup truck with a blond babe sitting beside him, her golden tresses blowing in the wind. He reaches over and puts his hand behind her neck, pulling her gently closer to him. She cuddles up, leans against him, licks his face. Yep, I love my black Labs, but there is nothing more affectionate than a golden retriever. And nothing sweeter than a dog enjoying a good ride with a human driver. I frequently run across our friend Bob Peterson here in town, driving along with his wonderful Lab

Oscar at his side, or I see Bob's pickup sitting somewhere with Oscar patiently looking out the window, waiting for his return. (It's become a tradition: I then say, "Hey, nice day! Who's your ugly buddy?" whereupon Bob says, "Well, that's Oscar," and I then say, "I was talking to Oscar.")

Just about as traditional in this part of America as pickup trucks with gun racks in the back window are pickup trucks with a big dog or two—usually black or chocolate Labs, for some reason—in the bed of the truck. I suppose it shouldn't bother me. In the event of an accident I imagine a dog is just as likely to be hurt flying around the inside of a truck cab as from the bed. Still, I worry about flying gravel, bugs, and debris, dogs losing footing and falling from the truck during a sharp turn or hard braking. Then there's always the possibility of the dog getting excited at a passing rabbit and jumping from the bed, but I also know I am not going to change the general ethic and habit of an entire population. Moreover, I suppose if you were to take a poll of 1,000 black and chocolate Labs asking whether they would rather: (1) ride in the open bed of a pickup truck or (2) stay at home and watch television. The results would read something like #1: 99.9 percent, #2: 0.1 percent (and that was actually a Chihuahua trying to pass as a Lab).

I can imagine that there are people (although not many men I know) who are offended by various things dogs might do in a closed truck cab, like track in mud, smell bad, fart, or otherwise expel various doggy fluids. On the other hand, the great majority of my friends have pickup trucks like mine where the driver, passenger, or dog are likely to get dirtier simply by getting into the cab than to diminish the tidiness of the truck in any way. But I just think it would be neat to have a dog to travel to town with to get the mail, a dog that would wait quietly and patiently for me while I have an extra beer with my buddies in the tavern (Linda: note!).

Alas, all my dogs to date have been ricocheters. I have no idea how you teach a dog to sit quietly and patiently in a pickup truck box, whether it is moving or standing still. I most assuredly can't imagine how you train a dog to sit in an open cab with absolutely nothing between him and passing cats, children, or slutty town doggy temptresses as if he were inside an electrified wire cage. But that's what dogs do around here. You can walk right past them sitting there in the truck bed, and while they might say howdy or stand up and acknowledge your presence, they never bust loose and run like idiots, which is to say, like my dogs.

Before we moved, we commuted to our cabin by the river from our home in Lincoln. At that time we had Slump. Slump was impossible in a car. He went nuts. He literally screamed. He flailed and flew. He was uncontrollable. He wasn't frightened, he was just frantic. Too much input. We put him in a comfortable dog travel cage. Didn't do a bit of good. We covered it to keep it dark and quiet for Slump. Nothing. Despite our reservations (I understand they are hard on a dog's system), we got doggy downers to calm him. No matter how drugged he was, Slump still struggled against the idea of calm and civilized travel. As I remember, I think that's why we moved out here—so we wouldn't have to commute with Slump anymore.

About the only time our dogs enjoy a ride in the car is when they are very sick or hurt and we have to take them to the veterinarian in our county seat, about 15 miles away. I'm sure that doesn't help matters for us in making car travel comfortable and interesting for our dogs. For them, car travel equals torture at the vet's. Since we have multiple pets—at this point two dogs and two cats—and since our vet is accommodating and congenial, we now have someone from the clinic simply load up a carrier of ampoules and syringes and come out here for the annual shots and physical exams. That seems to work pretty well but still doesn't speak at all to my personal and painful wish to have, and frustration in lacking, a pickup travel buddy.

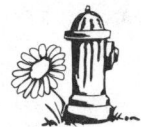

CHAPTER EIGHTEEN

# YOU GOTTA EE-LIM-I-NATE THE NEGATIVE

*Here, Gentlemen, a dog teaches us a lesson in humanity.*

—NAPOLEON BONAPARTE

While we're here at the point of painful confessions, I guess it's time to approach a part of this book I knew I would have to deal with sooner or later. You know now that I adore dogs. I think dogs are some of the most wonderful creatures on this Earth. I prefer dogs to people. Which is not to say that dogs are perfect. Yes, dogs have their faults and flaws. And I don't see how I can write my book about dogs without addressing those faults and flaws. So here it goes. . . .

Let's get the worst part over quickly. You can teach a dog to pee and poop outdoors, and with relative ease. Even that has its problems, which we will discuss later, but I don't know of a single dog owner who has ever trained his dog to fart outdoors. And believe me, if you have ever owned a dog, you know that it is neither the unsociability of the behavior nor the noise that is offensive. Almost all dogs' farts are SBD (you'll recall that means silent but deadly), although my daughter Joyce does insist that her friend Bob's dog Harley rips off foghorn farts regularly, so I can't pretend any authority here.

I think it is significant that the German language has a special word for the phenomenon, actually a portmanteau word—a couple words in one—that indicate to me that the idea of dog farts (or "dogfarts" in German) is so striking a phenomenon that it needs a special linguistic expression all its own: *Hundsfotz*. Let's be honest and serious for just one moment about this, and then let's move along to something less offensive, which is to say, anything else. Truly now, is there anything you have smelled in your life more offensive than a dog fart? Remarkable, isn't it?

I have already addressed the nature of canine poopology elsewhere in these pages, but while we are cataloging canine offenses, we can scarcely omit bringing it up again. Even dogs are embarrassed and disgusted by dog poop. If your dog is a digger, all you have to do to stop the practice is to scoop up a yardful of poop and put it in that hole. He won't be interested in it again for a long time. For reasons only dogs can understand, they are very fastidious about getting poop on their paws, even if they are not all that fussy about eating it.

Dogs are usually very self-conscious about pooping, seeking out some privacy, a quiet hour, a corner well away from open viewing. And when possible, on someone else's property. But not Thud. He just stops wherever he happens to feel the urge, even if it's only 10 feet away and in full view of you while you're eating a Braunschweiger sandwich. But most dogs I've known are private about their evacuations.

If dogs are driven by an insatiable covetousness for whatever it is that another dog has (and they are), then they are similarly obsessed with the notion of leaving their mark in the form of poop on another dog's territory. (Wow! It just occurred to me: do you suppose that's why ol' Coyote poops on the road below our place? Not to express his appreciation for our company and shared food scraps but to declare his contempt for our sissy dogs? I feel my world crumbling around me.)

Dog owners are often blamed for leading their dog(s) on a leash to relieve themselves on the lawns of neighbors, but it has been my experience that any dog given a chance will always elect to befoul someone else's property. I have no idea if this is a matter of leaving it elsewhere, of *not* beshatting their own territory? Or is this behavior motivated by a malicious pleasure dogs take in beshatting the landscaping of others? It's one of those things for sure.

Dog peeing habits are easier to understand, especially if you're a man. There's no secret that for dogs peeing is a matter of marking territory and leaving little messages, viz, to wit: "Yep, I'm that beagle you see now and then just west of you and up the hill at that split-level brick ranch-style house. I am cute and studly. I find your leavings here on this lamppost absolutely delicious and would be honored if only once we could meet somewhere around here and I could sniff your butt. The reciprocal of course is also offered, should you be so inclined. My name is Buford, by the way, and tonight at precisely 2 A.M. I will set up a howling like you've never heard before. Bark back 15 times if you hear me and would like to converse long-distance until someone drags one of us into the house and hits us with a newspaper, okay?"

Men do this a lot too. It must have been women who passed laws against it, that's all I can figure.

And yet there *are* mysteries about dog peeing customs. I have had two male dogs in a row that don't understand that male dogs lift a leg jauntily and pee up against a tree or post. Now, we do live in Nebraska where there are fewer trees in the whole state than some Iowans have in their backyards, but we do have trees in our yard, and, God knows, plenty of fence posts and other suitable verticalities. And I have done my share of demonstrations to show them exactly how it is to be done, including the three-point stance. While my example seems to amuse them, it does not instruct them.

Lucky did a kind of half-hearted leg lift when he peed, but unfortunately the target of his whiz was all too often Goldie. While Goldie didn't seem to mind being peed on all that much, it was pretty disgusting for those of us she then expected to pet, scratch, and brush her. This unfortunate but well-intentioned golden-shower arrangement came to be, as we recall now that we try to reconstruct the history, when Lucky and then Thud followed the customary although equally inexplicable habit of peeing *immediately and precisely* where the other dog, i.e., Goldie, peed.

Goldie would hustle out to the yard with her distinctive heading-out-to-take-a-leak saunter, which the two male dogs came to recognize. They would follow her, observe her toileting with interest but distant courtesy, and then immediately after a good sniff, pee on exactly the same spot (insofar as their male aiming mechanisms would allow, of course). The time between Goldie finishing and Lucky and Thud following up with their cover-pee became ever shorter, however, until eventually they overlapped. And then they became simultaneous. Goldie went out to pee, the two males went out at the same time, and perhaps just to save time, while she peed on the ground, they tried to pee on the very same spot but quite bluntly peed on her. We really worked hard to discourage this, we really did, but none of the three ever seemed to fully grasp what the big deal was.

Just yesterday I enjoyed a visit from a couple of old friends, Thunderbucket and Ricky Lee Anderson, Jr. (Thunderbucket is the guy and Ricky is his dog.) It was their first visit here to our farm, and of course there was a lot for both of them to explore. They were both relatively well behaved, but thankfully, in this case, the human handled himself, his manners, and his functions better than his canine counterpart. This is not—let's face it—always the case. It would have been enough that right in the middle of a perfectly civil conversation Ricky strolled over to a couch and took a leak up against it. That gaffe could have been dismissed as a momentary lapse, jet lag, preoccupation, West Coast casualness—or boredom with the conversation Bucket and I were having. But pretty soon, here came Ricky carrying a jar of my patented cheese stink bait-sandwich spread in his mouth; Thunderbucket explained that Ricky has a particular fondness for cheese. Okay, so we relieved Ricky of his treasure and suggested he was not behaving very well as a guest. So he drifted off, and pretty soon here he came with a bottle of my apple cider in his mouth. Bucket said that this too was understandable because they have an apple tree near their home in California and Ricky has developed a taste for apples. Okay, again, an understandable lapse, perhaps.

But then—and I am not exaggerating the least little bit—here comes Ricky Lee Anderson, Jr., with a bottle of my stash of Jack Daniels Green Label, a special favorite of mine, in his mouth. And that he was not all that eager to surrender. Thunderbucket had no explanation for this event. None at all.

And now that I think about it, it was *after* this series of events that Ricky peed on my couch.

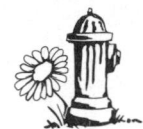

CHAPTER NINETEEN

# DISGUSTING IS AS DISGUSTING DOES

*Cats are the ultimate narcissists.*
*You can tell this because of all the time*
*they spend on personal grooming.*
*Dogs aren't like this. A dog's idea of personal grooming*
*is to roll on a dead fish.*

—JAMES GORMAN

One of the great mysteries of all time is why dogs eat poop. (You may want to skip this section of the book if you have a weak stomach or are eating a Braunschweiger sandwich.) I love lutefisk, which is widely held to be one of the most repulsive foods ever devised by man. It is cod, soaked in lye (I'm not joking . . . *lye*!) and then dried. When boiled and reconstituted, it takes on the consistency of mucousy gristle and stinks to high heaven. I cook it only in my outdoor summer kitchen when Linda is out of town, and usually when the wind is away from town so I don't run afoul of the Environmental Protection Agency. Then I drag a bucket of it to town and call my buddy Eric, the only other human being I know who actually likes lutefisk. And we eat it over in a corner of the tavern, while everyone else holds their noses, makes offensive comments about us, and throws things like wet bar napkins at us.

Well, I did that once a couple years ago and wound up with a pretty good bowl of it left over. I thought, you know, they say fish is good for dogs' diets, makes their fur shiny or something, so I carried it back down here and put it out for the dogs. They sniffed and sniffed at the bowl, slinked around it like it was a bucket of live rattlesnakes, and then . . . and then . . . and then they *rolled in it*! Dogs considered *my* food too disgusting to eat and good for nothing but rolling in. They eat cat poop! But they were disgusted by my supper! I have never felt so utterly insulted in my life, and by my dogs.

We have had to fence off a portion of dusty waste ground under one of our home's overhangs because that's where the cats have decided to poop. And that's what our dogs have come to consider a marvelous buffet of gustatory delights. Cat poop. They eat cat poop. And there's not a thing we can do to talk them out of it. They simply do not care about the clear message conveyed by a rolled-up newspaper. Not when it comes to cat poop. Nope, cat poop is waaaaaaay too good to turn down, even while a lout three times your size is pounding on your head with a newspaper. Gobble gobble gobble. Yum yum yum.

Okay, so we can avoid this social offense by building a solid wire fence isolating the cat poop zone, but this is not the kind of thing a human being keeps constantly at the forefront of his attention. We don't like to give a lot of thought to poop eating, I suppose, but even where it is an issue, it tends to slip inevitably into the subconscious. Our house is built on a truly wretched piece of ground. There is no dirt, for one thing. It's all sand. When we scraped off a patch on which to put our house and yard, the white sand the bulldozer piled up was as pure and clean as the stuff you see in movie house or hotel cigarette disposal containers. I dig this stuff up directly out of the ground to feed into my sandblaster out in the shop.

Well, it's nice to have a ready source of sandblasting material like that, but it sure as hell isn't the kind of thing that encourages the growth of bluegrass, I can tell you for a fact. We've had monstrous truckloads of actual *dirt* brought in here to give water and roots something to cling to, but it tends to work its way down through the sand to some subterranean rock layer miles beneath us in only a matter of a year or so. So, I was talking with a friend up at the tavern about this problem one day, and he said he was cleaning out a bunch of stables and what we needed was to put a good layer of well-rotted manure onto that barren ground. Hey! That sounds like a great idea, right? So the very next day he started hauling a manure spreader full of the stuff to our place with his tractor on an hourly basis, ton after ton of sodden, rotten horse poop.

The dogs couldn't believe it. They were certain they had died and gone to canine heaven. It wasn't enough that here was more stinky stuff than they had ever seen in their lives—complete with the occasional horse hoof trimming to gnaw on!—nor that it was the most obnoxious stinky stuff they had ever enjoyed. No, here it was, being delivered right to the very entrance of their own home, a kind of gourmet meals-on-wheels. Once they got past their slack-jawed amazement, they went nuts. They ran through the stuff. They ate it until they could hold no more. They rolled in it until they were all a shiny green that glowed in the dark. And their delight beyond imagination was our disgust in equal degree. Our family went into diaspora for many weeks, a generation and species gap like I've never seen. We wanted absolutely nothing to do with these disgust-o-wads and frankly, they simply didn't care. They were like teenagers gone crazy.

Eventually the sun dried out all the horse poop, the rains worked it down in the sand, and the Grand Era of Abundant Horse Shit faded and disappeared, now only a legend in the Welsch dogs' cosmogony. And I can tell you damn certain, we will never again open that yard gate for a manure spreader.

But we also went through a period of a few weeks when the dogs for some reason decided to eat their own and each other's poop. (I told you this was going to get disgusting.) We did some impressive hustling to pick it up before they could get at it, but there's only so much you can do along that line. And there's only so much we can put up with socially, even if it is clear and instinctive canine behavior; we are simply not going to sit on our patio sucking on a gin and tonic, watching the dogs eat poop.

So, we asked our veterinarian what might be the problem: a dietary deficiency, some kind of pathology, a gastric problem? He said sometimes dogs just get into doing this and while there may be a physiological explanation for it, sometimes they just do it.

So, what could we do? We can't just let them eat poop! And then he said something so stunning, I am still reeling from it almost a year later. He said yes, he could help us. He would give us something to put in the dogs' food that would make dog poop taste bad. He would give us something to put in their food . . . that would make dog poop . . . *taste bad*. Dog poop taste bad. Am I missing something here? Wouldn't we all pretty much guess that dog poop tastes bad to begin with? And if it doesn't, who figured out (1) that it doesn't taste bad and (2) that if you put this stuff in their food it *will* taste bad? This is science I really don't want to know much more about. I can't even remember if we did it. The dogs don't eat poop anymore and that's all I need to know, thank you very much.

Moreover, a dog that is offered a perfectly dandy meal of prime products especially blended for keeping a dog healthy and his coat shiny will, given the option, choose poop every time. Or at a minimum, the *other* dog's food, even if it is the very same commercial dog food. Or the very same poop. The canine cuisine priority system seems to be:

1. Whatever the other dog is eating;.
2. Anything disgusting but especially (a) cat poop or (b) dog poop.
3. Commercial dog food.

Someone is eventually going to get rich marketing a packaged product called either "Cat Poop Dog Food" or "The Other Dog's Food."

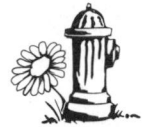

## CHAPTER TWENTY

# IN THE CASE OF DOGS, THEY ARE WHAT THE *OTHER* DOG EATS

*Outside of a dog, a book is man's*
*best friend.*
*Inside of a dog, it's too dark to read.*

—GROUCHO MARX

Even given no choices about what's for supper, a dog will make his or her choices. Thud doesn't care. He inhales whatever is in his bowl, or whatever was in his bowl before he jumped up and knocked it out of your hand. It simply doesn't matter. You could put cardboard scraps in his bowl and put it down in front of him and they would be gone in seconds. He instantly devours, no, *inhales* whatever is in his bowl. He does that in part, I should note, because he instantly then checks to see if there is any chance at all of getting to the other dogs' bowls—that is to say, *the other dogs' food*! Thud isn't at all mean about it. He doesn't growl or bite. He just eats it without discussion or argument.

Abbie, in yet another eerily precise way echoes her predecessor Goldie (whom, by the way, she never met): she doesn't even get up when we bring her food to the dog porch and throw the bars and deadlocks that will keep Thud from eating his food, and then hers, and then if he doesn't notice, her. We then set down Thud's food outside the door, where it instantly disappears, and turn back onto the porch, where Abbie still eyes us suspiciously.

Sometimes if we leave her to her own devices for 10 or 15 minutes, she will deign to examine what we are offering on her altar. Or maybe she won't. Sometimes we take a little bit of the best of what she is getting—the wet food or maybe a bit of ham or chicken we have sweetened the pot with—and put it carefully right in front of her nose. She sniffs. She may lick. If we are really, really polite and say something like, "Please, little sweet abbie, won't you favor us by at least sampling our meager, pathetic offering?" she may taste it.

Now, this is the truth: rarely, however, will she actually rise from her bed and agree to eat the meal we have prepared and brought to her until we say the words, "If you don't eat it we're going to take it away and give it to Thud!" Then she'll eat it. Then she will eat what could potentially become—yes!—*the other dog's food*!

Just moments ago I conducted a scientific experiment with my dogs. (See? I said this book wasn't really an expert sort of thing but down underneath there's a lot of heavy-duty research here.) If there is anything better than the other dog's food, I have always guessed, it would be "whatever the humans are eating." No matter what a dog is doing or eating—even in flagrante delicto, I imagine, although I've never conducted *that* particular part of the experiment—he will stop immediately at the sight, sound, or scent of a human being ingesting something. Anything.

Or at least that's what I thought. But then I read somewhere that you can cure a dog of constantly bothering you while you are eating if you simply eat something a dog cannot possibly like and give him some when he comes a-begging. So, I just stepped outside with a big, gorgeous, juicy orange. Dogs won't eat oranges. To a dog, oranges taste terrible. A dog will eat cat poop, but a dog will not eat an orange. I sat down on the patio swing and peeled my orange. Of course I was instantly besieged by two big, black Labs. They panted and flicked spit as only black Labs can do, they moaned, and begged, and generally insisted there is nothing they have ever wanted more in this world than that orange.

So I gave them each a hunk of the peel. There was some hesitation. Even a bit of confusion. Abbie dropped her peel. Thud saw that and trotted off smartly with his, not really convinced that orange peels are good eating but now sublimely pleased that he had an orange peel, and even better, that Abbie had none. Abbie looked at me. She looked at her orange peel. She looked at Thud, now reclining luxuriously in the shade of a maple tree, wallowing in the previous inexperienced pleasures of dining on an orange peel.

Now, Abbie realized what a mistake she'd made. Not only had she dropped her orange peel, what's worse, Thud had an orange peel. And an orange peel was obviously a wonderful thing to have. She went over to his shady spot and did the little trick she does of lying down just as close to him as she can, her nose only fractions of an inch from whatever he is enjoying . . . and not sharing. Sometimes she whimpers, but this time she didn't have a chance because Thud finished his orange peel and came trotting to me for more. Which I gave him.

Now Abbie came for her share. I gave her some. And Thud now had to deal with the fact that Abbie's orange peel was clearly better than his orange peel. And thus I learned something very important about dog priorities when it comes to food: While human food may, or may not, be any good, it is always desirable. But—and this is an enormous "but"—the bottom line truly is, what is best in this world of all bests is whatever the other dog is eating. Nothing could possibly be more desirable.

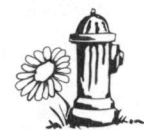

## CHAPTER TWENTY-ONE

# A BARK IS WORSE THAN A BITE ONLY IF YOU'RE NOT BEING BIT

*I have a great dog. She's half Lab, half pit bull.*
*A good combination. Sure, she might*
*bite off my leg, but she'll bring it back to me.*

—JIMI CELESTE

Probably the most feared flaw in a dog's personality is biting. Some dogs are bred to this defense mechanism, and some people depend on their dogs to resort to violence in protecting person and property. There have been occasions when we were very glad to have big, barking dogs in our yard because of uninvited and unwelcome guests who showed up at our yard. I'm certainly not *famous*, but I do have something of a public personality, especially from my years with CBS News *Sunday Morning* doing my "Postcards from Nebraska" with Charles Kuralt, and later Charles Osgood. While it's flattering for people to feel they know me from my television work and writing, the fact of the matter is, this place is not only where I live and enjoy my family, it's also where I work. And while some businesses depend on customers dropping in and spending some time, the business of writing depends on people *not* dropping in and spending time. So, sometimes it's nice to have big, barking dogs to discourage overly enthusiastic visitors from marching right past the sign saying No Visitors Please, coming through the front gate, and knocking at our front door.

We have solved the problem of uninvited guests largely by putting that sign out at our gate, and by asking folks in town—it's a small town, so it's not hard to get the word around—not to tell visitors to our village where we live. We don't ask them to lie; we just want them to tell curious travelers that we prefer not to have visitors. That seems to do the job with most people. It's only a courtesy, after all.

There was a time when despite our efforts and the help of our neighbors in town, drop-in got to be a real problem here, and we were almost at our wits' end. We put up all kinds of signs: a stop sign at the entrance of our place, an orange barrel smack in the middle of our drive, and finally a sign saying: "*Caution: Security Dogs on Duty.*" People walked right past that sign, by our big barking dogs—I suppose their wagging tails were too much of a giveaway that any threat they offered was a sham—and right up to our front door. (I wanted to get to biting dogs, but Linda found a much cleverer way to solve our problem. Quite by accident one night while she was thumbing through a mail catalog from Gempler's Farm Supply Store, she spotted among their dozens of commercially produced signs one saying: "*Danger These Monkeys Bite And Cause Serious Injuries. Do not approach. Peligro!*" That did the job. People who had no reluctance about driving past the "*No Visitors Please*" sign, the "*Keep Out— No Trespassing*" sign, the "*Caution: Security Doges on Duty*" sign, through the gate, past the dogs, and down to our door, took one look at the dangerous monkey sign, searched the cottonwood trees in our yard for those vicious monkeys, and decided maybe they didn't want to talk with me all that bad after all.)

Our inside joke here and among our friends was of course that Goldie, Thud, and Lucky offered no threat at all. The worst thing they would do is get snot on your leg while sniffing or maybe jostle you while arguing which of them needed an ear scratching worst. We told invited visitors that if they were met by the dogs and were at all worried, the operative passwords were "Where's your Frisbee?" whereupon the dogs would all go dashing madly off in search of something for you to throw.

And that always worked. Until the day our friend and neighbor who runs the flower shop in town came to our gate to deliver a bouquet I had ordered for Linda, being the romantic guy I am and all. Who knows what it was: the van she was driving, the fact that she was wearing a heavy coat (she had just returned from a run with the volunteer fire department), the fact that she was carrying those flowers—perhaps that we weren't home and a stranger entered our yard. I don't know, but what counts is that one of our dogs bit her.

These gentle guys had never bitten anyone. All we can figure is that they got excited and in their enthusiasm—certainly not in anger—got carried away. And it wasn't just a couple of nips. Marna (that's our flower lady's name) was very understanding about it, but she got a couple of good, hard bites, one on an arm (through the fire coat!) and again on her fanny. (She said that it was the most action she'd had since her husband had his operation, but still. . . . ) She showed us the bites on her arm, ignoring my offer to also check the ones on her bottom side, and we were definitely alarmed. (And it didn't help that Scott, our UPS man, told us the next week that he had told Marna that while her arm seemed to have returned to normal fairly quickly, her rear end sure still seemed to be swelled up. That's the way this town operates: everyone's a comedian.)

Marna was sure it was Lucky that bit her but, it was very hard for someone not very familiar with them to tell the difference between Lucky and Thud. The sociology of the situation was certain: as usual, Goldie had barked at Marna and got the other two dogs excited, and one of them had bitten her. Marna took another look at them and confirmed her first report that yep, it was Lucky.

Well, Linda instantly called the veterinarian, and the next day we hauled poor Lucky in to be "customized," in the hope it would diminish any further aggressive tendencies he might have. Which on the spot certainly gave me plenty of pause about biting Marna on the ass if I'd ever been so inclined.

At least one friend of ours who is pretty good with dogs uses fear to discourage dogs from such misbehavior as biting. You get someone the dog doesn't know to approach and then raise all kinds of hell with stones in cans, noisemakers, rolled-up newspapers, that kind of thing, but I really have my doubts about this approach. Do we really want our dogs terrified of visitors? Some trainers in fact use this very same approach to teach dogs to be *aggressive* toward strangers. I don't know. I'm not a canine training expert and, heaven knows, my animals are scarcely a model for suitable behavior.

Abbie has always been oral. I suppose most dogs are. Their mouth is what they have, after all. Their mouth is their hands. Abbie is ferociously oral, the most mouthy of any dog I've had. She insists on putting her mouth on everything and anything. It's as if she simply needs to touch you, or anything, with some part of her mouth to establish contact. Linda still has a nasty scar on the back of her leg where the newly arrived Abbie gave her a friendly nip with those puppy stilettos in her mouth. She no longer bites (Abbie, not Linda) but I'm not sure she can be broken of her need to, well, *kiss*. She understands that I don't want to be *licked*. That's just too gooey for me and I know where that mouth has been! (again, Abbie's), but I don't want to stifle her intense desire to express her affection either (and that goes for Linda too).

We have had absolutely wonderful luck with the toys called Kongs. Kongs come in various sizes and shapes, the most common being a kind of rounded pyramid of red rubber. They are incredibly tough. We have bought any number of "indestructible" toys, beds, leashes, blah blah blah for our dogs, all of which have been dismantled, destroyed, or eaten within hours if not minutes. And Abbie is the absolute master of destruction. She can take a hard rubber, "indestructible" chew-toy and peel pieces off of it as if it were a cheap Styrofoam cooler. She's amazing. And expensive.

But not so with Kongs. And our dogs love them. They are made so you can stuff goodies into them, making them even more desirable and enjoyable, but we've never found that necessary. We *have* found that running a short length of rope through a Kong makes it much more interesting to our dogs, easier for them to compete for and play tug-of-war with, and easier for us to throw long distances.

We have always had trouble with Abbie chewing on things we don't want chewed on. I don't know how many "indestructible" beds she has chewed to shreds. We tried putting murderously hot jalapeno sauces on the chewed spots. Apparently she has appreciated the added flavor, because it sure hasn't discouraged her. She loves helping Linda haul water hoses around the yard when Linda is irrigating our trees. Then Abbie settles down to a pleasant and cool afternoon in the shade of those trees, chewing the ends off the hoses. I now buy hose end replacements in gross lots. It is a constant struggle. The one effective way we have found to combat her destructiveness is to give her something acceptable to destroy. It's not that she wants to damage anything of value, or probably even damage anything. She just wants something that feels good to chew, and she is quite content when we provide her with that . . . for 10 minutes. The short length of rope through a Kong serves that purpose very nicely. And when that has been reduced to random threads, she moves on. More than likely to the hoses.

At first we added the rope to make it easier for the dogs to play with the Kong and to help us throw it, so we were not all that happy to find that Abbie was constantly dismantling them. But at some point I had an old rope hammock I was about to throw away and I thought, hey, here's one heck of a lot of rope I'm about to throw away. I wonder if Ab would enjoy it? So I sat on our patio pulling apart the hammock and gathering up all the short lengths of rope. They're not good for much else—too short, too ratty for anything practical—but they are perfect for a Kong rope. I pull a doubled length through the Kong, tie it, throw it. It takes Ab a day or two to chew through it, enjoying it as thoroughly as if it were a fresh cow bone, a commercial rawhide chewie, or—okay—her bed. And then we just throw away the gummy remnants and pull a new length of rope through while Abbie watches appreciatively. The moral is, sometimes with dogs as with people, it's just easier to accommodate immoderation than fight it.

## CHAPTER TWENTY-TWO

# "I YAM WHAT I YAM"

*A dog is not almost human,*
*and I know of no greater insult to the canine race*
*than to describe it as such.*

—JOHN HOLMES

It's been my firm conviction for a long time that white people are pretty dumb sometimes about what they can and can't control. For tens of thousands of years, the Indians lived comfortably on the Plains, for example, considering it just about as perfect a place to live as they could imagine, with more food than they could possibly use, both of the plant and animal varieties. They considered themselves to be part of the landscape, participants, partners, one of the many from corn to bison who shared the same ground very compatibly. All in all, they considered thc whole setup a gift from God.

Then came the *conquering* of the West by the white man. "Conquering?" How and why would one conquer one's own mother, the Indians asked? And the white man is still fighting against everything that is natural here, in the meanwhile destroying the water supply, exhausting the soil, killing off the wild life, and, of course, eventually causing his own removal from this "hostile" landscape. It was, for example, prairie dogs that worked as enormous, constant plowmen, circulating and tilling the soil to keep it rich and alive. Under their stewardship it fed millions of bison, after all. Now ranchers and farmers want to wage war and eradicate the prairie dog because they think that way they can graze one, two, six more cattle on the same range, never noting or caring that they are dooming the land to a sterility that in the long run—or maybe not so long run—will make it unsuitable for the cattle they have grazing now, much less the ones they want to add.

On occasion we keep chickens here on our tree farm and inevitably we lose some to the coyotes and red foxes. We had a chicken hawk for a while that sat in a huge old ash tree not far from our yard and, as if checking the menu, looked over our flock for his delectation. We wound up putting chicken wire *over* as well as around our chicken yard to cut down on his depredations. And on one incredible occasion I watched a bald eagle swoop down into our yard and take one of our hens.

Okay, that was not cause for celebration but jeez, if I were a chicken I think that's the way I'd want to go: soaring with the eagles. But more than that, it's the nature of things. If you are going to grow animals in these wild places, you simply need to assume you are going to lose an occasional bit of your domestic livestock to Mother Nature's wild herds. There's no need to get all riled up about it. It's no call for general warfare. If nothing else, it is a wonderfully philosophical example of how this world works. Besides, what do we need more in our lives: chickens or bald eagles?

More and more as I've gotten older (and that may be the key to this newly acquired sense of moderation, I suppose: "as I've gotten older"), I've decided that sometimes there are things that are more easily accepted than fought. Goldie had the incredible ability to detect moles working under our lawn. We have a very large fenced yard—maybe an acre or more—and we live out in the country, so we have moles. And they make a mess of our puny efforts to grow grass. (I suppose I am obligated at this point to include the note that Linda put in the margin of the manuscript: "'*we*,' white man?" This is a nasty allusion to the fact that I am waaay too busy a fellow to fuss with things like a lawn and so she does indeed generally do all the yard work around here. But I was of course referring to the generic, cultural "we." Let us continue with my point.) The moles lift up tunnels and the grass over them dies. They pile up dirt here and there in great mounds. While we never did spot her in action, it was nonetheless evident that Goldie could spot them moving in their tunnels. The evidence for this was (1) holes in the lawn where she attacked the moles' subterranean network, sometimes following a tunnel for 10 or 12 feet, digging up the whole mess of our yard in pursuit of this hidden intruder, and (2) the dead, mangled, soggy corpse of the mole in the dog porch after the capture and interrogation.

(One night after Goldie shrugged off her earthly shrouds, we were horrified to look into the dog porch and see a hideous echo of her dead-mole-on-the-dog-porch routine. There it was, a small brownish, soggy wad with a pathetic string of a tail sticking out. Jeez, it appeared that Abbie had posthumously picked up this habit of Goldie's too. I got a newspaper and with great disgust daintily lifted the gory, mangled mess from the bed. Hmmm . . . this isn't a dead mole! It's . . . it's . . . it's a tea bag Abbie had purloined from the end table where we had put it after brewing some tea for our evening relaxation! She must have sneaked the prize out the door and abandoned it when she discovered yet once again that not everything the big two-legs eat and relish is pleasant to the canine palate!)

The equation would at first seem to be heavily weighted against Goldie: tunnels and mounds of naked dirt in our yard on one hand, huge holes in the lawn and a horrible mess in the dog porch on the other. But that premise omits a crucial element: Goldie. Goldie was a sweet, smart, and timid lady. She wanted to please and she wanted to participate in the affairs of this home. Killing moles was her way of doing that. It was her special trick and talent. And it was her nature just as surely as being complicated and difficult is in the nature of being a teenage girl. The fact of the matter is, we could have scolded, yelled, fought, waved folded newspapers, rubbed noses into dirt piles, argued, and struggled all we wanted. Goldie was going to be Goldie. (And teenage daughter Antonia, correspondingly, was inevitably teenage daughter Antonia, of course.) Tossing the dirt back into Goldie's excavations, carrying mangled corpses out of the dog porch three or four times a year was small compensation for good old Goldie's passionate wars against the Mole People and her occasional triumph.

Which is not at all to say that we simply cave in on whatever it is that our dogs do. Not even for dear souls like

Goldie. Linda's passion is love apples—which is to say, tomatoes. She loves tomatoes above all other produce. So she has for years planted a few tomato plants around the house. While our friends in town wind up hauling around boxes of giveaway tomatoes from their *two* tomato plants, Linda is lucky to get three tomatoes from her six plants. So what's the deal? Are we really that bad at gardening?

It was more complicated a mystery than it might seem: we got flowers on our tomato plants, then small tomatoes, and even some fairly decent-looking green tomatoes. But none managed to make it to maturity before vanishing. They simply disappeared from the bush and vine. The mystery was solved one afternoon, as you've probably already guessed, while we were sitting on the patio looking out over the yard, watching the dogs lounge in the shade. Goldie got up, strolled over to a tomato plant, nosed around among the small green fruit, found one suitable for her taste, pulled it off, took it back to her shady spot, and ate it. Linda and I sat there, looking at each other in total amazement. And sudden understanding.

Well, we could have scolded ourselves blue in the face and eventually Goldie would have understood probably that it was yet another one of those things human beings seem to be unreasonably fussy and selfish about. Who would have guessed that these people of hers would have denied her something as simple and basic as a miserable green tomato, after all? We gave up on in-the-yard tomatoes and the next year planted them outside the fence. That way they were safe from Goldie. And the raccoons and deer could get them.

I don't think dogs or children should be indulged to the point of being spoiled, but I do think we need to keep things in perspective. Some things are not worth fighting about.

Some things simply are not going to change. I can explain to Thud during every thunderstorm that rumbles through here for the next one 100 years that thunder is not going to hurt him, but it won't make one whit of a difference to him; he is absolutely convinced that thunder is a terrible thing meant specifically to punish him and he is going to cower and tremble pathetically in that huge, intimidating body of his no matter how often I explain the physics of the matter to him. It's easier just to comfort him and hope he lives through the horrible experience. And we can be grateful, I guess, that we live in central Nebraska where we don't have to worry all that often about crops getting wet.

Some bad habits don't do enough harm to be condemned. Some friends of ours own a wonderful commercial winery, and they have a wonderful dog, named suitably enough Baco, as in *baco noir*, a type of hybrid wine grape. Linda and I always carry dog goodies in our vehicles for any dogs we happen to run across that deserve a pleasant surprise in their lives, sort of like the pleasant European custom of taking a small bouquet to the lady of a house you might be visiting.

Whenever we go to the Cuthills Vineyard of northeast Nebraska, therefore, we are sure to carry along some goodies for Baco. Baco takes the offering, clearly flattered and pleased by our thoughtfulness. And then he takes his new prize, looks around nervously, makes a few feints, false starts, diversion moves this way and that, and then takes the doggy snack out to the soft ground of the vineyard to bury it. Where he never sees it again.

I suppose we could consider this a waste of good dog yummies but is it, really? I mean okay, so Baco doesn't *eat* the nibble. He clearly enjoys it. He gets a precious prize, he gets to do with it what he wants, and when he returns from the vineyard, he has a new spring in his step, new confidence in the fact that he is appreciated and loved, and the knowledge, albeit false, that he will someday enjoy that gift of delectable chewies. When it has aged. Like good wine.

It's hard to know exactly what it is that a dog is going to consider a treasure. Where, for example, do they get the idea that rolling in cow poop, a long dead fish, or anything else disgusting but unidentifiable is a good idea? I can't imagine that in all the history of the relationship between dog and man any human being has ever given even the slightest indication that this activity makes a dog attractive. How many times in the millenniums that dogs have shared man's habitat from cave to tipi, from wickiup to castle, has a recently redolented dog returned to the owner's hearth rich with the heavy smell of the long-dead or -digested only to be rejected, stoned, bathed, insulted? Every time, that's how many times. Whatever else a dog may do that is forgivable, the apparently inborn habit of rolling in putrid crap has to be the most repellant. Eating cat poop, sharing the foulest of dog breath, chewing on a dead bird, farting in a duck blind, farting in a campsite sleeping bag, nothing—*nothing*—approaches pure obnoxious incivility like the dog that has rolled in something.

What's worse, anyone who has ever had anything to do with a four-footed friend will tell you that there is nothing more clearly proud of itself in this world than a recently stink-basted dog. His eyes sparkle, he approaches with a light and lively prance. He is clearly and absolutely convinced that he has done something that not only he considers admirable but that—and this is the astonishing part—he knows for a fact *you* will consider one of his finest accomplishments. Every dog that rolls in a green, slimy, fresh cow pie or rancid puddle of decaying crawdad offal feels he deserves some kind of award for fancy grooming. It shows on his face, in his posture, in his voice. . . .

When Lucky greeted us at our front gate with Linda's dead banty hen in his mouth, he was very, *very* proud of himself and his accomplishment. While what he did was wrong, I could understand how he might think that ridding us of this constant annoyance and bringing it to us—a task for which his entire breed was especially developed, after all—would win him a special place in our hearts. A caveman, Pawnee tribesman, or even a modern camper might appreciate his dog bringing in a fresh chicken, praise him, even share the bounty, and thus reinforce this behavior. But why through that same period of time of every dog on Earth—not just *his* breed, but every dog through all eternity—being condemned, chastised, punished, exiled for rolling in stinky stuff, have dogs not learned or sensed in even the slightest way that this rolling in filth is not a laudable practice? I cannot for the life of me imagine. It flies in the face of all the logic of natural selection.

I don't talk a lot of philosophy with my buddies out here in America's rural countryside. They are mostly farmers, auto body repairmen, plumbers, the school janitor, barflies, ne'er-do-wells. We talk about basic things but sometimes nonetheless we touch on philosophy. Like, why do dogs roll in stinky stuff? The consensus is that it must be somehow primal and basic since they don't seem to grasp any sort of logic leading to *not* rolling in stinky stuff. Theories run to the idea, probably correct, that this was a way a dog could cover its own scent to avoid detection in the hunt. Okay, maybe so, but dogs have been earning their fare in the company of man by good behavior for a long time now. Wouldn't we hope that they would turn the evolutionary corner soon now and figure out that they have more to gain by way of room and board by smelling at least neutral (better, good) but never so rotten they bring tears to human eyes? We can only hope so, but until then I think creationists have missed a real opportunity in not acknowledging and making some substantial fuss about this obvious glitch in the theory of survival of the fittest. Jeez, even the most unrepentant male human has learned that as unpleasant a process as it might be, cleaning up now and then and smelling good is going to get you a lot more food, affection, and comfort than "going natural" ever did or will. Maybe a comfortable dog is like a well-married man, thinking "I'm safe here. Sure, I needed to observe social rules before but, hey, this guy isn't going to shoot me now just because I stink." Of course, he's wrong. But then so are a lot of husbands.

I'm still listing obnoxious canine behavior. I'm surprised by what a long list it's getting to be. I still love my dogs but, man, this inventory sure is getting to be depressing.

When your dog humps your leg or the sofa cushion, it is maybe annoying, perhaps disgusting; more often than not, however, it's embarrassing. Just as dogs choose to tidy up their personal hygiene while you are entertaining company, it is also more often than not a visitor's leg that becomes an object of a dog's amatory attention. I don't know why that is. Again, theories among my cronies up at the town tavern are varied. Perhaps it's because a visitor is more likely to smell better than you do. Or smell like another object of desire, which is always of more interest to any male. Dog, that is. Thud is our male black Lab-in-residence and he was "customized" early on. Nonetheless he has recently shown—how shall we put it politely?—*interest* in Abigail. She, of course, is blithely uninterested in him and his advances, if that's what we can call them since they are anything but advanced. He seems mostly bewildered by what is going on even by himself. He knows that something about Abbie really smells or looks good in a strange, unexpected sort of way. And it makes him all humpy all over. And jerky. He is confused and embarrassed, it is clear, but he can't stop.

Abbie thinks it's great that he's finally showing some tendencies toward fun. She bites his legs, then his face. She runs insanely around the yard (and in the process becoming all the more seductive in his eyes, apparently). Since he isn't sure what it is that he is supposed to be doing exactly, or even approximately for that matter, he simply aims his knees at her. Sometimes he seems to be trying to mount her rear, sometimes her front leg, sometimes her chest, rarely anywhere even close to *ground zero*, as it were. We have on occasion been witness to these thrustings, evasions, and frustrations and shouted to Thud by way of helpful suggestion, "Wrong end, Thud! Wrong end!" But even this kind of useful information seems to embarrass him even more.

We worry about Thud in all this. He's getting pretty banged up, so to speak. Abbie sometimes knocks him over when he is balanced delicately and lost in the theory of what it is that he is, he thinks, trying to do. He has to run a good deal more than he is used to in keeping up with her. His temporary physiological manifestations, if you catch my drift, make it hard for him to get around comfortably. Thud is for all the world like a teenager in love. I guess that's what he is too.

My own educated and anthropological perspective is that dogs don't know any more about why they do the things they do in the pursuit of romance than male humans do. That is, when it comes to love and courtship, dogs may be stupid, but that is relative when considered in the context of what men are likely to do in any tavern in this country as closing hour approaches.

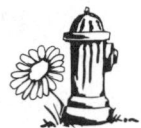

CHAPTER TWENTY-THREE

# BORN FREE, SORT OF

*A door is what a dog is perpetually on the wrong side of.*

—OGDEN NASH

A feature of doggy bad manners that bothers me just about more than any other is breaking loose. I try to understand and sympathize with just about every bad habit a dog might have, but escaping and running for the hills is for me one of the most painful because, while I can understand it completely, I fear the consequences more than anything else. None of the options are good: death on the highway, long separation from home and loved ones, injury, attack by other dogs, disease, starvation.

Generally speaking, I've been pretty lucky in this category. I've known and watched friends who have had a dog escape, or more accurately go lost, I guess. I can understand completely the dog's motivations: a life in a fenced yard, in a pen, on a leash, at the constant beck and call of a master. I'm not saying it's a bad life. Not at all. I suspect that even the dogs in question would admit that they have a darn good life. I taught in higher education for 30 years. I loved it. It wasn't really like a job. I loved the material I was working with, I loved my colleagues, I loved my job, I loved my students. But then I saw a little crack in the wall, an open gate, a flaw in the leash. I had the choice of safety in a comfortable situation where everything was just fine or a big, wide world out there with untold mysteries and wonders. I was through the open gate and running like an idiot in the streets in a flash of an eye.

My situation was even better/worse (it depends on what you think of freedom and its burdens) than a dog's: I knew quite precisely the chances I was taking in leaving a good job for the risk of living on my good looks. I knew that in surrendering security, I was risking not only my own welfare but that of my family. I knew that I had even less in the way of survival skills than even the most spoiled and housebound of city dogs. I had no illusions about the chances I was taking when I left that job that others fight, scramble, and beg for to move away from my lifelong home to the rural countryside, to an uncertain living, into a fairly dangerous jeopardy. But I ran through the open gate. Like any dog worthy of his breed.

Like a good dog, I may have had some people worried about what I was doing. A few even said as much. But at the bottom, I was responsible for the risk I was taking. That can't really be said of a dog. He doesn't know the dangers out there. He doesn't know how mean things can be. He probably doesn't even realize his own limitations. All he knows is the freedom, without regrets for what might have been, for the comforts he's not enjoying, without an understanding of the pain that comes, or is about to come.

I have had dogs bust loose on a number of occasions. Fleagle was incorrigible. No fence could hold him. But he was such a cool rambler that I was never afraid for him. I don't know that we ever went looking for him. He was one horny little rascal and most of his outbound adventures involved a female, so once that motivation had been resolved, so to speak, he came dragging home, tired but absolutely convinced that he'd done the right thing. Slump ran loose once in Lincoln when Mick the Brick left our gate open, but after he'd run full tilt for a couple of blocks he was ready to welcome Mick's offer of a truck ride back home. (Linda reminds me that there were other occasions when we had to search the city streets for Slump-on-the-run. My own memory mercifully fails.)

The toughest experiences we've had with loose dogs has been here at the farm. We live at the intersection of a highway with a river, which means that animals are often funneled onto this place because when they're on the move they don't want to cross the highway and they can't cross the river. So, along with a generous share of wild animals, everything from mountain lions to howling mice, we get our share of horses, cows, peacocks (no kidding!), and dogs drifting onto our place and eventually to the house or yard when they run out of energy and get hungry. We have had Great Pyrenees, Labs, spaniels, coon hounds, yappers, puppies, grizzled old mutts, everything. We do what we can to figure out who they belong to and give them a ride home or, if they have been taught not to accept rides from strangers, call their human partners to come and get them. In a small town, it's not hard to find out who the dogs belong to. (What's discouraging is how often it's the same people over and over who don't care for their animals often enough to protect them.) It's a fairly common event for us to get a call from a neighbor asking if we have seen their dog(s) running loose. I always make a point after a call like that to step outside, do a little calling and whistling, maybe drive down into our river bottoms to look around, check around the yard.

Nor is this an entirely altruistic action: we have to hope that if and when our dogs make their own mad dash for freedom, whoever winds up with them exhausted and filthy on their doorsteps will do the same favor and call us.

While I love this place of ours, it can be forbidding. There are dangers we know about but which a dog might not grasp, after all. For years we have had mountain lions off and on in our bottom ground, and I imagine a dog would make a tasty treat. We have lots of raccoons and they are skilled at getting a dog to water and drowning him. We once had a rabid coon come right into our yard, and while we keep our dogs' shot series current, it's still a scary issue. A pack of coyotes would tear our gentle and pacifist pups to shreds.

There are ugly people around here who would simply shoot a lost dog on sight. There are hunters who shoot anything that moves. There are trappers who set legal and illegal traps along the river that would maim or kill a dog just as surely as they cruelly maim and kill wild animals. There is the highway, populated especially at night by mindless drunks and teenagers who have no business running free, much less driving a car under any circumstances. The half-wit who ran down and killed our dog Blackjack on the highway was justified to the extent that our dog was running loose, having jumped a fence under repair, was black, and was on the highway at night. On the other hand, I would bet a month's income that the guy was speeding like every other self-important fool around here who leaves late and then drives like an idiot, half-asleep, half-drunk, half-witted, slugging down a beer or a coffee, tuning the radio, adjusting his underwear, going nowhere important, whatever.

I think of two occasions other than Blackjack's breakout when we had dogs on the loose. I can't remember the circumstances, which means that I probably left a gate open somewhere along the way. As usual, we didn't detect the dogs' absence until shortly after sundown. That meant that there wasn't light to find the dogs and that they were all the more in jeopardy. Black dogs at night—not a good combination. At night we are tired, we can't ask anyone to help us, and the dogs will have even more hours to travel even farther.

It's not just a matter of dogs running loose either. Things are getting more congested around here: more people move in, more strangers come to the bridge to enjoy the river, more irresponsible fools run the river in all-terrain vehicles (a device that *must* be outlawed as a toy and restricted to use as a tool before it destroys everything beautiful in this country). We used to take our dogs, walk them down to the river running loose. They would stick with me. They'd run maybe 50 feet from me, Thud more like one hundred. But they would come when I called, they never got far from me, and were rarely out of sight. We'd go to the river and they'd run down there, up and down the sandbars, swim almost to the bridge and back. And then, beat to a frazzle, they would drag ass back behind me up to the house, utterly exhausted, utterly happy. (And sometimes if I weren't watching, one or more would find something disgusting to roll in before we got back.)

But it was obviously a very different issue when they exited the gate without us. They were gone. We didn't know where, and what's worse, neither did they. They were just free and running. Our hope always was that they would follow the course they knew best: down to the river and back. That would keep them away from the highway, away from town, away from real trouble. A factor that was both positive and negative is that in the opposite direction from our home, toward the uplands and town and away from the river, is an area of native grass . . . and a miserable infestation of thoroughly evil prickly pear cactus.

You simply can't imagine how miserable this stuff is. Its spines will penetrate any canvas shoes, even some leather footwear. It not only hurts to beat billy hell when the spines stick in you—they have microscopic barbs facing back like the barbs on a harpoon or fishhook—but what they go into, they do not come out of easily. It gets worse: even when you pull out these demonic spines, for some reason the teeny little pinprick of a wound doesn't just heal. Your flesh reacts and builds a kind of callous over it that hurts for weeks and takes many more weeks to disappear. I have worked like a madman to get rid of this stuff but it's like the wind: you're not going to get rid of it. The most we can hope for is a couple good wet years so the grass we planted 30 years ago will take over and crowd out the cactus. Yeah, sure. Won't happen until the glaciers come back down, melt and retreat, and leave enough water around here to ensure plenty of cactus control.

Thing is, any dog that wanders into that minefield of cactus is in for major pain. And once they wander in, they can't figure out how to wander back out. They don't want to go back through the hell they've just gone through, but what they don't know is that the hell ahead of them is even worse. So, on one hand we worry that our loose dogs have wandered into those dreaded uplands. On the other hand, we have to hope that they have the sense of retreating once they have tasted the bite of that infernal botany.

The first breakout was by puppy Goldie and Blackjack. I can only imagine their utter glee when they found that open gate, tentatively stepped out, heard no recriminations, tasted freedom, and then . . . ran! It must have been an exhilarating rush. As became clear later, they eventually headed east, across the highway, maybe as far as the creek 300 yards east. The creek is shallow enough that they could have gotten across it easily, but since it was unfamiliar territory, they evidently didn't try it. My guess is that they simply ran and ran around the riverbed and riverbanks and then across the ground of our neighbors across the highway because they are the people who eventually called us.

When we discovered the escape, we jumped into vehicles and set out on the highway across the bridge, up the highway to town, down to the river bottoms, yelling and honking (they know my truck's horn), peering over our headlights into the approaching dusk. It was only when we gave up and returned home that we got the call. Our dogs were collapsed at our neighbors' place. We jumped into the pickup and drove the short distance to their place.

The dogs were too exhausted even to rise to their feet. We had to carry them to the truck. Which wasn't all that easy. They were so completely footsore and snarled with burrs and briers, they had become themselves huge, mobile cockleburs. Blackjack with his short hair was one thing—a mess for sure—but Goldie, with her long, fine hair, was one huge snarl, utterly beyond redemption. We wanted to be furious with these idiots, but we couldn't. We understood their glee and enthusiasm for freedom for one thing, no matter what frustration it had caused us, but mostly the consequences of their adventure were so evident and immediate, we just didn't have the heart to land on them any harder. We could only offer solace, be as gentle as possible so that we didn't drive the burrs any farther into their flesh, and get them home where we could currycomb them and, in the case of puppy Goldie, shave off every thread of hair on her body, so completely matted with cockleburs, beggar ticks, and sticktights as it was. She was so relieved to be found, so thankful for the medical and grooming care that you could see the gratitude in her eyes: "Home again, at last!"

Goldie must have learned something from that particular misadventure, because the next time the dogs made a break through the gate, she stayed back and let the idiot Labs run on their own. By this time Blackjack was gone, so it was Lucky and a very young Thud that decided to visit the river on their own. All we knew was when we checked the backyard, the gate was open, and the black guys were gone. And, of course, it was shortly before sundown, so time was at a premium. I drove to the bottoms, figuring that especially since it was our *back* gate, that would have been the natural direction for them to head. Linda ripped off for the highway and town to make sure they hadn't taken that route. We drove and drove, yelled, honked: nothing. And slowly but surely the night began to settle in, along with our despair. Goldie comforted us and said we were probably better off without those half-wits anyway. She didn't mean it; she was only trying to cheer us up.

Resigned, we collapsed on the backyard swing, wondering what we could do the next morning to find them. And, suddenly, dragging up to the back gate came Lucky, worn to a frazzle and full of cockleburs, but far more meaningfully, wet and with a barbed-wire cut on his leg. That, along with the direction from which Lucky came, said that they had almost assuredly gone west to the river . . . and away from the highway. Now, all we needed to do was find Thud, at that time just a little puppy. He hadn't really had time to get to know the place, so he might really be lost. And he was so small, he might have gotten himself into even more dire circumstances than a grown dog might.

I started walking into the growing darkness, west, toward the river. And I heard a pathetic cry. Both elated and fearful, I tried to get Thud to cry more so I could find him, and moved as quickly as I safely could in the dim light toward a *black* dog in the trees and high grass. When I found him, he couldn't move. His fat little legs were so completely worn out he couldn't even stand. He would have come home with Lucky if he could have, but he was so completely exhausted, he was having trouble generating his cries for help. So, I had to pick up this pathetic lump and carry him back to the house, like all parents are in all such situations, furious to the hilt, and as relieved as could be.

This has nothing to do with dogs—I'll get back to another Thud-on-the-run adventure—but in this way dogs really are like kids. My son, Chris, now a grown, professional travel writer with the Minneapolis–St. Paul *Star Tribune*, once "ran away from home" when he was just a tot. I should have seen his future in writing when we discovered the escape note he left on his pillow, something to the effect of, "I have runned away forever. Don't bother to look. . . ." The writing trickled off the page as surely as he had himself trickled off.

We searched and searched for him—this was in the city, so we were rightfully racked with worry about traffic and perverts—drove and drove and drove the neighborhood streets, called all the neighbors, finally called the police. Nothing. As with our dog hunts, we watched nightfall come with our child still missing. The police finally told us there was nothing more to be done so we should get some rest and resume our search first thing in the morning. I went to the bathroom to get ready for bed, opened the shower stall to take a quick wash, and there was Chris, huddled in the corner. His grand escape had taken him as far as our shower stall.

I should have known better, therefore, the day Thud made his most recent break for freeeeeeedooooooom, just a couple years ago now. It was even more a mystery than usual because no gates were open, there were no holes dug under the fence. Thud was gone, but we could find no clear avenue of his escape. All we could figure was that the garage door that sometimes does not close firmly might have been ajar just enough for him to nose his way out, which he had been known to do on previous occasions. We searched the grounds completely. We combed the bottom ground, the woods, the uplands around our place. We called the neighbors. We called the sheriff's office. Six hours later and still nothing.

And once again we faced that horrible moment of going to a restless night in bed, worrying about our baby. I went to our back bathroom, an adjunct to a room with a hot tub and shower added to our old farmhouse after we had been here awhile. As I went through our back porch area toward the gym, as we call it, I heard a funny, mechanical sound: "Thumpthumpthumpthump." It sounded like a bad tire, maybe out on the highway? No, it was coming from the direction opposite the highway. "Thumpthumpthump-thump." It got louder as I approached the door of the gym. Jeez, maybe on top of all the other disasters of the day the pump was now going out on the hot tub. Just what I need, I thought.

I opened the door to the gym and there was the source of the strange thumping noise. It was Thud's tail hitting the wall as he awaited someone to rescue him. He had found the outside door to the gym ajar, had come in, and then found that he couldn't push the door back open to get out. He probably got bored after awhile, until we discovered he was missing and started calling for him, whereupon he more than likely got a little frantic wanting to answer our call. So he approached the huge double windows of the gym the only way he could find access: over the Styrofoam cover on the hot tub. Which, of course, collapsed under his enormous weight, sending him into the tub. He then scrambled to get out—we could see from the evidence—pulling all the potted plants on the windowsills into the hot tub. He managed to get out, now nicely cleaned by his warm bath, but leaving behind him a complete mess of potting soil and plants floating in the hot tub.

It was another of those moments only dogs and children can provide us: a curious combination of incredible relief and joy with fury and frustration. It took me three days to clean out the mess in the hot tub. Thud watched the process safely from outside the gym.

CHAPTER TWENTY-FOUR

# CLEANLINESS IS NEXT TO DOGGINESS

*They say a reasonable number of fleas is good fer a dog—keeps him from broodin' over bein' a dog.*

—EDWARD NOYES WESTCOTT

One of the reasons we were surprised that Thud had ventured into the gym on his own is that this is the usual site of the most hideous tortures he can imagine being inflicted on any loyal dog: a bath. I have no idea why our dogs go into paroxysms of glee at the mere prospect of going to the river, where they will get a soaped-down bath and swim until they can barely gather the energy to walk back to the house, but fight with every ounce of energy they can muster to avoid a nice warm shower in *my* shower stall. But they do. Even at the river everything is running crazy and frolicking and swimming and diving in and out of the current . . . until there is some hint that the activities have mutated from "fun and games" to "getting clean." At that point, the fun is over. Water = good; bath = bad.

It is clear that the dogs really do like the scrubbing, the slightly warm water, and the attention of a directed bath. There is just something about the idea of a *bath* that offends them. I usually dress in overalls for the occasion but with the full intention of sitting inside the shower with them, one at a time, and getting thoroughly soaked in the process.

We start our dog-bathing procedure by gathering the commercial flea and tick soaps, putting a towel on the shower floor so they won't slip and slide uncomfortably, and picking up anything from the gym floor that might prove attractive to a snooping dog. Thing is, we have to lure all three at once into the gym for a shower, because if we only showered one and then tried to get the others to come in, they'd know what was up and would stay as far away from us and that door to the gym as possible for weeks. Goldie was always the worst: she knew all too well whenever showers were in the offing, and she wouldn't come close to us or the house. The Labs are slower to realize what's up and are much more easily lured in. A dog goodie treat will usually do it.

There is some strategy too in who goes into the shower first. One theory is to take the most tractable dog first because the less fuss we can raise with the first participant, the less trouble we are likely to have with the next. On the other hand, we have to consider if maybe it wouldn't be better to get the worst-case scenario over first, hoping that the second dog will be busy sniffing around and not be prepared to enter the Chamber of Death him- or herself. Those considerations usually fade away, however, because of a curious phenomenon I have no explanation for: the doggy shower group-support system. Whichever dog goes into the stall first is always uncertain, a little trembly, maybe a bit on the skittish side, looking for some way to escape the hideous fate that almost surely is going to result in being clean. Whereupon the other dog, whichever it may be (except for Goldie), takes a great interest in the process and comes right to the shower stall where I and the victim are now wrestling. The still-dry, next-in-line dog is then not simply interested in what is going on but seems genuinely concerned. And comforting. There is nose touching, licking, close contact, even with the soap flying and shower spray ricocheting. It's really very touching.

Now, that doesn't mean that the dog that gave comfort is any more prepared to face the horrors of cleanliness. It's the same struggle with the second dog, who only a moment before was telling the now clean dog "Oh, calm down! It's okay. It's just a little water and soap. Being clean and smelling good never hurt anyone." "Just-relax-and-enjoy" is now trembling, straining to get out, maybe even moaning piteously.

I should note that the previous dog, now clean but wet, never sticks around the shower stall long enough to return the favor of sympathetic compassion. No, he is without any question whatsoever going to do what a good dog always does right after a bath, when he smells clean and pretty and his coat is nice and shiny: go out into the yard and find something to roll in. Every time. It never fails.

Increasingly we have taken to hauling a few buckets of warm water out to our patio to wash the dogs. While it is harder to corner a dog on an open patio than in a shower stall, they seem to tolerate the experience more easily, and we compensate for the problems of having to haul warm water for washing and first rinses by using a garden hose to finish off the soapy parts. Moreover, outdoor bathing lets us quickly divert doggy attentions following a bath by throwing a Kong, dangling goodies, even doing a quick chase around the yard with Dad in pursuit, thus avoiding to at least some degree that dog inclination to apply as an after-bath talc a good dose of grass clippings, garden dirt, or the ever-popular *après le bain stinque*.

CHAPTER TWENTY-FIVE

# OF HOUSE AND HOME

*It is nought good a slepyng hound to wake ...*

—GEOFFREY CHAUCER,
*TROILUS AND CRISEYDE*

Throughout these pages I have mentioned our dog porch. To my mind, it is a perfect solution to a constant question: where is the dog going to live? Or simply sleep? There are people whose dogs are inseparable parts of the family; they live *in* and *with* the household. And that's fine. I even know people who sleep with their dogs. I did that when I was a kid, when I had Toodles, and, as reported above, I once did it with the dogs in their quarters just to see what their nights are like. On the other hand, I have a very attractive friend whose dog sleeps with her and her husband. Between them. In the same bed. I guess that if I were that husband, I'd have some questions about that arrangement.

While some dogs are fragile enough, far enough from their feral nature that they need the full-blown shelter of a heated or cooled house, shelter from the wind, and protection from dangerous animals like other dogs, cats, or, well, crickets, most dogs are much hardier than we give them credit for. Dogs are remarkably adaptable and carry a full set of survival clothing with them at all times. I think, for example, of the wonderfully happy and healthy sled dogs I saw far north of the Arctic Circle, sleeping outside in the driving wind and snow, on the open sea ice where no amount of shelter would seem enough. I noticed one north-facing yard of dogs, maybe 20 of them, chained in place with nothing more than some plywood boxes to house them. I asked one of the owners if the dogs could be comfortable with such meager protection from exposure. He laughed and explained that actually the wooden boxes were not shelter at all. They were the caches: crates of food and supplies for the dogs. The dogs had the south side of those boxes to get out of the wind as shelter, and that was pretty much it.

And, he noted, the dogs do just fine. They have developed their own physical systems and behavior devices to deal with the cold and wind. They curl up into tight balls with everything covered by their luxuriant coats, the final closure being their tails cleverly tucked over their nose and face. The dogs seemed fine, and obviously much better adapted to the environment than we near-naked, shivering people looking on at them with amazement.

I saw Inuit sled dogs housed in snow and ice igloos in the village of Qaanaaq and I asked about that. The explanation was that those luxurious quarters were for a mother and her pups, who *do* need extra protection. Thus, I could see that the lack of "housing" for the dogs was not a matter of careless disregard on the part of the owners but an honest realization of the facts of the matter: Arctic sled dogs can handle Arctic weather.

When I worry about dogs out here in rural America having as their only shelter a corner in a barn or machine shed, I recall that the coyotes that howl around those same buildings at night don't even have that and they prosper. I wouldn't ask that of my own dogs, but I know that I'm probably harder on them, inviting them in and out of a heated or cooled house during the winter or summer, than if I simply let them live their lives closer to the natural circumstances in which they would do as well as their sled dog cousins far to the north. What I'm saying is that some basic shelter for family pets is a darn good idea, but dogs and cats are likely to do better than we suspect with far less than we offer. A dry floor, some clean straw, protection from the wind and rain, perhaps some bales to retain their own heat, maybe a mate or two to add to their own warmth, and dogs do fine. Same with cats.

Our dog porch is an unheated adjunct to the main floor of our house. There is a hardwood door from our kitchen area to the dog area, but it is open more often than not, a screen door keeping out the dogs and insects that might follow them into their porch. There is also a door leading to the outdoors and into our yard, and perhaps most importantly, when we built the house, we had a permanent dog (and cat) door installed through the brick wall and the foundation so they can come and go as they please. A frame anteroom cuts off the wind, heat, and cold from that door, and they exit onto an open but shaded and floored patio. Since the main part of our house is a walk out basement kind of arrangement, the dog porch is also largely subterranean. The dog porch never freezes in the winter or reaches the ferociously hot temperatures we get around here in the summer. When we leave the door to the kitchen open or ajar, their quarters are really quite moderate.

Nice digs!

The biggest problem we have had with our dogs' shelter is bedding. Old coats or blankets are promptly seen as toys and are hauled out into the yard to be thrown around and torn to shreds. Abbie is, as noted above, a chewer, and bedding is her most favorite chewie. We have bought I-don't-know-how-many commercial beds, all advertised as extraordinarily tough, chew resistant, indestructible, tested to the point of perfection. Linda even reinforced the beds with two layers of heavy canvas sewn with stout ties, accented with demonically hot Tabasco sauce. Ha! Abbie always accepts the challenge. I have never seen a bed make it through one night with Abbie without suffering the fury of her Velociraptor teeth.

After reading an article somewhere about dogs, chewing, bedding, and housing, I thought that one suggestion might be just the solution we needed—clean straw. Abbie's not going to chew straw, right? Straw is cheap and clean. We easily obtained six bales at a farm supply store not far from here. The first lesson we learned was how much straw is in a bale. You cut the wires or cord and straw expands like the luggage of a girl packing for college. I brought two bales into the dog porch for starters. The porch measures about 10 by 5 feet. I cut the cords, and started separating the straw, spreading it out, and fluffing it up. Within minutes I was up to my waist in loose straw. And I wasn't even through the first half of the first bale. Man, there's a lot of straw in a bale! I hauled all the rest out to the summer kitchen for storage.

Well, the dogs loved the straw. It was soft, smelled good, was warm . . . just about perfect. But because the dog porch is attached to our home, and the dogs do occasionally come in from that porch into our living area, there was a constant tracking of straw into the house. And pretty soon we noticed a constant cloud of dust; the straw was breaking up into small pieces. The dogs had bits of straw stuck in their hair and carried that in. And then they started sneezing as the dust got worse. And then Linda started sneezing. And pretty soon Rog carried all the straw outside, threw it on the yard, and went back to the drawing board on dog bedding.

At this writing, the dogs' bedding is a thin pad of foam rubber sewn into a heavy canvas cover, then covered with a double layer of carpeting. It's not as comfortable as a real dog bed, but so far there hasn't been a lot of chewing on it either. We built a plain wooden pen out of one-by-eights that sits on the pad, thus making casual chewing of the edges and corners impossible. Linda tries to keep the puckers and folds stretched and flattened out to prevent easy access for the family nibbler. It's not the best of beds for them—it really can't be all that comfortable—and it's not going to be warm enough for next winter. I don't know what we'll do come fall. We are hoping Abbie forgets about how much fun it is to chew by then.

Meanwhile, in the house, in the front room, we have two large, soft commercial dog beds that they can enjoy when they come in for evening visits. They love the luxury, and we can keep an eye on destructive activities, although dogs being smart as they are, they are not about to chew on anything while we are watching.

GUARD
DOG
WORKING
DO NOT
ENTER

CHAPTER TWENTY-SIX

# ALL WORK AND NO PLAY

*DOG, n. A kind of additional or subsidiary Deity designed to catch the overflow and surplus of the world's worship. This Divine Being in some of his smaller and silkier incarnations takes, in the affection of Woman, the place to which there is no human male aspirant. The Dog is a survival—an anachronism. He toils not, neither does he spin, yet Solomon in all his glory never lay upon a door-mat all day long, sun-soaked and fly-fed and fat, while his master worked for the means wherewith to purchase the idle wag of the Solomonic tail, seasoned with a look of tolerant recognition.*

—AMBROSE BIERCE,
*A DEVIL'S DICTIONARY*

About that thing of not chewing while we are watching: it's not a police action sort of thing. Nor is it a matter of exerting authority and fear over a dog. They don't chew when they are with us because they don't feel the need to chew. I would say that the single most important thing in having and enjoying a dog and ensuring that they are happy and enjoying living with us is us making some time to play with them. That's a double-edged sword. Not only do they feel better if we have a little time together every day, I feel better if we have time together every day. I guess I feel less of a need to chew on my bedding too when I find the time—*make* the time—to throw something for them out in the yard, sit on the porch bench and scratch an ear or two, discuss world events with them, walk the perimeters of our territory and pee together through the fence, or even lie in the hammock and sleep.

One of the most remarkable things about "playing with the dogs" is that I don't have to do anything. The usual course of events during our play time is that I go out to the back porch and they both jump around like idiots for just a minute or two to show that they celebrate my arrival. Then one of them goes to the toy box and fishes out something that strikes them as being eminently throwable. I throw it five or six times. Abbie usually reaches it first, grabs it, dashes about the yard insanely making close passes by Thud's nose to show him quite clearly that she has it and he doesn't and he's not going to get it without a chase. She then makes a mad dash and leaps for the porch seat where I am sitting, an old Chevy van backseat, whereupon I yell, "She runs, she dodges . . . She scores!" She sits with me a moment or two, growls, shakes the Kong or ropie or bonie, sits on her head so I can scratch her rear and try to get the toy from her. She surrenders the toy and I throw it again. That happens maybe three or four times.

Then Thud gets the idea that there must be something pretty neat-o about that Kong, so he sashays over and tries to take it away from her. They growl and snarl and play tug of war. Abbie takes it away from Thud, he decides she plays too rough, he goes to the toy box and gets his own chewie, and they both drift off to some shady spot to work on their treasures.

At this point I've been in the yard with them maybe 5 minutes, at the most 10. And they are done with me. But if I go inside at this point, they will show clear disappointment and retreat to the porch themselves to lie in their bed and groan their displeasure. What they want to do, no kidding, is exactly what little kids like to do: they want to say "Hey, Dad! Watch this!" and then do some sort of half-baked circus act on the playground monkey bars. The dogs are just as happy if I am sitting there smoking a cigar or reading—or for that matter, lying in the hammock nursing a gin and tonic or sleeping—as they would be if I were rolling around on the ground with them. It is my presence that is important to them, not my participation or even my attention. They are pack animals. They just don't want to be alone. They want to be with the alpha male. They want him to share their time and space. It's a matter of noblesse oblige, or maybe alpha male oblige.

If I manage to drag myself out into the yard and make a few tentative, feeble efforts to chase them or grab whatever toy they happen to have at the moment, their eyes brighten and they are suddenly switched up to hyper-warp speed. "Wow! Dad is actually playing with us! Let's run in huge, sweeping circles as if we're insane and show him how much we appreciate the effort!"

But there is also a sinister side to these moments together in play: the "*other* woman" syndrome! Should Linda come out and sit beside me on the car seat, oh, man, that's not permissible. Abbie clearly feels that it is not only *her* seat, it is *her* alpha male! While she would never do anything violent, she instantly insinuates herself in no uncertain terms onto that car seat, between Linda and me, and makes it quite clear that she is not at all ready to relinquish her role as my favorite. It's all very touching and endearing.

In fact, the bottom line is that as smart as dogs are, they don't actually *know* when you are playing and when you are not. They can't imagine not playing. Labs being sporting dogs, they can't imagine working, so, well, everything must be sport. If I am in the backyard with a shovel moving dirt around, or if Linda is mowing—or better yet weed whacking—they presume that we are there playing somehow and are interested more than anything else in amusing *them*. No matter what we are doing, they follow us around gleefully, doing what they can to "help." As tempted as we might be to get mad at them for being in the way, most of the time they wind up winning the argument and making us take a new look at what we are doing. We reconsider if, well, we aren't actually playing after all when we get right down to looking at it.

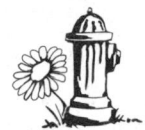

CHAPTER TWENTY-SEVEN

# PERMISSION GRANTED... ENTER!

*I was desperate. The swine who stole my dog doesn't realize what he did to me!*

—HITLER, 1917, AFTER A RAILROAD WORKER IN ALSACE STOLE HIS DOG

I imagine that's one of the reasons too that the time the dogs have our permission to come into the house and join us for an evening must be special to them. Sure, it would be more polite for us to spend an equal number of evenings with them in their porch, but they know how inconsiderate people can be, so they put up with us. So they do what they can to enjoy to the hilt the times they have inside.

Again the ritual is predictable. They sense immediately, the moment one of us gets up to let them in, what is impending. They are at the door and ready. We let them in. There is an acceptably brief moment of unrestrained delight, jumping, and prancing, and then Thud heads to the kitchen to see if any treasures might have been missed on the floor while Abbie takes advantage of the diversion to make a dash to the laundry room, where—if someone has foolishly left the door open—she grabs a sock or, on special occasions, some underclothing and drags it out to the front room. (As annoying as this can be, it is also touching. I was recently on assignment in Bosnia and during my absence, Ab made a special point of sorting through the offerings in the laundry room and bringing out one of *my* soiled socks. Isn't that touching . . . in a disgusting sort of way?)

She jumps up on the couch—she is allowed—to deliver the prize to me. There is some gnawing on their indoor chewies—rubber bones—and then they settle down to sleep. It's an instant and deep sleep, with lots of loud snoring, occasional SBD farting, and dreams that involves running, chasing, growling, and snapping.

Abbie occasionally watches some television. She is the only dog I've ever had that will look up into the sky at migrating geese or cranes. Thud never does. Goldie used to watch television occasionally; she would get up and leave when there were canine-corps stories on shows like *Cops*. She just didn't like the violence. I suppose the sound of a dog tearing a hunk out of some miserable, sweat-soaked perp is not a pretty thing for a dainty lady like Goldie to listen to. With Abbie and Thud it's the sirens that drive them nuts. Sometimes they will even howl if I don't turn down the sound to save them the agony. Or maybe dogs just have trouble watching dumb people getting into stupid situations over and over again.

On the other hand, human beings are total suckers when it comes to watching dogs on the screen. I won't even start listing all the movies and television shows in which the heroes are dogs—Lassie, Rin Tin Tin, Scooby Doo—the names are legion. In the interest of family serenity, I'm not mentioning the movie about an ol' dog that's, uh, yellow, if you catch my drift. See, when Linda was a little girl in parochial school she was once accorded the honor and responsibility of picking out a movie for her class to enjoy on a very special occasion. She thought *Old Yeller*, this movie about an ancient, off-white dog, would be just the ticket. As you probably know, the dog dies. And of course the entire class collapsed in sobbing and howling. Linda's classmates and the nuns never forgave her, although dozens of counselors and psychologists in eastern Nebraska have elected a monument to her and her choice in movies.

So, while the subject of dogs on screen is too broad and too sensitive to deal with here in any depth, I simply cannot put together a book on dogs without mentioning the movie *Best in Show*. It is about dogs or, more precisely, about dog people. If you have not seen this film, you are hereby ordered to. Even if you hate dogs. Especially if you hate dogs. But whatever you do, go to the bathroom before this movie starts or you are going to have a big cleaning bill coming up. Trust me on this one: see *Best in Show*.

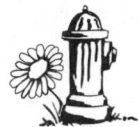

CHAPTER TWENTY-EIGHT

# IN SICKNESS AND IN HEALTH

*The greatness of a nation*
*and its moral progress can be judged*
*by the way its animals are treated.*

—GANDHI

I can't stand a dog having pain even to the extent of being discomfited by whatever television show I am watching. My dream as a child was to be a veterinarian. Early on I figured out that you can't treat sick and dying animals if sick and dying animals reduce you to a shuddering lump. It's not that I don't want to help. I just don't have the backbone for it. I was once at the home of some friends in the western Nebraska countryside when there was a frantic knock at the door. It was the veterinarian whose office was across the road; he needed some help. A rancher had brought in five dogs that had tangled with porcupines. I'm not trained in animal care, but I knew what that meant. We all ran across the road to do what we could. The vet anesthetized the dogs, and with pliers we all started pulling the ferocious spines from dog mouths and noses. It was a bloody, horrible mess. While I felt good knowing that I was participating in the treatment of the dogs that would lead to their eventual recovery and good health—and I hoped a well-learned lesson about the business end of porcupines—the idea of those dogs suffering was enough to haunt my dreams for a long time to come.

God bless those who treat animals and their ailments, and God bless friends of pets who do what they can to make their lives healthy and happy. We are only doing unto them, after all, what they would surely do unto us.

One of the things I like about me is that I don't often pretend to know what I don't know. In fact, if anything, I tend to do the opposite. I learned this one time while traveling in Germany: I found that it was much more advantageous to pretend to know no German and maybe surprise people when they found I knew a little bit than to pretend to know German well and surprise them with how little I actually knew.

Later I discovered that there is a good deal of money to be made by admitting and even embracing ignorance. I wrote a book about my misadventures in starting, way too late in life, to work at being an antique tractor mechanic and restorer. It turned out that this burgeoning hobby already had way too many experts. Guys like me who made a living doing one thing—teaching, doctoring, working with computers, nursing—but only dabbled in banging on old iron by way of personal therapy were sick and tired of the know-it-alls who sniffed because we didn't know a rod cap from an intake valve, apparently forgetting that there was every possibility that in another, maybe much more important endeavor, we could make them look like half-wits. It become evident very quickly that there were a lot of readers who wanted some reassurance that there are other aspiring restorers and mechanics who know even less than they do, and, man, could I ever demonstrate my lack of knowledge convincingly! No one could know less than I did, at least when I started. I made a pretty good living for a lot of years writing columns and books admitting my ignorance freely and with some good cheer.

Then I did the same thing with a couple of books about something about which I know even less: women, relationships, romance, marriage. So I'm something of an enthusiast, if not an expert, at being inept. No, what I know about dogs is only what I know about the dogs I've known. It's all anecdotal. I've done no studying on the subject beyond sitting in my backyard hammock, smoking a cigar or downing a cold drink, and watching my own dogs in action. So, I don't know much about dogs.

But I really don't know anything about people. And it's not just a passive ignorance, that is, the kind of ignorance that comes out of not having learned something. In the case of human beings, I really have tried to understand them. And the only thing I've learned from some considerable effort is that I still don't know anything about people, and I probably never will. I don't understand how men and women get along together, they being two totally different species with apparently totally different thought processes.

More than that, I don't understand how men *don't* get along together. I mean, in contrast to men and women, we men have so much in common: for example, *not* understanding women. So, why do men get into arguments? Fights?

Wars? I don't understand what seems to me a modern, increasing lack of civility in our lives. It seems to me to be so easy to get along, to be pleasant, to accommodate the usually fairly simple and understandable hopes and wishes of others. But more and more, people—maybe even not just men—seem to be all too ready to jump to offense, to insult, to slander and libel, to attack. If you have any doubts at all, listen to any AM radio talk show or go to any chat room on the Web. Even a site that deals with something as innocuous as tractors seems this day to be a place for bullying, insulting, snide superiority, superpatriot (actually, super *hate*riot) arrogance, religious and racial intolerance. I don't get it. Why start this kind of trouble in the first place? Why does one person care what another person believes about religion or politics? Why would one person try to muscle someone else into praying a prayer he doesn't want to pray? It's nuts, that's what it is.

I bet you wonder what I'm getting at, right? Well, what I'm getting at is that if I don't understand why men can't get along, even though individual men can sometimes be such asses, what I really can't understand in this world is how there can possibly be even the slightest hint of inconsideration toward someone as utterly innocent, wonderful, loving, compliant, friendly, loving, devoted, faithful, beautiful as a dog. And yet there is.

A man I considered a friend once pulled into our filling station at the pump beside mine. We struck up a conversation and at some point he motioned me to the back of his pickup truck. There were two coyotes he had shot. Two beautiful, wild, and free dogs, now bloodied and dead, their bright eyes now clouded, their lifeless tongues lolling out.

This man who I suddenly could only see as a pathological nut was not ashamed or embarrassed by his mindless brutality. No, he was actually proud. He had no livestock to protect, no interest in the animals he was killing other than his own pleasure in watching them die. Now, if you are a coyote hunter and this offends you, I really don't give a diddly damn. If you kill dogs for fun and profit, then in my book you are one sick cookie and I frankly don't care what you think about me, or about anything else. I lump your kind right down there with child molesters. I think forehead branding should be reconsidered.

And don't pull that usual zealot's stunt of trying to stick all kinds of other labels on me: antigun, antihunting, blah blah blah. I have more guns than you do. I eat meat. I don't hunt but I understand that it is to some extent necessary. But even in the hunt I have to wonder about someone who kills for fun. And when it comes to someone who kills dogs for fun, man, that is creepy beyond my ability to imagine.

Not much worse are those who don't care for their dogs or breed them for money, who don't feed them well or provide medical attention, those who chain their dogs and neglect them as a matter of course. In the same despicable category as those who kill dogs are those who abandon them. If there is any reason left in what we laughingly call a civilized world for the death penalty, now we are getting close to a deserving class of subhumans.

Can you tell I take this fairly seriously? I do. You don't see any human beings named Fido—"I am faithful"—because so damned few of our species have ever displayed enough of that virtue to deserve the label, I suspect.

CHAPTER TWENTY-NINE

# GOD BLESS THE CAREGIVERS

*Whoever said you can't buy happiness forgot little puppies.*

—GENE HILL

We don't just have to gnash our teeth in fury and frustration, however. There are mechanisms by means of which we can in a small way at least repay our canine friends, protect them from those who are less benevolent, fix the wounds and wrongs inflicted on them by the least of our own sorry ilk. Linda and I learned early on that the Humane Society in our area is as important to decent life here as the fire department and the emergency medical teams. What surprised us was that our closest Humane Society is 25 miles away, in Grand Island, but when we showed up there with puppies or kitties some half-wit had abandoned down by the highway bridge to starve, they would take them and try to find a home for them.

That got to be a burden on our conscience. The Central Nebraska Humane Society is supported in part by taxes paid by the citizens of Grand Island, and yet here we were, using their services. So we started to make small donations to them of money, bleach, blankets, food, a couple of vacuum sweepers, that kind of thing. And then we decided that we would take whatever moneys we got for Christmas or our birthdays, money we couldn't really count on or expect or had any right to in the first place, and make it our Humane Society fund. It hasn't been a lot of money—a hundred dollars or so a year—but then we started finding other small amounts of loose money that came into our household from time to time—the change and cash, for example, that shows up sodden but clean in the bottom of the clothes washer and dryer.

And we worked out a deal with the Humane Society staff: I'd take their list of needed items and go to the store to buy them—pleasure #1. Then I'd bring them to the Humane Society—pleasure #2. And then—the biggie!—pleasure #3: They'd let me roll around on the floor with whatever puppies they happened to have at the time. They are so full of life and joy, they smell so wonderful. What is it that makes puppies smell so distinctive and so sweet?

But then came the real agony: leaving those puppies behind, knowing that while some of them might be adopted, some might not. Linda and I are now more active supporters of the Humane Society and wish we could win the lottery so we could pour money into that worthy agency so that no dogs would have to be killed because they have committed the terrible sin of not being adopted. Well, we don't, but maybe all of us together can do more. It truly is the least we can do.

Therefore I would like to start by encouraging you to locate and support your local Humane Society to the hilt. Do something like take that Christmas money and put it to an even better use, costing you absolutely nothing, doing worlds of good. I'm betting that an animal shelter near you is in desperate need of something, maybe anything, from office supplies to clean rags, from animal toys to old blankets. Just yesterday I dropped by our Humane Society with a big box of new but cheap blankets and left a little extra money to buy an ad looking for a home for some abandoned animal or another, a mere $45 but enough to save a life, I hope.

Better yet, why not check to see if they could use *you*? Of course you're not an expert in animal care, but just an hour or two a week exercising pets, cleaning pens, helping with office work, whatever. Why don't you give them a call and ask them what you could do to help out? And join the Humane Society so you can add your voice to the national cry for decency when it comes to our pets.

There are a lot of other agencies, I know. We support Green Peace and the Wildlife Fund because we want wild dogs protected too: our wolves and coyotes. My daughter Antonia supports PETA (People for the Ethical Treatment of Animals) and, while they are a bit extreme for my tastes, I understand her compassion and even her radicalism, because after all, in my part of the world, simply supporting the Humane Society and the Wildlife Fund is seen by some as bleeding-heart liberalism. (That's fine. I have no reluctance about saying what I think of them either, so . . . ) Another organization you might consider in looking for ways to defend the defenseless while maintaining your own ethical standards is the North Shore Animal League

America (25 Davis Avenue, Port Washington, New York 11050 or www.nsalamerica.org), which encourages adoption of mixed breeds.

My intention at this point of the book was to append a list of organizations where you can go to seek help in rescuing dogs or, better yet, where you can offer your support and help to them in their work of rescuing dogs. I mean, that would be a handy reference, and after all, how many such agencies can there be? Well, I'm not much of a veteran at searching for such things on the Web, so now and then I forget what an incredible resource we now have in this amazing network of resources and information. I put the words "dog rescue" into the Google search engine and was buried with possible sources of information. So I went to the first such resource, Kyler Laird's Animal Rescue Resources site, and was within this one site again buried in possibilities. It turns out there are a lot of us who care about our dogs and want to repay their generosity with a demonstration of support of our own.

The bottom line is, there is no way I can reproduce that list of sites on these pages, not to mention that like most such informational sites, there are constant changes, eliminations, and additions, so whatever I put down on paper here would instantly be outdated. If you are familiar with the web, go to www.ecn.purdue.edu/~laird/animal_rescue and prepare to be amazed. There are 30 pages of other websites where you can find specific organizations and agencies for rescuing everything from Afghan hounds to Yorkshire terriers—disabled, strays, elderly, puppies, you name it. (And while we're at it, what's an "Akbash dog"?) And that's just dogs. The site also can guide you to sites for caring for birds, camels, cats, snakes, and an amazing variety of creatures! For example, people seem especially eager to atone the wrongs done racing dogs, probably because they are so callously used and discarded as if they were used toilet paper. Want to be a hero and make a home for a used-up and discarded but thoroughly lovable and loving greyhound? Go to www.greyhounds.org for information about the Greyhound Protection League.

And that's just a start. Now, remember, www.ecn.purdue.edu/~laird/animal_rescue is not a website that will help you rescue dogs or obtain dogs that need rescue. It is a listing of (literally!) thousands of sites for organizations around the world that work at rescuing dogs (and other critters). You will be amazed. If you are interested in a specific breed, this is where you'll find a means to help it. If you would like to take in a dog that needs a home, even of a specific breed, you will find it here. Just go to the address listed above and then go down the well-organized list to find what you are interested in, click on that address, and you will find yourself where you want to be.

Another useful website for finding rescue organizations close to you is www.petfinder.com. This is the same kind of site: a resource that will take you where you want to go to find the agency closest to you or to your interest in rescuing an animal. To find rescue links for specific breeds, you will also find the American Kennel Club (AKC) site at www.akc.org/breeds helpful.

My own heart is with the underdog: mixed breeds, mutts, discards, the dregs of dogdom. I love my black Labs, no doubt about it, but I will never again invest in a purebred Lab because there are too many mutts out there that need the love and protection and aren't getting it. Thud is papered. He's a great dog. I love him. Abbie is a mutt. She's a great dog, and guess what? I don't love her any less than Thud, nor do I love her any less than if she were an AKC show dog. That's why I love the Humane Society and the American Society for the Prevention of Cruelty to Animals (ASPCA). They don't ask for papers. In fact, it's even better than that: they take care of dogs that need help, and that's good enough for me.

I would really like for you to consider the Humane Society or ASPCA the next time you're looking for a dog, or for that matter, for any pet. These are animals that don't have much of a future in front of them, simply because the Humane Society's resources are inevitably stretched to the limit as Americans demonstrate their utter lack of sense in controlling their pets and their pets' breeding. (I'll save my opinions about the American lack of sense in controlling their own breeding for another time and another book.) And when you get your dog from the Humane Society, be sure you have it "customized." We don't need any more unwanted dogs. If you find yourself wanting another dog, just go to the Humane Society and rescue some good soul that is the product of some other human being's stupidity, cruelty, carelessness, whatever. That way you are doing a bunch of good favors all at once . . . almost too many to count: supporting the Humane Society, rescuing a life, getting yourself a good pet, taking a dog out of limbo.

If you are new to the idea of having a puppy in the house, need brushing up, or simply want some resource by way of support, be sure to take a look at the *Newparentguide: A Resource for New Adopters of Cats and Dogs*, a terrific magazine from the ASPCA.

Your new pet will be grateful, the Humane Society will be grateful, society will be grateful, I will be grateful. I was surprised myself to find that the Humane Society and the ASPCA are not the same thing. I had always presumed they were until just today when I decided that while I have always made substantial contributions to our local chapters, I really need to join up with the national organizations to add to their clout. The Humane Society's publication, *Animal Sheltering*, is a very handsome magazine—interesting and heart-rending. A subscription is so cheap it's ridiculous. I suggest you ignore their listed prices and send them $100. What the heck. You can find out more about it and the society, even subscribe and join, at www.animal sheltering.org.

A wonderful resource from the Humane Society is the National Association for Humane and Environmental Education, its publication program for children and schools. A subscription provides 32 copies of the *KIND ("Kids in Nature's Defense") News* and a teacher's guide for each month of the school year, a real bargain in education. For more information, to subscribe, or to adopt a teacher online, go to www.kindnews.org or www.nahee.org.

The ASPCA's membership magazine, *Animal Watch,* is also a terrific resource and some genuinely interesting general reading. The issue I have in my hands at this moment (spring 2003) has articles on dealing with animal pain, keeping geese as pets, and how to raise money for animal rescue; reports on the law and animal cruelty, updates on political matters on the national level; and articles on recycling dog hair (no kidding) and the recurring problem of, uh, poop eaters. Worth the price of membership is the inside of the front page and the back cover. In the front of the magazine is a feature called "Ani-Med," a complete and free telephone (610-254-7900) and Web (www.aspca.org/animed) service with information for a host of animal health problems with specific extensions for each problem, from "dog allergies" to "cat spraying." We tore the page from our first copy and installed it permanently in our telephone book for immediate reference. You need to get this magazine just to get the index of the various ailments and problems. On the back cover is an equally important ASPCA service, the Animal Poison Control Center, guaranteeing free help within minutes should you encounter this terrible problem. Until you get your own copy of *Animal Watch*, write down this number and address for the service: 888-426-4435 and www.apcc.aspca.org.

# AFTERWORD

*Dogs are not our whole life,*
*but they make our lives whole.*

**—ROGER CARAS**

I guess that's all I have to say for the moment about dogs. I'm sure I'll think of more I should have told you once I close the cover on this one, and there's not a doubt in my mind that almost every day for the rest of my life some dog or another is going to give me new material. Like a good friend, a good child, or a good mate, dogs can surprise you day after day with the new wonders of their bodies, minds, and souls. Writing even this much has struck me occasionally as an irony: Me telling you that you should spend more time with your dogs and pay better attention to what lessons they have to teach you while I sit here in my study, watching my dogs lounging or romping in the backyard and probably wondering where the heck I am at this particular moment, when I should be out there lounging or romping with them.

In fact, now that I think about it, that's precisely what I am going to do with the rest of this spring afternoon. I'm going to grab a Kong or Frisbee, toss it a few times for Thud and Abbie, then do a little ear scratching, watching them wrestle in the grass or sleep with the deep breaths that can only come from innocence, and thank God for the best of all the gifts he has given us on this Earth: our friends, our dogs.

# INDEX

**ROGER WELSCH**

*Dog's best friend*

# EARLY CHILDHOOD ASSESSMENT

## WHY, WHAT, AND HOW

Committee on Developmental Outcomes and
Assessments for Young Children

Catherine E. Snow and Susan B. Van Hemel, *Editors*

Board on Children, Youth, and Families

Board on Testing and Assessment

Division of Behavioral and Social Sciences and Education

NATIONAL RESEARCH COUNCIL
*OF THE NATIONAL ACADEMIES*

THE NATIONAL ACADEMIES PRESS
Washington, D.C.
**www.nap.edu**

THE NATIONAL ACADEMIES PRESS 500 Fifth Street, N.W. Washington, DC 20001

NOTICE: The project that is the subject of this report was approved by the Governing Board of the National Research Council, whose members are drawn from the councils of the National Academy of Sciences, the National Academy of Engineering, and the Institute of Medicine. The members of the committee responsible for the report were chosen for their special competences and with regard for appropriate balance.

The study was supported by Award No. HHSP23320042509XI between the National Academy of Sciences and the U.S. Department of Health and Human Services. Any opinions, findings, conclusions, or recommendations expressed in this publication are those of the author(s) and do not necessarily reflect the view of the organizations or agencies that provided support for this project.

**Library of Congress Cataloging-in-Publication Data**

Early childhood assessment : why, what, and how / Committee on Developmental Outcomes and Assessments for Young Children ; Catherine E. Snow and Susan B. Van Hemel, editors.

p. cm.

Includes bibliographical references and index.

ISBN 978-0-309-12465-2 (hardcover) — ISBN 978-0-309-12466-9 (pdf) 1. Children with social disabilities—Education (Preschool—United States. 2. Child development—United States. 3. Competency-based education—United States. I. Snow, Catherine E. II. Van Hemel, Susan B. III. Committee on Developmental Outcomes and Assessments for Young Children.

LC4069.2.E37 2008

372.126--dc22

2008038565

Additional copies of this report are available from the National Academies Press, 500 Fifth Street, N.W., Lockbox 285, Washington, DC 20055; (800) 624-6242 or (202) 334-3313 (in the Washington metropolitan area); Internet, http://www.nap.edu.



Printed in the United States of America

Suggested citation: National Research Council. (2008). *Early Childhood Assessment: Why, What, and How.* Committee on Developmental Outcomes and Assessments for Young Children, C.E. Snow and S.B. Van Hemel, *Editors.* Board on Children, Youth, and Families, Board on Testing and Assessment, Division of Behavioral and Social Sciences and Education. Washington, DC: The National Academies Press.

# THE NATIONAL ACADEMIES

***Advisers to the Nation on Science, Engineering, and Medicine***

The **National Academy of Sciences** is a private, nonprofit, self-perpetuating society of distinguished scholars engaged in scientific and engineering research, dedicated to the furtherance of science and technology and to their use for the general welfare. Upon the authority of the charter granted to it by the Congress in 1863, the Academy has a mandate that requires it to advise the federal government on scientific and technical matters. Dr. Ralph J. Cicerone is president of the National Academy of Sciences.

The **National Academy of Engineering** was established in 1964, under the charter of the National Academy of Sciences, as a parallel organization of outstanding engineers. It is autonomous in its administration and in the selection of its members, sharing with the National Academy of Sciences the responsibility for advising the federal government. The National Academy of Engineering also sponsors engineering programs aimed at meeting national needs, encourages education and research, and recognizes the superior achievements of engineers. Dr. Charles M. Vest is president of the National Academy of Engineering.

The **Institute of Medicine** was established in 1970 by the National Academy of Sciences to secure the services of eminent members of appropriate professions in the examination of policy matters pertaining to the health of the public. The Institute acts under the responsibility given to the National Academy of Sciences by its congressional charter to be an adviser to the federal government and, upon its own initiative, to identify issues of medical care, research, and education. Dr. Harvey V. Fineberg is president of the Institute of Medicine.

The **National Research Council** was organized by the National Academy of Sciences in 1916 to associate the broad community of science and technology with the Academy's purposes of furthering knowledge and advising the federal government. Functioning in accordance with general policies determined by the Academy, the Council has become the principal operating agency of both the National Academy of Sciences and the National Academy of Engineering in providing services to the government, the public, and the scientific and engineering communities. The Council is administered jointly by both Academies and the Institute of Medicine. Dr. Ralph J. Cicerone and Dr. Charles M. Vest are chair and vice chair, respectively, of the National Research Council.

**www.national-academies.org**

## COMMITTEE ON DEVELOPMENTAL OUTCOMES AND ASSESSMENTS FOR YOUNG CHILDREN

CATHERINE E. SNOW (*Chair*), Graduate School of Education, Harvard University
MARGARET BURCHINAL, Department of Education, University of California, Irvine; University of North Carolina
HARRIET A. EGERTSON, Independent consultant, Temecula, California
EUGENE K. EMORY, Department of Psychology, Emory University
DAVID J. FRANCIS, Department of Psychology, University of Houston
EUGENE E. GARCIA, College of Education, Arizona State University
KATHLEEN HEBBELER, SRI International, Menlo Park, California
EBONI HOWARD, Herr Research Center, Erikson Institute, Chicago
JACQUELINE JONES, New Jersey Department of Education, Trenton
LUIS M. LAOSA, Educational Testing Service, Princeton, New Jersey
KATHLEEN McCARTNEY, Graduate School of Education, Harvard University
MARIE C. McCORMICK, School of Public Health, Harvard University
DEBORAH J. STIPEK, School of Education, Stanford University
MARK R. WILSON, Graduate School of Education, University of California, Berkeley
MARTHA ZASLOW, Child Trends, Washington, DC

**Liaison to the Board on Children, Youth, and Families**

BETSY LOZOFF, Center for Human Growth and Development, University of Michigan

SUSAN B. VAN HEMEL, *Study Director*
MATTHEW D. McDONOUGH, *Senior Program Assistant*

## BOARD ON TESTING AND ASSESSMENT

EDWARD HAERTEL (*Chair*), Stanford University
LYLE F. BACHMAN, Department of Applied Linguistics and TESOL, University of California, Los Angeles
STEPHEN B. DUNBAR, College of Education, University of Iowa
DAVID J. FRANCIS, Department of Psychology, University of Houston
MICHAEL T. NETTLES, Educational Testing Service, Princeton, New Jersey
JAMES W. PELLEGRINO, Department of Psychology, University of Illinois at Chicago
DIANA C. PULLIN, Lynch School of Education, Boston College

STUART W. ELLIOTT, *Director*

# Acknowledgments

This report is the result of over a year of effort by the Committee on Developmental Outcomes and Assessments for Young Children. The study was performed at the request of the Office of Head Start, Administration for Children and Families (ACF) of the U.S. Department of Health and Human Services. The committee gathered and reviewed literature on developmental outcomes and assessments for young children, listened to briefings and presentations by experts and stakeholders, and, using this information and its combined expertise, has attempted to provide its best advice on issues associated with assessing children from birth to age 5.

Members of the study committee, volunteers selected from several academic and professional practice specialties, found the project an interesting and stimulating opportunity for interdisciplinary collaboration.[1] They cooperated in work groups, learned each other's technical languages, and exemplified in their work the collegial qualities that are among the National Academies' unique strengths. I am grateful to them for their hard work, expertise, and good humor. Committee member biographies can be found in Appendix E. Background papers that were prepared

[1]One member, Cybele Raver, resigned from the committee in September 2007 because of increased professional responsibilities.

under contracts to Linda Espinosa, Aki Murata, E. Michael Foster, and David Rose (some written with the participation of co-authors) were also of great value in the committee's work.

On behalf of the committee, I would like to express appreciation to the many other people who contributed to this project. Lauren Supplee of ACF served as project monitor and provided guidance as needed. ACF staff were of great help to the committee, obtaining hard-to-find documents and materials, providing helpful explanations, and answering the committee's questions about the documents and their applicability. Among those at ACF who provided information and support are Mary Bruce Webb, Jennifer Brooks, and Naomi Goldstein, who provided the committee with background and context as well as the specifics of the National Reporting System (NRS) and ACF's objectives for the study. Catherine Hildum, staff to the Senate Committee on Health, Education, Labor and Pensions, Subcommittee on Children and Families; James Bergeron, staff to the House Committee on Education and Workforce (R); and Roberto Rodriguez, staff to Senator Edward Kennedy, chair of the Senate Committee on Health, Education, Labor and Pensions, provided briefings that helped the committee understand the objectives of Congress for the study. Nicholas Zill of Westat and Sam Meisels of the Erikson Institute also provided briefings on the NRS. We also wish to thank the participants who provided input to the committee at its public stakeholder forum (see Appendix B).

At the National Research Council (NRC), Susan Van Hemel was study director for the project. Rosemary Chalk, director of the Board on Children, Youth, and Families, and Stuart Elliott, director of the Board on Testing and Assessment, provided important management support and oversight for this work, and Naomi Chudowski provided research support. Matthew McDonough, senior program assistant, provided administrative and logistic support as well as literature research and manuscript preparation work. The executive office reports staff of the Division of Behavioral and Social Sciences and Education, especially Christine McShane and Yvonne Wise, provided valuable help with editing and production of the report. Kirsten Sampson Snyder managed the report review process, and Eugenia Grohman provided guidance during that process.

This report has been reviewed in draft form by individuals chosen for their diverse perspectives and technical expertise, in accordance with procedures approved by the Report Review Committee of the NRC. The purpose of this independent review is to provide candid and critical comments that will assist the institution in making the published report as sound as possible and to ensure that the report meets institutional standards for objectivity, evidence, and responsiveness to the study charge. The review comments and draft manuscript remain confidential to protect the integrity of the deliberative process.

We thank the following individuals for their participation in the review of this report: Stephen J. Bagnato, Early Childhood Partnerships, Children's Hospital of Pittsburgh; Virginia Buysse, Child Development Institute, University of North Carolina at Chapel Hill; Gayle Cunningham, Executive Director's Office, Jefferson County Committee for Economic Opportunity, Birmingham, AL; David Dickinson, Department of Teaching and Learning, Vanderbilt University; Walter Gilliam, The Edward Zigler Center in Child Development and Social Policy of the Yale Child Study Center, Yale University School of Medicine; Robert L. Linn, Department of Education, University of Colorado; Joan Lombardi, The Children's Project, Washington, DC; Helen Raikes, University of Nebraska, Lincoln; David M. Thissen, Department of Psychology, University of North Carolina; and Ross A. Thompson, Department of Psychology, University of California, Davis.

Although the reviewers listed above have provided many constructive comments and suggestions, they were not asked to endorse the conclusions or recommendations, nor did they see the final draft of the report before its release. The review of this report was overseen by Aletha C. Huston, Pricilla Pond Flawn Regents Professor of Child Development, University of Texas at Austin, and Jack P. Shonkoff, Center on the Developing Child, Harvard University, as review coordinator and monitor, respectively. Appointed by the NRC, they were responsible for making sure that an independent examination of this report was carried out in accordance with institutional procedures and that all reviewers' comments were considered carefully. Responsibility for the final content of this report, however, rests entirely with the authoring committee and the institution.

Catherine E. Snow, *Chair*
Committee on Developmental Outcomes and Assessments for Young Children

# Contents

# EARLY CHILDHOOD ASSESSMENT

# Summary

The assessment of young children's development and learning has recently taken on new importance. Private and government organizations are developing programs to enhance the school readiness of all young children, especially children from economically disadvantaged homes and communities and children with special needs. These programs are designed to enhance social, language, and academic skills through responsive early care and education. In addition, they constitute a site where children with developmental problems can be identified and receive appropriate interventions.

Societal and government initiatives have also promoted accountability for these educational programs, especially those that are publicly funded. These initiatives focus on promoting standards of learning and monitoring children's progress in meeting those standards. In this atmosphere, Congress has enacted such laws as the Government Performance and Results Act and the No Child Left Behind Act. School systems and government agencies are asked to set goals, track progress, analyze strengths and weaknesses in programs, and report on their achievements, with consequences for unmet goals. Likewise, early childhood education and intervention programs are increasingly being asked to prove their worth.

In 2006, Congress requested that the National Research Council (NRC) conduct a study of developmental outcomes and appropriate assessment of young children. With funding from the Office of Head Start in the U.S. Department of Health and Human Services, the specific charge to this committee was the identification of important outcomes for children from birth to age 5 and the quality and purposes of different techniques and instruments for developmental assessments.

The committee's review highlights two key principles. First, the purpose of an assessment should guide assessment decisions. Second, assessment activity should be conducted within a coherent system of medical, educational, and family support services that promote optimal development for all children.

Our focus on the need for purposefulness and systematicity is particularly important at this time, because young children are currently being assessed for a wide array of purposes, across a wide array of domains, and in multiple service settings. The increase in the amount of assessment raises understandable worries about whether assessments are selected, implemented, and interpreted correctly. Assessments of children may be used for purposes as diverse as determining the level of functioning of individual children, guiding instruction, or measuring functioning at the program, community, or state level.

Different purposes require different types of assessments, and the evidentiary base that supports the use of an assessment for one purpose may not be suitable for another. As the consequences of assessment findings become weightier, the accuracy and quality of the instruments used to provide findings must be more certain. Decisions based on an assessment that is used to monitor the progress of one child can be important to that child and her family and thus must be taken with caution, but they can also be challenged and revisited more easily than assessments used to determine the fate or funding for groups of children, such as those attending a local child care center, an early education program, or a nationwide program like Head Start. When used for purposes of program evaluation and accountability, often called high stakes,[1]

[1]We have adopted the following definition of high-stakes assessment (see Appendix A): Tests and/or assessment processes for which the results lead to sig-

assessments can have major consequences for large numbers of children and families, for the community served by the program, and for policy.

If decisions about individual children or about programs are to be defended, the system of assessment must reflect the highest standards of evidence in three domains: the psychometric properties of the instruments used in the assessment system; the evidence supporting the appropriateness of the assessment instruments for different ethnic, racial, language, functional status, and age group populations; and the domains that serve as the focus of the assessment. In addition, resources need to be directed to the training of assessors, the analysis and reporting of results, and the interpretation of those results. Such attention is especially warranted when making decisions about whether programs will continue to be funded by tax monies.

The purpose and system principles apply as well to the interpretation, use, and communication of assessment data. Collecting data should be preceded by planning how the data will be used, who should have access to them, in what decisions they will play a role, and what stakeholders need to know about them. Ideally, any assessment activity benefits children by providing information that can be used to inform their caregivers and teachers, to improve the quality of their care and educational environments, and to identify child risk factors that can be remedied. But assessments may also have adverse consequences. Direct assessments may make children feel anxious, incompetent, or bored, and indirect assessments may constitute a burden on adults. An assessment activity may also deflect time and resources from instruction, and assessments cost money. It is therefore important to ensure that the value of the information gathered through assessments outweighs any negative effects on adults or children and that it merits the investment of resources.

Purposeful and systematic assessment requires decisions about what to assess. In this study, the committee focuses on five

---

nificant sanctions or rewards for children, their teachers, administrators, schools/programs, and/or school systems. Sanctions may be direct (e.g., retention in grade for children, reassignment for teachers, reorganization for schools) or unintended (e.g., narrowing of the curriculum, increased dropping out).

domains that build on the school readiness work of the National Education Goals Panel (1995):

1. physical well-being and motor development,
2. social and emotional development,
3. approaches toward learning,
4. language development (including emergent literacy), and
5. cognition and general knowledge (including mathematics and science).

This list reflects state early learning standards, guidelines from organizations focused on the welfare of young children, and the status of available assessment instruments. The domains are not specific about many areas of potential interest to parents, to educators, and to society, such as art, music, creativity, prosocial behavior, and morality. Also, for some purposes and for some children, including infants and preschool children with disabilities, a functional rather than a domain-specific approach to assessment may be appropriate.

Once a purpose has been established and a set of domains selected, the next challenge is to identify the best assessment instrument; this may be one that is widely used, or an adaptation of a previously used instrument, or in some cases a newly developed instrument. The varied available approaches, which include conducting direct assessments, interviewing parents or teachers, observing children in natural or slightly structured settings, and analyzing their work, all constitute rich sources of information. Issues of psychometric adequacy, in particular the validity of the instrument chosen for all the subgroups of children to be considered, are paramount, for observational and interview instruments as well as direct assessments.

The remainder of this summary presents guidelines for assessment related to four issues: purposes, domains and measures, implementation, and systems. The summary concludes with key points for a future research agenda.

## GUIDELINES ON PURPOSES OF ASSESSMENT

(P-1) Public and private entities undertaking the assessment of young children should make the purposes of assessment explicit and public.

(P-2) The assessment strategy—which assessments to use, how often to administer them, how long they should be, how the domain of items or children or programs should be sampled—should match the stated purpose and require the minimum amount of time to obtain valid results for that purpose. Even assessments that do not directly involve children, such as classroom observations, teacher rating forms, and collection of work products, impose a burden on adults and will require advance planning for using the information.

(P-3) Those charged with selecting assessments need to weigh options carefully, considering the appropriateness of candidate assessments for the desired purpose and for use with all the subgroups of children to be included. Although the same measure may be used for more than one purpose, prior consideration of all potential purposes is essential, as is careful analysis of the actual content of the assessment instrument. Direct examination of the assessment items is important because the title of a measure does not always reflect the content.

## GUIDELINES ON DOMAINS AND MEASURES OF DEVELOPMENTAL OUTCOMES

(D-1) Domains included when assessing child outcomes and the quality of education programs should be expanded beyond those traditionally emphasized (language, literacy, and mathematics) to include others, such as affect, interpersonal interaction, and opportunities for self-expression.

(D-2) Support is needed to develop measures of approaches to learning and socioemotional functioning, as well as other currently neglected domains, such as art, music, creativity, and interpersonal skills.

(D-3) Studies of the child outcomes of greatest importance to parents, including those from ethnic minority and immigrant groups, are needed to ensure that assessment instruments are available for domains (and thinking about domains) emphasized in different cultural perspectives, for example, proficiency in the native language as well as in English.

(D-4) For children with disabilities and special needs, domain-based assessments may need to be replaced or supplemented with more functional approaches.

(D-5) Selecting domains to assess requires first establishing the purposes of the assessment, then deciding which of the various possible domains dictated by the purposes can best be assessed using available instruments of proven reliability and validity, and considering what the costs will be of omitting domains from the assessment system (e.g., reduction of their importance in the eyes of practitioners or parents).

## GUIDELINES ON INSTRUMENT SELECTION AND IMPLEMENTATION

(I-1) Selection of a tool or instrument should always include careful attention to its psychometric properties.

A. Assessment tools should be chosen that have been shown to have acceptable levels of validity and reliability evidence for the purposes for which they will be used and the populations that will be assessed.

B. Those charged with implementing assessment systems need to make sure that procedures are in place to examine validity data as part of instrument selection and then to examine the data being produced with the instrument to ensure that the scores being generated are valid for the purposes for which they are being used.

C. Test developers and others need to collect and make available evidence about the validity of inferences for language and cultural minority groups and for children with disabilities.

D. Program directors, policy makers, and others who select instruments for assessments should receive instruction in how to select and use assessment instruments.

(I-2) Assessments should not be given without clear plans for follow-up steps that use the information productively and appropriately.

(I-3) When assessments are carried out, primary caregivers should be informed in advance about their purposes and focus. When assessments are for screening purposes, primary caregivers should be informed promptly about the results, in particular whether they indicate a need for further diagnostic assessment.

(I-4) Pediatricians, primary medical caregivers, and other qualified personnel should screen for maternal or family factors that might impact child outcomes—child abuse risk, maternal depression, and other factors known to relate to later outcomes.

(I-5) Screening assessment should be done only when the available instruments are informative and have good predictive validity.

(I-6) Assessors, teachers, and program administrators should be able to articulate the purpose of assessments to parents and others.

(I-7) Assessors should be trained to meet a clearly specified level of expertise in administering assessments, should be monitored systematically, and should be reevaluated occasionally. Teachers or other program staff may administer assessments if they are carefully supervised and if reliability checks and monitoring are in place to ensure adherence to approved procedures.

(I-8) States or other groups selecting high-stakes assessments should leave an audit trail—a public record of the decision making that was part of the design and development of the assessment system. These decisions would include why the assessment data are being collected, why a particular set of outcomes was selected for assessment, why the particular tools were selected, how the results will be reported and to whom, as well as how the assessors were trained and the assessment process was monitored.

(I-9) For large-scale assessment systems, decisions regarding instrument selection or development for young children should be made by individuals with the requisite programmatic and technical knowledge and after careful consideration of a variety of factors, including existing research, recommended practice, and available resources. Given the broad-based knowledge needed to make such decisions wisely, they cannot be made by a single individual or by fiat in legislation. Policy and legislation should allow for the adoption of new instruments as they are developed and validated.

(I-10) Assessment tools should be constructed and selected for use in accordance with principles of universal design, so they will be accessible to, valid, and appropriate for the greatest possible number of children. Children with disabilities may still need accommodations, but this need should be minimized.

(I-11) Extreme caution needs to be exercised in reaching conclusions about the status and progress of, as well as the effectiveness of programs serving, young children with special needs, children from language-minority homes, and other children from groups not well represented in norming or validation samples, until more information about assessment use is available and better measures are developed.

## GUIDELINES ON SYSTEMS

(S-1) An effective early childhood assessment system must be part of a larger system with a strong infrastructure to support children's care and education. The infrastructure is the foundation on which the assessment systems rest and is critical to its smooth and effective functioning. The infrastructure should encompass several components that together form the system:

A. ***Standards:*** A comprehensive, well-articulated set of standards for both program quality and children's learning that are aligned to one another and that define the constructs of interest as well as child outcomes that demonstrate that the learning described in the standard has occurred.

B. ***Assessments:*** Multiple approaches to documenting child development and learning and reviewing program quality that are of high quality and connect to one another in well-defined ways, from which strategic selection can be made depending on specific purposes.

C. ***Reporting:*** Maintenance of an integrated database of assessment instruments and results (with appropriate safeguards of confidentiality) that is accessible to potential users, that provides information about how the instruments and scores relate to standards, and that can generate reports for varied audiences and purposes.

D. ***Professional development:*** Ongoing opportunities provided to those at all levels (policy makers, program directors, assessment administrators, practitioners) to understand the standards and the assessments and to learn to use the data and data reports with integrity for their own purposes.

E. ***Opportunity to learn:*** Procedures to assess whether the environments in which children are spending time offer high-quality support for development and learning, as well as safety, enjoyment, and affectively positive relationships, and to direct support to those that fall short.

F. ***Inclusion:*** Methods and procedures for ensuring that all children served by the program will be assessed fairly, regardless of their language, culture, or disabilities, and with tools that provide useful information for fostering their development and learning.

G. ***Resources:*** The assurance that the financial resources needed to ensure the development and implementation of the system components will be available.

H. ***Monitoring and evaluation:*** Continuous monitoring of the system itself to ensure that it is operating effectively and that all elements are working together to serve the interests of the children. This entire infrastructure must be in place to create and sustain an assessment subsystem within a larger system of early childhood care and education.

(S-2) A successful system of assessments must be coherent in a variety of ways. It should be *horizontally coherent*, with the curriculum, instruction, and assessment all aligned with the early learning and development standards and with the program standards, targeting the same goals for learning, and working together to support children's developing knowledge and skill across all domains. It should be *vertically coherent*, with a shared understanding at all levels of the system of the goals for children's learning and development that underlie the standards, as well as consensus about the purposes and uses of assessment. It should be *developmentally coherent*, taking into account what is known about how children's skills and understanding develop over time and the content knowledge, abilities, and understanding that are needed for learning to progress at each stage of the process. The California Desired Results Developmental Profile provides an example of movement toward a multiply coherent system. These coherences drive the design of all the subsystems. For example, the development of early learning standards, curriculum, and the design of teaching practices and assessments should be guided by the same framework for understanding what is being attempted in the classroom that informs the training of beginning teachers and the continuing professional development of experienced teachers. The reporting of assessment results to parents, teachers, and other stakeholders should also be based on this same framework, as should the evaluations of effectiveness built into all systems. Each child should have an equivalent opportunity to achieve the defined goals, and the allocation of resources should reflect those goals.

(S-3) Following the best possible assessment practices is especially crucial in cases in which assessment can have significant consequences for children, teachers, or programs. The 1999 NRC report *High Stakes: Testing for Tracking, Promotion, and Graduation* urged extreme caution in basing high-stakes decisions on assessment outcomes, and we conclude that even more extreme caution is needed when dealing with young children from birth to age 5 and with the early care and education system. We emphasize that a primary purpose of assessing children or classrooms is to improve the quality of early childhood care and education by identifying where more support, professional development, or funding is needed and by providing classroom personnel with tools to track children's growth and adjust instruction.

(S-4) Accountability is another important purpose for assessment, especially when significant state or federal investments are made in early childhood programs. Program-level accountability should involve high stakes only under very well-defined conditions: (a) data about input factors are fully taken into account, (b) quality rating systems or other program quality information has been considered in conjunction with child measures, (c) the programs have been provided with all the supports needed to improve, and (d) it is clear that restructuring or shutting the program down will not have worse consequences for children than leaving it open. Similarly, high stakes for teachers should not be imposed on the basis of classroom functioning or child outcomes alone. Information about access to resources and support for teachers should be gathered and carefully considered in all such decisions, because sanctioning teachers for the failure of the system to support them is inappropriate.

(S-5) Performance (classroom-based) assessments of children can be used for accountability, if objectivity is ensured by checking a sample of the assessments for reliability and consistency, if the results are appropriately contextualized in information about the program, and if careful safeguards are in place to prevent misuse of information.

(S-6) Minimizing the burdens of assessment is an important goal; being clear about purpose and embedding any individual assessment decision into a larger system can limit the time and money invested in assessment.

(S-7) It is important to establish a common way of identifying children for services across the early care and education, family support, health, and welfare sectors.

(S-8) Implementing assessment procedures requires skilled administrators who have been carefully trained in the assessment procedures to be implemented; because direct assessments with young children can be particularly challenging, more training may be required for such assessments.

(S-9) Implementation of a system-level approach requires having services available to meet the needs of all children identified through screening, as well as requiring follow-up with more in-depth assessments.

(S-10) If services are not available, it can be appropriate to use screening assessments and then use the results to argue for expansion of services. Failure to screen when services are not available may lead to underestimation of the need for services.

## RESEARCH AGENDA

Among the tasks of the committee was the development of a research agenda to improve the quality and suitability of developmental assessment, across a wide array of purposes and for the benefit of all the various subgroups of children who will eventually be entering kindergarten. References to the need for research on assessment tools and the building of an assessment system are distributed throughout this document. Major topics of recommended research, with details in Chapter 11, are

- research related to instrument development,
- research related to assessment processes,
- research on the use of assessment tools and processes with special populations, and
- research related to accountability.

## CONCLUSION

Well-planned and effective assessment can inform teaching and program improvement, and contribute to better outcomes for children. Current assessment practices do not universally reflect the available information about how to do assessment well. This report affirms that assessments can make crucial contributions to the improvement of children's well-being, but only if they are well designed, implemented effectively, developed in the context of systematic planning, and are interpreted and used appropriately. Otherwise, assessment of children and programs can have negative consequences for both. The value of assessments therefore requires fundamental attention to their purpose and the design of the larger systems in which they are used.

# Part I

## Early Childhood Assessment

In this part of the report, we present an introduction to the work, in Chapter 1, with an explanation of the policy context for the study, the committee's charge, the committee's approach to the work, and the structure of the report.

In Chapter 2, we discuss purposeful assessment, emphasizing the importance of determining the purposes of any assessment before proceeding to design, develop, or implement it. We review some common purposes for assessing young children, and introduce some guidelines for such assessments developed by respected organizations concerned with the care and education of young children. We also introduce the special issues attendant to using assessment of young children for accountability purposes.

In Chapter 3, we provide some historical context for this study. We review the recent history of the development of early childhood learning standards and assessments, especially in the states and the federal government, with a discussion of the societal and governmental changes that have motivated some of these efforts.

# 1

# Introduction

Every society nurtures a set of goals for its children, although the balance among those goals may be contested within societies and may vary across them. People want their children to be safe and healthy, to be happy and well-adjusted, to be competent in some array of domains and accomplished in one or two of those, to be trustworthy, to have good friends and to establish loving relationships, to be guided by ethical commitments, and to be prepared cognitively and morally to contribute to society in small or large ways. Each of those goals encompasses wide variation: some parents value accomplishment in athletics highly, while others value music, and yet others value academics above all. Ethical commitments for some parents imply the adherence to a particular creed, and for others mean wrestling to develop one's own moral imperatives. Happiness for some means ongoing membership in family or clan, and for others means increasing individualization and independence. Nonetheless, at least at the general level sketched here, these societal goals for childhood are widely shared.

## THE POLICY CONTEXT

Policies focused on child development connect to a subset of these goals rather well and have largely ignored others. Policies promote infant and child safety and physical health, but societal attention to children's mental health is much less universal. Education policies, starting with the common school and continuing through the No Child Left Behind Act of 2001, have been designed to ensure adequate accomplishments in particular domains; reading and mathematics are almost always included, but science, history, literature, art, music, and athletics receive more intermittent and contested support. American society has largely avoided making policies related to "positive ethics"—how one should act—consistent with the separation of church and state. The criminal code can be seen as a set of ethical guidelines focusing on the negative side—what one should *not* do—but here as well the policies relevant to children typically exempt them from full responsibility even for wrongful actions.

The largest body of child-oriented federal, state, and local policies focuses on a subset of goals for child development: It is fairly uncontroversial that society should legislate and appropriate funding to ensure safety and health and to promote academic achievement. Much less attention has traditionally been devoted to happiness; trustworthiness; friendship and social relationships; membership in family, society, or nation; moral development; or leading a productive life.

One might conceptualize the policies as a map that provides a distorted representation of the underlying landscape, much as the Mercator projection of the earth greatly overestimates the areas of land masses at the poles. The "policy projection" of child development has often shrunk the size of social, emotional, and relational domains to focus on health and academics. This perspective directly reflects (and may indeed result from) the "researcher's projection" and the associated "measurement projection." Somewhat more attention has been given by the field of child development to language, literacy, and cognition than to happiness, emotional health, friendship, or morality (although some of these goals are beginning to attract research attention and to be represented in states' early childhood standards), and the tools available to measure development in that first set of domains are more numerous and more precise.

Assessment strategies also traditionally have focused on rather discrete aspects of a child's functioning, such as vocabulary or fine motor skills, because these lend themselves more readily to measurement. Discrete skills are valuable and valued because they allow children to carry out meaningful and important functions in day-to-day life, such as having conversations and forming friendships, understanding family stories and stories in books, and taking care of their own feeding and dressing needs. How children put discrete skills together to be able to carry out important day-to-day life functions is important from an outcomes perspective, but measurement strategies have not typically focused on more global functioning.

It goes far beyond the charge of this committee to analyze the history of this situation or to investigate the direction of causality; perhaps the ease of measurement in some domains has led to greater interest in them, or perhaps interest in them has led to better measurement. Nonetheless, we wish to emphasize that we are acutely aware of the danger of writing a report about "developmental outcomes and assessments" that takes for granted the outcomes and assessments available, without at least inquiring what the impact might be of a different or expanded set.

We also wish to emphasize our view, consistent with that of most developmental theorists, that understanding children's development of any outcome requires having information not just about a child's performance on the assessment but also about the conditions that have led to that performance and the conditions under which the performance is assessed. Many early childhood educators prefer indirect forms of assessment, such as observation of the child in a natural environment or parent or caregiver reports, to direct assessment. Nonetheless, direct assessments are widely used and offer rich information about individual children and groups of children. When they are used, however, the scores obtained should be richly contextualized. A child's score on a vocabulary test reflects not just the child's capacity to learn words, but also the language environment in which the child has lived since birth, the child's ease with the testing procedure, and the child's relationship with the tester. The younger the child, the more important are these considerations.

Policy makers recognize the importance of the environment in determining child outcomes; many of the initiatives they propose and support are designed to change that environment in order to influence the outcomes, for example by preventing malnutrition in pregnant women and infants, or increasing resources for early childhood education, or promoting time for recess and active play to reduce obesity. Social policy makers are committed environmentalists when designing programs, but they too often forget their environmentalist convictions when dictating ways of assessing the outcomes of those programs.

Assessment of young children is crucial in meeting a variety of purposes. It provides information with which caregivers and teachers can better understand individual children's developmental progress and status and how well they are learning, and it can inform caregiving, instruction, and provision of needed services. It helps early childhood program staff determine how well they are meeting their objectives for the children they serve, and it informs program design and implementation. It provides some of the information needed for program accountability and contributes to advancing knowledge of child development.

Furthermore, the tools available for assessing young children and their environments have increased vastly in number and variety in recent years. Advances in child development research and demands from educators, evaluation researchers, and policy makers have converged to provide a dizzying array of assessment options—thus enhancing the urgency of providing some guidelines for deciding when and what to assess, choosing and using assessment tools, and interpreting assessment data.

The assessment of young children's development and learning has taken on new importance as investment in early childhood education rises. Private and government organizations are increasingly implementing programs for young children, many of them targeted toward those from disadvantaged homes and communities. These programs attempt to improve children's chances for optimal development by compensating in various ways for perceived deficiencies. Some of the more intensive interventions include teaching parenting skills through home visits, providing child care services that nurture development, and offering such preschool programs as Head Start and state prekindergarten (pre-K) programs.

At the same time, the last decade or so has seen societal and government initiatives promoting accountability for such programs, especially those that are publicly funded. In this atmosphere, laws like the Government Performance and Results Act and the No Child Left Behind Act have been passed. School systems and government agencies are being asked to set goals, track progress, analyze strengths and weaknesses, and report on their achievements, with consequences when goals are not met. It is therefore not surprising that there is now considerable demand for early childhood intervention programs to prove their worth.

This desire for accountability in early childhood programs may lead quite directly to the proposition that it is possible (and reasonable) to measure program quality and hold programs accountable by measuring the "outputs" or "products" of the programs—that is, assessing the children. After all, that is what is being done for school-age children to satisfy the requirements of the No Child Left Behind Act, and pressures for standards, assessment, and accountability have multiplied for young children as well. We argue in this volume, though, that thinking about accountability for early childhood programs requires an understanding of much more than just how well children score on tests. Interpreting outcome scores collected from children in an early childhood program requires the presence of a larger system, in the context of which particular assessments are selected, implemented, and interpreted. Using child outcome scores properly requires that a number of conditions be met:

1. a clearly articulated purpose for the testing,
2. identification of why particular assessments were selected in relation to the purpose,
3. a clear theory connecting the assessment results and quality of care,
4. observation of the quality of instruction and specification of what would be needed for improvement,
5. a clear plan for following up to improve program quality,
6. strategizing to collect the required information with a minimum of testing, and
7. appropriate preparation of testers to minimize disruptive effects on children's responses.

On one hand, we recognize that having all these conditions in place is challenging. Doing assessment well is difficult, and designing assessment systems that serve the purpose of ensuring optimal outcomes for young children requires the investment of time, money, and considerable expertise. Failing to make those investments risks negative effects on children, on those responsible for care and education of young children, and ultimately on society. On the other hand, implementing assessment as a crucial, though neither simple nor inexpensive, part of a well-articulated early childhood care and education system offers the possibility of improved programs, better informed parents and care and education providers, happier and more accomplished children, and more solid evidence concerning program effectiveness.

## THE COMMITTEE'S CHARGE

In the context described above, the U.S. Department of Health and Human Services Office of Head Start implemented the Head Start National Reporting System (NRS) in 2003. (This assessment and its origins are discussed more fully in Chapter 3.) The NRS met with a great deal of well-publicized critical reaction from early childhood researchers and advocates, some of it based on the belief that such an assessment was inappropriate, and some criticizing the NRS design, development, and implementation process. Partly in response to this criticism, Congress included a requirement for an independent study by the National Research Council (NRC) of developmental outcomes and their assessment in funding legislation for the Administration for Children and Families (ACF) in fiscal year (FY) 2006.

In September 2006, the NRC, an operating arm of the National Academies, entered into a contract with the Office of Head Start of the ACF in the U.S. Department of Health and Human Services, at the request of the House Subcommittee on Education, to perform this study. The study was overseen jointly by the Board on Children, Youth, and Families (a joint activity of the NRC and the Institute of Medicine) and the NRC's Board on Testing and Assessment. The Committee on Developmental Outcomes and Assessments for Young Children was appointed following the procedures mandated for all NRC committee appointments. Those procedures are designed to ensure that committee members are chosen for their expertise, independence, and diversity and that the committee's membership is balanced and without conflicts of interest. Brief biographies of the committee members appear in Appendix E.

The committee's charge as described in the Academies proposal, incorporated by reference in the contract with the ACF reads:

> The committee will respond to a congressional mandate for a National Research Council panel to "review and provide guidance on appropriate outcomes and assessments for young children." The committee will focus on two key topics: (1) the identification of key outcomes associated with early stages of child development for children ages 0-5, and (2) the quality and purpose of different state-of-the art techniques and instruments for developmental assessments.
>
> In the first area, the committee will review the research base associated with developmental outcomes for children ages 0-5 in different domains, including physical, cognitive, social, psychobiological, and emotional. This review will include consideration of the range of variation associated with developmental outcomes in different child populations according to gender, SES status, race/ethnicity, and age. Special attention will be given to outcomes that are specified as the focus of early childhood programming, such as Head Start, as well as outcomes that allow states to monitor the developmental capacities of young children and to support programs that make positive contributions to these outcomes.
>
> In the second area, the committee will examine the available range of techniques and instruments for assessing these outcomes, paying particular attention to the empirical evidence available about the reliability, validity, fairness and other considerations related to the quality and use of the developmental assessments. The review will consider issues related to the use of assessments in screening the developmental status of special populations of children (such as children with developmental disabilities, children from minority cultures, and children whose home language is not English).
>
> The committee will also examine the criteria that should guide the selection of assessment techniques for different purposes, such as guiding curriculum and instructional decisions for individual children, or program evaluation and program accountability, and the ability to link early childhood interventions such as Head Start with wider community goals for young children. Special consideration will be given to the training requirements that are necessary for the use of assessments in different program settings and with different child populations. The committee will, to the extent possi-

ble, identify opportunities to link measurement improvement strategies within diverse settings (such as educational, developmental, and pediatric programs for young children) to avoid duplication and to maximize collaboration and efficiencies.

The committee will provide recommendations to practitioners and policy makers about criteria for the selection of appropriate assessment tools for different purposes, as well as how to collect and use contextual information to interpret assessment results appropriately for young children. The committee will also develop a research agenda to improve the quality and suitability of developmental assessment tools that can be used in a variety of early childhood program and service environments.

## THE COMMITTEE'S APPROACH

At the first meeting, the committee identified information needs in several domains and developed plans for obtaining and analyzing the needed information and for organizing the report. After reviewing the charge and the time available to complete the work, the committee discussed the scope of the tasks and determined what would and would not be attempted. We did not think it appropriate to perform in-depth technical reviews of existing instruments, nor to attempt to develop a list of "approved" assessment instruments. We chose instead to develop principles and criteria for the selection of appropriate instruments for various assessment purposes.

The committee gathered information from a broad range of sources on a number of issues:

- Appropriate purposes for assessing young children and uses for assessment results
  - —Defining appropriate uses and identifying user groups
  - —Identifying potential misuses of assessment results
  - —Using children's assessment results to make decisions about programs
- Decisions to be made in assessing young children
  - —Choosing domains that should be assessed
  - —Selecting direct versus observational, in-context, or "authentic" assessment
  - —Deciding when to sample children or items (or both) versus administering all items to all children

- Reviewing psychometric criteria
  - —Defining reliability and validity in assessments for young children
  - —Reviewing a sample of available assessments for their psychometric adequacy
  - —Seeking information about validity in less frequently studied populations
- Information and opinions about the NRS
- Special challenges of assessing language-minority children and children with disabilities in a fair and useful manner

We used several methods to gather the information needed, including literature review, briefings by the ACF and congressional staff and others, and a public forum for stakeholders.

The committee and staff searched for and reviewed a large number of ACF documents and online information relevant to Head Start and Early Head Start programs and to the NRS, the assessment effort instituted by Head Start in 2003 that was a major impetus for the commissioning of this report. Committee members drew on their expertise and professional experience in child development, early childhood care and education, and assessment in reviewing and evaluating these materials. The ACF materials reviewed include

- documents describing Head Start and Early Head Start programs, standards, frameworks, and research projects;
- documents describing the NRS, as well as its development and implementation; and
- web pages maintained by ACF organizations, including Head Start, the Office of Planning, Research and Evaluation, the Early Childhood Learning and Knowledge Center, the National Head Start Association, and others.

The committee also reviewed reports of the U.S. Government Accountability Office, the U.S. Department of Education, and other agencies relevant to early childhood assessment. In addition to all of these materials, some of the stakeholders and other sources provided documents for our review. Some of these were clearly opinion pieces advocating specific points of view or courses of action and were evaluated as such.

The committee reviewed scientific and professional literature in early childhood development and assessment, as well as information on early learning guidelines, standards, and frameworks developed by states and by organizations active in early childhood education. We were especially interested in materials on developmental outcomes, assessment methods, and instruments, including existing reviews of early childhood assessment instruments and material on children in special populations and with special needs. Previous NRC reports including *From Neurons to Neighborhoods: The Science of Early Childhood Development* (National Research Council and Institute of Medicine, 2000) and *Eager to Learn: Educating Our Preschoolers* (National Research Council, 2001), also provided much useful information. We read with special interest the report of the National Early Childhood Accountability Task Force, released about halfway through our work, and received a briefing on that report from the task force chair.[1]

We invited ACF personnel and staff members of the House and Senate education subcommittees to brief the committee at our first meeting. Some ACF personnel also attended the stakeholder forum, described below. The committee also asked for and received briefings from some individuals representing organizations involved with the NRS, to better understand the issues surrounding that assessment. Nicholas Zill of Westat, the contractor with major responsibility for its development and implementation, briefed the committee at the first meeting, as did Samuel Meisels, a prominent child development researcher and critic of the NRS.

In order to better understand the issues in the child development and early education community concerning assessments, the committee decided it would be useful to hear from various stakeholders involved in or affected by early childhood assessments. It was also important to ensure that the relevant groups had the opportunity to tell the committee about their views on the issues important to them and about their specific concerns.

---

[1]Two members of this committee, Eugene Garcia and Jacqueline Jones, were also members of the task force.

After consultation with ACF staff and general discussion in the committee, a number of stakeholders were identified. Representatives from these organizations were invited to speak briefly at an open meeting of the committee structured as a public forum and to submit written responses to questions posed by the committee. We invited a total of 55 organizations to participate in a public forum on July 6, 2007. Appendix B includes the agenda for the meeting, a list of participants, and the list of questions the stakeholder groups were asked to consider.

The committee made a good-faith effort to reach a broad sampling of stakeholders, although several interest groups whose inputs we solicited chose not to participate. We understand that we may not have heard all relevant points of view but worked with the information obtained from those who agreed to participate.

## STRUCTURE OF THE REPORT

This report is organized into four parts. Part I includes this introduction, Chapter 2, on purposes of assessment, and Chapter 3, a brief history of early childhood standards.

Part II concentrates on what should be assessed and why. Chapter 4 discusses screening assessments, particularly for infants and young toddlers; Chapter 5 focuses on the domains typically assessed in young children and approaches to assessing them; and Chapter 6 discusses methods for measuring the quality of early childhood environments.

Part III focuses on assessment methods. Chapter 7 addresses psychometric issues in assessment, and Chapter 8 deals with issues in assessing ethnic/racial minority and language-minority children and children with disabilities. Chapter 9 discusses the implementation of assessments.

Part IV, on assessing systematically, has two chapters. Chapter 10 is a discussion of the need for systems of assessment and how that need might be satisfied, and Chapter 11 provides the committee's guidance on assessments, including a proposed research agenda.

The report has five appendixes. Appendix A is a glossary of some important terms used in our discussions. Appendix B has information on the stakeholder forum held as part of the committee's information-gathering efforts. Appendix C has information on the domains included in state pre-K learning standards, as well as a description of recent state standards development. Appendix D provides sources for detailed information on assessment instruments. Appendix E contains brief biographical sketches of the committee members and staff.

# 2

# Purposeful Assessment

Assessment, defined as gathering information in order to make informed instructional decisions, is an integral part of most early childhood programs. By the mid-elementary level, children in some school systems may spend several weeks every year completing district and state assessments, and those in troubled schools probably spend even more time in more formal test preparation activities designed to ensure that their high-stakes assessment outcomes are acceptable. Since assessment is such a fact of educational life, it is important to step back and ask: Why is this assessment being done? What purpose does it have? Is this particular assessment optimal for meeting that purpose?

For younger children, thinking about purpose is equally central. Done well, ongoing assessment can provide invaluable information to parents and educators about how children grow and develop. Developmentally appropriate assessment systems can provide information to highlight what children know and are able to do. However, inappropriate testing of young children runs the risk of generating insufficient information for the tester and discomfort (or just wasted time) for the testee; such risks are unacceptable and can be avoided only if it is very clear why people are engaging in the activity and what benefit will accrue from it.

Furthermore, specifying the purpose of an assessment activity should guide all the decisions that we write about in this volume:

what domains to assess, what assessment procedures to adopt, and how to interpret and use the information derived from the assessments. We make the case throughout this report that the selection and use of assessments, in early childhood as elsewhere, should be part of a larger system that specifies the infrastructure for distributing and delivering medical or educational services, maintaining quality, supporting professional development, distributing information, and guiding further planning and decision making. Thus, while in this chapter we focus on the purposes for which one might choose and use an assessment tool, we return to the theme of purpose in thinking about designing the *systems* for assessment in Part IV.

A wide range of tools can be used to collect information about children, classrooms, homes, or programs, and thinking about mode of assessment along with purpose is crucial. Assessment modes include medical procedures, observation of natural behavior, participant reports using checklists or surveys, performance in structured versions of natural tasks, and performance on standardized tests. Given the challenges of direct assessment with very young children, it is worth first considering less intrusive modes of assessment if they also meet the purposes formulated.

In the following sections we discuss many purposes for which assessment of children's learning and development is employed, beginning with several purposes associated with determining the level of functioning of individual children, and progressing to the purpose of guiding instruction, and then measuring program or societal performance. After briefly mentioning research uses—employing assessment to learn more about child development—we present guidance to be kept in mind when assessing for individual child-focused or accountability purposes, drawing on the wisdom of many previous reports from organizations interested in promoting the education and welfare of young children.

## DETERMINING AN INDIVIDUAL CHILD'S LEVEL OF FUNCTIONING

### Individual-Focused Screening[1]

Many assessments, particularly in the infancy and toddler period, are designed to screen children for medical risks. For example, within a few days of birth, infants in the United States are screened for phenylketonuria (PKU)—a genetic disorder characterized by an inability of the body to use the essential amino acid, phenylalanine—and in the first year of life infants are screened for vision and hearing deficits. These screening assessments are typically carried out in pediatric settings. Because their purpose is to ensure delivery of care or appropriate services to all children with an identified problem or risk, the screening is designed to minimize false negatives. False positives are less harmful; they may alarm a parent or generate a costly follow-up, but such mistakes are less severe in consequence than missing a child who could benefit from early intervention or medical treatment. It is important to ensure that individual children who fail the screen are followed up with further assessment, both to confirm the identification and in many cases to specify the source of the difficulty. In Part II we document many of the domains for which screening instruments are available and widely used.

### Community-Focused Screening

Although community-focused screening may use the same tools and procedures as individual-focused screening, its purpose is not individual, but rather to give a picture of risk at the community level. Thus, for example, if screening for toxic levels of lead is done in an individual-focused way, the response would be to counsel parents about ways to protect children from lead exposure, as well as to treat them directly. If done in a community-focused way, the goal might be to identify neighborhoods with a high risk of lead toxicity, in order to guide the distribution of services or to plan the provision of compensatory education in those locations, or perhaps even to influence public policy; this could

[1]Screening, assessment, and other terms are defined in Appendix A.

co-occur with the individual-focused screening goal of informing parents about their children's health.

### Diagnostic Testing

If screening assessments indicate a child's performance is outside the expected range, then often further diagnostic assessment is needed to better describe the problem, to locate a cause, or both. Sometimes the screening and diagnostic instruments are the same; for example, high blood levels of lead strongly suggest a diagnosis of lead poisoning. But sometimes the screening is uninformative about a diagnosis. For example, a child who is identified by a language screening assessment as possibly having delayed language development needs further assessment to determine whether an actual delay exists, whether there are other, related delays (e.g., intellectual functioning, cognitive processing), and whether there are obvious causes (e.g., hearing loss).

A particular purpose for which individual diagnostic assessment is increasingly being used is to determine "response to intervention," in other words, to test whether interventions are successful in moderating developmental problems by using diagnostic probes.

### Establishing Readiness

A widely used purpose of individual assessment has been to establish the readiness of individual children to participate in particular educational programs. The concept of readiness in early childhood is complicated, as are the consequences of a finding that a child is "not ready" (Graue, 2006). Readiness tests (a form of achievement test) have often been used prior to kindergarten entrance to ascertain children's likelihood of success in kindergarten and as a basis on which to make recommendations to parents about whether to enroll their children in the regular program or in some form of extra-year program or to postpone kindergarten entry. Using tests for this purpose supersedes the legal establishment of kindergarten eligibility in state law based on age (Education Commission of the States, 2005). To the extent that readiness assessments focus on readiness to benefit from reading instruction, they have also been criticized as embodying a discredited model of literacy development (National Research Council, 1998).

Most of the instruments used to establish readiness have been found to be wanting, leading to incorrect recommendations about half the time (Meisels, 1987; Shepard, 1997). Using readiness tests to make recommendations about children's access to kindergarten is especially troublesome because many of the children recommended for delayed entry are the ones who would most benefit from participation in an educational program. Researchers and advocates have consistently recommended against the use of readiness tests for this purpose (National Association of Early Childhood Specialists in State Departments of Education, 2000; Shepard and Smith, 1986).

More recently, readiness has become a construct of interest to policy makers as they consider the needs of children with regard to access to prekindergarten education and as a measure of their status at the time of entry to kindergarten (Brown et al., 2007). A number of states now measure the readiness of children once they have entered kindergarten. It is important to distinguish this useful application of readiness assessment from that of testing for eligibility.

## GUIDING INTERVENTION AND INSTRUCTION

Using ongoing assessment information to guide instructional decisions is a primary purpose of early childhood assessment and should be a component of a high-quality early childhood program (National Association for the Education of Young Children and National Association of Early Childhood Specialists in State Departments of Education, 2003). Similarly, the instructional and therapy services provided to children receiving early intervention and early childhood special education should be based on the results of initial assessment information and regularly revised using subsequently collected information on the child's progress (Neisworth and Bagnato, 2005).

A case study in the value of reliance on assessment in planning and differentiating instruction is offered by the Reading First classrooms. Providing primary grade teachers with tools that are relatively easy to administer and to interpret, as a basis for grouping children and selecting instructional activities, has massively changed the nature of early literacy instruction in U.S. schools (Center on Education Policy, 2007). A similar shift to an "assessment culture" in preschool classrooms will enable teachers to identify the learning needs of their students, to provide activities optimally designed to promote their development across the crucial domains (described in Part II), and to allocate time optimally to the various domains, improving children's progress and promoting their engagement. For example, data from Head Start about children's proficiency at the beginning of the year in the domains of emergent literacy, numeracy, and oral language skills would help teachers decide how much time should be spent in teaching letter recognition and counting versus promoting vocabulary and sharing books.

In addition to using assessment information to establish a descriptive picture of children's strengths and needs and to plan for instruction at program entry, teachers and others working with young children need to collect ongoing assessment information to track their learning over time. In addition, assessment information on how children are progressing in each area of the curriculum or with regard to individualized goals can be aggregated across children to see whether the program as implemented is, for the children as a group, meeting the needs identified and the goals defined.

### Using Assessments for Planning and Monitoring Children's Progress

Assessment data used for planning activities and tracking learning collected individually about all children in a program or classroom can be used at the individual child level (e.g., to identify a child's strengths and areas of need) or aggregated across children and used at the classroom level (e.g., to check the appropriateness and effectiveness of the educational program; to identify strengths and weaknesses of the group as a whole) and at the center or school level. Teachers and parents are the primary audiences for assessment information collected to guide instruction. For the potential value of assessment to improve children's learning to be realized, teachers also need adequate time to review assessment information and reflect on its implications for practice. It is now widely recognized that those working in early childhood classrooms and programs should be purposeful in their educational planning and thus need to use assessments for planning and monitoring what children are learning.

Criterion-referenced or curriculum-based measures are used to plan instructional activities and monitor what children are learning. Assessment data can be collected through observation, collection of children's work, and talking to them (Dodge et al., 2004). The National Association for the Education of Young Children (NAEYC) and the Division for Early Childhood (DEC) have formulated recommendations about assessments for use in educational planning and progress monitoring. Examples of tools for this purpose include the Creative Curriculum's Developmental Continuum, the High/Scope Child Observation Record (COR), and the Work Sampling System. Teachers and other staff must receive training and follow-up on the use of any assessment tool to be able to obtain valid and reliable information about children's performance.

## Response to Intervention: A New Application of Assessment for Instruction and Intervention

Response to intervention (RTI) is an approach for identifying and providing systematic intervention for school-age children who are not making satisfactory progress (Fuchs and Fuchs, 2006). RTI models vary somewhat but common components include the use of multiple tiers of increasingly intense interventions, a problem-solving approach to identifying and evaluating instructional strategies, and an integrated data collection and assessment system to monitor student progress and guide decisions at every level (Coleman, Buysse, and Neitzel, 2006). The tiers refer to the levels of support a child needs to succeed in the classroom. The base tier addresses the needs of children who make adequate progress in a general program, the next tier refers to supports provided to children who need additional general assistance, and the third tier refers to more specialized assistance for children not succeeding in the previous tiers. Universal screening with a tool designed for this purpose is implemented in the base tier to identify children who are not meeting established educational benchmarks in a high-quality instructional program. Those identified as not making progress are provided with additional empirically supported interventions or instructional strategies and their progress is monitored on a regular basis to determine the effectiveness of the intervention, with additional intervention provided to those who continue to show limited progress.

Although there is considerable interest in applying tiered models to preschool, how the principles would be applied has not been thoroughly developed, and there has been very little research to date on the application to early education (Coleman, Buysse, and Neitzel, 2006; VanDerHayden and Snyder, 2006). An example of an RTI application for children under age 5 is a model called Recognition and Response; it is under development as an approach to early identification and intervention for children with learning disabilities (Coleman, 2006). The developmental and experiential variation in young children presents challenges for the strict application of RTI's prescribed universal screening, identification of low-performing children, and tiered intervention. One concern is whether the early and frequent use of assessment to single some children out as requiring additional assistance is necessary, or even potentially harmful, before the children have had the opportunity to benefit from a high-quality preschool experience. Much more research is needed on how to apply the assessment and intervention practices of multitiered models in a way that is consistent with what is known about young children's development.

## EVALUATING THE PERFORMANCE OF A PROGRAM OR SOCIETY

Perhaps the most talked-about of the many purposes for which assessment can be used, especially since the passage of the No Child Left Behind Act (NCLB) in 2001, is accountability. It is important to note that the term "accountability" encompasses a number of distinct purposes, which we attempt to distinguish here.

### Program Effectiveness

If a government or an agency is investing money in a program, it makes sense to ask the questions "Is this program effective? Is it meeting our goals?" Assessment designed to evaluate program effectiveness against a set of externally defined goals is one form of accountability assessment. This may look a lot like progress monitoring assessment, and indeed the selection of tools for the two purposes might be identical. But evaluation differs from progress monitoring in two key ways. First, progress monitoring assessment is meant to be useful to those inside the program who are responsible for day-to-day decisions about curriculum and pedagogy, whereas evaluation of program effectiveness is useful to those making decisions about funding, extending, or terminating programs. Second, progress monitoring requires data on all relevant domains from all children in a program, whereas in many cases it is possible to evaluate a program's effectiveness by sampling children rather than testing them all, or by using a matrix design to sample different abilities in different children.

Using assessments for accountability purposes may seem simple, but in fact interpreting test data as reflecting the value of a program can be risky. There are many challenges to the conclusion that a program in which children perform poorly at the end of the year should be terminated. What if they were extremely low scorers at program entry and made notable progress, just not enough to reach the norm or criterion? What if the program is basically sound but disruptions to financing or staffing led to poor implementation in this particular year? What if the program is potentially good but investments in needed professional development or curricular materials were denied? What if the alternative program in which the children would end up if this one is terminated is even worse? Challenges like this have been widely discussed in the context of accountability consequences for school-age children under NCLB, and they are equally applicable to programs for preschoolers.

In other words, establishment of program-level accountability is a legitimate and important purpose for assessment, but not one that can be sensibly met by sole reliance on child-focused assessment data. Accountability is part of a larger system and cannot be derived from outcome data alone, or even from pre- and posttest data, on a set of child assessments. We say more about the importance of the larger system in Chapter 10.

### Program Impacts

A more specific purpose for assessing children participating in a particular program is to evaluate the impact of that program, ideally in comparison to another well-defined treatment (which might be no program at all), and ideally in the context of random assignment of individuals or classrooms to the two conditions. Under these circumstances, it is possible to evaluate the impact of the program on children's performance on the assessments used. Under these (relatively rarely encountered) ideal experimental circumstances, it is appropriate to sample children in programs rather than testing them all, and it is possible, if one is willing to limit claims about program effectiveness to subsets of children, to exclude groups of children (English language learners, for example, or children with disabilities) from the assessment regimen.

### Social Benchmarking

Another purpose for early childhood assessment that relates to accountability at a societal level is social benchmarking—answering questions like "Are 3-year-olds healthier than they were 20 years ago?" or "How do American 4-year-olds perform compared with Australian 4-year-olds on emergent literacy tasks?" Social benchmarking efforts include projects like those launched by the National Center for Education Statistics (the Birth Cohort Study, the Early Childhood Longitudinal Study-Kindergarten) and individual states (California's Desired Results Developmental Profile).

These efforts provide profiles of "expectable development" that can be used for comparisons with smaller groups in particular studies and also as a baseline for comparison with data collected at a later time. Furthermore, these studies provide policy makers and the public with a view of what the society is doing well and not so well at. The movement to develop early learning guidelines can be seen as a contribution to the social benchmarking effort;

early learning guidelines represent a set of aspirations about what children should be able to do, and the social benchmarking assessments provide information about the reality.

## ADVANCING KNOWLEDGE OF CHILD DEVELOPMENT

Finally, a major purpose of assessment—and a major source of the assessments widely used for the purposes discussed in this chapter—is for research to advance knowledge of child development. It goes far beyond our charge to discuss in any detail the use of assessments for research purposes. Furthermore, there exist robust mechanisms—peer review of journal articles, peer review of grant proposals, institutional review boards for the use of human subjects—for providing guidance to researchers in selecting, administering, and interpreting the results of assessments of young children. Nonetheless, because researchers of child development have indeed innovated and in many cases refined the tools adopted for use by education practitioners and policy makers, it seems churlish not to acknowledge this important and generative line of work.

## GUIDELINES FOR ADMINISTERING AND USING CHILD ASSESSMENTS APPROPRIATELY FOR VARIOUS PURPOSES

Organizations concerned with early childhood development and learning have recognized the potential good that can come of child assessment as well as the harm that incorrect uses or interpretations of such assessments can cause. Several of them have developed position statements or guidelines for the use of assessments with young children, with the intention of maximizing the benefits and preventing harm. Some of these documents are listed in Box 2-1.

The more recent of them incorporate and expand on earlier ones to a large extent. Thus, the entire set represents a relatively coherent set of guidelines for selection, use, and interpretation of early childhood assessments. Several of these documents agree, for example, on the following important guidelines for individual assessment:

**BOX 2-1**
**Guidelines of Documents Promulgated by Major Early Childhood Professional Groups**

- *Principles and Recommendations for Early Childhood Assessments* (Shepard, Kagan, and Wurtz, 1998). Goal 1 Early Childhood Assessments Resource Group document.
- *Early Childhood Curriculum, Assessment, and Program Evaluation* (and an accompanying extension for English language learners), a position statement promulgated by the National Association for the Education of Young Children and the National Association of Early Childhood Specialists in State Departments of Education (2003).
- *Promoting Positive Outcomes for Children with Disabilities: Recommendations for Curriculum, Assessment, and Program Evaluation* from the Division for Early Childhood (2007).
- Council of Chief State School Officers set of documents on *Building an Assessment System to Support Successful Early Learners* (undated, but circa 2003a, 2003b).

- Assessments should benefit children: National Education Goals Panel (NEGP), NAEYC, DEC.
- Assessments should meet professional, legal, ethical standards: NAEYC, DEC.
- Assessments should be designed for a specific purpose and be shown to be psychometrically sound for that purpose: NEGP, NAEYC, DEC.
- Assessments should be age-appropriate or developmentally/individually appropriate: NEGP, NAEYC, DEC.
- Parents/family should be involved in assessment when possible: NEGP, NAEYC, DEC.
- Assessments should be linguistically and culturally appropriate/responsive: NEGP, NAEYC, DEC.
- Assessments should assess developmentally/educationally significant content: NEGP (in narrative), NAEYC, DEC.

- Assessment information should be gathered from familiar contexts (NEGP), realistic settings and situations (NAEYC), or be "authentic" (DEC).
- Information should be gathered from multiple sources: NEGP, NAEYC, DEC.
- Assessment results should be used to improve instruction and learning: NAEYC, DEC, NEGP.
- Screening should be linked to follow-up assessment: NEGP, NAEYC.

## SPECIAL CONSIDERATIONS WHEN USING CHILD ASSESSMENTS FOR ACCOUNTABILITY

Particular care is needed in moving from child-focused to accountability-focused purposes for assessment. Data collected for accountability purposes are never meant as a basis for drawing conclusions or informing program personnel about individual children. Instead, they are meant to be useful to funders, state and federal policy makers, and others responsible for making decisions about a program or policy, and for this purpose it is completely appropriate to use sampling. However, in many cases, states are attempting to use the same data for accountability and for progress monitoring purposes. The wisdom of this approach is questionable, although the apparent efficiencies are understandably seductive. Progress monitoring, however, requires data at the individual child level from all children.

Decisions about accountability should never rest solely on findings from child-directed assessments. Information about the conditions under which the program is operating and about the characteristics of the families and children it is serving are crucial to making valid inferences from child performance to program quality. (Many other safeguards must also be in place, which are discussed in Part III.) Considerable guidance about accountability assessment is available from the documents listed in Box 2-1, as well as from a recent Pew Foundation report (National Early Childhood Accountability Task Force, 2007).

The tools used for various accountability purposes are often adaptations of tools developed for other purposes. The large-scale, large-sample assessment sweeps needed for accountability purposes impose a particular set of requirements: relatively brief assessments that can be administered and interpreted in standardized and straightforward ways. These requirements are particularly difficult to meet when assessing young children. Standardization of administration conflicts with establishing a trusting relationship with a child, for example, and standardization of interpretation conflicts with using all the information available. The reliability of standardized tests is threatened when they are shortened for use with large groups, and brief forms may generate information too sparse to be interpretable, in particular for children from language and cultural minorities and children with disabilities. Thus such abbreviation or adaptation requires careful evaluation of the psychometric properties of the adapted or abbreviated instruments. Nonetheless, tools developed for other purposes (e.g., Peabody Picture Vocabulary Test—Dunn and Dunn, 2007; Bayley Scales of Infant and Toddler Development—Bayley, 2005; MacArthur-Bates Communicative Development Inventories—Fenson et al., 1993) are often adapted for use in large-scale evaluations and social benchmarking efforts.

As noted above, the validity of conclusions about accountability, evaluation, and social benchmarking extends only to groups that are represented in sufficient numbers among those on whom the instruments were normed and among those assessed. Language and cultural-minority children and children with disabilities must typically be either oversampled or excluded from consideration; neither solution is entirely without problems. Conclusions about the status or development of children in these groups are also of concern in large-scale assessments because they are highly standardized and often norm-referenced. Some children with disabilities may not be included because they need accommodations or because the floor of the assessment is too high. English language learners may not be included because the assessment is given or exists only in English. Any conclusion about program accountability requires data about initial as well as final performance.

Another key issue in accountability-related assessment is the selection of the assessment tools to be used. This step should be as purposeful as the other decisions—when to assess, whom to assess, how to assess—involved in establishing accountability.

Too often these decisions are made by committees or with input from multiple stakeholders; even with the best intentions, multiple parties may end up compromising on poor tests. We hope this report provides some guidance to groups making decisions about instruments to choose for any of the purposes they may be addressing.

# 3

# Perspectives on Early Childhood Learning Standards and Assessment

In a perfect world, participants in the development of a set of early childhood services at either a local or system level would begin by thinking about what is needed to improve the physical well-being and developmental competence of young children. They would decide what outcomes could be anticipated for children who participate in a particular well-designed program or set of services. They would subsequently concern themselves with what standards and processes would be needed to ensure that participating children would benefit from the program. The planners would select formative assessments to track children's progress toward the standards and use this information to guide instructional adjustments. And finally, reliable and valid processes to assess whether children's overall development and learning have met the expectations of the planners would be selected and employed. The results of such assessment would be used to refine the program practices with the expectation that the outcomes for children would improve even further.

In the real world, this rarely happens. The underresourced complex of early childhood care and education settings in the United States is seldom able to implement the ideal sequence of steps at the local, state, or national level. The federal government, individual states, and local providers usually find themselves working at least partially backward to create workable processes to determine what the expectations for children and their families should be, what program standards lead to the accomplishment of those outcomes, and how to assess children's status related to the standards as a function of program participation.

That picture is changing as the early childhood field, as never before, is influenced by and actively reconfigures itself in response to the burgeoning development of state prekindergarten (pre-K) programs and accompanying expectations for documentation of children's progress, the development of learning standards in K-12 education, the parallel development of state assessment systems, and the accompanying development of quality rating systems across the early care and education sector.

This chapter describes the development of well-defined expectations for child outcomes—that is, early learning standards—as a function of participation in an early childhood setting of some kind, how these learning standards are being used, and how practitioners are able to access information about how to use them. We use the term "early learning standards," as defined by the Early Childhood Education Assessment Consortium of the Council of Chief State School Officers, in collaboration with several early childhood organizations. Early learning standards are statements that describe expectations for the learning and development of young children across the domains of health and physical well-being, social and emotional well-being, approaches to learning, language development and symbol systems, and general knowledge about the world around them (Council of Chief State School Officers and Early Childhood Education Assessment Consortium, 2007).

Until recently the very idea of defined expectations for what children should know and be able to do at particular times in these very early years of their lives was rejected by many in the early childhood field. Policy makers, researchers, program leaders, and teachers have historically depended on structural program and process standards (e.g., the qualifications of staff, group size and ratio, nature of the curriculum, provisions for parental involvement, the nature of adult and child interaction) to assess whether a program was offering a quality experience for children. These sets of program and process standards exist in forms as diverse as the minimum regulations each state requires for child care settings, to requirements for operating the federal Head Start program, to regulations for state prekindergarten programs, to standards for National Association for the Education of Young Children accreditation (National Association for the Education of Young Children, 2006). Program standards can reflect the minimum floor under which a program cannot operate, such as in the case of the states' child care regulations, or they can be the highest quality requirements, as in the case of the new Accreditation Standards of the National Association for the Education of Young Children (2006).

## DEVELOPMENT OF EARLY LEARNING STANDARDS

Decades of research on effective programs have demonstrated that children participating in programs adhering to high-quality program and process standards exhibit improved developmental and learning outcomes compared with children with no program or those experiencing a low-quality program (Ackerman and Barnett, 2006; High/Scope Educational Research Foundation, 2002). Many states making an investment in prekindergarten conduct evaluations of program quality and, in some cases, assess child outcomes. These studies are in addition to the regular program monitoring done to ensure that programs meet state standards, and they have increased in number as more and more states have begun to invest public money in prekindergarten (Gilliam and Zigler, 2001). Michigan, for example, has compelling longitudinal program evaluation data on the link between program quality and child outcomes in the Michigan School Readiness Program (High/Scope Educational Research Foundation, in press; National Institute for Early Education Research, 2005). Few other public or private programs (e.g., child care, private preschools) are subject to either quality-driven program standards or requirements for assessing child outcomes.

The earliest state early learning standards were developed by states operating pre-K programs (typically for 3- and 4-year-olds or just 4-year-olds). Such standards were developed on the premise that evaluation of child outcomes could not be done without a set of early learning standards against which to measure children's progress. Since the early 1990s, there has been an explosion of activity around the development of state learning standards, and every state now has them except North Dakota (where they exist in draft form). National early learning standards, such as those developed for Head Start and by subject-specific professional organizations, have also been created (Council of Chief State School Officers and Early Childhood Education Assessment Consortium, 2003a; U.S. Department of Health and Human Services, Administration for Children and Families, 2003). A set of model early learning standards has been developed by a national committee of experts (Pre-kindergarten Standards Panel, 2002), although a 2003 study found that few states made specific reference to this document (Council of Chief State School Officers and Early Childhood Education Assessment Consortium, 2003b).

Virtually every report or article about states and their development of early learning expectations begins with an expression of surprise about how quickly the development process unfolded across the nation (see Box 3-1). The development and implementation of these standards reflect a significant shift in how the field has viewed the usefulness of setting expectations for young children's learning and development. Appendix C provides more information about state early childhood standards.

While acknowledging that adherence to high-quality program standards substantially increases the likelihood that participating children will benefit from the program, advocates have been forceful in expressing reservations about creating these sets of expectations (Hatch, 2001; National Association for the Education of Young Children and National Association of Early Childhood Specialists in State Departments of Education, 2002). Such reservations include a number of concerns:

- The threat of ignoring the variability of children's development and learning and of their experiences.
- Worry that early labeling of the most vulnerable children as "failures" puts their access to appropriate instruction and thus their future development at risk.
- Unfairly judging programs on the basis of whether participating children meet standards, without taking into account their status at entry to the program or information about the resources available to the program.

**BOX 3-1**
**The Development of Major Early Learning Standards**

| | |
|---|---|
| 1989 | Goal 1, "All children ready to learn," articulated by the nation's governors at education summit |
| 1995 | Publication of *Reconsidering Children's Early Development and Learning* (Kagan, Moore, and Bredekamp, 1995) |
| 1998 | Publication of *Preventing Reading Difficulties* (National Research Council, 1998) |
| | Publication of *Principles and Recommendations for Early Childhood Assessments* (Shepad, Kagan, and Wurtz, 1998) |
| 1999 | **10 states have standards for children ages 3-4** |
| 2000 | Publication of *From Neurons to Neighborhoods* (National Research Council and Institute of Medicine, 2000) |
| | Publication of *Head Start Child Outcomes Framework* (U.S. Department of Health and Human Services, Administration for Children and Families, 2000) |
| 2001 | Publication of *Eager to Learn* (National Research Council, 2001) |
| 2002 | **17 states have standards for children ages 3-4; 4 states have standards for children ages 0-3** |
| | *Good Start, Grow Smart* initiative (White House, 2002) launched |
| | Head Start National Reporting System launched |
| 2007 | **49 states have standards for children ages 3-4; 18 states have standards for children ages 0-3** |
| | Publication of *Taking Stock: Assessing and Improving Early Childhood Learning and Program Quality* (National Early Childhood Accountability Task Force, 2007) |
| | States now required to report outcomes data for children with disabilities served through Part C and Part B of the Individuals with Disabilities Education Act as part of their Annual Performance Report |

- The risk of children being unfairly denied program participation based on what they do or do not know.
- The risk that responsibility for meeting the standards will shift from the adults charged with providing high-quality learning opportunities to very young children.
- Whether high-quality teaching will be undermined by the pressure to meet standards, causing the curriculum to become rigid and focused on test content and the erosion of a child-centered approach to curriculum development and instructional practices.
- Whether switching to child outcome standards as the sole criterion for determining the effectiveness of programs or personnel is unfair. Early childhood services continue to be underresourced, and poor child outcomes may reflect the lack of resources.
- Misunderstanding of how to achieve standards frequently appears to engender more teacher-centered, didactic practices.

Although these concerns cannot be dismissed, it is important to note that early learning standards were developed as a tool to improve program quality for all children. Their rapid development has resulted from a combination of policy shifts and an emerging practitioner consensus, influenced by a number of factors:

- The standards-setting activity in K-12 education, which gained momentum after the 1990 establishment of the National Education Goals Panel and the subsequent passage of Goals 2000 by Congress in 1994. This act and its accompanying funding led states to develop or refine K-12 standards in at least the areas of English language arts, mathematics, science, and history.
- Greater understanding about the capabilities of young children. Earlier work of the National Research Council (NRC) has played a key role in informing and developing that understanding and thereby supporting the development of early learning standards. The most influential NRC document influencing the development of standards for

preschool-age children has been *Eager to Learn: Educating Our Preschoolers* (National Research Council, 2001). Other important influences include *From Neurons to Neighborhoods: The Science of Early Childhood Development* (National Research Council and Institute of Medicine, 2000) and *Preventing Reading Difficulties in Young Children* (National Research Council, 1998).

- Linking of the development of early learning standards with receipt of federal funds from the Child Care and Development Fund for each state (U.S. Department of Health and Human Services, Administration for Children and Families, 2002). The requirement that all states develop voluntary early learning guidelines in language, literacy and mathematics followed the release of the 2002 early childhood initiative, Good Start, Grow Smart (White House, 2002).

## HEAD START CHILD OUTCOMES FRAMEWORK

Head Start is a large, well-known federally funded early childhood services program, serving over 909,000 children in FY 2006. Actions taken by Head Start are highly visible and embody federal policies toward early childhood services. The following narrative provides some background for understanding the evolution of the Head Start National Reporting System.

### Development of the Framework

The Head Start Child Outcomes Framework was developed in response to an unfolding set of congressional mandates beginning with the 1994 reauthorization of the Head Start Act, which mandated the development of measures to assess services and administrative and fiscal practices, to be usable for local self-assessment and peer review, to identify Head Start strengths and weaknesses, and to identify problem areas (Section 641A).

The earliest response to this mandate by the Head Start Bureau was the creation of a Pyramid of Services diagram that local programs could use to support and inform continuous program improvement efforts (see Figure 3-1). The pyramid was also used in the formulation of the Family and Child Experiences Survey (FACES) (McKey and Tarullo, 1998).[1]

When Head Start was reauthorized in 1998, programs were required to include specific child outcomes in their self-assessment process. This requirement led in 2000 to the development of the Child Outcomes Framework (U.S. Department of Health and Human Services, Administration for Children and Families, 2000). The development process was informed by the participation of a committee of outside experts (the Head Start Bureau Technical Work Group on Child Outcomes), who used the Pyramid of Services as a basis for their deliberations.

Bureau staff also consulted standards documents from professional associations and the existing state early learning standards, of which 10 sets existed at the time.[2] Although those sets of state standards displayed some common elements, great disparity was reflected in the ways the developmental domains were described and in which domains were included. Some included only a few domains, such as language and literacy; others reflected the five dimensions described by the National Education Goals Panel Goal 1 Technical Planning Group (Kagan, Moore, and Bredekamp, 1995) or additional content-related domains (e.g., social studies, science, mathematics, arts).

As had the state leaders, the developers of the Head Start Child Outcomes Framework struggled with how to organize learning expectations for Head Start children. They settled on eight broad categories that include the domains in the Goal 1 document (Kagan, Moore, and Bredekamp, 1995), with the addition of the content categories of mathematics, science, and the arts. Expectations related to social studies were included under the social emotional domain as "knowledge of families and com-

---

[1]FACES employs direct assessment items from several nationally normed early childhood instruments, along with teacher reports, parent reports, and observation, to assess numerous cognitive and socioemotional outcomes. It follows children from their Head Start experiences through kindergarten and through the 1997 cohort into first grade (U.S. Department of Health and Human Services, Administration for Children and Families, 2006a, available: http://www.acf.hhs.gov/programs/opre/hs/faces/index.html).

[2]From Thomas Schultz via personal communication with committee member Harriet Egertson.

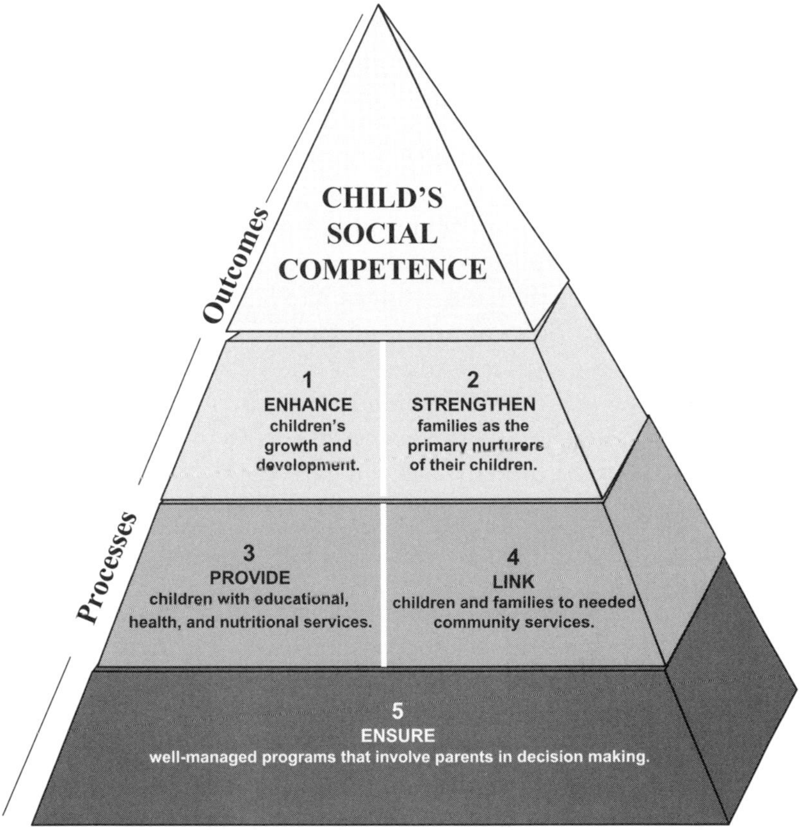


**FIGURE 3-1** Head Start Program performance measures conceptual framework.
SOURCE: U.S. Department of Health and Human Services, Administration for Children and Families (2006).

munities."[3] The eight general domains in the final document—language development, literacy, mathematics, science, creative arts, social and emotional development, approaches to learning, and physical health and development—were divided further into 27 domain elements, and 100 examples of more specific indicators of children's skills, abilities, knowledge, and behaviors considered to be important for school success (U.S. Department of Health and

[3]From S.A. Andersen via personal communication with committee member Harriet Egertson.

Human Services, Administration for Children and Families, 2003). Among the 100 indicators were 13 specific, legislatively mandated domain elements or indicators in various language, literacy, and numeracy skills. Two indicators are specific to the desired outcomes for young children learning English.

The framework was clearly intended to provide guidance for ongoing child assessment and program improvement efforts. Several caveats are specified in the introduction: the framework is intended to focus on children ages 3 to 5 rather than younger children and to guide local programs in selecting, developing, or adapting an assessment instrument or set of assessment tools.

The framework is not intended to be an exhaustive list of everything a child should know or be able to do by the end of preschool or to be used directly as a checklist for assessing children. There is no mention of its relationship to curriculum development. The introduction further attempts to broaden practitioner understanding of the use of the framework: "Information on children's progress on the Domains, Domain Elements and Indicators can be obtained from multiple sources, such as teacher observations, analysis of samples of children's work and performance, parent reports, or direct assessment of children. Head Start assessment practices should reflect the assumption that children demonstrate progress over time in development and learning on a developmental continuum, in forms such as increasing frequency of a behavior or ability; increasing breadth or depth of knowledge and understanding; or increasing proficiency or independence in exercising a skill or ability" (U.S. Department of Health and Human Services, Administration for Children and Families, 2000).

## GOOD START, GROW SMART INITIATIVE

The next step in the federal effort to prepare children to succeed in school with improved Head Start programs came in 2002. President George W. Bush mandated the Good Start, Grow Smart initiative to help states and local communities strengthen early learning for young children. As described in the executive summary of the initiative, President Bush directed the Department of Health and Human Services (HHS) to develop a strategy for assessing the standards of learning in early literacy, language, and numeracy skills in every Head Start center. Every local program was required to assess all children between the ages of 3 and 5 on these indicators at the beginning, middle, and end of each year and to analyze the assessment data on the progress and accomplishments of all enrolled children. Federal program monitoring teams were to conduct onsite reviews of each program's implementation of these requirements.

HHS was also directed to design a national reporting system to collect data from every local program. This system, combined with ongoing Head Start research and onsite program monitoring reviews, was envisioned as a source of comprehensive information on local program effectiveness. Local program data would be used to target new efforts in staff training and program improvement to enhance the capacity of Head Start to increase children's early literacy and school readiness. In addition, data on whether a program is successfully teaching standards of learning would be used in HHS evaluations of local Head Start agency contracts (White House, 2002).

## HEAD START NATIONAL REPORTING SYSTEM

The Administration for Children and Families (ACF) responded to the mandate of the Good Start, Grow Smart initiative to assess children's progress against uniform national standards by developing the National Reporting System (NRS), an instrument to be used to assess all 4- and 5-year-olds in Head Start.

The NRS was developed by a contractor, Westat, on an accelerated schedule. Work began in August 2002. Westat recruited a Technical Work Group of experts in child development, assessment, measurement, and program evaluation as advisers and also used focus groups and other methods to gather information and plan the NRS. After a field test in spring 2003, ACF approved a 15-minute assessment battery, trained Head Start program personnel as assessors, and implemented the NRS for the first time in fall 2003.

The NRS in its original form assessed skills in four areas: (1) comprehension of spoken English, tested with a "language screener," (2) vocabulary, (3) letter naming, and (4) early mathematical skills. Westat and its advisers did not include other domains because of the difficulty in finding high-quality instruments that would meet NRS requirements. Most of the items in the NRS battery were taken from existing assessment instruments that had been used in Head Start research or in local Head Start assessment programs.

A Spanish-language version of the assessment was developed as well. In the first year of implementation, it was administered after the English version to children whose home language was Spanish and who passed a Spanish language screener. Thus all children were assessed in English or Spanish only if they had passed the screener for that language.

The NRS aroused much concern on the part of some early childhood experts.[4] More than 200 educators, researchers, and practitioners signed letters to Congress in early 2003 laying out their concerns about the NRS, along with some suggested ways to improve it. The letters ended with the following words: "If we can move ahead on adopting a matrix sampling design for the proposed Reporting System; if we can ensure that the System is composed of subtests that are reliable, valid, and fair; and if we can have adequate time to learn how to mount this historically largest-ever effort to test young children without creating chaos and confusion, then we will have created a system that has a chance of assisting young, at-risk children" (Meisels et al., 2003).

In May 2005, the Government Accountability Office (GAO) released a report on the first year of implementation of the NRS (U.S. Government Accountability Office, 2005). In it, the GAO identified several weaknesses in the system and its implementation, noting: "Currently, results from the first year of the NRS are of limited value for accountability purposes because the Head Start Bureau has not shown that the NRS meets professional standards for such uses, namely that (1) the NRS provides reli-

---

[4]Among the other criticisms of the NRS was dissatisfaction with the omission of any measure of socioemotional development. A socioemotional component, based on teacher observations over a 1-month period, was added to the NRS as of the fall 2006 administration. For that administration, teachers were asked to assess only children who had been in the program for at least 4 weeks. It included items asking the teacher to report on approaches to learning, cooperative classroom behavior, relations with other children, and behavior problems (U.S. Department of Health and Human Services, Administration for Children and Families, 2006b).

able information on children's progress during the Head Start program year, especially for Spanish-speaking children, and (2) its results are valid measures of the learning that takes place" (U.S. Government Accountability Office, 2005, "Highlights").

The American Educational Research Association, along with a smaller group of experts, went on record with their reservations about the NRS later in 2005, when legislation was under consideration to suspend its implementation (American Educational Research Association, 2005; Yoshikawa and McCartney, 2005, personal communication to U.S. House of Representatives). The National Head Start Association expressed its concerns in a letter to the Office of Management and Budget (OMB) in 2006, after plans for continuing implementation of the NRS were submitted for OMB clearance. Believing that the burden of the reporting system on Head Start programs had been underestimated by ACF and that the results to be gained by continuing it did not justify the burden, the National Head Start Association requested that implementation of the NRS be suspended.

Reactions like these were among the factors that led to the congressional request for this National Academies study. The reauthorization of the Head Start program (P.L. 110-134, 2007) was signed into law in December 2007, while the current study was under way. It requires ACF to discontinue administration of the NRS in its current form, directing it to take into account the results of this National Academies report and of other scientific research in any new assessment design, development, and implementation.

At the time of this writing, administration of the NRS has been terminated, and ACF is under a requirement to follow a more rigorous process as it develops new assessment tools for Head Start. Other early childhood programs and funders, including state and local agencies charged with overseeing child development programs, are also working to devise assessments that can serve to improve the provision of services to children and to ensure better outcomes. This committee's challenging task is to provide useful guidance for all these efforts.

# Part II

# Child-Level Outcomes and Measures

The question of what outcomes are worthy of attention is in part one of values rather than an issue to be resolved with empirical evidence. The outcomes of interest vary to some extent as a function of a child's age; it is harder to distinguish domains of functioning in infants and toddlers than older preschoolers, and likewise younger preschoolers are exposed to more similar demands across settings than older preschoolers. In addition, the domains usually assessed for older children are more heavily influenced by the constraints of the traditional school curriculum. In selecting a domain or a measure, it is crucial to start with a well-defined purpose and to explore whether the outcomes and measures chosen are well suited for that specific purpose.

In our efforts to select domains of importance, the committee reviewed three kinds of evidence:

1. Evidence of substantial consensus on the value of a domain, as shown by its recurrence in theories of and research on child development or its inclusion in federal, state, or program standards or other such expressions of policy relevance.
2. Evidence for continuity within a domain over development or that it links to other current or later emerging outcomes of

importance, such as school achievement, life satisfaction, or avoidance of the criminal justice system.

3. Evidence that the domain is a frequent target of investment or intervention and that child performance in it is affected by changed environmental conditions.

None of these by itself settles the matter, and it is not always the case that all three are available, but convergence among them suggests that a domain deserves attention in this report.

In categorizing the domains, for the sake of simplicity we adapt the distinctions adopted by the National Education Goals Panel (Kagan, Moore, and Bredekamp, 1995), since these map onto both the developmental research literature (McCartney and Phillips, 2006; National Research Council and Institute of Medicine, 2000) and state and federal standards and policies. The boundaries between the domains discussed are, we acknowledge, artificial, as is the way constructs are categorized within them. Vocabulary, for example, is categorized here under Language and Literacy, but is also often included in Cognition as it is so directly relevant to performing well in mathematics, science, and other domains of general knowledge. Similarly, some researchers include constructs identified in this report as part of Approaches to Learning in the category of Socioemotional Functioning. Thus, we offer this categorization as a heuristic for discussing constructs and their measurement, not as a grand theory of child development. We differentiate and discuss five domains in the following chapters:

1. physical well-being and motor development,
2. socioemotional development,
3. approaches to learning,
4. language (and emergent literacy), and
5. cognitive skills, including mathematics.

This categorization provides an initial mapping of what might be considered important enough aspects of children's development to deserve systematic scrutiny from pediatricians, early childhood educators, parents, researchers, and policy makers. Some of these domains are better conceptualized and better instrumented than others; language, for example, has long been a target of interest for scholars of early childhood, and thus research-based descriptions, theories, and instruments for language have a long history. Such domains as socioemotional development and approaches to learning, which have come more recently to the center of research and educational interest, are not yet supplied with so many well-tested assessment instruments.

We recognize with regret that our categorization omits entirely domains of potentially great importance to the optimal development of children; there simply was not a basis in theory, research, or practice to include such domains as art, music, creativity, science, or ethics, despite their obvious importance. We emphasize that our omission of them in this discussion should in no way be interpreted as a license to diminish or omit them from the curriculum.

We are interested not just in identifying the domains of importance, but also in summarizing information about the availability of measures that reflect variation and change in these domains (as well as the ideal qualities of measures that might be developed in the future). Thus, we take as further support for the importance of attention to any domain the existence of widely used measures of it, coupled with evidence that those measures can be used reliably and validly.

We divide the treatment of domains and measures into those most commonly used in pediatric versus educational settings, and those most commonly implemented for purposes of screening and diagnosis versus providing instructional guidance, progress monitoring, and evaluation. Although Chapter 4 deals mostly with assessment typically done in the first year of life, we recognize that pediatric assessment continues throughout childhood. Furthermore, although many of the instruments discussed in Chapter 4 are used most widely with older preschoolers, we realize that many infants and toddlers (especially those enrolled in prevention or intervention programs) experience assessment that is more "educational" in nature.

In Chapter 5, we turn to a justification of the five domains. While it may be obvious that those domains should include the developmentally and educationally relevant ones of physical well-being, language and literacy, mathematics, and socioemotional development, a closer examination of each of these domains reveals considerable internal complexity, as well as some controversy about the actual subskills of greatest importance in those domains.

In Chapter 6, we turn from child measures to review measures that reflect aspects of the context in which young children spend their time. These context measures are, we argue, as important as the child-specific measures, because a child's score on any measured outcome cannot be interpreted without knowing something about the familial and educational contexts in which that child has developed and the opportunities to learn those contexts have provided. Measures of context can also serve as interim markers of program quality for both formative and summative assessments.

# 4

# Screening Young Children

In this chapter we review procedures for the screening of young children for both health-related and developmental purposes. We discuss the uses of assessment for infants and toddlers and the contexts in which they are assessed. We describe various screens performed on infants and toddlers to detect possible physiological, sensorineural, (micro)nutritional, and environmental threats to healthy development, and then we review assessments of developmental status and their use for screening purposes. We discuss two sorts of challenges to effective screening: the difficulties of assessing very young children and the societal conditions that need to be in place. Finally, we present a set of summary tables of some of the assessment instruments available for use with children age 3 years and younger.

We realize that this review is not exhaustive. We have focused on screening for conditions that have implications for educational outcomes, in line with our charge, the primary audience for this report, and acknowledging the limitations on the committee's resources. The issues central to the committee's charge pertain chiefly to instruments used with children in early childhood care and educational programs, so our major focus was on the preschool age group, which forms the majority of the children served by these programs. For the same reasons, we have focused our discussion here on screening rather than on in-depth diagnostic assessment for infants and toddlers, although we do list widely used diagnostic instruments in our tables. The diagnostic instruments are most often used by specialists after screening-based referral. In lieu of more extensive discussion, we provide references to recent reviews of infant and toddler instruments in which more detailed information can be found.

## ASSESSING INFANTS AND TODDLERS

The traditional model for assessment of infants in the first several months of life was primarily medical. It focused on using assessments for pediatric appraisal of normative physical and neuromotor development. Attention to behavioral and psychosocial factors was secondary, although most pediatricians acknowledged the importance of developmental factors over those of a purely physical or biological nature. Over the past half-century, behavioral development has become an integral part of regular pediatric evaluation, and pediatricians routinely provide clinical information on behavioral, cognitive, and psychosocial factors, thus providing a more comprehensive picture of each child's overall growth and development. The integration of biophysical examination with cognitive and socioemotional assessment links early infant assessment with the developmental outcomes of interest in this report.

### Uses of Assessment

The uses and purposes of assessment in the infant-toddler period determine to some extent the domains assessed. One source suggests four purposes of infant assessment (Wyly, 1997):

1. to identify infants who may be at risk for developmental delay,
2. to diagnose the presence and extent of developmental problems,
3. to identify an infant's specific abilities and skills, and
4. to determine appropriate intervention strategies.

This list does not include many purposes typical of assessment for older preschoolers, such as evaluation of intervention strategies, prediction of future competencies, or assessment of skills that are fundamental for success in a classroom environment, such as ease of gaining the child's attention and ability to sustain it. The focus is on the identification of possible developmental problems at an early age—in part, we argue, because of the relatively undifferentiated nature of developmental organization in early infancy and the associated difficulty of making precise predictions to later abilities. We note also that in spite of wide agreement that screening and monitoring of the development of these youngest children is important, pediatricians still do not fully agree on the most important domains to measure or the best measures to use (McCormick, 2008).

Most of the assessment conducted in this age range is actually screening to identify potential problems, to be followed by more definitive diagnostic assessment. The principles of a good screening program are thus relevant (Wilson and Jungner, 1968):

- a valid and reliable measure,
- acceptability to the population being screened and their parents or guardians,
- facilities to conduct the screening,
- facilities to ensure follow-up and treatment, and
- cost-effectiveness.

## Contexts and Assessment

As noted, assessment of infants and toddlers often takes place in pediatric settings, with screening as a primary goal. Screening may also take place in early childhood education and intervention settings, such as Early Head Start and home visiting programs. Interpreting results from such assessments must take into account the effects of a wide variety of inputs into the child's development, for example, safety of the residence, care practices of parents and other caregivers, exposure to substances that might hamper normal development, and consistency of care settings, as well as information about the infant's state of health and alertness during the assessment.

There is an explicit assumption that child care practices, caregiver stability, and infant-caregiver attachment provide the basis for optimal social and cognitive development. However, for many children, including those under age 3, substantial variability exists in the types, extent, and number of forms of out-of-home care available (Johnson, 2005); this variability may be even greater for children at risk of developmental delay, who may also be eligible to receive community-based early intervention services (Widerstrom, 1999). Understanding the quality of these variable settings, as well as the impact of the child's exposure to different settings, is crucial in interpreting child-based outcomes.

Because of the variety of the settings in which infants and toddlers are cared for, the equivalent of the older child's classroom as a place for administering developmental assessments is available only for the minority of children now reached by infant and toddler intervention and education programs like Early Head Start. However, because the vast majority of children under age 4 are monitored by pediatricians or family practitioners (Freed, Nahra, and Wheeler, 2004) and regular developmental assessment is recommended for well-child care, the pediatric setting thus becomes the most likely site for infant and toddler screening. This fact has implications for the training of pediatric personnel, for the design of organized data systems useful in ensuring that all children are screened for developmental problems, and for an integrated service delivery system that spans medical and educational settings.

## ASSESSING THREATS TO NORMATIVE DEVELOPMENT

We focus here on threats that are susceptible to prevention or amenable to postnatal intervention. There is a much longer list of factors associated with increased risk to normative development, ranging from child-specific (low birth weight, prematurity) to societal (poverty) factors; the ones discussed here are merely a selection.

### Genetic/Metabolic Screening

Currently, every newborn in the United States is screened at birth for certain genetic conditions and metabolic disorders, although the number of conditions varies by state (Kaye and Committee on Genetics, 2006; Lloyd-Puryear et al., 2007). Many of these conditions result in significant nervous system damage, leading to severe developmental delays, which early treatment may prevent or ameliorate (Kaye and Committee on Genetics, 2006). In the past, such screening depended on chemical analyses of a spot of blood taken at the time of discharge from the hospital nursery, limiting the number of conditions for which screening could be done. More recently, the use of tandem mass spectrometry (MS/MS) has greatly expanded the number of conditions for which screening is possible (Schulze, 2003). Although this technology is expensive to implement, its use has been argued to be very cost-effective (Carroll and Downs, 2005). Moreover, since neonatal metabolic screening has been so well incorporated into care following birth, it is generally well accepted by both providers and parents.

Estimating the effect of newborn genetic/metabolic screening is made difficult by several factors (Botkin, 2004; Kaye and Committee on Genetics, 2006). First, when newborn screening programs were initiated, the assumption was that an affected gene led to disease. Advances in modern genetics have revealed that many mutations may occur in a single gene, not all of them leading to significant disease, and it often is unclear whether treatment is needed. Second, the expanded MS/MS techniques reveal biochemical abnormalities that may or may not be associated with specific disease states, so the natural history of some of these abnormalities is unknown. Infant maturation may affect detection; for example, congenital hypothyroidism may be difficult to detect in preterm infants. Moreover, these tests, while having some power of detection, are not a proxy for functional outcomes related to behavior. The prevention of developmental disability requires a system of detection, validation, and treatment, and the treatments may be onerous, thereby affecting compliance. Finally, many more infants test positive on the screening tests than have the disease, and assessing these infants adds to the costs without preventing disability. In addition to the costs, simply identifying the infants who test falsely positive may have unintended consequences on their development (Fisher and Welch, 1999; Newman, Browner, and Hulley, 1990). Despite these concerns, neonatal metabolic screening has proven to be an effective screening process.

## Newborn Hearing Screening

Most states have introduced neonatal screening for congenital hearing loss (Kaye and Committee on Genetics, 2006). Such screening has been made possible by the development of relatively portable, computerized equipment. One approach, automated auditory brainstem response, a variant on electroencephalography, detects within 10 milliseconds the speed and amplitude of 5-7 component waves from the auditory nerve through structures along the auditory pathway in response to specific sounds. The screening test consists of soft clicks delivered through earphones and the detection of an auditory brainstem response through electrodes on the infant's forehead. Another approach, otoacoustic emissions, involves using a tiny microphone to detect the sounds made by the outer hair cells of the cochlea (National Center for Hearing Assessment and Management, 2007).

Proponents argue that children with hearing loss who receive intensive early intervention do better on school performance measures and have improved receptive language and less developmental delay (Blake and Hall, 1990; Moeller, 2000; Yoshinaga-Itano et al., 1998). However, unlike genetic/metabolic screening, in which specimens are sent to a central laboratory, offering greater control over technical quality, newborn hearing screening is conducted in the newborn nursery by a variety of personnel using a variety of protocols (Kaye and Committee on Genetics, 2006). The evidence does not appear to favor one protocol over another, and some hearing-impaired infants are still being missed (Gravel et al., 1999). Thus, a 2001 review of newborn hearing screening by the U.S. Preventive Services Task Force concluded that the evidence at that time was incomplete as to the benefit of newborn hearing screening, but an updated review is in progress (U.S. Preventive Services Task Force, 2001).

## Vision Screening

Vision screening is a recurrent and routine part of the pediatric physical examination. Early assessments focus on ensuring that there is a clear pathway from the front of the eye to the retina, where images are received; that the connection between the retina and the relevant part of the brain is intact, indicated by pupillary responses to light; and that the eyes move in a coordinated fashion. Between ages 2 and 4 years, it becomes possible to test for visual acuity—that is, the size of objects that can be seen at certain distances (American Academy of Pediatrics, 1996).[1] The goal of these procedures is to reduce poor vision or risk factors that lead to abnormal visual development. Recent evidence supports the effectiveness of intensive screening for the reduction of amblyopia and improved visual acuity. The U.S. Preventive Services Task Force concluded that the routine screening currently done has not been shown to be effective, although the potential benefit outweighed the minimal risk of the screening (U.S. Preventive Services Task Force, 2004).

### Iron Deficiency Screening

A lengthy literature addresses the effect of nutritional deficiency and child development (Grantham-McGregor, 1984). Since poor nutrition and micronutrient deficiency are more likely in the context of poverty and ill health, disentangling the effect of specific nutritional deficiencies on development is sometimes difficult. However, evidence from developing and industrialized countries supports a relation between iron deficiency and poorer socioemotional, sensorimotor, and cognitive development and school performance (Lozoff et al., 2000, 2003). Recommendations for screening for iron deficiency are consistent with this body of research (American Academy of Pediatrics, 2003). However, substantial questions about the specificity of using blood hemoglobin levels to assess the presence of iron deficiency led the U.S. Preventive Services Task Force to conclude that the evidence is insufficient to recommend for or against such screening (U.S. Preventive Services Task Force, 2006).

---

[1] Acuity tests, such as Teller Acuity Cards, are available for infants and toddlers, and they can be useful for at-risk (e.g., premature) infants, but they are not suitable for general screening and good predictive validity has not been demonstrated (National Research Council, 2002).

### Lead Screening

Lead absorbed from the environment has long been recognized as a neurotoxicant, and major efforts have been undertaken to reduce environmental lead (Grandjean and Landrigan, 2006). The success of these efforts has led to a sharp decline in the blood lead levels of children in America: as of 2006, only slightly more than 1 percent had blood lead levels above the cutoff of 10 micrograms/deciliter (Centers for Disease Control and Prevention, 2007). Nonetheless, certain populations, such as minority children and those living in older housing stock, remain at risk, and thus a targeted screening strategy has been recommended by the American Academy of Pediatrics (2005). Several studies have reported that children with low-level prenatal lead exposure (< 10 mg/dl) have intellectual deficits as measured by standard IQ tests (Banks, Ferrittee, and Shucard, 1997; Lanphear et al., 2000, 2002; Needleman and Gatsonis, 1990) reflected in poorer performance on specific items on the Neonatal Behavioral Assessment Scale (Brazelton and Nugent, 1995; Emory et al., 1999) and on infant intelligence at age 7 months (Emory et al., 2003; Shepherd and Fagan, 1981). The study by Emory et al. (2003) characterized the effects found as lowered optimal performance rather than an increase in impaired performance across the board.

## DEVELOPMENTAL ASSESSMENT

### Newborns

Developmental assessments provide useful information about overall physiological status and risk. Neurodevelopmental examinations initially focused on neurological reflexes and postural reactions that can be elicited in the newborn, which emerge and disappear within fairly specific time periods, as a means of assessing central nervous system integrity, especially early signs of cerebral palsy (Zafeieriou, 2003). Primitive reflexes are mediated by the brainstem and consist of complex, automatic movement patterns that emerge from 25 weeks of gestation and disappear by age 6 months. Postural reactions are infant responses to being held in different standardized positions and probably reflect more complex stimuli, such as those from joints, muscles, and other proprioceptors. Persistence of primitive reflexes and postural reactions or asymmetry in response tend to suggest central nervous system problems. In his review, however, Zafeieriou (2003) notes that there is considerable controversy about which reflexes or reactions, or combination thereof, provide the best clinical prediction. It should be noted that the major outcome being predicted is cerebral palsy.

More recently, neurodevelopmental assessment has also focused on behavioral attributes of the infant, particularly as they reflect organizational state and the ability to interact with the environment. The premise of this approach is that the infant is an active learner from birth and that his or her ability to change states or control his or her state in response to internal and external stimuli facilitates that learning. The Neonatal Behavioral Assessment Scale (NBAS) evaluates the self-regulatory capacity of the newborn infant to achieve two sleep states, two awake states, and one distress state. Within states, the infant may modify his or her response to external or internal stimuli by either habituating (i.e., not responding to a stimulus) or processing information from various sensory inputs (Tronick, 1987). The items on the NBAS cluster into seven areas: habituation, motor performance (tone and maturity), range of state, regulation of state, autonomic regulation, and reflexes (Tronick, 1987). The NBAS relies on well-trained examiners, and it is unclear to what extent variations in examiner ability influence its predictive validity.

The NBAS has been used to assess the effects of a variety of prenatal exposures, including obstetric medications, recreational drug use, and environmental toxins (Tronick, 1987). It has proven sensitive to normal and abnormal variations in fetal responses to labor (Emory, Walker, and Cruz, 1982), birth weight difference independent of gestational age (Emory and Walker, 1982), and clinical conditions with known neurological and neurobehavioral consequences (Emory, Tynan, and Davé, 1989). The NBAS is also used as a tool to educate parents about the skills of their newborn infants and to improve infant-parent interactions (Beeghly et al., 1995). A meta-analysis by Das Eiden and Reifman (1996) concluded that interventions using this scale during the neonatal period have a small to moderate positive effect on the quality of later parenting.

Using the model of the NBAS, Als et al. (2005) have developed the Assessment of Preterm Infants' Behavior (APIB). The scale assesses what are theorized to be five interacting systems of functioning: autonomic, motor, state organization, attention, and self-regulation. Like the NBAS, the APIB forms the basis of an intervention, the Newborn Individualized Development Care and Assessment Program, intended to improve the developmental outcomes of preterm infants by teaching caregivers in the neonatal intensive care unit how to interact more sensitively with the infant. If the intervention improves performance on the APIB and leads to better long-term outcomes in early childhood, then one might argue that the APIB has predictive validity, and Als et al. (2003) have argued for such an effect. However, a recent meta-analysis of individualized developmental interventions in the neonatal intensive care unit suggests that the data do not support this argument (Jacobs, Sokol, and Ohlsson, 2002).

### Infants and Toddlers

Developmental assessment of infants and toddlers occurs routinely in medical care settings and is carried out by a variety of people; some children receive this service through infant-toddler care/education/intervention programs. In view of the time pressures in primary care settings, the approach has been to rely on brief screening instruments, with more complete assessments of children who do not seem to be developing at the usual pace. Since most young children are monitored by pediatricians or other primary medical care personnel, it seems reasonable to use the clinical guidelines from the American Academy of Pediatrics (American Academy of Pediatrics, Committee on Children with Disabilities, 2001; American Academy of Pediatrics, Council on Children With Disabilities, 2006) as a template for this process.

The first step is developmental surveillance performed as part of the regular well-child visit. Surveillance is considered to include "eliciting and attending to the parents' concerns, documenting and maintaining a developmental history, making accurate observations of the child, identifying risk and protective factors, and . . . documenting the process and findings" (American Academy of Pediatrics, Council on Children with Disabilities, 2006). If developmental concerns are identified or the visit occurs at 9, 18, or 30 months, then a more structured developmental screen is recommended, and several examples are provided. If the screening results are positive, then the child should be referred for formal developmental assessment and early intervention services.

There are three general types of infant and toddler developmental assessments (see Appendix Tables 4-1 through 4-7 for some examples). First, screening tests may take the form of questionnaires for the primary caregiver about the child's activities, either soliciting the achievement of specific developmental milestones (smiling, walking, specific words) (Glascoe, Martin, and Humphrey, 1990) or eliciting more general assessments of child development (Glascoe, 2003). Second, developmental assessment may take the form of observations of child activities on a limited number of items. No matter which of these approaches is used initially, any child found to have developmental difficulties requires access to the third type, a more refined assessment with a professionally administered developmental tool.

The large number of available assessment instruments has been summarized in several publications (Buros Institute of Mental Measurements, 2007; Child Trends, 2004; Glascoe, 2003, 2005; Glascoe et al., 1990; Mathematica Policy Research, 2003). The website (http://www.dbpeds.org) of the American Academy of Pediatrics, in the section on Developmental and Behavioral Pediatrics, provides information on developmental screening and assessment. The Educational Testing Service also maintains an online catalog of instruments (http://sydneyplus.ets.org/search.asp?). The National Institute for Early Education Research (NIEER) has a similar database (http://nieer.org/assessment/). A new document from the National Early Childhood Technical Assistance Center covers instruments with a focus on social and emotional measures. Appendix D provides more information on these sources for detailed descriptions of instruments.

The instruments tend to cover similar domains of development, such as general cognitive skills; language, motor, and socioemotional development; and functional abilities appropriate to the age of the child. Appendix Tables 4-1 through 4-7 list some of the available instruments. Each table identifies the domain assessed, the type of instrument (usually screening or diagnostic), and the method by which data are gathered: caregiver report, direct observation of the child, or both methods.

The tables are *not* meant as an endorsement of any instruments, but rather as a way to categorize instruments that are frequently used and to lead the reader to references, like those listed above, that provide more detailed information on each.

## CHALLENGES IN EFFECTIVE INFANT SCREENING

There are two sets of challenges to be faced in generating an optimal system of infant assessment for screening purposes. The first set has to do with the inherent difficulty of assessing very young children reliably and validly, and the second with the many societal conditions that need to be in place to ensure effective infant assessment and use of infant assessment information

### The Difficulty of Assessing Young Children

Very young children are hard to assess reliably and validly because of the relatively undifferentiated nature of their capabilities. Infants are less differentiated than older children—that is, children express their developmental status in increasingly differentiated ways as they mature (National Research Council and Institute of Medicine, 2000). Moreover, the environment in which abilities are expressed changes drastically from infancy to preschool and beyond, thus requiring changes in the child's adaptive capacity as well.

Young children also show enormous variability within and across individuals, reflecting the emerging differentiation of functional systems. This developmental state gradually gives way in later childhood to narrower windows of performance considered to be "within normal limits." Embedded in this concept of "normal limits" is an expectation that, as children mature, their behavior will conform to the increasingly stringent standards and expectations associated with social and academic success.

In infancy, biological homeostasis, autonomic regulation, and organizational properties of behavioral development are important indicators. These might be informally assessed by observing how long it takes for an infant to calm down after a stressful event, such as an injection; whether an infant turns away from highly stimulating events before becoming overexcited; or whether a 14-month-old turns to a caregiver when confronted by an unfamiliar or frightening stimulus. By the time a child reaches age 2 years, autonomic regulation is typically under control, so the developmental challenges associated with gross and fine motor control, receptive and early expressive communication skills, and socioemotional regulation of affective states are now more important and more susceptible to assessment. By age 5, the child's major developmental challenges include expressive language and social communication skills, affect regulation in the context of broader social and peer relations, and cognitive maturation commensurate with instruction in a formal educational setting.

The child's expanding repertoire of behavioral and social abilities, including linguistic communication skills, opens up more options for assessment during the toddler years. Assessing infants permits only a relatively global appraisal of level of functioning. Infant assessment is therefore focused on optimal performance and the testing of limits more than on assessing whether the infant can pass a minimum threshold of performance in any particular domain. For infants even more than older children, optimal performance is dependent on state of arousal.

For infants and toddlers as for older preschoolers, effective assessment of behavioral functioning presupposes that the child attends to the relevant information. If the child is not attending, assessment results are typically viewed as invalid. The ability to sustain attention for information-processing purposes can itself be assessed from birth through age 5.

Prediction of later outcomes would be much easier if developmental assessments used with infants had a one-to-one correspondence to measures taken later. Under such circumstances, the timing of early developmental milestones—such as when the child sits unassisted, begins to grasp objects, crawl, babble, and declare wants and intentions—would lead to accurate predictions of later walking, handedness, speech development, and emotion regulation. There is no practical or reliable measure of any specific domain in early infancy that gives a precise prediction about the child's performance in that domain several years later; in part this fact reflects the enormous plasticity of the developing child and susceptibility to environmental influences. Thus, though screening measures of infant functioning can be very important in identifying the need for further diagnostic assessment to reveal conditions that represent risk for poor performance later on, as well as in allowing early access to prevention or intervention, assessment for purposes of tracking development or predicting later outcomes is less likely to be useful.

### Conditions Required for Effective Screening

A second set of challenges to effective screening arises from the complexity of putting together the societal conditions required to do it well. Several problems limit the potential usefulness of the current system for infant and toddler developmental screening. First, there are concerns about the validity of the instruments themselves. The sample sizes on which many tests were validated may be insufficient to provide robust estimates of their sensitivity—that is, their ability to identify those affected—and specificity—the ability to avoid identifying those not affected (Camp, 2007). Sensitivity may be further affected when the reference test is given to all who score in the abnormal range but to only a sample of those in the normal range. Some screening tests have used reference tests with outdated norms, resulting in inflated scores. In addition, several have procedural problems that could lead to biased results, and often the reported results do not indicate the predictive validity (Camp, 2007).

A second issue is that responsibilities for screening are dispersed across individuals and settings, and that a standard procedure for administering screenings has not been established. Thus, the screening assessments may not be administered and, if they are, may not provide comparable information across providers. A recent assessment of the quality of pediatric ambulatory care revealed that children received fewer than half of the recommended procedures and that screening procedures were particularly unlikely to be performed (Mangione-Smith et al., 2007). These results parallel those for specific screening tests (Biondich et al., 2006; Wasserman, Croft, and Brotherton, 1992). Clearly, if administration procedures are to be standardized and well implemented, medical and education practitioners working with infants and young children need training and support in the appropriate procedures.

Finally, the effectiveness of screening may be further limited by the fact that the system of access to screening settings and of response to abnormalities found may be as diffuse and unstandardized as the assessment process itself. Unlike the classroom setting, in which more standardized and local approaches to developmental and learning problems may be taken, response to abnormalities of development in infants, toddlers, and older preschoolers not already enrolled in intervention programs typically requires referral to other services for diagnosis and management. In part, this variability in response reflects the diversity of state and other policies regarding young children. This means that some infants and toddlers are not screened, and that those who are identified as requiring diagnostic assessments and other services may not receive them. As noted above, much of the early screening is accomplished in health care settings, and access to care is heavily dependent on having health insurance. Children without health insurance are more likely to have low family income, to come from minority families, to use medical care less intensely, and to be referred to other settings for services (Simpson et al., 2005). Even with insurance, access to some services is more difficult than others. Although the Individuals with Disabilities Education Act does mandate testing for all children suspected of developmental disability or delay and requires the provision of appropriate services to children so identified, there remains considerable local variation in the capacity to respond to this mandate. A recent chapter by Gilliam, Meisels, and Mayes (2005) proposes a system of screening and surveillance that uses many available community resources to provide a more integrated screening, referral, and assessment system.

Finally, even if the current assessment of infant and toddler development were more universally effective, fitting well into a larger system and building continuity with the assessment of slightly older preschoolers would improve its usefulness. The focus of infant-toddler assessment procedures is primarily on monitoring development and risks to development for purposes of ensuring adequate progress and to rule out health-related challenges to normal development. For example, the vision examinations conducted by health care providers may focus less on the visual acuity needed for classroom work and more on detecting opacities in the eye (e.g., cataracts) that may hamper visual development or muscle imbalances that might signal other neurological problems. Likewise, screening for iron deficiency should attend to the cognitive deficits associated with it as much as evaluating the child's nutritional status and addressing questions about the production and destruction of red blood cells and potential covert blood loss.

## CONCLUSION

Assessment of important behavioral and physiological outcomes for infants and toddlers is an increasing focus of pediatricians, primary medical care providers, and providers of care and education to infants and toddlers. Ideally, these individuals recognize the full array of information—child performance, caregiver report, observation—that can be used and are well trained to collect information systematically. While screening for risk is a key goal of assessment during this developmental period, an equally important goal is tracking well-child developmental indicators and focusing on what children can do as well as what they have problems with. For children with disabilities that have already been identified in this early period, a focus on functional capacities may be more important than a delineation of limitations. Although screening for risk and assessment for well-child functioning are widely practiced, the system of infant and toddler assessment needs to be expanded in a number of ways.

First, it is important that children living in poverty and children from cultural and language-minority groups are included in these assessments. Second, the system linking assessment results to other resources—referrals, follow-up, access to services—is at this time far from seamless. Identifying risk or disability in a young child does little good if no provisions have been made to remedy or mediate the problem, to help caregivers understand and address it, or to link the early available information to decisions about interventions, schooling, and ongoing attention. We raise again the importance of thinking systematically if the potential of assessment to improve child learning and welfare is to be realized.

# APPENDIX TABLES: SUMMARY OF ASSESSMENT INSTRUMENTS FOR CHILDREN 0-3 YEARS OF AGE

**APPENDIX TABLE 4-1** Domain: Cognition

| | Data-Gathering Method | | |
|---|---|---|---|
| **Instrument Type** | **Caregiver Report** | **Observation** | **Mixed/Both** |
| **Screening** | Ages and Stages[a] | Developmental Indicators for Assessment of Learning-Revised | Battelle Developmental Inventory Screening Test[a] |
| | Infant Development Inventory | Slosson Intelligence Test | Developmental Profile-II |
| | NCHS/NLSY Questionnaire (U.S. Department of Health and Human Services, National Center for Health Statistics, 1981) | Lexington Developmental Scales[a] | Preschool Screening System |
| | Parents' Evaluation of Developmental Status[a] | Bayley Infant Neurodevelopmental Screener (BINS) (Aylward, 1995) | Denver Developmental Screening Test II[a] |
| | Infant Monitoring System[a] | | Brigance Screens |
| | Denver Prescreening Developmental Questionnaire[a] | | Fagan Test of Infant Intelligence |

*continued*

**APPENDIX TABLE 4-1** Continued

| | Data-Gathering Method | | |
|---|---|---|---|
| **Instrument Type** | **Caregiver Report** | **Observation** | **Mixed/Both** |
| | Child Development Inventory and Child Development Review-Parent Questionnaire (Ireton, 1992) | | |
| | Parents/Evaluation of Developmental Status (PEDS)[a] | | |
| | Capute Scales (CAT/CLAMS) (Voigt et al., 2003) | | |
| **Diagnostic** | | Bayley Scales of Infant Development, Third ed. | |
| | | McCarthy Scales of Children's Ability | |
| | | Mullen Scales of Early Learning | |

[a]Includes questions on behavioral issues or personal-social development.

**APPENDIX TABLE 4-2** Domain: Language

| | Data-Gathering Method | | |
|---|---|---|---|
| **Instrument Type** | **Caregiver Report** | **Observation** | **Mixed/Both** |
| **Screening** | The Quick Test | Peabody Picture Vocabulary Test | |
| | Communication and Symbolic Behavior Scales (Wetherby and Prizant, 2002) | Expressive One-Word Picture Vocabulary Test | |
| | Early Language Milestone Scale (Coplan, 1993) | | |
| **Diagnostic** | Receptive Expressive Emergent Language Scale (REEL)[a] | Reynell Developmental Language Scales | Sequenced Inventory of Communication Development |
| | MacArthur-Bates Communicative Development Inventories | Preschool Language Scale | |
| | | Test of Early Language Development | |

[a]Requires trained interviewer/observer.

**APPENDIX TABLE 4-3** Domain: Motor

| | Data-Gathering Method | | |
|---|---|---|---|
| **Instrument Type** | **Caregiver Report** | **Observation** | **Mixed/Both** |
| **Screening** | Early Motor Pattern Profile (EMPP) (Morgan and Aldag, 1996) | | |
| | Motor Quotient (Capute and Shapiro, 1985) | | |
| **Diagnostic** | | Bayley Scales of Infant Development, Third ed. (see above) | |
| | | Movement Assessment of Infants (Chandler, Andrews, and Swanson, 1980) | |
| | | Peabody Developmental Motor Scales (Folio and Fewell, 1983) | |
| | | Alberta Infant Motor Scale (Piper and Darrah, 1994) | |

**APPENDIX TABLE 4-4** Domain: Social-Emotional

| | Data-Gathering Method | | |
|---|---|---|---|
| Instrument Type | Caregiver Report | Observation | Mixed/Both |
| **General** | Eyberg Child Behavior Inventory | Bayley Scales of Infant Development, Third ed. | Vineland Social-Emotional Maturity Scale[a] |
| | Infant-Toddler Social Emotional Assessment, ITSEA | | |
| | Brief Infant-Toddler Social Emotional Assessment, BITSEA | | |
| | Achenbach System of Empirically Based Assessment | | |
| | Devereux Early Childhood Assessment | | |
| | Temperament and Atypical Behavior Scale (TABS) (Bagnato et al., 1999) | | |
| **Screens for Specific Developmental Disabilities** | Modified Checklist of Autism in Toddlers (Dumont-Mathieu and Fine, 2005) | | |
| | Checklist for Autism in Toddlers (CHAT) (Baird et al., 2000) | | |

*continued*

**APPENDIX TABLE 4-4** Continued

| | Data-Gathering Method | | |
|---|---|---|---|
| **Instrument Type** | **Caregiver Report** | **Observation** | **Mixed/Both** |
| | Pervasive Developmental Disorders Screening Test-II (PDDST-II) (Siegel, 2004) | | |
| | Screening Tool for Autism in Two-Year-Olds (STAT) (Stone, Coonrod, and Ousley, 2000) | | |
| | Social Communication Questionnaire (SCQ) (Rutter, Bailey, and Lord, 2003) | | |

[a]Requires trained interviewer/observer.

**APPENDIX TABLE 4-5** Domain: Function/Activities of Daily Living

| | Data-Gathering Method | | |
|---|---|---|---|
| **Instrument Type** | **Caregiver Report** | **Observation** | **Mixed/Both** |
| **All** | | | Vineland Adaptive Behavior Scale-II[a] |

[a]Requires trained interviewer/observer.

**APPENDIX TABLE 4-6** Domain: Temperament

| | Data-Gathering Method | | |
|---|---|---|---|
| **Instrument Type** | **Caregiver Report** | **Observation** | **Mixed/Both** |
| **All** | Toddler Behavior Assessment Questionnaire (Carey Scales) | | |
| | Children's Behavior Questionnaire (Putnam and Rothbart, 2006) | | |
| | Infant Characteristics Questionnaire (Bates, Freeland, and Lounsbury, 1979) | | |
| | Pictorial Assessment of Temperament (PAT) (Clarke-Stewart et al., 2000) | | |

**APPENDIX TABLE 4-7** Domain: Attachment/Caregiver-Child Interaction

| | **Data-Gathering Method** | | |
|---|---|---|---|
| **Instrument Type** | **Caregiver Report** | **Observation** | **Mixed/Both** |
| **All** | | Ainsworth Strange Situation Procedure<br>Preschool Assessment of Attachment (Teti and Gelfand, 1997)<br>Nursing Child Assessment Satellite Training | |

# 5

# Assessing Learning and Development

Assessments for purposes other than screening and diagnosis have become more and more common for young children. Some of these assessments are conducted to answer questions about the child (e.g., monitoring progress during instruction or intervention). Other assessments are conducted to provide information about classrooms and programs (e.g., to evaluate a specific curriculum or type of program) or society in general (e.g., to describe the school readiness of children entering kindergarten). Many of the assessments widely in use in educational settings are designed primarily to inform instruction by helping classroom personnel specify how children are learning and developing and where they could usefully adapt and adjust their instructional approaches. Thus, the goals of much testing in this later period are more closely related to educational than to medical or public health issues, and the nature of the assessments as well as the domains assessed are modified accordingly.

The greater role of education in these assessments means that the settings for assessing children may be different, and the range of domains toward which assessments are directed is expanded. Assessment that is educationally oriented often takes school-age achievement as the ultimate target and thus is organized into domains that are highly relevant to K-12 schooling (e.g., literacy, science, social studies). Understanding the developmentally relevant conceptualization of these skills for preschool-age children is a task for researchers as well as test developers; nonetheless, it is clear that precursors to academic literacy, mathematics, and general knowledge can be measured long before formal instruction in these domains has commenced.

The domains of relevance to schooling extend well beyond cognition and knowledge. Children being educated or cared for in groups are expected to be able to regulate their emotions and attention; to form social relationships with peers and with nonfamilial adults; to learn from observation, participation, and direct instruction; and increasingly to direct their own learning. All these capacities are crucial if children are going to function well in preschool and child care or in K-12 programs, and promoting these capacities is also a primary goal of adults in group care and educational settings. Thus, assessments of such capacities are seen to reflect not only child skills but also the adequacy of the settings in which children spend their time. In addition, group care and educational settings vary in quality and in design, although state and local guidelines for teacher-child ratios, number of children served, and the preparation required of preschool teachers and caregivers limit the degree of variation to some extent.

Screening and diagnosis remain crucial purposes in assessment of older preschoolers, as well as infants and toddlers. In addition, such purposes as tracking the progress of children with an individualized education program or of groups of children exposed to a particular program or curriculum become particularly salient for older preschoolers. The measures discussed in this chapter are typically more appropriate for progress monitoring or program evaluation than for individual screening or diagnosis. Nonetheless, we recognize that all these domains raise assessment issues for the full range of purposes.

The chapter covers five domains: (1) physical well-being and motor development, (2) social and emotional development, (3) approaches to learning, (4) language and literacy, and (5) cognitive skills, including mathematics as a particular case. These are widely accepted domains differentiated in various policy statements, such as the "all children ready for school" goal of the National Education Goals Panel (Kagan, Moore, and Bredekamp,

1995) and in the analysis of state learning standards by Scott-Little, Kagan, and Frelow (2006). For each of the domains, we first discuss how it is defined and how its internal structure has been delineated. We then present evidence for the importance of the domain: that it is widely mentioned in child achievement standards, that it is a focus of developmental theory and research, or that it relates to other outcomes important in the short or long term. We also consider evidence that the developmental domain is malleable, that is, amenable to change through interventions, since the capacity to change is another source of evidence for the importance of assessing it. We then describe some of the assessment approaches and tools that have been widely used to reflect status or progress in that domain. Appendix Tables 5-1 through 5-7 provide a summary listing of the major instruments discussed here, with a table for each domain. For each table, the first column indicates the subscale or specific domain assessed, and the second through fifth columns list the instruments that offer the relevant subscales, categorized by the measurement method(s) used by each: direct assessment, questionnaire, observation, or interview. Because many useful instruments do not quite fit into the domains we discuss, we have also included a table for general knowledge (sometimes categorized under cognitive skills), and have included science in the table with mathematics.

For more detailed information on instruments, including evaluative reviews, specific age range, time to administer, administrator qualifications required, as well as psychometric information, we have listed and described a variety of print and online instrument compendia and reviews in Appendix D.

## PHYSICAL WELL-BEING AND MOTOR DEVELOPMENT

### Defining the Domain

This domain encompasses issues of health, intactness of sensory systems, growth, and fitness, as well as motor development. Motor development has long been a topic of interest in pediatric and developmental studies, and it also is one of the areas used in screening children for possible developmental problems. The component of this domain attracting particular policy interest recently is fitness, with evidence that increases in obesity and lack of exercise in childhood are coming to constitute public health challenges.

### Evidence of Consensus

Healthy children are a goal of every society, and indicators of health are included in standards promulgated by states as well as in Head Start standards and other documents reflecting policy. Piotrkowski, Botsko, and Matthews (2000) found in a survey of kindergarten teachers that good health was one of the factors perceived to be essential to school readiness. Surprisingly, issues of physical fitness are rarely addressed in state standards items, despite their clear importance to long-term health outcomes. Half of the physical well-being and motor development items cataloged by Scott-Little, Kagan, and Frelow (2005) addressed motor skills, but only 11.5 percent addressed fitness.

Perhaps because physical fitness and health have traditionally been considered of medical rather than educational relevance, they are not richly represented in the measures typically used in developmental assessment. An interest in the general welfare of children, however, dictates more focus on them in ongoing assessment. In particular, levels of childhood obesity constitute a recognized crisis (American Academy of Pediatrics, 2005; Institute of Medicine, 2005). Given the potential influences of early childhood care and education settings (which provide meals and organize physical activities that can influence obesity and fitness) and the evidence that preschool status on these dimensions predicts later health indices (Quattrin et al., 2005; Weiss et al., 2004), more attention is warranted to these indicators as part of developmental assessment. Many general developmental measures (e.g., the Bayley Scales of Infant Development and the Denver II) have subscales reflecting motor development, but greater attention to easily obtained measures of fitness (height, weight, body-mass index) as part of early childhood assessment in care and education settings is clearly merited.

## SOCIAL AND EMOTIONAL DEVELOPMENT

### Defining the Domain

Research on young children's social and emotional development has focused on three broad issues: (1) social competence, which reflects the degree of effectiveness the child has in social interactions with others (Fabes, Gaertner, and Popp, 2006); (2) self-regulation, which involves the modulating thought, affect, and behavior by means of deliberate as well as automated responses (Rothbart, Posner, and Kieras, 2006); and (3) maladjustment, consisting of clusters of symptoms that emerge over time, in more than one context, in more than one relationship, and that may impede the child's ability to adapt and function in the family and the peer group (Campbell, 2006). Although there is general agreement on these three dimensions, different researchers parse the field somewhat differently, with the result that the various measures that have been developed reflect different emphases in defining the domain.

### Importance in Practice and Policy

Although there is a lack of agreement as to how this domain should be subdivided, there is substantial agreement on the importance of the social and emotional development of young children to those working directly with them before and after the transition to formal schooling. In addition, a number of state consensus documents defining what young children should know and be able to do include a strong focus on their social and emotional skills, reflecting a recognition of the importance of this domain among policy makers as well.

Many states have addressed social and emotional development in their early learning guidelines. In reviews of state early learning guidelines, Scott-Little and colleagues conclude that guidelines for preschool-age children focus more on language and cognition than on physical and social and emotional development, whereas guidelines for infants and toddlers are more balanced across domains, with the guidelines for infants focusing especially on social and emotional development (Scott-Little,

Kagan, and Frelow, 2006). California's "Preschool Learning Foundations in Social and Emotional Development for Ages 3 and 4" (http://www.cde.ca.gov/re/pn/fd/documents/preschoollf.pdf) is an excellent example of the development of a consensus document regarding expectations for children's social and emotional skills in the preschool years. Relying heavily on the research on young children's social and emotional development, the document "describes benchmarks for the behavior of 3- and 4-year-olds in central domains of social and emotional development. . . . In focusing on social and emotional foundations of school readiness, a central assumption—well supported by developmental and educational research—is that school readiness consists of social-emotional competencies as well as other cognitive competencies and approaches to learning required for school success" (p. 1). The standards for social and emotional development in California's early learning standards identify the dimensions of self (self-awareness and self-regulation, social and emotional understanding, empathy and caring, and initiative in learning), social interaction (including interactions with familiar adults, interaction with peers, group participation, and cooperation and responsibility) and relationships (attachments to parents, close relationships with teachers and caregivers, and friendships). The perspective that social and emotional development and early learning are closely linked is reflected in the inclusion of "Initiative in Learning" as a component of social and emotional development, involving the child's interest in activities in the classroom, enjoyment of learning and exploring, and confidence in his or her ability to make new discoveries.

## Importance for Later Development

The social and emotional demands of formal schooling on young children differ from those of early childhood settings, and children's skills in this area at school entry are predictors of how well they make the adjustment to the new setting and progress academically (see Bierman and Erath, 2006; Campbell, 2006; Ladd, Herald, and Kochel, 2006; Mashburn and Pianta, 2006; Raver, 2002; Thompson and Raikes, 2007; Vandell, Nenide, and Van Winkle, 2006). Early childhood care and educational settings usually involve a choice of activities for portions of the day, many activities involve small rather than large groups, and children tend to have access to adult caregivers and teachers not only for guidance on activities but also when they are upset or experiencing difficulty with peers. Studies of kindergarten classrooms indicate a shift toward large group activities, which are structured, directed by teachers, and involve less choice. Lower adult-child ratios and more structured activities result in more limited access to adults. Not only do children need to learn to navigate interactions in larger groups and in tasks with more structure, but they also need to form new relationships with peers and teachers.

The domains of socioemotional development and executive function—the cognitive processes used in response to novel stimuli—are of central importance in early childhood, although a final decision about exactly which subskills in this area are most important to measure and most predictive would be somewhat speculative at this point. Nonetheless, providing a full picture of a young child's development or of the impact of a care and educational setting requires attending at least to the measurement of social competence, attention regulation, and behavior problems. Studies in these areas illustrate evidence of linkages between early social and emotional development and behavioral adjustment to school as well as academic performance.

*Social competence*: A series of studies by Ladd and colleagues provides evidence for how different facets of social engagement in the kindergarten classroom combine to predict participation in the classroom and achievement. In one, the researchers concluded that findings were consistent with the hypothesis that "children's classroom participation, particularly the ability to behave in a cooperative/independent manner in the kindergarten milieu, is a powerful precursor of early achievement" (Ladd, Birch, and Buhs, 1999).

The connection between a child's socioemotional characteristics and teacher-child relationships is well established. Teachers report more conflicts with children who exhibit antisocial behaviors, such as interpersonal aggression or tantrums (e.g., Birch and Ladd, 1998; Hamre and Pianta, 2001; Howes, Phillipsen, and Peisner-Feinberg, 2000; Ladd and Burgess, 2001; Ladd, Birch, and

Buhs, 1999; Pianta and Steinberg, 1992; Silver et al., 2005). Closeness, conflict, and dependence have been identified as three features of teacher-child relationships that are important to children's development (Mashburn and Pianta, 2006).

While relationships with teachers as well as peers during the transition to formal schooling appear to be central to positive engagement in school and thereby achievement, positive teacher and peer relations in turn appear to rest at least in part on children's knowledge of emotions and their ability to regulate the expression of their own emotions (Bierman et al., under review; Denham, 2006; Vandell, Nenide, and Van Winkle, 2006).

*Self-regulation*: Recent research on self-regulation acknowledges that some aspects of it involve emotion (e.g., modulation in the expression of negative emotions) and behavior (e.g., inhibition of aggressive impulses), and other aspects focus more on attentional and cognitive skills (e.g., the ability to maintain a set of instructions actively in working memory over time and despite distractions, taking the perspective of another, switching attention as task demands change) (Diamond et al., 2007; McClelland et al., 2007; Raver, 2002, 2004).

Socioemotional development is of importance during the early childhood period because it relates to children's capacities to form relationships, both trusting relationships with adults and friendships with peers, and these relationships in turn seem to be related to the speed of learning in early care and educational settings. These markers of positive relations with peers and teachers have implications for children's engagement and participation in the classroom. Children learn to regulate the expression of emotion in a variety of ways, including turning to others with whom they have secure relationships for comfort and support, using external cues, and, increasingly with age, managing their own states of arousal (Thompson and Lagattuta, 2006).

*Behavior problems*: Serious behavior problems are apparent early in some children. Research summarized by Raver (2002) indicates that children with early and serious problems of aggression who are rejected by peers are at elevated risk in terms of poor academic achievement, grade retention, dropping out of school, and eventually delinquency. Raver notes that children who are disruptive tend to get less instruction and positive feedback from teachers, to spend less time on task, to engage less with peers in learning tasks, and to show lower levels of school engagement overall, as reflected in part by lower attendance.

With respect to evidence relating to early social and emotional competencies, two notes of caution are needed. First, social and emotional competencies are worthy developmental goals in their own right, independent of their relationship to academic outcomes. Second, research in this area is not all in accord with the perspective that early social and emotional development predicts more positive academic achievement.

We note that, in a recent study, Duncan and colleagues (2007) carried out coordinated analyses of six major data sets looking at early predictors of later academic achievement. They found that early measures of achievement were strong predictors of later academic achievement, that measures of attention were moderately strong predictors of later achievement, but that measures of early social and emotional development, gleaned from parent and teacher reports, showed no or almost no predictive relationship to later achievement. The findings of this important study clearly differ from those of the reviews and findings summarized earlier. However, as the authors of this article themselves note, "our analysis is focused on behavior during the years just before and at the point of school entry. If some types of socioemotional skills are well established before the preschool years, and unchanging during these years, then we will not be able to detect their effects" (p. 1442). A further issue with this set of analyses is that the extensive set of control variables in the analyses includes many of the documented predictors of early social and emotional development, such as maternal education, family structure, family income, and, in some of the data sets, also parenting and home environment as well as participation in early care and education. This extensive set of controls may have diminished the capacity to detect relationships between early social and emotional development and later achievement. Finally, there was differential attrition in a number of the data sets included in the analyses, with greater attrition among families at greater risk. Selective attrition also works against detecting patterns of relationship between social and emotional development and academic achievement.

In summary, a number of recent reviews summarize evidence

confirming the relation of early social and emotional competencies, self-regulation, and absence of serious behavior problems to early participation in learning activities and to academic achievement. While it is important to note that social and emotional development predicts later academic outcomes, at the same time we insist that children's social and emotional well-being and competencies are worthy developmental goals in their own right, independent of their relationship to academic outcomes.

### Evidence of Malleability

According to a review by Raver (2002), there is substantial evidence from experimental evaluations that it is possible to improve young children's social and emotional development at the point of school entry or earlier, helping them to develop and stay on a positive course in their relationships with teachers and peers and to engage positively in learning activities. While the evidence summarized points to program effects across all the levels of intensity and the setting of the interventions considered (in the classroom, with parents, or both), findings are stronger when interventions engage parents as well as teachers and are more intensive. More recent reviews contribute to understanding the complexity of this domain (Bierman and Erath, 2006; Fabes, Gaertner, and Popp, 2006).

Several recent developments in intervention research on young children's social and emotional development are noteworthy. First, very recent work has focused explicitly on interventions targeting children's self-regulation skills. In recent work by Diamond and colleagues (Diamond et al., 2007), the Tools of the Mind curriculum, which embeds direct instruction in strengthening executive function in play activities and social interactions, was experimentally evaluated in prekindergarten programs in low-income neighborhoods. This intervention takes a Vygotskian approach—that is, it encourages extended dramatic play, teaches children to use self-regulatory private speech, and provides external stimuli to support inhibition. Results showed significant improvements in direct assessments of children's executive function. By the end of the school year, children in classrooms implementing Tools of the Mind did not need help staying on task or redirecting inappropriate behavior. This study provides important evidence that aspects of self-regulation are malleable.

## Measurement Issues

An ongoing challenge in the research on social and emotional development of young children is to forge agreement about specific constructs, measures, and the mapping of constructs to measures (Fabes, Gaertner, and Popp, 2006; Raver, 2002). The internal complexity of the domain is reflected in the fact that different measures parse it differently. The lack of agreement impedes the capacity to look across studies at accumulating patterns of findings (Zaslow et al., 2006).

Another challenge is that some see measures of social and emotional development as reflecting in part the early childhood environment and the teacher-child relationship, rather than as pure measures of the child. For example, a teacher who requires 3-year-olds in an early childhood classroom to sit still for long periods to do seat work is likely to assess many children as inattentive or disruptive (Thompson and Raikes, 2007). Her rating of a child as having behavior problems may actually be a reflection of her inappropriate expectations, rather than a child's enduring behavior problem.

Another measurement challenge is the heavy reliance in this domain on teacher and parent reports. In development are direct assessments of children's behavioral self-regulation (Emotion Matters II Direct assessments developed by Raver and modeled after work by Kochanska and colleagues); of the executive function aspects of self-regulation (the Head to Toe Task described by McClelland and colleagues, 2007); and of the Dots Task from the Directional Stroop Battery and the Flanker Task described by Diamond and colleagues (2007). Further work with these measures may generate important evidence about their reliability and validity, as well as their sensitivity to intervention approaches and their relation to teacher and parent reports and direct observations.

## Testing All Children

Much developmental research has assumed universality of many measures tapping socioemotional processes in child development (Phinney and Landin, 1998). More recently, investigators have begun to challenge this assumption by testing whether measures show a similar or different factor structure and different patterns of predictive validity across groups of children who vary by race, ethnicity, and culture (Knight and Hill, 1998; Mendez, Fantuzzo, and Cicchetti, 2002; Phinney and Landin, 1998; Raver, Gershoff, and Aber, 2007). Measures and constructs should be reviewed carefully for the presence or absence of consistent psychometric properties across groups of black, Hispanic, and European American children. More often than not, measurement equivalence for Asian and Pacific Islander children, American Indian children, and biracial children has been all but ignored (see Chapter 8 for more on assessing special populations).

## Available Measures

Existing measures of socioemotional development address two large groups of constructs: socioemotional functioning and self-regulation. Socioemotional functioning, in turn, can be divided into measures of positive functioning (prosocial behavior, relations with peers, attachment to caregiver, acceptance of authority) and problematic functioning (aggression, resisting authority, loneliness, depression). Self-regulation measures typically tap such domains as delayed gratification, sustained attention, behavioral persistence, and problem-solving skills—measures that may overlap with those classified under "approaches to learning" by some researchers.

A relatively well-articulated inventory of measures that can be used to capture constructs in the socioemotional domain now exists, although approximately half of those measures are newly developed and thus are not yet endowed with high levels of certainty about the full spectrum of psychometric properties. That said, the field has developed enough experience using these measures in experimental and nonexperimental research with low-income preschool-age children that solid estimates of their reliability, predictive validity, and distributional properties exist, as does information about the costs of collecting these assessments and their relative costs and benefits. Appendix Table 5-2 lists many of these measures.

## APPROACHES TO LEARNING

### Defining the Domain

The developmental domain of approaches to learning includes such constructs as showing initiative and curiosity, engagement and persistence, and reasoning and problem-solving skills (U.S. Department of Health and Human Services, Administration for Children and Families, 2003b). These skills are viewed separable from both socioemotional adjustment and overall cognitive skills (Fantuzzo et al., 2007), although it will be clear from the preceding section that the distinction from socioemotional skills is sometimes hard to draw. Approaches to learning are defined as "distinct, observable behaviors that indicate ways children become engaged in classroom interactions and learning activities," according to a recent review (Fantuzzo et al., 2007). Such behaviors are viewed as an essential component of school readiness (National Education Goals Panel, 1997; U.S. Department of Health and Human Services, Administration for Children and Families, 2003b), although they are less understood or researched than other components (Fantuzzo et al., 2007).

### Evidence of Consensus

There is general consensus that children need to be able to engage in classroom activities in order to learn in a classroom setting. The National Education Goals Panel (1997) underscored the importance of such learning behaviors. Subsequently, Head Start included indicators regarding approaches to learning in its Child Outcomes Framework (U.S. Department of Health and Human Services, Administration for Children and Families, 2003a). And 16 states have included indicators in this area in their early learning guidelines. Furthermore, elementary school teachers in the early grades believe that these behaviors are important (Foulks and Morrow, 1989; Lewit and Baker, 1995), claiming that many children, especially from low-income homes, enter kindergarten lacking them (Rimm-Kaufman, Pianta, and Cox, 2000).

## Evidence of Continuity and Associations with Important Outcomes

Aspects of infant behavior, such as giving attention and the ability to sustain attention, appear to show continuity over time and relate to educational outcomes. Learning behaviors, such as persistence and attention in the classroom, have been shown to be related to specific academic skills in early childhood, such as early mathematics and literacy skills, across a number of studies (Fantuzzo, Perry, and McDermott, 2004; Green and Francis, 1988; McDermott, 1984; McWayne, Fantuzzo, and McDermott, 2004), even when measures of emotional adjustment were also considered. Approaches to learning as rated by the kindergarten teacher at entry to school predicted growth in mathematics from kindergarten to third grade in a national sample, the Early Childhood Longitudinal Study-Kindergarten Cohort (ECLS-K) (DiPerna, Lei, and Reid, 2007).

Several studies have found significant associations between young children's learning-related behavior and their academic performance. Normandeau and Guay (1998) reported that first graders' "cognitive self-control" (the ability to plan, evaluate, and regulate problem-solving activities; attend to tasks; persist; resist distraction) was associated with their academic achievement, net of their intellectual skills assessed in kindergarten. Howse et al. (2003) found that teachers' ratings of kindergarteners' (but not second graders') motivation (e.g., "is a self-starter," "likes to do challenging work") predicted concurrent reading achievement, with receptive vocabulary (but not previous reading achievement) held constant.

In a longitudinal study of children from kindergarten through second grade by McClelland, Morrison, and Holmes (2000), teachers' ratings of kindergarten children's work-related skills (compliance with work instructions, memory for instructions, completion of games and activities) were significantly associated with children's academic performance in kindergarten, with IQ controlled. Work-related skills in kindergarten also predicted academic performance at the end of second grade, with kindergarten academic scores controlled. In a more recent study, McClelland, Acock, and Morrison (2006) found that learning-related behavior in kindergarten predicted reading and mathematics scores in sixth grade and growth in reading and mathematics between kindergarten and second grade, but not between second and sixth grades. They controlled for IQ, age, ethnicity, and maternal education. The measure they used was very broad, including social interaction and participation in play activities as well as task behavior (such as working independently and organizing work products). In one of the few other longitudinal studies, Green and Francis (1988) found that learning style (e.g., settles down well at an activity that needs concentration, willing to try on his or her own, copes with something new without getting nervous or upset) in 5- and 6-year-olds predicted reading scores 4 years later, when the children were 9 and 10 years old. The study did not, however, hold constant previous reading scores.

### Evidence from Interventions and Malleability

A number of observational studies have examined the extent to which approaches to learning in the fall predicted emotion regulation and peer play (Fantuzzo et al., 2005), mathematics and literacy skills at the end of the Head Start year (Fantuzzo, Perry, and McDermott, 2004; Fantuzzo et al., 2007), and gains in mathematical skills during the first 4 years of elementary school (DiPerna, Lei, and Reid, 2007).

Efforts to promote children's approaches to learning are inherent in many of the components of center-based education. Specific tests of their effectiveness, however, have been few. As noted above, a recently published experimental study (Diamond et al., 2007) showed effects for the Vygotskian play-based preschool curriculum called Tools of the Mind (Bodrova and Leong, 2001) on aspects of children's executive functioning related both to socioemotional development and to approaches to learning, such as maintaining attention and controlling behavior.

### Testing All Children

Many of the studies that have specifically focused on approaches to learning during early childhood appear to have been conducted in Head Start classrooms, which serve low-income children, including many black children and English language learners.

### Available Measures

Appendix Table 5-3 lists many measures of approaches to learning. The most widely used measures are questionnaires completed by the teacher. The Preschool Learning Behavior Scale (McDermott et al., 2000) asks the teacher about observable learning behaviors of children ages 3- to 5½-year-olds in the classroom context. The Teacher Rating Scale, an adaptation of the Social Skills Rating Scale for the ECLS-K study, includes a scale measuring approaches to learning for 5-year-olds, including items asking about engagement in learning, organization, creativity, and adaptability. These measures show good internal consistency and some content-specific validity, in that they predict academic outcomes even when other teacher ratings of emotional adjustment are also considered. Other measures include observations of behaviors during testing conditions appropriate for children as young as 3 months through entry to kindergarten and specific tasks measuring attention or inhibitory control (see the section on cognitive skills), as well as measures of motivation.

## LANGUAGE AND LITERACY

### Defining the Domain

Development of language and emergent literacy has long been targeted for research, with the result that many assessment procedures have been developed not only for use in research, but also for clinical and educational purposes. The increasing emphasis on school readiness as a target of early childhood programs has motivated the development of formative assessments for various domains of emergent literacy. The domain of language and literacy is complex because of the many component skills that can be assessed and because disagreement persists about how these component skills relate to one another and to long-term outcomes of importance.

The classic approach to child language assessment for purposes of research and diagnosis involves eliciting a sample of child speech, transcribing it, and then analyzing it to generate such indices as amount of talk per minute, variety of words produced, mean length of utterance, correctness of morphological markers, and responsiveness to adult talk. The use of automated analysis tools makes this approach relatively efficient and reliable, but it remains too time-consuming for purposes of evaluation or progress monitoring.

Aspects of language development can be assessed more efficiently as early as 1 year of age, typically with instruments that rely on structured parent or caregiver reports of the words and phrases children understand and produce, and for which norms are now available based on relatively large numbers of children tested in English, Spanish, and a number of other languages (MacArthur-Bates Communicative Development Inventories—Fenson et al., 1993). Standardized assessments involving one-on-one testing of receptive vocabulary have norms for children as young as 18 months, but the validity of a child's score on these tests is greatly threatened by such factors as shyness, familiarity with the examiner, and familiarity with the activity of responding on demand to adult requests. Vocabulary is the component skill that is most widely assessed in educational as well as research contexts, for a number of reasons: it is relatively straightforward to assess, it shows strong relationships with other aspects of oral language (syntax, discourse skills) and emergent literacy (phonological awareness, early conventional reading), and it has been well instrumented in several modes, including the calculation of lexical diversity measures based on spontaneous speech samples (Malvern and Richards, 1997), the use of parent and teacher reports (http://www.sci.sdsu.edu/cdi/), and the use of direct assessments (e.g., Peabody Picture Vocabulary Test—Dunn and Dunn, 2007; Woodcock-Johnson, Schrank, Mather, and Woodcock, 2006; Expressive One-Word Vocabulary Test—Gardner and Brownell, 2000).

Beyond vocabulary, the aspects of language skill that are considered important depend very much on the goal. Identifying and diagnosing children with language delay or disorder requires information about their skills with phonology and grammar, as deficits in these domains are often helpful in specifying the disorder and in guiding intervention. For these purposes, direct assessments, such as the TOLD-P:3, the TELD-3, or the Preschool Language Assessment (PLA) are needed (Blank, Rose, and Berlin, 1978; Hammill and Newcomer, 1997; Hresko, Reid, and Hammill, 1999); these are typically administered by speech and language clinicians with special training. Tracking outcome attainment for accountability, in contrast, typically requires less detailed information, because for normally developing children the various components of the language system develop in synchrony and thus a measure of vocabulary is a good proxy for language in general. Vocabulary is also a robust predictor of emergent and conventional literacy skills, but increasing evidence now suggests the importance of including measures of extended discourse (comprehension or production of stories and explanations) to provide a complete picture of language development, especially because producing connected discourse is more vulnerable to mild clinical problems than is skill in conversational contexts (e.g., Hemphill et al., 2002).

Emergent literacy is seen as encompassing a general understanding of what print is—that it represents spoken language, that books are sources of pleasure and information, that writing can be used for various purposes, as well as specific skills, such as book handling, letter recognition, "reading" environmental print, "reading" familiar storybooks, "writing" with intention to communicate, and recognizing the analyzability of spoken words into smaller units (phonological awareness) (National Research Council, 1998). Widely used approaches to collecting information about children's skills in these domains exist. Typically, they involve the systematic use of information collected during slightly structured versions of natural interactive settings, such as looking at a book with an adult (Marie Clay's Concepts of Print task; Clay, 1979), retelling a story (Sulzby's Familiar Storybook Reading scale; Sulzby, 1985), or scribbling/drawing/writing (developmental scales for judging the sophistication of children's scribbling and emergent writing with invented spelling; Bear et al., 1999). Somewhat more direct testing is typically involved in assessing children's phonological awareness (among the most widely used is the Comprehensive Test of Phonological Processing; Wagner, Torgesen, and Rashotte, 1990).

### Evidence of Associations with Important Outcomes

Many would argue that language and literacy are outcomes of obvious importance in their own right, and thus that arguments about their relationship to other or later developmental outcomes are unnecessary. However, given the internal complexity of this domain, it is perhaps worth considering which of the many components that one might assess are most likely to provide information of long-term interest. This task is made more complex by the fact that all these components are, at least in normally developing children, highly intercorrelated, in part because they are all likely to be supported by the same kinds of environments and interactive experiences (see the next section). Nonetheless, in terms of outcomes related to school success, there is now very strong evidence supporting the power of vocabulary at school entry in predicting literacy outcomes, for early as well as later reading outcomes (Craig, Connor, and Washington, 2003; Dickinson and Tabors, 2001; Poe, Burchinal, and Roberts, 2004; Roth, Speece, and Cooper, 2002; Snow et al., 1995, 2007).

Some have argued that early reading outcomes are better predicted by the emergent literacy skills of letter recognition and phonological awareness (Schatschneider et al., 2004), and indeed it is clear that these "inside-out" (Whitehurst and Lonigan, 1998) skills predict early reading growth better than they predict later reading growth, while the power of kindergarten vocabulary and discourse skills to predict first grade reading outcomes is somewhat less than for later reading outcomes (Mason et al., 1992; Sénéchal and LeFevre, 2002). Some of the disagreement about the relative strength of the various predictors may have to do with the impact of threshold effects in either the emergent literacy or the language domains, or perhaps with the interaction between children's skills and the approaches to early reading instruction they encounter (Juel and Minden-Cupp, 2000). Nonetheless, there is little disagreement that, ultimately even if not immediately upon school entry, the oral language skills developed during the preschool period are closely associated with success in literacy (de Jong and van der Leij, 2002; Dickinson et al., 2003; Sénéchal and LeFevre, 2002).

### Evidence of Malleability

Language and emergent literacy skills are prime targets of most early childhood programs, and in particular of programs designed to serve children from low-income or non-English-speaking families. There is abundant evidence that these skills are sensitive to the quality of the language and literacy environment both in the home (e.g., Barone, 2001; Vernon-Feagans, 1996) and in out-of-home settings (McCartney, 2002; NICHD Early Child Care Research Network, 2000, 2005). There is also evidence that they can be influenced by interventions, such as Early Head Start or the Abecedarian Project, designed to improve the overall richness of the language and literacy environment (National Institute for Early Education Research, 2002; Reynolds and Temple, 1998; U.S. Department of Health and Human Services, Administration for Children and Families, 2004; Wasik, Bond, and Hindman, 2006) and to increase the language focus in parent-child interactions (Jordan, Snow, and Porche, 2000) or by more targeted interventions focused on improving the quality of book-reading interactions (Whitehurst et al., 1994) or on teacher talk in the classroom (Beck, McKeown, and Kucan, 2002; Silverman, 2007).

### Testing All Children

The challenges of collecting interpretable data on the language skills of children from non-English-speaking or bilingual backgrounds are significant. Of course, spontaneous speech samples can be collected in any language, but information about the normal course of development is available for only a minority of the languages represented among children in American early care and educational settings. The testing industry has focused on English language assessments, and although language and literacy assessments are available in other languages, the range of such assessments is likely to be much narrower, their applicability to children growing up in the United States is likely to be limited, and their availability in the languages of immigrants (except for Spanish) nonexistent. Even assessments developed in Spanish-speaking countries should be used with caution for assessing Spanish speakers in the United States, who are probably exposed to English from an early age and are decreasingly likely to have access to emergent or conventional literacy experiences in Spanish. Thus, tests normed on monolinguals are unlikely to adequately reflect the knowledge of bilinguals growing up in complex socio-linguistic settings. Yet testing children only in English if they are growing up bilingual clearly threatens to vastly underrepresent their language capacities. One promising approach that has been funded by the Head Start University Partnership Measurement Development Grants Program involves eliciting reports on the Bates-MacArthur Communicative Development Inventory from mothers about the home language and from classroom personnel about English; teacher reports add crucial information about these children's language skills (Pan, Mancilla-Martinez, and Vagh, 2008).

Even if one resolved the challenge of the paucity of direct tests appropriate for a large portion of the non-English-speaking population, the challenges of administering those tests well would be daunting, and those challenges overlap to a large extent with the challenges of testing speakers of nonstandard varieties of English or members of minority English-speaking groups. Particularly when directly assessing young children, ensuring trust and mutual understanding is absolutely crucial. Thus, having well-trained testers who understand and value the child's language and language variety, who can speak that language variety in a way that is understandable to the child, and who can interact with the child in a way that is familiar is prerequisite to getting interpretable results. When a typical urban preschool might be serving children from a dozen different language backgrounds, this is no easy task.

Although the emergent literacy measures are somewhat more tractable, the validity of conclusions drawn from them can also be threatened by differences of language, language variety, orthography, and literacy experience. For example, what if a child being tested in English knows letter names only in Spanish? What if she or he adopts the natural Spanish approach to syllable segmentation, producing pa–n instead of p–an when asked to divide up a syllable? What if she or he hears Spanish phonemes and thus segments the word "day" into d–a–I, counting three phonemes (correct in Spanish) instead of the expected two? None of these responses would lead to difficulty if the tester were bilingual or well informed about the likelihood of these responses, but under normal circumstances these responses are likely to be counted wrong, if not actually deviant.

### Available Measures

Many measures are available for assessing the components of language, ranging from those used primarily for research purposes, to researcher measures that have been developed into scales or report forms with norms, to formal tests. Many are listed in Appendix Table 5-4. The domains of vocabulary and phonological awareness have been the most richly populated with formal tests, although indices, report forms, and assessments for other domains exist as well. A language test of particular note—because it was designed specifically to resolve the problem of dialect differences in identifying children with language disorders and has been provided with norms—is the Diagnostic Evaluation of Language Variation (DELV; Seymour et al., 2003). The DELV focuses on sentence processing, in particular the comprehension of constructions that are universal and least likely to be affected by lexical, morphological, or syntactic differences among different varieties of English. Because the DELV focuses on aspects of the language system selected to be present among normally developing children, it is more useful as a diagnostic than a progress monitoring instrument.

## COGNITIVE SKILLS

### Defining the Domain

This wide-ranging domain encompasses general intellectual functioning; knowledge of specific topics, such as mathematics, science, and social studies; and more specific cognitive skills, such as executive function, attention, and memory. Most measures of general cognitive skills in this area reflect the somewhat freighted construct of IQ, and many of the general knowledge constructs are difficult to differentiate from vocabulary, while many of the specific cognitive skills are difficult to differentiate from approaches to learning. In this section, we focus on the constructs and measures of general and specific cognitive skills because those measures are either widely used or viewed as crucial skills for social, language, and academic development. In the next section, we take mathematics as a specific case in which a large amount of developmental and assessment work has been done; it is considered an example of cognition, in particular of declarative knowledge.

We recognize and endorse the growing attention to the need to teach science, social studies, and the arts in early childhood in addition to the traditional domains of language, literacy, and mathematics; see, for example, the National Child Care Information Center website, which provides links to many resources for teaching science and social studies (http://www.nccic.org/poptopics/mathscience.html). Although we do not treat these topics here because of the paucity of research-based information about or assessment approaches to them, we hope they will merit inclusion in a future report dealing with early childhood assessment.

Although concepts of general cognitive skills vary widely, all include the ability to "understand complex ideas, to adapt effectively to the environment, to learn from experiences, to engage in various forms of reasoning, and to overcome obstacles by taking thought" (Neisser et al., 1996). The American Psychological Association convened a task force after the book, *The Bell Curve* (Herrnstein and Murray, 1994), sparked intense debate about intelligence. The task force report summarized existing theory and research, indicating that these conceptualizations vary in the extent to which different types of systems of intellectual abilities are differentiated and in the role attributed to culture in defining and acquiring intellectual skills. It also reported a general consensus that psychometric measures of cognitive skills tend to be highly correlated and are strongly influenced by an individual's genetic background and individual experiences (American Psychological Association Task Force on Intelligence, 1996).

The role of individual experiences in the development of general cognitive skills is especially evident in early childhood. On one hand, measures of early cognitive skills show only low to moderate correlations with measures from school age or later, with stronger correlations emerging as children become adept at using language (McCall, 1977). Somewhat stronger associations obtain when measures of infant habituation are used to assess infant cognitive skills (McCall and Carriger, 1993). On the other hand, correlations with measures of the child's environment are stronger in early childhood than subsequently (McCall, Appelbaum, and Hogarty, 1974).

In contrast to the long history of research on the development of general cognitive skills, research on the development of memory, attention, executive function, and emotional regulation has grown dramatically in the past 10-20 years. As mentioned earlier, evidence from both psychological and neuroscience research indicates that emotional regulation and executive function skills play an important role in developing self-regulation and social and academic competence during early childhood in both typically and atypically developing populations of children (Blair, 2002; Blair and Razza, 2007). Similarly, considerable research on the acquisition of memory skills shows the crucial role memory plays in the acquisition and retention of knowledge (Gathercole, 1998).

Executive function (EF), also known as fluid cognitive ability to distinguish it from crystallized cognition, or knowledge of declarative information, comprises cognitive processes utilized in response to novel stimuli. As investigated in a range of cognitive psychological research from information processing (Miyake et al., 2000), psychometric (Flanagan and McGrew, 1997; Woodcock, 1990), and neuropsychological and neurobiological perspectives (Norman and Shallice, 1986; Posner and Rothbert, 2000; Welsh, Pennington, and Groisser, 1991), the cognitive processes involved in executive function include the ability to hold information in mind in working memory, inhibit incorrect responses, and sustain or switch attention for the purposes of goal-directed action. Generally speaking, executive function refers to effortful cognitive processes as opposed to relatively automatic aspects of cognition associated with crystallized knowledge and declarative memory (memory for information that has been learned).

Executive function consists of distinct but moderately interrelated cognitive functions, including working memory, inhibitory control, and attention shifting components (Espy et al., 1999, 2004; MacDonald et al., 2000; Miyake et al., 2000; Robbins, 1996) that are related to, but distinct from, general intelligence (Blair, 2006; Bull and Scerif, 2001; Espy et al., 1999; Lehto, 2004). Working memory refers to the process of holding information in mind for the purpose of goal-directed activity. Attention shifting refers to the switching of the focus of attention between distinct but often closely related aspects or dimensions of a given object or objects within a task. Inhibitory control refers to the ability to inhibit or override a prepotent or previously well-learned stimulus-response association in favor of a subdominant response.

Memory is also viewed as multidimensional. During early childhood, children develop short-term memory, autobiographical memory, episodic memory, and metamemory (Gathercole, 1998). Short-term memory includes phonological memory and visual spatial memory and is often considered part of executive function.

## Evidence of Consensus

There is consensus that general cognitive skills are important, regardless of whether they are viewed holistically or as multiple types of academic or practical intelligence (Neisser et al., 1996) and that executive function plays a critical role in the development of social, language, and academic skills (Blair and Razza, 2007). Developmental psychologists have long recognized the importance of cognitive capacities as a crucial aspect of children's development, an aspect of importance in its own right, and one that interacts with health, language, academic, approaches to learning, and socioemotional adjustment.

## Evidence of Continuity and Associations with Important Outcomes

Cognitive skills measured in early childhood show increasing levels of stability and associations with important outcomes as children age. Developmental assessments of preverbal infants show very modest associations with subsequent IQ measures, whereas measures of infant habituation have shown moderate levels of associations with later cognitive scores (Neisser et al., 1996). In contrast, IQ scores of 3- to 5-year-olds show high levels of continuity with school-age assessments, although individual children can show substantial changes in scores over time (McCall, Appelbaum, and Hogarty, 1974). Standardized measures of general cognitive skills, such as IQ scores, provide very good prediction by ages 3-5 of academic achievement and modest correlations with adult outcomes, such as occupations (see Neisser et al., 1996, for a comprehensive review). However, the overlap between general cognitive skills and language remains. Attempts to develop culture-free and language-free measures of cognitive ability have had limited success (Neisser et al., 1996).

Measures of specific cognitive skills have also demonstrated continuity and associations with important outcomes. Executive function and attention have been measured in children as young as 2.5 years, and these skills appear to become more stable during early childhood, until they reach strong levels of stability by age 8 (Olson et al., 2005; Posner and Rothbert, 2000). Memory functioning shows substantial qualitative change during infancy and the preschool years, stabilizing around age 7 into adult-like structures of continuity (Gathercole, 1998). Measures of effortful control, inhibitory control, and attention-shifting in preschool predicted mathematical and literacy skills in kindergarten in a study of Head Start children. Similarly, both working memory and especially inhibitory control were related to mathematical skills in a sample of 4-year-olds (Blair and Razza, 2007). A computerized task measuring sustained attention provided moderately strong prediction of reading and mathematical skills in primary school in the Study of Early Child Care and Youth Development of the National Institute of Child Health and Human Development (Duncan et al., 2007). Phonological memory and processing is thought to play a critical role in reading and other academic skills.

## Evidence of Malleability

The theory of change for most early childhood intervention programs is that some form of preschool enrichment will lead to more rapid growth in cognitive skills for participants, often children from low-income families. Most often, cognitive skills are measured via individual direct assessments using standardized tests administered by trained staff members. A recent RAND Corporation study (RAND Labor and Population, 2005) examined programs implemented in the United States that provide services to children and families during early childhood and reported effect sizes (d) for cognitive outcomes for successful programs that ranged from .13 to 1.23.

The largest effect sizes were obtained in the most intensive interventions in assessments of children after age 2. The Abecedarian Project, a single-site experimental intervention that delivered 5 years of full-time quality child care, yielded effect sizes of d = .50 at 18 months, d = .83 at 24 months, d = 1.23 at 36 months, and d = .73 at 54 months on standardized infant developmental or IQ tests (note that the reduction in effect sizes between ages 3 and 5 appears to be related to the fact that control children were attending quality child care centers) (Burchinal, Lee, and Ramey, 1989). The High Scope/Perry Preschool Project, a single-site program that delivered 2 years of preschool between ages 3 and 5 and included a home visit/parenting education component, yielded effect sizes of d = 1.03 at age 5 on standardized IQ tests. The Infant Health and Development Project, a large multisite research project that delivered 3 years of home visiting and 2 years of full-time high-quality child care from birth, yielded an effect size of d = .83 on an IQ test at the end of the program at 36 months. The Early Training Project (Gray and Klaus, 1970), which included both home visiting and child care for preschoolers, reported an effect size of d = .70 in an IQ test.

In contrast, much weaker effect sizes were obtained for interventions that were less intense: d = .27 for the Ypsilanti Carnegie Infant Education project, which provided home visiting (Epstein and Weikart, 1979); d = .13 at 36 months for Early Head Start, a large multisite research site that delivered 2-3 years of home visiting and high-quality child care in some sites (U.S. Department of Health and Human Services, Administration for Children and

Families, 2004); d = .13 for the Prenatal Early Infancy Project-Elmira site (Olds et al., 1993), another home visiting project; and d = .12 at 48 months for the Head Start Impact Study, which evaluated the impact of a year of Head Start involving both center care and home visiting (U.S. Department of Health and Human Services, Administration for Children and Families, 2005). Finally, the relatively frequent need to renorm cognitive tests provides further evidence of mutability for general cognitive scores (Neisser et al., 1996). As the average level of education rose in this country, IQ tests had to be renormed to ensure that the mean score did not rise substantially.

A growing literature also demonstrates mutability in executive functioning. Experimental studies have demonstrated that children who participated in "brain training" activities and curricula exhibited improved neurocognitive abilities (including executive function) and, in some cases, behavior relative to peers who did not participate in the training activities (Diamond et al., 2007; Dowsett and Livesey, 2000; Klingberg et al., 2005; Rueda et al., 2005; Semrud-Clikeman et al., 1999).

## Testing All Children

The challenges of collecting interpretable data on the cognitive skills of children from non-English-speaking or multicultural backgrounds have been hotly debated. Overall, recent IQ and general cognitive tests have been developed using diverse populations in their norming samples, and scores on these tests tend to show similar patterns of prediction with academic achievement and other criteria for different ethnic and economic groups (Neisser et al., 1996). However, insufficient evidence exists to draw definitive conclusions regarding the use of these measures with infants, toddlers, and preschoolers. Similarly, many measures of specific cognitive skills were developed using middle-class white children but have been used recently in studies in Head Start classrooms or other programs serving low-income, ethnically diverse children. There is growing attention to the psychometric properties of these measures as the research moves away from documenting normative development to examining individual differences (Blair and Razza, 2007).

## Available Measures

Measures of general cognitive skills during early childhood include psychometrically developed developmental and IQ tests, questionnaires, specific tasks, and curriculum-based assessments. Many of these are listed in Appendix Table 5-4. The Bayley Scales of Infant Development measure the mental and motor development and test the behavior of infants from 1 to 42 months of age. The Wechsler tests may be the most widely used measures of 3- to 8-year-olds, although other psychometric tests are also widely used for children age 2 years and older, including the Stanford Binet Intelligence Scales, the Woodcock-Johnson III (WJ-III) Tests of Cognitive Abilities, and the Kaufman Assessment Battery for Children (K-ABC) (Bayley, 2005; Kaufman and Kaufman, 2006; Roid, 2003; Wechsler, 2003; Woodcock, McGrew, and Mather, 2001). The K-ABC assesses sequential and simultaneous processing skills as well as achievement. Similarly, the WJ-III assesses specific cognitive and achievement skills.

In contrast, most measures of executive function involve laboratory-based tasks. The continuous performance task is widely used to measure sustained attention for typically developing children in research and for children referred for cognitive delays or disorders. Assessments of executive skills were reviewed recently (Carlson, 2005), listing tasks appropriate for toddlers and preschoolers. Perhaps the most widely used measures include the continuous performance task, shape Stroop, snack delay, day/night, and Simon says (note that these are also used as measures of constructs defined under socioemotional development, again pointing out the porous boundaries between emotional and cognitive development). Assessments of memory include scales on psychometrically developed assessments and a wide variety of laboratory assessments (Gathercole, 1998). Ceiling and floor effects have limited the use of many of the laboratory tasks across a variety of ages, and concerns about the extent to which tasks require multiple specific cognitive skills result in measures that cannot provide pure assessment of a single executive function or memory skill.

## MATHEMATICS

In this section we discuss the development of mathematical understanding, concepts, and skills during early childhood as a particular aspect of the cognitive skills domain.

### Defining the Domain

Researchers emphasize that very young children can and should be acquiring knowledge that provides the foundations for later mathematics learning in number sense, spatial sense and reasoning (geometry), measurement, classification and patterning (algebra), and mathematical reasoning. Each of these subdomains of mathematics is described briefly below.

Research suggests that children begin developing *number sense* in early infancy (Clements, 2004; Clements, Sarama, and DiBiase, 2004; Feigenson, Dehaene, and Spelke, 2004; Xu, Spelke, and Goddard, 2005) and much of what young children know about numbers depends on their understanding and mastery of counting (Fuson, 1992a; National Research Council, 2001). Studies suggest that the three major basic skills required for counting are knowing the sequence of number words, one-to-one correspondence, and cardinality (Becker, 1989; Clements, 2004; Fuson, 1988, 1992a, 1992b; Hiebert et al., 1997; National Research Council, 2001). Following initial acquisition of counting, children begin to acquire an understanding of number operations (Clements, 2004; Hiebert et al., 1997; National Council of Teachers of Mathematics, 2000; National Research Council, 2001) and then simple operations and word problems (Fuson, 1992a). Number operations for preschoolers mainly involve understanding additive number relationships in which two (or more) small numbers make up one larger number (e.g., 2 and 3 make 5), which will develop into addition and subtraction concepts in the future. In acquiring these skills related to number sense, young children and students of nonmajority backgrounds tend to be influenced by the context of the problem and perform better with more contextual information (Boaler, 1994; Cooper and Dunne, 1998; Lubienski, 2000; Means and Knapp, 1991).

*Geometry* is the study of space and shape (Clements, 1999).

Shape knowledge involves not only recognition and naming, but also an understanding of shape characteristics and properties. Spatial reasoning involves location, direction, distance, and identification of objects (Clements, 1999). Based on Van Hiele's theory (1986), children are believed to learn about geometry on a progression of levels—visualization, analysis, abstraction, deduction, and rigor—and many geometry curricula and assessments follow this hierarchy.

*Measurement* involves assigning numbers to a set of continuous quantities (Clements and Stephan, 2004). To understand the concept of measurement, children must be able to decide on the attribute of objects to measure (e.g., width or length), select the units to measure the attribute, and use measuring skills and tools to compare the units (Clements, 2004). A typical developmental trajectory involves children first learning to use words that represent quantities or magnitude of a certain attribute (e.g., big and small); second, demonstrating an ability to compare two objects directly and recognize equality or inequality; and finally, learning to measure, connecting numbers to attributes of objects, such as length, weight, amount, area, and time (Clements, Sarama, and DiBiase, 2004; Ginsburg, Inoue, and Seo, 1999).

In the early childhood years, children develop beginning *algebraic concepts* as they sort and classify objects, observe patterns in their environment, and begin to predict what comes next based on a recognized pattern. Sorting, classifying, and working with patterns help them to bring order, organization, and predictability to their world. Classification and the analysis of patterns provide a foundation for algebraic thinking as children develop the ability to recognize relationships, form generalizations, and see the connections between common underlying structures (Clements, 2004; National Council of Teachers of Mathematics, 2000). Classification, defined as the systematic arrangement of objects into groups according to established criteria, involves categorizing, sorting, and grouping. Understanding a pattern involves the ability to identify similarities and differences among elements of a pattern, note the number of elements in the repeatable group, identify when the first group of elements begins to replicate itself, and make predictions about the order of elements based on given information. Acquisition of these skills appears to depend on identifying the core unit of the pattern, which, in turn, is dependent on the types of experiences the child experiences at home or in care and educational settings (Klein and Starkey, 2004; Starkey, Klein, and Wakeley, 2004).

Most young children can solve problems involving simple *mathematical reasoning* by age 3, often by modeling with real objects or thinking about sets of objects. Alexander, White, and Daugherty (1997) propose three conditions for reasoning in young children: (1) the children must have a sufficient knowledge base, (2) the task must be understandable and motivating, and (3) the context of the task must be familiar and comfortable to the problem solver. Although these conditions probably apply to problem solvers of all ages, they may be particularly important for young children who are not motivated to complete tasks for external reasons (e.g., good grades).

### Importance of the Domain

The case for assessing mathematics in early education programs is easy to make. Looking across international comparative studies, U.S. students' performance in mathematics is in the bottom third (American Institutes for Research, 2005). And recent analyses of longitudinal studies have shown that mathematical concepts, such as knowledge of numbers and ordinality, at school entry are the strongest predictors of later academic achievement, even stronger than early literacy skills (Duncan et al., 2007). Efforts clearly need to be made to improve opportunities for mathematics learning and carefully monitor children's learning. Furthermore, all the state early childhood standards mention mathematical development as a target for attention.

### Testing All Children

The ability to articulate thinking and problem-solving approaches in mathematics is currently recognized as an important skill (National Council of Teachers of Mathematics, 2000), although this may prove difficult for children who are not proficient in English or have not yet learned mathematics vocabulary. Mathematical skills therefore need to be assessed in multiple ways, with objects that can be manipulated and questions requiring verbal explanations.

### Available Measures

Each of the domains in mathematics discussed above has measures associated with it, although of varying quality and degrees of development. Both formative and summative assessments should measure children's skills in the different subdomains and not focus only on number sense. Because children's mathematical experiences and learning are grounded in their everyday lives, often in practical situations, it is also important that the problems, even in formal and structured assessments, be familiar and involve materials that children can use to solve the problem and show their thinking. Young children need to be able to touch and move objects to give an accurate demonstration of their understanding of the concepts. Assessments using still pictures on a piece of paper are likely to underestimate their mathematical understanding, as they may be better able to solve problems when they are allowed to move actual objects around physically. Some of the skills that should be examined in each domain are listed below.

Since young children's primary experience with numbers focuses on counting, any assessment of number sense should examine how children count groups of objects. Assessments should include asking the child to count to measure their knowledge of number sequence names and rote counting, assessing the child's understanding of one-to-one correspondence between objects and counting and of cardinality. Similarly, assessment of spatial sense and reasoning (geometry) should involve observation of children engaged in activities using shapes. Assessment of children's understanding of measurement in early childhood should begin with asking them to make direct comparisons of different attributes of objects. For classification and sorting, children should be provided with materials or objects and asked to create their own groups and describe their reasoning. Their reasoning should be carefully noted and their understanding should be evaluated based on their reasoning, not solely by the evaluator's criteria. Assessment items for mathematical reasoning should be embedded in other content topics. Because children's lives involve much problem solving, the more the assessment task is embedded in their everyday plays and activities, the better. When an assessment task is given, children's approaches should be observed carefully, and if they modify their approach in the process, the modification should be noted, because changing and adjusting strategies often provide information about their reasoning.

A growing number of assessment instruments is now available. Appendix Table 5-6 lists some of these measures as examples, and we give examples of tools that are useful for formative and summative evaluations of young children. Assessments are embedded in curricula, like Everyday Mathematics, providing tools for the teacher to monitor each child's progress. The Desired Results Developmental Profile, California's prekindergarten evaluation tool, has teachers rate preschoolers based on observation. Psychometrically developed standardized tests, like the Woodcock-Johnson, used for evaluation and diagnosis, are individually administered by a trained adult to children ages 2 to 5. Each of these tools assesses number sense, but only the teacher report tools also assess geometric, measurement, and algebraic skills.

## CONCLUSION

In this chapter, we have attempted to bring some organization to the very complicated question of what to assess in young children, taking into account not only the domains of importance to parents and preschool educators, but also those that predict long-term academic success. Although an exhaustive analysis of the theories of change that underlie prevention and intervention services was beyond the scope of work we could complete, we did use information about the design and effectiveness of such programs to help refine our list of domains. Inevitably, the discussion of domains to assess is influenced by the availability of assessment instruments for each of the domains, their quality, and the ease of using them. Identifying a domain as of high importance has little immediate effect on assessment activities if there are no tools available to measure it. Such identification, however, can serve as an important motivation for the development of better measurement tools for use in the future. As the history of instrument development in the domains of approaches to learning and social/emotional development shows, identifying a domain as important can generate researcher and practitioner interest that translates itself initially into informal assessments, which are refined and expanded to meet the psychometric criteria of importance from wider use.

The default when thinking about assessment is to think about direct, formal testing—the familiar scenario of an adult sitting down with a child and presenting prescribed questions or challenges for him or her to solve, in a prescribed sequence. It is important to emphasize that, although many of the assessment tools discussed in this chapter have that character, the repertoire of usable, reliable, and informative assessments is in fact much larger, including observation of the child in natural or somewhat structured settings, collecting information from primary caregivers and from adults in child care and educational settings about the child's behavior, and interacting with the child directly but without formal test items or materials. The reliability and validity of such measures for young children needs more study, and such research is beginning to be done. For example, Meisels, Xue, and Shamblott (in press) studied the Work Sampling for Head Start (WSHS) measure, derived from the Work Sampling System, which has observers complete a checklist of children's demonstrated capabilities. They reported moderate correlations with direct assessment instruments for language, literacy, and mathematics, but did not recommend use of the WSHS for accountability purposes.

# APPENDIX TABLES:
# 5-1 THROUGH 5-7—TABLES OF PRESCHOOL INSTRUMENTS[1]

**APPENDIX TABLE 5-1** Physical Well-Being and Motor Development Instruments

| Assessment | Data-Gathering Method | | | |
|---|---|---|---|---|
| **Subscales** | **Direct Assessment** | **Questionnaire** | **Observation** | **Interview** |
| **Physical development** | Denver II | Creative Curriculum Development Continuum for Ages 3-5<br>The Work Sampling System (WSS) | Growth Charts<br>Creative Curriculum Development Continuum for Ages 3-5<br>The Work Sampling System (WSS) | Denver II |
| **Motor development** | Bayley Scales of Infant Development (BSID), Third ed.<br>Denver II | | | Denver II |
| **Well-being** | | | Indices of Obesity | |
| **Nutrition** | | Toddler-Parent Mealtime Behavior Questionnaire | Toddler-Parent Mealtime Observation | |
| **Motor control** | NEPSY<br>Bayley Scales of Infant Development (BSID), Third ed. | | Games as Measurement for Early Self-Control (GAMES) | |

| | | | | |
|---|---|---|---|---|
| **Impulse control/ delay gratification** | | | Games as Measurement for Early Self-Control (GAMES) | |
| **Processing speed** | Woodcock-Johnson III (WJ-III) | | Clinical Evaluation of Language Fundamentals (CELF)-Preschool Behavioral Observation Checklist | |
| **Physical activity** | | | | |
| **Perceptual motor development** | | The Galileo System for the Electronic Management of Learning (Galileo) | The Galileo System for the Electronic Management of Learning (Galileo) | |
| **Music and movement** | | High/Scope Child Observation Record (COR) | High/Scope Child Observation Record (COR) | |
| **Motor quality** | Bayley Scales of Infant Development (BSID), Third ed., Behavioral Rating Scale (BRS) | | | |
| **Play and leisure time** | | | | Vineland Social-Emotional Early Childhood Scales (SEEC) |

[1]These listings do not imply any approval or endorsement by the committee of particular instruments. They are included to provide examples of instruments available for measuring various domains and outcomes. Appendix D provides information on where reviews of the instruments may be found.

**APPENDIX TABLE 5-2** Social-Emotional Development Instruments

| Assessment Subscales | Data-Gathering Method | | | |
|---|---|---|---|---|
| | **Direct Assessment** | **Questionnaire** | **Observation** | **Interview** |
| **Attachment** | | | Strange Situation | Attachment Q-Sort |
| **Behavior problems** | | Child Behavior Checklist | The Work Sampling System (WSS) | Social Skills Rating Scale (SSRS) |
| | | Social Skills Rating Scale (SSRS) | | |
| **Emotion regulation** | Bayley Scales of Infant Development (BSID), Third ed., Behavioral Rating Scale (BRS) | | Delay-of-Gratification Task | |
| **Social skills** | | Social Skills Rating Scale (SSRS) | The Work Sampling System (WSS) | Social Skills Rating Scale (SSRS) |
| | | ECLS-K Adaptation of the Social Skills Rating System (SSRS), Task Orientation/Approaches to Learning Scale | | |
| | | Adaptive Social Behavior Index | | |
| **Negative reaction tendency** | | Adapted EZ-Yale Personality/Motivation Questionnaire (Adapted EZPQ) | | |

| | | | |
|---|---|---|---|
| **Outer directedness** | | Adapted EZ-Yale Personality/Motivation Questionnaire (Adapted EZPQ) | |
| **Self-regulation tasks** | | | Games as Measurement for Early Self-Control (GAMES) |
| **Behavior rating scale** | Bayley Scales of Infant Development (BSID), Third ed. | | |
| **Fatigue/ boredom/ frustration** | | | Clinical Evaluation of Language Fundamentals (CELF)-Preschool Behavioral Observation Checklist |
| **Social-emotional development** | | Creative Curriculum Development Continuum for Ages 3-5 | Creative Curriculum Development Continuum for Ages 3-5 |
| **Social development** | | The Galileo System for the Electronic Management of Learning (Galileo) | The Galileo System for the Electronic Management of Learning (Galileo) |

*continued*

**APPENDIX TABLE 5-2** Continued

| Assessment Subscales | Data-Gathering Method | | | |
|---|---|---|---|---|
| | **Direct Assessment** | **Questionnaire** | **Observation** | **Interview** |
| **Social relations** | | High/Scope Child Observation Record (COR) | High/Scope Child Observation Record (COR) | |
| **Personal and social development** | | The Work Sampling System (WSS) | The Work Sampling System (WSS) | |
| **Attention/ arousal** | Bayley Scales of Infant Development (BSID), Third ed., Behavioral Rating Scale (BRS) | | | |
| **Clinical scales** | | Behavioral Assessment System for Children (BASC) | | |
| **Composites** | | Behavioral Assessment System for Children (BASC) | | |
| **Syndromes** | | Child Behavior Checklist (CBCL) and Caregiver-Teacher Report Form (C-TRF) | | |

| | | |
|---|---|---|
| **Summary scales** | Child Behavior Checklist (CBCL) and Caregiver-Teacher Report Form (C-TRF) | |
| **DSM-oriented scales** | Child Behavior Checklist (CBCL) and Caregiver-Teacher Report Form (C-TRF) | |
| **Factor analytically derived subscales** | Connor's Rating Scales-Revised (CRS-R) | |
| **Auxiliary scales** | Connor's Rating Scales-Revised (CRS-R) | |
| **Protective factors scale** | Devereux Early Childhood Assessment (DECA) | |
| **Behavioral concern** | Devereux Early Childhood Assessment (DECA) | |
| **Externalizing symptoms** | Infant-Toddler Social and Emotional Assessment (ITSEA) | Infant-Toddler Social and Emotional Assessment (ITSEA) |

*continued*

**APPENDIX TABLE 5-2** Continued

| Assessment | Data-Gathering Method | | | |
|---|---|---|---|---|
| **Subscales** | **Direct Assessment** | **Questionnaire** | **Observation** | **Interview** |
| **Internalizing symptoms** | | Infant-Toddler Social and Emotional Assessment (ITSEA) | | Infant-Toddler Social and Emotional Assessment (ITSEA) |
| **Dysregulation** | | Infant-Toddler Social and Emotional Assessment (ITSEA) | | Infant-Toddler Social and Emotional Assessment (ITSEA) |
| **Competence** | | Infant-Toddler Social and Emotional Assessment (ITSEA) | | Infant-Toddler Social and Emotional Assessment (ITSEA) |
| **Overall adjustment scales** | | Social Competence and Behavioral Evaluation (SCBE), Preschool Ed. | | |
| **Peer social interactions scales** | | Social Competence and Behavioral Evaluation (SCBE), Preschool Ed. | | |
| **Adult social interactions scales** | | Social Competence and Behavioral Evaluation (SCBE), Preschool Ed. | | |
| **Social competence** | | Social Competence and Behavioral Evaluation (SCBE), Preschool Ed. | | |

| | | |
|---|---|---|
| **Internalizing problems** | Social Competence and Behavioral Evaluation (SCBE), Preschool Ed. | |
| **Externalizing problems** | Social Competence and Behavioral Evaluation (SCBE), Preschool Ed. | |
| **General adaptation** | Social Competence and Behavioral Evaluation (SCBE), Preschool Ed. | |
| **Interpersonal relationships** | | Vineland Social-Emotional Early Childhood Scales (SEEC) |
| **Coping skills** | | Vineland Social-Emotional Early Childhood Scales (SEEC) |
| **Personal and social skills** | | Denver II |

**APPENDIX TABLE 5-3** Approaches to Learning Instruments

| Assessment Subscales | Data-Gathering Method | | | |
|---|---|---|---|---|
| | **Direct Assessment** | **Questionnaire** | **Observation** | **Interview** |
| | | The Galileo System for the Electronic Management of Learning (Galileo) | The Galileo System for the Electronic Management of Learning (Galileo) | |
| **Executive functioning** | NEPSY | | Tower of Hanoi | |
| **Inhibitory control** | NEPSY, CPT | | | |
| **Emotion regulation** | | | Delay-of-Gratification Task | |
| **Academic mastery motivation** | | Adapted EZ-Yale Personality/Motivation Questionnaire (Adapted EZPQ) | | |
| **Engagement in learning** | | ECLS-K Adaptation of the Social Skills Rating Scale (SSRS), Task Orientation/ Approaches to Learning Scale | | |
| **Organization** | | ECLS-K Adaptation of the Social Skills Rating Scale (SSRS), Task Orientation/ Approaches to Learning Scale | | |

| | | | |
|---|---|---|---|
| **Creativity** | | ECLS-K Adaptation of the Social Skills Rating Scale (SSRS), Task Orientation/ Approaches to Learning Scale | |
| **Adaptability** | | ECLS-K Adaptation of the Social Skills Rating Scale (SSRS), Task Orientation/ Approaches to Learning Scale | |
| **Visuospatial processing** | NEPSY | | |
| **Attention to task** | | | CELF-Preschool Behavioral Observation Checklist |
| **Self-help** | | The Galileo System for the Electronic Management of Learning (Galileo) | The Galileo System for the Electronic Management of Learning (Galileo) |
| **Initiative** | | High/Scope Child Observation Record (COR) | High/Scope Child Observation Record (COR) |
| **Orientation/ engagement** | Bayley Scales of Infant Development (BSID), Third ed., Behavioral Rating Scale (BRS) | | |
| **Adaptive behavior scales** | | Behavioral Assessment System for Children (BASC) | |

**APPENDIX TABLE 5-4** Cognitive Skills Instruments

| Assessment Subscales | Data-Gathering Method | | | |
|---|---|---|---|---|
| | **Direct Assessment** | **Questionnaire** | **Observation** | **Interview** |
| | Expressive One-Word Picture Vocabulary Test (EOWPVT)<br>Woodcock-Johnson III (WJ-III) | | | |
| **Intelligence** | Bayley, Stanford-Binet, Wechsler Preschool and Primary Scale of Intelligence (WPPSI), WISC | | | |
| **Executive functioning** | NEPSY | | Tower of Hanoi | |
| **Cognitive control** | | | Games as Measurement for Early Self-Control (GAMES) | |
| **Sustained attention** | | | Games as Measurement for Early Self-Control (GAMES) | |
| **Memory and learning** | NEPSY | | | |
| **Sequential processing** | Kaufman Assessment Battery for Children (K-ABC) | | | |

| | | |
|---|---|---|
| **Simultaneous processing** | Kaufman Assessment Battery for Children (K-ABC) | |
| **Mental processing** | Kaufman Assessment Battery for Children (K-ABC) | |
| **Achievement scale** | Kaufman Assessment Battery for Children (K-ABC)<br>Woodcock-Johnson III (WJ-III) | |
| **Spatial** | | Primary Test of Cognitive Skills (PTCS) |
| **Memory** | | Primary Test of Cognitive Skills (PTCS) |
| **Concepts** | | Primary Test of Cognitive Skills (PTCS) |
| **Short-term memory** | Stanford-Binet Intelligence Scale, Fourth ed. (SB-IV)<br>Woodcock-Johnson III (WJ-III) | |
| **Long-term retrieval** | Woodcock-Johnson III (WJ-III) | |

*continued*

**APPENDIX TABLE 5-4** Continued

| Assessment Subscales | Data-Gathering Method | | | |
|---|---|---|---|---|
| | **Direct Assessment** | **Questionnaire** | **Observation** | **Interview** |
| **Visual-spatial thinking** | Woodcock-Johnson III (WJ-III) | | | |
| **Auditory processing** | Woodcock-Johnson III (WJ-III) | | | |
| **Fluid reasoning** | Woodcock-Johnson III (WJ-III) | | | |
| **Response latency** | | | Clinical Evaluation of Language Fundamentals (CELF)-Preschool Behavioral Observation Checklist | |
| **Phonological awareness** | Woodcock-Johnson III (WJ-III) | | | |
| **Cognitive development** | | Creative Curriculum Development Continuum for Ages 3-5 | Creative Curriculum Development Continuum for Ages 3-5 | |
| **Early cognitive development** | | The Galileo System for the Electronic Management of Learning (Galileo) | The Galileo System for the Electronic Management of Learning (Galileo) | |

**APPENDIX TABLE 5-5** General Knowledge Instruments

| Assessment Subscales | Data-Gathering Method | | | |
|---|---|---|---|---|
| | **Direct Assessment** | **Questionnaire** | **Observation** | **Interview** |
| | Woodcock-Johnson III (WJ-III), Peabody Individual Achievement Test (PIAT), Peabody Individual Achievement Test-Revised (PIAT-R) | | Work Sampling Plans, Portfolio, Summative Instructional Tools (e.g., COR) | |
| **Mental scale** | Bayley Scales of Infant Development (BSID), Third ed. | | | |
| **Colors** | Bracken Basic Concept Scale-Revised (BBCS-R) | | | |
| **Performance IQ** | Wechsler Preschool and Primary Scale of Intelligence, Third ed. (WPPSI-III) | | | |
| **Full-scale IQ** | Wechsler Preschool and Primary Scale of Intelligence, Third ed. (WPPSI-III) | | | |

*continued*

**APPENDIX TABLE 5-5** Continued

| Assessment Subscales | Data-Gathering Method | | | |
|---|---|---|---|---|
| | **Direct Assessment** | **Questionnaire** | **Observation** | **Interview** |
| **Sizes** | Bracken Basic Concept Scale-Revised (BBCS-R) | | | |
| **Comparisons** | Bracken Basic Concept Scale-Revised (BBCS-R) | | | |
| **Shapes** | Bracken Basic Concept Scale-Revised (BBCS-R) | | | |
| **Direction/position** | Bracken Basic Concept Scale-Revised (BBCS-R) | | | |
| **Self-/social awareness** | Bracken Basic Concept Scale-Revised (BBCS-R) | | | |
| **Texture/material** | Bracken Basic Concept Scale-Revised (BBCS-R) | | | |
| **Quantity** | Bracken Basic Concept Scale-Revised (BBCS-R) | | | |
| **Time/sequencing** | Bracken Basic Concept Scale-Revised (BBCS-R) | | | |
| **Abstract/visual reasoning** | Stanford-Binet Intelligence Scale, Fourth ed. (SB-IV) | | | |

| | | | |
|---|---|---|---|
| **Academic progress** | Expressive One-Word Picture Vocabulary Test (EOWPVT) | | |
| **Creative arts** | | The Galileo System for the Electronic Management of Learning (Galileo) | The Galileo System for the Electronic Management of Learning (Galileo) |
| **Creative representation** | | High/Scope Child Observation Record (COR) | High/Scope Child Observation Record (COR) |
| **Social studies** | | The Work Sampling System (WSS) | The Work Sampling System (WSS) |
| **The arts** | | The Work Sampling System (WSS) | The Work Sampling System (WSS) |

**APPENDIX TABLE 5-6** Math and Science Instruments

| Assessment Subscales | Data-Gathering Method | | | |
|---|---|---|---|---|
| | **Direct Assessment** | **Questionnaire** | **Observation** | **Interview** |
| **Mathematics** | Woodcock-Johnson III (WJ-III), Peabody Individual Achievement Test (PIAT), Peabody Individual Achievement Test-Revised (PIAT-R), Test of Early Mathematics Ability (TEMA) | | Work Sampling Plans, Portfolio, Summative Instructional Tools | |
| **Science** | Woodcock-Johnson III (WJ-III), Peabody Individual Achievement Test (PIAT) | | Work Sampling Plans, Portfolio, Summative Instructional Tools | |
| **Quantitative reasoning** | Stanford-Binet Intelligence Scale, Fourth ed. (SB-IV) | | | |
| **Number/ counting** | Bracken Basic Concept Scale-Revised (BBCS-R)/SRC | | | |
| **Sizes** | Bracken Basic Concept Scale-Revised (BBCS-R)/SRC | | | |
| **Shapes** | Bracken Basic Concept Scale-Revised (BBCS-R)/SRC | | | |

| | | | |
|---|---|---|---|
| **Quantity** | Bracken Basic Concept Scale-Revised (BBCS-R) | | |
| **Achievement scale–arithmetic subtest** | Kaufman Assessment Battery for Children (K-ABC) | | |
| **Formal mathematics** | Test of Early Mathematics Ability, Second ed. (TEMA-2) | | |
| **Informal mathematics** | Test of Early Mathematics Ability, Second ed. (TEMA-2) | | |
| **Achievement–broad mathematics** | Woodcock-Johnson III (WJ-III) | | |
| **Achievement-mathematical calculation skills** | Woodcock-Johnson III (WJ-III) | | |
| **Achievement–mathematical reasoning** | Woodcock-Johnson III (WJ-III) | | |
| **Early mathematics** | | The Galileo System for the Electronic Management of Learning (Galileo) | The Galileo System for the Electronic Management of Learning (Galileo) |

*continued*

**APPENDIX TABLE 5-6** Continued

| Assessment Subscales | Data-Gathering Method | | | |
|---|---|---|---|---|
| | Direct Assessment | Questionnaire | Observation | Interview |
| **Nature and science** | | The Galileo System for the Electronic Management of Learning (Galileo) | The Galileo System for the Electronic Management of Learning (Galileo) | |
| **Logic and mathematics** | | High/Scope Child Observation Record (COR) | High/Scope Child Observation Record (COR) | |
| **Mathematical thinking** | | The Work Sampling System (WSS) | The Work Sampling System (WSS) | |
| **Scientific thinking** | | The Work Sampling System (WSS) | The Work Sampling System (WSS) | |

**APPENDIX TABLE 5-7** Language and Literacy Instruments

| Assessment | Data-Gathering Method | | | |
|---|---|---|---|---|
| **Subscales** | **Direct Assessment** | **Questionnaire** | **Observation** | **Interview** |
| | | The Galileo System for the Electronic Management of Learning (Galileo)<br>High/Scope Child Observation Record (COR)<br>The Work Sampling System (WSS) | The Galileo System for the Electronic Management of Learning (Galileo)<br>High/Scope Child Observation Record (COR)<br>The Work Sampling System (WSS) | |
| **General language** | Clinical Evaluation of Language Fundamentals (CELF),<br>MacArthur-Bates Communicative Development Inventories (CDI), Test of Language Dominance (TOLD), Woodcock-Johnson III (WJ-III), NEPSY | Creative Curriculum Development Continuum for Ages 3-5 | Creative Curriculum Development Continuum for Ages 3-5 | |
| **Vocabulary** | Peabody Picture Vocabulary Test (PPVT), Expressive One-Word Picture Vocabulary Test (EOWPVT) | MacArthur-Bates Communicative Development Inventories (CDI) | | |

*continued*

**APPENDIX TABLE 5-7** Continued

| Assessment | Data-Gathering Method | | | |
|---|---|---|---|---|
| **Subscales** | **Direct Assessment** | **Questionnaire** | **Observation** | **Interview** |
| **Phonological awareness** | Comprehensive Test of Phonological Processing (CTOPP), Woodcock-Johnson III (WJ-III) | | | |
| **Grammar** | Diagnostic Evaluation of Language Variation (DELV) | | | |
| **Literacy** | Test of Early Reading Ability (TERA), Woodcock-Johnson III (WJ-III), Peabody Individual Achievement Test (PIAT) Concepts About Print (Clay) Sulzby Classification Schemes: Emergent Storybook Reading (1985) | | Work Sampling Plans, Portfolio, Summative Instructional Tools | |
| **Reading recognition** | Peabody Individual Achievement Test-Revised (PIAT-R) | | | |
| **Reading comprehension** | Peabody Individual Achievement Test-Revised (PIAT-R) | | | |
| **Spelling** | Peabody Individual Achievement Test-Revised (PIAT-R) | | | |

| | | | | |
|---|---|---|---|---|
| **Verbal reasoning** | Stanford-Binet Intelligence Scale, Fourth ed. (SB-IV) | | | |
| **Verbal** | | Primary Test of Cognitive Skills (PTCS) | | |
| **Letters** | Bracken Basic Concept Scale-Revised (BBCS-R) | | | |
| **Verbal IQ** | Wechsler Preschool and Primary Scale of Intelligence, Third ed. (WPPSI-III) | | | |
| **Receptive language** | Clinical Evaluation of Language Fundamentals-Preschool (CELF-Preschool) Test of Early Language Development, Third ed. (TELD-3) | | Sequenced Inventory of Communication Development-Revised (SICD-R) | Sequenced Inventory of Communication Development-Revised (SICD-R) |
| **Expressive language** | Clinical Evaluation of Language Fundamentals-Preschool (CELF-Preschool) Reynell Developmental Language Scales: U.S. Edition (RDLS) Test of Early Language Development, Third ed. (TELD-3) | | Sequenced Inventory of Communication Development-Revised (SICD-R), Reynell Developmental Language Scales, U.S. ed. (RDLS) | Sequenced Inventory of Communication Development-Revised (SICD-R) |

*continued*

**APPENDIX TABLE 5-7** Continued

| Assessment Subscales | Data-Gathering Method | | | |
|---|---|---|---|---|
| | **Direct Assessment** | **Questionnaire** | **Observation** | **Interview** |
| **Total language** | Clinical Evaluation of Language Fundamentals-Preschool (CELF-Preschool) | | | |
| **Quick-test** | Clinical Evaluation of Language Fundamentals-Preschool (CELF-Preschool) | | | |
| **Recall ability** | Kaufman Assessment Battery for Children (K-ABC), Expressive Vocabulary Subtest | | | |
| **Verbal expression** | Kaufman Assessment Battery for Children (K-ABC), Expressive Vocabulary Subtest | | | |
| **Words and gestures** | | | | MacArthur-Bates Communicative Development Inventories (CDI) |
| **Words and sentences** | | | | MacArthur-Bates Communicative Development Inventories (CDI) |

| | | |
|---|---|---|
| **Expressive communication** | | Preschool Language Scale, Fourth ed. (PLS-4) |
| **Auditory comprehension** | | Preschool Language Scale, Fourth ed. (PLS-4) |
| **Verbal comprehension** | Reynell Developmental Language Scales, U.S. ed. (RDLS) | |
| **Spoken language quotient** | Test of Early Language Development, Third ed. (TELD-3) | |
| **Initial sound fluency** | Dynamic Indicators of Basic Early Literacy Skills, Sixth ed. (DIBELS) | |
| **Letter naming fluency** | Dynamic Indicators of Basic Early Literacy Skills, Sixth ed. (DIBELS) | |
| **Word use fluency** | Dynamic Indicators of Basic Early Literacy Skills, Sixth ed. (DIBELS) | |
| **Phoneme segmentation fluency** | Dynamic Indicators of Basic Early Literacy Skills, Sixth ed. (DIBELS) | |

*continued*

**APPENDIX TABLE 5-7** Continued

| Assessment Subscales | Data-Gathering Method | | | |
|---|---|---|---|---|
| | **Direct Assessment** | **Questionnaire** | **Observation** | **Interview** |
| **Nonsense word fluency** | Dynamic Indicators of Basic Early Literacy Skills, Sixth ed. (DIBELS) | | | |
| **Oral reading fluency and retell fluency** | Dynamic Indicators of Basic Early Literacy Skills, Sixth ed. (DIBELS) | | | |
| **Alphabet** | Test of Early Reading Ability-3 (TERA-3) | | | |
| **Conventions** | Test of Early Reading Ability-3 (TERA-3) | | | |
| **Meaning** | Test of Early Reading Ability-3 (TERA-3) | | | |
| **Letter-word identification** | Woodcock-Johnson III (WJ-III) | | | |
| **Writing samples** | Woodcock-Johnson III (WJ-III) | | | |
| **Word attack** | Woodcock-Johnson III (WJ-III) | | | |
| **Language skills** | Denver II | | | Denver II |

# 6

# Measuring Quality in Early Childhood Environments

The domains of importance in early childhood all show mutability as a result of aspects of the environment. In this chapter, we review measures of quality in family and in early care and educational environments. Sometimes the family or the quality of the early care and educational setting is an outcome in its own right—the target of an intervention, for example. In other cases, it is a mediator of the effects of an intervention (e.g., improving family financial resources, introducing a new preschool curriculum, providing professional development) on child-level outcomes. In both these cases, it is crucial to have reliable and usable instruments from which one can draw valid inferences about the quality of the environment.

Infants, toddlers, and young children need supportive, responsive, and stimulating relationships with caregivers and stimulating and safe environments to thrive (McCartney and Phillips, 2006; National Research Council and Institute of Medicine, 2000). The National Academies synthesis of research on early development *From Neurons to Neighborhoods* concluded that "early environments matter and nurturing relationships are essential" (National Research Council and Institute of Medicine, 2000, p. 4). Families provide the primary care for children and are often the focus of early intervention programs. Home visiting programs are designed to promote positive, supportive parenting and to reduce harsh negative parenting of infants, thereby indirectly enhancing their cognitive and social development (Wasik and Bryant, 2001). State or federally funded child care and educational programs are designed to promote children's cognitive, academic, and social skills directly (National Institute for Early Education Research, 2006). Parents and policy makers want to know about the quality of programs or family environments to ensure that they are enhancing, or at least not harming, children's development. Accordingly, assessing children's home and center-based environments, as well as child outcomes, has become an important part of assessment systems for young children (Adams, Tout, and Zaslow, 2007; Mitchell, 2005).

## OBSERVATIONAL MEASURES FOR MULTIPLE PURPOSES

Many observational measures have been developed to assess the quality of home or early childhood care and education programs. Selection of a measure requires consideration of the child population, the purpose of the observations, and the domains of most interest. For a program serving English language learners, for example, opportunities for children to develop language and vocabulary in their native language as well as English would be particularly important.

Observational measures serve a number of purposes. First, they can be used for caregiver and teacher professional development. They can call administrators' and caregivers' or teachers' attention to their own behaviors and practices that might promote positive child outcomes. Having caregivers and teachers evaluate their own or each other's classrooms and home-based care settings, as well as having two people (either an administrator and a caregiver/teacher or two caregivers/teachers) evaluate the same setting, can be instructive and can provide good material for discussion. Administrators of formal early care and education programs—such as child care centers, preschools, prekindergartens, and Head Start programs—can also use classroom observation measures as part of their teacher/caregiver evaluation strategy, as a more objective, sharable set of criteria for observation. Several promising professional development programs use observational measures as the basis for improving quality of child care. For example, Pianta and colleagues use their tool, the CLASS (Pianta, La Paro, and Hamre, 2007), to promote more intentional instruction, classroom management, and emotional support in the classroom through their professional program, My Teaching Partner (Kinzie et al., 2006). The Quality Interventions for Early Care and Education (QUINCE) intervention and evaluation, which uses on-site technical assistance to improve the quality of home-based as well as center-based child care, uses the environmental ratings scales, the Family Day Care Environment Rating Scale, or FDCERS (Harms and Clifford, 1989), and the Early Childhood Environment Rating Scale-Revised, or ECERS-R (Harms, Clifford, and Cryer, 1998), to promote the use of age-appropriate activities and enhance teacher-child interactions in their program, which follows the Partners for Inclusion model (Bryant, 2007; Wesley, 1994).

Second, observational measures can be used in formative assessment of programs that are striving to improve their quality. Periodic observations and examination of scores on different dimensions can help identify weaknesses that require further attention. Fourteen states now have quality ratings systems available to the public, with summary ratings of the quality of early care and education, and many more states are developing such systems, with the aim of improving information to consumers and providing supports to improve quality (Tout, Zaslow, and Martinez-Beck, forthcoming). Local communities as well are developing such systems. In most fully developed state quality ratings systems, an observational measure of the quality of the early care and education environment—usually the ECERS-R, FDCERS, or the infant and toddler version of this measure, the Infant/Toddler Environment Rating Scale (Harms, Cryer, and Clifford, 1990)—is used as one component of the overall rating of the environment, which usually includes multiple components, selected and weighted differently in each state or community. The rating of the environment is used not only as a contributor to the summary rating of quality, but also as a source of detailed information about the facets of quality that need improvement and in which changes will help progress to the next quality rating.

Third, classroom observations can be used for accountability purposes, instead of or as a supplement to child outcome measures. Child care quality has been a consistent modest to moderate positive predictor of children's cognitive and language skills in large, multisite studies and smaller local studies (Howes et al., 2008; Lamb, 1998; NICHD Early Child Care Research Network, 2006; Peisner-Feinberg et al., 2001; Vandell, 2004) and a somewhat consistent predictor of social skill (NICHD Early Child Care Research Network, 2006; Peisner-Feinberg et al., 2001; Vandell, 2004). Using early childhood assessments as part of an aligned system requires the capacity to juxtapose information about quality in the early care and education setting with change scores on children's development (along with other key components). Thus, a complete system will require both ratings of the environment and assessments of children at multiple points in time, although this is expensive.

In some federal and state efforts, observations of early care and education settings serve both a monitoring and accountability function and a formative function, providing information to improve quality. Thus, for example, as part of monitoring and accountability, the Head Start Impact Study collected observations of the quality of Head Start programs as well as of formal early care and education programs serving children in the control group (U.S. Department of Health and Human Services, Administration for Children and Families, 2005). Similarly, the Head Start Family and Child Experiences Survey (FACES) regularly collects observational data on a nationally representative sample of Head Start programs. The observational data are used in combination with child outcome data as part of ongoing program monitoring. However, the observational ratings and child outcomes together are also used to inform ongoing program improvement (see discussion in Zaslow, 2008). As one example, information from Head Start FACES was instrumental in shaping an increased focus in Head Start programs on early literacy development. Information from the Head Start Impact Study has also been instrumental in increasing professional development for Head Start teachers, focusing on early mathematics development in young children and how best to foster it.

Fourth, classroom observations are useful for research. Indeed, most measures were originally developed as part of a research initiative. An extensive body of work looks at the relationship of observational measures to child outcomes, especially in classroom-type early care and educational settings, and to a lesser extent in home-based care (Bryant, forthcoming; Burchinal, forthcoming; Burchinal et al., 2008). In addition, observational measures are used in evaluation studies to assess whether an intervention to improve practice in home-based or center-based early care and educational settings has affected caregiver/teacher practice or overall quality (for example, Bryant, 2007, and Pianta, 2007). An observational measure designed to assess parenting skills as a tool in caregiver or teacher professional development or for formative assessment should be detailed and descriptive so that it can help to direct improvement. In contrast, a measure used for research, summative assessment, or for accountability purposes, even if detailed, should be easily summarized in quantifiable ratings, so that scores can be compared over time and across settings.

Purposes, in turn, have implications for who conducts the observation. If the goal is professional development or formative assessment, observations might be done by individuals directly involved. For example, observations of parenting skills might be done by a home visitor; a child care program teacher or administrator could do observations of early care and education. If summative assessment or accountability is a goal, it is preferable that observation measures be administered by someone who is not directly connected to the program being evaluated, although program staff may sometimes perform this role if sufficient safeguards are in place to ensure the reliability and validity of the observations.

Most existing measures assess the social environment well and the learning environment at a very general level, but only a few adequately assess practices designed to teach academic or social skills specifically. Development of observational measures is just beginning to catch up with the increased political emphasis on academic preparation in programs for young children (National Institute for Early Education Research, 2006). We summarize below some existing observational measures of the home and center-based environments, without attempting to be exhaustive. For all of these measures, there is some evidence for their reliability and validity, and many include demonstrated associations with child outcomes.

Note that although home or classroom observations may not be as labor-intensive or expensive as assessing individual child outcomes, all of these measures require a fair amount of assessor/observer training for the results to be valid and reliable. Developers of observational systems should provide clear and sufficiently intensive training criteria. Publishers of some instruments, like the CLASS (Pianta, La Paro, and Hamre, 2007), require training to be conducted by a publisher-trained and certified trainer, with different training for different user purposes.

As specified by the developers, many natural observations of center-based or home settings require a minimum of 3 hours to ensure that sufficient sampling of the environment has occurred. Semistructured observations or interviews can require less time because they draw on specific kinds of interactions across all participants. Recommended times for the measures in Appendix Table 6-1 range from 1.5 hours to 2 half-days.

Details on these measures can be found in the literature cited and, for many, in a compendium profiling observational measures for early childhood care and education environments prepared by Child Trends (Child Trends, 2007). Appendix Table 6-1 is a summary of some important characteristics of each measure discussed. The stars indicate that the dimension is represented somewhat (one star) or substantially (two stars).

## ASSESSING HOME ENVIRONMENTS

Parents "structure the experiences and shape the environments within which early development unfolds" (National Research Council and Institute of Medicine, 2000, p. 226). Children's early cognitive, social, and physical development are all clearly linked to their relationships with their primary caregivers and the kinds of experiences available in their home environments (McCartney and Phillips, 2006). Theories of development focus on two overlapping dimensions related to assessing families in early childhood. The quality of relationships between the child and his or her primary caregivers is viewed as central for all forms of development, especially socioemotional skills (Bornstein and

Sawyer, in McCartney and Phillips, 2006, pp. 381-398). And the quality of cognitive stimulation clearly plays a critical role for cognitive, language, and social development (Bradley et al., 2001; Fuligni, Han, and Brooks-Gunn, 2004).

There have been many theoretical and empirical systems developed for describing how families affect children's cognitive, language, and social development. These systems almost always include at least three dimensions: (1) the quality of the parent-child relationships and more distally of mother-father and whole-family relationships, (2) the quality of stimulation provided directly by caregivers in interactions with the child and by the objects that are available in the family environment, and (3) provision of basic needs and safety monitoring. These dimensions are listed below with a set of characteristics that are believed to be important for each dimension:

1. Relationships (mother-child, father-child, other primary caregiver-child, and more distally mother-father), emotional climate, social interactions, support for social skills development, and discipline strategies:
   - A. Degree to which adults are affectionate, supportive, attentive, and respectful toward children.
   - B. Explicit support for social skills (e.g., encouraging children to "use their words," modeling and engaging children in conversations about social problem-solving skills, encouraging the use of learned strategies to solve real social conflicts).
   - C. Degree to which primary caregivers use consistent behavior management techniques that are not harsh or demeaning.
2. Cognitive stimulation:
   - A. Extent to which primary caregivers use the home environment to provide and scaffold learning activities for the child.
   - B. Degree to which primary caregivers provide stimulating activities in the community.
   - C. Degree to which primary caregivers talk to the child, engage the child in conversation, and use elaborated language in those verbal interactions.

D. Frequency with which children are exposed to books and have books read to them.
E. Literacy resources (e.g., books, magazines, writing materials, computers) in the home.

3. Provision of basic needs and safety monitoring:
A. Degree to which the home environment is free of hazards, clean, and organized.
B. Degree to which toys, books, and other child-friendly materials are available to the child without adult mediation.
C. Presence of or access to outdoor play areas or areas in which gross motor play can occur.

**Primary Caregiver-Child Interactions**

Primary caregiver-child interactions typically either are coded from videotapes of semistructured 10- to 20-minute observations in which the primary caregiver is asked to engage the child in age-appropriate activities or are rated live during longer observations in the home. An example is a measure used in the National Institute of Child Health and Human Development (NICHD) Study of Early Child Care and Youth Development (SECCYD) (NICHD Early Child Care Research Network, 1999, 2003) and the Early Head Start study (U.S. Department of Health and Human Services, Administration for Children and Families, 2004); different procedures are used for the youngest infants, toddlers, and preschoolers. Mothers of 6-month-olds were asked to play with their infants for 7 minutes and were told that they could use any toy or object available in the home or none at all. For the remaining 8 minutes, mothers were given a standard set of toys they could use in play.

At 15, 24, and 36 months, the observation protocol followed a three-boxes procedure in which mothers were asked to show their children age-appropriate toys in three containers in a set order. The mother was asked to have her child play with the toys in each of the three containers and to do so in the order specified, but she was told she could spend as long or as little time on each activity as she wished. Videotapes were coded by research assistants who had attended centralized training sessions. At 6, 15, and

24 months, mothers were rated on a 4-7 point scale (ranging from "not at all characteristic" to "highly characteristic") to describe maternal sensitivity to child nondistress, cognitive stimulation, intrusiveness, positive regard, and negative regard. At 36 and 54 months, the mothers were rated on 7-point ratings of supportive presence, hostility (reversed), and respect for autonomy.

The composite scores were the strongest predictor of children's cognitive, language, academic, and social outcomes when considered with demographic, parental attitude, and schooling characteristics in the NICHD SECCYD (NICHD Early Child Care Research Network, 2006). Similar observational systems have been developed and used for attachment (e.g., Egeland and Deinard, 1975), special education (e.g., Yoder and Warren, 2001), and effects of differing welfare reform policies on children (Weinfield, Egeland, and Ogawa, 1998). These observation procedures can also be used in assessing the quality of out-of-home care for infants and toddlers.

### Cognitive Stimulation

Cognitive stimulation is reflected in a dimension called quality of instruction, which is often measured using a videotaped laboratory procedure in which mother and child pairs participate in a series of developmentally appropriate problem-solving situations (Englund et al., 2004). The mother's instructional behavior is rated on a 7-point scale that reflects how well she structured the situation and coordinated her behavior to the child's activity and needs for assistance. The scale ranges from 1, indicating poor quality of instruction (uninvolved or unstructured), to 7, indicating effective instruction throughout the session. The rating from this measure correlated with subsequent scores on standardized achievement tests in several studies (see, e.g., Connell and Prinz, 2002; Englund et al., 2004; Pianta and Egeland, 1994; Pianta and Harbers, 1996; Pianta, Egeland, and Sroufe, 1990; Pianta, Nimetz, and Bennett, 1997). Other observational rating systems focus on the quality of cognitive (DeTemple and Snow, 1998) or affective (Frosch, Cox, and Goldman, 2001) interaction specifically surrounding book reading.

Recently the Child/Home Early Language and Literacy

Observation (CHELLO) observation measure was developed to assess the quality of early childhood language and literacy practices in mixed-age home-based child care settings (Neuman, Dwyer, and Koh, 2007). The measure complements a classroom observation measure (ELLCO) described below. A checklist is used to assess the literacy environment (books, writing materials, and cognitively stimulating toys) and a 1-5 rating scale includes items that assess the physical environment for learning, support for learning, and teaching strategies (e.g., vocabulary building, use of print, storytelling). The CHELLO total score has been shown to be correlated with growth in children's language skills (PPVT), phonological skills, and ability to do language-oriented mathematical problems.

### Home Observation for Measurement of the Environment

We single out the Home Observation for Measurement of the Environment (HOME; Caldwell and Bradley, 1984) for discussion because it is such a widely used assessment of the home environment. The focus is on the child *in* the environment, experiencing objects, events, and transactions occurring in connection with the family surroundings. There are separate forms for assessing infants and toddlers and older children. The infant/toddler version of the inventory (IT-HOME) focuses on infancy (birth to age 3 years). It is composed of 45 items clustered into 6 subscales: (1) parental responsivity, (2) acceptance of child, (3) organization of the environment, (4) learning materials, (5) parental involvement, and (6) variety in experience. Each item is scored in binary fashion (yes/no). Information used to score the items is obtained during the course of the home visit by means of observation and semistructured interview.

The early childhood version of the inventory (EC-HOME) is used during early childhood (ages 3 to 6). It is composed of 55 items clustered into 8 subscales: (1) learning materials, (2) language stimulation, (3) physical environment, (4) responsivity, (5) academic stimulation, (6) modeling, (7) variety, and (8) acceptance. Each item is scored in binary fashion (yes/no). Information on items is obtained either through observation or through asking the mother. Typically the total score is used, although a recent factor analysis (Fuligni et al., 2004) produced scales that appear to differentiate between stimulation in the home environment for language and literacy and for social development.

As with parental sensitivity, the quality of the home environment has been shown to be a moderate to strong predictor of academic and social outcomes for young children regardless of income or ethnicity (Bradley et al., 2001). Zaslow et al. (2006) found that the HOME, direct observations of mother-child interaction, and maternal self-report measures collected during the preschool years all predicted child outcomes during middle childhood in a low-income sample with family background characteristics controlled. However, direct observations showed the strongest pattern of prediction.

## CENTER-BASED EARLY CHILDHOOD ENVIRONMENTS

Early childhood care and education programs are increasingly being held accountable for their effects on children's development, and thus assessments of quality are needed. As noted earlier, measures of quality are also being used to inform efforts to improve quality at the community and state levels, and in research evaluating specific quality improvement efforts. The specific dimensions measured will vary as a function of program goals, as discussed throughout this report. It is important for measures of the environment to be used in conjunction with measures of child outcomes to provide a context for understanding the extent to which children show positive development during the time they are participating in early care and education. This section describes strategies for assessing program quality directly.

Many indicators that have been connected to child outcomes are fairly easy to quantify. Examples are staff-child ratios, number of children in a classroom, amount spent per child, the training and experience of teachers, and teacher turnover. Other quality variables are less easily quantifiable but are nonetheless important, such as opportunities for professional development for staff and the nature of the curriculum. Information on these variables is best obtained by interviews with program directors, surveys, or inspection of records. Some of these indicators, such as teacher/

caregiver education, staff-child ratio, and group size are related to better child outcomes across a number of studies (Howes, 1997; NICHD Early Child Care Research Network, 2002; Phillipsen et al., 1997; Vandell, 2004), although recent evidence has raised questions about whether teacher/caregiver education is related to child outcomes in publicly funded center-based child care settings, such as prekindergarten and Head Start programs (Early et al., 2006). Recent work suggests that teacher/caregiver education may play a different role in early care and educational settings with more versus less supports, requirements, and monitoring. A study in California by Vu, Jeon, and Howes (in press) found that teacher education contributed to quality in the *less* supported early care and education settings (such as private child care) but not in the more supported settings (such as state-sponsored prekindergarten).

## CLASSROOMS

Earlier we presented a list of dimensions on which parents and caregivers influence the development of young children. A similar set of dimensions of quality that are observable in the classroom are believed to contribute to children's physical, socio-emotional, and cognitive development. For some of them, there is good empirical evidence linking quality on the dimension to children's development (see Box 6-1).

### Observation Measures

Most existing measures assess the social environment well and the learning environment at a very general level, but only a few adequately assess practices related to cognition or academic skill domains. Development of observation measures is just beginning to catch up with the increased political emphasis on academic preparation. Early measures included only a few very general items related to practices designed to promote language and cognitive development. Thus, for example, many measures include items assessing the degree to which children choose activities, but few provide very much information on the degree to which children are given specific kinds of opportunities to develop literacy, mathematical, or science skills.

We summarize below selected observational measures that have been developed and used to assess early childhood programs. For each of these measures, there is some evidence for their reliability and validity. (Evidence on the reliability and validity of these and other observational measures is summarized by Child Trends, 2007, in a compendium providing profiles of measures of quality in early childhood care and educational settings.) Few measures have demonstrated effects on child outcomes, although most assess practices that have been associated with positive child outcomes. Note that although classroom observations may not be as labor-intensive or expensive as assessing individual child outcomes, a fair amount of training is necessary to use all of these measures reliably. Observations generally should be done for a minimum of 3 hours before a classroom is rated. For full-day programs, a full-day observation is preferable, and observations on two separate days are always desirable. The developers of some measures require their own training and certification.

**Assessment Profile for Early Childhood Programs**

The Assessment Profile for Early Childhood Programs (APECP; Abbot-Shinn and Sibley, 1992) is an observational checklist with dichotomous items that provides a global assessment of overall preschool classroom environment; it includes subscales that address specific aspects of the dimensions thought to define global quality. These scales include (1) learning environment (provisions for and accessibility of materials, space conducive to child independence), (2) scheduling (written plans assessed for balance and variety of activities), (3) curriculum (degree to which alternative techniques are used to facilitate learning, based on assessment of children in class; degree to which children are encouraged to be active in guiding their own learning; the role of the teacher in facilitating learning), (4) interacting (teachers' positive interactions, responsiveness, and management of children), and (5) individualizing (support for individualized learning experiences through assessment, parent communication, and referrals; plans for children with special needs).

## BOX 6-1
## Dimensions of Quality Observable in the Classroom

1. Emotional climate, social interactions, support for social skills development, and discipline strategies:
   A. Degree to which adults are affectionate, supportive, attentive, and respectful toward children.
   B. Explicit support for social skills (e.g., encouraging children to "use their words," modeling and engaging children in conversations about social problem solving skills, encouraging use of learned strategies to solve real social conflicts).
   C. Conversations about feelings.
   D. Collaboration and cooperation opportunities.
   E. Clarity and developmental appropriateness of rules.
   F. Teachers' use of redirection, positive reinforcement, encouragement, and explanations to minimize negative behavior.
2. Instructional activities—an explicit curriculum with specified learning goals for children.
3. General—individualized (adjusted to children's skills and interests); purposeful, planned instruction; integration of content areas; children actively interacting with materials.
4. Language—adults engage in conversations with children; activities that encourage conversation among children; explicit efforts to develop vocabulary and language skills in the context of meaningful activities.
5. Literacy—children read to and given opportunities to read; rhyming words, initial sounds, letter–sound links, and spellings of common words pointed out and practiced; functions and features of print pointed out; opportunities to dictate and write using invented spelling made available.
6. Mathematics—activities that involve counting objects, measuring, identifying shapes, creating patterns, telling time, classifying and seriating objects; instruction on concepts (e.g., big, bigger, equal, one-to-one correspondence, spatial relationships).
7. Science—active manipulation of materials (e.g., sink and float) with adult engaging children in prediction, systematic observation and analysis; instruction on scientific concepts linked to active exploration (e.g., care and observations of live animals).

8. Interactions with parents—activities and opportunities for parents to be informed about the program and their child.
9. Cultural responsiveness:
   A. Evidence of supports for linguistic and cultural diversity (e.g., pictures, books, language).
   B. Activities that expose children to diverse languages and cultural practices.
   C. Support for native language development.
   D. Support for learning English.
10. Safety:
    A. Adult-child ratio.
    B. Absence of broken furniture, any objects that could cause physical harm.
    C. Sufficient space; open pathways.
    D. Place for personal hygiene (e.g., teeth brushing, hand washing).
11. Materials:
    A. Technology (e.g., computers).
    B. Music (e.g., CD player).
    C. Creativity (e.g., art supplies, easels, play dough).
    D. Dramatic play (e.g., store, post office, kitchen, clothes).
    E. Science (e.g., sand, water, plants, live animals).
    F. Literacy (e.g., books, writing materials).
    G. Math (e.g., counting objects, blocks, measuring instruments).
    H. Fine motor (e.g., materials for drawing, scissors).
12. Physical arrangement:
    A. Space and equipment for gross motor activities (e.g., climbing equipment, swings, balls).
    B. Place for quiet and rest (e.g., rugs and pillows out of the center of activity).
    C. Children's access to materials.
13. Adaptations for children with disabilities.

The 75 items are scored on a yes/no basis according to whether or not they characterize a program during each time interval observed. Typically, programs are observed in 15- to 20-minute time periods over a course of 3 hours (e.g., one time period per hour), thus yielding up to 3 yes/no scores for each item. Although the measure includes items related to academic instruction, the yes/no format is a major limitation. Thus, for example, the caregiver/teacher asking only one open-ended question or writing down one word dictated by a child during an observation period gets a "yes" score for that observation period. The measure also does not differentiate among kinds of instructional approaches. For example, scores go up whether children are asked questions that require remembering specific facts (such as who, what, when questions), or questions that are open-ended or problem-solving (such as why and how questions). Scores on the learning environment are also substantially affected by the number of materials of a particular kind rather than the quality of their use. Also, some of the items require inspection of records (e.g., lesson plans, daily schedule).

The APECP scores have been related to child outcomes in both program improvement and observational studies (Lambert, Abbott-Shinn, and Sibley, 2006).

## Caregiver Interaction Scale

The Caregiver Interaction Scale (CIS; Arnett, 1989) provides a global rating of caregiver/teacher sensitivity and responsiveness to all children in the setting. It has been used in both center and home-based care and for infants, toddlers, and preschoolers. It focuses on caregiver/teacher interactions with children, especially on responsiveness and emotional tone. The measure consists of 26 items measuring teachers': (1) sensitivity (e.g., "seems enthusiastic about the children's activities and efforts"), (2) harshness (e.g., "seems unnecessarily harsh when scolding or prohibiting children"), (3) detachment (e.g., "spends considerable time in activity not involving interventions with the children"), and (4) permissiveness (e.g., "expects the children to exercise self-control"). Each item is rated on a 4-point Likert scale with 1 being "not at all" to 4 being "very much." The focus on teacher-child interaction is a strength if that is the primary goal. The measure must be supplemented with another measure if other dimensions of the classroom context need to be assessed.

### Classroom Assessment Scoring System

The Classroom Assessment Scoring System (CLASS; Pianta, La Paro, and Hamre, 2007) provides an assessment of the overall preschool classroom in terms of the teacher's sensitivity, quality of instruction across all academic areas, and classroom management. It assesses 10 domains of teacher-child interaction that form three subscales: (1) emotional support: (a) positive climate, (b) negative climate, (c) teacher sensitivity, (d) regard for children's perspectives; (2) classroom organization: (a) behavior management (proactive, nondisruptive, reinforcing positive behavior), (b) productivity (efficient use of time), (c) instructional learning formats (teacher enabling of children's experience, exploration and manipulation of materials); and (3) instructional support: (a) concept development, (b) quality of feedback, (c) language modeling. Each dimension is rated on a 7-point Likert-type scale. Observers rate all dimensions after at least four 20-minute intervals. The measure assesses instruction, but only at a very general level. There are no specific items related to literacy or mathematical instruction. A limitation is that there are only nine items focused on classroom practice, which include many different practices.

The CLASS, developed relatively recently, was used in an 11-state evaluation of prekindergarten programs. The instructional climate score provided the best, albeit modest, prediction of gains in children's language and literacy skills relative to scores from other widely used instruments (Howes et al., 2008).

### Classroom Practices Inventory

The Classroom Practices Inventory (CPI; Hyson, Hirsh-Pasek, and Rescorla, 1990) was developed to differentiate between developmentally appropriate practices, according to 1987 guidelines of the National Association for the Education of Young Children (NAEYC), and highly didactic practices. It focuses on the teaching practices the teacher uses with the entire preschool classroom. The measure contains 26 items divided into two subscales. The emotional climate subscale assesses the teacher's warmth, encouragement, and positive guidance. In the program focus subscale, half of the 20 items refer to didactic, teacher-directed practices (e.g., large-group instruction; workbooks, ditto sheets, and flashcards; memorization and drill; art projects that involve copying; focus on getting the right answer), which were considered developmentally inappropriate by NAEYC. Of the 10 items that describe positive activities, most concern child choice and initiative and diversity of activities and materials that children can manipulate. Three of the items refer to positive instructional approaches (e.g., "teachers ask questions that encourage children to give more than one right answer").

The CPI described center-based child care preschool programs in the 10-site NICHD Study of Early Child Care and Youth Development. The program focus score predicted children's language and academic outcomes at 4.5 years in analyses that adjusted for family characteristics in unpublished analyses (available from the authors on request).

### A Developmentally Appropriate Practices Template

A Developmentally Appropriate Practices Template (ADAPT; Van Horn and Ramey, 2004) has 19 items based on the 1987 NAEYC guidelines. It also focuses on the teaching practices the teacher uses with the entire preschool classroom. Items are anchored on a 1 (developmentally inappropriate) to 5 (developmentally appropriate) scale, with descriptions for each anchor. The items form three scales: (1) integrated curriculum (e.g., "teacher adapts instruction to children's interests, needs, and prior knowledge"; "literacy integrated across content areas with literacy materials of social relevance"), (2) social-emotional emphasis (e.g., "children's social and emotional development consistently supported by peers and teachers"; "children and teacher collaborate, classroom exemplifies community of learners with shared goals"), and (3) child-centered approaches (e.g., "children encouraged to choose and interact with materials to create and problem-solve"; "children work interdependently to complete task or project and make joint decisions"). Instructional practices are described at a fairly general level and focus primarily on integration and child-centeredness.

**Early Childhood Environment Rating Scale-Revised Edition**

The Early Childhood Environment Rating Scale-Revised Edition (ECERS-R; Harms, Clifford, and Cryer, 1998) is the most widely used measure of early childhood environments for both evaluation and research purposes. Its goal is to describe the overall quality of the preschool classroom based on the quality of teacher-child interactions and types of activities available in the classroom. The original scale was published in 1980 (Harms and Clifford, 1980) and was revised in 1998 (Harms, Clifford, and Cryer, 1998). The two measures have been compared (Sakai et al., 2003), with the scores on the revised version being highly correlated with those on the original scale but also being on average about .5 points lower. Developers of other scales frequently use correlations with the ECERS as a check on the validity of the new scale. The ECERS primarily focuses on the structural quality of early childhood programs as defined by 43 items that make up 7 subscales: (1) space and furnishings, (2) personal care routines, (3) language-reasoning, (4) activities, (5) interaction, (6) program structure, and (7) parents and staff. Each item is rated on a 1-7 scale with descriptions anchored at odd numbers, such that 1 represents an "inadequate situation," 3 is "minimal," 5 is "good," and 7 is an "excellent situation." The ECERS assesses the quality and quantity of books and mathematical materials in the classroom and assesses very global practices in the language-reasoning subscale (e.g., "a wide selection of books are accessible for a substantial portion of the day"; "children are asked questions to encourage them to give longer and more complex answers"). It does not measure instructional practices. Factor analyses of the instrument have consistently yielded two dimensions (National Association for the Education of Young Children, 2005). The first dimension describes the quality and quantity of teacher-child interactions across multiple types of activities, and the second dimension describes the extent to which a variety of age-appropriate activities are provided.

The ECERS or ECERS-R child-related total scores have been

modestly to moderately related to children's language and social skills across a large number of studies (Bryant et al., 1994; Burchinal, Peisner-Feinberg, et al., 2000; Burchinal, Roberts, et al., 2000; Howes, Phillips, and Whitebrook, 1992; McCartney, 1984; Peisner-Feinberg and Burchinal, 1997; Phillips, McCartney, and Scarr, 1987). The magnitude of these associations tends to be modest, with partial correlations of $0.06 < r < 0.17$ across studies. While most of these studies focused on total scores, a recent prekindergarten evaluation study reported that summary scores describing caregiver-child interactions were stronger predictors of child outcomes than summary scores describing the types and quality of activities available in the setting (Howes et al., 2008).

**Early Childhood Environment Rating Scale-Extension**

The Early Childhood Environment Rating Scale-Extension (ECERS-E; Sylva, Siraj-Blatchford, and Taggart, 2003; Sylva et al., 2006) was developed to supplement the ECERS-R, which was deemed by the authors to be insufficiently sensitive to important teaching practices that support children's intellectual development. Focusing on the quality of instruction for the preschool classroom, it has 4 separate subscales consisting of 18 items: (1) literacy (e.g., adult reading with child, attention paid to sounds in words, books, and print available and discussed), (2) mathematics (e.g., counting encouraged, number games, reading and writing numbers, shapes, matching and comparing), (3) science/environment (e.g., science resources, exploration of natural materials, scientific concepts introduced), and (4) diversity (e.g., planning for individual needs, race and gender equality addressed). The measure was tailored to tap the dimensions of quality defined by a new curriculum in England. Following the format of the ECERS-R, detailed descriptions are provided for each item; items are scored 1 (inadequate) through 7 (excellent). The measure is conservative in the sense that there are stringent rules for getting a relatively high score; a lower score could be given if one very specific practice was not seen. The measure would also favor better resourced programs because many items require the presence of specific learning materials. Reports of studies by the ECERS-E developers (Sylva et al., 2006) claim that the instrument has predictive validity for pre-reading scores, early number concepts, and nonverbal reasoning.

## Early Childhood Classroom Observation Measure

The Early Childhood Classroom Observation Measure (ECCOM; Stipek and Byler, 2004) also focuses on the quality of the preschool classroom in terms of both teacher sensitivity and classroom management style. It contains 32 highly descriptive items with 3 subscales: (1) management (teachers provide children with choices both in the context of teacher-planned activities and during free time; rules and routines are clear but flexible; children are given developmentally appropriate responsibilities; discipline is brief and nondisruptive, often involving explanations or assisting children in their own social problem solving); (2) social climate (teachers are warm, responsive, attentive, and respectful of children; tasks and activities are flexible and adapted to children's individual skill levels, interests, and experiences outside the classroom; social and communication skills are taught directly and in the context of naturally occurring social conflicts); and (3) learning climate and instruction (individualized but clearly articulated standards; coherent lessons; focus on understanding; children are active participants in instructional conversations; broad array of literacy experiences; mathematical instruction emphasizes processes and problem solving). Each of the items is rated at the end of the observations using a scale of 1 (practices are rarely seen) to 5 (practices predominate). A "classroom resources" checklist is also included to document materials in views that are related to technology, literacy, mathematics, dramatic play, art, gross motor equipment, and real-life objects. One limitation of the measure is that each item includes a number of different practices. As a consequence, the item score does not provide information on exactly which of the practices were observed.

## Early Language and Literacy Classroom Observation

The Early Language and Literacy Classroom Observation (ELLCO; Smith and Dickinson, 2002) focuses on the quality of the language and literacy experiences in a preschool classroom. It is one of the few measures that provides detailed information on literacy instruction and could be combined with a measure that includes items on other dimensions of classroom practice. It can be administered in as little as 1.5 hours. The Literacy Environment Checklist assesses the visibility and accessibility of such literacy-related materials as books, an alphabet, word cards, teacher dictation, alphabet puzzles, and writing tools. There are also 14 ratings that are made at the end of a classroom observation, using a rubric on a 1 (deficient) to 5 (exemplary) scale. The scale includes a few items on classroom management and climate, but most items focus on language-learning opportunities (e.g., oral language facilitation; book reading and discussion; instruction in and opportunities to write meaningful text; frequent and various approaches to assessment). Accompanying the observation measure is a teacher interview designed to clarify aspects of the observation. Finally, the Literacy Activities Rating Scale asks observers to record the amount of time spent on nine literacy behaviors related to book reading and writing.

Studies have shown that the ELLCO explained a significant amount of the between-classroom variation in children's receptive vocabulary (Peabody Picture Vocabulary Test) and early literacy skills (Dickinson et al., 2000; Smith and Dickinson, 2002) as well as social skills (Dickinson et al., 2001).

### Emerging Academics Snapshot

The Emerging Academics Snapshot (EAS; Ritchie et al., 2001) focuses on social and academic experiences of individual children in the preschool classroom. The experiences of selected children are often tallied to form a classroom composite, although the individual experiences are also used as predictors of that child's outcomes. It is a time-sampling observational instrument designed to describe children's exposure to instruction and engagement in academic activities, as well as to describe activities and adult responsive involvement. It includes 27 items that are coded as present or absent in 20-second periods, followed by a 40-second coding period. The instrument can be used in either a traditional time-sampled procedure—one child at a time—or as a snapshot.

When one child at a time is sampled, at least three 5-minute periods divided into 20-second intervals should be collected across a 1- to 2-hour period. When used in snapshot fashion, up to four children can be sampled in succession. To assess a program, a subset of randomly identified children could be observed and their data averaged. Subcategories include (1) children's activity setting, for example (a) routines (standing in line, cleanup, waiting for materials, etc.); (b) whole group; (c) small group time; (d) centers/free choice; (2) engagement with adults (didactic, scaffolds, uses home language of child); (3) engagement with activities (being read to, copying, engaged in mathematics, science, fantasy play, on the computer); and (4) peer interaction (e.g., solitary, parallel, cooperative pretend). The measure is descriptive and does not yield quality scores. It would not be appropriate for accountability purposes, but it can be instructive in teacher professional development and as a formative assessment tool to provide descriptive information on how children are spending their time.

At least some evidence suggests that the EAS measures aspects of the child care environment related to children's outcomes. It was used in the 11-state evaluation of prekindergarten programs. Gains in literacy outcomes were predicted by time spent in literacy-related activities (Howes et al., 2008).

### Family Day Care Rating Scale

The Family Day Care Rating Scale (FDCRS), designed for family day care programs, uses the same format as the ECERS-R. The 38 items form seven subscales: (1) space and furnishings, (2) personal care routines, (3) listening and talking, (4) activities, (5) interaction, (6) program structure, and (7) parents and provider.

A growing focus on the quality of home-based child care has resulted in greater use of the FDCRS, but few studies have measured both the quality of care and child outcomes. In perhaps the largest study, FDCRS scores predicted children's social and language skills (Kontos, Howes, and Galinsky, 1996).

## Infant and Toddler Environmental Rating Scale

The Infant and Toddler Environmental Rating Scale-Revised (ITERS-R; Harms et al., 1990) uses the same format as the ECERS-R, but it is designed to assess center-based child care programs for infants and toddlers. The 43 items are organized to cover seven categories: (1) space and furnishings, (2) personal care routines, (3) listening and talking, (4) activities, (5) interaction, (6) program structure, and (7) parents and staff.

While many studies have used the ITERS to document the quality of infant/toddler center care (e.g., Helburn, 1995), relatively few studies have also measured the infants or toddlers themselves. In one study that measured both the classroom and home environments and infant outcomes, the ITERS total score predicted both the level and rate of change in infant and toddler's language and IQ scores in a study of black children attending center-based care (Burchinal, Roberts, et al., 2000).

## Observation Measure of Language and Literacy Instruction

The Observation Measure of Language and Literacy Instruction (OMLIT; Abt Associates Inc., 2006) focuses on measuring the quality of the literacy practices in preschool classrooms. It is a battery of observation instruments that assess instructional practices and qualities of the environment in early childhood education classrooms that have been shown to support the development of oral language and emergent literacy skills. A classroom description is also included that provides contextual information, such as the number of children, their ages, and the languages they speak and that are used in instruction. There are five instruments:

1. The Classroom Literacy Opportunities Checklist is an inventory of 54 classroom literacy resources in 7 categories (e.g., text material and reading/listening areas; writing materials and writing area; diversity in the literacy materials). Items are coded either on a 3-point scale (minimally supplied, adequately supplied, well-supplied) or a 2-point scale (minimally supplied or well-supplied).

2. The Snapshot of Classroom Activities identifies literacy activities and integration of literacy materials in other activities, languages spoken, and count of adults and children present.
3. The Read Aloud Profile assesses dialogic reading practices on seven dimensions (e.g., pre-reading "set up," strategies used while reading, language(s) used).
4. The Classroom Literacy Instruction Profile describes the literacy activities and the instructional methods used by staff. Staff in the classroom are followed for 10 minutes at 15-minute intervals over the observation period, coding literacy "events." Codes are both descriptive (the strategies used) and evaluative (e.g., the cognitive challenge presented by the dialogue/discussion between the staff member and the children).
5. The Quality of Instruction in Language and Literacy measure rates the frequency and quality of literacy instruction and support for language and literacy development. Each of the 11 items is rated on a 5-point scale.

The OMLIT is extraordinarily detailed and comprehensive, and accompanying materials provide an extensive rationale for the choice of items. It is unlikely that all of the scales would be used, but specific selections could be made.

### Observation Record of the Caregiving Environment

The Observation Record of the Caregiving Environment (ORCE; National Institute of Child Health and Human Development, NICHD Early Child Care Research Network, 2000) focuses on the sensitivity and responsiveness of the caregiver to an individual child. It can be used in home- or center-based settings for infants, toddlers, and preschoolers. It is collected in one or two 3-hour visits to the child's home- or center-based care. The observer collects time-sampling observations of behaviors and completes ratings of the child's caregiver. The behavior scales provide a record of the occurrence or quantity of specific acts, and the qualitative scales take into account the quality (and nuances) of the caregiver's behavior in relation to the child's behavior. The most frequently used quality measure, the positive caregiving composite, is calculated slightly differently for each age level. At 6, 15, and 24 months, positive care-giving composite scores are the mean of five 4-point qualitative ratings (sensitivity to child's nondistress signals, stimulation of cognitive development, positive regard for child, emotional detachment [reflected], flatness of affect [reflected]). At 36 months, these five scales plus two additional subscales, "fosters child's exploration" and "intrusive" [reflected], are included in the composite. At 54 months, the positive caregiving composite is the mean of 4-point ratings of caregivers' sensitivity/responsivity, stimulation of cognitive development, intrusiveness (reflected), and detachment (reflected). The behaviors observed include language stimulation, positive talk (e.g., praise, encouragement), positive physical contact and other behaviors (e.g., positive affect, stimulation of social development, restricting activity, speaking negatively to child, etc.) as well as the amount of time the child positively or negatively interacted with the caregiver and other children.

The ORCE composite quality ratings predicted concurrent and later child outcomes in the 10-site NICHD Study of Early Child Care and Youth Development in analyses that adjusted for family demographic and parenting characteristics. Children who experienced more responsive and stimulating care according to the ORCE consistently had high language and cognitive scores and tended to have better social skills while in child care (NICHD Early Child Care Research Network, 2006) and to demonstrate better language skills through fifth grade (Belsky et al., 2007) and better academic skills through third grade (NICHD Early Child Care Research Network, 2005).

### Preschool Classroom Mathematics Inventory

The Preschool Classroom Mathematics Inventory (PCMI; National Institute for Early Education Research, 2007) was created to assess the quality of mathematics instruction for the preschool classroom and is modeled after Supports for the Early Literacy Assessment (see below). The 17 items assess instruction and learning opportunities related to (1) number (e.g., materials for counting, comparing number, and estimating; teachers encourage children to recombine and count); (2) mathematical concept (e.g., measuring and comparing amounts, time, classifying, seriation); and (3) parents (efforts to involve parents in supporting children's mathematical development). A 5-point scale is used, with a score of 5 representing strong evidence of a developmentally appropriate mathematics program. The one item on parents could not be given a score without a conversation with a teacher or director. This is the only measure that focuses entirely on mathematical learning opportunities. A limitation is that scores may not reflect the instructional program accurately because on any given day an observer is not likely to see the full range of mathematical activities that a program provides. To accurately reflect children's opportunity to learn, it would be necessary to visit the program more than once or to rely on teacher or administrator reports.

**Preschool Program Quality Assessment**

The Preschool Program Quality Assessment (PQA; High/Scope, 2003) provides an overall quality rating of the preschool classroom as well as descriptions of dimensions thought to define overall quality. It includes 63 5-point scales describing a broad array of program characteristics, with the endpoints (1 and 5) and the midpoint (3) defined and illustrated with examples. There are seven sections: (1) learning environment (e.g., defined interest areas, varied and open-ended materials, diversity-related materials); (2) daily routine (e.g., consistent, time for child-initiated activities, small-group time); (3) adult-child interaction (e.g., warm and caring atmosphere, adults as partners in play); (4) curriculum planning and assessment (e.g., team teaching, comprehensive child records); (5) parent involvement and family services (e.g., opportunities for involvement, staff-parent informal interactions); (6) staff qualifications and development (e.g., ongoing professional development, instructional staff background); and (7) program management (e.g., program licensed, operating policies and procedures). Some of the items are rated following observations. Others require information provided by administrators. The observation items tend to emphasize efforts to promote children's personal initiative, problem solving, and explorations.

The PQA manual (High/Scope, 2003) states that scores for

preschool classrooms have been shown to predict concurrent measures of children's language, and change in scores on the High/Scope child observation record, but gives little information on the studies that underlie these assertions.

### Supports for Early Literacy Assessment

The Supports for Early Literacy Assessment (SELA; Smith and colleagues, in development) focuses on literacy learning opportunities in the preschool classroom. It consists of 20 items concerning: (1) the literacy environment (print used for a purpose, such as labeling; inviting places to look at books; array of books; writing materials available; literacy items and props in pretend area); (2) language development (encouragement to use and extend oral language; introduction of new words, concepts, and linguistic structures; activities to promote oral language; books shared); (3) print/books concepts (calling attention to functions and features of print); (4) phonological awareness; (5) letters and words (promoting letter recognition and interest in writing); (6) parent involvement (home-based supports for literacy; regular communication with parents); and (7) sites with English language learners, promoting maintenance and development of children's native language. Scores range from 1 to 5, with 1 considered very low quality and 5 ideal quality. The measure is one of the few that provides substantial information on the literacy environment. One limitation is that some items require an interview with the teacher to complete.

### Supports for English Language Learners Classroom Assessment

The Supports for English Language Learners Classroom Assessment (SELLCA; National Institute for Early Education Research, 2005) consists of 8 items, with scores ranging from 1 (minimal evidence) to 5 (strong evidence). It assesses the degree to which the teacher incorporates the cultural backgrounds of the children in the classroom and encourages parent participation; provides literacy materials and encourages children to use their native language; and supports English language development.

Observations need to be supplemented with an interview of the director or a teacher to complete the scale.

## STRATEGY FOR ASSESSING PROGRAM QUALITY

We have described direct observation as a strategy for assessing program quality, focusing particularly on systematic assessments of practices that are believed or known to be associated with child outcomes and that yield numerical scores, allowing comparisons over time and across classrooms. Such measures can serve several related purposes.

Many classroom observation measures exist that can be used or adapted to meet the specific needs of a program. Prior to selecting a measure, it is necessary to be clear about the goals of the program and the criteria for quality. Available measures vary along several dimensions. First, they vary in whether they focus on the child care or educational experiences of the individual child or the entire classroom. Second, some measures provide a global assessment of the child care experiences, whereas other measures are designed to focus more closely on a specific aspect of those experiences. Third, they vary in how much they focus on various program qualities—the socioemotional context versus opportunities for children to develop academic skills, for example. Finally, many measures were designed for preschool classrooms, but some were designed to measure home-based child care or child care for infants and toddlers.

We note here that there is research underway examining current quality rating systems. One recent study by the RAND Corporation (2008) addressed aspects of the validity of the "Qualistar" rating system, implemented in child care centers and family care sites serving over 1,300 children. Centers showed improvement in measured program quality during the course of the study, but the authors found little evidence that quality ratings predicted child outcomes, and problems were found with the data used for some of the component measures in the system. The study had significant technical problems, including high child attrition, which limited the conclusions that could be drawn. More work examining existing quality rating systems could provide welcome information for those charged with assessing program quality.

**APPENDIX TABLE 6-1** Environmental Observation Instruments

| | Used for | | Features of Environment Observed | | | | | |
|---|---|---|---|---|---|---|---|---|
| **Instrument** | **Age Group** | **Type of Setting** | **Physical Environment, Materials**[a] | **Social/ Emotional Climate**[b] | **Learning Environment/ Opportunities** | **Language and Literacy** | **Math** | **Descriptive Detail**[c] |
| **Ratings of Parent-Child Interactions** | 6 months-11 years | Home or lab | | ** | | ** | | |
| **Quality of Instruction** | 2-5 years | Home or lab | | | ** | | | |
| **Home Observation for Measurement of the Environment** | 6 months-5 years | Home | ** | ** | ** | ** | | |
| **Assessment Profile for Early Childhood Programs (APECP)** | Infant, toddler, preschool | Center | ** | ** | ** | * | | * |
| **Caregiver Interaction Scale (CIS)** | Infant, toddler, preschool | All child care | | * | | | | |
| **Child/Home Early Language and Literacy Observation (CHELLO)** | Preschool | Home-based child care | ** | * | ** | ** | | |
| **Classroom Assessment Scoring System (CLASS)** | Preschool-3rd grade | Center/ school | | ** | ** | | | ** |

| | | | | | | | | |
|---|---|---|---|---|---|---|---|---|
| **Classroom Practices Inventory (CPI)** | 4-5 years | Center | | ** | ** | * | | * |
| **A Developmentally Appropriate Practices Template (ADAPT)** | 1st-3rd grades | School | | ** | * | * | | * |
| **Early Childhood Environment Rating Scale-Revised (ECERS-R)** | 2.5-5 years | Center | ** | * | * | * | | ** |
| **Early Childhood Environment Rating Scale-Extension (ECERS-E)** | 2.5-5 years | Center | * | | ** | ** | ** | ** |
| **Early Childhood Classroom Observation Measure (ECCOM)** | 4-7 years | Center/ school | * | ** | ** | * | * | ** |
| **Early Language and Literacy Classroom Observation (ELLCO)** | Pre-K-3rd grade | Center/ school | * | * | | ** | | * |
| **Emerging Academics Snapshot (EAS)** | 10 months- 8 years | Center/ school | | | * | * | * | * |

*continued*

**APPENDIX TABLE 6-1** Continued

| | Used for | | Features of Environment Observed | | | | | |
|---|---|---|---|---|---|---|---|---|
| Instrument | Age Group | Type of Setting | Physical Environment, Materials[a] | Social/ Emotional Climate[b] | Learning Environment/ Opportunities | Language and Literacy | Math | Descriptive Detail[c] |
| **Family Day Care Rating Scale (FDCERS)** | Infant-12 years | Home-based child care | * | | | | | |
| **Infant and Toddler Environmental Rating Scale-Revised (ITERS-R)** | Birth-30 months | Center | ** | * | * | * | | ** |
| **Observation Measure of Language and Literacy Instruction (OMLIT)** | Preschool | Center | | | * | ** | | ** |
| **Observation Record of the Caregiving Environment (ORCE)** | Available for 6-54 months | All child care | | ** | | | | |
| **Preschool Classroom Mathematics Inventory (PCMI)** | Preschool | Center | | | | | ** | ** |

| | | | | | | | |
|---|---|---|---|---|---|---|---|
| **Preschool Program Quality Assessment, 2nd ed. (PQA)** | Preschool | Center | ** | * | * | * | ** |
| **Supports for Early Literacy Assessment (SELA)** | 3-5 years | Center | | | | ** | ** |
| **Supports for English Language Learners Classroom Assessment (SELLCA)** | Preschool | Center | | | | ** | ** |

NOTES: Single asterisk = Instrument provides some representation of this feature. Two asterisks = Instrument provides substantial representation of this feature.

[a]Safety, physical arrangement, materials.

[b]Emotional climate, social interactions with adults, support for social skill development.

[c]Level of detail in descriptions.

# Part III

## How to Assess

In this part, we turn to the question of how to select and administer assessments, once purposes have been established and domains selected. Some of the issues dealt with here are the technical ones defined by psychometricians as key to test quality: the reliability and validity of inferences, discussed in Chapter 7. Others have to do with the usability and fairness of assessments, issues that arise when assessing any child but in particular children with disabilities and children from cultural and language minority homes; these are discussed in Chapter 8. In Chapter 9, and in particular with regard to direct assessments, we discuss the many ways in which the test as designed may differ from the test as implemented. Testing a young child requires juggling many competing demands: developing a trusting relationship with the child, presenting the test items in a relatively standardized way that is nonetheless natural, responding appropriately to both correct and incorrect answers and to other child behaviors (signs of fear, anxiety, sadness, shyness). While it may not be possible to manage all these demands optimally, it is important that they are at least acknowledged when interpreting test results.

# 7

# Judging the Quality and Utility of Assessments

In this chapter we review important characteristics of assessment instruments that can be used to determine their quality and their utility for defined situations and purposes. We review significant psychometric concepts, including validity and reliability, and their relevance to selecting assessment instruments, and we discuss two major classes of instruments and the features that determine the uses to which they may appropriately be put. Next we review methods for evaluating the fairness of instruments, and finally we present three scenarios illustrating how the process of selecting assessment instruments can work in a variety of early childhood care and educational assessment circumstances.

Many tests and other assessment tools are poorly designed. The failure of assessment instruments to meet the psychometric criteria of validity and reliability may be hard for the practitioner or policy maker to recognize, but these failings reduce the usefulness of an instrument severely. Such characteristics as ease of administration and attractiveness are, understandably, likely to be influential in test selection, but they are of less significance than the validity and reliability considerations outlined here.

Validity and reliability are technical concepts, and this chapter addresses some technical issues. Appendix A is a glossary of words and concepts to assist the reader. Especially for Chapter 7, many readers may want to focus primarily on identifying the questions they need to ask about assessments under consideration and understanding the concepts well enough to appreciate the responses, rather than on a deep understanding of the statistical processes that determine how those questions can be answered.

## VALIDITY AND RELIABILITY OF ASSESSMENTS

Before an assessment instrument or test is used for the purpose of making decisions about children, it is necessary to have evidence showing that the assessment does what it claims to do, namely, that it accurately measures a characteristic or construct (or "outcome" as we are referring to it in this report). The evidence that is gathered to support the use of an assessment is referred to as *validity* evidence. Generally, when one asks the question "Is the assessment doing what it is supposed to do?" one is asking for validity evidence. A special kind of validity evidence relates to the consistency of the assessment—this may be consistency over repeated assessment or over different versions or forms of the assessment. This is termed *reliability* evidence.

This chapter reviews the history and logic of validity and reliability evidence, especially as it pertains to infants and young children. It is important to note that, first, when judging validity or reliability, one is judging a weight of evidence. Hence, one does not say that an assessment is "valid" or is "reliable"; instead, one uses an accumulation of evidence of diverse kinds to judge whether the assessment is suitable for the task for which it is intended. Second, when mustering evidence for validity or reliability, the evidence will pertain to specific types of uses (i.e., types of decisions). Some forms of evidence inform a wider range of types of decisions than others. Nonetheless, one should always consider evidence as pertaining to a specific set of decisions.

### Brief Overview of the History of Validity Evidence

The field of assessment of human behavior and development is an evolving one and has undergone many changes in the last half-century. Some changes are the result of developments in the field itself; others are responses to the social and political context in which the field operates. Validity is an enduring criterion of the quality and utility of assessments, although conceptions of what constitutes validity of assessments have changed over time.

## Criterion Validity

Originally, the conception of assessment validity was limited to prediction—specifically, to the closeness of agreement between what the assessment actually assesses or measures and what it is intended to assess or measure (Cureton, 1951). Put differently, at the core of this definition of validity is the relationship between the actual scores obtained on a test or other assessment instrument and the score on another instrument considered to be a good assessment of the underlying "true" variable or construct. Under this model of validity—the *criterion* model—if there already exists a criterion assessment that is considered to be a true measure of the construct, then a test or other measurement instrument is judged to be valid for that construct if the latter instrument provides accurate estimates of the criterion (Gulliksen, 1950). The accuracy of the estimates is usually estimated using a correlation coefficient.

Among the advantages of the criterion model of validity are its relevance and potential objectivity. After a criterion has been specified, data can be collected and analyzed in a straightforward manner to ascertain its correlation with the measure being validated. It is not always easy, however, to identify a suitable or adequate criterion. When one considers criterion-related validity evidence, for example, the size of the correlation between test scores and criterion can differ across settings, contexts, or populations, suggesting that a measure be validated separately for every situation, context, or population for which it may be used. In many instances, criterion-related evidence is quite relevant to the interpretations or claims that can be made about the uses of assessments. In addition, questions about the validity of the criterion itself often remain unanswered or are difficult to answer without resorting to circular reasoning—for example, when scores on a test of cognitive development are the validity criterion for scores on a different test of cognitive development. Moreover, decisions involving the choice of a criterion involve judgments about the value of the criterion.

## The "Three Types of Validity" Approach

If agreement with a criterion were the only form of validity evidence, then one could never validate a measure in a new area, because there is no preexisting criterion in the new area. Thus, new and broader types of evidence were needed. The criterion model of validity was followed by a more nuanced and amplified view of validity, which identified three types: *content, construct,* and *criterion* validity.

*1. Content validity.* The content model of validation seeks to provide a basis for validation without appealing to external criteria. The process of establishing content validity involves establishing a rational link between the procedures used to generate the test scores and the proposed interpretation or use of those scores (American Educational Research Association, American Psychological Association, and National Council on Measurement in Education, 1999; Cronbach, 1971; Kane, 2006). In developing an assessment procedure or system, a set of specifications of the content domain is usually set forth describing the content areas in detail and the item types. Content here refers to the themes, wording, and format of the assessment items (e.g., tasks, questions) as well as the guidelines and procedures for administration and scoring.

Defining the content domain becomes critical because validity inferences can be challenged by suggestions that the domain definition is incomplete, irrelevant, or inappropriate. It is important to evaluate the appropriateness of an assessment tool's content domain with respect to the proposed uses of that tool. For example, an off-the-shelf test that is used for the purposes of evaluating an educational program may cover content that is part of the program's curriculum as well as material that was not part of that curriculum. It is then up to those who interpret the program evaluation results to evaluate the children's achievement with respect to both the content-represented and content-unrepresented parts of the test. Studies of alignment between early learning standards (e.g., state early learning standards, the Head Start Child Outcomes Framework) and assessments are a new variant of content-related validity evidence. Such *standards* are descriptions of what children should know and be able to do; *benchmarks*, a related concept, refer to descriptions of knowledge and skills that children should acquire by a particular age or grade level.

It is generally agreed by measurement professionals that content-related validity evidence is necessary but insufficient for validation. Other forms of validity evidence—such as empirical evidence based on relationships between scores and other variables—are also essential. The current shift in emphasis toward learning standards and aligned assessments does not alter this necessity for additional forms of validity evidence, and the growing consequences of assessments increase the importance of empirical evidence (Koretz and Hamilton, 2006).

2. *Construct validity*. Construct validity was originally introduced by Cronbach and Meehl (1955) as an alternative to content and criterion validity for assessments that sought to measure attributes or qualities that are theoretically defined but for which there is no adequate empirical criterion or definitive measure nor a domain of content to sample. They went on to emphasize, however, that "determining what psychological constructs account for test performance is desirable for almost any test" (p. 282). In other words, even if an assessment is validated through content- and criterion-related evidence, a deeper understanding of the construct underlying the performance on the test requires construct-related evidence (Kane, 2006).

Construct validity is also concerned with what research methodologists refer to as "confounding" (Campbell and Stanley, 1966; Cook and Campbell, 1979). This refers to the possibility that an assessment procedure that is intended to produce a measure of a particular construct, such as a child's level of quantitative knowledge, produces instead a measure that can be construed in terms of more than one construct. For example, a measure of a child's quantitative knowledge might be confounded with the child's willingness to cooperate with the stranger who is conducting the assessment. This reaction of the child to the assessor is thus a rival interpretation of that intended by the assessment procedure. To circumvent this rival interpretation, the assessment procedure might include more efforts to establish rapport between the child and the assessor, paying special attention to the fact that some children are temperamentally shyer than others. If no correlation can be observed between a measure of shyness or willingness to cooperate and the measure of quantitative knowledge, then the rival interpretation can be ruled out.

It is a mistake to think that construct validity applies only to measures of theory-based constructs. In this report we depart from some historical uses of the term "construct," which limit the term to characteristics that are not directly observable but that are inferred from interrelated sets of observations. As noted in the *Standards for Educational and Psychological Testing* (1999), this limited use invites confusion because it causes some tests but not others to be viewed as measures of constructs. Following the *Standards*, we use the term "construct" more broadly as "the concept or characteristic that a test is designed to measure" (American Educational Research Association, American Psychological Association, and National Council on Measurement in Education, 1999, p. 5).

3. *Integrated views of validity.* Current conceptions of assessment validity replace the content/criterion/construct trinitarian model and its reference to types of validity by a discussion of sources, or strands, of validity evidence, often including evidence regarding the consequences of the use of assessments. Cronbach (1971) argued that in order to explain a test score, "one must bring to bear some sort of theory about the causes of the test performance and about its implications" (p. 443). While recognizing the practicality of subdividing validity evidence into criterion, content, and construct, he called for "a comprehensive, integrated evaluation of a test" (p. 445). He emphasized that "one validates not a test, but an interpretation of data arising from a specified procedure" (p. 447). Messick (1989) echoed this emphasis. The aim of current conceptions of assessment validity is to seek information relevant to a specific interpretation and use of the assessments; many strands of evidence can contribute to an understanding of the meaning of assessments.

## Validity as Argument

Kane's (2006) treatment of validity is consonant with Messick's approach, although Kane emphasizes a general methodology for validation based on validity conceptualized as argument. In Kane's formulation, "to validate a proposed interpretation or use of test scores is to evaluate the rationale for its interpretation for use" (2006, p. 23). In Kane's approach, validation involves two kinds of argument. An *interpretive argument* specifies the proposed interpretations and uses of test results. This argument consists of articulating the inferences and assumptions that link the observed behavior or test performance to the conclusions and decisions that are to be based on that behavior or performance. The *validity argument* is an evaluation of the interpretive argument. "To claim that a proposed interpretation or use is valid is to claim that the interpretive argument is coherent, that its inferences are reasonable, and that its assumptions are plausible" (Kane, 2006, p. 23). In other words, the validity argument begins by reviewing the interpretive argument as a whole to ascertain whether it makes sense. If the interpretive argument is reasonable, then its inferences and assumptions are evaluated by means of appropriate evidence. Any interpretive argument potentially contains many assumptions. If there is any reason for not taking for granted a particular assumption, that assumption needs to be evaluated. The interpretive argument makes explicit the reasoning behind the proposed interpretations and uses, so that it can be clearly understood and evaluated. It also indicates which claims are to be evaluated through validation.

For example, a child assessment procedure or instrument usually takes some performances by or observations of the child that are intended to be a sample of all possible performances or observations that constitute the instrument's target content domain. The procedure assumes that the child's score on the instrument can be generalized to the entire domain, although the actual observed behaviors or performances may be only a small subset of the entire target domain. In addition, they may or may not be a representative sample of the domain. Standardization typically further restricts the sample of performances or observations by specifying the conditions of observation or performance. Although standardization is necessary to reduce measurement error, it causes the range of possible observations or performances to be narrower than that of the target domain. In other words, it can be seen that the interpretation of the child's observed behavior or performance as an indicator of his or her standing in the target domain requires a complex chain of inferences and generalizations that must be made clear as a part of the interpretive argument.

An interpretive argument for a measure of children's cognitive development in the area of quantitative reasoning, for example, may include inferences ranging from those involved in the scoring procedure (Is the scoring rule that is used to convert an observed behavior or performance by the child to an observed score appropriate? Is it applied accurately and consistently? If any scaling model is used in scoring, does the model fit the data?); to those involved in the generalization from observed score to universe of scores (Are the observations made of the child in the testing or observation situation representative of the universe of observations or performances defining the target cognitive domain? Is the sample of observations of the child's behavior sufficiently large to control for sampling error?); to extrapolation from domain score to level of development (or level of proficiency) of the competencies for that domain (Is the acquisition of lower level skills a prerequisite for attaining higher level skills? Are there systematic domain-irrelevant sources of variability that would bias the interpretation of scores as measures of the child's level of development of the target domain attributes?); to the decisions that are made, or implications drawn, on the basis of conclusions about developmental level on the target outcome domain (e.g., children with lower levels of the attribute are not likely to succeed in first grade; programs with strong effects on this measure are more desirable than those with weak effects).

The decision inference usually involves assumptions that rest on value judgments. These values assumptions may represent widely held cultural values for which there is societal consensus, or they may represent values on which there is no consensus or even bitter divisions, in which case they are readily identifiable for the purposes of validation. When the underlying decision assumptions represent widely held values, they can be difficult to identify or articulate for validation through scientific analysis.

The interpretive argument may also involve highly technical inferences and assumptions (e.g., scaling, equating). The technical sophistication of measurement models has reached such a high degree of complexity that they have become a "black box" even for many measurement professionals (Brennan, 2006, p. 14). Moreover, as Brennan further points out, many measurement models are operationalized in proprietary computer programs that can sometimes make it difficult or impossible for users to know important details of the algorithms and assumptions that underlie the manner in which measurement data are generated.

Ideally, the interpretive argument should be made as a part of the development of the assessment procedure or system. From the outset, the goal should be to develop an assessment procedure or system congruent with the proposed interpretation and use. In addition, efforts to identify and control sources of unwanted variance can help to rule out plausible alternative interpretations. Efforts to make the assessment system or procedure congruent with the proposed interpretation and uses provide support for the plausibility of the interpretive argument. In practice, this developmental stage is likely to overlap considerably with the appraisal stage, but at some point in the process "a shift to a more arm's-length and critical stance is necessary in order to provide a convincing evaluation of the proposed interpretation and uses" (Kane, 2006, p. 25). Kane views this shift as necessary because it is human nature (appropriate and probably inevitable) for the developers to have a confirmationist bias since they are trying to make the assessment system as good as it can be. The development stage thus has a legitimate confirmationist bias: its purpose is to develop an assessment procedure and a plausible interpretive argument that reflects the proposed interpretations and uses of test scores.

After the assessment instrument or system is developed but still as a part of the development process, the inferences and assumptions in the interpretive argument should be evaluated to the extent possible. Any problems or weakness revealed by this process would indicate a need for alterations in either the interpretive argument or the assessment instrument. This iterative process would continue until the developers are satisfied with the congruence between the assessment instrument and the interpretive argument. This iterative process is similar to that of theory development and refinement in science; here the interpretive argument plays the role of the theory.

When the development process is considered complete, it is appropriate for the validation process to take a "more neutral or even critical stance" (Kane, 2006, p. 26). Thus begins the appraisal stage. If the development stage has not delivered an explicit, coherent, detailed interpretive argument linking observed behavior or performance to the proposed interpretation and uses, then the development stage is considered incomplete, and thus a critical evaluation of the proposed interpretation is premature (Kane, 2006).

The following events should occur during the appraisal stage:

1. Conduct studies of questionable inferences and assumptions in the interpretive argument. To the extent that the proposed interpretive argument withstands these challenges, confidence in the claims increase. "If they do not withstand these challenges, then either the assessment procedure or the interpretive argument has to be revised or abandoned" (Kane, 2006, p. 26).
2. Search for hidden assumptions, including value judgments, seeking to make such assumptions explicit and subject them to scrutiny (e.g., by individuals with different values).
3. Conduct investigations of alternative possible interpretations of the scores. An effective way to challenge an interpretive argument is to propose an alternative, more plausible argument. The evaluation of plausible competing interpretations is an important component in the appraisal of the proposed interpretive argument.

**Ruling Out Plausible Alternative Hypotheses**

It is important to recognize that one never establishes the validity of an assessment instrument or system; rather, one validates a score, and its typical uses, yielded by the instrument (Messick, 1989). For example, depending on the circumstances surrounding an assessment (e.g., the manner of test administration, the characteristics of the target population), the same instrument can produce valid or invalid scores.

The essence of validity, then, can be stated in the question, "To what extent is an observed score a true or accurate measure of the construct that the assessment instrument intends to measure?" Potential threats to validity are extraneous sources of variance—or construct-irrelevant variance—in the observed scores. These extraneous or irrelevant sources of variance are typically called measurement error. As in the process of conducting scientific research, the validity question can be stated in the form of a hypothesis: "The observed score is a true or accurate reflection of the target construct." The task of validating is to identify and rule out plausible alternate hypotheses regarding what the observed score measures. In a very fundamental sense, as is the case in science, one never "proves" or "confirms" the assessment hypothesis—rather, the successful assessment hypothesis is tested and escapes being disconfirmed. (The term *assessment hypothesis* is used here to refer to the hypothesis that specifies what the intended meaning of the observed score is, i.e., what the assessment instrument is intended to measure.) In this sense, the results of the validation process "probe" but do not prove the assessment hypothesis (Campbell and Stanley, 1966; Cook and Campbell, 1979). A valid set of scores is one that has survived such probing, but it may always be challenged and rejected by a new empirical probe. The task of validation, then, is to expose the assessment hypothesis to disconfirmation.

In short, varying degrees of confirmation are conferred upon the assessment hypothesis through the number of plausible rival hypotheses (Campbell and Stanley, 1966) available to explain the meaning of the observed scores. That is, the smaller the number of such rival hypotheses remaining, the greater the degree of confirmation of the assessment hypothesis. Thus, the list of potential sources of assessment invalidity is essentially a list of plausible hypotheses that are rival to the assessment hypothesis that specifies what the meaning of the observed score is intended to be. Studies need to be designed and conducted to test the tenability of each plausible rival hypothesis in order to determine whether each can be ruled out as a plausible explanation of the observed scores. Where the assessment procedure properly and convincingly "controls" for a potential source of invalidity, the procedure renders the rival hypothesis implausible.

**The Contemporary Synthesis of Views About Validity Evidence**

The current *Standards for Educational and Psychological Testing* (American Educational Research Association, American Psychological Association, and National Council on Measurement in Education, 1999) lays out five sources of evidence for validity, which need to be combined to form the basis for a validity argument. These are based on the discussions above and are only briefly described here. For an extended account of how to use these types of evidence in the validity argument for a particular assessment, see Wilson (2005).

1. ***Evidence Based on Instrument Content.*** To compose the evidence based on an assessment's content, the measurer must engage in "an analysis of the relationship between a test's content and the construct it is intended to measure" (American Educational Research Association, American Psychological Association, and National Council on Measurement in Education, 1999, p. 11) and interpret that analysis in an argument concerning the validity of using the instrument. This is generally not an empirical argument in itself, although it may well be based on the results of earlier empirical studies. This is what has been described above in the section on content validity.
2. ***Evidence Based on the Response Process.*** If one chooses to assemble evidence based on response processes, one must engage in a detailed analysis of children's responses to the assessment, either while they are taking the assessment or just after, in an exit interview.

   In the standard think-aloud investigation (also called "cognitive labs"; American Institutes for Research, 2000), children are asked to talk aloud about what they are thinking while they are actually responding to the item. What the respondent says is recorded, transcribed, and analyzed. Asking a child to think aloud is of limited value with infants, but children in the preschool years can provide useful information. However, in a variant of this, observation rather than questioning may be the source of the evidence. Children may be videotaped and other characteristics may be recorded, such as having their eye movements tracked. Children must be familiarized with such observational situations and allowed to explore the environment so that they are comfortable. The results can provide insights ranging from the very plain—"the children were very distracted when responding"—to the very detailed, including evidence about particular behaviors and actions that were evident when they were responding.

The exit interview is similar in aim but is timed to occur after the child has made his or her responses. It may be conducted after each item or after the assessment as a whole, depending on whether the measurer judges that the delay will or will not interfere with the child's memory. Again, limitations with infants and toddlers are obvious. The types of information gained will be similar to those from the think-aloud, although generally it will not be so detailed. It may be that a data collection strategy that involves both think-alouds or observations and exit interviews will be best.

3. ***Evidence Based on Internal Structure.*** To collect evidence based on internal structure, the measurer must first ensure that there is an intention of internal structure. Although this idea of intended structure may not always be evident, it must always exist, even if it is treated as being so obvious that it need not be mentioned or only informally acknowledged in some cases. We refer to this internal structure as the *construct*. This is what has been described above in the section on construct validity. Note that the issue of differential item functioning (DIF), discussed later in this chapter, is one element of this type of evidence, specifically one related to fairness of the assessment.
4. ***Evidence Based on Relations to Other Variables.*** If there are other "external" variables that the construct should (according to theory) be related to, and especially if another instrument is intended to measure the same or similar variable, a strong relation (or lack of a strong relation) between the assessment under scrutiny and these external variables can be used as validity evidence. Typical examples of these external variables are (a) caregiver judgments and (b) scores on other assessments. Another source of external variables is treatment studies: if the measurer has good evidence that a treatment does indeed change the construct, then the contrast on the assessment between a treatment and a control group can be used as an external variable. (One

has to be careful about circularity of argument here; it should not be the case that the evidence for the treatment's efficacy is the same data as being used to investigate validity of the assessment.) Note that the relationship predicted from theory may be positive, negative, or null—that is, equally important that the instrument be supported by evidence that it is measuring what it should measure (*convergent* evidence, which may be positive or negative depending on the way the variables are scored), as it is that it is not measuring what it shouldn't (*divergent* evidence, which would be indicated by a null relationship).

Evaluations of early childhood interventions have the potential to provide important information regarding the validity of assessments for young children. Rather than using assessment instruments to evaluate the effectiveness of interventions, psychometricians use interventions as one means to evaluate the validity of assessments. For example, evidence of validity for a specific instrument of social skills is obtained when intervention effects on that instrument emerge from interventions designed to improve social skills. Typically one uses assessment instruments to evaluate the effectiveness of an intervention based on the assumption that those instruments have sufficient psychometric reliability and validity to be useful. In contrast, in the validity context, one is using successful interventions to evaluate the external validity of assessment instruments.

The logic of using intervention data to establish validity involves several conditions. First, it assumes that the intervention is based on a theory of change in specific child characteristics or outcomes. These outcomes are the child's abilities, skills, or beliefs targeted for change by the intervention. Second, the intervention successfully changes those outcomes. Third, the outcomes are measured with assessment instruments that are aligned (i.e., directly measure the designated outcomes). When these conditions are met, then the magnitude of the difference between treated and untreated children can be used as an index of external validity. Under this logic, more intensive interventions should yield larger treatment effects than less intensive interventions.

5. ***Evidence Based on Consequences of Using an Assessment Instrument.*** Under an integrated, comprehensive approach to

validity, information regarding the consequences of the assessment becomes part of the evidentiary basis for judging the validity of the assessment. An illustration can be drawn from high-stakes assessments in education, through which policy makers have sought to establish accountability. As with any form of assessment, these can have intended or unintended, desirable or undesirable consequences. An alleged potential consequence of high-stakes assessments is that they can drive instructional decisions in unintended and undesirable ways, usually by over-emphasizing the skills tested ("teaching to the test"). They can also possibly have a corrupting influence, since the motivation to misuse or misrepresent test scores can be compelling. In addition, the psychometric characteristics of the test can vary depending on whether it is administered under low- or high-stakes conditions (e.g., level of motivation or anxiety as construct-irrelevant sources of variance in test performance). It is also possible that new and future technologies used to administer, score, or report assessments will have unintended, unanticipated consequences—as many new technologies have had.

## Social Consequences of Assessment

As in the field of medicine, in assessment there is an obligation to do no harm to those assessed. As such, it is important to inquire into the intended as well as unintended consequences of assessment. Validity theoreticians differ from one another in the extent to which they incorporate the consequences of assessment under the purview of validity. Thus, although evidence about consequences can inform judgments about validity, it is important to distinguish between evidence that is directly relevant to validity and consequences that may inform broader concerns, such as educational or social policy.

For example, concerns have been raised about the impact of certain forms of assessment on narrowing the curriculum. (That is, it is often said that assessments should not have the effect of unduly narrowing the early childhood program's focus to the detriment of the program's wider or comprehensive goals.) For example, an educational assessment system should not lead teachers to concentrate instruction on a few or narrowly defined learning objectives merely for the sake of the children's passing a test, or to concentrate on a few discrete skills that can be achieved through routine drill, to the exclusion of coverage of other of the program's goals for learning and development. Similarly, the assessment should not cause children to acquire habits of mind that emphasize shallow learning and quick forgetting, it should not take away the joy and excitement of engaging in intellectual inquiry, and it should not have the effect of discouraging them from taking responsibility for their own expanded learning. Such impact, if it occurs, may not in itself necessarily diminish the validity of an assessment score, although it raises issues surrounding test use.

If, however, a consequence of an assessment is the result of a threat to assessment validity—for example, if there is construct-irrelevant variance, such as children's language skills, affecting their performance on a test intended to measure only quantitative reasoning, a situation resulting in English language learners scoring as a group lower than other children on that test—then the social consequence is clearly linked to validity.

When claims are made about the benefits or harms of assessment that go beyond the uses of assessment—for example, claims that the use of assessments will encourage better classroom instruction by holding educators accountable—then the validation process should be informed by whether or not those claims hold true.

The relevance of unintended consequences is not always easily ascertained. For example, there can be confusion about whose intent is under consideration (e.g., the test developer's intent or the user's) and about whether a consequence is positive or negative. Moreover, the user is often an individual with little or no technical knowledge to determine the validity of a score interpretation that she or he might make (e.g., newspaper readers' trying to make sense of newspaper reports based on test data).

### Validity of Assessments Used for Judging Program Quality

Concerning assessment instruments that are to be used for the purposes of judging program quality, a fundamental question is,

"Can the instrument adequately gauge program quality?" This is really a threefold question: (1) Do the scores (or other data that are derived from the instrument) have the technical characteristics (e.g., reliability) to show measurable improvement in children's developmental level on the program's intended outcomes? (Popham, 2007). (2) Is there evidence available that the scores (or other data that are derived from the instrument) have appropriate validity characteristics (e.g., internal construct validity, external variable validity, etc.) for measuring the program's intended outcomes? (Popham, 2007). (3) Is the evaluation design strong enough that improvement can be attributed to program effects?

The program may or may not specify targets for attaining particular developmental levels on its intended outcomes. If the program has specific developmental outcome targets, then questions that should be asked in relation to the assessment instrument include (a) "What are those targets?" and (b) "Can the instrument accurately measure those targets?" It is important, for example, to ensure that the instrument does not have a ceiling short of those targets.

One should also ask, "What is the yardstick used to measure a program's success?" For example, is the outcome target the percentage of children who score at or above the chronological age norms for that outcome? If so, are those norms for the nation as a whole or are they subgroup norms—such as state norms, ethnic or language minority or socioeconomic group norms? If subgroup norms are used, it may be important to establish the metrics of correspondence between them (Popham, 2007). For example, a 1-decile improvement at the lower tail of the distribution may or may not mean the same thing as a 1-decile improvement at the higher tail end. Thus, more program resources may be required to obtain improvements for one group of children than for another group—or for one portion of the normative curve than for another.

Moreover, in making judgments about program effectiveness on the basis of assessment data, one should also ask, "Are those program targets realistic?" Although this question does not bear on the quality of the assessment instrument per se, it nevertheless bears on the appropriateness of its use. What is a realistic level of expectation for children's attaining a particular level of development on a program's intended outcomes? What is the timeline for attaining a program's outcome targets?

If assessment results are used for the purposes of accountability, it is important that the assessment should reflect the domains or areas of development or learning that the program or policy was intended to influence. For example, a pre-K program that was not designed to provide nutrition should not be held accountable for children's nutritional status. This is discussed further in Chapter 10 on assessment systems.

## Reliability Evidence

The traditional quality-control approach to score consistency has been to find ways to measure the consistency of the scores—this is the so-called reliability coefficient. There are several ways to do this, for example as (a) how much of the observed variance in scores is attributable to the underlying "true" score (as a proportion), (b) the consistency over time, and (c) the consistency over different sets of items (i.e., different "forms"). These constitute three different perspectives on measurement error and are termed internal consistency, test-retest, and alternate forms reliability, respectively.

The *internal consistency* reliability coefficients are calculated using the information about variability that is contained in the data from a single administration of the instrument—effectively they are investigating the proportion of variance accounted for by the "true" score. This "variance explained" formulation is familiar to many through its use in analysis of variance and regression methods. Examples are the Kuder-Richardson 20 and 21 (Kuder and Richardson, 1937) for dichotomous responses and coefficient alpha (Cronbach, 1951) for polytomous responses.[1]

As described above, there are many sources of measurement error beyond a single administration of an instrument. Each such source could be the basis for calculating a different reliability coefficient. One type of coefficient that is commonly used is the

---

[1]Dichotomous means there are two possible responses, such as yes/no, true/false. Polytomous means there are more than two possible responses, as in partial-credit items.

*test-retest* reliability coefficient. In a test-retest reliability coefficient, the respondents give responses to the questions twice, then the reliability coefficient is calculated simply as the correlation between the two sets of scores. On one hand, the test and the retest should be so far apart that it is reasonable to assume that the respondents are not answering the second time by remembering the first but are genuinely responding to each item anew. This may be difficult to achieve for some sorts of complex items, which may be quite memorable. On the other hand, as the aim is to investigate variation in the scores not due to real change in respondent's true scores, the measurements should be close enough together for it to be reasonable to assume that there has been little real change. Obviously, this form of reliability index will work better when a stable construct is being measured with forgettable items, compared with a less stable construct being measured with memorable items.

Another type of reliability coefficient is the *alternate forms* reliability coefficient. With this coefficient, two sets of items are developed for the instrument, each following the same construction process. The two alternate copies of the instrument are administered, and the two sets of scores are then correlated to produce the alternate forms reliability coefficient. This coefficient is particularly useful as a means of evaluating the consistency with which the test has been developed.

Other classical consistency indices that have also been developed have their equivalents in the construct modeling approach. For example, in the so-called split-halves reliability coefficient, the instrument is split into two different (nonintersecting) but similar parts, and the correlation between them is used as a reliability coefficient after adjustment with a factor that attempts to predict what the reliability would be if there were twice as many items in each half. The adjustment is a special case of the Spearman-Brown formula:

$$r' = \frac{Lr}{1+(L-1)r},$$

where $L$ is the ratio of the number of items in the hypothetical test to the number of items in the real one (i.e., if the number of items were to be doubled, $L = 2$).

These reliability coefficients can be calculated separately, and the results will be quite useful for understanding the consistency of the instrument's measures across each of the different circumstances. In practice, such influences will occur simultaneously, and it would be better to have ways of investigating the influences simultaneously also. Such methods have indeed been developed—for example, generalizability theory (e.g., Shavelson and Webb, 1991) is an expansion of the analysis of variance approach mentioned above.

One of the issues in interpreting reliability coefficients is the lack of any absolute standards for what is acceptable. It is certainly true that a value of 0.90 is better than one of 0.84, but not so good as one of 0.95. At what point should one say that a test is "good enough"? At what point is it not? One reason that it is difficult to set a single uniform acceptable standard is that instruments are used for multiple purposes. A better approach is to consider each type of application individually and develop specific standards based on the context. For example, when an instrument is to be used to make a single division into two groups (pass/fail, positive/negative, etc.), then a reliability coefficient may be quite misleading, using, as it does, data from the entire spectrum of the respondent locations. It may be better to investigate false positive and false negative rates in a region near the cut score.

## MEASUREMENT CHOICES: DIRECT ASSESSMENT AND OBSERVATION-BASED ASSESSMENT

Choosing what type of assessment to use is a critical decision for the design of an early childhood program evaluation or an accountability system. As others have noted, it is a decision for which there are no easy answers because there are serious shortcomings in all currently available approaches (Meisels, 2007). Two sharply contrasting measurement approaches (which we have discussed in other chapters) can be used with children under age 5: direct assessments and observation-based (often called authentic) measures.

A direct assessment involves an adult, possibly a familiar adult but sometimes a stranger, sitting with a child and asking him or her to respond to a number of requests, such as pointing to picture, or counting objects. The conditions for administration, such as the directions and how the materials are presented, are standardized to ensure that each child is being presented with identical testing conditions.

Observation-based measures, such as those involving observation of children's behaviors or a portfolio collecting records of observations together with products of children's work, use regularly occurring classroom activities and products as the evidence for what children know and can do. Observation-based measures encompass a variety of tools, including checklists of a series of items that a teacher or parent completes based on general knowledge of the child, and classroom-based observation tools, with which the teacher is expected to make extensive annotations based on what the child is doing in the classroom and use that documentation to complete the observation items. Portfolio assessment involves collecting and analyzing records of such observations or samples of children's work.

Both direct assessment and observation-based assessment have strengths and weaknesses. Direct assessments, however, have been used far more frequently in large-scale research projects, such as the Early Childhood Longitudinal Study; program evaluations, such as the evaluation of Early Head Start; and accountability efforts, such as the Head Start National Reporting System. Consequently, there is more known about both the strengths and weaknesses of this approach. Observation-based and performance methods are routinely recommended as tools for teachers to use to plan and guide instruction (National Association for the Education of Young Children and National Association of Early Childhood Specialists in State Departments of Education, 2003). Even the recommendation to regularly use such measures to assess children's progress in early childhood classrooms is a relatively new development, so there is much yet to be learned about the large-scale use of authentic tools for any purpose and that certainly includes program evaluation and accountability.

In an extensive review of assessment approaches, researchers at Mathematica Policy Research (2007) noted challenges associated with using both direct assessment and observation-based measures for program evaluation and accountability purposes.

Direct assessments often have been found to be predictive of school achievement. However, they are strongly associated with socioeconomic status and may not show whether a program is supporting children across all developmental domains. The dilemma is that as a direct measure gets longer and more comprehensive, it also taxes the energy and attention span of young children. The limitations of direct assessment derive from the nature of the young child; that nature is not well matched to the demands of a standardized testing situation. Potential problems include the following:

- The child may not be familiar with this type of task or be able to stay focused.
- Young children have a limited response repertoire, being more likely to show rather than tell what they know.
- Young children may have difficulty responding to situation cues and verbal directions.
- Young children may not understand how to weigh alternative choices, for example, what it means for one answer to be the "best" answer.
- Young children may be confused by the language demands, such as negatives and subordinate clauses.
- Young children do not respond consistently when asked to do something for an adult.
- In some cultures, direct questioning is considered rude.
- The direct, decontextualized questioning about disconnected events may be inconsistent with the types of questions children encounter in the classroom.
- Measurement error may not be randomly distributed across programs if some classrooms typically use more direct questioning, like that found in a standardized testing situation.

These problems may not be shown in traditional ways of assessing validity, which compare children's performance on one type of direct assessment with their performance on a similarly structured test—so-called external validity evidence. Mathematica Policy Research reports on a study by La Paro and Pianta (2000) that found that about 25 percent of the variance in academic achievement in primary grades was predicted by assessments administered in preschool or kindergarten. This provides a ceiling for possible external validity evidence. Observation-based measures present an entirely different set of issues. They do not present any of the problems associated with the young child's ability to understand and comply with the demands of a structured testing situation, since the child's day-to-day behavior is the basis for the inference of knowledge and skills. Teachers and caregivers collect data over a variety of contexts and over time to gain a more valid and reliable picture of what children know and can do. Observation-based assessment approaches also are consistent with recommended practices for the assessment of young children. The challenges associated with observation-based measures are centered around the caregiver or teacher as the source of the information. Mathematica Policy Research (2007) has summarized challenges related to observation-based assessments:

- There is a need to establish trust in teachers' and caregivers' judgments. Research has identified the conditions under which their ratings are reliable, but there is an ongoing need to monitor reliability.
- Teachers and caregivers must be well trained in the administration of the tool to achieve reliable results. More research is needed to specify the level of training needed to obtain reliable ratings from preschool teachers. (Assessors of direct assessments need to be trained as well, but the protocol may be more straightforward.)
- The assessment needs to contain well-defined rubrics and scoring guides.
- Teachers and caregivers may be inclined to inflate their ratings if they know the information is being used for program accountability.
- Not all teachers or caregivers will be good assessors.
- Measurement carried out by teachers and caregivers requires that additional steps be taken to ensure the validity and reliability of the data, such as periodic monitoring.

A strength of observation-based measures is that the information has utility for instructional as well as accountability purposes.

This means the time invested in training teachers to become good observers and the time teachers spend collecting the information are of direct benefit to classroom practice, which is not true for direct assessment. Mathematica Policy Research concludes that it is wiser "to invest in training teachers to be better observers and more reliable assessors than to spend those resources training and paying for outside assessors to administer on-demand tasks to young children in unfamiliar contexts that will provide data with the added measurement error inherent in assessing young children from diverse backgrounds" (Mathematica Policy Research, 2007).

More research needs to be done on the use of observation-based assessment tools for program evaluation and accountability. If teachers or caregivers are not well trained or do not complete the tool reliably because they want their programs to look good for accountability, then the information is useless for both accountability and instructional purposes. Several states have elected to use observation-based measurement in their preschool accountability systems, but it is so new that very limited data are available. One large program evaluation was able to document that early childhood teachers could be trained to use observation-based measures reliably. Bagnato and colleagues (Bagnato, Smith-Jones, et al., 2002; Bagnato, Suen, et al., 2002) used an authentic assessment approach to document improved outcomes for 1,350 preschoolers participating in an innovative community-based urban preschool initiative. The highest level of education was a high school diploma for 42 percent of the teachers working with the children and thus providing the child outcomes data. To ensure the outcomes data were valid and reliable, the evaluation team provided initial, booster, and follow-up training until mastery was reached; supervised caregiver assessments during a set week each quarter; and once a year conducted random, authentic assessments on children as a concurrent validation of teacher and parent assessments.

Although we have presented direct assessments and observation-based assessments as distinct choices in the paragraphs above, a more recent perspective sees them as constituting different parts of an assessment system or net (Wilson, 2005; Wilson and Adams, 1996). In this perspective, no single type of assessment is seen as being fully satisfactory, hence a multipart assessment system is developed, which uses a combination of specific assessment types to ensure that the measures are useable under a range of circumstances and the entire system can adapt to changing circumstances. The strengths of item response modeling are used to establish both the validity and the usefulness of this approach. In a classic example drawn primarily from K-12 education, the two assessment types were multiple-choice items and open-response items (Wilson and Adams, 1996), but in the context of early childhood education, a more likely combination would be a mixture of direct assessment and observation-based assessments, such as teacher observations and portfolios. The judicious deployment of such a combination allows the different assessment types to "bootstrap" one another in terms of validity, going a long way to helping establish (a) whether the direct assessments did indeed suffer from problems of unfamiliarity and (b) whether observation-based assessments suffered from such problems as teacher bias. Moreover, systematic use of a combination of assessments enables the monitoring of assessments as an ongoing possibility, not just a special study carried out during initial implementation.

## METHODS FOR ASSESSING TEST AND ITEM BIAS

Developing tests for educational and psychological purposes requires a thorough consideration of the populations for which the test is appropriate. Specifically, the test development process should include several phases designed to ensure that tests and items are free from bias across the populations for which the test is intended. These steps include the subjective review of items and test content by subject matter and bias review panels, as well as more objective or quantitative examination of item and test properties. In modern test development, the examination of test bias favors these more quantitative examinations of item and test bias for their ability to quantify the extent to which items and tests may function differently across populations of interest, and because of the strong psychometric theory that supports their development and use, but interpretation will still rely heavily on qualitative approaches.

The following section is an overview of these quantitative

methods for examining (a) test bias and (b) DIF. These issues are most relevant for three populations of young children, which are the subject of the next chapter: minority children, English language learners, and children with disabilities.

## Differential Item Functioning

Assessments are typically made of children from a variety of backgrounds. One standard requirement of fairness in assessment practice is that, for children who are at the same level of ability on the variable being measured, the items in the instrument behave in a reasonably similar way across different subgroups. That is, the items should show no evidence of bias due to DIF (American Educational Research Association, American Psychological Association, and National Council on Measurement in Education, 1999, p. 13). Typically these subgroups are gender, ethnic and racial, language, or socioeconomic groups, although other groupings may be relevant in particular circumstances.

First, it is necessary to make an important distinction. If the responses to an item have different frequencies for different subgroups, then that is evidence of differential impact of the item on those subgroups. Although such results may well be of interest for other reasons, they are not generally the focus of DIF studies. Instead, DIF studies focus on whether children *at the same locations on the score distribution* give similar responses across the different subgroups.

DIF is not always indicated when different groups perform differently on an assessment or on particular items. For example, suppose that more English language learners got a particular item wrong from an assessment of "speaking in English" than children who are native speakers; that would constitute differential impact on the results of the assessment and could well be an interesting result in itself. But the issue of DIF would not necessarily be raised by such a result—it is to be expected that someone learning a language will find it harder to speak that language than native speakers, and hence the result does not challenge the contention that the instrument was accurately measuring that difference in their speaking performance.

However, if children from the two groups who scored at

around the same level on the whole assessment had response rates on that item that were very different, that would be evidence of DIF for that item. The item is sensitive to some special characteristic of the children that goes beyond what is being assessed generally across the range of the items in the assessment (e.g., interest in the topic or content of the item). In order to be more fair to children from different subgroups, one would wish to reduce the influence of items from the assessment that had notable amounts of DIF, or perhaps amend them to eliminate this characteristic.

Second, one must be careful to distinguish between DIF and item bias. For one thing, it is possible that a test may include two items that exhibit DIF between two groups, but in opposite directions, so that they tend to "cancel out." Also, DIF may not always be a flaw, since it could be due to "a kind of multidimensionality that may be unexpected or may conform to the test framework" (American Educational Research Association, American Psychological Association, and National Council on Measurement in Education, 1999, p. 13). However, despite these considerations, most test developers seek to reduce or eliminate instances of DIF in their tests. The Educational Testing Service has developed criteria for judging DIF effects (Longford, Holland, and Thayer, 1993).

Several techniques are available for investigating DIF, among them techniques based on linear and logistic regression and techniques based on log-linear models (see Holland and Wainer, 1993, for an overview).

For example, consider the results of a (hypothetical) DIF analysis examining the differences between males and females on one item (item "Z") of a certain test, shown in Figure 7-1. For each score on the test as a whole, the proportions of boys and girls who responded correctly to the item have been plotted separately. If there were no DIF, those proportions would be the same (except for sampling error) for all scores.

Looking at the figure, we see that for most whole-test scores boys are more likely to respond correctly to this item than are girls. That is DIF, and it means that this item indicates a larger difference in proficiency between boys and girls on this item than on the test as a whole. Examination of item Z may well reveal that

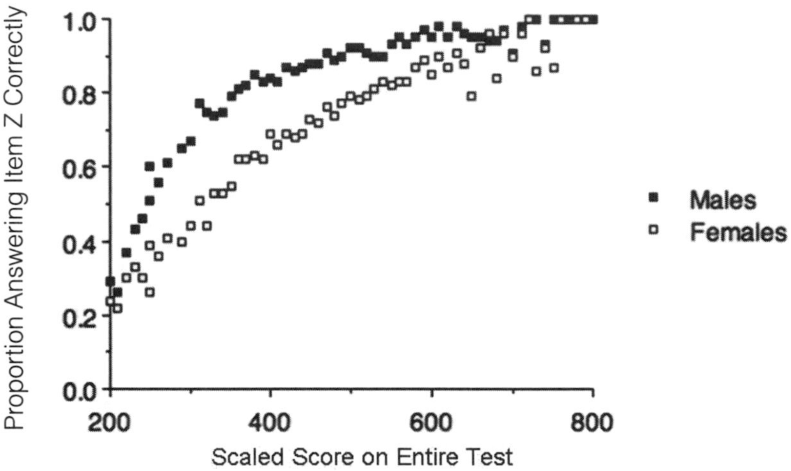


**FIGURE 7-1** Examining differential item functioning—Proportion answering item Z correctly vs. score on entire test, for male and female subjects (hypothetical data).

there is something about it that unintentionally favors boys. There are many statistical procedures available to judge whether there is statistically sound evidence of DIF that are useful for different kinds of test items and sample sizes; see Wilson (2005), Dorans and Holland (1993), and Thissen, Steinberg, and Wainer (1993) for examples.

Consider an example involving Chinese and U.S. children who were administered a test of cognitive development in their own languages (see Huang, 2007). Applying effect size criteria like those mentioned above (Longford et al., 1993) to the statistically significant difference found shows that indeed the DIF for several items is "large." One such item concerns the use of comparatives—for example, "more" and "fewer" in English and their equivalents in Chinese. It is easier for Chinese children than U.S. children (at the same overall cognitive development status) to get the comparative item correct. (Remember that this applies to just that item, but not the other items.) In fact, it turns out that this effect is common to five other items involving both comparatives and superlatives (Huang, 2007). In investigating this, we note that the Chinese language has some interesting differences in comparison to English. For example, the two languages differ greatly in the formation of comparatives and superlatives. In English, the words for comparatives and superlatives often used are "more," "most," "less/fewer," "least/fewest," "as many," and "equal." Some of these words are used differentially depending on whether the nouns they are applied to are countable or not. For example, we say "less butter" but "fewer sheep," "the least of the butter" but "fewest of the sheep," and "as many sheep" but "as much butter." But note that one can say "more sheep" as well as "more butter," so the rule is not a consistent one. In contrast, in Chinese, nouns are not differentiated to be countable or not. Moreover, instead of using different words, the same two characters (*duo* and *shao*) and the same comparative (*geng*) and superlative (*zui*) are used. The function is morphologically easier in Chinese than in English. Zhou and Boehm (1999) found Chinese and U.S. elementary children developed differently on those concepts. So it is not surprising that the five DIF items testing children's ability to compare quantities all favored Chinese children. To get an idea of the effect size of this difference, the relative odds of getting the item correct for children in the two groups can be calculated and they are 1:2.77 (U.S.:Chinese)—that is, for respondents at the same level of cognitive development, approximately 1 U.S. child for every 3 Chinese children would be predicted to get the item correct. This effect size needs to be embedded in a real-world context to decide whether it is important or not. However, it seems to be reasonable to say that the difference is quite noticeable and likely to be interpretable in many contexts.

Once an item exhibiting DIF has been identified, one must decide what to do about it. Recall that not all instances of empirical DIF threaten the item—as mentioned earlier, the grouping characteristics may not be ones of concern for issues determined to be important, such as fairness. It is sobering to realize that, for each item, it is almost inevitable that there will be some grouping that could be constructed for which the item will exhibit DIF. It is first necessary to establish that the DIF is indeed not a result of random fluctuations, and then the same steps are needed: (a) repeated samplings and (b) development of a "theory of DIF" for that particular item. If one is indeed confident that DIF is established, then the best strategy is to develop alternative items that do not exhibit DIF. However, it may not be possible to replace the DIF item in the instrument—in the case above, the question would be whether comparatives and superlatives were indeed considered necessary to one's conception of cognitive development. Then the measurer must make a judgment about the best way to address the issue. Note that a technical solution is available here—the measurer can use the two different calibrations for the two groups, but this is seldom a chosen strategy, as it involves complex issues of fairness and interpretation.[2]

## Validity Generalization

As described earlier, the validity of inferences based on test data is critical to the selection and use of tests. Test users need to know the extent to which the inferences that they make on the basis of test performance would still apply if the child had been tested by a different examiner, on a different day of the week, in a different setting, using an alternate form of the same test, or even using a different assessment of the same skill or ability. Whether a particular test will function in the same way for different populations (e.g., for minority and nonminority children) in different settings (e.g., in a Head Start program and a private, for-profit, preschool program) are questions for research. However, because there are virtually infinite ways in which to characterize subpopulations of interest, and there are infinitely many settings across which one might wish to use assessments, it is impractical to consider that all tests might be studied on all populations in all settings of interest. Even if it were practical, doing so might not provide the best answer to questions about the validity of specific assessments, because individual studies can suffer from methodological shortcomings that can affect the estimation of validity coefficients in ways that do not affect the validity of inferences based on the test. Put another way, the information one seeks con-

---

[2]To carry this out, one would use item estimates anchored (for the non-DIF items) on the whole sample to estimate different difficulties for the DIF items, then make sure that the two metrics are equated.

cerns population properties of the test but the individual research studies provide only imperfect estimates of these quantities. Even well-designed studies can provide only imperfect information about the test properties.

A number of methodological factors can affect estimates of test validity. Several obvious candidates include sampling error, unreliability in the specific test being studied, unreliability in the specific criterion being used (e.g., another test measure, performance in a course, success at the next grade level), and restriction of range in the study sample. When assessing whether tests function similarly across different settings, such as in one preschool compared with another, or for different populations, such methodological factors that affect the size of the validity coefficients must be taken into consideration. The portability of test validity across different settings and populations has come to be known as validity generalization (Murphy, 2003). Studies of validity generalization rely on the methods of meta-analysis to examine the factors affecting variability in validity coefficients. The basic logic of the validity generalization argument rests on the ability of meta-analysis techniques to adjust validity coefficients for sampling error and other methodological artifacts that affect sample estimates of validity coefficients and then to estimate the magnitude of the remaining variance in validity coefficients. If the variability in the validity coefficients is statistically not different from zero once sampling error and other methodological study artifacts have been controlled, then one would conclude that validity will generalize to other settings and populations.

Validity generalization has been widely used in the industrial and organizational psychology literature to examine the portability across employment settings of the validity of cognitive ability tests and other assessments used in employee selection. In the employment context, there are many studies providing data on the use of tests to measure specific ability domains. Interest often centers on the role of specific domains of assessment in predicting job performance more than on the validity evidence for specific tests. However, the techniques of validity generalization can also be used to study the validity evidence for specific tests and the use of specific tests in different populations. In studying test properties, validity generalization techniques are statistically preferable to isolated comparisons across populations. Because such statistical artifacts as sampling error, unreliability in the test and criterion, restriction of range in study samples, and other study design features can be controlled through the techniques of meta-analysis, validity generalization studies can provide better inferences about the comparability or noncomparability of test properties across settings and populations than simple comparisons of test correlations in individual studies or from narrative research reviews.

Although the concept of validity generalization has been used most widely in employment research, related concepts have been discussed in other contexts. For example, the concept of population generalizability (Laosa, 1991) has been used to describe the extent to which inferences about tests or treatment effects in the normative population will also apply to other populations of interest. Although much of the literature on validity generalization is focused on the use of tests in employment settings, its relevance to educational and early childhood settings is clear.

## Limits of Validity Generalization

There are significant limitations to the use of validity generalization to infer the absence of test bias. In part, these limitations are inherent in the use of meta-analysis and the logic of statistical hypothesis testing. The inference that validity generalization holds is based on a test of the statistical hypothesis that validity coefficients (i.e., population correlations) do not vary across populations or contexts. Practically speaking, this is based on a test to determine that the variability in observed validity coefficients is not different from zero once sampling error and other methodological artifacts have been controlled. Thus, the inference of validity generalization is tantamount to accepting a null hypothesis in statistical hypothesis testing. As in other hypothesis-testing contexts, one cannot prove that validity generalization holds; one can only disprove it. Consequently, one can really infer only that the current evidence does not disprove the validity generalization.

There are many reasons why the evidence might not support rejecting the validity generalization hypothesis even though validity coefficients vary across populations or contexts. Just as in the case of DIF and differential test functioning, the statistical power of the hypothesis test must be considered. In DIF, power is primarily a function of the sample size in each subgroup and the magnitude of the difference in item parameters across populations. In meta-analysis, the power of the variance test is principally affected by the number of studies, the sample sizes in those studies, and the magnitude of differences in the validity coefficients across populations. If the number of studies in the meta-analysis is small, or the magnitude of the variability in validity coefficients is small, or the sample sizes in the included studies in the meta-analysis are small, power may be low for the test of variability in the validity coefficients.

A complete discussion of the validity generalization literature or the use of meta-analysis to study validity generalization is beyond the scope of this volume. Interested readers are referred to Goldstein (1996), Hunter and Schmidt (1990), and Murphy (2003). For considerations about the use of validity generalization techniques in the study of test bias, see National Research Council (1989).

## SELECTING ASSESSMENTS AND DEVELOPING SYSTEMS: EXAMPLE SCENARIOS

In the following section we describe three scenarios in which an individual or organization has decided to develop an assessment component for an early childhood program. These scenarios are intended to demonstrate the processes that the individual or organization might establish for achieving its objectives. They are illustrative and are not intended to be definitive or comprehensive. They apply to assessments of children and of early care and education environments, though we have focused mostly on child assessments. When designing an assessment system to accomplish multiple purposes involving multiple domains (e.g., assessing children's status; guiding intervention; or measuring program improvements in language, arithmetic, and socioemotional development), one must replicate many of the processes involved in selecting a test to measure performance in a single domain. Consequently, we begin with a simple scenario in which a program director wishes to assess children's language skills at entry into an early childhood educational program. We then consider a more complex scenario in which a consortium of early childhood programs seeks to establish an assessment system that can be used across all programs in the consortium to make instructional decisions for the children in the consortium's care. Finally, we consider the situation in which the local school board of a large urban school district has decided to incorporate child assessments into its evaluation of the district's new preschool initiative aimed at improving children's school readiness, socio-emotional development, and physical health. All of the scenarios are fictitious and any resemblance to actual people or programs is entirely coincidental.

We understand that assessment circumstances vary in the real world. A local program may have constraints on time, money, knowledge, and/or autonomy that limit its freedom in selecting assessment designs and instruments. A state-sponsored program may have state standards to meet, may need assessments that will provide information on how well those standards are being met, and may have to use assessments selected by the state. A federally sponsored program, similarly, operates in the context of standards imposed and assessment decisions made at the federal rather than the local level. We discuss these possibly conflicting requirements in Chapter 10. In the scenarios we mention some constraints on assessment design and implementation, (e.g., cost). The following scenarios therefore, represent cases in which people at the program levels specified have assessment needs that they wish to satisfy, within the constraints of their particular situations.

### Selecting One or More Tests to Meet a Local Need

Jane Conway is the director of the Honeycomb Early Childhood Center, serving a small rural community. The child population at Honeycomb has historically been largely Caucasian, but in more recent years the population has become increasingly diverse, with more African American and Latino families. Ms. Conway has decided that, in order to better serve the families and children at Honeycomb, she wishes to evaluate the language proficiency of children at the time of their enrollment. In order to achieve her objective, she establishes a test selection committee that is comprised of herself, her best teacher, a parent, and Rebecca Thompson, a retired school psychologist. She asks Dr. Thompson to chair the committee, because of her experience working in school settings with diverse child populations, including children who are not native speakers of English.

Dr. Thompson and Ms. Conway meet and agree to complete the committee's work in 45 days. To achieve this goal, they will need to rely on information about specific assessments from external sources, such as *Tests in Print* (Murphy, Spies, and Plake, 2006) and the *Buros Mental Measurements Yearbook* (Buros Institute of Mental Measurements, 2007); products of the Buros Institute of Mental Measurements at the University of Nebraska; publications focused on preschool assessment, such as the Child Trends (http://www.childtrends.org) compendium, *Early Childhood Measures Profiles* (Child Trends, 2004), and the compendium developed by Mathematica Policy Research for Head Start (Mathematica Policy Research, 2003); and online databases, such as those provided by Buros, the Educational Testing Service, and others.[3]

The first committee meeting is focused on clarifying the purpose for using the test. Ms. Conway explains that her desire is to have information about the incoming language skills of all of the children and to be able to gauge how much language skill the children gain over the course of their time at Honeycomb. Thus, she would like a test that measures both receptive and expressive language, including vocabulary and the ability to follow directions, and children's knowledge and understanding of grammar (e.g., the ability to form the simple past tense of common verbs). She wants to know how the children at Honeycomb compare with other typically developing 3- and 4-year-old children. She is especially concerned to know the overall language skills, not just the English language skills, of the English language learners. This will help her teachers provide the necessary visual and linguistic supports to their children and opportunities to develop language skills through their interactions with the teacher, the environment, and the other children, as well as to measure their progress

[3]See Appendix D for a list and descriptions of useful sources of information on instruments.

over the course of the year to ensure that their language skills are developing at an appropriate pace and that they will be ready for kindergarten when they finish at Honeycomb.

The committee discusses these purposes and works to further clarify the assessment setting. They discuss who will administer and score the assessments, who will interpret the assessments, what specific decisions will be made on the basis of the assessment results, when these decisions will need to be made and how often they will be reviewed and possibly revised, which children will participate in the assessments, and what the characteristics of these children are: their ages, their race/ethnicity, their primary language, their socioeconomic status, and other aspects of their background and culture that might affect the assessment of their language skills. Dr. Thompson concludes, on the basis of the answers to these questions and refinement of their purposes in assessing children's language, that either a direct assessment or a natural language assessment might be used. Ms. Conway likes the idea of using a natural language assessment but considers that such an assessment may be too costly. The committee decides not to preclude any particular form of assessment until they have more information on the available assessments; their reliability and validity for the purposes they have specified with children like those at Honeycomb; and the specific costs associated with using each of them, including the costs of training personnel to administer, score, and interpret the assessments and the costs associated with reporting and storing the assessment results so that they will be useful to teachers.

The committee next considers how they will go about identifying suitable tests. They consider what tests are being used in other programs like Honeycomb. In one nearby program, the director has adopted the use of a locally developed assessment. Ms. Conway considers that perhaps Honeycomb could also use this assessment, since the other program appears to be obtaining excellent results with it. However, Dr. Thompson points out that such a locally developed test, because it has not been normed with a nationally representative sample, will not meet at least one of the stated purposes for assessment, namely, to provide the teacher with information about how each assessed child is doing relative to other typically developing children. Knowledge about how the children at Honeycomb compare with typically developing children is a sufficiently important purpose that the committee rejects the idea of using any locally developed assessments that do not support this kind of inference.

Having clarified their purposes for collecting language assessments and given careful consideration to the requirements and limitations of their specific setting, the committee collects information on specific assessments. They search online publishers of major commercial tests for new and existing assessments and search and gather information from the print and online resources mentioned above, to gather general descriptive information about the skills measured by each assessment, its format (both stimuli and response formats), training requirements or skills of examiners, costs, and the kinds of scores and interpretive information that are provided. Because they anticipate finding a large number of assessments that meet their general needs, they decide not to examine specific review information until after they have narrowed the field to a manageable number (e.g., 10). They do agree, however, to consider tests that measure only some of the language skills of interest, although they believe that it would be preferable to have one assessment that measures all of the skills of interest.

Dr. Thompson has developed an electronic form on which to record this information for each test that they identify as meeting their primary needs. Committee members arrange the information to be collected and the general characteristics to be rated in a hierarchy from most important to least important. Information on the name of the test and the publisher is to be obtained on all potentially suitable tests, including those that will ultimately be eliminated, in order that the committee has a record of each test examined at any level and the reason that it was rejected or not given further consideration. They arrange the criteria in the following order: (1) measures some or all of the language skills of interest, (2) has been normed on a nationally representative sample and provides normative information for each subgroup of interest to Honeycomb, (3) is suitable for use with children in the age range found at Honeycomb, and (4) is suitable for administration by preschool teachers. For each characteristic, the individual gathering the information is to mark "Yes," "No," or

"?" A test obtaining a "No" response to any characteristic will not be given further consideration, as it clearly fails to meet at least one important purpose. Tests with a "Yes" for all characteristics are highly valued, but it is expected that at least some information may not be available through online sources and will require further research. Because of the potential time required to complete this research, the committee can undertake this research only for tests that are otherwise highly promising. Thus, tests with "?" can remain in the pool for now, and, depending on what the characteristics of the set of tests that remain in the pool, they may be further researched or dropped.

At the second committee meeting, the spreadsheets are assembled and the collection of tests is reviewed to see which tests show the most promise on the basis of the first-stage review. The ultimate objective of this meeting is to reduce to a manageable size the number of tests on which more detailed information will be sought. The committee reviews rejected tests to ensure that everyone agrees with the reason that the reviewer rejected those tests. Disagreements are settled at this point by keeping tests in the pool. The final disposition of these assessments may depend on the number of clear winners in the pool. If there are many outstanding options to choose from, then there is little or no need to give further consideration to tests that may be marginal, but if there is a limited number of tests that have been scored positively across all dimensions, then these "iffy" tests might merit further examination and review. (Two committees confronted with the same information may make different decisions about the disposition of such tests, and there is no single right answer to the number of tests to consider for more detailed review.) Thus, at this stage there are at least three groups of assessments: those for which additional review information will be sought, those that have been clearly rejected because of one or more "No" responses on the primary dimensions, and those that are seen as less desirable than tests in the top group but that are nevertheless not clearly rejected. It is helpful to rank-order the best of the tests in this last group. Occasionally, the more detailed review process may eliminate all of the top candidates, necessitating that one give further consideration to tests that were in this middle category.

Having rank-ordered these tests as alternates can save time in this situation.

After the second meeting, the committee members collect, distribute, and read detailed review information on the top assessments prior to the next meeting. The committee chair assembles technical information, including any information on test reliability relevant to each test, adding it to the spreadsheet. The most relevant information is kept for each test. For example, if specific information is available on reliability for 3- and 4-year-old children, this information is preferred over reliability information that is not delineated by age group. Similarly, information that is provided for specific subgroups of children, such as Spanish-speaking children, African American children, and children with disabilities, is recorded separately. For some tests, this information must be found in technical manuals or in published research that uses the test. Thus, for tests that look promising, an effort will be made to seek out this information through a broader search of the literature and technical documents from the publisher. If this information cannot be secured in time for the next meeting, the committee will consider extended efforts to get it, if the test otherwise looks promising.

Following the collection and distribution of the detailed review information, the committee meets for a third time to narrow down the list of acceptable tests to a set of top contenders. Factors to consider at this point include the technical information from the reviews as well as cost information. For each of the tests that fare well in this stage of the review process every reasonable effort will be made to obtain a copy of the test,[4] so that the full technical manual and administration procedures can be reviewed in-house. The review materials on each test will be examined to ensure that the test supports the kinds of inferences that Ms. Conway and her teachers wish to make about their children's language skills and development. This judgment will be based on the information

[4]We know it may be difficult or expensive to obtain copies of tests and manuals, and it may not always be practical to do this. Workarounds may be possible, for example by tapping the expertise of committee members, bringing in a consultant familiar with the test and its manual, or relying on sample items or limited access arrangements on publisher websites. It is always preferable for decision makers to see the full instrument and its manual.

about reliability and validity that has been accumulated from all available sources. It is tempting to think that the best decision will be obvious and that everyone would make the same decision in the face of the same information, but each setting is somewhat different, and choosing between tests is a matter of balancing competing objectives. For example, reviewers may differ in how much weight they put on the desire for short testing times compared with the desire for high reliability and validity for all subgroups of children, or the desire for a single assessment compared with the desire to measure all of the identified skills. Thus, decisions may vary from setting to setting, or even between members of the same committee in a given setting. These differences can be reduced by deciding on specific weights for each criterion that all reviewers will use, but in most situations these differences of opinion will need to be resolved by the committee.

It is important to keep in mind that, at this point, the goal is simply to settle on a small slate of possible tests to review directly. The committee can always decide to keep an extra test in the review when opinions about it are divided. Some information will prevent a test from further consideration, such as a test that has been shown to function differently for language-minority children, children with disabilities, or other important subgroups (see the section on differential item and differential test functioning), or a test found to have poor reliability for one or more subgroups, or a test that is found to have special requirements for test administrators that cannot be met in the current setting.

Lack of information is not, in and of itself, a reason to reject a test. For example, a test that appears strong on all other criteria may have no information on its functioning for language-minority children. Specifically, the published information may not discuss the issue of test bias, and there may be no normative information or validity studies that focus on the use of the test with this population. The decision that one makes about this test may depend largely on: (1) the strength of other tests in the pool with respect to their use with language-minority children, (2) the ability to locate information from other sources that can provide the missing information on the test in question, and (3) the capacity of the center to generate its own information on how the test functions with this population of children through systematic use of the test and collection of data that can address this question. In the absence of strong alternatives, a center that has the capacity to use the test in a research mode prior to using the test operationally to make decisions on individual children might choose to do so.

There are two critical points to continue to keep in mind here. First, lack of information is not the same thing as negative information. Second, each suggests different courses of action. Negative information indicates that the test does not function as desired and should not be used for a particular purpose with a particular population. In contrast, lack of information simply indicates that it is not yet known how the test functions. Lack of information does not necessarily imply that the test is biased or functions poorly when used with the target population, but it also does not imply that the test can be assumed to function well in this population or to function comparably across populations of interest. Often, lack of information will lead to rejection of a test; rather, it should lead to a suspension of judgment about the test until relevant information can be located or generated. For a center that lacks the capacity to locate or generate such information, there may be no practical difference in these two situations for choosing an assessment at a given point in time. In either case, the test is of no use to the center at that point in time.

Having compiled all of the collected information on each of the tests, the committee evaluates the information to identify the top two or three tests that best meet the purposes that they detailed at the outset. This process amounts to weighing the strengths and weaknesses of each test, taking into account the dimensions that the committee has agreed are most important for their purposes, and taking into account when information might be lacking for a particular test. Those tests rated as the top two or three will be obtained from the publisher (see note 4, above), along with the technical manuals and any supporting materials that accompany the test. All of this information will be examined firsthand by the committee. This review will typically involve a thorough and direct examination of test items and administration procedures, review of the rationale behind the format of the test and the construction of test items, and a complete reading of the administration guidelines and scoring procedures and information on the interpretation of test scores. The committee may also elect to show the tests to the teachers who will use them, to have teachers rate the difficulty of learning to administer the test, and to pilot the tests with a few children in order to get a sense of how they react to the procedures. This information will be compiled, along with the technical and descriptive information about the test, the information on cost, and the committee's best judgment about any special infrastructure that might be needed to support a particular test (e.g., a test may require computerized scoring to obtain standard scores).

At this point, the committee can choose the test or tests that will best meet the assessment needs of the center. The decision about which test or tests to adopt will boil down to a compromise across the many criteria agreed on by the committee. In this case, these included the desire to have an assessment process that is both child and teacher friendly, minimizes lost instructional time, meets the highest standards of evidence for reliability and validity for the purposes for which assessment is being planned and with the particular kinds of children that comprise the center's population, and that can be purchased and supported within the budgetary limits set out by the director. To no one's surprise, no test has emerged that is rated at the top on all of the committee's dimensions. Nevertheless, the committee's diligence in collecting and reviewing information and in their deliberations has given them the best possible chance of selecting a test that will best meet their needs.

## Selecting Tests for Multiple Related Entities

In this scenario we consider a consortium of early childhood programs that seeks to establish an assessment system to guide instructional decisions that can be used across all programs in the consortium. The process is similar in many respects to the process followed by Ms. Conway and the team at Honeycomb. Unique to this situation are the facts that the consortium wishes to use assessment to guide instructional decision making and that the consortium would like to use the assessment system across all members of the consortium. These differences suggest that the processes adopted by Honeycomb should be modified in specific ways, namely, in the construction of the committee and in the criteria for distinguishing among the tests.

The expansion of the test setting to multiple members of a consortium has specific implications for the constitution of the selection committee. It is critical that the committee that will clarify the purposes of assessment, gather and review test information, and ultimately select the test should be expanded to include representation from across the consortium. It may not be possible to have representation from each member on the committee, but some process should be put in place to ensure that the differing needs and populations across the member programs of the consortium are adequately represented on the committee. It is equally, if not more, important to ensure that the necessary expertise is present on the committee for clarifying assessment purposes, gathering and reviewing the technical information, and choosing among the tests. Just as choosing among the tests will involve weighing advantages and disadvantages and making compromises, with some elements nonnegotiable, establishing the committee to carry out the process will involve choices, compromises, and nonnegotiable elements to be decided on by the leadership of the consortium.

The expansion of the assessment setting to cover all members of a consortium also has implications for implementing the assessment plan. In the case of a single entity, it is immediately obvious who will be responsible for each phase of the assessment plan, from purchasing the assessment, to training those who will administer the test, to scoring, interpreting, and acting on the test. When a consortium is involved and the desire exists to have all entities using the same assessment, a number of other questions must be addressed and the consortium must decide if only a single answer will be allowed to each question, or if individual members will be allowed to answer the question different ways. For example, when will testing be conducted? Who will be responsible for conducting the assessment? Who will train the assessors, and who will coordinate the training? What steps will be taken to ensure that training quality is uniformly high and that all assessors have been trained and meet the same standards? Will results of assessments be shared across members of the consortium, and if so, in what way? Who will be responsible for collecting the data, in what form will the data be collected, and how will the data be stored and aggregated for reporting purposes? Who will decide on report formats and the process of disseminating the results? This list is not exhaustive, but it highlights some of the additional challenges that arise when more than one entity is involved in the testing enterprise.

Another major difference between the current scenario and the Honeycomb scenario is the focus on using assessment results to guide instructional decisions. Using assessments to guide instructional decisions implies that assessments will occur at intervals throughout the year, which may imply that different assessments are used at different times during the year, or that different forms of the same assessments are used at different times during the year. In part this distinction hinges on the nature of the instructional decisions to be made throughout the year. Decisions that relate to monitoring progress in a single domain would generally argue for the use of different forms of the same assessment over time, whereas decisions that relate to the introduction of instruction in a new domain or transitioning from one form of instruction to another (e.g., from native language instruction to English instruction) might argue for the use of a different assessment.

Several questions must be considered when the focus is on guiding instruction. The first is whether or not the assessment is expected to assess progress against a specific set of standards set forth by the state, the district, the consortium, or some other entity. Ideally, there will not be multiple sets of standards against which performance must be gauged, as each set of standards potentially increases the number of behaviors that have to be assessed and monitored, and the more standards that exist, the more likely it becomes that sets of standards will come into conflict with one another.

A second major question that must be addressed is the distinction between status and growth. If the assessment is to monitor growth over time, it should be clear in what domain growth is being measured, whether growth in that domain is captured through quantitative change (i.e., change in level of performance), or whether growth in that domain is captured through qualitative change (i.e., change in type), or both. Measuring quantitative change requires that additional psychometric work has been done on the instruments to develop a scale for tracking performance gains over time, and that it is clear how to interpret differences between scores at different points on the score scale. Major tests have begun introducing such *developmental scales*, as they are often called, but these are by no means ubiquitous, and the lack of a strong, psychometrically sound developmental scale can seriously hinder accurate interpretation of performance gains over time. Finally, unlike the Honeycomb scenario, which focused on status at entry relative to national norms, the focus on using assessment to guide instruction suggests that the members of the consortium might well be interested in, and best be served by, a locally developed assessment. To the extent that the standards and instructional decisions are mostly local, then it is far more likely that a locally developed assessment, tailored to reflect local standards and approaches to instruction, will meet the needs of the consortium. However, this likelihood also has implications for the test review and selection committee. In particular, locally developed tests are not likely to be covered in the available assessment reviews, and are not likely to have been developed to the same rigorous psychometric standards as tests that are intended for use on a broader audience. Thus, the committee may need to gather technical information on more assessments, and may find little or no technical information is available for many of them. Information about test bias in particular is likely to be missing, with the result that it will have to be investigated in the local setting for the selected assessments.

Except for these major differences, the process for the consortium is much the same as the process for Honeycomb. The consortium's committee must spend time clarifying their purposes for assessment and determining the precise reasons for using assessment, the kinds of decisions to be made on the basis of assessment results, and the domains to be assessed. The potential focus on multiple domains of assessment adds complexity to their task, namely, the need to differentiate between domains that may be highly related to one another, and the necessity of restricting the domains to a number that can be reasonably assessed. The process of gathering information about tests and the steps required to adequately review and choose between tests are essentially the same for the consortium committee and the Honeycomb committee. Although the consortium committee may decide to give priority to tests that can assess all of the domains that they have chosen to measure, it is unlikely that they will be able to restrict the review to such tests until later in the review process, when it is clear what tests are available to address their needs. Because the process of gathering information, reviewing it, and selecting among the tests is essentially the same as in the first scenario, that information is not repeated here.

### Selecting Tests in a Program Evaluation Context

Finally, we consider Novatello School District, a large urban school district in which the school board has decided to incorporate child assessments into the evaluation of its new preschool initiative, which is aimed at improving children's school readiness, socioemotional development, and physical health. Novatello has a diverse population of children from many ethnic and linguistic backgrounds with considerable economic diversity in all ethnic groups and approximately 140 home languages other than English. In addition, Novatello provides kindergarten instruction either in English or in the native language for children whose primary language is either Spanish or Farsi, the two predominant languages among Novatello's school population. The Spanish language kindergartens are located throughout the district, whereas the Farsi programs are located in a small region, reflecting the housing patterns of the community.

Novatello's situation differs in important ways from the two previous scenarios. The program evaluation or accountability purpose of the assessment has the greatest implications for the design of the assessment system. The context of multilingual instruction carries further implications, which must be taken into account if the assessments are to enable valid inferences about the program's effects on children's school readiness, socioemotional development, and physical health.

Program evaluation or accountability carries with it significant implications for the use of assessments that were not present in the first two scenarios. In particular, in the prior scenarios, the assessments were decidedly low stakes; the decisions being made on the basis of the children's performance on the assessments had minor consequences, if any, for the children and teachers. In the program evaluation context, one cannot assume that the consequences for children and teachers will be negligible. If program closure is a potential consequence of a poor evaluation outcome, then the consequences for both children and teachers are very high. If children might be prevented from entering kindergarten on the basis of the results of school readiness assessments, then the consequences for children are high. Similarly, if teachers' employment with the district or pay raises are tied to children's performance, then the consequences for teachers are high.

As the consequences associated with decisions based on assessment scores become greater, there is a correspondingly greater burden to demonstrate the validity of inferences that are based on those assessment scores, which in turn requires greater precision in assessment scores. Precision can be increased with uniformity in the assessment setting, standardization of instructions and scoring, and security of assessment information. However, with young children, efforts to standardize assessment conditions can create artificiality in the assessor-child interactions, which may negatively affect the validity of the assessment scores. More importantly, the program evaluation context requires that scores obtained from children support inferences about the programs in which the scores were obtained, even though such assessments are designed to support inferences about children, not necessarily the programs that serve them.

Determining whether these same assessment scores support valid inferences about the educational context in which the scores were obtained requires a level of abstraction beyond the inference from the score to the child. The validity of the inference from the score to the program cannot be assumed on the basis of the validity of inferences about children's abilities. The validity of inferences about programs must also be demonstrated, just as the validity of inferences about children's knowledge, skills, and abilities must be demonstrated and cannot be assumed on the basis of assessment construction or other properties of assessment scores.

Reliance on child assessments in program evaluations carries an explicit assumption that differences between programs in child outcomes at the end of the year can be attributed to differences in the educational quality of the programs. Unambiguous inferences about program differences on the basis of end-of-year differences in child performance are most justifiable when the assignment of children to programs has been controlled in some meaningful way, which is not generally the case. In the absence of controlled assignment, inferences about program differences require considerable care and caution, especially when those inferences are based, in part, on the results of child assessments. In particular, in the absence of controlled assignment, one must justify any assumption that differences between programs in child assessments are attributable only to differences between programs in factors that are under the control of the programs. Support for this assumption is context specific, and it may or may not be defensible in a single district, let alone in a single state. Thus, developing a suitable context for program evaluation will require substantial dialogue among program leaders to identify and address factors that differ among programs and that relate to differences in child outcomes but that are, nonetheless, outside the control of the programs. Failure to account for such differences will negatively affect the validity of inferences about differences in program quality that are based on differences in child outcomes.

In the current context, two factors that could affect the validity of inferences about programs based on child assessment results are the primary language of the child and the language of instruction used in the preschool program. The committee developing the assessment program for Novatello must determine the conditions governing whether children should be assessed in English or in their primary language. Because the language of instruction model varies across programs that will be evaluated, and because children differ in their primary language within and between programs, there are several factors to consider. In Novatello, children are allowed primary language instruction prior to kindergarten along with English language development if they speak either Farsi or Spanish. These children will receive their instruction in kindergarten in their primary language, and thus there is consistency between the language of instruction prior to and during kindergarten. Because primary language instruction is not available in other languages, speakers of languages other than Spanish and Farsi are instructed prior to and during kindergarten in English.

The Novatello assessment development committee decides that children should be assessed in the language in which they are instructed for all assessment domains that link directly to skills and abilities related to instruction. At the same time, all children, including those instructed in a language other than English, will be assessed for English language acquisition because of the programs' focus on English acquisition for all children. The committee agrees that near-term outcome expectations for children must be adjusted to reflect their status as nonnative speakers of English and to reflect the language of instruction. These adjustments are agreed on in order to ensure that short-term performance expectations adequately reflect the different developmental trajectories of children who are at different stages of acquiring English. Although Novatello expects that all children who enter school at preschool or kindergarten will reach proficiency with English by the end of elementary school, they have established outcome expectations for preschool and kindergarten that reflect children's different backgrounds in order to set realistic and comparable performance expectations for all programs. Without these adjustments, programs in areas with high concentrations of nonnative speakers of English or children with the greatest educational needs would be disadvantaged by the evaluation system.

The Novatello assessment committee faces all the same challenges that were faced by Honeycomb and the consortium. They must define the domains of interest and all of the purposes of assessment. They must consider whether they are collecting child assessments for purposes other than program evaluation, such as to assess the different educational needs of entering children, to monitor learning and progress, and to make instructional decisions regarding individual children. If their singular purpose is program evaluation, then it is not necessary to assess all children at all occasions; rather, a sampling strategy could be employed to reduce the burden of the assessment on children and programs, while still ensuring accurate estimation of the entry characteristics of the child population and program outcomes. Challenges of sampling include controlling the sampling process, ensuring that sampling is representative, and obtaining adequate samples of all subpopulations in each program, to the extent that outcomes for subgroups will be monitored separately. If, however, program evaluation is not the primary purpose for collecting child assessment data, then the committee must clarify all of the primary purposes for assessing children and ensure that the instrument review and selection process adequately reflects all of these purposes, prioritizing them according to their agreed-on importance.

The expansion of the assessment framework to include such domains as socioemotional functioning and physical well-being do not fundamentally alter the instrument review and selection process. The committee will have to expand its search to identify available assessments and to locate review information on those assessments. However, the process itself of identifying assessments, gathering and reviewing technical information, considering training needs and challenges, and addressing issues of assessment use with learners from different cultural and linguistic backgrounds is not fundamentally different from the process used by Honeycomb to evaluate language assessments. Of course, the expansion to multiple domains and to domains outside of academic achievement makes the total scope of work much greater, and decreases the chances that a single assessment can be found that will address all of the committee's needs. Thus, issues relating to total assessment time across the set of selected assessments will likely lead to compromises in choosing assessments for any particular domain; the most thorough assessment of each domain may generate time demands and training requirements that are excessive when considering multiple domains.

Unlike the consortium context, in which aggregation of data and centralized reporting were an option to be discussed and decided on by the members of the consortium, the program evaluation context by definition requires that child assessment results will flow to a centralized repository and reporting authority. Precisely what information will be centralized and stored and the process whereby such information will flow to the central agency can be a matter of discussion, but clearly there must be some centralization of child assessment results. The creation of an infrastructure that can support the collection and reporting of this information must be addressed by Novatello. This infrastructure may not fall under the purview of the assessment review and selection committee, but decisions made regarding the infrastructure most definitely affect the committee's work. Some assessments may lend themselves more readily to use within the planned infrastructure than others, and this information should be considered in evaluating the usefulness of assessments. While ease of integration with the infrastructure would not drive a choice between two instruments that differ substantially in their technical adequacy, it could be a factor in choosing between two instruments of comparable technical merit. When examining the costs associated with the two assessments, the costs of incorporating the assessments into the reporting infrastructure must also be considered.

**Summary**

This section provides three different assessment scenarios that might arise in early childhood settings. They are intended to highlight the kinds of processes that one might establish to identify suitable instruments, gather information about those instruments, compile and evaluate the information, and ultimately select the instruments and make them operational for the stated purposes. While each new scenario introduces elements not present in the preceding ones, there is considerable overlap in key aspects of the process of refining one's purpose; identifying assessments; gathering, compiling, and reviewing information; and ultimately selecting instruments and making them operational in the particular context. One other way in which all of the scenarios are alike is in the need for regular review. Like most educational undertakings, assessments and assessment programs should be subject to periodic review, evaluation, and revision. Over time, the effectiveness of assessment systems for meeting their stated purposes may diminish. Regular review of the stated purposes of assessment, along with regular review of the strengths and weaknesses of the assessment system and consideration of alternatives—some of which may not have been available at the time of the previous review—can ensure that the individual assessments and the entire assessment system remain effective and efficient for meeting the organization's current purposes. If the process for selecting tests in the first place is rigorous and principled, the review and evaluation process will be greatly simplified.

# 8

# Assessing All Children

All children deserve to be served equitably by early care and educational services and, if needed, by intervention services. This requires that there be fair and effective tools to assess their learning and development and identify their needs. In this chapter we address the challenges to assessment posed by groups of children who differ from the majority population in various ways. For all of the groups discussed here, assessment has been problematic.

This chapter has three major sections. In the first section, we review issues around the assessment of young children who are members of ethnic and racial minority groups in the United States and the research that has been done on them, chiefly on black children. The next section deals with assessment of young children whose home language is not English, to whom we refer as English language learners. The final section treats the assessment of young children with disabilities.

## MINORITY CHILDREN

Conducting assessments for all children has both benefits and challenges, but when it comes to assessing young children from a cultural, ethnic, or racial minority group, unique concerns apply related to issues of bias. There is a long history of concern related to the potential for, and continued perpetuation of, unfair discriminatory practices and outcomes for minority children. The topic has struck political, legal, and emotional chords, with many in the minority population holding deep-seated skepticism about the positive benefits of assessing their children (Green, 1980; Reynolds, 1983). Some of the features that distinguish minority children in United States include racial/ethnic background, socioeconomic status (SES), cultural values, dialect/linguistic differences, historical and current discrimination, current geographic isolation, and other characteristics that marginalize a population to the majority society. In this section we provide a brief overview of the concerns about assessment of young minority children and examine the available empirical evidence on potential bias in assessing young children from birth to age 5.

## Fairness

The primary concerns about the assessment of this population are fairness and equality across groups. That is, there is concern that assessment tools, by their inherent properties, could contribute to the over- or underidentification of children differently across different minority population groups. Since the first assessment tools were developed, there has been long-standing concern that test scores may not necessarily reflect differences in ability or developmental milestones among children and the populations they represent, but rather demonstrate problems in the construction, design, administration, and interpretation of the assessment tests that lead them to be unfair and untrustworthy (Brown, Reynolds, and Whitaker, 1999; Garcia and Pearson, 1994; Gipps, 1999; National Association of Test Directors, 2004; Skiba, Knesting, and Bush, 2002). Most of what is known about potential bias in assessing minority children is based on school-age children and youth. Less is known about children younger than age 5 and assessment score differences between whites and blacks (Brooks-Gunn et al., 2003). Children ages 5-14 are the most extensively examined for cultural bias, mostly in intelligence testing, with most of the empirical focus on ages 7-11 (Valencia and Suzuki, 2001).

It is important for us to clarify the many definitions of "unfair" and "untrustworthy" assessment problems that are typically termed "bias," because they are often confused by researchers and the public alike (Reynolds, Lowe, and Saenz, 1999). There is bias as in being unfair or as "partiality toward a point of view or prejudice," and there is bias defined as a statistical term: "systematic error in measurement of a psychological attribute as a function of membership in one or another cultural or racial subgroup" (Reynolds, Lowe, and Saenz, 1999, p. 550). Many of the definitions of bias as defined by statistical terms are tied to psychometric validity and reliability theory (discussed in Chapter 7); however, they are often confounded with philosophical definitions of bias related to fairness and views of prejudice (Brown, Reynolds, and Whitaker, 1999).

## Types of Biases

Several categories of biases are particularly relevant for minority populations (Reynolds, 1982; Reynolds, Lowe, and Saenz, 1999).

### Inappropriate Content and Measuring Different Constructs

Bias may arise when the content of the test is unfamiliar to or inappropriate for minority children; test content is inappropriate for a population as a result of contextual differences (Neisworth and Bagnato, 2004). The assumption is that since tests are designed for cultural values and practices of middle-class white children, minority children will be at a disadvantage and more likely to perform poorly because of a lack of exposure to, and a mismatch with, content included in the testing situation. A lack of success in an assessment may be due to the fact that the assessment instrument does not reflect the local and cultural experiences of the children taking the test, resulting in flawed examinations and misrepresentation of minority children's true ability and performance (Hagie, Gallipo, and Svien, 2003).

For example, differences in culture between racial minority and white majority groups in communication patterns, child-rearing practices, daily activities, identities, frames of reference, histories, and environmental niches may influence child development and how development is assessed (Gallimore, Goldenberg, and Weisner, 1993; Hiner, 1989; Ogbu, 1981, 2004; Slaughter-Defoe, 1995; Weisner, 1984, 1998). Hilliard (1976, 2004) has provided several conceptual arguments about the role of contextual factors that differ among racial/ethnic groups, such as reasoning styles, conceptions of time and space, and dependence on and use of nonverbal communication (Castenell and Castenell, 1988).

The dominant, majority group members may stigmatize the food, clothing, music, values, behaviors, and language or dialect of minorities as inferior to theirs or inappropriate, creating a collective group of "minorities" as a separate segment of society that is "not like" the majority (Ogbu, 2004). Variations in ecological circumstances suggest that assessments may be culturally loaded because they reflect the (typically white, majority) developers' experiences, knowledge, values, and conceptualizations of the developmental domains being examined (intelligence, aggressive behavior, etc.). This can lead to a mismatch between the cultural content of the test and the cultural background of the person being assessed, so test items are not accurately reflective of the developmental experiences of the minority population.

The idea that all children have been exposed to the same constructs that the assessment tries to measure, regardless of different socialization practices, early literacy experiences, and other influences, is a fallacy (Garcia and Pearson, 1994; Green, 1980; Laing and Kamhi, 2003; Valencia and Suzuki, 2001). So, for example, bias may arise on the Peabody Picture Vocabulary Test-III (PPVT-III) because of a lack of familiarity with pointing at pictures to communicate, unfamiliarity with English vocabulary, or a combination of these (Laing and Kamhi, 2003). Not all children are exposed to the unspoken expectations for communication and behavior in school settings, such as the early exposure to oral and written linguistic experiences of the mainstream. As such, children who may have cultures with strong oral traditions for learning (American Indians, Haitian Creoles) may be at risk for biased assessments (Notari-Syverson, Losardo, and Lim, 2003).

Evidence has long suggested that children from many minority racial groups do not, as a group, perform as well as children from the majority white group on school achievement and formal, standardized tests, even controlling for socioeconomic background and proficiency in standard American English (Garcia and Pearson, 1994; Rock and Stenner, 2005). The list of theories related to such disparities is long; however, one reason relevant to this report is that differences in test scores (e.g., between black and white children) may be due to striking disparities in ecological conditions and to instruments that are not designed to be sensitive to those cultural variations. Such contextual variations, if not considered in the assessment instrument design, can lead to systematic biases (Brooks-Gunn et al., 2003). Such a bias may actually perpetuate or increase social inequalities because it legitimates them by designing a test that has content and measures reflecting the values, culture, and experiences of the majority (Gipps, 1999).

### Inappropriate Standardization Sample and Methods

Hall (1997) argues that Western psychology tends to operate from an ethnocentric perspective that research and theories based on the majority, white, population are applicable to all groups. These paradigms are seen as templates to be used on all groups to derive parallel conclusions. As such, often the standardization samples of tests are primarily drawn from white populations, and often minorities are included in insufficient numbers for them to have a significant impact on item selection or to prevent bias. For example, there is a great deal of concern about accurate identification of language disorders among black children using standardized, norm-referenced instruments, because many literacy tests are developed based on mainstream American English and do not recognize dialect differences. The tests have been normed on children from white, middle-class backgrounds (Fagundes et al., 1998; Qi et al., 2003; Washington and Craig, 1992). Often validity and sampling tests do not include representative samples of nonmainstream English speakers, so the statistical ability to find items that are biased is limited (Green, 1980; Seymour et al., 2003).

It may be that the large proportion of minority children who score poorly on some standardized language assessment tools may have to do more with the fact the tests have been normed on children from primarily white, middle-class language backgrounds than with true differences in children's language abilities (Qi et al., 2003). Minority groups may be underrepresented in standardization samples relative to their proportions in the overall population, or their absolute number may be too small to prevent bias. Standardized tests based on white middle-class normative data have inevitable bias against children from minority and lower SES groups, providing information on their status in comparison to mainstream children. They do not take into account cultural differences in values, beliefs, attitudes, and cultural influences on assessment content; contextual influences of measuring behavior; or alternative pathways in development (Notari-Syverson et al., 2003, p. 40).

In addition, the fact that a minority group is included in a normative sample does not mean the assessment tool is unbiased and appropriate to use with that group (Stockman, 2000). It is a common misconception that, because a test is "normed," it is unbiased toward minorities. The norming process, by its nature, leans toward the mainstream culture (Garcia and Pearson, 1994). When test companies draw strict probability samples of the nation, very small numbers of particular minorities are likely to be included, increasing the likelihood that minority group samples will be unrepresentative. Even if a test is criterion-referenced instead of norm-referenced, the performance standards (cutoff scores) by which the children's performance is evaluated are likely to be based on professional judgments about what typical (that is, mainstream) children know and can do at a particular developmental level (Garcia and Pearson, 1994).

### Inappropriate Testing Situation and Examiner Bias

Rarely examined is the assessor's influence on child assessments and whether assessor familiarity or unfamiliarity exerts a bias against different population groups. For example, situational factors may systematically enhance or depress the performance of certain groups differently, such as familiarity with the testing situation, the speed of the test, question-answer communication style, assessor personal characteristics, and the like (Green, 1980, p. 244). Assessor and language bias is present particularly if the assessor speaks only standard English, which may be unfamiliar, intimidating, or confusing to minority children (Graziano, Varca, and Levy, 1982; Sharma, 1986; Skiba, Knesting, and Bush, 2002). For example, a meta-analysis by Fuchs and Fuchs (1986) of 22 empirical studies on assessor effects on intelligence tests for children ages 4-16 suggested that children scored higher when tested by familiar assessors. SES was a vital variable: children from low SES backgrounds performed much better with a familiar assessor, whereas high SES children performed similarly across assessor conditions (Fuchs and Fuchs, 1986).

Some researchers have suggested that assessment format and test-taking style can be threatening to some minority populations by its unusual or foreign format and procedure, leading to direction bias (directions for the test misinterpreted by the child) (Castenell and Castenell, 1988; Fagundes et al., 1998). These characteristics may not be equally present in all test-taking populations. Also, the test-taking style dictated by standardized procedures may influence the performance of children from diverse cultural backgrounds, such that their performance may not represent their true ability because they lack familiarity with the test-taking situation (Qi et al., 2003).

### Inequitable Social Consequences

Use of assessments that are not free from bias may result in minority groups being over- or underrepresented in services or educational tracks. Most often the conversation is focused on inappropriate overrepresentation in services (e.g., special education) or on minorities being relegated to inferior programs or services because of test performance (Hilliard, 1991). Historically, test scores have been used to keep black and Hispanic children in segregated schools (Chachkin, 1989). More recently, excessive reliance on test scores for placement purposes has sent disproportionate numbers of minority children into special education programs and low tracks in middle and high school (Chachkin, 1989; Garcia et al., 1989; Rebell, 1989), cited in Garcia and Pearson (1994). Also, the opposite is possible: some children (e.g., Asians) may be overrepresented in advanced programs and high tracks. As Gopaul-McNicol and Armour-Thomas (2002) write: "The challenge for equity in assessment is to ensure that the judgments made about behavior of individuals and groups are accurate and that the decisions made do not intentionally or unintentionally favor some cultural group over another" (p. 10).

### Differential Predictive Validity

To ensure the absence of bias requires that errors in prediction are independent of group membership, and that tests predict important outcomes or future behaviors for minority children. Claims have been made that tests do not accurately predict relevant criteria for minorities and that the criteria against which tests are typically correlated, being from the majority culture, are themselves biased against minority group members (Brown, Reynolds, and Whitaker, 1999; Reynolds, Lowe, and Saenz, 1999). The psychometric methods described in Chapter 7 are among those that may be used to detect such bias in existing instruments and to avoid them when developing and norming new instruments.

## EMPIRICAL EVIDENCE ABOUT POTENTIAL BIAS

In 1983 Reynolds laid out the types of assessment test bias that may occur with minority populations and the need for empirical testing of assessment instruments. Twenty-five years later, this call for empirical research about bias has largely gone unanswered.

Empirical evidence does not provide a consistent answer about the potential bias of assessments of minority populations. In addition, most of the work examining test bias has been focused on school-age and adult populations (e.g., intelligence testing, entrance exams, employment tests; Reynolds, 1983). As Reynolds quipped (1983, p. 257), "For only in God may we trust; *all* others *must* have data." What empirical evidence is available about the potential bias of assessments for minority children from birth to age 5? The quick answer: very little.

### A Search for Evidence

Despite a wealth of conceptual and theoretical arguments and the need to be cautious using assessments with minority populations (e.g., Hilliard, 1979, 1994, 2004), the availability of published empirical evidence testing potential bias for minority populations, particularly in assessment tools used for children between birth and age 5, is sparse. In our search, we developed a list of commonly used early childhood measures from several comprehensive sources (Child Trends, 2004; National Child Care Information Center, 2005). We used the EBSCO search engine (also called Academic Search Premier) to find empirical studies that examined bias and fairness assessment for minority children. Search results were filtered on the basis of four criteria: (1) an empirical design, (2) examination of an individually administered assessment tool, (3) testing of minority participants, and (4) a focus on children from birth to age 5. Only studies published in refereed scholarly journals were examined. All studies were assessed by reading the title and abstracts. If the abstract didn't provide enough information to judge the article's match to the established criteria, the full article was reviewed. Table 8-1 lists the number of empirical articles found on test bias with minority populations by core developmental domains. A total of 64 assessment tools were searched across a number of developmental domains for empirical evidence about potential bias or fairness of the tool with English-speaking, minority populations. In all, 30 empirical articles were found that meet the committee's criteria.

In addition to searching for empirical evidence, the committee reviewed several test manuals of child assessment tools, looking at the empirical approaches test developers reported to consider the potential for bias for different ethnic and minority populations. Some findings: (1) There was little reported evidence that the performance of minority children was examined separately from the larger standardization group. (2) Sometimes detailed data from the normative sample of the current assessment tool version are not available. (3) Standardization samples of minority children are small. (4) Race and class may be confounded in the normative sample.

### Methodological Issues

In our review of the 30 empirical studies, several key methodological issues emerged that may contribute to why there is no

**TABLE 8-1** Peer-Reviewed Articles Found on Test Bias with Minority Populations Across Major Developmental Domains

| Developmental Domain | Number of Assessment Tools Searched | Number of Bias Testing Articles Found | Assessment Tools with Articles Meeting Committee Criteria |
|---|---|---|---|
| **Cognitive** | 11 | 16 | • Kaufman Assessment Battery for Children (K-ABC) (n = 5)<br>• Peabody Individual Achievement Test-Revised (PIAT-R) (n = 2)<br>• Stanford-Binet Intelligence Scales, Fourth ed. (SB-IV) (n = 3)<br>• Wechsler Preschool and Primary Scale of Intelligence, Third ed. (WPPSI-III) (n = 3)<br>• Woodcock-Johnson III (WJ-III) (n = 3) |
| **Language** | 15 | 9 | • Expressive Vocabulary Test (n = 3)<br>• Peabody Picture Vocabulary Test III (n = 5)<br>• Preschool language scale (n = 1) |
| **Socioemotional** | 21 | 5 | • Behavioral Assessment System for Children (n = 1)<br>• Bayley Scales of Infant Development (n = 1)<br>• Child behavior checklist 1½-5 (n = 1)<br>• Attachment Q-set (n = 1)<br>• Peen Interactive Peer Play Scale (n = 1) |
| **Approaches to learning** | 4 | 0 | 0 |

unified conclusion about the role of bias in assessment tests for children.

1. The lack of agreement on the definition of bias. Often it is not clearly specified what type of bias and validity is being tested for, and, if it is, only one type of bias may be addressed. Most of the attention is focused on construct validity and testing for biases related to inappropriate content, followed by biases related to an improper normative sample. Cultural groups may have conceptions or meanings of constructs that are not aligned with what is represented in the assessment (Gopaul-McNicol and Armour-Thomas, 2002). Or there is no commonly agreed-on use of the term "bias" from a multicultural testing perspective or agreement on how to measure it (Stockman, 2000, p. 351). Psychometric tests alone cannot address all potential issues of construct threats—problems about the validity of the constructs themselves, not just whether they are being assessed equivalently. These include contextual nonequivalence, conceptual nonequivalence, and linguistic nonequivalence.
2. A related issue is mono-operation of bias and measures of bias. That is, many studies use only a single variable or a single technique to examine bias effects (Cook and Campbell, 1979).
3. Methods used to empirically test for bias vary widely, from simple comparisons of means and standard deviations with the normative sample, partial correlation between subgroups and item scores to conduct t-tests, to multiple regression and methodological approaches controlling for potential confounding variables. Depending on what type of bias is being examined, the simple presence or absence of differences in mean scores between two different minority groups does not directly say anything about the fairness of the test (Qi et al., 2003; Reynolds, Lowe, and Saenz, 1999).
4. Lack of consistent use of psychometric research and theory in testing for bias. Empirical evidence for potential bias with minority groups may be a result of the type of psychometric

property studied and type of statistical method employed (Valencia and Suzuki, 2001). For example, the significant difference in performance between minority samples and the normative sample of an assessment test prompts one to consider whether this is evidence for test bias (Qi et al., 2003). There is no agreement about which psychometric procedures that deal with or test for bias are most effective (Crocker and Algina, 1986, cited in Fagundes et al., 1998). In item analysis, a normal distribution alone does not indicate whether items differed in difficulty in a sequential manner equally for minority and nonminority populations (Qi et al., 2003). For example, if items are placed in order of increasing difficulty based on a white-normed population, it is possible that this sequence is not appropriate for black children (Qi et al., 2003).

5. Examining or testing for content validity or bias tends to focus on individual item bias. Subjective techniques to overcome such bias usually involve panels of experts from diverse backgrounds who say the question is "valid" and statistical techniques that are based on item test differences—and these experts often disagree.
6. Small sample sizes, limited representation of minority groups, and monolithic conceptualization of minority groups. For example, there is often an assumption that all American Indians, Asian Americans, or African Americans represent a similar culture and language (Helms, 1992). Most studies examine only black-white differences. Most existing studies are based on small samples and provide limited power to examine the relationship between various environmental factors and the reliability or validity of test outcomes.
7. The empirical evidence available about bias for minority populations is almost entirely based on African American and Mexican American children (Madhere, 1998; Valencia and Suzuki, 2001). Given the growing presence of other minority groups, particularly Hispanic and Asian groups, the lack of attention to these groups in bias testing is problematic, and combining various ethnic groups into a single rubric is a serious flaw in the empirical testing of

assessment validity and potential bias (Cho, Hudley, and Back, 2002).

8. Few studies examine potential bias with proper control for potential confounding variables. The most obvious omissions are the age and gender of the child. Few studies report gender or consider gender differences in testing for cultural bias. Many fail to report or control for socioeconomic status as well.
9. Most of the research on test bias, particularly cultural bias with minority populations, was conducted in the late 1970s and 1980s, with very few studies in the 1990s or later. Also, the subjects were mostly older children. For example, Valencia and Suzuki's (2001) review found that 92 percent of empirical, peer-reviewed articles on cultural bias in intelligence tests for children of preschool age or older were conducted in the 1970s and 1980s.
10. Limitation of the type of assessment instruments examined for bias. What is known about cultural bias in assessment instruments is confined mostly to intelligence and cognitive tests, mostly the WISC, WISC-R, and K-ABC. The WISC and WISC-R have now been replaced by the WISC-III, yet this new version has not been examined, so most of what is known about cultural bias in intelligence tests is thus based on two obsolete instruments (Valencia and Suzuki, 2001). Tests that measure other aspects of child development have not received much attention, yet they are also likely to be culturally influenced, as intellectual and cognitive tests are. An example is culturally defining and measuring dimensions of socioemotional development. Such dimensions as creativity, attention, approaches to learning, and aggression may well be contextually, ecologically, and culturally dependent.
11. Little empirical work has been done on the effects of the assessor, the rater, or the testing situation. The questions of whether some children systematically perform worse under testing situations, and whether assessor effects operate by increasing the distress or anxiety associated with a testing situation, merit further research attention (Brooks-Gunn et al., 2003). Few empirical tests have exam-

ined variations across subjects relative to the race of the assessor or interactions between the race of the assessor and the race of the child (Sharma, 1986).

The lack of current available empirical evidence exploring test bias in early childhood assessment suggests that the subject has become peripheral among both policy makers and researchers. But, as was stated so clearly at a National Association of Test Directors Symposium in 2003, "those of us who work in testing should not be lulled into a false sense of calm. The issues raised in the earlier go-around have not been fully addressed" (National Association of Test Directors, 2004, p. 7). The issues raised in the policy arena about the fairness of testing, particularly for young children, have not been informed by sufficient systematic information.

## ENGLISH LANGUAGE LEARNERS[1]

The increasing demand for evaluation, assessment, and accountability in early education comes at a time when the fast-ing growing population of children in the country consists of those whose home language is not English. This presents several challenges to school systems and practitioners who may be unfamiliar with important concepts, such as second language acquisition, acculturation, and the role of socioeconomic status as they relate to the development, administration, and interpretation of assessments.

Because assessment is key to effective curricular and instructional strategies that promote children's learning, young English language learners (ELL) have the right to be assessed. Through individual assessments, teachers can personalize instruction, make adjustments to classroom activities, assign children to appropriate program placements, and have more informed communication with parents. System administrators need to know how young English language learners are performing in order to make proper adjustments and policy changes. However, there is

[1]This section is informed by a paper prepared for the committee by Espinosa (2007).

a lack of adequate instruments to use with them, especially considering the hundreds of languages spoken in the United States. Some tests exist in Spanish, but most lack the technical qualities of a high-quality assessment tool. In addition, there is a shortage of bilingual professionals with the skills necessary to evaluate these children, and a shortage as well of conceptual and empirical work systematically linking context with child learning. In this section we discuss these challenges, review important principles associated with high-quality assessments of young English language learners, and discuss further needs in the field so that research and practice work together to see that such principles are implemented.

Several terms are used in the literature to describe children from diverse language backgrounds in the United States. A general term describing children whose native language is other than English, the mainstream societal language in the United States, is "language minority." This term is applied to nonnative English speakers regardless of their current level of English proficiency. Other common terms are "English language learner" and "limited English proficient." These two terms are used interchangeably to refer to children whose native language is other than English and whose English proficiency is not yet developed to a point at which they can profit fully from English instruction or communication. In this report, the term "English language learner" is used, rather than "limited English proficient," as a way of emphasizing children's learning and progress rather than their limitations. Given the charge of the committee, the focus is particularly on children from birth to age 8—young English language learners.

### Young English Language Learners: Who Are They?

Young English language learners have been the fastest growing child population in the country over the past few decades, due primarily to increased rates in both legal and illegal immigration. Currently, one in five children ages 5-17 in the United States has a foreign-born parent (Capps et al., 2005), and many, though not all, of these children learn English as a second language. Whereas the overall child population speaking a non-English native language in the United States rose from 6 percent in 1979 to 14 percent in

1999 (National Clearinghouse for English Language Acquisition, 2006) and the number of language-minority children in K-12 schools has been recently estimated to be over 14 million (August and Shanahan, 2006), the representation of English language learners in U.S. schools has its highest concentration in early education. This is because most ELL children attending U.S. public schools since entry develop oral and academic English proficiency by grade 3. The ELL share of children from prekindergarten to grade 5, for example, rose from 4.7 to 7.4 percent from 1980 to 2000, while the ELL share of children in grades 6 to 12 rose from 3.1 to 5.5 percent over this same time span (Capps et al., 2005).

Assessing the development of young English language learners demands an understanding of who these children are in terms of their linguistic and cognitive development, as well as the social and cultural contexts in which they are raised. The key distinguishing feature of these children is their non-English language background. In addition to linguistic background, other important attributes include their ethnic, immigrant, and socioeconomic histories (Abedi et al., 2000; Capps et al., 2005; Figueroa and Hernandez, 2000; Hernandez, 2006). Although diverse in their origins, ELL children, on average, are more likely than their native English-speaking peers to have an immigrant parent, to live in low-income families, and to be raised in cultural contexts that do not reflect mainstream norms in the United States (Capps et al., 2005; Hernandez, 2006).

Decades of research support the notion that children can competently acquire two or more languages (García, 2005). Currently, among the available theoretical approaches, transfer theory best explains the language development of young children managing two or more languages (Genesee et al., 2006), asserting that certain linguistic skills from the native language transfer to the second. In like manner, errors or interference in second language production occur when grammatical differences between the two languages are present. In the process of cross-linguistic transfer, it is normal for children to mix (or code-switch) between languages. Mixing vocabulary, syntax, phonology, morphology, and pragmatic rules serves as a way for young bilingual children to enhance meaning. Because language use is context-driven, the bilingual child's choice of language depends on characteristics of and the particular relationship with the addressee as well as the child's own attitudinal features.

Young English language learners represent diverse ethnic backgrounds. According to the U.S. Department of Education (2008), in recent years approximately four in five English language learners were from Spanish-speaking homes, followed by Vietnamese (2 percent), Chinese languages (2 percent), Hmong (1.6 percent), Korean (1 percent), and many more native and foreign languages. While a majority of Hispanic English language learners are of Mexican origin (approximately 7 in 10), substantial proportions have origins in Puerto Rico, Central America, South America, Cuba, and the Dominican Republic (Hernandez, 2006). Within and among these groups, ELL children represent diverse social and cultural customs and histories, which are essential to consider thoroughly when assessing their linguistic, cognitive, social, and emotional development in home and school contexts.

Finally, it is important to consider the socioeconomic status of English language learners, including family income as well as the amount of educational capital (i.e., parental education) in the home. In 2000, 68 percent of English language learners in prekindergarten to grade 5 lived in low-income families (defined as family income below 185 percent of the federal poverty level), compared with 36 percent of English-proficient children in the same grades (Capps et al., 2005). Moreover, nearly half of ELL children in elementary school had parents with less than a high school education in 2000, compared with 9 percent of parents of English-proficient children. A quarter of ELL elementary schoolchildren had parents with less than a ninth grade education, compared with 2 percent of parents of English-proficient children (Capps et al., 2005). Parent education levels are important indices, as they influence language and educational practices in the home and therefore the development of skills valued in U.S. schools.

## Assessment Issues

Young English language learners have the right to benefit from the potential advantages of assessment. The current empirical knowledge base and the legal and ethical standards are limited yet sufficient to improve ways in which they are assessed.

Improvements will require commitments from policy makers and practitioners to implement appropriate assessment tools and procedures, to link assessment results to improved practices, and to use trained staff capable of carrying out these tasks. Researchers and scholars can facilitate the improvement of assessment practices by continuing to evaluate implementation strategies in schools and by developing systematic assessments of contextual factors relevant to linguistic and cognitive development. Assessments of contextual processes will be necessary for current assessment strategies, which largely focus on the individual, to improve classroom instruction, curricular content, and therefore children's learning (Rueda, 2007; Rueda and Yaden, 2006).

### Legal and Ethical Precedents

The impetus for appropriate and responsive assessment practices of young English language learners comes from a number of legal requirements and ethical guidelines, which have developed over time. Case law, public law, and ethical codes from professional organizations support the use of sound assessment tools, practices, and test interpretations. A widely cited set of testing standards is *Standards for Educational and Psychological Testing* (American Educational Research Association, American Psychological Association, and National Council on Measurement in Education, 1999). This volume offers a number of ethical standards for assessing the psychological and educational development of children in schools, including guidelines on test development and application. It includes a chapter on testing children from diverse linguistic backgrounds, which discusses the irrelevance of many psychoeducational tests developed for and normed with monolingual, English-speaking children. Caution is given to parties involved in translating such tests without evaluating construct and content validity and developing norms with new and relevant samples. It also discusses accommodation recommendations, linguistic and cultural factors important in testing, and important attributes of the tester. Similar, though less detailed provisions are found in the *Professional Conduct Manual* of the National Association of School Psychologists (2000).

It has been argued that *Standards for Educational and Psychologi-*

*cal Testing* (American Educational Research Association, American Psychological Association, and National Council on Measurement in Education, 1999) has outpaced present policy, practice, and test development (Figueroa and Hernandez, 2000). However, the Individuals with Disabilities Education Act (IDEA) of 2004 has specific requirements related to the assessment of English language learners. It requires, for example, the involvement of parents or guardians in the assessment process as well as a consideration of the child's native language in assessment. Unlike ethical guidelines, which often represent professional aspirations and are not necessarily enforceable, public law requires compliance. The Office of Civil Rights (OCR) is given the charge to evaluate compliance to federal law and, when necessary, audit public programs engaged in assessment practices and interpretations of English language learners and other minority children.

## Assessment Practice: Use and Misuse

In addition to the concerns surrounding the assessment of all young children, there are central issues inherent in the assessment of young children from non-English language backgrounds. Implementation research suggests that assessment practices with young English language learners continue to lag behind established legal requirements and ethical standards set forth by professional associations (American Educational Research Association, American Psychological Association, and National Council on Measurement in Education, 1999). In part, this is because of a lack of available instruments normed on representative samples of English language learners, inadequate professional development and training, and insufficient research to inform best practice. Such is the case for the assessment of language, cognitive skills, academic achievement, among other areas. Each of these areas is visited briefly.

### *Assessment Instruments*

Language is the key distinguishing feature of English language learners. Assessments of language in early childhood and elementary school settings are used to identify and place children into programs (including special education), to determine oral English proficiency, to determine first- and second-language vocabulary skills, and to predict literacy performance (Garcia, McKoon, and August, 2006). The Language Assessment Scales (LAS; De Avila and Duncan, 1990; Duncan and De Avila, 1988) and Pre-Language Assessment Scales (Pre-LAS; Duncan and De Avila, 1998) are currently among the most commonly used instruments to measure oral language proficiency. These scales, however, have not been found to predict academic language proficiency in English on their own (Garcia, McKoon, and August, 2006). Available research findings indicate that native language academic and reading performance, combined with oral English proficiency, and teachers' judgments, are better predictors of academic English proficiency (Gutiérrez-Clellen, 1999; Gutiérrez-Clellen and Kreiter, 2003).

Issues of test bias are important to consider when assessing the vocabulary development of young English language learners. The Peabody Picture Vocabulary Test (PPVT; Dunn and Dunn, 2007) and the Test de Vocabulario en Imágenes Peabody (TVIP; Dunn et al., 1986) have been reported to be the most commonly used vocabulary tests in English and Spanish (Garcia, McKoon, and August, 2006). The Woodcock-Johnson (Woodcock, McGrew, and Mather, 2001) and the Preschool Language Scale, Fourth ed. (PLS 4) (Zimmerman, Steiner, and Pond, 2002) are also used. These tests are structured so that increasingly difficult and less frequent words are used to test the child's vocabulary awareness, relative to the normative sample. However, unlike the English version, the TVIP was not developed using word frequency measures from Spanish, but was simply translated from English. This creates problems when interpreting the Spanish scores, even when the English scores are useful to compare the oral skills of English language learners with those of their English-speaking, monolingual peers.

Many of the other native language assessments used with young English language learners focus on receptive vocabulary or provide a limited view of their development. Because of the limited availability of instruments to test the native language development of young English language learners, including receptive and expressive skills, school personnel are often forced to rely on informal assessments by teachers, aides, or other informants.

This can undermine efforts to build a suitable curriculum and recognize a child's linguistic strengths and weaknesses. Further research is needed to develop psychometrically sound native language assessments for English language learners. This will require the expertise of several disciplines, including linguistics, cognitive psychology, education, and psychometrics.

Cognitive (or intellectual) assessments are also very common in early childhood education settings. Because of the inherent problems in assessing the cognitive skills of English language learners with language-loaded tests like the Wechsler Intelligence Scales for Children, Fourth ed. (WISC-IV; Wechsler, 2003), two options for intellectual assessment have been made available in recent years. One is the emergence of "nonverbal" intelligence tests. The Universal Nonverbal Intelligence Test (UNIT; Bracken and McCallum, 1998), a commonly used nonverbal cognitive test, has received positive reviews (Borghese and Gronau, 2005; Fives and Flanagan, 2002), although it is designed for children from age 5 to about age 18, not for preschoolers. The standardization of the UNIT was conducted with 2,100 children from diverse backgrounds, and the test manual provides normative scores of several subpopulations. The main complaint about the UNIT is that it is difficult to use and requires a great deal of training and practice to administer.

The second option to traditional cognitive measures is intelligence tests developed for specific ELL populations. To date, these tests are available only for Spanish-speaking children, and most are for school-age children. One is the Spanish version of the WISC-IV (Wechsler, 2004). This test was calibrated to the WISC-IV English with a U.S. sample drawn from several areas of origin—Mexico, Cuba, the Dominican Republic, Puerto Rico, Central America, and South America. Some test items were modified to minimize cultural bias across groups. The test is given in Spanish, and children earn credit for answers in either Spanish or English. It is designed for children from ages 6 to 16. Spanish versions of the Woodcock-Johnson-Revised Tests of Cognitive Ability (WJ-R COG, 3; Woodcock and Johnson, 1989), which can be used with children as young as age 2 years, are also available. Further empirical research evaluating the reliability and validity of these instruments is needed.

The instruments and practices used to assess achievement often depend on the purpose of assessment. Assessments for accountability purposes tend to rely on criterion-referenced tests developed by state departments of education (Abedi, Hofstetter, and Lord, 2004; Abedi et al., 2000; National Research Council, 2000). Debates have continued over the past decades regarding the inclusion of English language learners in large-scale child assessment programs. Due to antidiscrimination laws, court cases, and standards-based legislation, there has been a push to include all children in state assessments, including young English language learners. This has led to the use of accommodations—changes in the test process, in the test itself, or in the test response format—to more accurately portray the performance of English language learners and not discriminate against language background (Abedi, Hofstetter, and Lord, 2004). Currently, however, decisions about which accommodations to use, for whom, and under what conditions are based on little empirical evidence.

Assessments of academic achievement are also used to improve children's learning and identification for special services. For children in early education, these tend to assess early literacy (e.g., sound and letter recognition, sight words) and numeracy (e.g., numbers, shapes, relative size, ordinality) skills. A large variety of tools and practices is used for these purposes, which can be categorized by two general types of performance assessment. First, commercial (mostly norm-referenced) tests are used. Some of the same concerns with regard to normative cognitive assessment are relevant to normative academic assessment. That is, many of the tests have been developed essentially as back-translations or adaptations of existing English language measures, without evaluating their construct and content validity. Moreover, the normative samples often do not reflect the ethnic, socioeconomic, or linguistic backgrounds of ELL children.

Even when these obstacles are overcome and when bilingual achievement tests have been produced with representative samples, the argument is made that the content of standardized tests does not necessarily predict success in the curriculum. The base case for this argument is that test content often does not reflect classroom content, and that academic outcomes do not inform instructional or curricular interventions per se. For these reasons, a second option for the achievement assessment to improve children's learning and to determine identification for special services, known as curriculum-based measurement, has accumulated evidence and attention over the past few decades (Fuchs, 2004; Rhodes, Ochoa, and Ortiz, 2005). Conceptualized initially as an approach to child progress monitoring (Deno, 1985), curriculum-based measurement tasks are used to assess child performance in the curriculum on a weekly basis. Results are used simultaneously to monitor child progress and to inform instructional or curricular interventions. The slope of scores over time is used to monitor progress and the rate of growth toward a determined goal or standard. The IDEA of 2004 allows curriculum-based measurement approaches to replace traditional testing approaches (i.e., normative testing) of academic achievement to determine special education eligibility for learning disabilities, something the IDEA of 1997 did not allow.

Other areas of child development important to and assessed in early educational settings include socioemotional (or behavioral), motor, and adaptive (or daily living) skills, as well as hearing, vision, and health factors. As mentioned previously, these developmental areas are of interest in early education and pre-K–12 schooling insofar as they impact children's learning and educational well-being. Some issues have been raised in the research literature regarding assessment instruments and practices used with culturally and linguistically diverse children in these areas as well (Carter, Briggs-Gowan, and Ornstein Davis, 2004; Figueroa and Hernandez, 2000). For example, when Spanish translations of the Behavior Assessment System for Children, Second ed. (BASC-2; Reynolds and Kamphaus, 2003), a set of rating scales measuring the socioemotional development of children, were produced, the test was not standardized with Spanish-speaking populations. Moreover, the construct and content validity of this tool and those like it need to be evaluated in light of cultural differences regarding definitions of behavior appropriateness and abnormality. Optimally, these assessment instruments would be developed in a culturally and linguistically responsive manner, specific to each of the different groups.

*Professional Development and Training*

A number of problems arise when school personnel are engaged in the assessment of young English language learners without the necessary competence, tools, and therefore practices. The literature on disproportional representation of language-minority children in special education programs, for example, has pointed to culturally and linguistically unresponsive referral, assessment, and eligibility determination practices in schools as causes of disproportionality (Coutinho and Oswald, 2000; Rhodes et al., 2005). Moreover, although the research and legal and ethical declarations mandate responsive practice, several studies have documented referral, assessment, and interpretation practices that are below standard. These studies have highlighted language barriers and the low expectations of teachers (McCardle, Mele-McCarthy, and Leos, 2005), questionable intellectual assessment practices (Bainter and Tollefson, 2003), questionable language assessment practices (Ochoa, Galarza, and Amado, 1996; Yzquierdo, Blalock, and Torres-Velasquez, 2004), invalid or irrelevant interpretations (Harry and Klingler, 2006), and inappropriate translation and interpretation practices (National Research Council, 2000; Ochoa et al., 1996; Paredes Scribner, 2002; Santos et al., 2001).

This has several implications for ongoing implementation research in the area of professional development and training for assessing young English language learners. This research will need to focus on strategies to improve staff competencies necessary to work as a part of a professional team, to work with interpreters, and to choose and administer appropriate assessment batteries. Moreover, implementation research should highlight strategies to train practitioners to develop their competence in second language acquisition, acculturation, and the evaluation of educational interventions.

*Practice and Research*

There is a gap between current assessment practice of young English language learners and what the research and the legal and ethical standards suggest is best practice. It is therefore important that research and practice continue an ongoing dialogue to improve this scenario. Support and necessary funding should be provided by policy makers, institutions of higher education, and other research programs to pursue this course. Researchers can engage assessment scholarship to this end in three ways.

First, the field needs more tests developed and normed especially for young English language learners. This will require a bottom-up approach, meaning that assessment tools, procedures, and factor analytic structures are aligned with the cultural and linguistic characteristics of ELL children, as opposed to top-down approaches in which, for example, test items are simply translated from their original language to the native languages of young English language learners. Norm-based tests should also take into account important characteristics of the children, including their linguistic, ethnic, and socioeconomic histories.

Second, it is time for conceptual and empirical work on child assessment to move beyond the individual level. Most of the discussion in this section reflects the extant literature, which has focused heavily on the assessment of processes and outcomes for the individual—assessing language, cognitive development, academic learning, and so forth. With this knowledge base, teachers and schools are expected to adjust aspects of the environment to improve learning. It has become clear that processes outside the individual—including in the classroom (e.g., teacher-child interactions, peer-to-peer interactions), the home (e.g., frequency of words spoken, number of books), and the school (e.g., language instruction policies)—affect learning. The field lacks conceptual frameworks and the measures necessary to move this research forward to systematically improve children's learning.

Preliminary research on the role of context in learning suggests that variations in environmental factors can increase children's engagement and participation (Christenson, 2004; Goldenberg, Rueda, and August, 2006), which in turn can lead to increased learning—and that the influence of contextual contingencies on learning outcomes is mediated by children's motivation to learn (Rueda, 2007; Rueda and Yaden, 2006; Rueda et al., 2001). Conceptual frameworks should account for the multilevel nature of contexts, including the nesting of individuals within classrooms and families, classrooms within schools, and schools within school districts, communities, and institutions. Moreover, the role of culture and the feasibility of cultural congruence across both in-school and out-of-school contexts will be important to this work. Meaningful empirical work in this area will require the convergence of research methods (e.g., multilevel statistics and the mixing of qualitative approaches with quasi-experimental designs) and social science disciplines (e.g., cognitive psychology, educational anthropology, sociology of education).

Finally, more research documenting the current scenario of the assessment of young English language learners across the country is needed. As the population of these young children continues to grow and to disperse to states with historically low representations of ELL children, more work will be needed to evaluate assessment practices in their localities. Both survey research and observational approaches will be needed in this documentation. This work will aid the development of strategies to train professionals with the skills necessary to serve young ELL children.

## Principles of Assessment

Given the large and increasing size of the young ELL population in the United States, the current focus on testing and accountability, and the documented deficits in current assessment practices, improvements are critical. Improvements are necessary at all phases of the assessment process, including preassessment and assessment planning, conducting the assessment, analyzing and interpreting the results, reporting the results (in written and oral formats), and determining eligibility and monitoring (implementation issues are discussed in Chapter 9).

Researchers and organizational bodies have offered principles for practitioners engaged in the assessment of young English language learners. Among the most comprehensive is a list from the National Association for the Education of Young Children (2005). In a supplement to their 2003 position statement on early childhood curriculum, assessment and program evaluation, the NAEYC presents seven detailed recommendations "to increase the probability that all young English language learners will have the benefit of appropriate, effective assessment of their learning and development" (p. 1). The last of these recommendations concerns further needs (i.e., research and practice) in the field, the subject of the following section. Because these recommendations—presented here as principles—were a collaborative effort of a committee comprised of over a dozen researchers in the field, they are quite representative of recommendations found in the literature.

First, screening and assessment instruments and procedures should be used for appropriate purposes. Screening tools should result in needed supports and services and, if necessary, further assessment. Assessments should be used fundamentally to support learning, including language and academic learning. For evaluation and accountability purposes, young English language learners should be included in assessments and provided with appropriate tests and accommodations.

Second, screenings and assessments should be linguistically and culturally appropriate. This means that assessment tools and procedures should be aligned with the cultural and linguistic characteristics of the child. When tests are translated from their original language to the native language of the ELL child, they should be culturally and linguistically validated to verify the relevance of the content (i.e., content validity) and the construct purported to be measured (i.e., construct validity). Moreover, in the case of norm-based tests, the characteristics of children included in the normative sample should reflect the linguistic, ethnic, and socioeconomic characteristics of the child.

Third, the primary purpose of assessment should be to improve instruction. The assessment of child outcomes using appropriate tools and procedures should be linked closely to classroom processes. This means relying on multiple methods and measures, evaluating outcomes over time, and using collaborative assessment teams, including the teacher, who is a critical agent for improved learning and development. Assessment that systematically informs improved curriculum and instruction is the most useful.

Fourth, caution ought to be used when developing and interpreting standardized formal assessments. As discussed, standardized assessments are used for at least three purposes: to identify disabilities and determine program eligibility, to monitor and improve learning, and to further accountability. It is important that young English language learners are included in large-scale assessments and that these instruments continue to be used to improve educational practices and placements. However, those administering and interpreting these tests ought to use caution. Test development issues—including equivalence, translation, and norming—must be scrutinized, and evidence-based accommodations should be provided during accountability assessments.

Fifth, those administering assessments should have cultural and linguistic competence. This may be the most challenging of the principles. Professional development and training of teachers, school psychologists, speech pathologists, and school administrators constitute a long-term goal that will demand ongoing funding and implementation research. Those assessing young English language learners should be bicultural, bilingual, and knowledgeable about second language acquisition. In many cases, consultants and interpreters are used when the supply of school personnel possessing these qualifications is limited. Implementation research is needed to understand best practices in working with consultants and interpreters through the pre-assessment and assessment planning, conducting the assessment, analyzing and interpreting the results, reporting the results (in written and oral formats), and determining eligibility and monitoring.

Finally, families should play critical roles in the assessment process. Under federal law, parents have the right to be included in the decision-making process regarding the educational placement of their child. Moreover, the educational benefit of the assessment process for a given child is optimal when parents' wishes are voiced and considered throughout. Although family members should not administer formal assessments, they are encouraged to be involved in selecting, conducting, and providing information to contextualize results. The process and results of assessment should be explained to parents in a way that is meaningful and easily understandable.

## CHILDREN WITH SPECIAL NEEDS

Assessment historically has played a central role in the provision of services to young children with special needs, unlike the general early childhood community, for which assessment has been viewed with suspicion until relatively recently (McConnell,

2000). This diverse population of young children presents numerous challenges related to the validity of assessments, not only because they are young, but also because of their developmental or disability-related needs. The following pages address why young children with special needs are being assessed, the principles that should guide assessment, and some of the unique issues raised by conducting assessments for this population. The term "young children with special needs" is used to describe children from birth through age 5 years who have diagnosed disabilities, developmental delays, or a condition that puts them at risk for a delay or a disability.

Key to understanding the assessment issues in this area is understanding who makes up this population. Many children with special needs receiving services do so through programs supported under the Individuals with Disabilities Education Act, the primary law that provides funding and policy guidance for the education of children with disabilities. The IDEA is basically a grants program of federal funds going to states to serve students with special needs on the condition that the education provided for them is appropriate (National Research Council, 1997).

In 2006, nearly 1 million children with special needs under age 5 received services through programs governed by the IDEA. Specifically, almost 300,000 children under age 3 received early intervention services and more than 700,000 children ages 3 to 5 received special education and related services (https://www.ideadata.org/arc_toc8.asp#partbCC). Children under age 5 with special needs are served under two different sections of IDEA. Children from birth to age 3 receive services under Part C, Infants and Toddlers with Disabilities, whereas children ages 3 through 5 are served under Part B, which addresses special education and related services for children and youth ages 3 through 21.

Infants and toddlers receive services for a variety of developmental problems, with communication problems being the most frequent. A total of 64 percent of children served under age 3 have some kind of developmental delay. Nearly one in five (19 percent) have some kind of a prenatal or perinatal abnormality, and 18 percent have motor problems. Three-fourths of the children identified between ages 2 and 3 receive services for a communication problem. Smaller percentages have problems with movement (18 percent) (Scarborough, Hebbeler, and Spiker, 2006). Nearly half (47 percent) of children ages 3 to 5 are reported to have a primary disability of speech and language impairment, with 35 percent having a primary disability of developmental delay (https://www.ideadata.org/arc_toc8.asp#partbCC).

## Assessment Purposes

Young children with special needs are extremely diverse in the nature and extent of their competencies and needs, and this diversity has significant implications for assessment. The purposes of assessment include screening, diagnosis, and determination of eligibility for services, program planning, progress monitoring, and research, evaluation, and accountability (McLean, 2004; Neisworth and Bagnato, 2004).

### Screening

Screening, the process of identifying children who may need additional assessment, is the type of assessment that first suggests the presence of a possible developmental or physical problem, such as a mild communication delay or a hearing problem. A screening assessment may be focused on multiple areas of development, such as language, cognition, and socioemotional development, or specific body functions, such as vision or hearing. Some children, such as those with severe motor problems, would be unlikely to participate in a general developmental screening assessment intended to identify children at risk for poor development because the presence of a delay or disability is already apparent or documented from birth. A number of assessment measures are available with acceptable levels of sensitivity and specificity, indicating that, if conducted well with well-chosen measures, screening can be an accurate process (Meisels and Atkins-Burnett, 2000).

### Diagnosis and Eligibility Determination

Most young children with special needs participate in an assessment for diagnostic purposes and to establish their eligibility for early intervention or early childhood special education services. A diagnostic evaluation is conducted to determine whether the child's functioning is sufficiently outside the realm of typical development to warrant diagnosis of a disability or a developmental delay. The IDEA requires that children referred for early intervention services be assessed in five areas: physical development, cognitive development, communication development, social or emotional development, and adaptive development.

The IDEA requires that children ages 3 and older be assessed in the area of suspected disability, although recommended practice is for a comprehensive assessment in all areas (Neisworth and Bagnato, 2005). Children under 36 months of age are eligible for early intervention services under the IDEA if they have either a developmental delay or a condition likely to result in a delay if services are not provided (e.g., blindness). The IDEA requires that each state set its own criteria for determination of developmental delay. The criteria used by the states vary greatly (Shackelford, 2006), and some may require assessment precision or other psychometric qualities not available in current instruments. States also have the option to serve children under the IDEA who do not have an established condition but are at risk of developing a developmental delay.

The IDEA eligibility criteria for 3- through 5-year-olds are quite different from those for infants and toddlers, meaning that a child can be eligible for services in one age group and not the other. States are required to serve all children ages 3 through 5 who have one of the 13 IDEA-specified disabilities[2] and who have a demonstrated need for special education or related services. These are the same eligibility criteria that apply to children ages 5 through 21 with the exception of developmental delay, which can be used only with children through age 9.

An alternative approach for eligibility determination, response to intervention (RTI), is being used with school-age children and has potential for younger children. Discussed briefly in Chapter 2,

[2]Specific learning disabilities, speech or language impairment, mental retardation, emotional disturbance, multiple disabilities, hearing impairments, orthopedic impairments, other health impairments, visual impairments, autism, deaf-blindness, traumatic brain injury, developmental delay.

RTI involves a multitiered procedure for identifying children who are experiencing difficulties; however, the application of this approach with younger children has not yet been fully developed (Coleman, Buysse, and Neitzel, 2006; VanDerHayden and Snyder, 2006). With current eligibility assessment procedures, children are identified for special assistance on the basis of poor performance on a norm-referenced assessment. A multitiered model differs from traditional identification practices in that assessment is used first to identify children who are not benefiting from a high-quality program and then to monitor their progress when additional assistance is provided. If the amount of additional service deemed necessary for the child to show progress is beyond the scope of the regular program, then the child could be considered in need of special education (VanDerHayden and Snyder, 2006).

Assessment is central to implementation of a multitiered model, but, unlike current approaches to eligibility, the access to special services does not hinge on the outcome of assessment at a single point in time. Because assessment is ongoing in a multitiered model, children have regular opportunities to receive special services if they need them, or to no longer receive them when they are performing at expected levels. Although a well-researched and well-implemented RTI model in early childhood might be an additional way to identify some children who need additional assistance around learning or behavior challenges (Barnett et al., 2006; Hemmeter, Ostrosky, and Fox, 2006), identification for IDEA services in the near future is likely to continue to rely on more traditional assessment procedures for many children.

### Planning for Intervention or Instruction

The provisions of the IDEA require that each eligible child's education must be determined on an individualized basis and designed to meet his or her unique needs. The law uses the word "evaluation" to describe the process of determining eligibility for services and the term "assessment" to describe the process of gathering information for planning the child's program of services (McLean, 2004). The difference is not just a matter of semantics, because the norm-referenced assessments used to determine eligibility do not provide useful information for intervention planning, meaning that another type of assessment must be administered for this purpose (Bailey, 2004; Fewell, 2000; McCormick and Noonan, 2002; McLean, 2005).

For children and families, this means that additional assessments need to be conducted after the diagnostic evaluation substantiates that the child meets the eligibility criteria for services. Criterion-referenced or curriculum-based measures are generally used as part of the assessment process to identify objectives for the child and identify appropriate instructional or intervention strategies to achieve these objectives (Bagnato, 2007; Losardo and Notari-Syverson, 2001).

In addition, information about the family's daily routines and activities, the family's concerns and priorities, and the child's special interests is useful in planning (Wolery, 2003), as is information about classroom activities and goals for children in group care and educational settings (Pretti-Frontczak et al., 2007).

**Progress Monitoring**

The phrase "progress monitoring" is currently used to describe two different kinds of assessment processes for young children with disabilities. The first refers to tracking their progress through a set of objectives using any criterion or curriculum-based tool administered at regular intervals (Pretti-Frontczak et al., 2007; Wolery, 2003). The second involves the use of tools derived from a general outcomes model (Deno, 1997), in which key skills linked to general outcomes are assessed repeatedly over time, allowing for depiction of growth toward identified outcomes (Carta et al., 2002; McConnell, 2000).

Monitoring progress is related to planning the child's program, and the same assessments can be used for this purpose. The assessment process helps the teacher, interventionist, or therapist know whether they should continue to address this outcome or set of outcomes with the set of strategies being used or should identify higher level outcomes or new strategies (Pretti-Frontczak et al., 2007; Wolery, 2003). Note that for children making good progress, progress monitoring identifies the need for the teacher to address high-level outcomes. For children not making progress, progress monitoring may indicate the need for alternative intervention approaches to achieve outcomes not being met with current strategies. Whereas the IDEA has requirements addressing evaluation for eligibility determinations and assessment for program planning, it is silent on the use of ongoing assessment to monitor a child's progress toward a given set of outcomes. The law requires periodic review and updating of the child's plan, but it does not address how assessment tools are to be used in this process. The use of ongoing assessment for planning and progress monitoring, however, is considered one of the indicators of a quality program for all young children, including children with disabilities (Division for Early Childhood, 2007; National Association for the Education of Young Children and National Association of Early Childhood Specialists in State Departments of Education, 2003).

### Large-Scale Assessment: Research, Evaluation, and Accountability

Studies have examined multiple aspects of the development of young children with disabilities and the factors influencing their development, such as parent interaction or the effectiveness of a particular intervention strategy or curriculum model. A substantial body of research addresses the development of young children with particular kinds of disabilities or delays, for example, visual impairments or autism, and much of that evidence is based on the administration of assessment tools that track children's development (see, e.g., Hatton et al., 1997; Rodrigue, Morgan, and Geffken, 1991). Similarly, many studies have examined issues of intervention or program effectiveness for young children with special needs by looking at developmental gains on assessment measures (McLean and Cripe, 1997; Spiker and Hopmann, 1997).

The National Early Intervention Longitudinal Study and the Pre-Elementary Education Longitudinal Study are two national policy studies of IDEA services to young children with special needs that examined child outcomes and drew some of their findings from assessments (Hebbeler et al., 2007; Markowitz et al., 2006). Other national studies and evaluations, such as the Early Childhood Longitudinal Study-Kindergarten Cohort and the national evaluation of Early Head Start, have included children with special needs because they were included in the population of children from which the study sample was drawn (Hebbeler and Spiker, 2003).

The diversity of children with special needs, especially with regard to some who have limited response capabilities and lower overall functioning, is highly problematic when it comes to large-scale evaluations designed to look at the entire population of young children for research, evaluation, or accountability purposes. And the assessment of young children with special needs to address state or federal accountability requirements is a relatively recent phenomenon, either for programs specifically for children with special needs or for general early childhood programs in which they are served, such as Head Start or state-operated preschools (Division for Early Childhood, 2007; Harbin, Rous, and McLean, 2005; Hebbeler, Barton, and Mallik, 2008). Beginning in 2008, the U.S. Department of Education is requiring that all states provide data on progress made by young children during their time in IDEA-governed programs. States are employing a variety of approaches to obtain these data, including using a single assessment statewide, several online assessments, a summary process based on team decision making, and multiple sources of information that include formal assessment tools.

Much attention in the last 20 years has focused on making sure that children in special education are included in state K-12 accountability efforts, because previously they were not. The 1997 amendments to the IDEA require that children with disabilities be included in state and district assessment programs and provided with appropriate accommodations. The law also requires that states report their scores on these assessments in the same detail and with the same frequency as the scores of other children (Ysseldyke et al., 1998).

## Principles of Assessment

Several aspects of the assessment of young children with disabilities for eligibility and program planning are codified in the IDEA as described above and may be addressed in state laws and regulations as well. In addition, several organizations, including the National Association of the Education of Young Children, the National Association of Early Childhood Specialists in State Departments of Education, and the National Association of School Psychologists, have developed position statements on the assessment of young children (National Association for the Education of Young Children and National Association of Early Childhood Specialists in State Departments of Education, 2003; National Association of School Psychologists, 2005). The principles in these documents apply to all children, including those with special needs. Indeed, some of the principles apply to using assessment to identify children in need of special services. The Division for Early Childhood (DEC) of the Council for Exceptional Children has developed a set of recommended practices specifically addressing the assessment of young children with special needs (Neisworth and Bagnato, 2005). The DEC also has developed a companion document to NAEYC's position statement on curriculum, assessment, and evaluation that elaborates on these topics for children with disabilities (Division for Early Childhood, 2007).

A common theme across the professional organizations and echoed by many in the field is the importance of using multiple sources of information and never making a decision about a child based on a single assessment (Greenspan and Meisels, 1996; McCune et al., 1990; McLean, 2004; Meisels and Atkins-Burnett, 2000; Wolraich et al., 2005). This recommendation is especially important for children with special needs, whose performance and behavior across settings and situations can be even more variable than those of typically developing children.

A key principle of good assessment is that families of children with special needs should be included in the assessment process (Boone and Crais, 2002; Division for Early Childhood, 2007; Meisels and Atkins-Burnett, 2000; Meisels and Provence, 1989; Neisworth and Bagnato, 2005). Thinking of families as equal and contributing partners in the assessment has numerous implications for how an assessment process is to be carried out. Family members contribute to the assessment process by supporting the child during assessment, validating the findings suggested by other team members, identifying discrepancies between the child's performance on a formal assessment and what a child usually does, reporting on typical patterns of behavior, and conducting the assessment with team members to ensure the best performance of the child (Division for Early Childhood, 2007; Woods and McCormick, 2002). The variability in the performance of children with special needs across situations requires incorporating information from family members to obtain an accurate picture of the child's capabilities. Families are reliable reporters of information about their child's performance, and the validity of the assessment is enhanced by including it (Suen et al., 1993, 1995).

Another principle applicable to all children but of special relevance to children with special needs is the importance of providing them with multiple opportunities to demonstrate their competencies. The setting for the assessment, the child's relationship with the person conducting the assessment, and the ability of the assessor to establish rapport, fatigue, hunger, interest level in the materials and numerous other factors could result in a severe underestimate of the child's capabilities (Division for Early Childhood, 2007; Meisels and Atkins-Burnett, 2000). Besides offering multiple assessment opportunities, tapping multiple sources of information (family members' reports, observation of children in familiar settings) about the child's functioning helps reduce the chance of underestimating their functioning (McLean, 2004).

Qualities of good early childhood assessment, identified by Neisworth and Bagnato (2005), are that it is useful for its chosen purpose; acceptable to both families and professionals; authentic in that the circumstances and people involved in the assessment are familiar to the child; based on collaboration between families and professionals; reflects convergence of multiple sources of information; accommodates individual differences; sensitive to even small increments of change; and based on tools that have been validated for use with the population of children for whom the assessment is being used. Five practices addressing the assessment of children with special needs and recommended by the Division for Early Childhood of the Council for Exceptional Children reflect these qualities (Neisworth and Bagnato, 2005):

1. Professionals and families collaborate in planning and implementing assessment.

2. Assessment is individualized and appropriate for the child and family.
3. Assessment provides useful information for intervention.
4. Professionals share information in respectful and useful ways.
5. Professionals meet legal and procedural requirements and meet recommended practices guidelines.

## Assessment Challenges

Children with special needs are assessed in large numbers and by a varied array of practitioners, yet little information about actual assessment practices is available. It would be useful to know what tools are being used, how child behaviors are being judged, how eligibility decisions are being reached, to what extent children with special needs are included in accountability assessments, and so on. The use of norm-referenced standardized assessments for children with special needs creates particular challenges. Standardized assessments require that items be administered the same way to all children, requiring them to show competence on demand, possibly in an unfamiliar setting and at the request of a stranger. The structure and requirements of traditional norm-referenced measures present numerous problems for the assessment of young children in general, but especially for young children with special needs (Bagnato, 2007; Macy, Bricker, and Squires, 2005; McLean, 2004; Meisels and Atkins-Burnett, 2000; Neisworth and Bagnato, 2004). In fact, Bagnato concluded that "conventional testing has no valid or justifiable role in early care and education" (Bagnato and Yeh-Ho, 2006, p. 618). A discussion of some of these problems follows.

One of the problems is based on the extent and number of response demands that the testing situation makes on the child. Standardized testing often requires verbal fluency, expressive communication, fully functioning sensory systems, as well as comprehension of the assessment cues including the verbal and visual cues being given by the examiners (Bagnato, 2007; Division for Early Childhood, 2007; Meisels and Atkins-Burnett, 2000). Many young children with special needs are not capable of complying with all of the demands of the testing situation.

A national study of eligibility practices of over 250 preschool psychologists with over 7,000 children found that nearly 60 percent of the children would have been untestable if the psychologists had followed standardized procedures. Children could not respond as they were expected to because of lack of language, poor motor skills, poor social skills, and lack of attention and other self-control behaviors (Bagnato and Neisworth, 1995).

One of the basic principles of good assessments is that an assessment must have demonstrated validity for the purposes for which it is used (American Educational Research Association, American Psychological Association, and National Council on Measurement in Education, 1999). Norm-referenced measures are often used with young children to determine eligibility for IDEA services. As explained previously, state definitions for eligibility for early intervention services employ criteria (e.g., percent delay) that necessitate the use of norm-referenced measures. In 1987, a landmark paper examined the test manuals of 27 aptitude and achievement tests and found that publishers provided very little information on the use of the test with children with disabilities (Fuchs et al., 1987).

More recently, Bagnato and colleagues (Bagnato, McKeating-Esterle, and Bartolomasi, 2007; Bagnato et al., 2007a, 2007b) published syntheses of both published and unpublished research on testing and assessment methods for early intervention, with funding from the U.S. Department of Education, Office of Special Education Programs. They concluded that no research has been conducted to support the use of conventional tests for early intervention eligibility. Only three studies have been conducted to support the use of authentic assessment methods and clinical judgment methods for this purpose. Bailey (2004) suggests that the factor structure used to develop age levels for developmental assessments may not be appropriate for children with developmental delays. He cites a study that found only three factors for children with severe developmental disabilities rather than the five factors reported in the manual (Snyder et al., 1993). Weak or imprecise measurement during eligibility determinations may lead to denial of access to services.

One possible way to mitigate some of the limitations of using norm-referenced assessments for eligibility determinations is through the use of clinical judgment, which, in those states that allow it, can be used instead of or in conjunction with formal assessments. Dunst and Hanby (2004) compared the percentage of children served in the 28 states and the District of Columbia that allow the use of informed clinical opinion with those that do not and found no differences in the percentage of children served, suggesting that professionals in the states that allow for informed clinical opinion may not take advantage of this eligibility determination practice.

Another practice problem associated with standardized norm-referenced assessments is that they do not provide information that is relevant for program planning because the items are chosen for their ability to discriminate among children. In other words, ideal items on norm-referenced tests are passed by half the children and failed by half the children in the norming group. Because norm-referenced tests lack treatment or instructional validity (Bailey, 2004; Botts, Losard, and Notari-Syverson, 2007; Neisworth and Bagnato, 2004), service providers need to give additional assessments to develop intervention plans. One study, which represents a possible new direction for eligibility assessment, examined the use of a curriculum-based measure for eligibility as an alternative to norm-referenced assessment (Macy, Bricker, and Squires, 2005). It found support for the potential of alternative forms of assessment for making eligibility decisions.

All of the problems with using norm-referenced assessment notwithstanding, at least professionals administering traditional tools to young children for diagnostic purposes have the option to select a particular instrument on the basis of the characteristics of the individual child to be tested and should be augmenting that information with information from other sources. The examiner also can modify the assessment procedures to accommodate fatigue or lack of interest. Although such changes in administration violate the standard administration procedures, they may be the only way to get usable information from the assessment (Bagnato and Neisworth, 1995). Often no such option for individualization exists when children with disabilities are assessed for research, evaluation, or accountability purposes—the other reasons why children with special needs would be administered standardized assessments.

For the aggregated data to be meaningful, all children must be administered the same assessment according to the same guidelines. The issue of aggregating data is somewhat less problematic for researchers or program evaluators studying a homogeneous subpopulation of children with special needs, such as young children with blindness, because the study designers may have the option to select a measure that has been developed and validated with the subpopulation of interest (assuming such measures exist). For large data collections encompassing the entire range of young children with disabilities, the challenges related to instrument selection and administration are substantial, as are the challenges of recruiting assessment administrators and interpreters with the full range of relevant knowledge and experience.

Designers of large-scale data collections may respond to the assessment challenges posed by the diversity of children with special needs by excluding them from either the entire study sample or from one or more of the assessments. Another approach is to include only those children with special needs deemed capable of participating in the general assessments and either exclude or administer an alternate assessment to those who cannot take part in the regular assessment. The Early Childhood Longitudinal Study-Kindergarten Cohort, for example, included all children with special needs, provided a set of accommodations for those who needed them, and included an alternate assessment for children who could not participate in the regular assessment (Hebbeler and Spiker, 2003).

Given that the data in large-scale studies will be aggregated across children and possibly disaggregated by subgroups, it is imperative that accurate conclusions be drawn about the performance of children with special needs. Even though there are no data on the validity of using standardized norm-referenced assessments with children with special needs for this purpose, national and statewide evaluation efforts, including the Head Start's National Reporting System, have used such measures with this population for these purposes.

Currently, an assessment system developed by the state of California contains the only assessment tools that have been developed explicitly for large-scale data collection with young children, including those with special needs. These observation-based tools are unique because they were designed from the beginning to ensure that young children with disabilities could be included in the data collection (see http://www.draccess.org for more information).

In addition to these general problems, we describe below several challenges of special relevance to the assessment of children with disabilities.

### Construct-Irrelevant Skills and the Interrelatedness of Developmental Domains

For a young child to demonstrate competency on even a single item on an assessment requires a combination of skills, yet some of them may not be relevant to the construct being assessed. To the extent that items on an assessment require skills other than the construct being assessed (e.g., problem solving), construct-irrelevant variance exists in the scores. Some examples of this in assessments of young children with special needs are obvious. A child who cannot hear or who has no use of her arms will not be able to point to a picture of a cat when asked. The item requires hearing and pointing as well as knowledge of a cat, even though these are not the skills being tested. The child who cannot point will fail the item, regardless of what he or she knows about cats.

Other occurrences of construct-irrelevant variance may not be so obvious. All assessments that require children to follow and respond to the examiner's directions require some degree of language processing. Even though test developers attempt to address this by keeping instructions simple, all young children are imperfect language processors because they are still learning language. Many young children with special needs have impairments related to communication, meaning their capacity to process language is even less than the restricted capacity of a typical peer. Unlike deafness, blindness, or a motor impairment, language processing problems may present no visible signs of impact on the assessment process.

Construct-irrelevant variance is a major problem for the assessment of young children because many assessments are organized and scored around domains of development. Domains are a construct created to describe areas of development. They do not exist independently in the child, and therefore measurement tools that assume independence of domains will have some degree of construct-irrelevant variance due to overlap across domains. Ironically, the impact of construct-irrelevant skills is greater for children with disabilities, because their development across domains may be less connected than it is for typically developing children. For example, completing a two-piece puzzle requires both cognitive and motor skills, skills that develop in tandem in typically developing children. The puzzle is challenging for the same-age child with limited motor skills, even though that child may have a very solid understanding of how the pieces fit together.

**Functional Outcomes and Domain-Based Assessments**

For many years the emphasis in working with young children with special needs has been on identifying and improving functional, rather than domain-based, outcomes. The concept of an appropriate outcome of intervention for a young child with disabilities has evolved over time. One approach used previously by service providers was to write outcomes drawn from domain-based developmental milestones (Bailey and Wolery, 1984). Two examples of milestones as outcomes are "Places round piece in a form board" or "Nests two then three cans." Although some lists of milestones can provide useful skills, milestones do not make good instructional targets for numerous reasons. They are not derived from a theory of development. Many were originally developed because of their ability to differentiate the performance of children of different ages on standardized tests. And the sequence of development for typically developing children may not represent the best sequence for children with disabilities.

A contrasting approach to outcome identification, which is now considered recommended practice, is to develop outcomes that are functional (McWilliam, 2004). Functional outcomes (a) are immediately useful, (b) enable a child to be more independent, (c) allow a child to learn new, more complex skills, (d) allow a child to function in a less restrictive environment, and (e) enable a child to be cared for more easily by the family and others (Wolery,

1989). An example of a functional outcome is "Natalie will be able to sit in her high chair, finger feed herself, and enjoy dinner with her family." Outcomes like this are important because they allow a child to participate more fully in a variety of community settings (Carta and Kong, 2007). Unlike a set of developmental milestones that may have limited utility to a child on a day-to-day basis, functional skills are usable across a variety of settings and situations with a variety of people and materials that are part of the child's daily environment (Bricker, Pretti-Froniczak, and McComas, 1998).

Functional outcomes are at odds with domain-based assessments because they recognize the natural interrelatedness across domains as essential to children's being able to accomplish meaningful tasks in their daily lives. A functional outcomes approach does not try to deconstruct children's knowledge and skills into types of items reflected in many domains-based assessment frameworks; the units of interest are the more complex behaviors that children must master to be able to function successfully in a variety of settings and situations. The International Classification of Functioning, Disability and Health—Children and Youth Version (ICF-CY) (World Health Organization, 2007) is based on an emerging international consensus that characterization of individuals' health and ability or disability should be grounded in functions, activities, and participation and provide methods for characterizing these in children.

The emphasis in many assessment tools on discrete skills and their organization into domains can operate as a barrier to recommended practice for practitioners, who are to use the results in partnership with families to identify the child's areas of need and plan interventions addressing meaningful functioning.

### Universal Design and Accommodations

Universal design is a relatively new phenomenon that has direct application to assessment design for all children, especially young children with special needs. Ideally, all assessments should be designed in accord with principles of universal design, thereby minimizing the need for accommodations. Universal design has its origins in architectural efforts to design physical environments to be accessible to all. According to the Center for Universal Design (1997), universal design is "the design of products and environments to be usable by all people, to the greatest extent possible, without the need for adaptation or specialized design." Universal design is reflected in the community in sidewalks that have curb cuts, allowing people with wheelchairs to cross streets.

The goal in applying principles of universal design to assessments is to develop assessments that allow for the widest range of participation and allow for valid inferences about performance (Thompson and Thurlow, 2002). Applying the principles of universal design to the development of assessments for accountability for elementary and secondary school-age children, Thompson and Thurlow identified seven elements of universally designed assessments (Table 8-2).

Some of the principles, such as maximum readability and maximum legibility, are primarily applicable to assessments in which the child will be reading passages of text, but most of these principles can be applied to early childhood assessment design. A principle of special relevance for young children is the need for precisely defined constructs. Just as physical environments are to be designed to remove all types of barriers to access and use, assessments are to be designed so that cognitive, sensory, emotional, and physical barriers that are not related to the construct being tested are removed (Thompson, Johnstone, and Thurlow, 2002), which relates to the previous discussion on construct-irrelevant skills. Application of universal design principles is intended to minimize construct-irrelevance variance. Universal design principles are especially relevant for standardized assessments but also apply to criterion-based assessments. For example, objectives for children can be described with regard to "communication" rather than spoken language and "mobility" rather than walking. Many of the assessment tools in use today with young children predate the concept of universal design and thus were not developed to reflect these principles (California's Desired Results System being a notable exception).

Even with the application of universal design principles, the need may remain to develop accommodations to allow some children with special needs to be assessed with a particular instrument and for their scores to accurately reflect their capabilities.

**TABLE 8-2** Elements of Universally Designed Assessments

| Element | Explanation |
|---|---|
| **Inclusive assessment population** | Tests designed for state, district, or school accountability must include every student except those in the alternate assessment, and this is reflected in assessment design and field testing procedures. |
| **Precisely defined constructs** | The specific constructs tested must be clearly defined so that all construct-irrelevant cognitive, sensory, emotional, and physical barriers can be removed. |
| **Accessible, nonbiased items** | Accessibility is built into items from the beginning, and bias review procedures ensure that quality is retained in all items. |
| **Amenable to accommodations** | The test design facilitates the use of needed accommodations (e.g., all items can be Brailled). |
| **Simple, clear, and intuitive instructions and procedures** | All instructions and procedures are simple, clear, and presented in understandable language. |
| **Maximum readability and comprehensibility** | A variety of readability and plain language guidelines are followed (e.g., sentence length and number of difficult words are kept to a minimum) to produce readable and comprehensible text. |
| **Maximum legibility** | Characteristics that ensure easy decipherability are applied to text, to tables, figures, and illustrations, and to response formats. |

SOURCE: Thompson and Thurlow (2002).

An accommodation is never intended to modify the construct being tested. Accommodations can include modifications in presentation, in response format, in timing, and in setting. They are generally associated with standardized testing, with its stringent administration requirements. Criterion-based measures, which tend to be more observation-based, provide children with many and varied ways to demonstrate competence as part of the assessment procedures, an approach that reduces but may not eliminate the need for accommodations.

An extensive body of literature has developed in the last 20 years on the use of accommodations of various kinds with various subgroups of school-age children with disabilities, as states moved to include children with disabilities in statewide accountability testing programs (see http://www2.cehd.umn.edu/NCEO/accommodations). There is no corresponding literature for young children, probably because the process of building a system of ongoing large-scale assessment of young children for accountability is only beginning in many states (National Early Childhood Accountability Task Force, 2007), and it is the implementation of large-scale data collection that precipitates the need for accommodations.

## Other Assessment Characteristics

Individual assessment tools differ with regard to other features that have implications for their appropriateness for some children with special needs. The tool must have a low enough floor to capture the functioning of children who are at a level that is far below their age peers. Not having enough items low enough for children with severe disabilities can be a problem on a norm-referenced or curriculum-referenced measure. Similarly, the assessment must have sufficient sensitivity to capture small increments of growth for children who will make progress at far slower rates than their peers (Meisels and Atkins-Burnett, 2000).

Identifying a tool that has a sufficiently low floor, provides adequate sensitivity, and covers the target age range will be challenging for any large-scale assessment that includes young children with special needs. An assessment developed to be used with 3- through 5-year-olds that includes items only appropriate to that age span will not adequately capture the growth of a 3-year-old who begins the year with the skills of a 2-year-old and finishes with those of a 3-year-old.

One last consideration related to assessing young children with special needs is the extent to which the test's assumptions about how learning and development occur in young children are congruent with how development occurs in the child being assessed. Caution is needed in using assessments with children with special needs that were developed for a typically developing population, and in which children with special needs were not included in the design work or the norming sample (Bailey, 2004).

## Conclusion

The nearly 1 million young children with special needs are regularly being assessed around the country for different purposes. Although a variety of assessment tools are being used for these purposes, many have not been validated for use with these children. Much more information is needed about assessments and children with special needs, such as what tools are being used by what kind of professionals to make what kind of decisions. Assessment for eligibility determines whether a young child will have access to services provided under the IDEA. It is unknown to what extent these critical decisions are being made consistent with recommended assessment practices and whether poor assessment practices are leading to inappropriate denial of service. The increasing call for accountability for programs serving young children, including those with special needs, means that even more assessment will be occurring in the future. Yet the assessment tools available are often insufficiently vetted for use as accountability instruments, and they are difficult to use in standardized ways if children have special needs, and they focus inappropriately on discrete skills rather than functional capacity in daily life. Until more information about assessment use is available and better measures are developed, extreme caution is critical in reaching conclusions about the status and progress of young children with special needs. The potential negative consequences of poor measurement in the newest area of assessment, accountability, are especially serious. Concluding that programs serving young children with special needs are not effective based on flawed assessment data could lead to denying the next generation of children and families the interventions they need. Conversely, good assessment practices can be the key to improving the full range of services for young children with special needs: screening, identification, intervention services, and instruction. Good assessment practices will require investing in new assessment tools and creating systems that ensure practitioners are using the tools in accordance with the well-articulated set of professional standards and recommendations that already exist.

# 9

# Implementation of Early Childhood Assessments

As noted in earlier chapters, there is a substantial body of evidence on the importance of considering the reliability and validity of early childhood assessments in the selection of measures and in understanding and interpreting the information obtained from them. In addition to looking at the psychometric properties of the assessment tools themselves, there is emerging evidence that it is also important to attend carefully to the ways in which assessments are actually carried out.

Indeed, as noted in Chapter 7, problems with implementation can pose a challenge to the validity of the data obtained. A poorly trained assessor or a child so distracted that she does not engage with the assessment fully, for example, can lead to questionable data. Careful consideration of implementation issues can help to contribute to the underlying goals. For example, if the goal is to use ongoing monitoring or evaluation to strengthen early childhood programs, then planning for implementation can include consideration of how results will be summarized and communicated to programs. These issues may be particularly salient when early childhood assessments are implemented on a broad scale—for example, when assessments are carried out focusing on a population of children or of early childhood programs.

The purpose of this chapter is to summarize the emerging evidence on implementation issues in conducting early childhood assessments. That is, we complement the earlier summary of research that looks *within* the assessment tools by considering the evidence on *the way in which they are implemented*. Relative to the substantial body of work looking at the reliability and validity of specific early childhood assessments, there is much more limited research on issues of implementation. While summarizing available evidence, this chapter also identifies areas in which future research could contribute to the understanding of implementation issues in early childhood assessment.

The discussion of implementation issues is organized into three areas, moving sequentially from preparation for administration to the actual administration, and then to follow-up steps:

1. Preparation for administration: clarifying the purpose of assessment, communicating with parents, training of assessors, and protection against unintended use of data.
2. Administration of assessments: degree of familiarity of the child with the assessor, children's responses to the assessment situation, issues in administration of assessment to English language learners, adaptations for children with special needs.
3. Following up on administration: helping programs use the information from assessments and taking costs to programs into account in planning for next steps.

## PREPARING FOR ADMINISTRATION

### Determining and Communicating the Purpose of the Assessments

In a summary of principles of early childhood assessment that continues to serve as an important resource (see Meisels and Atkins-Burnett, 2006; Snow, 2006), the National Education Goals Panel (Shepard, Kagan, and Wurtz, 1998) identified four underlying purposes for conducting assessments of young children. They cautioned that problems can occur when there is lack of clarity or agreement as to the underlying purpose of carrying out assessments, because decisions about which assessment is used, the circumstances under which the information is collected, who is assessed, the technical requirements for the assessment, and how the information is communicated follow from the purpose. As one illustration, Shepard, Kagan, and Wurtz (1998) note that assessments for the purpose of improving instruction have the least stringent requirements for reliability and validity, while assessments with high stakes have the most stringent ones. Assessments to guide instruction can be gathered repeatedly over the course of the year through observations in the classroom, and instruction can be modified if the most recent observations update and change earlier information. This flexibility is not present for high-stakes assessment, in which information gathered in one or only a few assessments must provide a sufficient basis for important decisions. In a more recent discussion of this issue, Mathematica Policy Research (2008) similarly notes that while careful attention needs to be paid to standardization in the implementation of early childhood assessments when the goal is evaluation research, there is greater flexibility in administration when the goal is screening. For example, for screening purposes it may be warranted to repeat the administration of an item if this helps to be certain of the child's best possible performance. Chapter 7 includes a detailed explanation of the process of matching assessments to purposes.

Shepard and colleagues (1998) also cautioned against the inappropriate use of assessment resulting from poor understanding of the purpose. For example, screening assessments, intended to provide an initial indication of whether a child should receive in-depth diagnostic assessment by a specialist, are sometimes inappropriately used to make a final determination of children's special needs. Screening assessments are also sometimes used to guide instruction, without the further detailed information that is needed to glean how children's learning is progressing in relation to a set of goals or a curriculum.

Assessments carried out by teachers through ongoing observation in the classroom (such as work sampling) have sometimes been used for ongoing program monitoring, although it has been questioned whether data collection of this type is sufficiently reliable to be used for this further purpose. Use of data from ongoing observations in the classroom for a purpose other than informing instruction also has the potential to introduce bias, as incentives or consequences come to be connected to teacher reports (Snow, 2006).

Interviews carried out with staff in a small but nationally representative sample of Head Start programs regarding implementation of the Head Start National Reporting System (NRS) suggest that there was ambiguity as to whether the information from the child assessments was to be used for evaluation and monitoring purposes (with the intent of informing program improvement and tracking whether improvements were occurring over time) or whether it was intended for high-stakes purposes (to make determinations about program funding). Staff in 63 percent of the programs in this study indicated that they felt that it was not clear how the results of the assessment were going to be used (Mathematica Policy Research, 2006).[1] This study concluded that when systems of early childhood assessment are implemented, information should be shared with programs about how data will be used. Furthermore, if the intent is to guide program improvement, the results at the program level should be shared with sufficient time to guide decisions for the coming year, and guidance should be provided on how to use the results at the program level.

### Communicating with Parents

A further issue of importance in planning for the implementation of early childhood assessments is whether informed consent is required of parents and how they will be informed of results. Mathematica Policy Research (2006) reports that in the representative sample of Head Start programs studied to document implementation of the NRS, nearly all programs had informed parents that their children would be participating in the assessments. However, there was ambiguity as to whether informed consent was needed. In the second year of implementation, in this sample, two-thirds of programs had obtained written consent from parents. This represented a substantial increase over the proportion of programs collecting written consent in the first year of implementation.

Thus, in preparing for administration of early childhood assessments, a clear decision should be made about a requirement to obtain informed consent from parents, and it should be

[1]A report of the spring 2006 NRS administration was published in 2008 and received too late for inclusion here.

consistently implemented. Mathematica Policy Research notes in addition that the availability of written information for parents about planned assessments would help to ensure that parents receive uniform information to guide them both regarding their children's participation in an assessment and in interpreting results when they become available.

## Assessor Training

The quality of data obtained from child assessments relies heavily on the appropriate training of assessors. A process for certifying that assessors have completed training and are prepared to administer an assessment reliably has now been implemented in multiple large-scale studies involving early childhood assessments. These include FACES (the Family and Child Experiences Study), the Early Head Start Research and Evaluation Study, and the Early Childhood Longitudinal Study-Birth Cohort (Mathematica Policy Research, 2008; Spier, Sprachman, and Rowand, 2004). In the Early Head Start Research and Evaluation Study, for example, the certification process included videotaping interviewers administering the adaptation of the Bayley Scales of Infant Development developed for this study. The interviewers evaluated their own adherence to the administration protocol, and then their administration of the assessment was reviewed and rated by research staff. Interviewers were required to score 85 percent or above on a set of criteria on two tapes in order to be certified to administer the assessment.

Mathematica Policy Research (2006) describes the results of direct observations carried out as more than 300 assessments of Head Start children were conducted for the NRS. Each administration was coded using a set of criteria similar to those noted by Mathematica Policy Research (2008), such as coaching the child, deviations from the assessment script, and errors in scoring particular items. Results indicated that 84 percent of assessments were conducted in such a way that assessors would have been certified.

The use of a certification process with scoring of specific types of deviations from an assessment protocol allows for identification of the types of problems occurring in administration. According to

Mathematica Policy Research (2008), administration issues in the FACES early childhood assessment identified in the certification process included nonneutral encouragement of children, coaching, failure to allow for nonverbal responding, deviation from the script developed to standardize administration, and errors in scoring particular items in the assessment battery. Providing feedback to assessors on their errors can help establish and maintain adherence to the assessment protocol.

### Protection Against Unintended Use of Data

Maxwell and Clifford (2004) note that there is always a possibility that early childhood assessments may be used for high-stakes purposes even when that was not the original intent of data collection. For example, data collected for tracking and monitoring of the overall functioning of a program may be used to make decisions about the progress of individual children or teachers.

Maxwell and Clifford note that protections should be put in place against inappropriate uses of data for high-stakes decision making when that was not the intent and when the data do not have the technical characteristics needed for such purposes. One possibility for protection against the unintended use of data for high-stakes decisions about children is the collection of data for a sample of children rather than for all children in a program (with the caution that an appropriate sampling approach needs to be developed). Another possibility involves a data entry and reporting system that provides reports only at the level of analysis intended (such as at the program level) rather than for individual children or classrooms.

## ADMINISTRATION OF ASSESSMENTS

### Degree of Familiarity of the Assessor to the Child

A study by Kim, Baydar, and Greek (2003) raises the possibility that having a familiar person present during an assessment may influence children's assessment results. In this study, having someone familiar, such as a parent, present in the room in addition to the assessor was associated with higher scores for children ages 6 to 9 on a measure of receptive vocabulary assessed in the home as part of the National Longitudinal Survey of Youth-Child Supplement. This finding suggests that a familiar presence may help the child relax and focus during an assessment. It is also possible that the causal direction works in the opposite way, and that children who have closer, more supportive, and stimulating relationships with parents—and therefore may tend to score higher on a vocabulary assessment—also tend to have parents who want to stay with them and monitor a situation with an unfamiliar adult present. In addition, in this study, when there was a match between the child's and the assessor's race, the race-related gap in assessment scores on measures of vocabulary, reading, and mathematics was significantly reduced.

Counterbalancing these findings are reports from the study by Mathematica Policy Research (2006) indicating that familiarity of the assessor and child can also pose difficulties. In the small but representative sample of Head Start programs in which implementation of the NRS was studied, teachers were used as assessors in 60 percent of programs. Furthermore, teachers were often permitted to assess the children in their own classes (this was reported in 75 percent of programs that used teachers as assessors). According to the report, teacher assessors sometimes became frustrated when they felt that the child was responding incorrectly, because the teacher felt that the child knew the correct answer to an assessment question (for example, could name more letters than responded to correctly on the letter-naming task). Teachers sometimes felt uncomfortable with the standardization required for the assessments, especially not being able to provide praise when the child performed well. Some children also reportedly became concerned because of the discrepant behavior of their teachers in not providing positive feedback.

Systematic study of the effects of familiarity of the assessor on children's assessment scores would make an important contribution. While evidence to date concerns variation in children's scores and reactions to the assessment situation when familiarity with the assessor has varied naturally (that is, at the decision of families or programs regarding who should be present during an assessment), an important next step would be to randomly assign children to be assessed by someone familiar or unfamiliar. Such work should examine not only children's outcomes when familiarity with the assessor is varied, but also on how fidelity of administration may vary with familiarity with the assessor to the child and on observations of the child's reactions in the assessment situation.

## Children's Responses to the Assessment Context

Researchers have begun to study various factors that contribute to assessment burden in young children. For example, the length of assessments in relation to children's performance is a topic that is receiving increasing attention. Sprachman et al. (2007) observe that "researchers need to balance the desire to assess many domains of child development against the potential threats to measurement posed by long administrations. Minimizing child burden while maintaining high reliability of estimates of achievement is an ongoing objective" (p. 3919). Efforts have been made to develop abbreviated versions of assessments, such as the short form of the Bayley Scales of Infant Development developed for the Early Childhood Longitudinal Study-Birth Cohort, in order to minimize burden (Spier et al., 2004). That abbreviation process involves multiple empirical steps. Shortening an assessment or using only selected items always requires great care in ensuring the validity and reliability of the abbreviated measure, as explained in Chapter 7.

Another approach to reducing respondent burden when young children are involved focuses on limiting the duration of assessment or splitting assessments into multiple sessions. As a starting point, research to date has examined children's performance under naturally occurring variation in the length of assessments. It is important to note, as do the researchers involved in these early studies, that this is only a starting point for examining this set of issues. It needs to be followed by research intentionally varying duration of assessment and examining child response to the assessment context as well as child performance. As the researchers note, when studying duration as it occurs naturally, length of assessment may reflect how many items a child can complete or how long a child can persist in an assessment task.

One recent study examined variations in children's performance associated with session length on the assessments carried out for the Preschool Curriculum Evaluation Research Study (PCER; Rowand et al., 2005). While the FACES early childhood assessments and the assessments carried out for the Head Start Impact Study required about 20 minutes to administer, and the NRS took approximately 15 minutes, the PCER assessment battery was substantially longer, requiring about 60 minutes. Because the PCER study was designed to evaluate the full range of impacts of different early childhood curricula, it was important that multiple domains of development be assessed. However, an important question was whether the longer assessment was having implications for the children's performance.

Rowand et al. (2005) found that children who took longer to complete the PCER assessments scored higher, probably because these children were administered more items to reach their ceiling. These researchers also asked whether children generally scored as well on subtests focusing on literacy that were administered earlier versus later in the assessment battery. They found that 63 percent of children showed consistent performance on the early- and late-administered literacy assessments. The 37 percent of children whose performance varied on earlier versus later subtests of the same domain, however, included 21 percent who scored worse as the assessment proceeded (perhaps reflecting fatigue with the long assessment) but 16 percent who scored better on the related assessment carried out later in the session. In a sample of 1,168 preschool-age children, 228 needed two sessions instead of one to complete the assessment. Performance on four key outcomes did not differ significantly according to the number of sessions required to complete the assessment. However, interviewers rated children as more persistent, more likely to sit still, and less likely to make frequent comments if they completed the assessment in one session. These results suggest that long assessment batteries may be difficult for some young children to complete, and that it is important to train assessors to identify when to take breaks or split administration. The authors of this study note the need for a random assignment study in which children are assigned to complete the same battery of assessments in one versus two sessions. This would eliminate issues of self-selection in the research to date, with children who need to complete the assessment in two sittings showing differing initial characteristics.

In another study focusing on data from the PCER study, researchers asked whether scores would have differed systematically if different "stop rules" had been used—that is, whether different requirements had been used for the number of incorrect responses needed before discontinuing the Woodcock-Johnson Letter Word Identification subtest or the Applied Problem mathematics subtest (Sprachman et al., 2007). According to these researchers, "the WJ III tests use stop rules that often take children into questions that are well beyond their ability, which can result in frustration for both the child and the assessor. Although these rules add just a few minutes to the assessment on any one test, the extra minutes have a cumulative effect"(p. 3919). The researchers note that because the Woodcock-Johnson assessments were intended to assist in determining if individual children needed special services, care was taken to build in conservative rules regarding when a child could no longer respond correctly, requiring six incorrect responses as well as going to the bottom of the items on a particular easel. While not varying administration, this study looked at scores if the stop rule had instead been six incorrect items but not going to the bottom of an easel, or three incorrect items.

Stop rule procedures were important particularly to the scores on the Applied Problem subtest. For example, there was an exact score match in only 64 percent of children's scores in the fall preschool administration and 56 percent of children's scores in the spring administration when the stop rule of three items was used as opposed to standard scoring. While the match was better for the Letter-Word Identification subtest, scores matched closely in both the spring and fall assessment for only about three-fourths of the children (74 percent in the fall and 77 percent in the spring). At the same time, however, the cross-time stability of scores, correlations across the two subtests, and prediction from the subtest scores to other measures in the same domain were very similar whether the standard stop rule or an abbreviated stop rule was used. Caution appears to be needed in assuming that scores will be similar with the use of differing stop rules. Yet, as the researchers note, further work will be needed to examine whether systematically varying stop rules can affect overall performance by diminishing the total length of assessments or the sense of frustration in answering questions that are difficult for a child.

Length of assessment was sometimes a concern in the substantially shorter NRS assessment. Head Start staff in the selected sites of the study of implementation were asked about their perceptions of the children's reactions to the NRS assessment (Mathematica Policy Research, 2006). The responses were mixed. Staff in 63 percent of the programs sampled indicated that "most children responded positively" to the assessment. And 43 percent of the staff members interviewed felt that the assessment protocol was too long, and that this contributed to behavioral issues in the children. Behaviors that were of concern to staff included children becoming bored or restless during the Peabody Picture Vocabulary Test (PPVT) or letter-naming tasks and needing redirection. Children sometimes pointed again and again to the same quadrant of the PPVT rather than varying their responses to respond to the word provided. By staff report, however, some children enjoyed the one-on-one time that the assessment permitted. Staff members also often reported that children's comfort level with the assessment situation increased from the fall to the spring assessment. It would be valuable to examine children's assessment scores in light of assessor perceptions of child comfort in order to examine whether children's comfort level might be associated with higher scores.

### Administration for Children Who Are Learning English

Multiple implementation issues arise in administering early childhood assessments to children who are learning English. These include the order of assessments if they will be carried out in two languages; length and potential burden to the children of receiving the assessment in two languages; the availability of skilled bilingual assessors; and the adequacy of training for conducting assessments in two languages. The assessment of children who are learning English also requires a reconsideration of the purposes of assessment. We note that issues pertaining to the content, reliability, and validity of assessments in a language other than English are covered in Chapter 8.

**Revisiting the Issue of Underlying Purpose When Assessing in More Than One Language**

The decision to administer an assessment in both the home language and English to a child who is learning English is clearly tied to the purpose of the assessment for English language learners and the goals of instruction for these children in their early care and education program (Espinosa, 2005). For example, if the intent is to measure how far along a child is in learning English, it might suffice to assess only in English once he or she has passed a screener in English. Another possible purpose for assessing children who are English language learners is to assess their maintenance of and progress in their home language while they are learning English. If this is the goal, then it would be important to assess the child in both languages, and analyses would report on both. Yet another possibility is that the aim of the assessment is to measure the child's mastery of certain concepts or of overall vocabulary, irrespective of which language this is in. If this is the goal, an appropriate assessment practice would be to encourage a child to respond to assessment questions in either the home language or in English and to feel free to use both.

The availability of new approaches both to screening and to administration of assessments to children who are learning English will help make it possible to select procedures that are in alignment with the underlying purpose. Thus, for example, new language routing procedures have been developed for the First Five LA Universal Preschool Child Outcomes Study, a study that needed to address the challenge of having many children in the study population learning English with a range of different home languages (Mathematica Policy Research, 2007). The new routing procedures involve three steps: asking parents about the child's language use, examining the child's performance on two subtests from the Oral Language Development Scale or the Pre-Language Assessment Scale (Pre-LAS) (Duncan and De Avila, 1998), and observing the language in which the child tends to respond on a conceptually scored receptive vocabulary test. The routing procedures provide for the possibility that the initial language of assessment may be revised during the course of administration in response to the child's spontaneous language use.

The conceptual scoring on the receptive vocabulary assessment is intended to acknowledge that children learning English may have mastered particular words in one or another language, giving the child the opportunity show mastery of vocabulary across languages. This matches with the purpose noted above of assessing overall mastery of concepts and vocabulary rather than vocabulary in a particular language, an approach that will not be appropriate if the underlying purpose is to assess retention of home language or progress in English. The important point to note here is that the range of options for routing and of approaches to assessment for children learning English is expanding and will enable better matching with the underlying purpose of assessment.

**Order of Administration**

Questions about the order of administration of assessments for children learning English arose in the initial year of the NRS and resulted in a change in practice (Mathematica Policy Research, 2006). In the first year, all children receiving the assessment in both Spanish and English started with the English assessment. However there was feedback that this was discouraging to children whose mastery of English was still limited. There was concern that scores on the Spanish language assessment were being affected by these children's initial negative experience with the English assessment.

In the second year of administration, the order of administration was reversed, so that the Spanish version of the assessment was always to be given first to children receiving the assessment in both Spanish and English. Interestingly, this too caused some problems, particularly in the spring administration. By this point, children who were accustomed to speaking only in English in their Head Start programs were not always comfortable being assessed in Spanish. According to Mathematica Policy Research, the children's discomfort may have arisen for several different reasons: they may have been taught not to speak Spanish in their Head Start programs, their Spanish may never have been very strong, or their Spanish may have been deteriorating. There were also some observed deviations from the sequencing of the assessments in the small observational study of assessments conducted in both Spanish and English. Three of 23 programs that participated in this study were observed continuing to administer the assessment in English prior to the Spanish version after the change in guidelines for administration.

These findings indicate that when the decision is to administer assessments in two languages, a decision about order of administration is not an easy one to make because there are potential issues with either ordering. Decisions about ordering may need to take into account the nature and goals of the early childhood program, especially whether the primary goal is to maintain two languages or to introduce English. There is a need for systematic study of whether scores for young children learning English vary according to order of administration of home language and English versions of assessments.

### Length of Administration

The NRS implementation study found that administration of the Spanish assessment took several minutes longer than the English assessment (18.6 compared with 15.8 minutes). In addition, children who received the assessments in two languages had to spend double the time or a little more in the assessment situation. The guidance that sites received was to try to administer both assessments the same day, but to reserve the English language assessment for another day if the child seemed bored or tired. Interviews with program staff about their experiences in administering the NRS assessment indicated concern with the burden to Spanish-speaking children of taking the assessment in two languages (Mathematica Policy Research, 2006). There is a need for systematic study of whether children's assessment scores are related to whether assessments in two languages are conducted as part of a single session or broken up into two sessions.

### Availability of Bilingual Assessors and Trainers

A further issue may be finding assessors who are sufficiently bilingual to administer assessments in both Spanish and English. Although the study conducted of assessments in both Spanish and

English as part of the NRS was small, it helps to identify issues that other large-scale systems of early childhood assessment may face. Thus, for example, results reported by Mathematica Policy Research (2006, p. 29) indicate that "observers at about half the sites with observed Spanish assessments reported that some Spanish-language assessors either were not very fluent in Spanish or knew Spanish to speak but not to read; they had difficulty reading or pronouncing words in the assessment, and in rare cases, had difficulty communicating with the children (for example, they had trouble understanding questions in Spanish)."

In addition, 17 percent of the programs in the study sample administering the assessment in Spanish indicated that there was a problem with finding certified trainers who could provide training on the Spanish version of the assessment. Overall, while 84 percent of the observed English language administrations of the NRS protocol achieved a certification score of 85 percent of higher and would have been certified, the portion who attained or surpassed the certification criterion for observed Spanish language administrations was 78 percent. Analyses have not been reported on whether children's assessment scores are related to assessors' fluency in Spanish nor on the degree to which assessors would have met certification criteria.

These results indicate that an important set of issues for those setting up a system of early childhood assessment with an increasingly diverse population of children will be not only finding appropriate assessments but also finding those qualified to administer the assessments in Spanish and other languages, as well as ways to ensure that there is an appropriate process for training on the administration of the assessment in languages other than English.

### Inclusion of Children with Disabilities in a System of Assessment

The 2008 Mathematica Policy Research report identifies as a key issue in training assessors their preparation in working with children with disabilities. In preparing to conduct assessments at a particular site, assessors need to be trained to collect information on appropriate accommodations for individual children—for example, to ascertain whether an aide should be present, if children need to take frequent breaks, or if it is important to confirm that hearing aids or other assistive devices are working properly. It is possible that certification on assessments could include a requirement to tape an assessment with a child who has a disability. Such a procedure would help to ensure that assessors are aware of and are implementing appropriate practices for children with special needs.

In the small study of NRS implementation, 30 of 35 programs reported carrying out assessments with children with disabilities. Staff in these programs usually indicated that they were comfortable with the accommodations made for these children. However, about one in six programs would have liked additional information on when to include children with disabilities in the assessment process and when to exempt them and on the kinds of accommodations that were appropriate during the assessments. Some direct observations of assessments carried out as part of the study indicated that children who could have been exempted were nonetheless being assessed. These findings suggest that in implementing a system of early childhood assessments, it is a high priority to articulate clearly the decision rules for including children with disabilities in the assessments as well as to provide appropriate training for assessors on the use of accommodations.

## FOLLOWING UP ON ADMINISTRATION

### Guiding the Use of Information from Assessments

Key implementation decisions for a system of early childhood assessments do not stop once the assessments have been administered and the data analyzed and summarized. Decisions have to be made about *how* assessment results will be reported back to programs and program sponsors/funding agencies, and *what guidance* will be provided on how programs should use the information from the assessments. Fundamental decisions need to be made about how results will be used if the purpose of carrying out assessments is for program monitoring and evaluation or for high-stakes purposes.

Turning again to the study of implementation carried out as part of the NRS, problems with the guidance provided to programs on how to use the results of the assessments often concerned the unit of analysis. In more than half of the sample programs in the study, respondents felt that it would have been more useful to report on results at the classroom or center level rather than the program level (which may have involved multiple centers), because those were the units in which quality improvement efforts were most meaningful. Furthermore, about half of the programs participating in the study indicated that local assessments (such as ongoing observational assessment through work sampling) were more useful for program improvement purposes than the program-level results of the NRS because results were available more quickly, covered a wider range of domains of children's development, and could be summarized at the classroom level or even for individual children.

Thus, when designing a system of assessment, it is important to look forward in time to the point of communicating results and to consider in advance the extent to which results are appropriate for use in program improvement, as well as how best to summarize them so that implications for programs are clear.

### Assessing the Costs of Implementing a System of Assessment

Finally, a key follow-up step involves taking stock of the costs of the assessments to programs. There is limited information from research available on this issue. Direct examination of the costs of purchasing material, conducting training, and implementing early childhood assessments would be extremely valuable. Some pertinent findings come from program directors participating in the NRS who reported their perceptions of the costs of implementation (Mathematica Policy Research, 2006). These data should be seen as a starting point in the examination of this issue not only because of the small sample size, but also because director perceptions were not accompanied by direct measures of costs. In this study, 77 percent of the program directors interviewed indicated that there had been substantial in-kind as well as monetary costs to their programs of implementation of the NRS assessments. An in-kind cost they reported was the cost of having staff taken away from their usual activities, including instruction of children, to conduct assessments. A monetary cost they reported was the need to hire substitute teachers so that teachers could carry out the assessments or to hire contract staff to conduct the assessments.

Information on costs to programs can be used as input into decisions for the future about the frequency of assessments (for example, whether to conduct them at one or multiple time points), whether assessments are conducted universally or for a sample of children, and whether resources need to be made available to programs to cover the additional costs of assessments.

## CONCLUSION

Emerging evidence indicates that implementing a reliable and valid system of early childhood assessment requires careful consideration not only of which assessments to use but how they are prepared for, how they are put into practice, and how results are communicated to programs. In the next chapter we stress the particular importance of these issues in large-scale systemwide implementation of assessments. However, such issues as clear communication of the purpose of the assessments, consistent practices regarding communication with parents and obtaining informed consent, training of assessors, circumstances of administration to children, appropriate training and assessment practice for children learning English as well as children with disabilities, and communication of results to programs are important whether the assessments occur only within specific programs or at a broader level, such as across a state or for a national program. There is a clear need for research focusing explicitly on such issues as how child performance may vary as a function of variations in the length of assessment, familiarity of the assessor, and procedures for assessing children who are learning English.

# Part IV

## Assessing Systematically

In this part, we present our ideas about how to design, develop, and implement systems of assessment. We strongly believe that assessment of young children should be an integral part of a larger system of early childhood development services, and should be designed to be coherent with the objectives and approaches the system embraces and should be complementary to the other components of the system. We realize that today such comprehensive systems to support children's development are more commonly aspirations than realities, but we see them as an important goal that should be pursued. Thus in Chapter 10 we present our vision of an ideal early childhood services system, its components and infrastructure, and describe the roles that assessments play in such a system. In Chapter 11, we present our guidelines for developing and implementing assessments within such a system.

# 10

## Thinking Systematically

In this volume we have discussed the dimensions of assessment, including its purposes, the domains to be assessed, and guidelines for selecting, implementing, and using information from assessments. Beyond this, however, one cannot make use of assessments optimally without thinking of them as part of a larger system. Assessments are used in the service of higher level goals—ensuring the well-being of children and their families, ensuring that societal resources are deployed productively, distributing scarce educational or medical resources equitably, facilitating the relevance of educational outcomes to economic challenges, making informed decisions about contexts for the growth and development of children, and so on. Assessments by themselves cannot achieve these higher goals, although they are a crucial part of a larger system designed to address them. Only when the entire system is considered can reasonable decisions about assessment be made.

This chapter argues that early childhood assessment needs to be viewed not as an isolated process, but as integrated in a system that includes a clearly articulated higher level goal, such as optimal growth, development, and learning for all children; that defines strategies for achieving the goal, such as adequate funding, excellent teaching practices, and well-designed educational environments; that recognizes the other elements of infrastructure instrumental to achieving the goal, such as professional development and mechanisms for monitoring quality in the educational environment; and that selects assessment instruments and procedures that fit with the other elements in service of the goal. We begin by noting the multiple state and federal structures in which early childhood assessments are being implemented.

These structures have emerged from different sources with different funding streams (e.g., federally funded Head Start, state-funded prekindergarten, foundation-funded intervention programs) and rarely display complete convergence of performance standards, criteria, goals, or program monitoring procedures. Thus, referring to "a larger system of early care and education" is slightly deceptive, or perhaps aspirational. Furthermore, even the well-established programs in the "system" may lack key components—for example, they may assess child outcomes but not relate those outcomes to measures of the environment, or they may not have a mechanism in place for sharing child outcome data in helpful ways with caregivers and teachers.

We use recent National Research Council reports, state experiences with the No Child Left Behind Act, and the recent work of the Pew Foundation–sponsored National Early Childhood Accountability Task Force—a national effort focused on accountability in early childhood—as a basis for articulating the components needed in order for early childhood assessment to be part of a fully integrated system. We also provide some examples of progress toward this goal at the state level. Although we did not find any examples of fully integrated systems, in which services are provided by a single source and the assessment infrastructure is fully aligned and developed, the three states we describe are moving toward integrating early childhood assessment in a well-articulated system.

## WHAT DO WE MEAN BY A SYSTEM?

The idea of a system comes up often in education discussions and analyses—there are education systems, instructional systems, assessment systems, professional development systems—but it is not always clear what the word actually means. Systems have a number of important features, which are enumerated in *Systems for State Science Assessment* (National Research Council, 2006).[1] In particular, they are organized around specific goals; they are made up of subsystems, each of which serves its own purposes; the subsystems must work well both autonomously and in harmony with one another for the larger system to work well; and a missing or poorly operating subsystem may cause a system to function poorly or not at all. In our use of the term with reference to early childhood assessment, the committee intends

- that assessments be seen as a part or subsystem[2] of a larger system of early childhood care and education, which addresses the multiple aspects of child development and influences discussed in this volume;
- that selection of assessments be intimately linked to goals defined by that larger system;
- that procedures for sharing information about and using information from assessments be considered as part of the process of selecting and administering assessments; and
- that different parts of the assessment system itself (standards, constructs, measures, indicators) work together.

Systems need to have well-developed feedback loops to prevent over- or undercompensation for changes in a single part. Feedback loops occur whenever an output of some subsystem connects back to one of its inputs. For example, a fundamental feedback loop occurs in the classroom when a teacher identifies problems that children are having with an idea or skill and adjusts his or her instructional techniques and the learning environment in response. When this causes the children to learn the idea or skill successfully, one would say that the feedback loop has worked effectively. Implementation of a similar feedback loop at the level of the program takes child performance as the input for identifying classrooms in which teachers need additional

[1]This section and the following one on infrastructure draw heavily on the content of the National Research Council's 2006 report, *Systems for State Science Assessment*.

[2]Although assessment is here defined as a *subsystem* of a larger system, throughout this chapter we refer to the "assessment system" for the sake of simplicity, except when the distinction is important.

assistance in implementing instructional activities. These two subsystems—the individual- and the program-level feedback from child performance to teacher supports—function well as part of a larger system if the same or consistent information is used in both loops. However, if, for example, the teacher is responding to child performance so as to enhance creative problem solving, whereas the institution is encouraging teachers to focus on children's rote memorization capacity, then the subsystems conflict and do not constitute a well-functioning system.

In a well-designed program, the assessment subsystem is part of a larger system of early childhood care and education comprised of multiple interacting subsystems. These other systems include the early learning standards, which describe what young children should know and be able to do at the end of the program; the curriculum, which describes the experiences and activities that children will have; and the teaching practices, which describe the conditions under which learning should take place, including interactions among the teachers and children as well as the provisioning and organization of the physical environment (National Research Council, 2006). The relationships among these four subsystems are illustrated in Figure 10-1, adapted from the "curriculum, instruction, assessment (CIA) triangle" commonly cited in the educational assessment community. Each of these subsystems is also affected by other forces, for example, laws intended to influence what children are expected to learn, professional development practices, and teacher preparation policies influenced by professional organizations and accrediting agencies. We argue in this chapter that all these components must be thought of as part of a larger system, and that they must be designed so as to be coherent with one another, as well as with the policy and education system they are a part of, and with the goals for child development that the entire system is meant to be promoting. We reframe these arguments as a conclusion to this chapter.

## INFRASTRUCTURE FOR AN ASSESSMENT SYSTEM

An early childhood assessment subsystem should be part of a larger system with a strong infrastructure that is designed to

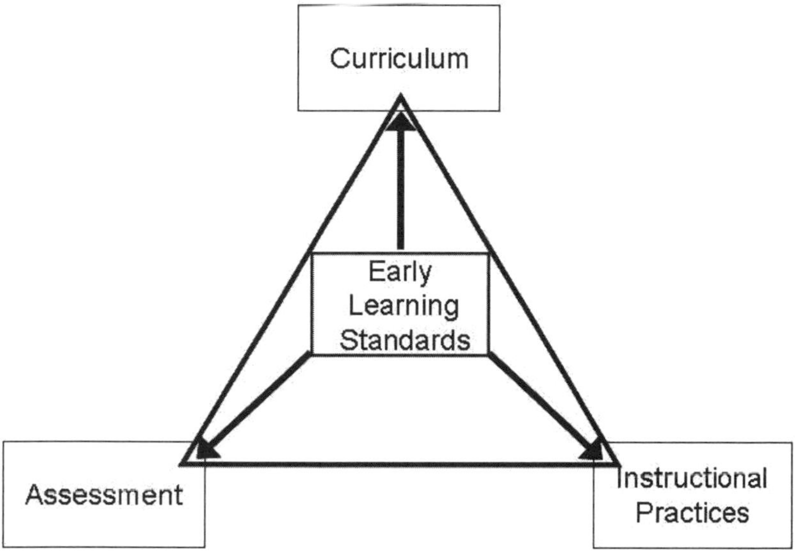


**FIGURE 10-1** A schematic relationship (the "CIA Triangle") among early learning standards, curriculum, instructional practices, and assessment.

provide high-quality early care and education. The infrastructure is the foundation on which the assessment subsystem rests and is critical to its smooth and effective functioning (National Early Childhood Accountability Task Force, 2007). The infrastructure encompasses several components that together form the system:

1. ***Standards:*** A comprehensive, well-articulated set of standards for both program quality and children's learning that are aligned to one another and that define the constructs focused on in assessment as well as the performance levels identified as acceptable.
2. ***Assessments:*** Multiple approaches to documenting child performance and reviewing program quality that are of high quality and connect to one another in well-defined ways, from which strategic selection can be made depending on specific purposes.
3. ***Reporting:*** A procedure, defined on the basis of the standards and the assessments, designed to maintain

an integrated, user-accessible database of assessment results, provide for quality assurance and integrity of data, and generate reports for the varied user audiences and purposes.

4. ***Professional development:*** Ongoing opportunities provided to those at all levels (practitioners, assessment administrators, program directors, policy makers) to understand the standards and the assessments and to learn to use the data and data reports with integrity for their own purposes.
5. ***Opportunity to learn:*** Procedures for ensuring that the environments in which children are spending time offer high-quality support for development and learning, as well as safety, enjoyment, and affectively positive relationships. This is crucial when decisions about children or programs are based on assessment outcomes.
6. ***Inclusion:*** Methods and procedures for ensuring that all children served by the program will be assessed fairly, regardless of their language, culture, or disabilities, and with tools that provide the most useful information for fostering their development and learning.
7. ***Resources:*** Assurance that the resources needed to ensure the development and implementation of the system components are available or will be recruited.
8. ***Monitoring and evaluation:*** Procedures for continuously monitoring the system itself to ensure that it is operating effectively and that all elements are working together to serve the interests of the children.

This infrastructure must be in place to create and sustain an assessment subsystem within a larger system of early childhood care and education. Ensuring the adequacy of each of these components raises some critical challenges. A challenge to the adoption of systems-level thinking about early childhood care and education, and thus about early childhood assessment, is the absence, under current U.S. policies, of a unified structure for early care and education. The current variety of separate programs segregated by setting, by agency, and by funding streams, with their numerous challenges to delivering uniformly high-quality early care and education services, also serves as a barrier to developing a unified system of assessment. While the suggestion that these many barriers to an integrated system must be vaulted may seem unrealistic, we argue that a vision of a well-integrated, coherent system is needed to guide the development of policy for young children. We expand on the importance of each component of a well-organized system below.

## Standards

The most fundamental aspect of the assessment system is the set of explicit goals for children's development and learning around which the larger system is organized, thus providing the basis for coherence among the various elements. In most educational settings, these are referred to as "standards," but in early childhood education sometimes other terms, such as "guidelines" or "foundations," have been used. Whatever they are named, these standards direct the design of curriculum, the choice of teaching practices, and the priorities of teachers in setting instructional goals, planning activities and experiences, and organizing the environment. They are the starting point for developing assessments, judging performance levels, and rating children's and the program's growth and performance.

Standards are also the framework for reporting children's performance to educators and the public and for focusing program improvement efforts. Note that, although these standards are to be applied to children's performance, they can be used as one input in establishing accountability for teachers, centers, and states (National Research Council, 2006). Thus, while some may see holding teachers, early care and education settings, and states to these standards for children's performance as potentially punitive, others argue that they constitute a defense of the right of children to a high-quality and fair early childhood environment. Note that when applying the same logic to the programs in which children are to be educated, an equivalent set of statements can be made regarding program standards.

For example, consider the No Child Left Behind Act (NCLB), which requires states to have reading, mathematics, and science standards for K-12 education that must be of "high quality," although the act says relatively little about what characterizes standards of high quality. While we are emphatically not recommending that the NCLB regime be extended to early childhood education, it is important to understand the NCLB framework, as it is the most common reference point on standards in the United States, and states are being asked by the federal government to align their preschool standards with their K-12 standards. Under the act, the word "standards" refers both to content standards and to achievement standards. The law requires states to develop challenging academic standards of both types, and a federal guidance document describes them as follows (U.S. Department of Education, 2004):

- Academic *content* standards must specify what all children are expected to know and be able to do; contain coherent and rigorous content; and encourage the teaching of advanced skills.
- Academic *achievement* standards must be aligned with the state's academic content standards. For each content area, a state's academic achievement standards must include at least two levels of achievement (proficient and advanced) that reflect mastery of the material in the state's academic content standards, and a third level of achievement (basic) to provide information about the progress of lower-achieving children toward mastering the proficient and advanced levels.

Note that achievement standards are often also referred to as performance standards.

The NCLB-driven standards apply to children in grades 3-12 and link directly to the explicitly defined academic content areas that are also assessed in determining adequate yearly progress for schools. It would be inappropriate to borrow this model unchanged and apply it to early childhood settings, in which explicit instruction in well-defined academic content areas is not characteristic of excellent care and education.

The Council of Chief State School Officers defines common standards and assessment-related terms in language relevant to the early childhood community (http://www.ccsso.

org/projects/SCASS/projects/early_childhood_education_assessment_consortium/publications_and_products/2838.cfm). It defines standards as "widely accepted statements of expectations for children's learning or the quality of schools and other programs." Of critical importance in this definition is the inclusion of program standards on equal footing with expectations for children's learning.

The report *Systems for State Science Assessment* (National Research Council, 2006) examines the role of standards in certain educational assessments and recommends that they be designed with a list of specific qualities in mind: standards should be clear, detailed, and complete; be reasonable in scope; be correct in their academic and scientific foundations; have a clear conceptual framework; be based on sound models of learning; and describe performance expectations and proficiency levels. State standards that have been developed for K-12 education do not meet these requirements as a whole, although some come closer than others. Recent analyses of states' early childhood standards also suggest some misunderstanding of the difference between content and performance (Neuman and Roskos, 2005; Scott-Little, Kagan, and Frelow, 2003a). Appendix C presents a brief description of the current status of state standards for early childhood education, and includes some discussion of the efforts to align early childhood with K-12 standards.

Standards should be arranged and detailed in ways that clearly identify what children need to know and be able to do and how their ideas and skills will develop over time. Learning progressions (also called "learning trajectories") and learning performances are two useful approaches to arranging and detailing standards so as to guide curriculum, teaching practices, and assessment.

Learning progressions are descriptions of successively more sophisticated ways of thinking and behaving that tend to follow one another as children mature and learn: they lay out in text and through examples what it means to move toward more mature understanding and performance.

A useful example of the ideas of learning progressions and learning performances in the preschool years is California's Desired Results Developmental Profiles-Revised (DRDP-R) and its learning progression for interpersonal skills. This learning progression has been viewed as being composed of six areas, for each of which a measure (or observational guide) has been constructed:

1. expressions of empathy,
2. building cooperative relationships with adults,
3. developing friendships,
4. building cooperative play with other children,
5. conflict negotiation, and
6. awareness of diversity in self and others.

The learning progression itself is summarized in the DRDP-R Preschool instrument (California Department of Education, 2005). Taking the interpersonal skills example further, we can examine one of the measures to see what the learning progression looks like. For example, consider the measure "building cooperative play with other children." For the chosen measure, the progression, expressed as four successive levels, is as follows (starting from the lowest):

(a) interacts with other children side-by-side as they play with similar materials,
(b) engages with another child or children in play involving a common idea or purpose,
(c) shows preference for particular playmates but plays cooperatively with a variety of children, and
(d) leads or participates in planning cooperative play with other children.

This measure in the learning progression is brought to life by examples of learning performances that could illustrate the different levels. Examples for the lowest level (a in the list above) are:

(i) plays blocks side-by-side with other children,
(ii) hands another child a toy that he or she is looking for, and
(iii) hands a bucket to a child sitting next to him or her in the sandbox.

Note that the teachers are encouraged to develop their own examples, so that these three do not become canonical. To illustrate changes to the second level in this measure, examples for the next level (b in the list) are as follows:

(i) plays with blocks with another child,
(ii) plays in sand to build a castle with several other children, and
(iii) joins another child to help look for a lost toy.

More examples of learning performances are shown in Figure 10-2, which is a copy of the scoring guide for the measure "building cooperative play with other children."

Learning progressions should be developed around the organizing principles of child development, such as self-regulation. Such organizing principles—which are sometimes referred to as the "big ideas" of a curriculum—are the coherent foundation for the concepts, theories, principles, and explanatory schemes for child development (National Research Council, 2006).

Organizing standards around these big ideas represents a fundamental shift from the more traditional organizational structure used in K-12 standards, in which standards are grouped under discrete topic headings. For example, instead of listing "knowledge of 10 letters" as a desirable outcome for a 4-year-old, one might list letter recognition and phonological awareness as examples of performances under a heading such as "emergent understanding of literacy forms." A likely positive outcome of reorganizing standards from many discrete topics to a few big ideas is a shift from breadth to depth of coverage, from long lists of goals to a relatively small set of foundational values, principles, and concepts. If those values, principles, and concepts are the target of instruction, they can develop naturally and be extended over time.

Specifying learning performances is a technique for elaborating on content standards by describing what children should be able to do if they have achieved a standard. Some examples of learning performances: children should be able to interact

**Desired Result 1: Children are personally and socially competent** **Preschool**

↓ Indicator: SOC – Preschoolers demonstrate effective social and interpersonal skills

↓ **Measure 6: Building cooperative play with other children**

Definition: Child interacts with other children through play that becomes increasingly cooperative and oriented towards a shared purpose

**1. Mark the highest developmental level the child has mastered.**

| Exploring | Developing | Building | Integrating |
|---|---|---|---|
| ◯ | ◯ | ◯ | ◯ |
| **Interacts with other children side-by-side as they play with similar materials** | **Engages with another child or children in play involving a common idea or purpose** | **Shows preference for particular playmates, but plays cooperatively with a variety of children** | **Leads or participates in planning cooperative play with other children** |
| ◯ Not yet at fi rst level | | | |
| **Examples** | | | |
| ▸ Plays blocks side-by-side with other children.<br>▸ Hands another child a toy that he or she is looking for.<br>▸ Hands a bucket to a child sitting next to him or her in the sandbox. | ▸ Plays with blocks with another child.<br>▸ Plays in sand to build a castle with several other children.<br>▸ Joins another child to help look for a lost toy. | ▸ Plays in blocks area with whomever happens to be there, then moves on to play with particular playmates on the climbing structure.<br>▸ Gets along easily with various playmates in different parts of the room or playground.<br>▸ Participates in short pretend play with several peers, but mostly interacts with one of them. | ▸ Succcessfully organizes playmates to build a city out of blocks.<br>▸ Participates in pretend play with peers, following the agreed-upon roles.<br>▸ Successfully helps to negotiate where and how a small group of children can play.<br>▸ "We can make one big spaceship with the LEGOS. Want to try?" |

**2. Record evidence for this rating here.**

**3. Mark here if the child is emerging to the next level** ◯

**4. If you are unable to rate this measure, explain why.**

**Measure 6** | **Building cooperative play with other children** | **SOC 4 (of 6)**



**FIGURE 10-2** An excerpt from the Desired Results Developmental Profile-Revised. Reprinted by permission from the California Department of Education, CDE Press 1430 N. Street, Suite 3207, Sacramento, CA 95814.

with their peers in a positive way, express their wishes, follow common teacher instructions, carry out basic personal hygiene, use different media for art. A clear understanding of what performance demonstrates that a child has attained a standard allows assessment developers to design activities or tasks to elicit those performances, and it provides teachers with explicit goals for instruction. This approach helps build coherence between what is taught and what is assessed (National Research Council, 2006).

## Assessments

Assessment, which includes everything from systematic child observations to nationally standardized tests, is an organized process for gathering information about child performance and early care and education environments. Assessments of all kinds make available information vital in allowing the early childhood education system to make decisions about choosing content and learning experiences, to hold preschool programs accountable for meeting development and learning goals, and monitor program effectiveness. Assessment is also a way for teachers, school administrators, program directors, and state and national education policy and decision makers to operationalize the goals for children's development and learning articulated in the standards. Although assessment can serve all of these purposes, no single assessment can.

To generate valid inferences, every assessment has to be designed expressly to serve its functions. An assessment designed to provide information about a child's problems with a single idea or skill, in order to guide a teacher in helping that child learn, would be constructed differently from an assessment designed to provide data to policy makers for evaluating the effectiveness of a statewide program. The former requires that children's understanding of the selected idea or skill be tested rigorously and completely; the latter requires that the assessment sample all of the topics the program is designed to teach. Results from either of these assessments would not be valid for the purposes of the other, although they may share certain characteristics as part of a common system of assessment.

## Reporting

The reporting of assessment results is frequently taken for granted, but deliberation on this step is essential in the design of assessment systems and for the sound use of assessment-based information. In fact, decisions about the scope and targets of reporting should be made before assessment design or selection proper begins, and, most importantly, before the assessment data themselves are collected (National Research Council, 2006).

Information about children's progress is useful for all tiers of the system, although different tiers need varying degrees of assessment frequency and varying degrees of detail. Parents, teachers, early childhood program administrators, policy makers, and the public need comprehensible and timely feedback about what is taking place in the classroom (Wainer, 1997). Furthermore, taking a systems perspective, many kinds of information need to be accessible, but not all stakeholders need the same types of information. Thus, very early in the process of system design, questions need to be asked about how various types of information will be accessed and reported to different stakeholders and how that reporting process can support valid interpretations.

Individual standards or clusters of standards can define the scope of reporting, as can learning progressions if they have been developed and made clear to the relevant audiences. Reports can compare one child's performance, or the performance of a group, with other groups or with established norms. They can also describe the extent to which children have met established criteria for performance (the current No Child Left Behind or NCLB option). If descriptions of the skills, knowledge, and abilities that were targeted by the tasks in the assessment are included, users will be better able to interpret the links between the results and goals for children's learning. It is important to recognize that many states lack the resources to design assessments that are perfectly aligned with their standards. They may have to resort to selecting existing assessments and cross-walking them to standards. While this may lead to a period of only partial alignment, the exercise leads to useful opportunities to refine both standards and assessment portfolios.

The reporting of assessment outcomes can take on many

appearances—from graphical displays to descriptive text, and from numbers to a detailed analysis of what the numbers mean. In some states, NCLB assessment results are reported on a standard-by-standard basis; others provide information keyed to learning objectives for a specific class. In some states in Australia, where learning continua serve as the basis for assessment at all levels of the system, progress maps are used to describe child achievement. Figure 10-3 is a progress map from a Government of Western Australia website (http://www.curriculum.wa.edu.au/ProgressMaps/english.htm). During the early childhood years, assessment results should be conveyed to parents in accessible

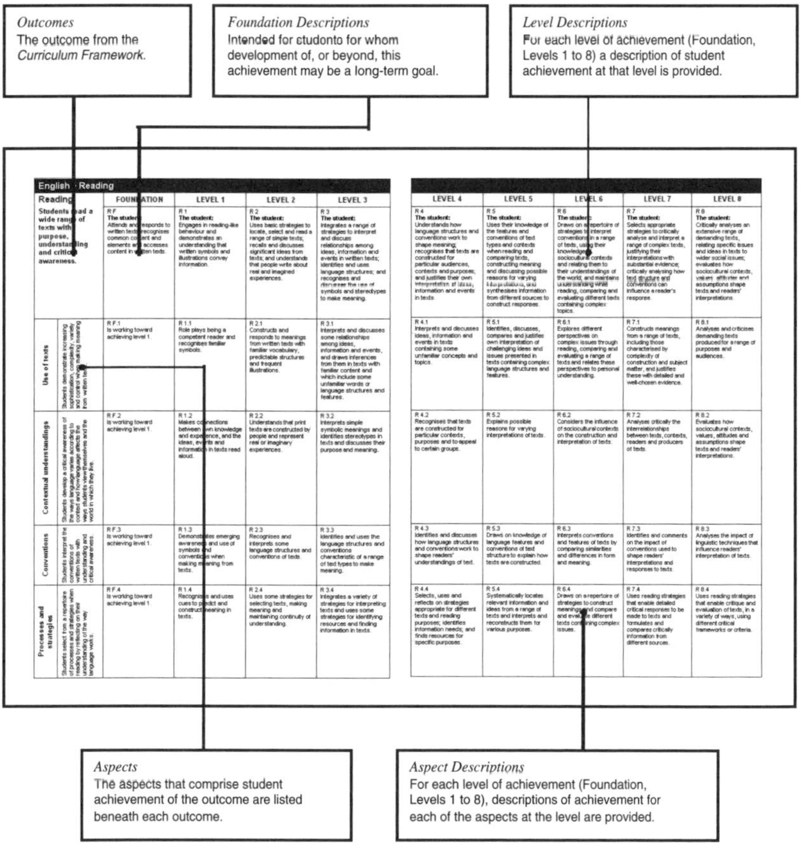


**FIGURE 10-3** Progress map and descriptive information.
SOURCE: http://www.curriculum.wa.edu.au/ProgressMaps/english.htm.

ways; this may occur during individual periodic conferences or by sending written reports.

It seems clear that interpretive material should always be included in reports. Interpretive material is accompanying text that explains, in a way that is appropriate to the technical knowledge of the intended audience, the relevance and importance of the results. According to *Systems for State Science Assessment,* interpretative material should

- specify the purposes of the assessment.
- describe the skills, knowledge, and abilities being assessed.
- provide sample assessment items and activities and sample child responses keyed to performance levels.
- provide a description of the performance levels.
- describe the skills, knowledge, and abilities that a child or group of children either have achieved or have not yet achieved.
- describe how the results should be interpreted and used, with a focus on ways to improve children's performance.
- describe and ward off common misinterpretations of results.
- indicate the precision of scores or classification levels.

Samples of children's work are a useful way of illustrating their accomplishments. When reports include such samples, users can gain further insight as to what it means for a child to be classified at a particular achievement level. Samples can also be used to illustrate the ways in which a child or group of children should improve (and, of course, following Figure 10-1, all of these should relate back to the early learning standards).

Background information—for example, about the characteristics of education and opportunities afforded to children, even such information as children's motivation—can further enhance the usefulness of assessment results. The Internet offers the possibility of making information available to stakeholders on a scale that might be impractical for paper-based reports. Information can be presented with guidance about its use and interpretation, and if the presentation is interactive, users can focus on the areas of greatest relevance to them. Any such facility must be designed with effective safeguards to protect the confidentiality of information and the privacy of the children being assessed, as well as to ensure that only authorized users have access to information.

Users of results need to recognize the degree of uncertainty or measurement error associated with all assessment results. This is an area that is critically misunderstood by many audiences of assessment data, and it is particularly important if a variety of measures are used in a system. Measurement error can be conveyed using standard error bands, a graphic display, or statements regarding the probability of misclassification (American Educational Research Association, American Psychological Association, and National Council on Measurement in Education, 1999). No matter how this is done, each time a score is reported, it should be accompanied by an indication of its margin of error or other indicators of the measure's degree of precision. This information should be supported by text that makes clear how the precision of the scores should be factored into inferences based on the results.

While there has been a great deal of research on the design of technically sound assessments, there is little research on ways of reporting results that promote accurate and meaningful interpretations (Goodman and Hambleton, 2003; Hambleton and Slater, 1997; Jaeger, 1998). Research has indicated that users' preference for a data display and their comprehension of it do not always coincide (Wainer, Hambleton, and Meara, 1999). Different reporting formats should be evaluated with usability studies to determine which are best understood and most likely to be used accurately by typical audiences.

## Professional Development

Professional development recognizes that all adults need ongoing opportunities to improve their skills and competencies as they carry out their roles and responsibilities. Recognizing the particular challenges facing the early childhood workforce, educators have designed many different kinds of professional development opportunities, most of them focused on the higher level goals of improving instruction and curriculum. The aim of professional development as related to assessment is to create consistency across the various practitioners working with young children, in a program or in a state, in their understanding of children's development and learning and in their expectations and goals for their accomplishments.

Professional development usually links informal training with formal education, seeks to improve the quality of training content through a training approval process, provides incentives (including compensation) for training, and offers training passports or career registries that chronicle the cumulative training and education individuals receive (e.g., the National Registry Alliance at http://www.registryalliance.org). According to Kagan, Tarrant, and Berliner (2005), 10 elements of high-quality professional development in a systems approach have been articulated by the early childhood community of practice: core knowledge; career path; professional development delivery mechanism; quality approval and assurance system; qualifications and credentials; incentives for professional development; access and outreach; financing; governance; and evaluation. Irrespective of the particular components one espouses, all elements of the professional development system must work together and reinforce each other.

Professional development is a crucial support for all forms of early childhood assessment. Successful implementation demands orientation and ongoing training of a host of contributors to the elements of early learning and program standards, assessment administration, and management of databases. Teachers and program managers require education and support to become capable and adept at understanding and using the varieties of reports and analyses of child assessment data. Early care and education programs, like school districts, require individuals with higher levels of expertise in assessment, data management, and data analysis than are widely available in the labor market at the moment. More broadly, each audience and consumer group can benefit from some form of support to enhance their assessment literacy as they strive to comprehend and interpret the implications of child assessments, program assessments, and other forms of data.

Moreover, an assessment system should provide for ongoing professional development opportunities to equip managers and practitioners to improve the quality of their services, implement best practice strategies, and foster children to enhanced progress and levels of accomplishment in relation to the standards. And as feedback reports roll out to different levels and units of the system, it is incumbent for system administrators to provide these same opportunities, resources, and supports for managers and practitioners.

### Opportunities for Development and Learning

An assessment of children's well-being cannot be understood without knowing the circumstances in which they reside, the opportunities afforded for development across the assessed domains, and the interaction of the individual child with those opportunities (Pianta, 2003). Therefore, relevant to any assessment of development and learning in an early childhood assessment system are program quality indicators to assess information that is uniform across programs despite their different funding, sponsorship, and regulatory standards. Although not implemented in most states currently, program assessments at various levels (the facility, the staffing, the social and intellectual features) can provide data that pertain to all programs and could serve as a vast repository of information in a systems approach. Moreover, linking the collection of program quality information to child-level assessment information would assist in the more appropriate interpretation and analysis of those assessments.

This vision for an assessment systems approach requires attention to the entire range of children's opportunities for development and learning. Participation in program quality reviews is one means to accomplish this for early childhood centers and providers. In addition, articulated linkages between quality levels, program standards, and development and learning standards are necessary. In this approach, currently disparate systems of program standards would be connected through a single comparable set of quality rating levels. It would then be possible to link the opportunities to develop and learn to an assessment that is more targeted at the child level. Certainly, efforts should be made to simplify and consolidate separate systems of program monitoring and licensing reviews to eliminate duplicative assessments, without sacrificing the capacity necessary to certify local program compliance with applicable legislative mandates and regulatory requirements.

There is a need for states and programs to continually examine and update the scope and quality of criteria and assessment tools for determining key elements of program quality. This is particularly important in a time when early learning and program quality standards require attention to growing populations of children with disabilities as well as of children and families from language and cultural minorities. Ensuring the appropriate assessment of quality of learning environments, instructional practices, and learning opportunities for the full range of children being served is crucial, and as these populations grow and shift in character (e.g., increased numbers of children identified as on the autism spectrum, new waves of immigration from parts of the world that did not historically send emigrants to North America), adaptations in the learning environments and instructional approaches may also be needed.

In short, an ongoing and linked system of appropriate assessments of development and early learning opportunities provides a central stream of assessment information on the quality of program services and supportive management practices, crucial for a number of reporting formats for different audiences and uses. It serves as a linchpin in the infrastructure for a system of early childhood assessment.

## Inclusion

In this report, we have articulated the challenges of early childhood assessment across the full range of development levels and emphases, and with populations that are culturally and linguistically diverse and those characterized by various aspects of disability. A solid system of early childhood assessment is inclusive of all children receiving services. As we have said, the assessments and the system must be concerned that:

- children's cultural and developmental variations are respected;
- the full range of developmental challenges—physical, social, emotional, linguistic, and cognitive—are embraced; and

- children's learning and development are not compromised for the sake of assessment.

Meeting these challenges requires a wide range of tools and requires individuals at all levels of the system to recognize when standard tools need to be adapted or substituted with more appropriate tools. The natural variability in children's performance on assessments is extended when the diversity of the learners increases. Developmental, situational, experiential, economic, cultural, linguistic, and measurement factors may differ across cultural and language groups (Espinosa and Lopez, 2007; García, 2005). This has implications for selecting types of assessment strategies to use as well as for the conditions under which those strategies should be implemented. Despite the inherent challenges and limitations associated with the assessment of young children, early childhood professionals agree that, if conducted properly, a good assessment can play a constructive role at various levels (Meisels, 2006) and that the challenges in using the existing assessment tools with subgroups of children do not justify excluding them from the assessment system.

## Resources

Early childhood programs use human, intellectual, and financial resources to address in some manner each of the elements described above. Clearly, existing early childhood systems benefit from the prior investment of resources in (a) articulating learning and program standards; (b) selecting, procuring, and developing assessments; (c) training individuals to administer and interpret assessment data; and (d) devoting time to the administration and analysis of those assessments. Some programs also manage to find the resources to provide professional development around assessment and to design or implement effective and inclusive early education opportunities.

However, these resources of time, money, and effort are distributed unevenly and not integrated in a systems approach (Bruner et al., 2004). Bringing these strands together systematically requires that resources be directed appropriately and that they be distributed over the various demands in the system in a strategic way. A systems approach must therefore include investment in the infrastructure necessary to provide timely, useful, high-quality assessment data. On the financial side, policy makers at all levels should anticipate and be prepared to support budget requests to cover the costs of enhanced child and program assessment efforts, data management, and professional development. With a focus on state-level accountability, the National Early Childhood Accountability Task Force (2007) estimated that 2 to 5 percent of all state program funding would be needed to provide such an infrastructure.

Acting systematically particularly requires identifying opportunities to invest resources to improve the technical quality of assessments and data systems, including the validity and reliability of tools, capacity for inclusion and appropriate assessment of special populations, and adequacy of quality assurance safeguards and supports (Espinosa, 2008). Similarly, resources are necessary for exploring opportunities to improve the coherence of standards, assessments, and other accountability elements across state and federal programs, as well as for gathering information about the multiple sets of standards, assessments, monitoring/licensing reviews, and reporting requirements imposed on programs with multiple funding streams. Resources are required to ensure consistency in defining and measuring program quality—the opportunities for development and learning, including child care licensing, state pre-K program standards, Head Start program performance standards, and federal legislative mandates and regulations (Mitchell, 2005). When resources are severely limited, difficult decisions about prioritization will be necessary.

## Monitoring and Evaluation

Any system will need monitoring and evaluation to maintain good functioning. We outline the role these important functions play in a systems approach: ensuring that the system is coherent, clearly communicates valued standards for teaching and learning, and provides accurate data for decision making (National Research Council, 2006).

An assessment system must, above all, provide sound and

useful information. Users expect the information to be valid, which is the term discussed in Chapter 7 and used by measurement experts for a quintessential feature of any assessment: the extent to which an assessment's results support meaningful inferences for certain intended purposes.

Collecting relevant data and carrying out appropriate validity studies for the specific types of decisions that are typical in a certain assessment system are imperative for justifying the continuation of that system, and any significant changes in the operation of the system should restart the process of data collection and validity review.

We list below some of the specific challenges of evaluating and monitoring each element of the assessment system. Discussing each aspect of the evaluation and monitoring system is beyond the scope here—see *Systems for State Science Assessment* (National Research Council, 2006) for a more comprehensive account. Some of the salient issues are

- alignment of assessment frameworks and specifications with standards.
- field testing of assessment tasks and tests, to include item analyses and investigations of evidence of score and interrater reliability; fairness; quality of scaling; and validity of scores.
- alignment of assessment tools with standards.
- maintenance of alignment and quality of the assessment tools over time.
- monitoring the success of the reporting system.
- monitoring the effects of the system, including investigations of whether it builds the capacity of staff to enable children to reach standards, builds the capacity of teachers to be effective assessors, influences the way resources are allocated to ensure that children will achieve standards, supports high-quality teaching aligned with standards, and supports equity in children's access to quality early childhood education (Baker et al., 2002).
- examining the feasibility of the system as a whole, including the burden on teachers, administrators, and children.

The process described here may go beyond the resources available in many programs. In particular, some programs may need to rely on selecting existing assessment tools and reporting strategies rather than developing new ones. Nonetheless, we describe here an ideal toward which programs should be moving.

## THE CURRENT LANDSCAPE OF EARLY CHILDHOOD SYSTEMS

An analysis of a systems approach for early childhood assessment starts with the somewhat utopian view presented in the previous section, but it also requires careful review of the current terrain: How are current early childhood assessment efforts linked to standards, learning opportunities, or both? The early childhood landscape reveals multiple forms and targets of service and assessment, varied sources of standards and mandates, numerous ways of reporting and using data, and different approaches to linking consequences with patterns of performance by children and programs (Gilliam and Zigler, 2004); in other words, it is at this moment very far from constituting a single system. The National Early Childhood Accountability Task Force (2007) concluded that early childhood agencies are implementing a great variety of child and program assessments.

Table 10-1 displays nine different forms of child and program assessments, including four forms of assessment used to document the quality of early childhood programs, four forms of assessments of young children, and one form of assessment that gathers information on both program quality and children's learning. Each form carries its own distinctive purposes, its procedure for reporting to different audiences, and its specific ways of using assessment data. Taken together, these multiple assessments are generating many different types of data on children and programs. They also require substantial time and effort from local practitioners and program administrators (National Early Childhood Accountability Task Force, 2007).

Beyond drawing attention to the large number of different forms of assessment, the Accountability Task Force Report notes that current assessment models, with the single exception of program evaluation studies, separate reports about child outcomes

**TABLE 10-1** Current Forms of Early Childhood Assessments

| Form | Population Assessed | Uses of Data |
|---|---|---|
| PROGRAM ASSESSMENTS | | |
| Quality rating systems | Providers seeking recognition for varied levels of quality | Consumer information on quality status<br>Higher reimbursement rates for higher quality<br>Program improvement |
| Program accreditation | Providers seeking recognition as above a threshold of quality | Consumer information on quality status<br>Program improvement |
| Program monitoring | Providers receiving state/federal program funding | Program improvement<br>Funding decisions |
| Program licensing | All providers serving young children | Determine compliance with health and safety standards |
| CHILD ASSESSMENTS | | |
| Kindergarten readiness assessment | All children at kindergarten entry | • Report to public<br>• Planning early childhood investments |
| State/federal pre-K child assessments | Children enrolled in a state or federal program | Reporting to funding sources |
| Assessment for instruction | All children | Planning curriculum<br>Informing parents |
| Developmental screening | All children | Referral to assess for eligibility for special education |
| CHILD + PROGRAM ASSESSMENTS | | |
| Program evaluations | Representative samples of children and local programs | • Report to legislatures and the public on program quality, outcomes, impacts<br>• Informs program improvement and appropriations decisions |

SOURCE: National Early Childhood Accountability Task Force (2007).

from reports on program quality. This means that information about the quality of a program's services is rarely integrated with information about progress and outcomes for the children served in that program and, conversely, data on children's learning is rarely juxtaposed with information about the quality of services, teaching, and learning opportunities provided to those children.

This chapter summarizes bold goals for early childhood assessment systems that transcend most contemporary practice in supporting both accountability and children's learning and development. Experience with the design requirements of effective assessment systems based on standards is still developing. Even in the K-12 system, which has a longer history of assessment and accountability, the methods for designing and guaranteeing alignment of assessments to standards and to learning opportunities are still evolving, with only a limited amount of research guidance. The research base on current theories of learning that should guide the development of assessments is also evolving (but see National Research Council, 2006). Thus, while current accountability practice is based on the premise that continuous cycles of assessment and improvement are key to helping all learners reach high standards, the means of making that goal a reality are still underspecified. Because very young children are at even greater risk than older ones of negative consequences from the misuse of assessment, great care must be taken not to impose the incomplete understandings in the K-12 system on this vulnerable population (National Research Council and Institute of Medicine, 2000).

Recent years have witnessed significant investments at the state and federal level in early childhood programming. Concomitantly, state and federal program offices are managing separate and varied approaches to standards and assessments for the growing populations of children they serve. Table 10-2 highlights different standards and assessments established by four major funding sources for early childhood services: child care, Head Start, state pre-K, and early childhood special education. These standards include frameworks of learning goals for young children and standards for programs. The table also provides information on the number of states that are currently implementing various types of standards and assessments.

This table highlights the fact that the nation's approach to

**TABLE 10-2** Standards and Assessments for Young Children by Funding Source

| | Child Care | Head Start | State Pre-K | Early Childhood Special Education |
|---|---|---|---|---|
| Standards for children's learning | Early learning guidelines (49 states) | Head Start Child Outcomes Framework (federal) | Early learning guidelines (49 states) | 3 functional goals (federal) |
| Child assessments | No current requirements | National Reporting System* (federal) | Pre-K assessments (12 states) Kindergarten assessments (16 states) | States report percent of children in 5 categories on 3 goals |

*The National Reporting System was discontinued after this table was published.
SOURCE: National Early Childhood Accountability Task Force (2007).

early childhood public policy and management entails multiple systems of assessment requirements and mechanisms. Each connected set of standards and assessments generates different information on the characteristics and performance of publicly funded early childhood services. Many local provider agencies receive funding from multiple state and federal sources and therefore are required to manage their programs to meet several different forms of standards for program quality; implement reporting or assessment procedures to respond to the demands of each funding source; and orient their curricula, teaching, and learning strategies to several overlapping frameworks of learning goals for children.

Early childhood assessment efforts in "systems" include a mix of long-standing and newly emerging strategies (Scott-Little, Kagan, and Frelow, 2003b). For example, two major clusters of new initiatives are state and federal efforts to articulate frameworks of learning goals for young children and efforts to develop, organize, and manage for varied purposes new large-scale assessments of young children. Frameworks of learning goals for state-initiated early learning guidelines, federal efforts in Head Start, and early childhood special education have all been generated in the past 8 years. During the same time period, assessment and reporting efforts have been launched by states collecting information on children participating in state pre-K programs or entering kindergarten, by the Head Start Bureau, and by the Office of Special Education Programs

These newer child-focused standards and assessments complement long-standing policies defining standards, assessments, and monitoring systems geared to aspects of program quality, program inputs, and management practices. Federal and state program offices as well as local provider agencies are thus currently engaged for the first time in explaining and interpreting child outcome standards and the potential uses and misuses of newly expanded child assessment data sets. These federal, state, and local managers have extensive experience and greater shared understanding of how program quality standards are applied in the context of various forms of licensing and monitoring reviews and enforcement decisions. Assessment strategies related to program quality standards have longer track records, a greater accumulation of data, and support systems that have been implemented and fine-tuned over the course of many years of research. Child-focused assessment systems are, in contrast, still in diapers.

In summary, an overview of current childhood assessment efforts reveals an array of different forms of child and program assessments, multiple sources of policy mandates in the areas of learning and quality standards, and a series of systems operating in parallel, based largely on the structures of state and federal programs or funding streams. Nonetheless, some states are working to confront these challenges and to develop coherent systems for early childhood care and education, supported by assessment systems and focused on promoting the development of all the children in the state.

## STATE EFFORTS

We briefly summarize the efforts of three states that are attempting to put systems together, documenting the progress they have made and the challenges they have encountered. California, Nebraska, and New Jersey have been chosen because they have focused in recent years on developing systematic approaches to early childhood education and assessment. We certainly do not mean to suggest that these three states constitute exemplars or models, although each does display some strengths (and some weaknesses), and all have made efforts to think systemically about early childhood. These brief portraits illustrate the general points made in this chapter.

## California

The California Department of Education (CDE) has revised its process-oriented compliance-based approach to evaluating the child development services it provides to focus on the results desired from the child care and development system. A strength of the new approach is its compatibility with CDE's accountability system for elementary and secondary education. Desired Results for Children and Families (DRCF) is a system by which educators can document the progress made by children and families in achieving desired results and by which managers can retrieve information to help practitioners improve child care and development services (California Department of Education, 2003).

A desired result is defined as a condition of well-being for children and families (e.g., children are personally and socially competent). Desired results reflect the positive effects of the child development system on the development and functioning of children and on the self-sufficiency and functioning of families. The desired results system has several goals:

- Identify the measures that demonstrate the achievement of desired results across the development areas for children from birth to age 13 in child care and development programs.
- Use the measures for monitoring children's progress in programs.
- Provide information that reflects the contributions made to child development by each of the various types of CDE-funded child development programs.

- Hold programs accountable to program standards that support the achievement of desired results and are used to measure program quality.
- Provide a data collection mechanism for evaluating the quality of individual child development programs.
- Create a base of information on the relationships between processes and results that can be used to target technical assistance to improve practice in all child development programs.

At the state level, educators use the desired results system to identify successes and areas for improvement so that CDE can provide support and technical assistance to increase program quality. At the program level, practitioners use the desired results system to determine the extent to which children and families are achieving the desired results, so that quality improvement activities may be effectively targeted to directly benefit program participants. The desired results system encourages differences in the structure and objectives of individual child development programs. It is culturally sensitive and linguistically responsive to the diverse populations of children and families served.

## Including Children with Disabilities

The desired results system is also being coordinated with a concurrent project, Desired Results: Access for Children with Disabilities Project (DR Access, http://www.draccess.org/index.html). The DR Access project is funded by the CDE Special Education Division and coordinates with the DCRF system in two ways. First, DR Access staff members worked with CDE staff members and CDE's contractors during the development of the desired results system to make the Desired Results Developmental Profile as inclusive and appropriate as possible for assessing the progress of young children with disabilities. Second, DR Access staff members have also developed a system of adaptations and guidelines for the Desired Results Developmental Profile that allows practitioners to assess children with disabilities in an appropriate manner within the structure of the desired results system.

Through these two approaches, DR Access staff members

ensured that the desired results system was responsive to the needs of young children with disabilities and was applicable to all settings in which they and their families were served. The vision held by the contributors to desired results and DR Access was that, through collaboration, a continuity of outcomes would be achieved for all children in CDE programs.

## Components of the System

The desired results system has six basic components: desired results, indicators, themes, measures, criteria for success, and measurement tools.

1. ***Desired results:*** The six desired results, to which all CDE-funded child care and development programs are expected to contribute, are that children are personally and socially competent, are effective learners, show physical and motor competence, are safe and healthy, and have families that support their learning and development, and achieve their goals. These desired results encompass the four developmental domains—cognitive, socioemotional, language, and physical development.
2. ***Indicators:*** An indicator defines a desired result more specifically so that it can be measured. For example, an indicator of the desired result "children are personally and socially competent" is that "children show self-awareness and a positive self-concept." Desired results are generally better measured by using multiple indicators; no single indicator gives full information on all aspects of achievement.
3. ***Themes:*** A theme describes the aspect of development that is being measured for each indicator (e.g., self-awareness: dependence and interdependence, understanding that one's self is a separate being with an identity of its own and with connectedness to others).
4. ***Measures:*** A measure quantifies achievement of a particular indicator and developmental theme (e.g., a preschooler can communicate easily with familiar adults).

5. ***Criteria:*** The criteria for success define the acceptable level of achievement for each indicator (e.g., English language learners who entered the program with no comprehension of English now participate in read-alouds by repeating key words).
6. ***Measurement tools:*** A measurement tool is the actual instrument or procedure used to capture or track information on indicators and standards of achievement (e.g., the Desired Results Developmental Profile).

### Professional Development

The training and implementation phase of desired results for center-based programs and family child care home networks is being carried out in a series of regional training sessions for local program administrators. Assisted by the California Institute on Human Services, CDE is providing comprehensive training designed to facilitate implementation of the desired results system in programs at the local level and to build the capacity of local programs to train staff members who work directly with children. Participation in the training is by invitation only, and sites are selected one year before they are due for a Coordinated Compliance Review or Contract Monitoring Review.

## Nebraska

Results Matter (http://ectc.nde.ne.gov/special_projects/results_matter/results_matter.htm) is designed to improve programs and child and family outcomes for all children in Nebraska from birth to age 5, whether they are served through school districts, the Early Development Network (Part C of the Individuals with Disabilities Education Act), newly implemented infant and toddler programs funded through the Early Childhood Endowment, or community partners. The system grew out of earlier efforts to monitor and evaluate state-funded preschool programs. Its broader application came as a result of recent federal requirements for reporting outcomes for children with disabilities. The system employs both program quality assessment and child outcome assessment to accomplish several purposes: improve experiences, learning, development, and lives of young children (birth to age 5) and their families; inform program practices; demonstrate program effectiveness; guide the development of local and state policies and procedures; and provide data to demonstrate results.

The system is administered through the Nebraska Department of Education. Major partners include the state's Early Childhood Training Center, Health and Human Services, the Munroe-Meyer Institute at the University of Nebraska Medical Center, and multi-county educational service units. The system operates with the advice of the Results Matter Child Measurement Task Force.

## Child Assessment

Child assessment tools were selected based on whether they employ ongoing observation of children engaged in real activities, with people they know, in natural settings; reflect evidence-based practices; engage families and primary care providers as active participants; integrate information gathered across settings; are individualized to address each child's unique ways of learning; inform decisions about day-to-day learning opportunities for children; and reflect the belief that development and learning are rooted in culture supported by the family.

The selected tools also reflect optimal congruence with Nebraska's Early Learning Guidelines (Birth to Three and Three to Five; http://ectc.nde.ne.gov/ELG/elg.htm) and are congruent with the program standards found in Rule 11, Regulations for Early Childhood Programs (http://www.nde.state.ne.us/LEGAL/RULE11.html). These tools are the High/Scope Child Observation Record (COR), the Creative Curriculum Developmental Continuum, and the Assessment, Evaluation and Programming System (AEPS).

The state has purchased licenses for the use of these tools; programs complete the assessment online. Some districts have chosen to use more than one assessment and thus more than one online system. Districts began entering data in 2006, and the first data were reported to the Office of Special Education Programs in the U.S. Department of Education in February 2008. The use of these tools supported through the online data system provides the state with unprecedented opportunities to compile needed data, not only for the required state and local reporting functions, but also for ongoing program improvement and curriculum planning. Nebraska's system is responsive to the federal mandate of the IDEA Part C (birth to age 3) and Part B, 619 (ages 3 to 5), as well as the state requirements of Nebraska Department of Education Rule 11, Regulations for Early Childhood Programs (http://www.nde.state.ne.us/LEGAL/RULE11.html), which apply to all pre-K programs operated through public schools.

### Program Quality Assessment

The system also includes regular evaluation of programs to ensure that they achieve and maintain overall high quality, employ qualified staff, and operate in compliance with federal and state guidelines. Programs receiving state funding are required to conduct an annual evaluation using one of the environment rating scales, such as the Infant/Toddler Environment Rating Scale-Revised, ITERS-R (Harms, Clifford, and Cryer, 1998); Early Childhood Environment Rating Scale-Revised, ECERS-R (Harms, Cryer, and Clifford, 1990); or the Early Language and Literacy Classroom Observation, ELLCO (Smith and Dickinson, 2002), and complete Nebraska's Rule 11 reporting and approval processes. Data obtained from these tools are used to develop improvement plans. In addition, programs are strongly encouraged to participate in the accreditation process of the National Association for the Education of Young Children and receive technical and financial assistance to do so.

### Professional Development

Programs receive continuous support to ensure that their participation in Results Matter does generate the highest quality data and knowledge about how to use it to improve program quality and child and family outcomes. The state's Early Childhood Training Center, in cooperation with the organizations that provide the program and child assessment tools, regularly offers training in their use. The state maintains a cadre of professionals who have achieved reliability in the use of the environment rating scales. In addition, each program provider is required to submit a Fidelity Process Plan to address how the reliability and validity of the child observational data will be monitored and recorded. These plans describe initial training and subsequent activities to strengthen the validity of the data.

## New Jersey

New Jersey's Abbott Preschool Program is designed to provide high-quality preschool education to children ages 3 and 4 in 31 of the state's poorest districts. The program has a mixed delivery system and is conducted in school districts and community-based centers, including Head Start programs.

### Curriculum and Instruction

The New Jersey State Department of Education (NJDOE) has developed a set of early learning standards—the Preschool Expectations: Standards of Quality (2004)—which outline what children should know and be able to do at the end of their preschool program across a comprehensive set of domains. Five curriculum models have been approved: Creative Curriculum, High/Scope, Tools of the Mind, Curiosity Corner, and Bank Street. Each is aligned to the Preschool Expectations. Each district is required to select one of these approved curriculum models and to provide early childhood educators with professional development related to appropriate curriculum implementation.

### Assessments

The NJDOE designed two performance-based assessments in the areas of literacy and mathematics that were linked directly to the Preschool Expectations: the Early Learning Assessment System-Literacy (ELAS-L; New Jersey Office of Early Childhood Education, 2004) and the Early Learning Assessment System for Mathematics (ELAS-M; New Jersey Office of Early Childhood Education, 2006). In the initial years of the preschool program, the state provided professional development for teachers in the observation and documentation of young children's learning and in administering and scoring the ELAS assessments. While these measures were originally intended to be used both for program evaluation and to inform instructional practice, state officials decided that they would be used only for instructional planning. In the ninth year of Abbott preschool implementation, the districts must select a commercially produced performance-based assessment that covers the entire range of domains in the Preschool Expectations. The ELAS instruments may still be used in the areas of literacy and mathematics.

### Assessment at Various Levels

At the classroom level, teachers administer a performance-based assessment that covers the range of domains outlined in the Preschool Expectations. These formative assessments are intended to inform instructional practice and to give teachers direct information on the learning and development of individual children. Up one level, a sample of the community-based and school district classrooms is assessed for quality on the ECERS-R. The results of these measures are used for teacher professional development. ECERS-R scores are also reported at the district level and used to monitor classroom quality across the 31 districts.

Statewide, a longitudinal study is tracking the progress of a sample of children who have participated in the Abbott preschool program on nationally normed measures of language, literacy, and mathematics. In addition, a regression discontinuity design is being used to estimate the impact of preschool on the performance of children who received it in comparison to those who did not.

## THINKING ABOUT ASSESSMENT AS A SYSTEM

Despite the clear advantages of a systems approach to early childhood care and education, there is no doubt that the move toward systematicity will encounter many obstacles. The states and the federal government often effect change in the early childhood system by introducing new programs, local or limited innovations, and underfunded mandates. These might well constitute good models or useful efforts, but they undermine efforts to build coherence across programs and funding sources at the same time.

Similarly, laudable efforts to increase accountability can lead to consequences that undermine coherence. For practical reasons, accountability efforts typically involve selection of a small number of assessment instruments that carry high stakes for the program. Concentrating attention on a specific test rather than on building a system can lead to unintended consequences. When the results of that test have significant repercussions, one consequence is often that the prevailing instruction and curriculum will come to be significantly affected by the particulars of that test—specifically, by the details of material tested or the formats used. In this situation, gains observed in test results may not represent true gains in learning or progress toward meeting standards. Instead, they may primarily reflect children's improved ability to respond to items on a particular kind of test. A typical pattern is that test scores in the first years after a new test is introduced will show significant—and publicly celebrated—increases, particularly if high stakes are involved, but these improvements tend to level off after that initial uplift (see Linn, 2003, for a general survey; see also Herman and Perry, 2002, for an example from California).

Further evidence of this phenomenon comes from cases in which alternate indicators of the tested skill fail to match the gains shown by the high-stakes test. If children have indeed improved in mathematics, for example, gains should be evident on other indicators of mathematical skill; if not, the gains are suspect. The disjunction between the high-stakes and alternate tests of the same skill has been observed with older children for mathematics (e.g., see Koretz and Baron, 1998, for an example from Kentucky) and is the typical pattern seen when comparing results on state tests to those on National Assessment of Educational Progress (Linn, 2003). Some observers believe that such patterns as these illustrate the limits of what can be achieved primarily through test preparation, and that continuing improvement over the long term will require more meaningful changes in the teaching, learning process, and assessment. These findings suggest the need for a systematic approach in which it is possible to validate gains and the meaning of test scores continuously over time.

Assessment by itself cannot improve children's learning—it is the correct use of assessment information that can bring about that aim. If they are to improve learning, assessments must be based on the early learning objectives and be set in contexts that relate to curriculum and teaching practices that are common in early childhood education. Assessment should appraise what children are being taught, and what is taught should embody the aims of learning described in the standards. Thus, all of the elements in the early childhood education system have to be built on a shared vision of what is important for children to know and understand, how teaching practices affect that knowledge and understanding over time, and what can be taken as evidence that learning and development have occurred (National Research Council, 2001).

The following criteria, developed by the committee, operationalize these somewhat abstract principles in important characteristics that child outcome measures should have if they are to provide useful evidence for the improvement of early care and education systems.

1. A clearly articulated purpose for the testing.
2. Identification of why particular assessments were selected in relation to the purpose.
3. A clear theory connecting the assessment results and quality of care.
4. Observation of quality of instruction and specification of what would need to be focused on for improvement.
5. A clear plan for following up to improve program quality.
6. Strategizing to collect the required information with a minimum of testing.
7. Appropriate preparation of testers to minimize disruptive effects on child responses.

Assessment systems must operate at multiple levels—individual child, classroom, center, school district, state, and national levels. An assessment system is thus sensitive to a variety of influences—some that originate from the top and spread down, and others that work from the bottom up (National Research Council, 2001).

Assessments of children must be based on an appreciation of the development and learning of typically developing children and of the typical range of variation for children of any age. This knowledge must be based on the best scientific evidence available, must be sensitive to the values inherent in choosing to concentrate on specific areas rather than others, and must be completed by sound professional expertise (National Research Council, 2001). An example of an instrument designed according to these principles is the Desired Results Developmental Profile-Revised, a part of which is illustrated in Figure 10-2.

Thus, a successful system of assessments must be coherent in a variety of ways (National Research Council, 2001, 2006).[3] It will be horizontally coherent when the curriculum, instruction, and assessment are all aligned with the early learning standards, target the same goals for learning, and work together to support children's developing knowledge and skill across all domains. It will be vertically coherent when there is a shared understanding at all levels of the system (classroom, center, school or program, and state) of the goals for children's learning and development that underlie the standards, as well as consensus about the purposes and uses of assessment. And it will be developmentally coherent when it takes into account what is known about how children's understanding develops over time and the content knowledge, abilities, and understanding that are needed for learning to progress at each stage of the process. Developmental coherence should extend across the boundaries between preschool and K-12 schooling, to ensure that the goals for young children's learning and development are formulated by taking into account later goals and expectations and with an understanding of how early accomplishments do and do not predict later achievement.

These coherences are necessary in the interrelationship of all the subsystems. For example, the development of early learning standards, curriculum, and the design of teaching practices and assessments should be guided by the same framework for understanding what is being attempted in the classroom that informs the training of beginning teachers and the continuing professional development of experienced teachers. The reporting of assessment results to parents, teachers, and other stakeholders should also be based on this same framework, as should the evaluations of effectiveness built into all systems. Each child should have an

---

[3]This section on coherence draws heavily upon the content of the National Research Council's 2006 report, *Systems for State Science Assessment*.

equivalent opportunity to achieve the defined goals, and the allocation of resources should reflect those goals. We emphasize that a system of assessment is only as good as the effectiveness—and coherence—of all of its components.

# 11

# Guidance on Outcomes and Assessments

This report centers around two key principles. First, all assessments should be integrated into a larger coherent system of early childhood care and education that they are designed to support. This is not a new idea, but the committee is convinced that it bears repeating, because it is fundamental to worthwhile assessment. A system of early childhood care and education must have well-articulated goals and objectives, documented in standards, guidelines, and frameworks, that can inform the design and implementation of early care and education programs. The same set of goals should drive all assessment of whether the objectives are being met—by programs, by teachers, and by children. This supports the coherence necessary for an effective system.

Second, and also a key point not new in this report, the purposes for assessment must be clearly articulated *before* the assessment is designed, developed, selected, or implemented. Different purposes require different types of assessments, and an assessment designed for one purpose should never be converted to another without careful consideration of its appropriateness to the new purpose. This is really an extension of the first principle, but it is especially important for building trust among the people and organizations involved in an assessment effort. Poorly articulated purposes and assessments used for inappropriate purposes can lead to decisions that are unfair or unclear, and they may do harm to programs, teachers, and, most importantly, children.

In this chapter, we present a set of guidelines that should be useful to a broad range of organizations charged with the assessment of children and of programs providing care and education to young children. These guidelines are organized around the major themes of the report and flow from the perspective that any assessment decision should be made in the context of a larger, coherent assessment system, which is in turn embedded in a network of medical, educational, and family support systems designed to ensure optimal development for all children.

Thus, though we briefly recap our rationale, based on our review of the literature, and present our guidelines following the order of topics in the volume, we hope the reader interprets our discussion of purposes, targets, and procedures for assessment as different specific topics subordinated to the notion of an assessment system. In compliance with our charge, we have also included a section presenting a recommended agenda for research on the assessment of young children, following the detailed guidelines.

These guidelines should be useful to anyone contemplating the selection or implementation of an assessment for young children, including medical and educational service providers, classroom practitioners, federal, state, and local governments and private agencies operating or regulating child care and early childhood education programs, and those interested in expanding the knowledge base about child development and the conditions of childhood. To make our guidance more pointed and practical, the chapter ends with a list of high-priority actions by members of specific groups engaged in the assessment of young children, which can be taken quickly and should provide maximum payoffs.

## PURPOSES AND USES OF ASSESSMENT

### Rationale

In recent years, the purposes for which young children are being assessed have expanded, with more children being assessed than ever before. Young children have been assessed to screen for and identify possible developmental problems for many years, but with advances in knowledge and new technologies the number of potential problems for which screening can be done has increased. The use of assessment to plan and guide instruction with young children also has been a recognized purpose of assessment for many years but has received more attention lately, as it has become widely acknowledged as a key component of a high-quality early childhood program. Making decisions about early childhood programs is a purpose for assessment for which an increasing number of children are being assessed lately, and for which even more children are likely to be assessed in the future. These decisions can be the result of a program evaluation or as part of ongoing accountability procedures. This last area has generated much discussion because of the technical challenges involved and because of the potential for misuse of assessment information.

Despite the greatly increased amount of assessment in which young children are engaged, it is not always clear why assessments are undertaken or what rationale exists for the form of assessment selected. Assessments are often chosen and used that do not match their purpose well. The process of developing any assessment system involving young children needs to begin with a clearly articulated statement of purpose.

Clearly thinking through the purpose involves defining the question the assessment process is designed to answer, as well as defining in advance how the information to be collected will be used. The problem of mismatch between assessment purpose and assessment use is evidenced in several ways:

- Assessments designed and developed for one purpose are adopted for different purposes, without consideration of the match of information generated to the goal or to the validity of inferences with the novel use. Whoever selects the assessment instrument should consider the goal and seek an instrument with proven validity when used for that goal. If such an instrument does not exist, then firm conclusions cannot be drawn.
- There are not many tools designed for large-scale program evaluation, so tools designed for other purposes often are adapted (e.g., shortened or administered differently) out

of necessity, without sufficiently investigating the validity of the adapted tools in their new form and for their new purpose.
- There is considerable worry in the field that an absence of the funding needed to develop effective measures is driving people to use simple, unaligned, poorly developed measures or to use well-developed psychometrically sound measures to assess constructs for which they are not well designed.

Purposes for assessment range widely, and some measures can be used for more than one purpose. Child-focused assessments can be used for child-specific purposes, such as screening and diagnosis, as well as for program monitoring and improvement purposes or for program evaluation. Similarly, with care, classroom quality assessments can be used for purposes of program monitoring, as formative input to guide program decisions, as an outcome in program evaluations, or in order to serve as moderating or mediating variables in predicting child outcomes in research. Nonetheless, not all instruments are appropriate for all purposes, and those selecting an assessment need to review the purposes for which it was designed to determine if it can be appropriately used for their intended purpose.

It is not uncommon that inferences about program effectiveness are based on end-of-program performance of individual children. Such inferences are inappropriate without attention to the environments children experience both inside and outside the program, as well as to the characteristics at entry of the children served by the program. In the systems perspective we adopt, child performance should be viewed developmentally, and the complexity of factors influencing child performance or growth in any particular domain should be understood. Threats to the validity of inferences about program effectiveness that are based purely on child performance are reduced if measures reflect child progress rather than just end-of-program status, as well as if direct indicators of quality in the environment are also collected. Of course, information from these various sources about program effectiveness then also needs to be contextualized in information about resources (funding, longevity, administrative support, professional development) available to the program before it could possibly justify any decisions about restructuring or defunding.

There is a responsibility to articulate the purpose of any assessment in a responsible way to those who participate and who might be influenced by outcomes. For example, if a program is being evaluated, program staff should understand whether there are plans to use the assessments to evaluate their performance on an individual level. They should also know whether the information will be made available to guide decisions about the program and individual children. Consequences of assessment vary. Ideally, of course, assessment information benefits children by providing information that can be used to inform their caregivers, to improve the quality of their care and education environments, and to identify child risk factors that could be remediated. Particularly in assessing young children, care is needed to ensure that they are not negatively affected (unintentionally frightened or made to feel incompetent) by the process of assessment, and that the value of the information gathered through assessment outweighs any negative effects (e.g., time taken away from instruction, disruption of normal routine, boredom or disengagement with the tasks, decisions that may negatively affect them).

### Guidelines on Purposes of Assessment

(P-1) Public and private entities undertaking the assessment of young children should make the purposes of assessment explicit and public.

(P-2) The assessment strategy—which assessments to use, how often to administer them, how long they should be, how the domain of items or children or programs should be sampled—should match the stated purpose and require the minimum amount of time to obtain valid results for that purpose. Even assessments that do not directly involve children, such as classroom observations, teacher rating forms, and collection of work products, impose a burden on adults and will require advance planning for using the information.

(P-3) Those charged with selecting assessments need to weigh options carefully, considering the appropriateness of candidate assessments for the desired purpose and for use with all the subgroups of children to be included. Although the same measure may be used for more than one purpose, prior consideration of all potential purposes is essential, as is careful analysis of the actual content of the assessment instrument. Direct examination of the assessment items is important because the title of a measure does not always reflect the content.

## DOMAINS AND MEASURES OF DEVELOPMENTAL OUTCOMES

### Rationale

During infancy and toddlerhood in particular, frequently assessed domains include those implicated by the agenda of screening for medical, developmental, or environmental risk. Across the entire preschool period, a critical issue is what aspect of young children's skills or behavior to measure. Research on the developing child has traditionally conceived of development as proceeding in different domains, for example, language or motor or socioemotional development. These distinctions have served science well and are helpful for assessment purposes, but in reality the distinctions among children's skills and behaviors are somewhat artificial and not as clear-cut as the organization of research or assessment tools would suggest. Developmental domains are intertwined, especially in the very young child, making it challenging or even impossible to interpret measures in some domains without also measuring the influence of others.

Health, socioemotional functioning and cognitive functioning are closely interconnected in infancy, as for example when sleeping difficulties affect both socioemotional and cognitive functioning. For somewhat older preschoolers, the domains may be more readily differentiated operationally and theoretically, but they remain interdependent; for example, socioemotional (e.g., capacity to regulate negative emotion) and cognitive measures are interrelated and appear to have linked neural bases.

Nevertheless, a conceptualization is needed that identifies the areas of development society wants to track and that programs and services for young children are trying to impact. Convergent sources of information suggest that five major domains of child functioning recur in discussions of development during the preschool period. Following the usage established by the National Education Goals Panel (1995) on school readiness, we use the following terms to describe them:

1. physical well-being and motor development,
2. social and emotional development,
3. approaches toward learning,
4. language development (including emergent literacy), and
5. cognition and general knowledge (including mathematics and science).

These domains are themselves at different levels of development in defining the constructs they encompass and in the range and sophistication of the associated measures, and they differ as well in the amount of attention they get in policies for young children. It is relatively easy to converge on a set of general domains, but disagreement is common when specifics are needed. Social and emotional development, for example, encompasses emotion labeling in some assessments, but not others. Attentiveness is classified as social/emotional in some assessments, but under approaches toward learning in others. Also, the operationalization of the larger constructs evolves over time; fitness as an aspect of physical well-being, for example, is only recently emerging as a focus of policy attention in the preschool period, and it is not widely included in state standards. For the domains of social and emotional development and approaches to learning and for the subdomain of fitness, this is a period of active measures development, including both direct assessment and further work on parent and teacher reports. While important work in these areas is under way, both measures development and consensus about key constructs remain less advanced than for such subdomains as language, literacy, and mathematics.

Some domains important to many parents and perhaps to others are minimally represented in standards, research, or assessment—such as art, music, morality. Those concerned with promoting good outcomes for children differ in their beliefs about what domains are most important, as evidenced by the variation among states' early learning standards and the focus on basic skills in the federal program Good Start, Grow Smart. Furthermore, a policy focus on a domain is likely to generate pressures to develop associated measures, which in turn increases the likelihood that the domain will be included in subsequent assessment activities.

One basis for identifying particular domains as outcomes worthy of being tracked in young children is the values of parents, educators, policy makers, and traditional forces in society; these forces are clearly historical, and thus the basis may need to be expanded as the composition of society changes. Another is predictive data that show relationships to school achievement or other important long-term outcomes (e.g., staying out of the juvenile justice system); these, too, represent relationships to traditionally valued outcomes, but as the goals of education change, they, too, might need to be adjusted. Evidence is not available about the relative relevance of the domains currently emphasized in assessment systems to groups increasing their representation in the society rather than those traditionally most numerous.

Although domains are an easy way to think about outcomes, they may not be the right approach for all purposes. A notable example is assessment of children with disabilities, for whom the recommended practice is to write functional rather than domain-based outcomes on individualized service plans (e.g., dressing oneself, participating in family mealtime). To support this emphasis in service provision, the Office of Special Education Programs in the U.S. Department of Education adopted three functional outcomes for national accountability reporting on programs serving children from birth to age 3 and ages 3 through 5 with delays and disabilities.

## Guidelines on Domains and Measures of Developmental Outcomes

(D-1) Domains included when assessing child outcomes and the quality of education programs should be expanded beyond those traditionally emphasized (language, literacy, and mathematics) to include others, such as affect, interpersonal interaction, and opportunities for self-expression.

(D-2) Support is needed to develop measures of approaches to learning and socioemotional functioning, as well as other currently neglected domains, such as art, music, creativity, and interpersonal skills.

(D-3) Studies of the child outcomes of greatest importance to parents, including those from ethnic minority and immigrant groups, are needed to ensure that assessment instruments are available for domains (and thinking about domains) emphasized in different cultural perspectives, for example, proficiency in the native language as well as in English.

(D-4) For children with disabilities and special needs, domain-based assessments may need to be replaced or supplemented with more functional approaches.

(D-5) Selecting domains to assess requires first establishing the purposes of the assessment, then deciding which of the various possible domains dictated by the purposes can best be assessed using available instruments of proven reliability and validity, and considering what the costs will be of omitting domains from the assessment system (e.g., reduction of their importance in the eyes of practitioners or parents).

## SELECTING AND IMPLEMENTING ASSESSMENTS

### Rationale

A wide array of instruments and approaches can be used to collect information about young children and their environments, ranging from interviews with caregivers to ratings of child performance by caregivers or observers, to observations in naturally occurring or structured settings to direct assessments. Assessments of any type must be selected and implemented with care, but special attention is needed when using direct assessments with young children. It requires greater attention to establishing a relationship with the child, to ascertaining whether the task is familiar and comprehensible to him or her, to limiting length of the session and the child's discomfort, to recognizing the role of conditions like hunger or fatigue, and to recognizing the possibility of bias if the tester is a caregiver or otherwise connected to the child. Instruments that have the most user-appeal often do not have the best psychometric properties. For example, portfolios of children's artistic productions contain rich information but are hard to rate reliably. In the experience of committee members, selection of instruments is often more influenced by cost, by ease of administration, and by use in other equivalent programs than by the criteria proposed here.

Those charged with selecting assessment instruments need to carefully review the information provided in the instrument's technical manual. Although test publishers may provide extensive psychometric information about their products, additional evidence beyond that provided in manuals should also be considered in instrument selection. Those selecting assessments should be familiar with the assessment standards contained in the standards document produced by the American Educational Research Association, American Psychological Association, and National Council on Measurement in Education (1999). Important questions to ask are: Has this assessment been developed and validated for the purpose for which it is being considered? If a norm-referenced measure is being considered, has the assessment been normed with children like those with whom it will be used? For example, if the assessment is to be used as part of a program evaluation with minority children, were like children included in the development studies, including any norming studies? There is typically more robust evidence for inferences based on early childhood measures when used for normally developing, white, English-speaking children than for children from ethnic or language minorities or children with disabilities. Validity evidence is quite sparse for these special groups on most extant measures. Conducting valid assessments with language-minority children and children with special needs is especially challenging, and the reader is referred to Part III for more discussion of these topics. As explained in Chapter 7, one cannot say that measurement instruments either possess or lack validity; rather, inferences from the use of particular measurements for particular purposes may be supported or not supported by validity evidence.

There are many special considerations when using existing

assessments for language-minority and cultural-minority children and children with disabilities.

Key issues for children learning English include whether to assess in both the child's home language and English and in what order the assessments should occur. If the child's primary caregivers intend to raise the child bilingually, or if the early care and education setting is intentionally bilingual, then assessing the child in both languages reflects both the goals and the context of development. Typically, a young child should be assessed first in the higher proficiency language, if that is known.

Information of importance in drawing inferences about young children's functioning can be derived from many sources: collection of children's work products (drawings or stories told), observation of the child in natural settings while engaged in a task or while interacting with peers, interviews with and surveys of parents and teachers, and direct child assessments. Each of these assessment modes has its own strengths and potential pitfalls. For example, work products are highly informative, but selecting equivalent "performances" across children is difficult. Teacher ratings reflect the ability to compare across children, but they are subject to bias if collected in circumstances in which there may be serious consequences for the teachers. Parent reports are based on rich knowledge of the child, but they are subject to social desirability biases. Observational measures provide information about real-world functioning, but they have to be contextualized in an understanding of how typical the observed behavior is. Direct assessments often provide information about norms or criteria for performance, but they can generate misleading results if the child being tested is shy, unfamiliar with the tester, or resistant to direction.

Implementing a state-level early childhood assessment system is a relatively new process for any state that has undertaken it. States have approached this task in different ways, with some making decisions that would be supported by research and recommended practice and others making decisions that would not. There is enormous variation across settings in the care with which decisions about early childhood assessments are made. New Jersey, for example, has developed effective assessment decision processes, which were described in Chapter 9.

### Guidelines on Instrument Selection and Implementation

(I-1) Selection of a tool or instrument should always include careful attention to its psychometric properties.

(a) Assessment tools should be chosen that have been shown to have acceptable levels of validity and reliability evidence for the purposes for which they will be used and the populations that will be assessed.

(b) Those charged with implementing assessment systems need to make sure that procedures are in place to examine validity data as part of instrument selection and then to examine the data being produced with the instrument to ensure that the scores being generated are valid for the purposes for which they are being used.

(c) Test developers and others need to collect and make available evidence about the validity of inferences for language and cultural minority groups and for children with disabilities.

(d) Program directors, policy makers, and others who select instruments for assessments should receive instruction in how to select and use assessment instruments.

(I-2) Assessments should not be given without clear plans for follow-up steps that use the information productively and appropriately.

(I-3) When assessments are carried out, primary caregivers should be informed in advance about their purposes and focus. When assessments are for screening purposes, primary caregivers should be informed promptly about the results, in particular whether they indicate a need for further diagnostic assessment.

(I-4) Pediatricians, primary medical caregivers, and other qualified personnel should screen for maternal or family factors that might impact child outcomes—child abuse risk, maternal depression, and other factors known to relate to later outcomes.

(I-5) Screening assessment should be done only when the available instruments are informative and have good predictive validity.

(I-6) Assessors, teachers, and program administrators should be able to articulate the purpose of assessments to parents and others.

(I-7) Assessors should be well trained to meet a clearly specified level of expertise in administering assessments, should be monitored systematically, and should be reevaluated occasionally. Teachers or program staff may administer assessments if they are carefully supervised and if reliability checks and monitoring are in place to ensure adherence to approved procedures.

(I-8) States or other groups selecting high-stakes assessments should leave an audit trail—a public record of the decision making that was part of the design and development of the assessment system. These decisions would include why the assessment data are being collected, why a particular set of outcomes was selected for assessment, why the particular tools were selected, how the results will be reported and to whom, as well as how the assessors were trained and the assessment process was monitored.

(I-9) For large-scale assessment systems, decisions regarding instrument selection or development for young children should be made by individuals with the requisite programmatic and technical knowledge and after careful consideration of a variety of factors, including existing research, recommended practice, and available resources. Given the broad-based knowledge needed to make such decisions wisely, they cannot be made by a single individual or by fiat in legislation. Policy and legislation should allow for the adoption of new instruments as they are developed and validated.

(I-10) Assessment tools should be constructed and selected for use in accordance with principles of universal design, so they will be accessible to, valid, and appropriate for the greatest possible number of children. Children with disabilities may still need accommodations, but this need should be minimized.

(I-11) Extreme caution needs to be exercised in reaching conclusions about the status, progress, and effectiveness of programs serving, young children with special needs, children from language-minority homes, and other children from groups not well represented in norming or validation samples, until more information about assessment use is available and better measures are developed.

## THE ASSESSMENT SYSTEM

### Rationale

In its use of the term "system," the committee intends that:

- the assessment system and assessing within that system be seen as part of the larger structure of early childhood care and education, including child outcomes as well as program standards, constructs, measures, indicators, decision making, and follow-up;
- selection of assessments be intimately linked to goals defined in the context of that larger system;
- procedures for sharing information about and using information from assessments be considered as part of the process of selecting and administering assessments; and
- different parts of the assessment system itself (standards, constructs, measures, indicators) work together.

Many, if not most, early childhood assessment programs currently in use lack elements of well-integrated systems. At least some partially integrated systems exist and constitute models for how to design assessment systems—in New Zealand and in New Jersey, for example—but there are many barriers to doing this universally. The knowledge and resources are available to do a better job of integrating information from a range of early child outcome and program assessments into efforts to improve the quality of services to young children.

Assessments that are not integrated into well-designed systems often are ill-suited to the purposes to which they are put, are not well aligned with program standards and goals, and they do not contribute as they should to the improvement of children's learning and development. Evaluation and accountability are separate goals; integrating them takes explicit planning and great care to avoid potential risks to children, teachers, and programs.

Good, systematic use of assessment for program improvement, evaluation, or accountability purposes implies integrating information from a range of assessments focusing on different elements of the system. It implies as well a procedure for providing assistance in addressing problems with classroom resources and challenges, as well as for providing resources and support (including corrective action) before the imposition of any negative consequences for teachers or programs. Furthermore, any use of assessment for drawing conclusions about program effectiveness requires meeting the criteria for a systematic and coherent approach to assessment-based decision making. These criteria include

1. Clearly articulated purpose for the testing. Identification of why particular assessments were selected in relation to the purpose.
2. Clear connection between the assessment results and quality of care.
3. Observation of quality of instruction and definition of what would need to be focused on for improvement.
4. Clear plan for following up to improve program quality.
5. Careful decisions about how to achieve the purposes of the assessment while minimizing the assessment burden, e.g., by sampling children, domains, or items.
6. Careful decisions about how to balance standardizing the administration of direct assessments with threats to optimal test performance because of unnaturalness or nonresponsiveness.

The NRC Committee on High Stakes (National Research Council, 1999) articulated a list of criteria that had to be met before any high stakes were imposed on students or on schools; that committee's work was primarily relevant to the K-12 system, but its general tone of caution about using assessments to make crucial decisions is equally applicable to the early childhood years. For example, its report concluded that educational decisions about individual children should never be based on a single test, that different kinds and sources of information about child performance were needed. Similarly, high-stakes decisions about teachers and programs should never be based on a single source of information. Information from child assessments should be contextualized in an understanding of their care and education environments, as well as child-specific factors (fatigue, hunger, illness) that may undermine the validity of inferences. Information about program effectiveness should be contextualized in an understanding of the resources and supports available. Decisions about teacher effectiveness cannot be validly based on information from child performance or even from direct observation without also knowing about access to resources, to professional development, to mental health consultation, to supervision, and so on.

Lack of further investigation and follow-up to screening are violations of good practice. There are high stakes associated with being identified for retention or special services, but also with failure to identify those with possible problems and follow up with appropriate in-depth diagnostic assessment and, when appropriate, services.

Doing accountability well for early childhood programs is expensive and occurs only if the accountability work is funded as part of funding the program. As states invest increasingly in prekindergarten programs, it is important to recognize that building in a process of accountability takes thoughtful planning as well as resources. There are models of carefully designed accountability processes built into a few such programs.

### Guidelines on Systems

(S-1) An effective early childhood assessment system must be part of a larger system with a strong infrastructure to support children's care and education. The infrastructure is the foundation on which the assessment systems rest and is critical to its smooth and effective functioning. The infrastructure should encompass several components that together form the system:

(a) ***Standards:*** A comprehensive, well-articulated set of standards for both program quality and children's learning that are aligned to one another and that define the constructs of interest as well as child outcomes that demonstrate that the learning described in the standard has occurred.

(b) ***Assessments:*** Multiple approaches to documenting child development and learning and reviewing program quality that are of high quality and connect to one another in well-defined ways, from which strategic selection can be made depending on specific purposes.

(c) ***Reporting:*** Maintenance of an integrated database of assessment instruments and results (with appropriate safeguards of confidentiality) that is accessible to potential users, that provides information about how the instruments and scores relate to standards, and that can generate reports for the varied audiences and purposes.

(d) ***Professional development:*** Ongoing opportunities provided to those at all levels (policy makers, program directors, assessment administrators, practitioners) to understand the standards and the assessments and to learn to use the data and data reports with integrity for their own purposes.

(e) ***Opportunity to learn:*** Procedures to assess whether the environments in which children are spending time offer high-quality support for development and learning, as well as safety, enjoyment, and affectively positive relationships, and to direct support to those that fall short.

(f) ***Inclusion:*** Methods and procedures for ensuring that all children served by the program will be assessed fairly, regardless of their language, culture, or disabilities, and with tools that provide useful information for fostering their development and learning.

(g) ***Resources:*** The assurance that the financial resources needed to ensure the development and implementation of the system components will be available.

(h) ***Monitoring and evaluation:***

Continuous monitoring of the system itself to ensure that it is operating effectively and that all elements are working together to serve the interests of the children. This entire infrastructure must be in place to create and sustain an assessment subsystem within a larger system of early childhood care and education.

(S-2) A successful system of assessments must be coherent in a variety of ways. It should be *horizontally coherent,* with the curriculum, instruction, and assessment all aligned with the early learning and development standards and with the program standards, targeting the same goals for learning, and working together to support children's developing knowledge and skill across all domains. It should be *vertically coherent,* with a shared understanding at all levels of the system of the goals for children's learning and development that underlie the standards, as well as consensus about the purposes and uses of assessment. It should be *developmentally coherent*, taking into account what is known about how children's skills and understanding develop over time and the content knowledge, abilities, and understanding that are needed for learning to progress at each stage of the process. The California Desired Results Developmental Profile provides an example of movement toward a multiply coherent system. These coherences drive the design of all the subsystems. For example, the development of early learning standards, curriculum, and the design of teaching practices and assessments should be guided by the same framework for understanding what is being attempted in the classroom that informs the training of beginning teachers and the continuing professional development of experienced teachers. The reporting of assessment results to parents, teachers, and other stakeholders should also be based on this same framework, as should the evaluations of effectiveness built into all systems. Each child should have an equivalent opportunity to achieve the defined goals, and the allocation of resources should reflect those goals.

(S-3) Following the best assessment practices is especially crucial in cases in which assessment can have significant consequences for children, teachers, or programs. The NRC report *High Stakes: Testing for Tracking, Promotion, and Graduation* (National Research Council, 1999) urged extreme caution in basing high-stakes decisions on assessment outcomes, and we conclude that even more extreme caution is needed when dealing with young children from birth to age 5 and with the early care and education system. We emphasize that a primary purpose of assessing children or classrooms is to improve the quality of early childhood care and education by identifying where more support, professional development, or funding is needed and by providing classroom personnel with tools to track children's growth and adjust instruction.

(S-4) Accountability is another important purpose for assessment, especially when significant state or federal investments are made in early childhood programs. Program-level accountability should involve high stakes only under very well-defined conditions: (a) data about input factors are fully taken into account, (b) quality rating systems or other program quality information has been considered in conjunction with child measures, (c) the programs have been provided with all the supports needed to improve, and (d) it is clear that restructuring or shutting the program down will not have worse consequences for children than leaving it open. Similarly, high stakes for teachers should not be imposed on the basis of classroom functioning or child outcomes alone. Information about access to resources and support for teachers should be gathered and carefully considered in all such decisions, because sanctioning teachers for the failure of the system to support them is inappropriate.

(S-5) Performance (classroom-based) assessments of children can be used for accountability, if objectivity is ensured by checking a sample of the assessments for reliability and consistency, if the results are appropriately contextualized in information about the program, and if careful safeguards are in place to prevent misuse of information.

(S-6) Minimizing the burdens of assessment is an important goal; being clear about purpose and embedding any individual assessment decision into a larger system can limit the time and money invested in assessment.

(S-7) It is important to establish a common way of identifying children for services across the early care and education, family support, health, and welfare sectors.

(S-8) Implementing assessment procedures requires skilled administrators who have been carefully trained in the assessment procedures to be implemented; because direct assessments with young children can be particularly challenging, more training may be required for such assessments.

(S-9) Implementation of a system-level approach requires having services available to meet the needs of all children identified through screening, as well as requiring follow-up with more in-depth assessments.

(S-10) If services are not available, it can be appropriate to use screening assessments and then use the results to argue for expansion of services. Failure to screen when services are not available may lead to underestimation of the need for services.

## RESEARCH AGENDA

Among the tasks of the committee was the development of a research agenda to improve the quality and suitability of developmental assessment, across a wide array of purposes and for the benefit of all the various children who will eventually be entering kindergarten. References to the need for research on assessment tools and the building of an assessment system, distributed throughout this volume, especially in connection with concerns about the adequacy of current instruments and processes, are gathered together here. These recommendations relate specifically to research needs in connection with assessment tools and the building of an assessment system, the committee's specific charge.

However, research related to assessment is dependent on continued support for other basic research in child development (especially as related to children of cultural and linguistic minorities), family functioning, effective programming for children and families, and community supports. The research base that can guide the development of assessments is based on theories of learning that are also evolving (see National Research Council, 2006); it would be short-sighted to proceed as though everything needed to do this well is already known. The relationship between assessment tools and knowledge of child development is highly intertwined. Advances in knowledge will proceed in tandem with advances in assessment because a primary way that researchers learn about what children know and can do or how one area of development relates to another involves administering the currently available assessment tools. As assessment tools improve, the knowledge base will expand; at the same time, innovations in assessment will emerge from the expanding knowledge base.

Given the current state of assessment tools and how much more understanding is needed about the development of young children, especially those from other cultures or who speak other languages, it is imperative that both the strengths and limitations of any given set of assessments be acknowledged. Because very young children are at even greater risk than older ones of bad consequences resulting from the misuse of assessment, great care must be taken not to impose the incomplete understandings in the K-12 system on this more vulnerable population (National Research Council and Institute of Medicine, 2000).

### Instrument Development

The various assessments available for use with young children have their origins in a variety of theoretical frameworks and purposes. Some were developed many years ago and thus do not incorporate what is now known about development and learning. Principles of assessment development and psychometric theory also have advanced in recent years and these are not reflected in older tools. Assessment development is a lengthy and resource-intensive process, but it is critically important that it be undertaken. Assessments are used to make a variety of decisions about young children, including screening, diagnosis, and instructional planning. With the emergence of more programs for young children and the need for accountability for those resources, assessment will become even more widespread. The quality of the assessment tools must match the various demands being placed on them, and that requires an investment in research on the development of new techniques.

**Basic Considerations About Assessment**

The field presently lacks conceptual frameworks and the measures necessary to move this research forward to systematically improve children's learning. Preliminary research on the role of context in learning suggests that environmental factors can increase children's engagement and participation (Christenson, 2004; Goldenberg, Rueda, and August, 2006), which in turn can lead to increased learning—and that the influence of contextual contingencies on learning outcomes is mediated by children's motivation to learn (Rueda, 2007; Rueda and Yaden, 2006; Rueda et al., 2001). Meaningful empirical work in this area will require the convergence of research methods (e.g., multilevel statistics and the mixing of qualitative approaches with experimental and quasi-experimental designs) and social science disciplines (e.g., cognitive psychology, educational anthropology, the sociology of education).

Conceptual and empirical research on child assessment is needed to move beyond the individual level to understand that processes outside the individual—in the classroom (e.g., teacher-child interactions, peer-to-peer interactions), the home (e.g., frequency of words spoken, number of books), and the school (e.g., language instruction policies) affect learning.

Research is needed to apply the latest technical advances, such as item response theory, to assessment development, to ensure that assessments are providing good measurement for all children. Most direct assessment tools and observations methods are developed conceptually, without sufficient attention to ensuring adequate measurement at all ranges of the scale and for children from diverse backgrounds.

Development research is needed on assessments that span a broader age range, ideally from birth to ages 6 or 7. Assessments with a broader age span are needed for research to allow children's learning and development to be tracked longitudinally, through the transition into the primary grades. They also are important for program continuity, as children move from one early childhood classroom to the next, and for relating children's learning to early learning guidelines. Finally, for children with developmental delays, assessments that span the entire early childhood period allow growth to be tracked on the same assessment, even if children are performing significantly below their age peers.

Recently developed tools for examining social emotional development need further work to generate evidence about their reliability, validity, and sensitivity to intervention approaches. More work is needed to develop key constructs within the domain of approaches to learning, as well as tools to measure those constructs and their role in children's learning and development. The shortcomings of current measures, especially standardized norm-referenced measures for young children and those with special needs, have been extensively documented, yet it is precisely these kinds of measures that are often employed in large-scale data collections. New measures are needed that accurately capture children's growth toward being able to meaningfully participate in the variety of settings that make up their day-to-day lives.

Research is needed on how to effectively use technology in all forms of early childhood assessment. Some assessments currently provide for online entry of data and computerized scoring and automatic report generation, but more work is needed. More research is needed on the use of computer adaptive procedures for establishing floor and ceiling levels, to allow more in-depth assessment at the child's current performance level. Computer-adaptive assessment could be applicable to both direct and observation-based measures.

## For the Improvement of Screening

Research is needed to validate screening tools for the full range of children represented in early childhood programs. There is a need to continue to collect information on who currently conducts screenings, including consideration of the barriers working against more widespread screening. There is a need for information on how many are screened, fail the screen, receive follow-up testing, and receive treatment or intervention based on whether a problem is verified. (Newborn hearing screening data is a model for this; the dismal results on measures of follow-up have become clear only because the data were systematically collected.)

### For the Improvement of Diagnostic Tests

More information is needed on the validity of currently available tools to identify the presence of a developmental delay or atypical development (Are the right children being identified?). Tools are needed for identifying developmental delay in children from other cultures and those who are speakers of other languages.

### For the Improvement of Observation-Based and Curriculum-Based Child Measures

More research is needed in the use of authentic assessment tools for program evaluation and accountability, including consideration of what level of training (and retraining) is necessary to ensure that teachers reliably administer the assessment initially and over time, whether the use of observation-based tools in an accountability system leads to inflated scores or otherwise reduces its usefulness in the classroom, and what level of monitoring and supervision is required to ensure that the assessment is administered consistently.

Information is needed about how to train teachers efficiently and effectively in the administration and use of curriculum-based assessments. Further work is needed to determine whether psychometric methods to address differences in how teachers use rating scales need to be routinely applied when these approaches are used for evaluation.

There is a need for research on the impact on practice of ongoing assessment in the classroom, on the barriers to effective implementation and use of ongoing assessment, and on the use of progress monitoring for ensuring that all children are receiving appropriate instruction.

## Assessment Processes

### Response to Intervention

Much more research and model development are needed on the application of response to intervention (RTI) to identification and service delivery in early childhood, especially as it relates to developmentally appropriate practice. These questions are critical:

- How can RTI be applied effectively to preschoolers?
- Will it allow for the earlier identification and intervention for children with learning problems?
- What type of assessment tools are needed to apply RTI to early childhood?
- Can these tools be used to plan instruction?
- How can screening for RTI be integrated with ongoing assessment for instructional planning? (The Institute of Education Sciences will be funding an RTI center for preschoolers; proposals are now under review.)

Research is needed on the types of tools and types of information most useful to teachers for ongoing assessment.

### Child Outcomes and Program Quality Standards

Research is needed on tools and processes to tap children's knowledge and skill in such domains as art, music, creativity, science, and ethics. There is need for consistent definitions and measures for key constructs in early social and emotional competencies, self-regulation, and the absence of serious behavior problems. Parallel work is needed to establish their relationship to early participation in learning activities and to academic achievement. Further research is needed to identify fruitful domain structures and optimal content and formats for early learning standards to serve as a model for states as they revise initial work. Research should continue to identify program quality elements that strengthen child outcomes.

### Use of Assessment Tools and Processes with Special Populations

#### Addressing Bias

Little work has been done to address the effect of bias in the assessment process for young children; such work is hampered by disagreement about what constitutes bias and how it operates with different populations. Research on how to address these issues is needed to be able to move forward. More work is needed to explore the influence of sampling and norming in reducing bias. More work is needed to understand the effects of the examiner, rater, or the testing situation on all children, but especially on populations subject to bias.

Work is needed to expand the universal design characteristics of extant testing instruments, to make them optimally useful for all children, including children with special needs and children from cultural and language minorities, and to consider universal design characteristics in the development of new instruments. Work is needed on the functionality of various instruments with different populations (e.g., for minority and nonminority children) in different settings (e.g., in a Head Start program and a private, for-profit, preschool program).

### English Language Learners

Research is needed to develop psychometrically sound native language assessments for English language learners (ELLs). This will require the expertise of several disciplines, including linguistics, cognitive psychology, education, and psychometrics. Further empirical research is needed to evaluate the reliability and validity of traditional cognitive measures for English language learners and intelligence tests developed for specific ELL populations. For English language learners, empirical research is needed to inform decisions about which accommodations to use, for whom, and under what conditions.

There is a need for ongoing implementation research in the area of professional development and training for assessing young English language learners. This research needs to identify the substance of professional development to improve staff competencies necessary to work as a part of a professional team; inform how staff works with interpreters; guide how to choose and administer appropriate assessment batteries; and train practitioners to develop their competence in second language acquisition, acculturation, and the evaluation of educational interventions.

More research documenting the current scenarios for the assessment of young ELLs across the country is needed, including more work to evaluate assessment practices in various localities; survey research and observational approaches to document practices in preassessment and assessment planning, conducting the assessment, analyzing and interpreting the results, reporting the results (in written and oral format), and determining eligibility and monitoring; and a focus on the development of strategies to train professionals with the skills necessary to serve young ELL children.

Research is needed to develop assessment tools normed especially for young English language learners using a bottom-up approach, so that assessment tools, procedures, and constructs assessed are aligned with cultural and linguistic characteristics of ELL children.

### Children with Special Needs

More research is needed on what the various practitioners who assess young children with special needs—early interventionists, special education teachers, speech therapists, psychologists, etc.—actually do.

More research is needed on the use of accommodations with children with disabilities. What are appropriate guidelines for decision making about what kind of accommodations to use with what kind of child under what conditions?

Research is needed on the impact of accommodations on the validity of the assessment results.

## Accountability and Program Quality

There is a need for the development of assessment instruments designed for the purpose of accountability and program evaluation. Instruments that are developed for federal studies such as the Early Childhood Longitudinal Study, Kindergarten-First Grade Waves (ECLS K) or national studies of Head Start should become publicly available, so they can used by others. There is a need for research on the implementation of accountability systems and the tracking of positive and negative consequences at all levels of the system:

- How strong is the research base for the accountability system? What is the impact on practice? Is that impact in line with what could be reasonably expected from the prior research?
- Does the system have the intended impact?
- Are there any negative consequences of the accountability system (e.g., narrowing of the curriculum, exclusion of high-risk children)?
- If data are meant to improve programs or direct allocation of resources, does this happen?
- How familiar are teachers and child care providers with the purpose of a program evaluation or a state accountability system?
- How does information need to be packaged to ensure it is understood by program administrators, teachers or child care providers, and parents?

There is a need for a compilation of experiences with different measures for accountability purposes. What are we learning about which measures or types of measures work well? There is a need for research on the development of accountability standards for types of information reported about assessments and accountability for early childhood programs. Increased consideration of and research on system-level effects of various assessment approaches are needed. Detailed case studies of coherent comprehensive assessment systems serving well-integrated systems of child care and education should be developed to serve as models for programs, districts, and states attempting to develop such systems.

There is a need for research on the overall validity and consequences of particular approaches, such as:

- Direct assessment with sampling—Where this has been used, what have been the program-level impacts?
- If data are provided at the center but not the classroom level, does this create negative reactions?
- What level of training and follow-up monitoring is required to ensure the assessment is administered consistently?

Different reporting formats should be evaluated with usability studies to determine which are best understood and most likely to be used accurately by typical audiences.

## PUTTING GUIDANCE INTO PRACTICE

We conclude this volume by addressing our most urgent advice to the most likely agents. Different agents almost inevitably have somewhat different purposes for assessment, as well as different responsibilities and different levels of control. Here we attempt to clarify what actions can be taken by each of the major agents to implement the guidelines we have provided. In this way we hope to jumpstart actions to improve the care and education of young children.

### Pediatricians and Primary Health Care Personnel

- Pediatricians and health care personnel should be aware of the full range of information sources useful in screening children for developmental and medical risk; those responsible for the education of such professionals should include such information in medical training and in-service training.
- Health care personnel should use effective strategies to convey information to parents and other caregivers of infants and children to whom they administer assessments.
- Health care personnel should be aware of the educational implications of the risks they might identify through screening assessment, in order to help guide the search for services.
- Health care providers need to be aware of the resources available in the community, such as Individuals with Disabilities Education Act Part C early intervention and preschool special education programs for children who are in need of additional developmental assessment and services.

### Classroom Teachers in Early Childhood Settings

- Teachers should work with colleagues and coaches/professional development personnel/program administrators to select or devise and implement formative (classroom- or curriculum-based) assessments to guide their own teaching.
- If assessment information of any kind is collected in the classroom, the teacher should be fully informed about why the assessment is being conducted and for what purposes the data will be used. The teacher should be able to explain the purpose, process, and results of the assessment to parents.
- Teachers should seek information about the psychometric properties of any assessments being used with children, in particular for direct assessments, and exercise caution in using direct assessment results from assessments with low reliability or tests not normed on children like those in their classrooms.
- Teachers should make sure that they understand the meaning of children's scores, both in relative terms (who is scoring highest, lowest in the class) and in relation to standards or expectations (who is scoring at or below expected levels for the age) if age-based norms are available.
- Teachers should work with colleagues and coaches/professional development personnel/program administrators to determine the best ways of sharing information about child performance with primary caregivers, and encourage the program they work in to be systematic about sharing assessment findings with parents.
- If the information collected as part of formal assessments (for program evaluation purposes, for example) ignores important domains, teachers should seek out ways to collect and record supplementary information on their own group of children. For example, if only early mathematical and literacy skills are formally tested, teachers should be systematic about collecting a wider array of developmental indicators, e.g., by using systematic observations during peer play sessions to collect information about children's

socioemotional development, ask the child to select artistic products for placement in an art portfolio, take 90 seconds to elicit and write down a story from each child to reflect oral language skills, or in other ways be systematic about collecting a wider array of developmental indicators.

### Early Childhood Program Administrators

- Program administrators should support their classroom personnel in selecting or developing and implementing formative (classroom- or curriculum-based) assessments to guide their own teaching.
- Program administrators should ensure that they are fully informed about any assessment information of any kind being collected in their program by external agents. It is their responsibility (and their right) to know why the assessment is being conducted and for what purposes the data will be used.
- Program administrators should seek information about the psychometric properties of any assessments being used with their children, in particular direct assessments, and exercise caution in using direct results from assessments with low reliability or tests not normed on children like those in their program.
- Program administrators should make sure they understand the meaning of children's scores, what they say both about how children in the program are progressing and whether they are meeting age-based or standards-based expectations.
- Program administrators should work to ensure that their own level of assessment literacy is appropriate to the types of assessment taking place in their classroom. They should promote the assessment literacy of their staff through professional development opportunities.
- Program administrators should work with the practitioners in their program to establish and practice the best ways of sharing information about child performance with primary caregivers and ensure that the program is systematic about sharing assessment findings.

- If the information collected as part of formal assessments ignores important domains, program administrators should encourage their staff to find assessments that cover the other domains or collect and record supplementary information on their own.
- Program administrators should make systematic observations of classrooms to assess the quality of teaching and the social context, using their own or an available measure, and use the findings to coach and provide professional support for teachers.
- If no information related to the effectiveness of the program is being collected by external agencies, program administrators should undertake their own regular systematic evaluation of the program and use the results to improve its overall effectiveness. The evaluation should include data on program quality (e.g., features of the classrooms, teacher-child interaction) and assessments that document the progress being made by children in the program.

### District, State, and Federal Officials with Responsibility for Early Childhood Programs

- Officials should ensure the availability of professional development to support program personnel in interpreting and using information from assessments and in selecting or developing formative (classroom- or curriculum-based) assessments to guide their own continual improvement.
- Officials should be clear about the purposes for which they are recommending or mandating assessments and ensure that the assessments and assessment strategies recommended or mandated fit those purposes well.
- When selecting or developing assessment instruments or strategies for use with any purpose in their programs, officials should maintain a record (audit trail) of the decisions made and the factors that influenced those decisions.
- Officials should ensure that the psychometric properties of any direct tests they select or develop are adequate, both

in general and in particular for children like those being served in their programs.

- Officials should build funding and planning for progress monitoring and evaluation into the budgets for program implementation.
- Officials should consider the larger system when making specific decisions about assessment. They should select assessment instruments that are aligned with standards and that complement one another in the kinds of information they provide, plan in advance for informing program personnel about the nature and the purposes of the assessments, and plan in advance how the information generated will be shared and used.
- Officials should reexamine regularly the standards to which their assessments are aligned, the domains that are included in their assessment system, and the degree of coherence (horizontal, vertical, and developmental) across the assessment system and early childhood care and education structure.
- Officials should become informed about the risks associated with assessing young children.
- Officials should not make high-stakes decisions for children or for programs unless a number of criteria have been met. These criteria include

1. A clearly articulated purpose for the testing.
2. Identification of why particular assessments were selected in relation to the purpose.
3. A clear connection between the assessment results and quality of care.
4. Observation of quality of instruction and definition of what would need to be focused on for improvement.
5. A clear plan for following up to improve program quality.
6. Careful decisions about how to achieve the purposes of the assessment while minimizing the assessment burden, for example by sampling children, domains, or items.
7. Careful decisions about how to balance standardizing the administration of direct assessments with threats to

optimal test performance because of unnaturalness or nonresponsiveness.

### Researchers

- Researchers should work with early childhood practitioners and programs to learn about the full array of child outcomes of interest to them, to analyze the adequacy of the extant array of assessment instruments, to improve existing assessment procedures, and to develop assessment procedures for understudied or poorly instrumented domains.
- Researchers should work to expand the universal design characteristics of extant testing instruments, to make them optimally useful for all children, including those with disabilities and cultural and language minority children.
- Researchers should study the development of linguistic and cultural minority children in order to inform the development of assessments that would adequately reflect their capacities.
- Researchers should develop detailed case studies of coherent comprehensive assessment systems serving well-integrated systems of child care and education, to serve as models for programs, districts, and states attempting to develop such systems.

## CONCLUSION

Writing a report about assessment, especially about assessment in early childhood, almost inevitably has to anticipate two quite different audiences. A significant proportion of the audience will start reading the report armed with a negative view of the idea of assessing preschoolers, alert to the complexities of assessing young children in ways that are informative and reliable, aware that testing can produce stress or discomfort in the child, and worried that the full array of skills and capacities the child has is unlikely to be represented. This portion of the audience will be integrating the new information in the report with assessment horror stories—children who were identified as low IQ when in fact they were second language learners, programs that were threatened with loss of funding because the children in them failed to meet some external standard even though they had progressed enormously, programs subjected to evaluation using tests of capacities that had not been included in the curriculum. Such readers will be particularly sensitive to the notion that child assessment might be included as a basis for program accountability.

Another large portion of the audience will filter the information in a report like this through a generally much more positive view of assessment in early (and later) childhood. These readers are thinking of the value to parents of the procedures for screening infants to identify those who need services. They would cite the value to taxpayers of evaluating early childhood programs to ensure they are of high quality and the value to practitioners, to parents, and to children of having both progress monitoring and formative assessments available to support program improvement. They would cite standards and associated assessments as levers for program improvement, as well as the need to hold publicly financed programs accountable for meeting their goals of providing young children with supportive and stimulating environments. They would point out how much has been learned about child development from assessment, and how much more we need to know.

Of course, quite a lot of the readers, like many members of this committee, constitute a third group—those who understand the opportunities that well-thought-out and effective assessment offers to inform teaching and program improvement, but who are simultaneously acutely aware that poor practices abound even in the face of the best information about how to do better. Representing the views of this latter group, this report attempts to take neither a positive nor a negative view of assessment, although we recognize the credibility of specific claims on both sides of the controversy. The committee members represent the full range of gut feelings about assessment. Some of us, reading early drafts of these chapters, wrote comments suggesting that more warnings and cautions were needed, whereas others wrote comments indicating that the view of assessment presented was much too bleak, that the value of assessment in educational improvement needed to be more robustly emphasized. We conclude, not that the very positive or the very negative views are wrong, but that both are correct and that both are limited. The final version of the report, thus, explicitly does not take the position that assessment is here to stay and we'd better learn to live with it. Rather, it takes the position that assessments can make crucial contributions to the improvement of children's well-being, but only if they are well designed, implemented effectively and in the context of systematic planning, and interpreted and used appropriately. Otherwise, assessment of children and programs can have negative consequences for both. We conclude that the value of assessments themselves cannot be judged without attention to the design of the larger systems in which they are used.

# References

## SUMMARY

National Education Goals Panel. (1995). *Reconsidering children's early development and learning: Toward common views and vocabulary*. Washington, DC: Author.

## CHAPTER 1

National Research Council. (2001). *Eager to learn: Educating our preschoolers*. Committee on Early Childhood Pedagogy, B.T. Bowman, M.S. Donovan, and M.S. Burns (Eds.). Commission on Behavioral and Social Sciences and Education. Washington, DC: National Academy Press.

National Research Council and Institute of Medicine. (2000). *From neurons to neighborhoods: The science of early childhood development*. Committee on Integrating the Science of Early Childhood Development, J.P. Shonkoff and D.A. Phillips (Eds.). Board on Children, Youth, and Families, Commission on Behavioral and Social Sciences and Education. Washington, DC: National Academy Press.

## CHAPTER 2

Brown, G., Scott-Little, C., Amwake, L., and Wynn, L. (2007). *A review of methods and instruments used in state and local school readiness evaluations*. (Issues and Answers Report, REL 2007–No. 004.) Washington, DC: U.S. Department of Education, Institute of Education Sciences, National Center for Education Evaluation and Regional Assistance, Regional Educational Laboratory Southeast.

Center on Education Policy. (2007). *Reading first: Locally appreciated, nationally troubled*. Washington, DC: Author.

Coleman, M.R., Buysse, V., and Neitzel, J. (2006). *Recognition and response: An early intervening system for children at-risk for learning disabilities*. Chapel Hill: University of North Carolina, FPG Child Development Institute.

Council of Chief State School Officers. (2003a). *Building an assessment system to support successful early learners: The role of child assessment in program evaluation and improvement*. Washington, DC: Author. Available: http://www.ccsso.org/Projects/scass/projects/early_childhood_education_assessment_consortium/publications_and_products/3002.cfm [accessed August 2008].

Council of Chief State School Officers. (2003b). *Key considerations building an assessment system to support successful early learners: Overview* (fact sheet). Washington, DC: Author. Available: http://www.ccsso.org/Projects/scass/projects/early_childhood_education_assessment_consortium/publications_and_products/3002.cfm [accessed August 2008].

Division for Early Childhood. (2007). *Promoting positive outcomes for children with disabilities: Recommendations for curriculum, assessment, and program evaluation.* Missoula, MT: Author.

Dodge, D.T., Heroman, C., Charles, J., and Maiorca, J. (2004). Beyond outcomes: How ongoing assessment supports children's learning and leads to meaningful curriculum. *Young Children, 59*(1), 20-28.

Education Commission of the States. (2005, February). *Access to kindergarten: Age issues in state statutes*. Available: http://www.ecs.org/clearinghouse/58/27/5827.doc [accessed February 1, 2008].

Fuchs, D., and Fuchs, L.S. (2006). Introduction to responsiveness to intervention: What, why, and how valid is it? *Reading Research Quarterly, 41*, 92-99.

Graue, E. (2006). The answer is readiness—Now what is the question? *Early Education and Development, 17*(1), 43-56.

Meisels, S.J. (1987). Uses and abuses of developmental screening and school readiness testing. *Young Children, 42*(2), 68-73.

National Association for the Education of Young Children and National Association of Early Childhood Specialists in State Departments of Education. (2003). *Early childhood curriculum, assessment, and program evaluation.* Washington, DC: National Association for the Education of Young Children.

National Association of Early Childhood Specialists in State Departments of Education. (2000). *Still! Unacceptable trends in kindergarten entry and placement: A position statement*. Available: http://naecs.crc.uiuc.edu/position/trends2000.html [accessed February 1, 2008].

National Early Childhood Accountability Task Force. (2007). *Taking stock: Assessing and improving early childhood learning and program quality*. Philadelphia: Author.

National Research Council. (1998). *Preventing reading difficulties in young children.* Committee on the Prevention of Reading Difficulties in Young Children, C.E. Snow, M.S. Burns, and P. Griffin (Eds.). Commission on Behavioral and Social Sciences and Education. Washington, DC: National Academy Press.

Neisworth, J., and Bagnato, S. (2005). DEC recommended practices: Assessment. In S. Sandall, M.L. Hemmeter, M. McLean, and B.J. Smith (Eds.), *DEC recommended practices book: A comprehensive guide for practical application in early intervention/early childhood special education* (pp. 45-70). Longmont, CO: Sopris West.

Shepard, L.A. (1997). Children not ready to learn? The invalidity of school readiness testing. *Psychology in the Schools, 34*(2), 85-97.

Shepard, L.A., and Smith, M.L. (1986). Synthesis of research on school readiness and kindergarten retention. *Educational Leadership, 44*(3), 78-86.

Shepard, L., Kagan, S.L., and Wurtz, C. (1998). *Principles and recommendations for early childhood assessments.* Goal 1 Early Childhood Assessments Resource Group. Washington, DC: National Education Goals Panel.

VanDerHayden, A.M., and Snyder, P. (2006). Integrating frameworks from early childhood intervention and school psychology to accelerate growth for all children. *School Psychology Review, 35*(4), 519-534.

## CHAPTER 3

Ackerman, D.J., and Barnett, W.S. (2006). Increasing the effectiveness of preschool programs. *Preschool Policy Brief, 11.*

American Educational Research Association. (2005). *Letter to Congress.* Washington, DC: Author.

Council of Chief State School Officers and Early Childhood Education Assessment Consortium. (2003a). *Key considerations: Building a system of standards to support successful early learners: The relationship between early learning standards, program standards, program quality measures and accountability.* Washington, DC: Author.

Council of Chief State School Officers and Early Childhood Education Assessment Consortium. (2003b). *Matrix of state early learning standards.* Washington, DC: Author.

Council of Chief State School Officers and Early Childhood Education Assessment Consortium. (2007). *The words we use: A glossary of terms for early childhood education standards and assessment.* Available: http://www.ccsso.org/Projects/scass/projects/early_childhood_education_assessment_consortium/publications_and_products/2892.cfm [accessed February 2008].

Gilliam, W.S., and Zigler, E.F. (2001). A critical meta-analysis of all impact evaluations of state-funded preschool from 1977 to 1998: Implications for policy, service delivery and program evaluation. *Early Childhood Research Quarterly, 15,* 441-473.

Hatch, J.A. (2001). Accountability shove down: Resisting the standards movement in early childhood education. *Phi Delta Kappan, 83*(6), 457-462.

High/Scope Educational Research Foundation. (2002). *Making validated educational models central in preschool standards.* Ypsilanti, MI: Author.

High/Scope Educational Research Foundation. (in press). *Michigan school readiness program evaluation, grades 6-8 follow-up.* Ypsilanti, MI: Author.

Kagan, S.L., Moore, E., and Bredekamp, S. (1995). *Reconsidering children's early development and learning: Toward common views and vocabulary*. National Education Goals Panel Goal 1 Technical Planning Group. Washington, DC: U.S. Government Printing Office.

McKey, R.H., and Tarullo, L. (1998). Ensuring quality in Head Start: The FACES Study. *The Evaluation Exchange, 4*(1).

Meisels, S.J., Barnett, W.S., Espinosa, L., Kagan, S.L., et al. (2003). *Letter to U.S. representatives concerning implementation of the National Reporting System*. Available: http://www.nhsa.org/download/research/headstart letterforsenate.doc [accessed July 2008].

National Association for the Education of Young Children. (2006). *NAEYC accreditation criteria*. Available: http://www.naeyc.org/academy/NAEYC AccreditationCriteria.asp [accessed February 2008].

National Association for the Education of Young Children and National Association of Early Childhood Specialists in State Departments of Education. (2002). *Early learning standards: Creating the conditions for success*. Washington, DC: Author.

National Early Childhood Accountability Task Force. (2007). *Taking stock: Assessing and improving early childhood learning and program quality*. Philadelphia: Author.

National Institute for Early Education Research. (2005). *The effects of the Michigan School Readiness Program on young children's abilities at kindergarten entry*. Rutgers, NJ: Author.

National Research Council. (1998). *Preventing reading difficulties in young children*. Committee on the Prevention of Reading Difficulties in Young Children, C.E. Snow, M.S. Burns, and P. Griffin (Eds.). Commission on Behavioral and Social Sciences and Education. Washington, DC: National Academy Press.

National Research Council. (2001). *Eager to learn: Educating our preschoolers*. Committee on Early Childhood Pedagogy, B.T. Bowman, M.S. Donovan, and M.S. Burns (Eds.). Commission on Behavioral and Social Sciences and Education. Washington, DC: National Academy Press.

National Research Council and Institute of Medicine. (2000). *From neurons to neighborhoods: The science of early childhood development*. Committee on Integrating the Science of Early Childhood Development, J.P. Shonkoff and D.A. Phillips (Eds.). Board on Children, Youth, and Families, Commission on Behavioral and Social Sciences and Education. Washington, DC: National Academy Press.

Pre-kindergarten Standards Panel. (2002). *Pre-kindergarten standards: Guidelines for teaching and learning*. New York: McGraw-Hill.

Shepard, L., Kagan, S.L., and Wurtz, E. (1998). *Principles and recommendations for early childhood assessments*. National Education Goals Panel Goal 1 Early Childhood Assessments Resource Group. Washington, DC: National Education Goals Panel.

U.S. Department of Health and Human Services, Administration for Children and Families. (2000). *Head Start child outcomes framework*. Washington, DC: Author.

U.S. Department of Health and Human Services, Administration for Children and Families. (2002). *Child care and development fund: Report of state plans FY 2002-2003*. Washington, DC: Author.

U.S. Department of Health and Human Services, Administration for Children and Families. (2003). Head Start child outcomes: Setting the context for the National Reporting System. *Head Start Bulletin, 76*. Available: http://eclkc.ohs.acf.hhs.gov/hslc/ecdh/eecd/Assessment/Child%20Outcomes/edudev_art_00090_080905.html [accessed August 2008].

U.S. Department of Health and Human Services, Administration for Children and Families. (2006a). *Head Start performance measures center: Family and child experiences survey (FACES 2000)*. (Technical report.) Washington, DC: Author.

U.S. Department of Health and Human Services, Administration for Children and Families. (2006b). *NRS social-emotional development rating webcast transcript*. Washington, DC: Author.

U.S. Department of Health and Human Services, Administration for Children and Families. (2006c). *Research to practice: Program performance measures for Head Start programs serving infants and toddlers*. Available: http://www.acf.hhs.gov/programs/opre/ehs/perf_measures/reports/prgm_perf_measures/perf_meas_4pg.html [accessed March 2008].

U.S. Government Accountability Office. (2005). *Head Start: Further development could allow results of new test to be used for decision making*. Washington, DC: Author.

White House. (2002). *Good start, grow smart: The Bush administration's early childhood initiative*. Washington, DC: Executive Office of the President.

## PART II

Kagan, S.L., Moore, E., and Bredekamp, S. (1995). *Reconsidering children's early development and learning: Toward common views and vocabulary*. National Education Goals Panel Goal 1 Technical Planning Group. Washington, DC: U.S. Government Printing Office.

McCartney, K., and Phillips, D. (Eds.). (2006). *Handbook of early childhood development*. Malden, MA: Blackwell.

National Education Goals Panel. (1995). *Reconsidering children's early development and learning: Toward common views and vocabulary*. Washington, DC: Author.

National Research Council and Institute of Medicine. (2000). *From neurons to neighborhoods: The science of early childhood development*. Committee on Integrating the Science of Early Childhood Development, J.P. Shonkoff and D.A. Phillips (Eds.). Board on Children, Youth, and Families, Commission on Behavioral and Social Sciences and Education. Washington, DC: National Academy Press.

## CHAPTER 4

Als, H., Butler, S., Kosta, S., and McAnulty, G. (2005). The assessment of preterm infants' behavior (APIB): Furthering the understanding and measurement of neurodevelopmental competence in preterm and full-term infants. *Mental Retardation and Developmental Disability Research Review, 11*, 94-102.

Als, H., Gilkerson, L., Duffy, F.H., McAnulty, G.B., Buehler, D.M., Vandenberg, K., Sweet, N., Sell, E., Parad, R.B., Ringer, S.A., Butler, S.C., Blickman, J.G., and Jones, K.J. (2003). A three-center, randomized, controlled trial of individualized developmental care for very low birth weight preterm infants: Medical, neurodevelopmental, parenting and caregiving effects. *Journal of Developmental and Behavioral Pediatrics, 24*(6), 399-408.

American Academy of Pediatrics. (1996). Eye examination and vision screening in infants, children and young adults. *Pediatrics, 98*(1), 153-157.

American Academy of Pediatrics. (2003). Iron deficiency. In *Pediatric nutrition handbook* (5th ed.). Elk Grove, IL: Author.

American Academy of Pediatrics. (2005). Lead exposure in children: Prevention, detection, and management. *Pediatrics, 16*(4), 1036-1046.

American Academy of Pediatrics, Committee on Children with Disabilities. (2001). Developmental surveillance and screening of infants and young children. *Pediatrics, 108*(1), 192-196.

American Academy of Pediatrics, Council on Children with Disabilities. (2006). Identifying infants and young children with developmental disorders in the medical home: An algorithm for developmental surveillance and screening. *Pediatrics, 118*(1), 405-420.

Bagnato, S.J., Neisworth, J.T., Salvia, J.J., and Hunt, F.M. (1999). *Temperament and Atypical Behavior Scale (TABS): Early childhood indicators of developmental dysfunction*. Baltimore, MD: Brookes.

Baird, G., Charman, T., Baron-Cohen, S., Cox, A., Swettenham, J., Wheelwright, S., and Drew, A. (2000). Screening for autism at 18 months of age: 6-year follow-up study. *Journal of the American Academy of Child and Adolescent Psychiatry, 39*(3), 694-702.

Banks, E.C., Ferrittee, L.E., and Shucard, D.W. (1997). Effects of low-level lead exposure on cognitive function in children: A review of behavioral, neuropsychological and biological evidence. *Neurotoxicology, 18*, 237-281.

Bates, J.E., Freeland, C.A., and Lounsbury, M.L. (1979). Measurement of infant difficultness. *Child Development, 50*, 794-803.

Beeghly, M., Brazelton, T.B., Flannery, K.A., Nugent, J.K., Barrett, D.E., and Tronick, E.Z. (1995). Specificity of preventative pediatric intervention effects in early infancy. *Journal of Developmental and Behavioral Pediatrics, 16*, 158-166.

Biondich, P.G., Downs, S.M., Carroll, A.E., Laskey, A.L., Liu, G.C., Rosenman, M., Wang, J., and Swigonski, N.L. (2006). Shortcomings in infant iron deficiency screening methods. *Pediatrics, 117*(2), 290-294.

Blake, P.E., and Hall, J.W. (1990). The status of state-wide policies for neonatal hearing screening. *Journal of the American Academy of Audiology, 1*, 67-74.

Botkin, J.R. (2004). Research for newborn screening: Developing a national framework. *Pediatrics, 116*, 862-871.

Brazelton, T.B., and Nugent, J.K. (1995). *The Neonatal Behavioral Assessment Scale*. Cambridge, England: MacKeith Press.

Buros Institute of Mental Measurements. (2007). *The seventeenth mental measurements yearbook*. Lincoln, NE: Buros Institute of Mental Measurements.

Camp, B.W. (2007). Evaluating bias in validity studies of developmental/behavioral screening tests. *Journal of Developmental & Behavioral Pediatrics, 28*(3), 234-240.

Capute, A.J., and Shapiro, B.K. (1985). The motor quotient: A method for the early detection of motor delay. *American Journal of the Diseases of Children, 98*, 692-697.

Carroll, A.E., and Downs, S.M. (2005). Comprehensive cost-utility analysis of newborn screening strategies. *Pediatrics, 117*, S287-S295.

Centers for Disease Control and Prevention. (2007). *Tested and confirmed elevated blood lead levels by state, year, and blood lead level group for children < 72 mos.* Atlanta: Author. Available: http://www.cdc.gov/nceh/lead/surv/stats.htm [accessed October 2008].

Chandler, L., Andrews, M., and Swanson, M. (1980). *The movement assessment of infants: A manual*. Rolling Bay, WA: Infant Movement Research.

Child Trends. (2004). *Early childhood measures profiles*. Washington, DC: Author.

Clarke-Stewart, K.A., Fitzpatrick, M.J., Allhusen, F.D., and Goldberg, W.A. (2000). Measuring difficult temperament the easy way. *Journal of Developmental and Behavioral Pediatrics, 21*, 207-220.

Coplan, J. (1993). *Early language milestone scale*. Austin, TX: Pro-Ed.

Das Eiden, R., and Reifman, A. (1996). Effects of Brazelton demonstrations on later parenting: A meta-analysis. *Journal of Pediatric Psychology, 21*(6), 857-868.

Dumont-Mathieu, T., and Fine, D. (2005). Screening for autism in young children: The Modified Checklist for Autism in Toddlers (M-CHAT) and other measures. *Mental Retardation and Developmental Disabilities Research Review, 11*, 253-262.

Emory, E.K., and Walker, E.F. (1982). Relationship between birth weight and neonatal behavior. In L.P. Lipsitt and T.M. Field (Eds.), *Infant behavior and development: Perinatal risk & newborn behavior* (pp. 21-31). New York: Ablex.

Emory, E.K., Ansari, Z., Pattillo, R., Archibold, E., and Chevalier, J. (2003). Maternal blood lead effects on infant intelligence at age 7 months. *American Journal of Obstetrics and Gynecology, 188*, S26-S32.

Emory, E.K., Pattillo, R., Archibold, E., Bayorh, M., and Sung, F. (1999). Neurobehavioral effects of low-level lead exposure in human neonates. *American Journal of Obstetrics and Gynecology, 181*, S2-S11.

Emory, E.K., Tynan, W.D., and Davé, R. (1989). Neurobehavioral anomalies in neonates with seizures. *Journal of Clinical and Experimental Neuropsychology, 11*(2), 231-240.

Emory, E.K., Walker, E.F., and Cruz, A. (1982). Fetal heart rate part II: Behavioral correlates. *Psychophysiology, 19*(6), 680-686.

Fisher, E.S., and Welch, H.G. (1999). Avoiding the unintended consequences of growth in medical care: How might more be worse. *The Journal of the American Medical Association, 281*(5), 446-453.

Folio, M.R., and Fewell, R.R. (1983). *Peabody developmental motor scales and activity cards: A manual*. Allen, TX: DLM Teaching Resources.

Freed, G.L., Nahra, T.A., and Wheeler, J.R.C. (2004). Which physicians are providing health care to America's children? *Archives of Pediatrics and Adolescent Medicine, 158*, 22-26.

Gilliam, W.S., Meisels, S.J., and Mayes, L. (2005). Screening and surveillance in early intervention systems. In M.J. Guralnick (Ed.), *The developmental systems approach to early intervention*. Baltimore, MD: Brookes.

Glascoe, F.P. (2003). Parents' evaluation of developmental status: How well do parents' concerns identify children with behavioral and emotional problems? *Clinical Pediatrics, 42*, 133-138.

Glascoe, F.P. (2005). Screening for developmental and behavioral problems. *Mental Retardation and Developmental Disabilities Research Reviews, 11*(3), 173-179.

Glascoe, F.P., Martin, E.D., and Humphrey, S. (1990). A comparative review of developmental screening tests. *Pediatrics, 86*, 5467-5554.

Grandjean, P., and Landrigan, P. (2006). Developmental neurotoxicity of industrial chemicals. *The Lancet, 368*(9553), 2167-2178.

Grantham-McGregor, S. (1984). Chronic undernutrition and cognitive abilities. *Human Nutrition-Clinical Nutrition, 38*(2), 83-94.

Gravel, J.S., Fausel, N., Liskow, C., and Chobot, J. (1999). Children's speech recognition in noise using omni-directional and dual-microphone hearing aid technology. *Ear & Hearing, 20*(1), 1-11.

Ireton, H. (1992). *Child development inventory manual*. Minneapolis, MN: Behavior Science Systems.

Jacobs, S.E., Sokol, J., and Ohlsson, A. (2002). The newborn individualized developmental care and assessment program is not supported by meta-analyses of the data. *Journal of Pediatrics, 140*, 699-706.

Johnson, J.O. (2005). Who's minding the kids? Child care arrangements: Winter, 2002. *Current Population Reports* (P70-101). Washington, DC: U.S. Census Bureau.

Kaye, C.I., and the Committee on Genetics. (2006). Introduction to the newborn screening fact sheets. *Pediatrics, 118*(3), 1304-1312.

Lanphear, B.P., Dietrich, K., Auinger, P., and Cox, C. (2000). Cognitive deficits associated with blood lead concentrations, 10Mg/dl in US children and adolescents. *Public Health Reports, 115*, 521-529.

Lanphear, B.P., Hornung, R., Ho, M., Howard, C., Eberli, S., and Knauf, D.K. (2002). Environmental lead exposure during early childhood. *Journal of Pediatrics, 140*, 40-47.

Lloyd-Puryear, M.A., Tonniges, T., van Dyck, P.C., Mann, M.Y., Brin, A., Johnson, K., and McPherson, M. (2007). American Academy of Pediatrics Newborn Screening Task Force recommendations: How far have we come? *Pediatrics, 117*(5 Pt. 2), S194-S211.

Lozoff, B., Jiminez, E., Hagen, J., Mollen, E., and Wolf, A.W. (2000). Poorer behavioral and developmental outcome more than 10 years after treatment for iron deficiency in infancy. *Pediatrics, 105*(4), e51. Available: http://pediatrics.aappublications.org/cgi/content/abstract/105/4/e51 [accessed August 2008].

Lozoff, B., Andraca, I.D., Castillo, M., Smith, J.B., Walter, T., and Pino, P. (2003). Behavioral and developmental effects of preventing iron-deficiency anemia in healthy full-term infants. *Pediatrics, 112*(4), 846-854.

Mangione-Smith, R., DeCristofaro, A.H., Setodji, C.M., Keesey, J., Klein, D.J., Adams, J.L., Schuster, M.A., and McGlynn, E.A. (2007). The quality of ambulatory care delivered to children in the United States. *The New England Journal of Medicine, 357*(15), 1515-1523.

Mathematica Policy Research. (2003). *Resources for measuring services and outcomes in Head Start programs serving infants and toddlers*. Princeton, NJ: Author.

McCormick, M. (2008). Issues in measuring child health. *Ambulatory Pediatrics, 8*(2), 77-84.

Moeller, M.P. (2000). Early intervention and language development in children who are deaf and hard of hearing. *Pediatrics, 106*, e43. Available: http://pediatrics.aappublications.org/cgi/content/full/106/3/e43 [accessed August 2008].

Morgan, A.M., and Aldag, J.C. (1996). Early identification of cerebral palsy using a profile of abnormal motor patterns. *Pediatrics, 98*(4), 692-697.

National Center for Hearing Assessment and Management. (2007). *Early hearing detection and intervention (EHDI) resources and information*. Available: http://www.infanthearing.org/ehdi.html [accessed July 2008].

National Research Council. (2002). *Visual impairments: Determining eligibility for Social Security benefits*. Committee on Disability Determination for Individuals with Visual Impairments, P. Lennie and S.B. Van Hemel (Eds.). Board on Behavioral, and Sensory Sciences, Center for Studies of Behavior and Development, Division of Behavioral and Social Sciences and Education. Washington, DC: National Academy Press.

National Research Council and Institute of Medicine. (2000). *From neurons to neighborhoods: The science of early childhood development*. Committee on Integrating the Science of Early Childhood Development, J.P. Shonkoff and D.A. Phillips (Eds.). Board on Children, Youth, and Families, Commission on Behavioral and Social Sciences and Education. Washington, DC: National Academy Press.

Needleman, H.L., and Gatsonis, C.A. (1990). Low-level lead exposure and the IQ of children: A meta-analysis of modern studies. *The Journal of the American Medical Association, 263*(2), 673-678.

Newman, T.B., Browner, W.S., and Hulley, S.B. (1990). The case against childhood cholesterol screening. *The Journal of the American Medical Association, 264*, 3039-3043.

Piper, M.C., and Darrah, J. (1994). *Motor assessment of the developing infant*. Philadelphia: W.B. Saunders.

Putnam, S.P., and Rothbart, M.K. (2006). Development of short and very short forms of the children's behavior questionnaire. *Journal of Personality Assessment, 87*, 102-112.

Rutter, M., Bailey, A., and Lord, C. (2003). *The social and communication questionnaire (SCQ) manual*. Los Angeles, CA: Western Psychological Services.

Schulze, A., Lindner, M., Kohlmuller, D., Olgemoller, K., Mayatepek, E., and Hoffman, G.F. (2003). Expanded newborn screening for inborn errors of metabolism by electrospray ionization-tandem mass spectrometry: Results, outcome, and implications. *Pediatrics, 111*, 1399-1406.

Shepherd, P.A., and Fagan, J.F. (1981). Visual pattern detection and recognition memory in children with profound mental retardation. In N.R. Ellis (Ed.), *International review of research in mental retardation*. New York: Academic Press.

Siegel, B. (2004). *Pervasive developmental disorders screening test-II (PDDST-II). Early childhood screener for autistic spectrum disorders*. San Antonio, TX: Harcourt Assessment.

Simpson, L., Owens, P., Zodet, M., Chevarley, F., Dougherty, D., Elixhauser, A., and McCormick, M.C. (2005). Health care for children and youth in the United States: Annual report on patterns of coverage, utilization, quality, and expenditures by income. *Ambulatory Pediatrics, 5*(1), 45-46.

Stone, W.I., Coonrod, E.E., and Ousley, O.Y. (2000). Brief report: Screening tool for autism in two-year-olds (STAT): Development and preliminary data. *Journal of Autism and Developmental Disorders, 30*, 607-701.

Teti, D.M., and Gelfand, D.M. (1997). The preschool assessment of attachment: Construct validity in a sample of depressed and nondepressed families. *Development and Psychopathology, 9*, 517-536.

Tronick, E.Z. (1987). The Neonatal Behavioral Assessment Scale as a biomarker of the effects of environmental agents on the newborn. *Environmental Health Perspectives, 74*, 185-189.

U.S. Department of Health and Human Services, National Center for Health Statistics. (1981). *National health interview survey-1981 child health supplement*. Washington, DC: Author.

U.S. Preventive Services Task Force. (2001). *Guide to clinical preventive services*. Washington, DC: Office of Disease Prevention and Health Promotion.

U.S. Preventive Services Task Force. (2004). *Screening for visual impairment in children younger than age 5 years: Update of the evidence.* Rockville, MD: Agency for Healthcare Research and Quality. Available: http://www.ahrq.gov/clinic/uspstf/uspsvsch.htm [accessed July 2008].

U.S. Preventive Services Task Force. (2006). *Screening for iron deficiency anemia—Including iron supplementation for children and pregnant women*. Washington, DC: Office of Disease Prevention and Health Promotion.

Voigt, R.G., Brown, F.R., Fraley, J.K., Liorente, A.M., Rozelle, J., Turcich, M., Jensen, C.L., and Heird, W.C. (2003). Concurrent and predictive validity of the Cognitive Adaptive Test/Clinical Linguistic and Auditory Milestone Scale (CAT/CLAMS) and the mental developmental index of the Bayley Scales of Infant Development. *Clinical Pediatrics, 42*(5), 427-432.

Wasserman, R., Croft, C., and Brotherton, S. (1992). Preschool vision screening in pediatric practice: A study from the Pediatric Research in Office Settings (PROS) network. *Pediatrics, 89*(5 Pt. 1), 834-838.

Wetherby, A.M., and Prizant, B.M. (2002). *Communication and symbolic behavior scales: Developmental profile*. Baltimore, MD: Brookes.

Widerstrom, A. (1999). Newborns and infants at risk for or with disabilities. In A. Widerstrom, B. Mowder, and S. Sandall (Eds.), *Infant development and risk* (2nd ed., pp. 3-24). Baltimore, MD: Brookes.

Wilson, J.M.G., and Jungner, G. (1968). *Principles and practice of screening for diseases*. Geneva: World Health Organization.

Wyly, M.V. (1997). *Infant assessment*. Boulder, CO: Westview Press.

Yoshinaga-Itano, C., Sedey, A.L., Coulter, D.K., and Mehl, A.L. (1998). Language of early- and later-identified children with hearing loss. *Pediatrics, 102*, 1161-1171.

Zafeieriou, D.I. (2003). Primitive reflexes and postural reactions in the neuro-developmental examination. *Pediatric Neurology, 31*, 1-8.

## CHAPTER 5

Alexander, P.A., White, C.S., and Daugherty, M. (1997). Analogical reasoning and early mathematics learning. In L.D. English (Ed.), *Mathematical reasoning: Analogies, metaphors, and images* (pp. 117-147). Mahwah, NJ: Lawrence Erlbaum Associates.

American Academy of Pediatrics. (2005). Lead exposure in children: Prevention, detection, and management. *Pediatrics, 16*(4), 1036-1046.

American Institutes for Research. (2005). *Reassessing U.S. international mathematics performance: New findings from the TIMSS and PISA*. Washington, DC: Author.

American Psychological Association Task Force on Intelligence. (1996). *Intelligence: Knowns and unknowns*. Washington, DC: Author.

Barone, T. (2001). The end of the terror: On disclosing the complexities of teaching. *Curriculum Inquiry, 31*(1), 89-102

Bayley, N. (2005). *Bayley Scales of Infant and Toddler Development*. San Antonio, TX: Psychological Corporation.

Bear, D.R., Invernizzi, M., Templeton, S., and Johnston, F. (1999). *Words their way: Word study for phonics, vocabulary, and spelling instruction*. Upper Saddle River, NJ: Prentice Hall.

Beck, I., McKeown, M., and Kucan, L. (2002). *Bringing words to life: Robust vocabulary instruction*. New York: Guilford Press.

Becker, J. (1989). Preschoolers' use of number words to denote one-to-one correspondence. *Child Development, 60*, 1147-1157.

Bierman, K.L., and Erath, S.A. (2006). Promoting social competence in early childhood: Classroom curricula and social skills coaching programs. In K. McCartney and D. Phillips (Eds.), *Handbook of early childhood development*. Malden, MA: Blackwell.

Bierman, K.L., Domitrovich, C.E., Nix, R.L., Gest, S.D., Welsh, J.A., Greenberg, M.T., Blair, C., Nelson, K.E., and Gill, S. (under review). *Promoting academic and social-emotional school readiness: The Head Start REDI program.* The Pennsylvania State University. Available: http://www.srcd.org/journals/cdev/0-0/Bierman.pdf [accessed July 2008].

Birch, S., and Ladd, G.W. (1998). Children's interpersonal behaviors and the teacher-child relationship. *Developmental Psychology, 34*, 934-946.

Blair, C. (2002). School readiness: Integrating cognition and emotion in a neurobiological conceptualization of children's functioning at school entry. *American Psychologist, 57*(2), 111-127.

Blair, C. (2006). How similar are fluid cognition and general intelligence? A developmental neuroscience perspective on fluid cognition as an aspect of human cognitive ability. *Behavioral and Brain Sciences, 29*, 109-125.

Blair, C., and Razza, R.P. (2007). Relating effortful control, executive function, and false belief understanding to emerging math and literacy ability in kindergarten. *Child Development, 78*(2), 647-663.

Blank, M., Rose, S., and Berlin, L. (1978). *Preschool Language Assessment Instrument (PLAI).* New York: Psychological Corporation.

Boaler, J. (1994). When do girls prefer football to fashion? An analysis of female underachievement in relation to "realistic" mathematics contexts. *British Educational Research Journal, 20*(5), 551-564.

Bodrova, E., and Leong, D.J. (2001). *Tools of the mind: A case study of implementing the Vygotskian approach in American early childhood and primary classrooms.* Geneva: UNESCO, International Bureau of Education.

Bull, R., and Scerif, G. (2001). Executive functioning as a predictor of children's mathematics ability: Inhibition, switching, and working memory. *Developmental Neuropsychology, 19*(3), 273-293.

Burchinal, M., Lee, M., and Ramey, C. (1989). Type of day-care and preschool intellectual development in disadvantaged children. *Child Development, 60*(1), 128-137.

Campbell, S.B. (2006). Maladjustment in preschool children: A developmental pschyopathology perspective. In K. McCartney and D. Phillips (Eds.), *Handbook of early childhood development* (pp. 358-378). Malden, MA: Blackwell.

Carlson, S. (2005). Developmentally sensitive measures of executive function in preschool children. *Developmental Neuropscyhology, 28*, 595-616.

Clay, M. (1979). *Concepts about print tests: Sand and stones.* Portsmouth, NH: Heinemann.

Clements, D.H. (1999). Geometric and spatial thinking in young children. In J.V. Copley (Ed.), *Mathematics in the early years.* Reston, VA: National Council of Teachers of Mathematics.

Clements, D.H, Sarama, J., and DiBiase, A.M. (Eds.). (2004). *Engaging young children in mathematics: Standards for early childhood mathematics education.* Mahwah, NJ: Lawrence Erlbaum Associates.

Clements, D.H. (2004). Major themes and recommendations. In D.H. Clements, J. Sarama, and A.-M. DiBiase (Eds.), *Engaging young children in mathematics: Standards for early childhood mathematics education.* Mahwah, NJ: Lawrence Erlbaum Associates.

Clements, D.H., and Stephan, M. (2004). Measurement in pre-K to grade 2 mathematics. In D.H. Clements, J. Sarama, and A.-M. DiBiase (Eds.), *Engaging young children in mathematics: Standards for early childhood mathematics education* (pp. 299-317). Mahwah, NJ: Lawrence Erlbaum Associates.

Cooper, B., and Dunne, M. (1998). Anyone for tennis? Social class differences in children's responses to national curriculum mathematics testing. *The Sociological Review*, 115-148.

Craig, H.K., Connor, C.M., and Washington, J.A. (2003). Early positive predictors of later reading comprehension for African American students: A preliminary investigation. *Language, Speech, and Hearing Services in Schools, 34*(1), 31-42.

de Jong, P.F., and van der Leij, A. (2002). Effects of phonological abilities and linguistic comprehension on the development of reading. *Scientific Studies of Reading, 6*(1), 51-77.

Denham, S.E. (2006). Emotional competence. In J.L. Luby (Ed.), *Handbook of preschool mental health: Development, disorders, and treatment* (pp. 23-44). New York: Guilford Press.

Diamond, A., Barnett, W.S., Thomas, J., and Munro, S. (2007). Preschool program improves cognitive control. *Science, 318*, 1387-1388.

Dickinson, D.K., and Tabors, P.O. (Eds.). (2001). *Beginning literacy with language: Young children learning at home and school.* Baltimore, MD: Brookes.

Dickinson, D.K., McCabe, A., Anastasopoulos, L., Peisner-Feinberg, E.S., and Poe, M.D. (2003). The comprehensive language approach to early literacy: The interrelationships among vocabulary, phonological sensitivity, and print knowledge among preschool-aged children. *Journal of Educational Psychology, 95*(3), 465-481.

DiPerna, J.C., Lei, P.W., and Reid, E.R. (2007). Kindergarten predictors of mathematical growth in the primary grades: An investigation using the Early Childhood Longitudinal Study Kindergarten Cohort. *Journal of Educational Psychology, 90*, 369-379.

Dowsett, S., and Livesey, D. (2000). The development of inhibitory control in preschool children: Effects of "executive skills" training. *Developmental Psychobiology, 36*, 161-174.

Duncan, G., Dowsett, C., Claessens, A., Magnuson, K., Huston, A., Klebanov, P., Pagani, L.S., Feinstein, L., Engel, M., Brooks-Gunn, J., Sexton, H., Duckworth, K., and Japel, C. (2007). School readiness and later achievement. *Developmental Psychology, 43*(6), 1428-1446. Available: http://www.apa.org/journals/releases/dev4361428.pdf [accessed July 2008].

Dunn, L.M., and Dunn, D.M. (2007). *Peabody Picture Vocabulary Test* (4th ed.). Upper Saddle River, NJ: Pearson Assessments.

Epstein, A., and Weikart, D. (1979). *The Ypsilanti-Carnegie Infant Education Project: Longitudinal follow-up*. Ypsilanti, MI: High/Scope.

Espy, K.A., Kaufmann, P.M., McDiarmid, M.D., and Glisky, M.L. (1999). Executive functioning in preschool children: Performance on A-not-B and other delayed response format tasks. *Brain and Cognition, 41*(2), 178-199.

Espy, K.A., McDiarmid, M.D., Cwik, M.F., Senn, T.E., Hamby, A., and Stalets, M.M. (2004). The contributions of executive functions to emergent mathematic skills in preschool children. *Developmental Neuropsychology, 26*, 465-486.

Fabes, R.A., Gaertner, B.M., and Popp, T.K. (2006). Getting along with others: Social competence in early childhood. In K. McCartney and D. Phillips (Eds.), *Handbook of early childhood development* (pp. 297-316). Malden, MA: Blackwell.

Fantuzzo, J., Bulotsky-Shearer, R., Fusco, R.A., and McWayne, C. (2005). An investigation of preschool classroom behavioral adjustment problems and social-emotional school readiness competencies. *Early Childhood Research Quarterly, 20*(3), 259-275.

Fantuzzo, J., Bulotsky-Shearer, R., McDermott, P.A., McWayne, C., Frye, D., and Perlman, S. (2007). Investigation of dimensions of social-emotional classroom behavior and school readiness for low-income urban preschool children. *School Psychology Review, 36*(1), 44-62. Available: http://repository.upenn.edu/gse_pubs/124/ [accessed July 2008].

Fantuzzo, J., Perry, M.A., and McDermott, P. (2004). Preschool approaches to learning and their relationship to other relevant classroom competencies for low-income children. *School Psychology Quarterly, 19*, 212-230.

Feigenson, L., Dehaene, S., and Spelke, E. (2004). Core systems of number. *Trends in Cognitive Sciences, 8*, 307-314.

Fenson, L., Dale, P., Reznick, J.S., Thal, D., Bates, E., Hartung, J.P., Pethick, S., and Reilly, J. (1993). *MacArthur-Bates Communicative Development Inventories*. San Diego, CA: Singular.

Flanagan, D.P., and McGrew, K.S. (1997). A cross-battery approach to assessing and interpreting cognitive abilities: Narrowing the gap between practice and cognitive science. In D.P. Flanagan, J.L. Genshaft, and P. Harrison (Eds.), *Contemporary intellectual assessment: Theories, tests, and issues* (pp. 314-325). New York: Guilford Press.

Foulks, B., and Morrow, R.D. (1989). Academic survival skills for the young child at risk for school failure. *Journal of Educational Research, 82*(3), 158-165.

Fuson, K.C. (1988). *Children's counting and concepts of number*. New York: Springer-Verlag.

Fuson, K.C. (1992a). Relationships between counting and cardinality from age 2 to age 8. In J. Bideau, C. Meljac, and J.P. Fischer (Eds.), *Pathways to number: Children's developing numerical abilities* (Chapter 6, pp. 127-150). Hillsdale, NJ: Lawrence Erlbaum Associates.

Fuson, K.C. (1992b). Research on whole number addition and subtraction. In D. Grouws (Ed.), *Handbook of research on mathematics teaching and learning*. New York: Macmillan.

Gardner, M.F., and Brownell, R. (2000). *Expressive One-Word Picture Vocabulary Test*. Novato, CA: Academic Therapy.

Gathercole, S.E. (1998). The development of memory. *Journal of Child Psychiatry, 39*, 3-27.

Ginsburg, H.P., Inoue, N., and Seo, K.H. (1999). Young children doing mathematics: Observations of everyday activities. In J.V. Cooper (Ed.), *Mathematics in the early years* (pp. 87-99). Reston, VA: National Council of Teachers of Mathematics.

Gray, S.W., and Klaus, R.A. (1970). The early training project: A seventh-year report. *Child Development, 7*(4), 909-924.

Green, L.F., and Francis, J. (1988). Children's learning skills at the infant and junior stages: A follow-on study. *British Journal of Educational Psychology, 58*(1), 120-126.

Hammill, D.D., and Newcomer, P.L. (1997). *Test of language development-primary* (3rd ed.). Austin, TX: Pearson Education.

Hamre, B.K., and Pianta, R.C. (2001). Early teacher-child relationships and the trajectory of children's school outcomes through eighth grade. *Child Development, 72*, 625-638.

Hemphill, L., Uccelli, P., Winner, K., Chang, C.-J., and Bellinger, D. (2002). Narrative discourse in young children with histories of early corrective heart surgery. *Journal of Speech, Language, and Hearing Research, 45*, 318-331.

Herrnstein, R.J., and Murray, C. (1994). *The bell curve: Intelligence and class structure in American life*. New York: Simon and Schuster.

Hiebert, J., Carpenter, T.P., Fennema, E., Fuson, K.C., Wearne, D., and Murray, H. (1997). *Making sense: Teaching and learning mathematics with understanding*. Portsmouth, NH: Heinemann.

Howes, C., Phillipsen, L., and Peisner-Feinberg, E. (2000). The consistency of perceived teacher-child relationships between preschool and kindergarten. *Journal of School Psychology, 38*, 113-132.

Howse, R.B., Lange, G., Farran, D.C., and Boyles, C.D. (2003). Motivation and self-regulation as predictors of achievement in economically disadvantaged young children. *Journal of Experimental Education, 71*(2), 151-174.

Hresko, W.P., Reid, D.K., and Hammill, D.D. (1999). *Test of early language development* (3rd ed.). Austin, TX: Pearson Education.

Jordan, G.E., Snow, C.E., and Porche, M.V. (2000). Project EASE: The effect of a family literacy project on kindergarten students' early literacy skills. *Reading Research Quarterly, 35*(4), 524-546.

Juel, C., and Minden-Cupp, C. (2000). Learning to read words: Linguistic units and instructional strategies. *Reading Research Quarterly, 35*(4), 458-492.

Kaufman, A.S., and Kaufman, N.L. (2006). *Kaufman Assessment Battery for Children (K-ABC)* (2nd ed.). Upper Saddle River, NJ: Pearson Assessments.

Klein, A., and Starkey, P.J. (2004). Fostering preschool children's mathematical knowledge: Finding from the Berkeley Math Readiness Project. In D.H. Clements, J. Samara, and A.-M. DiBiase (Eds.), *Engaging young children in mathematics: Standards for early childhood mathematics education* (pp. 343-360). Hillsdale, NJ: Lawrence Erlbaum Associates.

Klingberg, T., Fernell, E., Olesen, P.J., Johnson, M., Gustafsson, P., Dahlstrom, K., Gillberg, C.G., Forssberg, H., and Westerberg, H. (2005). Computerized training of working memory in children with ADHD—A randomized, controlled trial. *Journal of the American Academy of Child and Adolescent Psychiatry, 44*(2), 177-186.

Knight, G.P., and Hill, N.E. (1998). Measurement equivalence in research involving minority adolescents. In V.C. McLoyd and L. Steinberg (Eds.), *Studying minority adolescents: Conceptual, methodological, and theoretical issues* (pp. 183-210). Mahwah, NJ: Lawrence Erlbaum Associates.

Ladd, G.W., and Burgess, K. (2001). Do relational risks and protective factors moderate the linkages between childhood aggression and early psychological and school adjustment? *Child Development, 72*, 1579-1601.

Ladd, G.W., Birch, S., and Buhs, E. (1999). Children's social lives in kindergarten: Related spheres of influence. *Child Development, 70*, 1373-1400.

Ladd, G.W., Herald, S.L., and Kochel, K.P. (2006). School readiness: Are there social prerequisites? *Early Education and Development, 17*(1), 115-150.

Lehto, J.E. (2004). A test for children's goal-directed behavior: A pilot study. *Perceptual and Motor Skills, 98*(1), 223-236.

Lewit, E.M., and Baker, L.S. (1995). School readiness. *The Future of Children, 5*(2), 128-139.

Lubienski, S.T. (2000). Problem solving as a means toward mathematics for all: An exploratory look through a class lens. *Journal of Research in Mathematics Education, 31*(4), 454-482.

MacDonald, A.W., Cohen, J.D., Stenger, V.A., and Carter, C.S. (2000). Dissociating the role of the dorsolateral prefrontal and anterior cingulate cortex in cognitive control. *Science, 288*(5472), 1835-1838.

Malvern, D.D., and Richards, B.J. (1997). A new measure of lexical diversity. In A. Ryan and A. Wray (Eds.), *Evolving models of language*. Bristol, England: Multilingual Matters.

Mashburn, A.J., and Pianta, R.C. (2006). Social relationships and school readiness. *Early Education and Development, 17*(1), 151-176.

Mason, J., Stewart, J., Peterman, C., and Dunning, D. (1992). *Toward an integrated model of early reading development* (No. 566). Champaign, IL: Center for the Study of Reading.

McCall, R.B. (1977). Childhood IQ's as predictors of adult educational and occupational status. *Science, 197*(4302), 482-483.

McCall, R.B., and Carriger, M.S. (1993). A meta-analysis of infant habituation and recognition memory performance as predictors of later IQ. *Child Development, 64*(1), 57-79.

McCall, R.B., Appelbaum, M.I., and Hogarty, P.S. (1974). *Developmental changes in mental performance*. Chicago, IL: University of Chicago Press.

McCartney, K. (2002). Language environments and language outcomes: Results from the NICHD study of early child care and youth development. In L. Girolametto and E. Weitzman (Eds.), *Enhancing caregiver language facilitation in child care setting* (pp. 3-1–3-10). Toronto: The Hanen Centre.

McClelland, M.M., Acock, A.C., and Morrison, F.J. (2006). The impact of kindergarten learning-related skills on academic trajectories at the end of elementary school *Early Childhood Research Quarterly, 21*(4), 471-490.

McClelland, M.M., Cameron, C.E., Connor, C.M., Farris, C.L., Jewkes, A.M., and Morrison, F.J. (2007). Links between behavioral regulation and preschoolers' literacy, vocabulary, and math skills. *Developmental Psychology, 43*(4), 947-959.

McClelland, M.M., Morrison, F.J., and Holmes, D.L. (2000). Children at risk for early academic problems: The role of learning-related social skills. *Early Childhood Research Quarterly, 15*(3), 307-329.

McDermott, P.A. (1984). Comparative functions of preschool leaming style and IQ in predicting future academic performance. *Contemporary Educational Psychology, 9*, 38-47.

McDermott, P.A., Green, L.F., Francis, J.M., and Stott, D.H. (2000). *Preschool Learning Behaviors Scale*. Philadelphia: Edumetric and Clinical Science.

McWayne, C.M., Fantuzzo, J.W., and McDermott, P.A. (2004). Preschool competency in context: An investigation of the unique contribution of child competencies to early academic success. *Developmental Psychology, 40*, 633-645.

Means, B., and Knapp, M.S. (1991). Cognitive approaches to teaching advanced skills to educationally disadvantaged students. *Phi Delta Kappan, 7*, 282-289.

Meisels, S.J., Xue, Y., and Shamblott, M. (in press). *Assessing language, literacy, and mathematics skills with work sampling for Head Start*. Submitted to *Early Education and Development*.

Mendez, J.L., Fantuzzo, F., and Cicchetti, D. (2002). Personality and social development: Profiles of social competence among low-income African American preschool children. *Child Development, 73*(4), 1085-1100.

Miyake, A., Friedman, N.P., Emerson, M.J., Witzki, A.H., Howerter, A., and Wager, T.D. (2000). The unity and diversity of executive functions and their contributions to complex "frontal lobe" tasks: A latent variable analysis. *Cognitive Psychology, 41*(1), 49-100.

National Council of Teachers of Mathematics. (2000). *Principles and standards for school mathematics*. Reston, VA: Author.

National Education Goals Panel. (1995). *Reconsidering children's early development and learning: Toward common views and vocabulary*. Washington, DC: Author.

National Education Goals Panel. (1997). *Building a nation of learners*. Washington, DC: Author.

National Institute for Early Education Research. (2002). *A benefit-cost analysis of the Abecedarian early childhood intervention*. New Brunswick, NJ: Author.

National Research Council. (1998). *Preventing reading difficulties in young children*. Committee on the Prevention of Reading Difficulties in Young Children, C.E. Snow, M.S. Burns, and P. Griffin (Eds.). Washington, DC: National Academy Press.

National Research Council. (2001). *Adding it up: Helping children learn mathematics*. J. Kilpatrick, J. Swafford, and B. Findell (Eds.). Mathematics Learning Study Committee, Center for Education. Division of Behavioral and Social Sciences and Education. Washington, DC: National Academy Press.

Neisser, U., Boodoo, G., Bouchard, Jr., T.J., Boykin, A.W., Brody, N., Ceci, S.J., Halpern, D.F., Loehlin, J.C., Perloff, R., Sternberg, R.J., and Urbina, S. (1996). Intelligence: Knowns and unknowns. *American Psychologist, 51*(2), 77-101.

NICHD Early Child Care Research Network. (2000). The relation of child care to cognitive and language development. *Child Development, 71*(4), 960-980.

NICHD Early Child Care Research Network. (2005). Pathways to reading: The role of oral language in the transition to reading. *Developmental Psychology, 41*(2), 428-442.

Norman, D.A., and Shallice, T. (1986). Attention to action. In R.J. Davidson, G.E. Schwartz, and D. Shapiro (Eds.), *Consciousness and self-regulation: Advances in theory and research* (pp. 1-18). New York: Plenum Press.

Normandeau, S., and Guay, F. (1998). Preschool behavior and first-grade school achievement: The mediational role of cognitive self-control. *Journal of Educational Psychology, 90*(1), 111-121.

Olds, D.L., Henderson, C.R., Phelps, C., Kitzman, H., and Hanks, C. (1993). Effect of prenatal and infancy nurse home visitation on government spending. *Medical Care, 31*(2), 155-174.

Olson, S.L., Sameroff, A.J., Kerr, D.C.R., Lopez, N.L., and Weeman, H.M. (2005). Developmental foundations of externalizing problems in young children: The role of effortful control. *Development and Psychopathology, 17*, 25-45.

Pan, B.A., Mancilla-Martinez, J., and Vagh, S.B. (2008). *Tracking bilingual children's vocabulary development: Reporter- and language-related measurement challenges.* Poster presentation at the Head Start's Ninth National Research Conference, June 23-25, Washington, DC.

Phinney, J.S., and Landin, J. (1998). Research paradigms for studying ethnic minority families within and across groups. In V.C. McLoyd and L. Steinberg (Eds.), *Studying minority adolescents: Conceptual, methodological, and theoretical issues* (pp. 89-110). Mahwah, NJ: Lawrence Erlbaum Associates.

Pianta, R.C., and Steinberg, M. (1992). Teacher-child relationships and the process of adjusting to school. *New Directions for Child Development, 57*, 61-80.

Piotrkowski, C.S., Botsko, M., and Matthews, E. (2000). Parents' and teachers' beliefs about children's school readiness in a high-need community. *Early Childhood Research Quarterly, 15*(4), 537-558.

Poe, M.D., Burchinal, M.R., and Roberts, J.E. (2004). Early language and the development of children's reading skills. *Journal of School Psychology, 42*, 315-332.

Posner, M.I., and Rothbert, M.K. (2000). Developing mechanisms of self-regulation. *Development and Psychopathology, 12*, 427-441.

Quattrin, T., Liu, E., Shaw, N., Shine, B., and Chiang, E. (2005). Obese children who are referred to the pediatric endocrinologist: Characteristics and outcome. *Pediatrics, 115*, 348-351.

RAND Labor and Population. (2005). *Early childhood interventions: Proven results, future promise*. Santa Monica, CA: RAND Corporation.

Raver, C. (2002). *Emotions matter: Making the case for the role of young children's emotional development for early school readiness* (No. 3). Ann Arbor, MI: Society for Research in Child Development.

Raver, C. (2004). Placing emotional self-regulation in sociocultural and socioeconomic contexts. *Child Development, 75*(2), 8.

Raver, C., Gershoff, E.T., and Aber, J. (2007). Testing equivalence of mediating models of income, parenting, and school readiness for white, black, and Hispanic children in a national sample. *Child Development, 78*(1), 20.

Reynolds, A.J., and Temple, J.A. (1998). Extended early childhood intervention and school achievement: Age thirteen findings from the Chicago Longitudinal Study. *Child Development, 69*(1), 231-246.

Rimm-Kaufman, S.E., Pianta, R.C., and Cox, M.J. (2000). Teachers' judgment of problems in the transition to kindergarten. *Early Childhood Research Quarterly, 15*(2), 147-166.

Robbins, T.W. (1996). Refining the taxonomy of memory. *Science, 273*(5280), 1353-1354.

Roid, G.H. (2003). *Stanford-Binet Intelligence Scales for Early Childhood* (5th ed.). Rolling Meadows, IL: Riverside.

Roth, F.P., Speece, D.L., and Cooper, D.H. (2002). A longitudinal analysis of the connection between oral language and early reading. *Journal of Educational Research, 95*(5), 259-272.

Rothbart, M.K., Posner, M.I., and Kieras, J. (2006). Temperament, attention, and the development of self-regulation. In K. McCartney and D. Phillips (Eds.), *Handbook of early childhood development* (pp. 338-357). Malden, MA: Blackwell.

Rueda, M.R., Rothbart, M.K., McCandliss, B.D., Saccomanno, L., and Posner, M.I. (2005). Training, maturation, and genetic influences on the development of executive attention. *Proceedings of the National Academy of Sciences of the United States of America, 102*(41), 14931-14936.

Schatschneider, C., Francis, D.J., Carlson, C.D., Fletcher, J.M., and Foorman, B.F. (2004). Kindergarten prediction of reading skills: A longitudinal comparative analysis. *Journal of Educational Psychology, 96*(2), 265-282.

Schrank, F.A., Mather, N., and Woodcock, R.W. (2006). *Woodcock-Johnson III(r) Diagnostic Reading Battery*. Rolling Meadows, IL: Riverside.

Scott-Little, C., Kagan, S.L., and Frelow, V.S. (2005). *Inside the content: The depth and breadth of early learning standards.* Greensboro: University of North Carolina, SERVE Center for Continuous Improvement.

Scott-Little, C., Kagan, S.L., and Frelow, V.S. (2006). Conceptualization of readiness and the content of early learning standards: The intersection of policy and research? *Early Childhood Research Quarterly, 21*(2), 153-173.

Semrud-Clikeman, M., Nielsen, K.H., Clinton, A., Sylvester, L.H., Parle, N., and Connor, R.T. (1999). An intervention approach for children with teacher- and parent-identified attentional difficulties. *Journal of Learning Disabilities, 32*(6), 581-590.

Sénéchal, M., and LeFevre, J.-A. (2002). Parental involvement in the development of children's reading skill: A five-year longitudinal study. *Child Development, 73*(2), 445-460.

Seymour, H.N., Roeper, T.W., de Villiers, J., and de Villiers, P.A. (2003). *Diagnostic evaluation of language variation*. San Antonio, TX: Pearson Assessments.

Silver, R., Measelle, J., Armstrong, J., and Essex, M. (2005). Trajectories of classroom externalizing behavior: Contributions of child characteristics, family characteristics, and the teacher-child relationship during the school transition. *Journal of School Psychology, 43*, 39-60.

Silverman, R.D. (2007). Vocabulary development of English-language and English-only learners in kindergarten. *The Elementary School Journal, 107*, 365-384.

Snow, C.E., Porche, M., Tabors, P., and Harris, S. (2007). *Is literacy enough? Pathways to academic success for adolescents.* Baltimore, MD: Brookes.

Snow, C.E., Tabors, P.O., Nicholson, P., and Kurland, B. (1995). SHELL: Oral language and early literacy skills in kindergarten and first grade children. *Journal of Research in Childhood Education, 10*, 37-48.

Starkey, P., Klein, A., and Wakeley, A. (2004). Enhancing young children's mathematical knowledge through a pre-kindergarten mathematics intervention. *Early Childhood Research Quarterly, 19*, 99-120.

Sulzby, E. (1985). Children's emergent reading of favorite storybooks: A developmental study. *Reading Research Quarterly, 20*(4), 458-481.

Thompson, R.A., and Lagattuta, K. (2006). Feeling and understanding: Early emotional development. In K. McCartney and D. Phillips (Eds.), *Handbook of early childhood development* (pp. 317-337). Malden, MA: Blackwell.

Thompson, R.A., and Raikes, A.H. (2007). The social and emotional foundations of school readiness. In R.K. Kaufmann and J. Knitzer (Eds.), *Social and emotional health in early childhood* (pp. 13-35). Baltimore, MD: Brookes.

U.S. Department of Health and Human Services, Administration for Children and Families. (2003a). *Head Start child outcomes framework*. Washington, DC: Author.

U.S. Department of Health and Human Services, Administration for Children and Families. (2003b). Head Start child outcomes—Setting the context for the National Reporting System. *Head Start Bulletin, 76*. Available: http://www.headstartinfo.org/publications/hsbulletin76/cont_76.htm [accessed July 2008].

U.S. Department of Health and Human Services, Administration for Children and Families. (2004). *Early Head Start research: Making a difference in the lives of infants, toddlers, and their families. The impacts of early Head Start, volume 1: Final technical report*. Washington, DC: Author.

U.S. Department of Health and Human Services, Administration for Children and Families. (2005). *Head Start impact study: First year findings*. Washington, DC: Author.

Van Hiele, P.M. (1986). *Structure and insight: A theory of mathematics education*. Orlando, FL: Academic Press.

Vandell, D., Nenide, L., and Van Winkle, S.J. (2006). Peer relationships in early childhood. In K. McCartney and D. Phillips (Eds.), *Handbook of early childhood development* (pp. 455-470). Cambridge, MA: Blackwell.

Vernon-Feagans, L. (1996). *Children's talk in communities and classrooms*. Cambridge, MA: Blackwell.

Wagner, R., Torgesen, J., and Rashotte, C. (1990). *Comprehensive test of phonological processing*. Bloomington, MN: Pearson Assessments.

Wasik, B.A., Bond, M.A., and Hindman, A. (2006). The effects of a language and literacy intervention on Head Start children and teachers. *Journal of Educational Psychology, 98*(1), 63-74.

Wechsler, D. (2003). *The Wechsler Intelligence Scale for Children* (4th ed.). San Antonio, TX: Psychological Corporation.

Weiss, R., Dziura, J., Burgert, T.S., Tamborlane, W.V., Taksali, S.E., Yeckel, C.W., Allen, K., Lopes, M., Savoye, M., Morrison, J., Sherwin, R.S., and Caprio, S. (2004). Obesity and the metabolic syndrome in children and adolescents. *The New England Journal of Medicine, 350*(23), 2362-2374.

Welsh, M.C., Pennington, B.F., and Groisser, D.B. (1991). A normative-developmental study of executive function: A window on prefrontal function in children. *Developmental Neuropsychology, 7*, 131-149.

Whitehurst, G.J., and Lonigan, C.J. (1998). Child development and emergent literacy. *Child Development, 69*, 848-872.

Whitehurst, G.J., Arnold, D.H., Epstein, J.N., Angell, A.L., Smith, M., and Fischel, J.E. (1994). A picture book reading intervention in day care and home for children from low-income families. *Developmental Psychology, 30*, 679-689.

Woodcock, R.W. (1990). Theoretical foundations of the WJ-R measures of cognitive ability. *Journal of Psychoeducational Assessment, 8*(3), 231-258.

Woodcock, R.W., McGrew, K.S., and Mather, N. (2001). *Woodcock-Johnson III (WJ-III) Tests of Cognitive Abilities*. Rolling Meadows, IL: Riverside.

Xu, F., Spelke, E.S., and Goddard, S. (2005). Number sense in human infants. *Developmental Science, 8*(1), 88-101.

Zaslow, M., Halle, T., Martin, L., Cabrera, N., Calkins, J., Pitzer, L., and Margie, N.G. (2006). Child outcome measures in the study of child care quality: Overview and next steps. *Evaluation Review, 30*, 577-610.

## CHAPTER 6

Abbot-Shinn, M., and Sibley, A. (1992). *Assessment profile for early childhood programs: Research version*. Atlanta, GA: Quality Assist.

Abt Associates Inc. (2006). *Observation training manual: OMLIT early childhood*. Cambridge, MA: Author.

Adams, G., Tout, K., and Zaslow, M. (2007). *Early care and education for children in low-income families: Patterns of use, quality, and potential implications*. Washington, DC: The Urban Institute.

Arnett, J. (1989). Caregivers in day-care centers: Does training matter? *Journal of Applied Developmental Psychology, 10*, 541.

Belsky, J., Vandell, D.L., Burchinal, M., Clarke-Stewart, K.A., McCartney, K., Owen, M., and the NICHD Early Child Care Research Network. (2007). Are there long-term effects of early child care? *Child Development, 78*, 681-701.

Bornstein, M.H., and Sawyer, J. (2006). Family systems. In K. McCartney and D. Phillips (Eds.), *Handbook of early childhood development* (pp. 381-398). Malden, MA: Blackwell.

Bradley, R.H., Corwyn, R.F., Burchinal, M., McAdoo, H.P., and Garcia-Coll, C. (2001). The home environments of children in the United States: Part 2, Relations with behavioral development from birth through age 13. *Child Development, 72*, 1868-1886.

Bryant, D. (2007). *Delivering and evaluating the Partnerships for Inclusion model of early childhood professional development in a 5-state collaborative study*. Paper presented at the National Association for the Education of Young Children, November, Chicago, IL.

Bryant, D. (forthcoming). Observational measures of quality in center-based early care and education programs. Submitted to *Child Development Perspectives*.

Bryant, D.M., Burchinal, M.R., Lau, L.B., and Sparling, J.J. (1994). Family and classroom correlates of Head Start children's developmental outcomes. *Early Childhood Research Quarterly, 9*(4), 289-309.

Burchinal, M. (forthcoming). *The measurement of child care quality*. University of California, Irvine.

Burchinal, M., Kainz, K., Cai, K., Tout, K., Zaslow, M., Martinez-Beck, I., and Rathgeb, C. (2008). *Child care quality and child outcomes: Multiple studies analyses*. Paper presented at Developing a Next Wave of Quality Measures for Early Childhood and School-Age Programs: A Working Meeting, January, Washington, DC.

Burchinal, M.R., Peisner-Feinberg, E., Bryant, D.M., and Clifford, R. (2000). Children's social and cognitive development and child care quality: Testing for differential associations related to poverty, gender, or ethnicity. *Applied Developmental Science, 4*, 149-165.

Burchinal, M.R., Roberts, J.E., Riggins, R., Zeisel, S., Neebe, E., and Bryant, M. (2000). Relating quality of center child care to early cognitive and language development longitudinally. *Child Development, 71*, 339-357.

Caldwell, B.M., and Bradley, R.H. (1984). *Home observation for measurement of the environment*. Little Rock: University of Arkansas.

Child Trends. (2007). *Quality in early childhood care and education settings: A compendium of measures*. Washington, DC: Author.

Connell, C.M., and Prinz, R.J. (2002). The impact of childcare and parent-child interactions on school readiness and social skills development for low-income African American children. *Journal of School Psychology, 40*(2), 177-193.

DeTemple, J., and Snow, C.E. (1998). Mother-child interactions related to the emergence of literacy. In C.A. Eldred (Ed.), *Parenting behaviors in a sample of young single mothers in poverty: Results of the New Chance Observational Study* (pp. 114-169). New York: Manpower Demonstration Research.

Dickinson, D.K., Sprague, K., Sayer, A., Miller, C., Clark, N., and Wolf, A. (2000). Classroom factors that foster literacy and social development of children from different language backgrounds. In M. Hopmann (Chair) (Ed.), *Dimensions of program quality that foster child development: Reports from 5 years of the Head Start Quality Research Centers*. Poster presentation at the biannual National Head Start Research Conference, June, Washington, DC.

Dickinson, D.K., Sprague, K., Sayer, A., Miller, C.M., and Clark, N. (2001, April). *A multilevel analysis of the effects of early home and preschool environments on children's language and early literacy development*. Paper presented at the Biennial Conference of the Society for Research in Child Development, April, Minneapolis, MN.

Early, D.M., Bryant, D.M., Pianta, R.C., Clifford, R.M., Burchinal, M.R., Ritchie, S., Howes, C., and Barbarin, O. (2006). Are teachers' education, major, and credentials related to classroom quality and children's academic gains in pre-kindergarten? *Early Childhood Research Quarterly, 21*(2), 174-195.

Egeland, B., and Deinard, A. (1975). *Life stress scale and manual*. Minneapolis: University of Minnesota.

Englund, M.M., Luckner, A.E., Whaley, G., and Egeland, B. (2004). Children's achievement in early elementary school: Longitudinal effects of parental involvement, expectations, and quality of assistance. *Journal of Educational Psychology, 96*, 723-730.

Frosch, C.A., Cox, M.J., and Goldman, B.D. (2001). Infant-parent attachment and parental and child behavior during parent-toddler storybook interaction. *Merrill-Palmer Quarterly, 47*(4), 445-474.

Fuligni, A.S., Han, W.J., and Brooks-Gunn, J. (2004). The Infant-Toddler HOME in the 2nd and 3rd years of life. *Parenting, 4*(2&3), 139-159.

Harms, T., and Clifford, R. (1980). *Early Childhood Environment Rating Scale*. New York: Teachers College Press.

Harms, T., and Clifford, R.M. (1989). *Family Day Care Rating Scale*. New York: Teachers College Press.

Harms, T., Clifford, R., and Cryer, D. (1998). *Early Childhood Environment Rating Scale* (Revised ed.). New York: Teachers College Press.

Harms, T., Cryer, R., and Clifford, R. (1990). *Infant/Toddler Environment Rating Scale*. New York: Teachers College Press.

Helburn, S. (1995). *Cost, quality and child outcomes in child care centers*. Denver: University of Colorado, Department of Economics, Center for Research in Economic and Social Policy.

High/Scope. (2003). *Preschool Program Quality Assessment* (2nd ed.). Ypsilanti, MI: High/Scope Press.

Howes, C. (1997). Children's experiences in center-based child care as a function of teacher background and adult:child ratio. *Merrill-Palmer Quarterly, 43*, 404-425.

Howes, C., Mashburn, A., Pianta, R., Hamre, B., Downer, J., Barbarin, O., Bryant, D., Burchinal, M., and Early, D.M. (2008). Measures of classroom quality in pre-kindergarten and children's development of academic, language and social skills. *Child Development, 79*(3), 732-749.

Howes, C., Phillips, D.A., and Whitebrook, M. (1992). Thresholds of quality: Implications for the social development of children in center-based child care. *Child Development, 53*, 449-460.

Hyson, M., Hirsh-Pasek, K., and Rescorla, L. (1990). The classroom practices inventory: An observation instrument based on NAEYC's guidelines for developmentally appropriate practices for 4- and 5-year-old children. *Early Childhood Research Quarterly, 5*, 475-494.

Kinzie, M.B., Whitaker, S.D., Neesen, K., Kelley, M., Matera, M., and Pianta, R.C. (2006). Innovative web-based professional development for teachers of at-risk preschool children. *Educational Technology & Society, 9*(4), 194-204.

Kontos, S., Howes, C., and Galinsky, E. (1996). Does training make a difference to quality in family child care? *Early Childhood Research Quarterly, 11*(4), 427-445.

Lamb, M. (1998). Nonparental child care: Context, quality, correlates, and consequences. In W. Damon, I.E. Sigel, and K.A. Renninger (Eds.), *Handbook of child psychology* (Vol. 4: Child). London: Wiley.

Lambert, R., Abbott-Shinn, M., and Sibley, A. (2006). Evaluating the quality of early childhood education settings. In B. Spodek and O.N. Saracho (Eds.), *Handbook of research on the education of young children* (2nd ed.). Mahwah, NJ: Lawrence Erlbaum Associates.

McCartney, K. (1984). Effect of quality of day care environment on children's language development. *Developmental Psychology, 20*, 244-260.

McCartney, K., and Phillips, D. (Eds.). (2006). *Handbook of early childhood development*. Malden, MA: Blackwell.

Mitchell, A.W. (2005). *Stair steps to quality: A guide for states and communities developing quality rating systems for early care and education.* Alexandria, VA: United Way Success by Six.

National Association for the Education of Young Children. (2005). *Screening and assessment of young English-language learners: Supplement to the NAEYC and NAECS/SDE joint position statement on early childhood curriculum, assessment, and program evaluation*. Washington, DC: Author.

National Institute for Early Education Research. (2005). *Support for English language learners classroom assessment*. Rutgers, NJ: Author.

National Institute for Early Education Research. (2006). *The state of preschool.* Rutgers, NJ: Author.

National Institute for Early Education Research. (2007). *Preschool classroom mathematics inventory.* Rutgers, NJ: Author.

National Research Council and Institute of Medicine. (2000). *From neurons to neighborhoods: The science of early childhood development.* Committee on Integrating the Science of Early Childhood Development, J.P. Shonkoff and D.A. Phillips (Eds.). Board on Children, Youth, and Families, Commission on Behavioral and Social Sciences and Education. Washington, DC: National Academy Press.

Neuman, S., Dwyer, J., and Koh, S. (2007). *Child/Home Early Language & Literacy Observation Tool (CHELLO)*. Baltimore, MD: Brookes.

NICHD Early Child Care Research Network. (1999). Child care and mother-child interaction in the first three years of life. *Developmental Psychology, 35*, 1399-1413.

NICHD Early Child Care Research Network. (2000). The relation of child care to cognitive and language development. *Child Development, 71*(4), 960-980.

NICHD Early Child Care Research Network. (2002). Early child care and children's development prior to school entry: Results from the NICHD Study of Early Child Care. *American Educational Research Journal, 39*, 133-164.

NICHD Early Child Care Research Network. (2003). Does quality of child care affect child outcomes at age 4½? *Developmental Psychology, 39*, 451-469.

NICHD Early Child Care Research Network. (2005). Duration and developmental timing of poverty and children's cognitive and social development from birth through third grade. *Child Development, 76*(4), 795-810.

NICHD Early Child Care Research Network. (2006). Child care effect sizes for the NICHD Study of Early Child Care and Youth Development. *American Psychologist, 61*(2), 99-116.

Peisner-Feinberg, E.S., and Burchinal, M.R. (1997). Relations between child-care experiences and children's concurrent development: The cost, quality, and outcomes study. *Merrill-Palmer Quarterly, 43*(3), 451-477.

Peisner-Feinberg, E.S., Burchinal, M.R., Clifford, R.M., Culkin, M.L., Howes, C., Kagan, S.L., and Yazejian, N. (2001). The relation of preschool child-care quality to children's cognitive and social developmental trajectories through second grade. *Child Development, 72*(5), 1534-1553.

Phillips, D., McCartney, K., and Scarr, S. (1987). Child care quality and children's social development. *Developmental Psychology, 23*, 537-543.

Phillipsen, L., Burchinal, M., Howes, C., and Cryer, D. (1997). The prediction of process quality from structural features of child care. *Early Childhood Research Quarterly, 12*, 281-304.

Pianta, R.C. (2007). Preschool is school, sometimes: Making early childhood education matter. *Education Next, 7*, 44-49.

Pianta, R.C., and Egeland, B. (1994). Predictors of instability in children's mental test performance at 24, 48, and 96 months. *Intelligence, 18*(2), 145-163.

Pianta, R.C., and Harbers, K.L. (1996). Observing mother and child behavior in a problem-solving situation at school entry: Relations with academic achievement. *Journal of School Psychology, 34*(3), 307-322.

Pianta, R.C., Egeland, B., and Sroufe, L.A. (1990). Maternal stress and children's development: Prediction of school outcomes and identification of protective factors. In J. Rolf, A. Masten, D. Cicchetti, K. Neuchterlein, and S. Weintraub (Eds.), *Risk and protective factors in the development of psychopathology* (pp. 215-235). New York: Cambridge University Press.

Pianta, R.C., La Paro, K.M., and Hamre, B.K. (2007). *Classroom Assessment Scoring System*. Baltimore, MD: Brookes.

Pianta, R.C., Nimetz, S.L., and Bennett, E. (1997). Mother-child relationships, teacher-child relationships, and school outcomes in preschool and kindergarten. *Early Childhood Research Quarterly, 12*(3), 263-280.

RAND Corporation. (2008). *Qualistar Early Learning Quality Rating and Improvement System as a tool for improving child-care quality*. Santa Monica, CA: Author.

Ritchie, S., Howes, C., Kraft-Sayre, M., and Weiser, B. (2001). *Emerging academic snapshot*. Los Angeles: University of California.

Sakai, L., Whitebook, M., Wishard, A., and Howes, C. (2003). Evaluating the Early Childhood Environment Rating Scales (ECERS): Assessing differences between the first and revised edition. *Early Childhood Research Quarterly, 18*, 427-445.

Smith, M., and Dickinson, D. (2002). *User's guide to the early language & literacy classroom observation toolkit*. Available: http://www.brookespublishing.com/store/books/smith-ellco/index.htm [accessed July 2008].

Smith, S., Davidson, S., Weisenfield, G., and Katsaros, S. (in development). *Supports for early literacy assessment*. New York: New York University School of Education Child and Family Policy Center.

Stipek, D., and Byler, P. (2004). The early childhood classroom observation measure. *Early Childhood Research Quarterly, 19*, 375-397.

Sylva, K., Siraj-Blatchford, I., and Taggart, B. (2003). *Assessing quality in the early years: Early Childhood Environment Rating Scale-Extension (ECERS-E): Four curricular subscales.* Stoke-on Trent, Staffordshire, England: Trentham Books.

Sylva, K., Siraj-Blatchford, I., Taggart, B., Sammons, P., Melhuish, E., Elliot, K., and Totsika, V. (2006). Capturing quality in early childhood through environmental rating scales. *Early Childhood Research Quarterly, 21,* 76-92.

Tout, K., Zaslow, M., and Martinez-Beck, I. (forthcoming). Measuring the quality of early care and education programs at the intersection of research, policy, and practice. Submitted to *Child Development Perspectives.*

U.S. Department of Health and Human Services, Administration for Children and Families. (2004). *Early Head Start research: Making a difference in the lives of infants, toddlers, and their families. The impacts of early Head Start, volume 1: Final technical report.* Washington, DC: Author.

U.S. Department of Health and Human Services, Administration for Children and Families. (2005). *Head Start impact study: First year findings.* Washington, DC: Author.

Van Horn, M., and Ramey, S. (2004). A new measure for assessing developmentally appropriate practices in early elementary school, a developmentally appropriate practice template. *Early Childhood Research Quarterly, 19,* 569-587.

Vandell, D. (2004). Early child care: The known and the unknown. *Merrill-Palmer Quarterly, 50,* 387-414.

Vu, J.A., Jeon, H., and Howes, C. (in press). Formal education, credential, or both: Early childhood program classroom practices. Submitted to *Early Education and Development.*

Wasik, B.H., and Bryant, D.M. (2001). *Home visiting: Procedures for helping families* (2nd ed.). Newbury Park, CA: Sage.

Weinfield, N.S., Egeland, B., and Ogawa, J.R. (1998). Affective quality of mother-child interactions. In C.A. Eldred (Ed.), *Parenting behaviors in a sample of young single mothers in poverty: Results of the New Chance Observational Study* (pp. 71-113). New York: Manpower Demonstration Research.

Wesley, P.W. (1994). Providing on-site consultation to promote quality in integrated child care programs. *Journal of Early Intervention, 18*(4), 391-402.

Yoder, P.J., and Warren, S.F. (2001). Relative treatment effects of two prelinguistic communication interventions on language development in toddlers with developmental delays vary by maternal characteristics. *Journal of Speech Language and Hearing Research, 44,* 224-237.

Zaslow, M. (2008). Issues for the learning community from the Head Start Impact Study. *Infants and Young Children, 21*(1), 4-17.

Zaslow, M., Halle, T., Martin, L., Cabrera, N., Calkins, J., Pitzer, L., and Margie, N.G. (2006). Child outcome measures in the study of child care quality: Overview and next steps. *Evaluation Review, 30,* 577-610.

## CHAPTER 7

American Educational Research Association, American Psychological Association, and National Council on Measurement in Education. (1999). *Standards for educational and psychological testing*. Washington, DC: American Educational Research Association.

American Institutes for Research. (2000). *Voluntary national test, cognitive laboratory report, year 2*. Palo Alto, CA: Author.

Bagnato, S.J., Smith-Jones, J., McComb, G., and Cook-Kilroy, J. (2002). *Quality early learning—Key to school success: A first-phase 3-year program evaluation research report for Pittsburgh's Early Childhood Initiative (ECI)*. Pittsburgh, PA: SPECS Program Evaluation Research Team.

Bagnato, S.J., Suen, H., Brickley, D., Jones, J., and Dettore, E. (2002). Child developmental impact of Pittsburgh's Early Childhood Initiative (ECI) in high-risk communities: First-phase authentic evaluation research. *Early Childhood Research Quarterly, 17*(4), 559-589.

Brennan, R.L. (2006). Perspectives on the evolution and future of educational measurement. In R.L. Brennan (Ed.), *Educational measurement* (4th ed., pp. 1-16). Westport, CT: ACE/Praeger.

Buros Institute of Mental Measurements. (2007). *The seventeenth mental measurements yearbook*. Lincoln, NE: Author.

Campbell, D.T., and Stanley, J.C. (1966). *Experimental and quasi-experimental designs for research*. Chicago, IL: Rand McNally.

Child Trends. (2004). *Early childhood measures profiles*. Washington, DC: Author.

Cook, T.D., and Campbell, D.T. (1979). *Quasi-experimentation: Design & analysis issues for field settings*. Boston: Houghton Mifflin.

Cronbach, L.J. (1951). Coefficient alpha and the internal structure of tests. *Psychometrika, 16*(3), 297-334.

Cronbach, L.J. (1971). Test validation. In R.L. Thorndike (Ed.), *Educational measurement* (2nd ed., pp. 443-507). Washington, DC: American Council on Education.

Cronbach, L.J., and Meehl, P.E. (1955). Construct validity in psychological tests. *Psychological Bulletin, 52*, 281-302.

Cureton, E.E. (1951). Validity. In E.F. Lindquist (Ed.), *Educational measurement* (pp. 621-694). Washington, DC: American Council on Education.

Dorans, N.J., and Holland, P.W. (1993). DIF detection and description: Mantel-Haenszel and standardization. In P.W. Holland and H. Wainer (Eds.), *Differential item functioning*. Hillsdale, NJ: Lawrence Erlbaum Associates.

Goldstein, H. (1996). *Assessment: Problems, developments, and statistical issues: A volume of expert contributions*. New York: Wiley.

Gulliksen, H. (1950). *Theory of mental tests*. New York: Wiley.

Holland, P.W., and Wainer, H. (1993). *Differential item functioning*. Hillsdale, NJ: Lawrence Erlbaum Associates.

Huang, X. (2007). *Validity equivalence between the Chinese and English versions of the IEA Child Cognitive Developmental Status Test*. Berkeley: University of California.

Hunter, J.E., and Schmidt, F.L. (1990). Dichotomization of continuous variables: The implications for meta-analysis. *Journal of Applied Psychology, 75*(3), 334-349.

Kane, M.T. (2006). Validation. In R.L. Brennan (Ed.), *Educational measurement* (4th ed., pp. 17-64). Westport, CT: American Council on Education/Praeger.

Koretz, D.M., and Hamilton, L.S. (2006). Testing for accountability in K-12. In R.L. Brennan (Ed.), *Educational measurement* (4th ed., pp. 531-578). Westport, CT: American Council on Education/Praeger.

Kuder, G.F., and Richardson, M.W. (1937). The theory of the estimation of test reliability. *Psychometrika, 2*(3), 151-160.

La Paro, K., and Pianta, R. (2000). Predicting children's competence in the early school years. A meta-analytic review. *Review of Educational Research, 70*(4), 443-484.

Laosa, L.M. (1991). The cultural context of construct validity and the ethics of generalizability. *Early Childhood Research Quarterly, 6*, 313-321.

Longford, N.T., Holland, P.W., and Thayer, D.T. (1993). Stability of the MH D-DIF statistics across populations. In P.W. Holland and H. Wainer (Eds.), *Differential item functioning*. Hillsdale, NJ: Lawrence Erlbaum Associates.

Mathematica Policy Research. (2003). *Resources for measuring services and outcomes in Head Start programs serving infants and toddlers*. Princeton, NJ: Author.

Mathematica Policy Research. (2007). *Measuring children's progress from preschool through third grade*. Princeton, NJ: Author.

Meisels, S. (2007). Accountability in early childhood: No easy answers. In R.C. Pianta, M.J. Cox, and K. Snow (Eds.), *Schools readiness and the transition to kindergarten in the era of accountability* (pp. 31-47). Baltimore, MD: Brookes.

Messick, S. (1989). *Validity*. New York: Macmillan.

Murphy, K.R. (Ed.). (2003). *Validity generalization: A critical review*. Mahwah, NJ: Lawrence Erlbaum Associates.

Murphy, L.L., Spies, R.A., and Plake, B.S. (Eds.). (2006). *Tests in print* (vol. VII). Lincoln: University of Nebraska Press.

National Association for the Education of Young Children and National Association of Early Childhood Specialists in State Departments of Education. (2003). *Early childhood curriculum, assessment, and program evaluation: Building an effective, accountable system in program for children birth through age 8, A position statement*. Washington, DC: Author.

National Research Council. (1989). *Fairness in employment testing: Validity generalization, minority issues, and the General Aptitude Test Battery*. J.A. Hartigan and A.K. Wigdor (Eds.). Board on Mathematical Sciences and Their Applications, Division on Engineering and Physical Sciences. Washington, DC: National Academy Press.

Popham, W.J. (2007). Another bite out of the apple. *Educational Leadership, 64*(6), 83-84.

Shavelson, R.J., and Webb, N.M. (1991). *Generalizability theory: A primer (measurement methods for the social sciences)*. New York: Sage.

Thissen, D., Steinberg, L., and Wainer, H. (1993). Detection of differential item function using the parameters of item response models. In P.W. Holland and H. Wainer (Eds.), *Differential item functioning*. Hillsdale, NJ: Lawrence Erlbaum Associates.

Wilson, M. (2005). *Constructing measures: An item response modeling approach*. Mahwah, NJ: Lawrence Erlbaum Associates.

Wilson, M., and Adams, R.J. (1996). Evaluating progress with alternative assessments: A model for Chapter 1. In M.B. Kane (Ed.), *Implementing performance assessment: Promise, problems and challenges*. Hillsdale, NJ: Lawrence Erlbaum Associates.

Zhou, Z., and Boehm, A.E. (1999). *Chinese and American children's knowledge of basic relational concepts*. Paper presented at the biennial meeting of the Society for Research in Child Development, April, Albuquerque, NM.

## CHAPTER 8

Abedi, J., Hofstetter, C.H., and Lord, C. (2004). Assessment accommodations for English-language learners: Implications for policy-based empirical research. *Review of Educational Research, 74*(1), 1-28.

Abedi, J., Lord, C., Hofstetter, C., and Baker, E. (2000). Impact of accommodation strategies on English language learners' test performance. *Educational Measurement: Issues and Practice, 19*(3), 16-26.

American Educational Research Association, American Psychological Association, and National Council on Measurement in Education. (1999). *Standards for educational and psychological testing*. Washington, DC: Author.

August, D., and Shanahan, T. (Eds.). (2006). *Developing literacy in second-language learners: Report of the National Literacy Panel on language-minority children and youth*. Mahwah, NJ: Lawrence Erlbaum Associates.

Bagnato, S.J. (2007). *Authentic assessment for early childhood intervention: Best practices*. New York: Guilford Press.

Bagnato, S.J., and Neisworth, J. (1995). A national study of the social and treatment "invalidity" of intelligence testing in early intervention. *School Psychologist Quarterly, 9*(2), 81-102.

Bagnato, S.J., and Yeh-Ho, H. (2006). High-stakes testing with preschool children: Violation of professional standards for evidence-based practice in early childhood intervention. *KEDI International Journal of Educational Policy, 3*(1), 23-43.

Bagnato, S.J., Macey, M., Salaway, J., and Lehman, C. (2007a). *Research foundations for authentic assessments to ensure accurate and representative early intervention eligibility*. Washington, DC: U.S. Department of Education, Office of Special Education Programs, TRACE Center for Excellence.

Bagnato, S.J., Macey, M., Salaway, J., and Lehman, C. (2007b). *Research foundations for conventional tests and testing to ensure accurate and representative early intervention eligibility*. Washington, DC: U.S. Department of Education, Office of Special Education Programs, TRACE Center for Excellence.

Bagnato, S.J., McKeating-Esterle, E., and Bartolomasi, P. (2007). *Evidence-base for team assessment practices in early intervention*. Washington, DC: U.S. Department of Education, Office of Special Education Programs, TRACE Center for Excellence.

Bailey, D. (2004). Tests and test development. In M. McLean, M. Wolery, and D.B. Bailey, Jr. (Eds.), *Assessing infants and preschoolers with special needs* (3rd ed., pp. 22-44). Upper Saddle River, NJ: Pearson.

Bailey, D.B., and Wolery, M. (1984). *Teaching infants and preschoolers with handicaps*. Columbus, OH: Merrill.

Bainter, T.R., and Tollefson, N. (2003). Intellectual assessment of language minority students: What do school psychologists believe are acceptable practices? *Psychology in the Schools, 40*(6), 899-903.

Barnett, D.W., Elliott, N., Wolsing, L., Bunger, C.E., Haski, H., McKissick, C., and Vander Meer, C.D. (2006). Response to intervention for young children with extremely challenging behaviors: What it might look like. *School Psychology Review, 35*(4), 568-582.

Boone, H.A., and Crais, E. (2002). Strategies for achieving family-driven assessment and intervention planning. In M.M. Ostrosky and E. Horn (Eds.), *Assessment: Gathering meaningful information* (Vol. Monograph Series No. 4, pp. 1-14). Missoula, MT: Division for Early Childhood.

Borghese, P., and Gronau, R.C. (2005). Convergent and discriminant validity of the universal nonverbal intelligence test with limited English proficient Mexican-American elementary students. *Journal of Psychoeducational Assessment, 23*, 128-139.

Botts, D.C., Losard, A., and Notari-Syverson, A. (2007). Alternative assessment: The pathway to indivualized instruction for young children. *Young Exceptional Children Monograph Series, 9*, 71-85.

Bracken, B., and McCallum, R.S. (1998). *The universal nonverbal intelligence test*. Chicago, IL: Riverside.

Bricker, D., Pretti-Froniczak, K., and McComas, N. (1998). *An activity-based approach to early intervention* (2nd ed.). Baltimore, MD: Brookes.

Brooks-Gunn, J., Klebanov, P.K., Smith, J., Duncan, G.J., and Lee, K. (2003). The black-white test score gap in young children: Contributions of test and family characteristics. *Applied Developmental Science, 7*(4), 239-252.

Brown, R.T., Reynolds, C.R., and Whitaker, J.S. (1999). Bias in mental testing since "Bias in Mental Testing." *School Psychology Quarterly, 14*(3), 208-238.

Capps, R., Fix, M., Murray, J., Ost, J., Passel, J.S., and Herwantoro, S. (2005). *The new demography of America's schools: Immigration and the No Child Left Behind Act*. Washington, DC: The Urban Institute.

Carta, J.J., and Kong, N.K. (2007). Trends and issues in intervention for preschoolers with developmental disabilities. In S.L. Odom, R.H. Horner, M.E. Snell, and J. Blacher (Eds.), *Handbook of developmental disabilities* (pp. 181-198). New York: Guilford Press.

Carta, J.J., Greenwood, C.R., Walker, D., Kaminski, R., Good, R., McConnell, S., and McEvoy, M. (2002). Individual growth and development indicators (IGDIs): Assessment that guides intervention for young children. *Young Exceptional Children Monograph Series, 4,* 15-28.

Carter, A.S., Briggs-Gowan, M.J., and Ornstein Davis, N. (2004). Assessment of young children's social-emotional development and psychopathology: Recent advances and recommendations for practice. *Journal of Child Psychology and Psychiatry, 45*(1), 109-134.

Castenell, L.A., and Castenell, M.E. (1988). Testing the test: Norm-referenced testing and low-income blacks. *Journal of Counseling and Development, 67,* 205-206.

Center for Universal Design. (1997). *The principles of universal design.* Available: http://www.design.ncsu.edu/cud/about_ud/udprinciplestext.htm [accessed December 2007].

Chachkin, N.J. (1989). Testing in elementary and secondary schools: Can miscue be avoided? In B. Gifford (Ed.), *Test policy and the politics of opportunity allocation: The workplace and the law* (pp. 163-187). Boston: Kluwer Academic.

Child Trends. (2004). *Early childhood measures profiles.* Washington, DC: Author.

Cho, S., Hudley, C., and Back, H.J. (2002). Cultural influences on ratings of self-perceived social, emotional, and academic adjustment for Korean American adolescents. *Assessment for Effective Intervention; Special Issue: Assessment of Culturally-Linguistically Diverse Learners, 29*(1), 3-14.

Christenson, S.L. (2004). The family-school partnership: An opportunity to promote learning and competence of all students. *School Psychology Review, 33*(1), 83-104.

Coleman, M.R., Buysse, V., and Neitzel, J. (2006). *Recognition and response: An early intervening system for children at-risk for learning disabilities.* Chapel Hill: University of North Carolina, FPG Child Development Institute.

Cook, T.D., and Campbell, D.T. (1979). *Quasi-experimentation: Design & analysis issues for field settings.* Boston: Houghton Mifflin.

Coutinho, M.J., and Oswald, D.P. (2000). Disproportionate representation in special education: A synthesis and recommendations. *Journal of Child and Family Studies, 9,* 135-156.

Crocker, L., and Algina, J. (1986). *Introduction to classical and modern test theory.* New York: Holt, Rinehart and Winston.

De Avila, E., and Duncan, S. (1990). *Language Assessment Scales—Oral.* Monterey, CA: CTB McGraw-Hill.

Deno, S. (1985). Curriculum-based measurement: The emerging alternative. *Exceptional Children, 52,* 219-232.

Deno, S. (1997). Whether thou goest . . . Perspectives on progress monitoring. In J.W. Lloyd, E.J. Kameenui, and D. Chard (Eds.), *Issues in educating students with disabilities* (pp. 77-99). Mahwah, NJ: Lawrence Erlbaum Associates.

Division for Early Childhood. (2007). *Promoting positive outcomes for children with disabilities: Recommendations for curriculum, assessment, and program evaluation.* Missoula, MT: Author.

Duncan, S.E., and De Avila, E. (1988). *Language Assessment Scales—Reading and Writing*. Monterey, CA: CTB McGraw-Hill.

Duncan, S.E., and De Avila, E. (1998). *Pre-Language Assessment Scale 2000*. Monterey, CA: CTB McGraw-Hill.

Dunn, L.M., and Dunn, D.M. (2007). *Peabody Picture Vocabulary Test* (4th ed.). Upper Saddle River, NJ: Pearson Assessments.

Dunn, L.M., Padilla, E.R., Lugo, D.E., and Dunn, L.M. (1986). *Test de Vocabulario en Imágenes Peabody*. Circle Pines, MN: American Guidance Service.

Dunst, C., and Hanby, D.W. (2004). States' Part C eligibility definitions account for differences in the percentage of children participating in early intervention programs, *Snapshots, 1*, 1-5.

Espinosa, L. (2007). *A review of the literature on assessment issues for young English language learners.* Unpublished paper commissioned by the Committee on Developmental Outcomes and Assessments for Young Children, The National Academies, Washington, DC.

Fagundes, D.D., Haynes, W.O., Haak, N.J., and Moran, M.J. (1998). Task variability effects on the language test performance of southern lower socioeconomic class African American and Caucasian five-year-olds. *Language, Speech, and Hearing Services in Schools, 29*, 148-157.

Fewell, R. (2000). Assessment of young children with special needs: Foundations for tomorrow. *Topics in Early Childhood Special Education, 20*(1), 38-42.

Figueroa, R.A., and Hernandez, S. (2000). *Testing Hispanic students in the United States: Technical and policy issues.* Washington, DC: President's Advisory Commission on Educational Excellence for Hispanic Americans.

Fives, C.J., and Flanagan, R. (2002). A review of the Universal Nonverbal Intelligence Test (UNIT): An advance for evaluating youngsters with diverse needs. *School Psychology International, 23*(4), 425-448.

Fuchs, D., and Fuchs, L.S. (1986). Test procedure bias: A meta-analysis of examiner familiarity effect. *Review of Educational Research, 56*(2), 243-262.

Fuchs, D., Fuchs, L.S., Benowitz, S., and Barringer, K. (1987). Norm-referenced tests: Are they valid for use with handicapped students? *Exceptional Children, 54*(3), 263-271.

Fuchs, L.S. (2004). The past, present, and future of curriculum-based measurement research. *School Psychology Review, 33*(2), 188-192.

Gallimore, R., Goldenberg, C., and Weisner, T. (1993). The social construction and subjective reality of activity settings: Implications for community psychology. *American Journal of Community Psychology, 21*, 537-559.

García, E.E. (2005). *Teaching and learning in two languages: Bilingualism and schooling in the United States.* New York: Teachers College Press.

Garcia, G.E., and Pearson, P.D. (1994). Assessment and diversity. *Review of Research in Education, 20*, 337-391.

Garcia, G.E., McKoon, G., and August, D. (2006). Synthesis: Language and literacy assessment. In D. August and T. Shanahan (Eds.), *Developing literacy in second language learners.* Mahwah, NJ: Lawrence Erlbaum Associates.

Garcia, G.E., Stephens, D.L., Koenke, K.R., Pearson, P.D., Harris, V.J., and Jimenez, R.T. (1989). *A study of classroom practices related to the reading of low-achieving students: Phase one (Study 2.2.3.5).* Urbana: University of Illinois, Reading Research and Education Center.

Genesee, F., Geva, E., Dressler, C., and Kamil, M. (2006). Synthesis: Cross-linguistic relationships. In D. August and T. Shanahan (Eds.), *Report of the National Literacy Panel on Language Minority Youth and Children.* Mahwah, NJ: Lawrence Erlbaum Associates.

Gipps, C. (1999). Socio-cultural aspects of assessment. *Review of Research in Education, 24,* 355-392.

Goldenberg, C., Rueda, R., and August, D. (2006). Synthesis: Sociocultural contexts and literacy development. In D. August and T. Shanahan (Eds.), *Report of the National Literacy Panel on Language Minority Youth and Children.* Mahwah, NJ: Lawrence Erlbaum Associates.

Gopaul-McNicol, S., and Armour-Thomas, S.A. (2002). *Assessment and culture.* New York: Academic Press.

Graziano, W.G., Varca, P.E., and Levy, J.C. (1982). Race of examiner effects and the validity of intelligence tests. *Review of Educational Research, 52*(4), 469-497.

Green, R.L. (1980). Critical issues in testing and achievement of black Americans. *Journal of Negro Education, 49*(3), 238-252.

Greenspan, S.I., and Meisels, S.J. (1996). Toward a new vision for the developmental assessment of infants and young children. In S.J. Meisels and E. Fenichel (Eds.), *New visions for the developmental assessment of infants and young children* (pp. 11-26). Washington, DC: Zero to Three.

Gutiérrez-Clellen, V.F. (1999). Language choice in intervention with bilingual children. *American Journal of Speech-Language Pathology, 8,* 291-302.

Gutiérrez-Clellen, V.F., and Kreiter, J. (2003. Understanding child bilingual acquisition using parent and teacher reports. *Applied Psycholinguistics, 24,* 267-288.

Hagie, M.U., Gallipo, P.G., and Svien, L. (2003). Traditional culture versus traditional assessment for American Indian students: An investigation of potential test item bias. *Assessment for Effective Intervention, 23*(1), 15-25.

Hall, C.C.I. (1997). Cultural malpractice: The growing obsolescence of psychology with the changing U.S. population. *American Psychologist, 52*(6), 624-651.

Harbin, G., Rous, B., and McLean, M. (2005). Issues in designing state accountability systems. *Journal of Early Intervention, 27*(3), 137-164.

Harry, B., and Klingler, J. (2006). *Why are so many minority students in special education? Understanding race and disability in schools.* New York: Teachers College Press.

Hatton, D.D., Bailey, D.B., Burchinal, M.R., and Ferrell, K.A. (1997). Developmental growth curves of preschool children with vision impairments. *Child Development, 68*(5), 788-806.

Hebbeler, K., and Spiker, D. (2003). Initiatives on children with special needs. In J. Brooks-Gunn, A.S. Fuligni, and L.J. Berlin (Eds.), *Early child development in the 21st century: Profiles of current research initiatives.* New York: Teachers College Press.

Hebbeler, K., Barton, L., and Mallik, S. (2008). Assessment and accountability for program serving young children with disabilties. *Exceptionality*, 16(1), 48-63.

Hebbeler, K., Spiker, D., Bailey, D., Scarbourgh, A., Mallik, S., Simeonsson, R., Singer, M., and Nelson, L. (2007). *Early intervention for infants and toddlers with disabilities and their families: Participants, services, and outcomes*. Menlo Park, CA: SRI International. Available: http://www.sri.com/neils/pdfs/NEILS_Report_02_07_Final2.pdf [accessed July 2008].

Helms, J.E. (1992). Why is there no study of cultural equivalence in standardized cognitive ability testing? *American Psychologist, 49*(9), 1083-1101.

Hemmeter, M.L., Ostrosky, M., and Fox, L. (2006). Social and emotional foundations for early interventions: A conceptual model for intervention. *School Psychology Review, 35*(4), 583-601.

Hernandez, D. (2006). *Young Hispanic children in the U.S.: A demographic portrait based on Census 2000*. Tempe: Arizona State University.

Hilliard, A.G. (1976). *Alternatives to I.Q. testing: An approach to the identification of gifted minority students*. Sacramento: California State Department of Education.

Hilliard, A.G. (1979). Standardization and cultural bias impediments to the scientific study and validation of intelligence. *Journal of Research and Development in Education, 12*(2), 47-58.

Hilliard, A.G. (1991). *Testing African American students*. Morristown, NJ: Aaron Press.

Hilliard, A.G. (1994). What good is this thing called intelligence and why bother to measure it? *Journal of Black Psychology, 20*(4), 430-443.

Hilliard, A.G. (2004). Intelligence: What good is it and why bother to measure it? In R. Jones (Ed.), *Black psychology*. Hampton, VA: Cobb and Henry.

Hiner, N.R. (1989). The new history of children and the family and its implications for educational research. In W.J. Weston (Ed.), *Education and the American family*. New York: New York University Press.

Laing, S.P., and Kamhi, A. (2003). Alternative assessment of language and literacy in culturally and linguistically diverse populations. *Language, Speech, and Hearing Services in Schools, 34*(1), 44-55.

Losardo, A., and Notari-Syverson, A. (2001). *Alternative approaches to assessing young children*. Baltimore, MD: Brookes.

Macy, M., Bricker, D.D., and Squires, J.K. (2005). Validity and reliability of a curriculum-based assessment approach to determine eligibility for Part C services. *Journal of Early Intervention, 28*(1), 1-16.

Madhere, S. (1998). Cultural diversity, pedagogy, and assessment strategies. *The Journal of Negro Education, 67*(3), 280-295.

Markowitz, J., Carlson, E., Frey, W., Riley, J., Shimshak, A., Heinzen, H., Strohl, J., Klein, S., Hyunshik, L., and Rosenquist, C. (2006). *Preschoolers with disabilities: Characteristics, services, and results: Wave 1 overview report from the Pre-Elementary Education Longitudinal Study (PEELS)*. Rockville, MD: Westat. Available: https://www.peels.org/Docs/PEELS%20Final%20Wave%201%20Overview%20Report.pdf [accessed July 2008].

McCardle, P., Mele-McCarthy, J., and Leos, K. (2005). English language learners and learning disabilities: Research agenda and implications for practice. *Learning Disabilities Research and Practice, 20*(1), 69-78.

McConnell, S.R. (2000). Assessment in early intervention and early childhood special education: Building on the past to project into the future. *Topics in Early Childhood Special Education, 20*, 43-48.

McCormick, L., and Noonan, M.J. (2002). Ecological assessment and planning. In M.M. Ostrosky and E. Horn (Eds.), *Assessment: Gathering meaningful information* (pp. 47-60). Missoula, MT: Division for Early Childhood.

McCune, L., Kalmanson, B., Fleck, M.B., Glazewski, B., and Sillari, J. (1990). An interdisciplinary model of infant assessment. In S.J. Meisels and J.P. Shonkoff (Eds.), *Handbook of early childhood intervention* (pp. 219-245). New York: Cambridge University Press.

McLean, L., and Cripe, J.W. (1997). The effectiveness of early intervention for children with communication disorders. In M. Guralnick (Ed.), *The effectiveness of early intervention* (pp. 329-428). Baltimore, MD: Brookes.

McLean, M. (2004). Assessment and its importance in early intervention/early childhood special education. In M. McLean, M. Wolery, and D.B. Bailey, Jr. (Eds.), *Assessing infants and preschoolers with special needs* (3rd ed., pp. 1-21). Upper Saddle River, NJ: Pearson Assessments.

McLean, M. (2005). Using curriculum-based assessment to determine eligibility: Time for a paradigm shift. *Journal of Early Intervention, 28*(1), 23-27.

McWilliam, R.A. (2004). DEC recommended practices: Interdisciplinary models. In S. Sandall, M.L. Hemmeter, B.J. Smith, and M.E. McLean (Eds.), *DEC recommended practices: A comprehensive guide for practical application in early intervention/early childhood special education* (pp. 127-131). Longmont, CO: Sopris West.

Meisels, S.J., and Atkins-Burnett, S. (2000). The elements of early childhood assessment. In J.P. Shonkoff and S.J. Meisels (Eds.), *Handbook of early childhood intervention* (2nd ed., pp. 231-257). New York: Cambridge University Press.

Meisels, S., and Provence, S. (1989). *Screening and assessment: Guidelines for identifying young disabled and developmentally vulnerable children and their families*. Washington, DC: National Early Childhood Technical Assistance System/National Center for Clinical Infant Programs.

National Association for the Education of Young Children. (2005). *Screening and assessment of young English-language learners: Supplement to the NAEYC and NAECS/SDE joint position statement on early childhood curriculum, assessment, and program evaluation*. Washington, DC: Author.

National Association for the Education of Young Children and National Association of Early Childhood Specialists in State Departments of Education. (2003). *Early childhood curriculum, assessment, and program evaluation: Building an effective, accountable system in programs for children birth through age 8. A position statement*. Washington, DC: National Association for the Education of Young Children.

National Association of School Psychologists. (2000). *Professional conduct manual*. Bethesda, MD: Author.

National Association of School Psychologists. (2005). *Position statement on early childhood assessment*. Bethesda, MD: Author.

National Association of Test Directors. (2004). *The achievement gap: Test bias or school structures?* Paper presented at the National Council on Measurement in Education, San Diego.

National Child Care Information Center. (2005). *Federal and state funding for early child care and education.* Fairfax, VA: Author.

National Clearinghouse for English Language Acquisition. (2006). *The growing numbers of limited English proficient students: 1993/94-2003/04*. Washington, DC: Office of English Language Acquisition, U.S. Department of Education.

National Early Childhood Accountability Task Force. (2007). *Taking stock: Assessing and improving early childhood learning and program quality*. Philadelphia: Author.

National Research Council. (1997). *Educating one and all: Students with disabilities and standards-based reform.* Committee on Goals 2000 and the Inclusion of Students with Disabilities, L.M. McDonnell and P. Morison (Eds.). Board on Testing and Assessment, Center for Education, Commission on Behavioral and Social Sciences and Education. Washington, DC: National Academy Press.

National Research Council. (2000). *Testing English language learners in U.S. schools: Report and workshop summary*. Committee on Educational Excellence and Testing Equity, K. Hakuta and A. Beatty (Eds.). Board on Testing and Assessment, Center for Education, Division of Behavioral and Social Sciences and Education. Washington, DC: National Academy Press.

Neisworth, J.T., and Bagnato, S.J. (2004). The mismeasure of young children. *Infants and Young Children, 17*(3), 198-212.

Neisworth, J., and Bagnato, S. (2005). DEC Recommended practices: Assessment. In S. Sandall, M.L. Hemmeter, B.J. Smith, and M. McLean (Eds.), *DEC recommended practices. A comprehensive guide for practical application in early intervention/early childhood special education* (pp. 45-70). Longmont, CO: Sopris West.

Notari-Syverson, A., Losardo, A., and Lim, Y.S. (2003). Assessment of young children from culturally diverse backgrounds: A journey in progress. *Assessment for Effective Intervention, 29*(1), 39-51.

Ochoa, S.H., Galarza, S., and Amado, A. (1996). An investigation of school psychologists' assessment practices of language proficiency with bilingual and limited-English-proficient students. *Diagnostique, 21*(4), 17-36.

Ochoa, S.H., Gonzalez, D., Galarza, A., and Guillemard, L. (1996). The training and use of interpreters in bilingual psychoeducational assessment: An alternative in need of study. *Diagnostique, 21*(3), 19-40.

Ogbu, J.U. (1981). Origins of human competence: A cultural-ecological perspective. *Child Development, 52*, 413-429.

Ogbu, J.U. (2004). Collective identity and the burden of "acting white" in black history, community, and education. *Urban Review, 36*(1), 1-35.

Paredes Scribner, A. (2002). Best assessment and intervention practices with second language learners. In A.T.J. Grimes (Ed.), *Best practices in school psychology IV*. Bethesda, MD: National Association of School Psychologists.

Pretti-Frontczak, K., Jackson, S., Gross, S.M., Grisham-Brown, J., Horn, E., and Harjusola-Webb, S. (2007). A curriculum framework that supports quality early education for all children. In E.M. Horn, C. Peterson, and L. Fox (Eds.), *Linking curriculum to child and family outcomes* (pp. 16-28). Missoula, MT: Division for Early Childhood.

Qi, C.H., Kaiser, A.P., Milan, S.E., Yzquierdo, Z., and Hancock, T.B. (2003). The performance of low-income African American children on the Preschool Language Scale-3. *Journal of Speech, Language, and Hearing Research, 46*, 576-590.

Rebell, M.A. (1989). Testing, public policy, and the courts. In B. Gifford (Ed.), *Test policy and the politics of opportunity allocation: The workplace and the law*. Boston: Kluwer Academic.

Reynolds, C.R. (1982). Methods for detecting construct and prediction bias. In R.A. Berk (Ed.), *Handbook of methods for detecting test bias* (pp. 199-259). Baltimore, MD: Johns Hopkins University Press.

Reynolds, C.R. (1983). Test bias: In God we trust; all others must have data. *Journal of Special Education, 17*(3), 241-260.

Reynolds, C.R., and Kamphaus, R.W. (2003). *Behavior assessment system for children* (2nd ed.). Minneapolis, MN: Pearson.

Reynolds, C.R., Lowe, P.A., and Saenz, A.L. (1999). The problem of bias in psychological assessment. In C.R. Reynolds and T.B. Gutkin (Eds.), *Handbook of school psychology* (3rd ed., pp. 549-595). New York: Wiley.

Rhodes, R., Ochoa, S.H., and Ortiz, S. (2005). *Assessing culturally and linguistically diverse students: A practical guide*. New York: Guilford Press.

Rock, D.A., and Stenner, A.J. (2005). Assessment issues in the testing of children at school entry. *The Future of Children, 15*(1), 15-34.

Rodrigue, J.R., Morgan, S.B., and Geffken, G.R. (1991). A comparative evaluation of adaptive behavior in children and adolescents with autism, Down syndrome, and normal development. *Journal of Autism and Developmental Disorders, 21*(2), 187-196.

Rueda, R. (2007). *Motivation, learning, and assessment of English learners*. Paper presented at the School of Education, California State University, Northridge.

Rueda, R., and Yaden, D. (2006). The literacy education of linguistically and culturally diverse young children: An overview of outcomes, assessment, and large-scale interventions. In B. Spodek and O.N. Saracho (Eds.), *Handbook of research on the education of young children* (2nd ed., pp. 167-186). Mahwah, NJ: Lawrence Erlbaum Associates.

Rueda, R., MacGillivray, L., Monzó, L., and Arzubiaga, A. (2001). Engaged reading: A multi-level approach to considering sociocultural features with diverse learners. In D. McInerny and S.V. Etten (Eds.), *Research on sociocultural influences on motivation and learning* (pp. 233-264). Greenwich, CT: Information Age.

Santos, R.M., Lee, S., Valdivia, R., and Zhang, C. (2001). Translating translations: Selecting and using translated early childhood materials. *Teaching Exceptional Children, 34*(2), 26-31.

Scarborough, A.A., Hebbeler, K.M., and Spiker, D. (2006). Eligibility characteristics of infants and toddlers entering early intervention in the United States. *Journal of Policy and Practice in Intellectual Disabilities, 3*(1), 57-64.

Seymour, H.N., Roeper, T.W., de Villiers, J., and de Villiers, P.A. (2003). *Diagnostic evaluation of language variation*. San Antonio, TX: Pearson Assessments.

Shackelford, J. (2006). State and jurisdictional eligibility definitions for infants and toddlers with disabilities under IDEA. *NECTAC Notes, 21*, 1-16.

Sharma, S. (1986). Assessment strategies for minority groups. *Journal of Black Studies, 17*(1), 111-124.

Skiba, R.J., Knesting, K., and Bush, L.D. (2002). Culturally competent assessment: More than nonbiased tests. *Journal of Child and Family Studies, 11*(1), 61-78.

Slaughter-Defoe, D.T. (1995). Revisiting the concept of socialization: Caregiving and teaching in the 90s, a personal perspective. *American Psychologist, 50*(4), 276-286.

Snyder, P., Lawson, S., Thompson, B., Stricklin, S., and Sexton, D. (1993). Evaluating the psychometric integrity of instruments used in early intervention research: The Battelle Developmental Inventory. *Topics in Early Childhood Special Education, 13*(2), 216-232.

Spiker, D., and Hopmann, M. (1997). The effectiveness of early intervention for children with Down syndrome. In M. Guralnick (Ed.), *The effectiveness of early intervention* (pp. 271-306). Baltimore, MD: Brookes.

Stockman, I.J. (2000). The new Peabody Picture Vocabulary Test-III: An illusion of unbiased assessment? *Language, Speech, and Hearing Services in Schools, 31*(4), 340-353.

Suen, H.K., Logan, C.R., Neisworth, J.T., and Bagnato, S. (1995). Parent-professional congruence: Is it necessary? *Journal of Early Intervention, 19*(3), 243-252.

Suen, H.K., Lu, C.H., Neisworth, J.T., and Bagnato, S.J. (1993). Measurement of team decision making through generalizability theory. *Journal of Psychoeducational Assessment, 11*, 120-132.

Thompson, S., and Thurlow, M. (2002). *Universally designed assessments: Better tests for everyone!* Minneapolis: University of Minnesota, National Center on Educational Outcomes.

Thompson, S.J., Johnstone, C.J., and Thurlow, M.L. (2002). *Universal design applied to large-scale assessment.* Minneapolis: University of Minnesota, National Center on Educational Outcomes.

U.S. Department of Education. (2008). *Biennial report to Congress on the implementation of the Title II state formula grant program, school years 2004-2006.* Washington, DC: Author.

Valencia, R.R., and Suzuki, L.A. (2001). *Intelligence testing and minority students: Foundations, performance factors, and assessment issues*. Thousand Oaks, CA: Sage.

VanDerHayden, A.M., and Snyder, P. (2006). Integrating frameworks from early childhood intervention and school psychology to accelerate growth for all children. *School Psychology Review, 35*(4), 519-534.

Washington, J.A., and Craig, H.K. (1992). Performances of low-income, African American preschool and kindergarten children on the Peabody Picture Vocabulary Test-Revised. *Language, Speech, and Hearing Services in Schools, 23,* 329-333.

Wechsler, D. (2003). *The Wechsler Intelligence Scale for Children* (4th ed.). San Antonio, TX: Psychological Corporation.

Wechsler, D. (2004). *The Wechsler Intelligence Scale for Children—Spanish* (4th ed.). San Antonio, TX: Psychological Corporation.

Weisner, T.S. (1984). A cross-cultural perspective: Ecocultural niches of middle childhood. In A. Collins (Ed.), *The elementary school years: Understanding development during middle childhood.* Washington, DC: National Academy Press.

Weisner, T.S. (1998). Human development, child well-being, and the cultural project of development. In D. Sharma and K. Fischer (Eds.), *Socio-emotional development across cultures. New directions in child development, 81,* 69-85. San Francisco, CA: Jossey-Bass.

Wolery, M. (1989). Using assessment information to plan instructional programs. In D. Bailey and M. Wolery (Eds.), *Assessing infants and toddlers with handicaps* (pp. 478-495). Englewood Cliffs, NJ: Merrill/Prentice Hall.

Wolery, M. (2003). Using assessment information to plan intervention programs. In M. McLean, M. Wolery, and D.B. Bailey (Eds.), *Assessing infants and preschoolers with special needs.* Upper Saddle River, NJ: Prentice Hall.

Wolraich, M.L., Gurwitch, R.H., Bruder, M.B., and Knight, L.A. (2005). The role of comprehensive interdisciplinary assessments in the early intervention system. In M.J. Guralnick (Ed.), *The developmental systems approach to early intervention* (pp. 133-150). Baltimore, MD: Brookes.

Woodcock, R.W., and Johnson, M.B. (1989). *Woodcock-Johnson–Revised Tests of Cognitive Abilities.* Itasca, IL: Riverside.

Woodcock, R.W., McGrew, K.S., and Mather, N. (2001). *Woodcock-Johnson III (WJ-III) Tests of Cognitive Abilities.* Rolling Meadows, IL: Riverside.

Woods, J., and McCormick, K. (2002). Toward an integration of child- and family-centered practices in the assessment of preschool children: Welcoming the family. *Young Exceptional Children, 5*(3), 2-11.

World Health Organization. (2007). *The international classification of functioning, disability and health—Children and youth version, ICF-CY.* Geneva: Author.

Ysseldyke, J.E., Thurlow, M.L., Kozleski, E., and Reschly, D. (1998). *Accountability for the results of educating students with disabilities: Assessment conference report on the new assessment provisions of the 1997 amendments to the Individuals with Disabilities Education Act.* Available: http://education.umn.edu/NCEO/OnlinePubs/awgfinal.html [accessed January 2008].

Yzquierdo, Z., Blalock, G., and Torres-Velasquez, D. (2004). Language-appropriate assessments for determining eligibility of English language learners for special education services. *Assessment for Effective Intervention, 29*(2), 17-30.

Zimmerman, I.L., Steiner, V.G., and Pond, R.E. (2002). *Preschool Language Scale* (4th ed.). San Antonio, TX: Harcourt Assessment.

## CHAPTER 9


Duncan, S.E., and De Avila, E. (1998). *Pre-Language Assessment Scale 2000.* Monterey, CA: CTB McGraw-Hill.

Espinosa, L. (2005). Curriculum and assessment considerations for young children from culturally, linguistically, and economically diverse backgrounds. *Special Issue, Psychology in the Schools, 42*(8), 837-853.

Kim, H., Baydar, N., and Greek, A. (2003). Testing conditions influence the race gap in cognition and achievement by household survey data. *Applied Developmental Psychology, 23*, 16.

Mathematica Policy Research. (2006). *Implementation of the Head Start National Reporting System: Spring 2005 update.* Princeton, NJ: Author.

Mathematica Policy Research. (2007). *Language routing protocol developed for the First Five LA Universal Preschool Child Outcomes Study, 2007-2008.* Princeton, NJ: Author.

Mathematica Policy Research. (2008). *Introduction to conducting assessments as part of survey projects: Presentation for staff development trainings.* Princeton, NJ: Author.

Maxwell, K.L., and Clifford, R.M. (2004). School readiness assessment. *Young Children: Journal of the National Association for the Education of Young Children, January*, 10. Available: http://journal.naeyc.org/btj/200401/Maxwell.pdf [accessed February 2008].

Meisels, S.J., and Atkins-Burnett, S. (2006). Evaluating early childhood assessments: A differential analysis. In K. McCarney and D. Phillips (Eds.), *Handbook of early childhood development* (pp. 533-549). Cambridge, MA: Blackwell.

Rowand, C., Sprachman, S., Wallace, I., Rhodes, H., and Avellar, H. (2005). *Factors contributing to assessment burden in preschoolers.* Paper presented at the American Association for Public Opinion Research, May, Miami, FL. Available: http://www.allacademic.com/meta/p_mla_apa_research_citation/0/1/6/7/2/p16722_index.html [accessed July 2008].

Shepard, L., Kagan, S.L., and Wurtz, L. (1998). *Principles and recommendations for early childhood assessments.* Goal 1 Early Childhood Assessments Resource Group. Washington, DC: National Education Goals Panel.

Snow, K.L. (2006). Measuring school readiness: Conceptual and practical considerations. *Early Education and Development, 17*(1), 7-41.

Spier, E.T., Sprachman, S., and Rowand, C. (2004). *Implementing large-scale studies of children using clinical assessments.* Paper presented at the Children and the Mediterranean Conference, January, Genoa, Italy.

Sprachman, S., Atkins-Burnett, S., Glazerman, S., Avellar, S., and Loewenberg, M. (2007). *Minimizing assessment burden on preschool children: Balancing burden and reliability.* Paper presented at the Joint Statistical Meetings, September, Salt Lake City, UT.

## CHAPTER 10

American Educational Research Association, American Psychological Association, and National Council on Measurement in Education. (1999). *Standards for educational and psychological testing*. Washington, DC: American Educational Research Association.

Baker, E.L., Linn, R.L., Herman, J.L., and Koretz, D. (2002). *Standards for educational accountability systems*. Los Angeles: National Center for Research on Evaluation, Standards, and Student Testing, University of California.

Bruner, C., Wright, M.S., Gebhard, B., and Hubbard, S. (2004). *Building an early learning system: The ABC's of planning and governing structures*. Des Moines, IA: SECPTAN.

California Department of Education. (2003). *Desired results for children and families*. Sacramento: Author, Child Development Division.

California Department of Education. (2005). *Desired Results Developmental Profile-Revised (DRDP-R), Preschool Instrument*. Sacramento: Author, Child Development Division.

Espinosa, L.M. (2008). *A review of the literature on assessment issues for young English language learners*. Paper commissioned by the Committee on Developmental Outcomes and Assessments for Young Children, The National Academies, Washington, DC.

Espinosa, L.M., and López, M.L. (2007). *Assessment considerations for young English language learners across different levels of accountability*. Philadelphia: The National Early Childhood Accountability Task Force.

García, E.E. (2005). *Teaching and learning in two languages: Bilingualism and schooling in the United States*. New York: Teachers College Press.

Gilliam, W.S., and Zigler, E.F. (2004). *State efforts to evaluate the effects of prekindergarten: 1977-2003*. New Haven, CT: Yale University Child Study Center.

Goodman, D.P., and Hambleton, R.K. (2003). *Student test score reports and interpretive guides: Review of current practices and suggestions for future research*. Amherst: University of Massachusetts School of Education.

Hambleton, R.K., and Slater, S.C. (1997). Reliability of credentialing examinations and the impact of scoring models and standard setting policies. *Applied Measurement in Education, 10*, 19-38.

Harms, T., Clifford, R., and Cryer, D. (1998). *Early Childhood Environment Rating Scale* (Revised ed.). New York: Teachers College Press.

Harms, T., Cryer, R., and Clifford, R. (1990). *Infant/Toddler Environment Rating Scale*. (Revised ed.). New York: Teachers College Press.

Herman, J.L., and Perry, M. (2002). *California student achievement: Multiple views of K-12 progress*. Menlo Park, CA: Ed Source.

Jaeger, R.M. (1998). Evaluating the psychometric qualities of the National Board for Professional Teaching Standards' assessments: A methodological accounting. *Journal of Personnel Evaluation in Education, 22*, 189-210.

Kagan, S.L., Tarrant, K., and Berliner, A. (2005). *Building a professional development system in South Carolina: Review and analysis of other state's experiences*. New York: Columbia University National Center for Children and Families.

Koretz, D.M., and Baron, S.I. (1998). *The validity of gains in scores on the Kentucky Instructional Results Information System (KIRIS).* Santa Monica, CA: RAND Corporation.

Linn, R.L. (2003). Accountability: Responsibility and reasonable expectations. *Educational Researcher, 32*(7), 3-13.

Meisels, S.J. (2006). *Accountability in early childhood: No easy answers.* Chicago, IL: Erikson Institute.

Mitchell, A.W. (2005). *Stair steps to quality: A guide for states and communities developing quality rating systems for early care and education.* Alexandria, VA: United Way Success by Six.

National Early Childhood Accountability Task Force. (2007). *Taking stock: Assessing and improving early childhood learning and program quality.* Philadelphia: Author.

National Research Council. (2001). *Knowing what students know: The science and design of educational assessment.* Committee on the Foundations of Assessment, J. Pellegrino, N. Chudowsky, R. Glaser (Eds.). Board on Testing and Assessment, Center for Education, Division of Behavioral and Social Sciences and Education. Washington, DC: National Academy Press.

National Research Council. (2006). *Systems for state science assessment.* Committee on Test Design for K-12 Science Achievement, M.R. Wilson and M.W. Bertenthal (Eds.). Board on Testing and Assessment, Center for Education, Division of Behavioral and Social Sciences and Education. Washington, DC: The National Academies Press.

National Research Council and Institute of Medicine. (2000). *From neurons to neighborhoods: The science of early childhood development.* Committee on Integrating the Science of Early Childhood Development, J.P. Shonkoff and D.A. Phillips (Eds.). Board on Children, Youth, and Families, Commission on Behavioral and Social Sciences and Education. Washington, DC: National Academy Press.

Neuman, S.B., and Roskos, K. (2005). The state of state pre-kindergarten standards. *Early Childhood Research Quarterly, 20*(2), 125-145.

New Jersey Office of Early Childhood Education. (2004). *NJ early learning assessment system—Literacy.* Trenton: New Jersey Department of Education.

New Jersey Office of Early Childhood Education. (2006). *NJ early learning assessment system—Math.* Trenton: New Jersey Department of Education.

Pianta, R.C. (2003). *Standardized classroom observations from pre-K to third grade: A mechanism for improving quality classroom experiences during the P-3 years.* New York: Foundation for Child Development.

Scott-Little, C., Kagan, S.L., and Frelow, V.S. (2003a). Creating the conditions for success with early learning standards: Results from a national study of state-level standards for children's learning prior to kindergarten. *Early Childhood Research & Practice, 5*(2).

Scott-Little, C., Kagan, S.L., and Frelow, V.S. (2003b). *Standards for preschool children's learning and development: Who has standards, how were they developed, and how are they used?* Greensboro: University of North Carolina.

Smith, M., and Dickinson, D. (2002). *User's guide to the early language & literacy classroom observation toolkit.* Available: http://www.brookespublishing.com/store/books/smith-ellco/index.htm [accessed July 2008].

U.S. Department of Education. (2004). *Standards and assessments peer review guidance: Information and examples for meeting requirements of the No Child Left Behind Act of 2001.* Washington, DC: Author.

Wainer, H. (1997). Improving tabular displays: With NAEP tables as examples and inspirations. *Journal of Educational and Behavioral Statistics, 22,* 1-30.

Wainer, H., Hambleton, R.K., and Meara, K. (1999). Alternative displays for communicating NAEP results: A redesign and validity study. *Journal of Educational Measurement, 36,* 301-335.

## CHAPTER 11

American Educational Research Association, American Psychological Association, and National Council on Measurement in Education. (1999). *Standards for educational and psychological testing.* Washington, DC: Author.

Christenson, S.L. (2004). The family-school partnership: An opportunity to promote learning and competence of all students. *School Psychology Review, 33*(1), 83-104.

Goldenberg, C., Rueda, R., and August, D. (2006). Synthesis: Sociocultural contexts and literacy development. In D. August and T. Shanahan (Eds.), *Report of the National Literacy Panel on Language Minority Youth and Children.* Mahwah, NJ: Lawrence Erlbaum Associates.

National Education Goals Panel. (1995). *Reconsidering children's early development and learning: Toward common views and vocabulary.* Washington, DC: Author.

National Research Council. (1999). *High stakes: Testing for tracking, promotion, and graduation.* Committee on Appropriate Test Usage, J.P. Heubert and R.M. Hauser (Eds.). Center for Education, Division of Behavioral and Social Sciences and Education. Washington, DC: National Academy Press.

National Research Council. (2006). *Systems for state science assessment.* Committee on Test Design for K-12 Science Achievement, M.R. Wilson and M.W. Bertenthal (Eds.). Board on Testing and Assessment, Center for Education, Division of Behavioral and Social Sciences and Education. Washington, DC: The National Academies Press.

National Research Council and Institute of Medicine. (2000). *From neurons to neighborhoods: The science of early childhood development.* Committee on Integrating the Science of Early Childhood Development, J.P. Shonkoff and D.A. Phillips (Eds.). Board on Children, Youth, and Families, Commission on Behavioral and Social Sciences and Education. Washington, DC: National Academy Press.

Rueda, R. (2007). *Motivation, learning, and assessment of English learners.* Paper presented at the School of Education, California State University, Northridge, April.

Rueda, R., and Yaden, D. (2006). The literacy education of linguistically and culturally diverse young children: An overview of outcomes, assessment, and large-scale interventions. In B. Spodek and O.N. Saracho (Eds.), *Handbook of research on the education of young children* (2nd ed., pp. 167-186). Mahwah, NJ: Lawrence Erlbaum Associates.

Rueda, R., MacGillivray, L., Monzó, L., and Arzubiaga, A. (2001). Engaged reading: A multi-level approach to considering sociocultural features with diverse learners. In D. McInerny and S.V. Etten (Eds.), *Research on sociocultural influences on motivation and learning* (pp. 233-264). Greenwich, CT: Information Age.

# Appendixes

# Appendix A

# Glossary of Terms Related to Early Childhood Assessment

**Accommodations** Adaptations in assessment tools and standards to permit children with disabilities or English language learners to show what they know and can do. Adjustments may be made, for example, in the way a test is administered or presented, in the timing, in the language, or in how the child responds. The nature of the adjustment determines whether or not what is being measured or the comparability of scores is affected (Council of Chief State School Officers, 2008).

**Achievement test** A testing instrument, typically standardized and norm-referenced, used to measure how much a child has learned in relation to educational objectives (Council of Chief State School Officers, 2008).

**Alternative assessment** See Performance assessment.

**Assessment** A term sometimes used loosely to refer to any type of appraisal of young children. In a narrower sense, assessment refers to information from multiple indicators and sources of evidence that is organized and interpreted and then evaluated to make an appraisal (McAfee, Leong, and Bodrova, 2004).

**Authentic assessment** A type of performance assessment that uses tasks that are as close as possible to real-life practical and intellectual challenges and the child completes the desired behavior in a context as close to real life as possible (McAfee, Leong, and Bodrova, 2004).

**Construct-irrelevant variance** Variance in assessment results that reflects variables other than the construct the assessment is intended to measure. An example is the variance in a mathematics assessment that may occur if the child being assessed lacks the language skills to understand the assessment items.

**Criterion-referenced assessment** A testing instrument in which the test-taker's performance (i.e., score) is interpreted by comparing it with a prespecified standard or specific content and/or skills (Council of Chief State School Officers, 2008).

**Curriculum-based assessment** Form of criterion-referenced measurement wherein curricular objectives act as the criteria for the identification of instructional targets and for the assessment of status and progress (Bagnato and Neisworth, 1991).

**Developmental assessment** An ongoing process of observing a child's current competencies (including knowledge, skills, dispositions, and attitudes) and using the information to help the child develop further in the context of family and caregiving and learning environments (Council of Chief State School Officers, 2008).

**Developmentally appropriate** Developmentally appropriate practice is informed by what is known about child development and learning, what is known about each child as an individual, and what is known about the social and cultural contexts in which children live (adapted from National Association for the Education of Young Children, 1996, 2008).

**Dynamic assessment** Assessment approach characterized by guided support or learning for the purpose of determining a child's potential for change (Losardo and Notari-Syverson, 2001).

**Formal assessment** A procedure for obtaining information that can be used to make judgments about characteristics of children or programs using standardized instruments (Council of Chief State School Officers, 2008).

**Formative assessment** An assessment designed to monitor progress toward an objective and used to guide curricular and instructional decisions.

**High-stakes assessment** Tests or assessment processes for which the results lead to significant sanctions or rewards for children, their teachers, administrators, schools, programs, or school systems. Sanctions may be direct (e.g., retention in grade for children, reassignment for teachers, reorganization for schools) or unintended (e.g., narrowing of the curriculum, increased dropping out).

**Informal assessment** A procedure for obtaining information that can be used to make judgments about characteristics of children or programs using means other than standardized instruments (Council of Chief State School Officers, 2008).

**Naturalistic assessment** See Authentic assessment.

**Norm-referenced test** A standardized testing instrument by which the test-taker's performance is interpreted in relation to the performance of a group of peers who have previously taken the same test. The group of peers is known as the "norming" group (Council of Chief State School Officers, 2008).

**Performance assessment** Finding out what children know and can do by observing how they perform certain tasks. Usually uses tasks as close as possible to real-life practical and intellectual challenges (McAfee, Leong, and Bodrova, 2004).

**Portfolio assessment** A collection of work, usually drawn from children's classroom work, which, when subjected to objective analysis, becomes an assessment tool (Council of Chief State School Officers, 2008).

**Progress monitoring** Assessment conducted to examine students' academic performance and evaluate the effectiveness of instruction. Progress is measured on a regular basis (e.g., weekly or monthly) by comparing expected and actual rates of learning. Based on these measurements, teaching is adjusted as needed (Association for Supervision and Curriculum Development, 2008).

**Readiness test** A testing instrument designed to measure skills believed to be related to school learning tasks and to be predictive of school success (Council of Chief State School Officers, 2008).

**Reliability** The consistency of measurements, gauged by any of several methods, including when the testing procedure is repeated on a population of individuals or groups (test-retest reliability), or is administered by different raters (inter-rater reliability). There is no single, preferred approach to quantification of reliability (American Educational Research Association, American Psychological Association, and National Council on Measurement in Education, 1999).

**Screening** The use of a brief procedure or instrument designed to identify, from within a large population of children, those who may need further assessment to verify developmental and/or health risks (Council of Chief State School Officers, 2008).

**Standardized test** A testing instrument that is administered, scored, and interpreted in a standard manner. It may be either norm-referenced or criterion-referenced (Council of Chief State School Officers, 2008).

**Standards-based assessment** An assessment using criteria that are derived directly from content or performance standards (adapted from Council of Chief State School Officers, 2008).

**Summative assessment** An assessment that typically documents how much learning has occurred at a point in time; its purpose is to measure the level of child, school, or program success (Association for Supervision and Curriculum Development, 2008).

**Validity (of an assessment or tool)** The extent to which an instrument measures what it purports to measure; the extent to which an assessment's results support meaningful inferences for certain intended purposes.

## SOURCES


American Educational Research Association, American Psychological Association, and National Council on Measurement in Education. (1999). *Standards for educational and psychological testing*. Washington, DC: Author.

Association for Supervision and Curriculum Development. (2008). *Homepage*. Available: http://www.ascd.org [accessed June 2008].

Bagnato, S.J., and Neisworth, J.T. (1991). *Assessment for early intervention: Best practices for professionals*. New York: Guilford Press.

Council of Chief State School Officers. (2008). Glossary terms. Washington, DC: Author. Available: http://www.ccsso.org/projects/scass/projects/early_childhood_education_assessment_consortium/publications_and_products/2892.cfm [accessed August 2008].

Losardo, A., and Notari-Syverson, A. (2001). *Alternative approaches to assessing young children*. Baltimore, MD: Brookes.

McAfee, O., Leong, D.J., and Bodrova, E. (2004). *Basics of assessment: A primer for early childhood educators*. Washington, DC: National Association for the Education of Young Children.

# Appendix B

# Information on Stakeholder Forum

**Public Forum and Information-Gathering Session**
**July 6, 2007**

**AGENDA**

1:00 **Catherine Snow,** Committee Chair, and **Susan Van Hemel,** Study Director. Welcome and introduction of committee. Description of the study and purpose of the forum. Review of procedure and ground rules.

1:20 **Ben Allen,** National Head Start Association

1:32 **Tammy Mann,** Zero to Three

1:44 **Fasaha Traylor,** Foundation for Child Development

1:56 **Jerlean Daniel,** National Association for the Education of Young Children

2:08 **Joan Isenberg,** National Association of Early Childhood Teacher Educators

2:20 **Sally Flagler,** National Association of School Psychologists

2:32 **Andrea Browning,** Society for Research in Child Development (brief statement)

2:40 **Break**

3:00 **Willard Gilbert,** National Association for Bilingual Education

3:12 **Felicia DeHaney,** National Black Child Development Institute
3:24 **Miriam Calderon,** National Council of La Raza
3:36 **Michael Lopez,** National Center for Latino Child and Family Research
3:48 **Michaelene Ostrosky,** Center on the Social Emotional Foundations of Early Learning
4:00 **Mark Innocenti,** Division for Early Childhood, Council for Exceptional Children
4:12 **Noma Anderson,** American Speech-Language-Hearing Association
4:24 **Guest Comments** (sign up upon arrival), Maximum 3 minutes per speaker.
≈5:00 **Adjourn**

## BACKGROUND INFORMATION

Congress and the U.S. Department of Health and Human Services (HHS) have launched multiple initiatives to invest in early childhood interventions to improve healthy development for at-risk children. These initiatives include programs such as Head Start and Early Head Start, which serve low-income children from birth to age 5, pregnant women, and their families. The programs strive to provide services responsive to the children and their families' cultural, ethnic, and linguistic heritage.

Assessment of children's progress is a key feature of Head Start classrooms, since ensuring that children are ready for school requires systematic, comprehensive, and ongoing evaluation. Numerous types of assessments are used in Head Start programs. For example, performance standards for Head Start require that programs assess the progress of each child toward an array of positive outcomes, on an ongoing basis; programs are required to screen children to identify special needs; and children are assessed on their achievement of specific cognitive and language outcomes through the standardized National Reporting System. The challenges of assessing young children are numerous, and in Head Start these challenges are compounded by the multiple cultural- and linguistic-minority origins of the children who participate in these programs.

Concerns about the identification of relevant developmental outcomes for young children and selection of appropriate assessment instruments for the Head Start program are emerging within an increasingly crowded landscape of other early interventions, including state-based early childhood education programs. An evidence-based analysis of scientific research will help to inform these efforts as well as building consensus about the appropriate instruments, objectives, and frameworks that should guide standards-based assessment of young children.

### The Study

Congress included conference report language in the HHS FY2006 appropriations bill (H.Rpt. 109-300) directing HHS to sponsor a study by the National Academy of Sciences to address these issues. In response, the National Research Council (NRC) will organize an ad hoc committee to review research on developmental outcomes and assessment processes for young children (ages 0-5). The committee will focus on two key topics in conducting the study and preparing its report: (1) the identification of key developmental outcomes associated with children ages 0-5 that should be the focus of early childhood programming and (2) the identification of state-of-the art techniques and instruments for developmental assessments, including examination of areas where current assessment tools are inadequate. It is anticipated that the 20-month study will inform the development and implementation of future testing instruments for children enrolled in Head Start programs and other early childhood interventions as well as guiding training needs for staff involved in administering and interpreting various assessments. Explicit attention will be given in the study to identification of children with various disabilities as well as assessments of children from minority cultures and those whose home language is not English.

The study will be conducted through a collaboration between the NRC/IOM Board on Children, Youth, and Families and the NRC Board on Testing and Assessment. The study committee will convene several times, will conduct a literature review, and will commission a set of background papers to inform its deliberations. The final study report will include a research synthesis that highlights key developmental outcomes and the features associated with selected categories of assessment tools, lessons learned from their use in different program settings, and policy and research recommendations to improve the quality of developmental assessments and their use with diverse populations of young children. Dissemination efforts will include briefings for agency officials, congressional representatives, and officers for key stakeholder organizations, and the production of a report brief that will translate the study findings for practitioners and policy makers.

**Questions for Forum Participants**

Listed below are general topics and more specific questions based upon the issues that the Committee on Developmental Outcomes and Assessments for Young Children will be addressing in its work. We are interested in your views on any of these that you and your organization feel competent to address, but you should not feel obliged to answer all of the questions.

Please indicate clearly which questions you are responding to, and keep your written response to a maximum of **five pages** (11 pt. type or larger). If your organization has published position statements that address our questions, you may refer the committee to those, noting which questions are addressed in each. References, if you provide them, will not be included in the page count. Please send your responses to us (mmcdonough@nas.edu) as Word or PDF files no later than **June 29.** Thank you for your participation. Your materials will be deposited in the project's Public Access file and will be made available to interested parties upon request.

1. **General Issues: Why measure**
   What are the most important philosophical issues in assessing the development of children from birth to 5 years old? Do your answers differ with the age (within the birth to 5-year range) of the children being assessed? Questions you may want to address include:
   A. What are the most important benefits of such assessment?

B. What are the most important risks associated with such assessment?
C. What are appropriate purposes for such assessment?
D. What are appropriate uses of assessment results?
E. To whom should assessment results be reported? At what level of aggregation?
F. What is the proper role of child assessment in early childhood program accountability?

2. **Outcomes, Domains, Functions: What to measure**
What developmental outcomes, domains, or functions are appropriate for assessment, and why? Questions you may want to address include:
A. What domains/outcomes/functions best predict children's later development and learning outcomes?
B. What domains/outcomes/functions can be assessed most reliably and validly in this age group?

3. **Assessment Instruments: How to measure**
What are the most important considerations or criteria to use in designing or selecting assessment instruments for young children? Questions you may want to address include:
A. For what domains/outcomes/functions do we have useful, valid, reliable assessment tools at this time?
B. For what domains/outcomes/functions do we NOT have useful, valid, reliable assessment tools at this time?
C. What do you see as the relative merits of direct assessment versus assessment based on ongoing observation of children in their natural environments?
D. Where do you stand on the issue of administering all children all instruments and items versus some form of sampling?

4. **Assessment Implementation: How to perform assessments and use the results**
What do you see as the major issues for implementing assessment of young children? Questions you may want to address include:

A. Who should be assessing children? Teachers, caregivers, parents, others? What training and supervision do the assessors need?
B. What can be done to assure that results are used in beneficial ways? What training do users of assessment results need? How can results best be presented to various users or audiences?

5. **Special Populations (children with disabilities/delays, English language learners, children from minority cultures, etc.): Equity, fairness, inclusion**
What are the special concerns about the assessment of children from these groups and your recommendations for appropriate assessment of these children? Questions you may want to address include:
A. What suggestions would you offer for assuring that the assessment of all children is fair and useful?
B. Can universal design principles be employed in the design of assessments for young children? If so, should those principles be employed?

## FORUM SPEAKER LIST

**Ben Allen,** National Head Start Association
**Noma Anderson,** American Speech-Language-Hearing Association
**Andrea Browning,** Society of Research on Child Development
**Miriam Calderon,** National Council of La Raza
**Jerlean Daniel,** National Association for the Education of Young Children
**Felicia DeHaney,** National Black Child Development Institute
**Sally Flagler,** National Association of School Psychologists
**Willard Gilbert,** National Association for Bilingual Education
**Mark Innocenti,** Division for Early Childhood, Council for Exceptional Children
**Joan Isenberg,** National Association of Early Childhood Teacher Educators
**Michael Lopez,** National Center for Latino Child and Family Research
**Tammy Mann,** Zero to Three

**Michaelene Ostrosky,** Center on the Social Emotional Foundations of Early Learning
**Fasaha Traylor,** Foundation for Child Development

# Appendix C

# Development of State Standards for Early Childhood Education

Making generalizations across the states' early learning standards[1] is difficult. They differ on many dimensions, including diverse structures for naming the elements of the documents, diverse structures for organizing the content, varied intent for their use, multiple methods for defining and creating alignment with the states' K-12 standards, and a wide range of resources available to put them into practice.

One characteristic of the state documents that comes closer to congruency, especially in the development/revision of the standards following the launching of the federal Good Start, Grow Smart initiative is: Who was involved in the development of state early learning standards? Examination of the front material in the state documents reveals that the stakeholder groups that came

---

[1]For consistency the term "early learning standards" is used throughout this appendix to refer to child outcomes, guidelines, and other references to written sets of expectations for young children. This use of the term is consistent with the definition in the Glossary developed by the Early Childhood Education Assessment Consortium of the Council of Chief State School Officers in collaboration with several early childhood organizations. The definition of *early learning standards* is: statements that describe expectations for the learning and development of young children across the domains of health and physical well-being, social and emotional well-being, approaches to learning, language development and symbol systems, and general knowledge about the world around them (Council of Chief State School Officers and Early Childhood Education Assessment Consortium, 2007).

together to develop standards in the states have themselves been highly diverse. This diversity is a common element.

Prior to Good Start, Grow Smart, the departments of education were typically the lead agencies since those early standards were developed primarily to guide the development of the states' prekindergarten programs. After Good Start, Grow Smart spurred the development of early learning standards by additional states, leadership was often a joint enterprise of the state social services agencies having oversight of the child care program and the departments of education. In several cases, the Head Start State Collaboration Offices were also included in the leadership team. Stakeholder participants typically included representatives from a wide array of early childhood program sectors and support services (e.g., family- and center-based child care; state prekindergarten; Head Start and Early Head Start; associate- and bachelor-level higher education; resource and referral agencies; specialists in age levels, such as infant/toddler, preschool, kindergarten/primary; specialists in content areas; specialists in special needs; social services, mental health, medical professionals, nutritionists, parents). Participation by such a broad base of interested parties reflects a commitment on the part of state leaders to the creation of standards suitable for use across the field and reflective of reasonable expectations for the wide range of child characteristics during this developmental period.

## EARLY LEARNING STANDARDS DOCUMENTS

Differences among the state documents on this dimension are legion. The lack of consensus makes it difficult to make comparisons of actual content. The early learning standards documents represent a consensus process reflective of the often different emphases of the states. It is unlikely that states will move toward a common set of national standards, although the successive revision processes and the easy access that the Internet provides to the work of other states may tend to bring about a form of consensus over time.

Various scholars who have analyzed the documents recently have described or recommended structures and naming schemes (National Institute for Early Education Research, 2003; Neuman and Roskos, 2005; Scott-Little, Kagan, and Frelow, 2005). The scholars do not use consistent terminology or frameworks in analyzing the content of sets of standards. The National Institute for Early Education Research (2003) recommend a three-stage framework of content statements "categorized within a hierarchical structure of domains, standards, and benchmarks":

1. Domains are the seven general subject areas which statements may belong to.
2. Standards are familiar categories within a domain and help organize a collection of closely related benchmarks.
3. Benchmarks describe either student knowledge or skill; they do not describe student performance, student activities, or goals of the curriculum (Introduction to the State Standards Database at http://nieer.org/standards/).

Neuman and Roskos (2005) analyzed current naming and organizational structures in early learning standards documents. They argue for parsimony and clarity based on research and recommend a hierarchy organized by content domain, skill area, and indicators (exemplars).

By itself this disagreement about terminology is not harmful as long as the developers understand the hierarchy that they have chosen and can use it to communicate important ideas to practitioners and to families. The most serious problem is the confusion in many of the documents about the difference between content and performance standards. Use of more consistent schema may become more widespread as the state documents are revised to reflect what has been learned from their initial use and because of their increasing use as the basis for the development of state assessment systems.

## CONTENT

A more recent and complete compilation of information about the content of early learning standards and their use across the states is found in annual web-based surveys conducted by the members of the Early Childhood Education Assessment (ECEA) Consortium of the Council of Chief State School Officers

(CCSSO). The results of the 2005 survey are reported in an article, "Early Learning Standards: Results from a National Survey to Document Trends in State-Level Policies and Practices" in the online peer-reviewed journal *Early Childhood Research and Practice* (Scott-Little et al., 2007, pp. 1-22). A total of 49 states (96 percent of 51, including the District of Columbia) provided information about the development and use of their early learning standards. All indicated that the standards were intended as a resource to improve instruction and strengthen curriculum. Of the 49 states, 36 (73 percent) said that improving professional development was an important intent and 32 (65 percent) said that educating parents about children's development and learning was important.

With 49 of 51 states now having developed early learning standards (North Dakota standards continue to be in draft form), the following generalizations may be observed:

- All 49 have standards in the areas of Language and Early Literacy.
- 37 have standards in Mathematics; of the 12 which do not, mathematical concepts are included in standards on Cognition and General Knowledge.
- 42 states have standards in Physical/Motor Development and Health; the 7 that do not are that states with standards only in Language and Early Literacy and Mathematics (CO, MD, OH, PA, SC, VA) and in Language and Early Literacy only (NY).
    —15 of the 42 states address content in a general section on Cognition and General Knowledge. The remainder divides content areas into Mathematics, Science, Arts, and Social Studies.
    —Nearly half (21) have standards addressing Approaches to Learning.

Appendix Table C-1 provides these data for all the states.

**TABLE C-1** Domain/Content Areas Headings Included in National and State Pre-K Early Learning Standards Documents

| | Physical/ Motor/ Health | Social/ Emotional | Approaches Toward Learning | Language/ Comm-unication | Literacy | Cognition/ General Knowledge | Math | Science | Art/ Aesthetics | Social Studies | Other |
|---|---|---|---|---|---|---|---|---|---|---|---|
| **National** | | | | | | | | | | | |
| **Head Start COF** | x | x | x | x | x | | x | x | x | | |
| **Carnegie/ McGraw-Hill** | x | x | x | x | x | | x | x | x | x | World Languages |
| **States** | | | | | | | | | | | |
| AL | x | x | x | x | x | | x | x | x | | Technology Environmental Education |
| AK | x | | | x | x | | x | x | x | x | World Languages |
| AZ | x | x | | x | x | | x | x | x | | Safety |
| AR | x | x | | x | | x | | | | | |
| CA | x | x | | | | | | | | | Safety |
| CO | | | | x | x | | x | | | | |
| CT | x | x | | | | x | | | x | | |
| DE | x | x | x | x | | | x | x | x | | |
| FL | x | x | x | x | | x | | | | | |
| GA | x | x | | x | | | x | x | x | | |
| HI | x | x | | x | x | x | | | x | | |
| ID | x | | | x | x | | x | x | | x | Humanities |

*continued*

**TABLE C-1** Continued

| | Physical/ Motor/ Health | Social/ Emotional | Approaches Toward Learning | Language/ Comm- unication | Literacy | Cognition/ General Knowledge | Math | Science | Art/ Aesthetics | Social Studies | Other |
|---|---|---|---|---|---|---|---|---|---|---|---|
| IL | x | x | | x | | | x | x | x | x | Foreign Language |
| IN | x | | | x | x | | x | x | x | x | |
| IA | x | x | x | x | x | | x | x | x | | |
| KS | x | x | x | x | x | | x | x | x | x | |
| KY | x | | | x | x | | x | x | x | x | |
| LA | x | x | | x | x | x | x | x | x | x | |
| ME | | | | | | | | | | | LR: Career Preparation, Modern and Classic Languages, Technology |
| Learning Results | x | | | x | x | | x | x | x | x | |
| Early Learning Results | x | x | | x | | x | | | | | |
| MD | | | | x | x | | x | x | | x | |
| MA | x | | | x | x | | x | x | | x | Technology, Engineering |
| MI | x | x | | x | x | x | x | x | x | x | Nutrition, Self-Help |
| MN | x | x | x | x | | x | x | x | x | x | |
| MS | x | x | | x | | | x | x | | | |
| MO | x | x | | | x | | x | x | | | |
| MT | x | x | | x | x | | x | x | x | x | |
| NE | x | x | x | x | x | | x | x | x | | |

| | | | | | | | | | | | |
|---|---|---|---|---|---|---|---|---|---|---|---|
| NV | | | | | | | | | | | McGraw-Hill |
| NH | | | | | | | | | | | |
| NJ | x | x | | x | x | | x | x | x | x | World Languages |
| NM | x | x | | x | x | | | | x | | |
| NY | | | | x | x | | | | | | |
| NC | x | x | x | x | | x | | | | | |
| ND | | | | | | | | | | | |
| OH | | | | x | x | | x | x | | x | |
| OK | x | x | x | x | x | | x | x | x | x | |
| OR | | | | | | | | | | | |
| PA | | | | x | x | | x | | | | |
| RI | x | x | x | x | x | | x | x | x | | |
| SC | | | | x | x | | x | | | | |
| SD | x | x | x | x | x | | x | x | x | x | |
| TN | x | x | | x | x | | x | x | x | x | |
| TX | x | x | | x | x | x | x | x | x | x | Technology |
| UT | x | x | | x | x | x | x | x | x | | |
| VT | x | x | x | x | x | | x | x | x | x | Technology |
| VA | | | | x | x | | x | | | | |
| WA | | x | | x | x | | x | | | | Self-Help |
| | | | | x | x | | | | | | |
| WV | x | x | | x | x | | x | x | x | | |
| WI | x | x | x | x | | x | | | | | |

continued

**TABLE C-1** Continued

| | Physical/ Motor/ Health | Social/ Emotional | Approaches Toward Learning | Language/ Comm-unication | Literacy | Cognition/ General Knowledge | Math | Science | Art/ Aesthetics | Social Studies | Other |
|---|---|---|---|---|---|---|---|---|---|---|---|
| WY | x | x | x | x | x | | x | x | x | | |

NOTE: This table has been adapted with permission from a 2005 report by Scott-Little, Kagan, and Frelov, *Inside the Content: The Breadth and Depth of Early Learning Standards.* The table has been updated to include states that published their early learning standards document after this report was completed. Data were collected by simply reviewing the table of contents of each early learning standards document and noting the developmental domain areas and academic subject areas included in the table of contents. Results from analyses conducted by Scott-Little, Kagan, and Frelov (2005) on the content of the actual early learning standards included in the documents indicate that the table of contents is not always an accurate reflection of the content of the standards themselves. While the table of contents may reflect the intentions or overall mind set of the persons who developed the early learning standards, they do not necessarily give a complete or accurate indication of the areas of learning and development that have been addressed in the standards themselves.

## ALIGNMENT WITH THE HEAD START CHILD OUTCOMES FRAMEWORK

At the time the Head Start Child Outcomes Framework (HSCOF) was released in 2000, only 10 states had published early learning standards. It was at that time the only set of nationally recognized standards that could lay claim to a research base. In November 2007, the state early childhood specialists, all of whom had participated in the development of early learning standards in their respective states, were queried about the degree to which the HSCOF was consulted in the development of their early learning standards. Of the specialists who responded, all indicated that the HSCOF had been used in the formulation of their early learning standards. The depth of the use varied; however, it was clear that all of them had considered the organization and the content of the HSCOF in deciding how to create their own sets of standards.

In reexamining Appendix Table C-1, it appears that the majority of the states that have gone beyond Language, Early Literacy, and Mathematics have included all the domain and content areas included in the framework, with the exception of Approaches to Learning. Only about two-fifths of the states have that named category. A more thorough analysis of the entire corpus of standards might reveal that Approaches to Learning indicators are embedded in other areas, such as Social/Emotional Development and Cognition. Furthermore, the emphasis on this area in the 21st Century Learning Skills (Partnership for 21st Century Skills, 2007) suggests that Approaches to Learning might gain greater visibility in subsequent revisions.

## ALIGNMENT WITH LEARNING STANDARDS IN THE K-12 SYSTEM

While the major purpose of the 2005 CCSSO survey was to determine the extent to which standards were being implemented in the states, respondents also provided information about issues in their development. Chief among these was how states addressed the issue of alignment. How early learning standards are aligned to standards for children in the K-12 system is both important and of great interest. The ECEA CCSSO group, in their web-based glossary of assessment terms, *The Words We Use: A Glossary of Terms for Early Childhood Education Standards and Assessment* (2007), defines alignment as:

> The horizontal (coordination within an age/grade level), vertical (what came before and what will follow), and temporal (across the calendar year) relationships among early learning standards, curriculum, teaching practices, and assessment. Alignment at the early childhood level (birth through age 8) forms the basis for the formulation of standards and assessment for older students.

Since the Good Start, Grow Smart initiative (White House, 2002) called on states to address vertical alignment, it is not surprising that all the states reporting in the 2005 ECEA CCSSO survey indicated that their early learning standards were aligned in some way with the states' K-12 standards. The nature of that reported alignment is diverse and difficult to understand, given the way the question was framed. In the CCSSO ECEA survey, 27 states (66 percent) reported some form of vertical alignment using the states' kindergarten standards as a guide. The open-ended survey responses provided more understanding of this downward-mapping process, with states reporting greater or lesser direct connection between the early learning standards and the states' kindergarten standards. Some states duplicated the content areas in the kindergarten standards, and others included domains typically associated with descriptions of children's early development (e.g., social emotional, approaches to learning).

Clearly, connecting the work accomplished in the creation of standards and assessments at the pre-K level with that which exists in K-12 should be a priority at both state and local levels. Having now created standards for pre-K, many states are now looking more critically at the alignment between pre-K and kindergarten and are moving toward addressing that alignment in spite of the challenges involved.

The learning and development of young people are complex at all levels. In the early stages, how professionals decide to organize indicators of expected development and learning is informed both by what science tells us and by what seems to be a reasonable framework. Use of the developmental domains helps to accentuate the importance of areas such as social/emotional development and approaches to learning to children's development in the language and cognitive areas. In the K-12 system, attention to these areas occurs outside of the learning standards, if at all. Pre-K practitioners have given greater attention to content areas over the past decade, owing greatly to earlier NRC publications (National Research Council, 2001). A parallel effort to raise the attention of practitioners in the K-12 arena to the importance of social/emotional development and approaches to learning not only would improve the learning environment for elementary children, it would create a better environment to address alignment issues. Ohio and Massachusetts are among states with initiatives underway to harmonize pre-K and K-3 education systems.

In its infant toddler guidelines, the state of Michigan uses the image of a tree to explain how development and learning progress in the early years:

> . . . children's development is not a straight line; one discrete skill or milestone does not lead directly to another in a single chain of developments. For the very youngest, it is difficult to differentiate between developmental domains such as approaches to learning, social and emotional development, language and cognition. . . . One action falls in many domains—and that skill will later lead to a number of other skills in a variety of domains. . . . Perhaps the image is of a tree, where the roots are the strands in this document, and the skills we see later are the branches and leaves. It may not be possible to trace all the connections directly, but the early developments all contribute to the later accomplishments. (Michigan State Board of Education, 2006, pp. 2-3)

Building on this analogy, standards reflecting this view of development and learning might be conceived of as beginning with the less differentiated accomplishments, progressing to the domains represented in this document and branching out to include the content domains more commonly found in the early elementary years of schooling.

A few promising initiatives are re-emerging, led largely by the Foundation for Child Development. Its recent report, *PK-3rd: A New Beginning for American Education* (Foundation for Child Development, 2008) outlines a bold agenda for bringing the years that span pre-K through grade 3 into a cohesive unit to support children's early learning and development (http://www.fcd-us.org/initiatives/initiatives_show.htm?doc_id=447080).

## REFERENCES

Council of Chief State School Officers and Early Childhood Education Assessment Consortium. (2007). *The words we use: A glossary of terms for early childhood education standards and assessment.* Available: http://www.ccsso.org/Projects/scass/projects/early_childhood_education_assessment_consortium/publications_and_products/2892.cfm [accessed February 2008].

Foundation for Child Development. (2008). *PreK-3rd: A new beginning for American education.* Available: http://www.fcd-us.org/initiatives/initiatives_show.htm?doc_id=447080 [accessed May 2008].

Michigan State Board of Education. (2006). *Early childhood standards of quality for infant and toddler programs.* Lansing: Author.

National Institute for Early Education Research. (2003). *State standards database.* New Brunswick, NJ: Author.

National Research Council. (2001). *Eager to learn: Educating our preschoolers.* Committee on Early Childhood Pedagogy, B.T. Bowman, M.S. Donovan, and M.S. Burns (Eds.). Commission on Behavioral and Social Sciences and Education. Washington, DC: National Academy Press.

Neuman, S.B., and Roskos, K. (2005). The state of state pre-kindergarten standards. *Early Childhood Research Quarterly, 20*(2), 125-145.

Partnership for 21st Century Skills. (2007). *The intellectual and policy foundations of the 21st century skills framework.* Tucson, AZ: Author.

Scott-Little, C., Kagan, S.L., and Frelow, V.S. (2005). *Inside the content: The depth and breadth of early learning standards.* Greensboro: University of North Carolina, SERVE Center for Continuous Improvement.

Scott-Little, C., Lesko, J., Martella, J., and Milburn, P. (2007). Early learning standards: Results from a national survey to document trends in state-level policies and practices. *Early Childhood Research and Practice, 9*(1), 1-22.

White House. (2002). *Good start, grow smart: The Bush administration's early childhood initiative.* Washington, DC: Executive Office of the President.

# Appendix D

# Sources of Detailed Information on Test and Assessment Instruments

For specific information on the features and content of instruments for use with infants and young children, the committee refers the reader to the following sources. They provide information on the construct measured, the content of the instrument, the time to administer, how the instrument is administered (e.g., caregiver or teacher report, direct assessment, interview, observation), the age range and purpose (screening, diagnosis, assessment, etc.) for which each measure is appropriate, and the interpretation and use of results. In some cases they offer information on the instruments' psychometric properties: reliability, validity for various uses, research support for claims of validity, etc. Some also have specific information regarding use with special populations. The ones called "reviews" provide evaluations. Additional reviews of specific instruments may often be found by searching the ERIC (http://www.eric.ed.gov) and PsycInfo (http://www.apa.org/psycinfo/) databases.

## RECENT PRINT REVIEWS AND COMPENDIUM DOCUMENTS

**Title:** *The 17th Mental Measurements Yearbook* (Buros Institute of Mental Measurements, 2007)

**Source: Buros Institute of Mental Measurements**

**Notes:** Buros publishes periodic editions of its yearbook, the latest of which, the 17th, was released in 2007. The yearbook provides in-depth descriptions and critical reviews of current instruments.

**Titles:** *Early Childhood Measures Profiles* (Child Trends, 2004); *Quality in Early Childhood Care and Education Settings: A Compendium of Measures* (Child Trends, 2007)

**Source: Child Trends**

**Notes:** The Child Trends organization has published two recent compendia of instruments for use with young children, one for child assessment and one for assessment of care and education environments. These provide in-depth descriptive information on each instrument, including descriptions of the norming populations. The compendium of child measures has extensive information on reliability and validity, both from the manual and from other research. The environmental measures compendium describes ways in which each measure addresses diversity, a feature not addressed in many other sources.

**Title:** *Resources for Measuring Services and Outcomes in Head Start Programs Serving Infants and Toddlers* (Mathematica Policy Research, 2003)

**Source: Mathematica Policy Research**

**Notes:** Mathematica Policy Research developed this compendium of instruments for the Office of Head Start. It is oriented to the Head Start and Early Head Start programs, and its Appendix C has useful information on the measures used in the Early Head Start Research and Evaluation Project, including descriptions of psychometric properties. It covers measures of child development; parenting, the home environment, and parent well-being; and program implementation and quality.

**Title:** *Screening for Developmental and Behavioral Problems*

**Source: Glascoe (2005),** *Mental Retardation and Developmental Disabilities Research Reviews, 11*(3), 173-179

**Notes:** This recent review article by Glascoe describes screening tools and instruments for use with infants and young children and is focused chiefly on instruments for use in pediatric surveillance and screening programs. Similar information authored by Glascoe is available at the DBPeds website (see below).

**Title:** *Developmental Screening Tools: Gross Motor/Fine Motor for Newborn, Infants and Children*

**Source: (Beligere, Zawacki, Pennington, and Glascoe, 2007)** (available at DBPeds website)

**Notes:** Glascoe and colleagues provide a listing specifically of screening tools for gross motor and fine motor development, also available on the DBPeds website.

**Title:** *Assessing Social-Emotional Development in Children from a Longitudinal Perspective for the National Children's Study: Social-Emotional Compendium of Measures*

**Source: (Denham, 2005)** (available at The National Children's Study website)

**Notes:** Denham provides extensive information on content and psychometric characteristics of social-emotional instruments, with additional comments on their use for the national children's Study. She includes judgments on strengths and weaknesses of each measure reviewed, and references for research studies of each instrument. Many of the measures reviewed are not for young children.

**Title:** *Developmental Screening and Assessment Instruments with an Emphasis on Social and Emotional Development for Young Children Ages Birth Through Five*

**Source: National Early Childhood Technical Assistance Center (NECTAC) at the University of North Carolina** (Ringwalt, 2008)

**Notes:** A new resource, this document provides information, including psychometric properties, for a large number of multi-domain and socioemotional instruments. It is available at http://www.nectac.org/~pdfs/pubs/screening.pdf.

## ONLINE DATABASES OF MEASUREMENT INSTRUMENTS

**Site: Buros Center for Testing**

**URL: http://www.unl.edu/buros/**

**Notes:** This is a service of the organization that has for many years produced the venerable print-based Mental Measurements Yearbook (see above). It provides brief instrument descriptions available online at no cost. In-depth test reviews from the yearbook, including information on the psychometric properties of instruments and how they were established, are available for purchase online at $15 per title.

**Site: National Institute for Early Education Research (NIEER)**

**URL: http://nieer.org/assessment/**

**Notes:** NIEER maintains an assessment database (accessed from the "Facts and Figures" tab on the NIEER homepage by selecting Assessment Database) that provides detailed information on the short list of early childhood measures categorized as "verified," similar to that found at the Educational Testing Service (ETS) site. Much less information is given for "unverified" instruments. It does not provide much psychometric information but notes what information is available in instrument technical manuals. The site notes that much of its information was obtained from test publishers and other databases, including Buros, ETS, and ERIC.

(The ERIC database is no longer supported, but refers users to the ETS database.)

**Site: Educational Testing Service TestLink—"SydneyPlus Knowledge Portal"**

**URL: http://sydneyplus.ets.org**

**Notes:** This site provides a database of test and assessment instruments, including research instruments. For each instrument it provides a database record with fairly detailed descriptive information but does not review psychometric properties.

**Site: DBPeds**

**URL: http://dbpeds.org**

**Notes:** This website, the homepage of the American Academy of Pediatrics section on developmental and behavioral pediatrics, provides a great deal of information on developmental screening and assessment, including reviews of instruments, advice on incorporating screening into pediatric practice, and online learning modules for pediatric professionals. It focuses on instruments of use to pediatric professionals.

## REFERENCES

Beligere, N., Zawacki, L., Pennington, S., and Glascoe, F.P. (2007). *Developmental screening tools: Gross motor/fine motor for newborn, infants and children.* Available: http://www.dbpeds.org/articles/detail.cfm?TextID=%20738 [accessed June 2008].

Buros Institute of Mental Measurements. (2007). *The seventeenth mental measurements yearbook.* Lincoln, NE: Author.

Child Trends. (2004). *Early childhood measures profiles.* Washington, DC: Author.

Child Trends. (2007). *Quality in early childhood care and education settings: A compendium of measures.* Washington, DC: Author.

Denham, S.E. (2005). *Assessing social-emotional development in children from a longitudinal perspective for the National Children's Study.* Washington, DC: Battelle Memorial Institute.

Glascoe, F.P. (2005). Screening for developmental and behavioral problems. *Mental Retardation and Developmental Disabilities Research Reviews, 11*(3), 173-179.

Mathematica Policy Research. (2003). *Resources for measuring services and outcomes in Head Start programs serving infants and toddlers*. Princeton, NJ: Author.

Ringwalt, S. (2008). *Developmental screening and assessment instruments with an emphasis on social and emotional development for young children ages birth through five.* Chapel Hill: University of North Carolina, FPG Child Development Institute, National Early Childhood Technical Assistance Center.

# Appendix E

# Biographical Sketches of Committee Members and Staff

**Catherine E. Snow** (*Chair*) is the Henry Lee Shattuck professor of education at the Harvard Graduate School of Education. Her research interests include children's language development as influenced by interaction with adults in home and preschool settings, literacy development as related to language skills and as influenced by home and school factors, and issues related to the acquisition of English oral and literacy skills by language-minority children. She has coauthored books on language development (e.g., *Pragmatic Development* with Anat Ninio) and on literacy development (e.g., *Unfulfilled Expectations: Home and School Influences on Literacy* with W. Barnes, J. Chandler, I. Goodman, and L. Hemphill) and published widely on these topics in refereed journals and edited volumes. Her contributions to the field include membership on several journal editorial boards, codirectorship for several years of the Child Language Data Exchange System, and editorship of *Applied Psycholinguistics*. She served as a board member at the Center for Applied Linguistics and as president of the American Educational Research Association. At the National Research Council (NRC), she was a member of the Committee on Establishing a Research Agenda on Schooling for Language Minority Children, chair of the Committee on Preventing Reading Difficulties in Young Children, and a member of the board of the Division of Behavioral and Social Sciences and Education. A member of the National Academy of

Education, Snow has held visiting appointments at the University of Cambridge, England, Universidad Autonoma in Madrid, and the Institute of Advanced Studies at Hebrew University in Jerusalem. She has a Ph.D. in psychology from McGill University and worked for several years in the linguistics department of the University of Amsterdam.

**Margaret Burchinal** is a professor in the Department of Education at the University of California at Irvine and senior scientist at the Frank Porter Graham Child Development Institute, as well as a research professor in the Department of Psychology at the University of North Carolina at Chapel Hill. She has served as the primary statistician for many educational studies of early childhood, including the 11-state Pre-Kindergarten Evaluation for the National Center for Early Learning and Development; the longitudinal study of 1,300 children in the Study of Early Child Care of the National Institute of Child Health and Human Development; the 4-state evaluation of child care in the Cost, Quality, and Child Outcomes Study; the 3-site study of family child care homes in the Family Child Care and Relative Care Study; and the Abecedarian and CARE Projects. As an applied methodologist, she has helped to demonstrate that such sophisticated methods as meta-analysis, fixed-effect modeling, hierarchical linear modeling, piecewise regression, and generalized estimating equations provide education researchers with advanced techniques to address important educational issues, such as whether child care quality measures are biased. In addition, she has pursued a substantive interest in early education as a means to improve school readiness for at-risk children. She has a Ph.D. from the University of North Carolina at Chapel Hill.

**Harriet A. Egertson** is an independent early childhood education consultant. Until 2002, she was the administrator of the Office of Early Childhood Education in the Nebraska Department of Education. In that capacity, she also directed the Head Start–State Collaboration Project and the Even Start Family Literacy program and led the development of one of the first cross-auspice professional development initiatives in the nation. Currently she is contracted to work with the Council of Chief State School Officers and several state departments of education on various projects related to early learning guidelines, curriculum, and assessment. Prior to going to the Nebraska Department of Education in 1975, she taught at the primary level in Oakland, California, and Fremont, Nebraska, and worked with a rural Head Start program in Nebraska. She has held leadership positions in several state and national professional organizations and served on nonprofit boards. She was a member of the National Education Goal 1 Technical Panel, which produced *Principles and Recommendations for Early Childhood Assessments.* She has a bachelor's degree from San Francisco State University and a master's degree in elementary education and administration and a Ph.D. in early childhood development from the University of Nebraska.

**Eugene K. Emory** is professor of psychology at Emory University. His areas of expertise include clinical psychology, neuropsychology, behavioral perinatology, and fetal development. His primary research interests lie in such areas as prenatal brain, behavior, and cognition; perinatal stress and hypothalamic-pituitary-adrenal activation; maternal psychopathology (schizophrenia and depression) and fetal development; fetal brain imaging; and neurocognitive development. His secondary research interests include maternal psychopathology in expectant women, depression in welfare mothers, and effects of out-of-home and foster care on child psychological development. At the NRC, he was a member of the Board on Behavioral, Cognitive, and Sensory Sciences. He has a Ph.D. from the University of Florida.

**David J. Francis** is professor of quantitative methods and chair of the Department of Psychology at the University of Houston, where he also serves as director of the Texas Institute for Measurement, Evaluation, and Statistics. He has authored or coauthored numerous peer-reviewed articles and book chapters and is a fellow of Division 5 (Measurement, Evaluation, and Statistics) of the American Psychological Association. He currently serves on the independent review panel for the National Assessment of Title I, as well as the Reading and Writing Peer Review Panel of the Institute of Education Sciences. Previously he served as an official adviser to the U.S. Department of Education on assessment and accountability during negotiated rule-making for the No Child Left Behind Act, as a member of the National Technical Advisory Group of the What Works Clearinghouse, and as a member of the National Literacy Panel for Language Minority Youth and Children. He is a codeveloper of the Texas Primary Reading Inventory and Tejas Lee early reading assessments. At the NRC, he is a member of the Board on Testing and Assessment (BOTA) and was a member of the Committee on Promising Education Practices. He has a Ph.D. from the University of Houston.

**Eugene E. García** is vice president for education partnerships at Arizona State University. His role is to strengthen K-12 education in the state of Arizona by linking the university and the private sector, encompassing the coordination of teacher preparation across colleges and campuses in Arizona, as well as the implementation of the university–public school initiative to establish campus schools. He is also currently chairing the National Task Force on Early Education for Hispanics funded by the Foundation for Child Development and the Mailman Family Foundation. He has published extensively in the area of language teaching and bilingual development and is currently conducting research on effective schooling for linguistically and culturally diverse student populations. He is the author of *Hispanic Education in the United States: Raíces y Alas*; *Understanding and Meeting the Challenge of Student Diversity*; and *Teaching and Learning in Two Languages: Bilingualism and Schooling in the United States*. At the NRC, he served on the Committee on Scientific Principles in Educational Research: Exploration of Perspectives and Implications for OERI and the NRC/Institute of Medicine (IOM) Committee on Adolescent Health and Development. He has a Ph.D. in human development from the University of Kansas.

**Kathleen Hebbeler** is manager of the Community Services and Strategies Program in the Center for Education and Human Services at SRI International. She has more than 20 years of experience in research and evaluation of education, health, and social programs for children and adolescents. She has directed large-scale projects involving quantitative and qualitative methods and has extensive experience in longitudinal research. Since joining SRI in 1992, she has conducted evaluations for federal and state agencies and private foundations, as well as training in evaluation design for a variety of audiences, with a special focus on identification and measurement of child and family outcomes. Currently, she is directing the Early Childhood Outcomes Center, a 5-year project designed to build consensus and provide national leadership around issues related to the measurement of outcomes for young children with disabilities and their families. She also is directing the National Early Intervention Longitudinal Study, which is examining services and outcomes for more than 3,300 infants and toddlers with disabilities in early intervention programs around the United States. She recently completed a 10-year evaluation of the Community Partnerships for Healthy Children, an initiative that used community collaboration and mobilization to improve the well-being of young children. She has authored numerous papers and presented at many national meetings in the areas of early childhood development, general and special education, community collaboration, and children's health. She has a Ph.D. in human development and family studies from Cornell University.

**Eboni Howard** is director of the Herr Research Center for Children and Social Policy at the Erikson Institute and holds the Frances Stott chair in early childhood policy research. She has extensive experience in evaluating program implementation and outcomes in the areas of childhood education, early intervention, welfare, family support, child abuse prevention, and foster care practices. She oversees projects in the areas of children's mental health, social-emotional development, and quality of state-funded prekindergarten programs. She also is leading a pilot study that examines the family routines and resources of foster families. Before joining Erikson in January 2006, she was a senior researcher at Chapin Hall Center for Children at the University of Chicago. There she led evaluation studies related to families' social service use, early childhood programs, foster care services, and home visitation programs for families with young children. She has a Ph.D. from the Human Development and Social Policy Program at Northwestern University.

**Jacqueline Jones** is the assistant commissioner for early childhood in the Division of Early Childhood Education at the New Jersey Department of Education. Her expertise is in early childhood education research. She worked for 15 years at the Educational Testing Service (ETS) as senior research scientist and director of both Early Childhood Research and Development and Initiatives in Early Childhood and Literacy. This work focused on the study and implementation of appropriate early childhood assessment systems. She and her colleagues have worked with school districts and Head Start programs in New Jersey and nationally on assessment-related professional development projects. She also developed the Understanding Early Science Learning program, a set of videotape and print materials to help document the evidence of young children's science understanding. Part of the ETS Pathwise Professional Development Series, the program is for early childhood teachers, staff developers, and university teacher educators. She has a Ph.D. in communication sciences and disorders: learning disabilities from Northwestern University.

**Luis M. Laosa** is principal research scientist (emeritus) in the Center for Education Policy and Research at the ETS. His research has focused on children's learning and psychological development, academic achievement, families and schools as learning environments, cultural and linguistic diversity, assessment and testing, educational and social policies toward children, and psychosocial stresses of intercultural migration and their impact on human development and social adaptation. He is the author of numerous scientific and scholarly publications and has served on several professional committees, including the Board of Scientific Advisors of the National Institute of Child Health and Human Development, the Technical Planning Group of the National Education Goals Panel, and as chair of the Committee on Child Development and Social Policy of the Society for Research in Child Development. He is a former editor of *Revista Interamericana de Psicologia/Interamerican Journal of Psychology.* At the NRC, he was a member of the Committee on Child Development Research and Public Policy, BOTA, and the Committee on Goals 2000 and the Inclusion of Students with Disabilities. He received certification in school psychology and professional certification and license in general psychology, served as clinical assistant professor of psychology in the Department of Psychiatry of the University of Texas Medical School at San Antonio, and served on the faculty of the Graduate School of Education in early childhood development at the University of California, Los Angeles. He has a Ph.D. in psychology from the University of Texas at Austin.

**Kathleen McCartney** is the dean of the Faculty of Education and the Lesser professor in early childhood development at Harvard University. She is a developmental psychologist whose research informs theoretical questions on early experience and development as well as policy questions on child care, early childhood education, poverty, and parenting. For the past 15 years, she has served as a principal investigator on the National Institute of Child Health and Human Development Study of Early Child Care and Youth Development, a study of 1,350 children from birth through age 15. She is the editor (with Deborah Phillips) of *The Handbook of Early Childhood Development*. Her work has been informed by her experience as the director of the University of New Hampshire Child Study and Development Center, a laboratory school for children from birth through kindergarten. She has a Ph.D. from Yale University.

**Marie C. McCormick** is Sumner and Esther Feldberg professor of maternal and child health in the Department of Society, Human Development, and Health in the Harvard School of Public Health. She is also professor of pediatrics at the Harvard Medical School and senior associate director of the Infant Follow-up Program at Children's Hospital. Her research involves epidemiological and health services research investigations in areas related to infant mortality and the outcomes of high-risk neonates. She is currently conducting projects on the outcomes of infants experiencing neonatal complications like low birth weight, interventions potentially ameliorating adverse outcomes, and the evaluation of programs designed to improve the health of families and children. She is a member of IOM and has served on its Committee on Understanding Premature Birth and Assuring Health Outcomes and the Committee on Immunization Safety Review. She has an M.D. from the Johns Hopkins Medical School and an

Sc.D. from the Johns Hopkins University Bloomberg School of Public Health.

**Deborah J. Stipek** is dean of the School of Education at Stanford University. Her work concerns instructional effects on children's achievement motivation, early childhood education, elementary education, and school reform. She has worked in the U.S. Senate and with the Office of Head Start. While a professor at the University of California, Los Angeles, she served as director of the Corinne Seeds University Elementary School (pre-K through sixth grade) and the Urban Education Studies Center. At the NRC, she served for 5 years on the NRC/IOM Board on Children, Youth, and Families and chaired the NRC/IOM Committee for Increasing High School Students' Engagement and Motivation to Learn. She has a B.S. in psychology from the University of Washington and a Ph.D. in developmental psychology from Yale University.

**Susan B. Van Hemel** (*Study Director*) is a senior program officer in the Division of Behavioral and Social Sciences and Education at the NRC. Previous projects at the NRC include a study of behavioral modeling and simulation, a study of staffing standards for aviation safety inspectors at the Federal Aviation Administration, studies of Social Security disability determination for individuals with visual and hearing impairments, and workshops on technology for adaptive aging and on decision making in older adults. She has also done work for a previous employer on vision requirements for commercial drivers and on commercial driver fatigue, as well as many years of other work on human performance and training. She is a member of the Human Factors and Ergonomics Society and its technical groups on perception and performance and aging. She has a Ph.D. in experimental psychology from the Johns Hopkins University.

**Mark R. Wilson** is a professor in the Graduate School of Education at the University of California, Berkeley. His interests focus on measurement and applied statistics. His work spans a range of issues in measurement and assessment, from the development of new statistical models for analyzing measurement data; to the development of new assessments in subject matter areas, such as science education, patient-reported outcomes, and child development; to policy issues in the use of assessment data in accountability systems. He has recently published three books: *Constructing Measures: An Item Response Modeling Approach* is an introduction to modern measurement; *Explanatory Item Response Models: A Generalized Linear and Nonlinear Approach* (with Paul De Boeck) introduces an overarching framework for the statistical modeling of measurements that makes available new tools for understanding the meaning and nature of measurement; and *Towards Coherence Between Classroom Assessment and Accountability* explores the issues relating to the relationships between large-scale assessment and classroom-level assessment. At the NRC, he chaired the Committee on Test Design for K-12 Science Achievement. He is the founding editor of *Measurement: Interdisciplinary Research and Perspectives.* He has a Ph.D. in educational measurement and educational statistics from the University of Chicago.

**Martha Zaslow** is the vice president for research at Child Trends and area director for the early child development content area. Her research takes an ecological perspective, considering the contributions of different contexts to the development of children in low-income families, including the family, early care and education, and policy contexts. In studying the role of the family, she has focused especially on parenting, carrying out observational studies of mother-child interaction. In studying early care and education, her work has focused on patterns of child care use among low-income families and on strategies to improve child care quality. She has a particular interest in the professional development of those working in early childhood settings and its relation to quality and to child outcomes. With respect to the policy context, she has studied the use of funding from the Child Care and Development Fund to improve child care quality, state initiatives to improve children's school readiness, and impacts on children of different welfare reform policies. At the NRC, she was a member of the NRC/IOM Committee on Promoting Child and Family Well-Being Through Family Work Policies: Building a Knowledge Base to Inform Policies and Practice. She has a Ph.D. in psychology from Harvard University.

# Index

## D

## E

## F

## G



## H

## K



## L

## O

## P

## Q



## R

## W



## Y